Argentina

the Bradt Travel Guide

918·2

Erin McCloskey

with Tim Burford

edition

I

www.bradtguides.com

Bradt Travel Guides Ltd, UK
The Globe Pequot Press Inc, USA

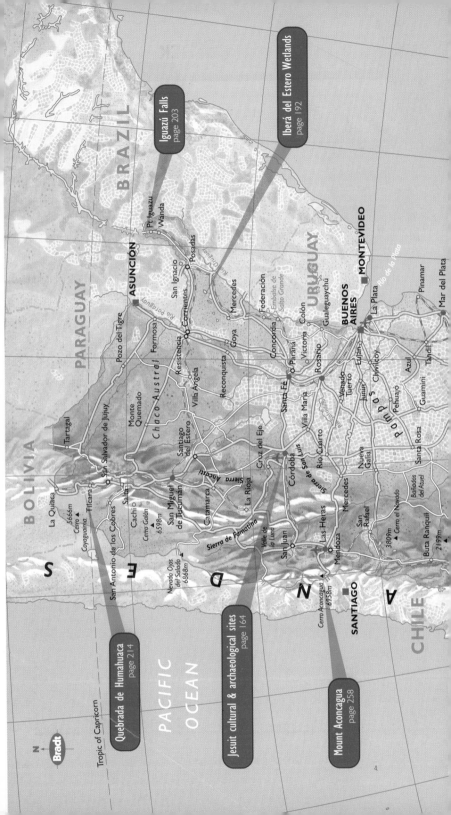

ATLANTIC

OCEAN

South Georgia

Falkland Islands
(Islas Malvinas)

West Falkland   East Falkland

Isla de los Estados

Cabo de Hornos
(Cape Horn)

Drake Passage

Peninsula Valdés
Punta Delgada

Puerto Madryn
Trelew
Rawson

Punta Tombo

Camarones

Comodoro Rivadavia

Golfo de San Jorge

Fitz Roy

Puerto Deseado

Punta Pozos

Puerto San Julián

Comandante Luis
Piedrabuena

Bahía
Grande

Río Gallegos

Cabo Virgenes

Río Grande

de Tierra

del Fuego

Ushuaia

Isla Grande

Esquel

José de
San Martín

Paso Río Mayo

Perito
Moreno

Cerro San Lorenzo
3699m

El Chaltén

El Calafate

Cerro Cojudo Blanco
1335m

Gran Altiplancie
Central

Cerro Colorado
1271m

Río Chico

Río Senguerr

D   I   U   O   B   D   D   d

**Perito Moreno,
Los Glaciares National Park**
page 329

0   500km
0   300 miles

KEY
■ Capital city
● Major city
○ Main town
○ Other town
✈ Airport
— Main road
— Other road
— Railway
--- International boundary

Argentina
Don't miss...

Buenos Aires
The obelisk, Plaza de la República
(AC/TIPS) page 91

Iguazú Falls
Designated a UNESCO World
Heritage Site in 1984
(EM) page 203

Plains of northern Patagonia
Rio Negro Province
(AM/TIPS) page 273

Peninsula Valdés
Elephant seal,
Mirounga leonina
(JG) page 351

Tango
Couple dancing the tango, Buenos Aires
(AP/TIPS) page 44

above left **Magellanic penguins,** *Spheniscus magellanicus*, **Peninsula Valdés** (EM) page 351

above right **Female elephant seal,** *Mirounga leonina*, **Peninsula Valdés** (EM) page 351

left **Peninsula Valdés** (FN/SAP) page 351

top **Guanaco combat,** *Lama guanacoe* (JG) page 382

above left **Capybara,** *Hydrochoeris hydrochaeris,* **Iberá del Estero wetlands** (EM) page 192

above right **Marsh deer,** *Blastocerus dichotomus,* **Iberá del Estero wetlands** (EM) page 192

below **Giant anteater,** *Myrmecophaga tridactyla* (TM/SAP)

Author/Contributor

Erin McCloskey was born in Canada, has lived several years in Italy and is a worldwide traveller. She is a writer and editor, with a degree in conservation biology from the University of Alberta. Her focus has been on socio-environmental issues, natural history, photography and dance, all well represented in Argentina. She owns a small property in Bariloche.

MAJOR CONTRIBUTOR

Tim Burford studied languages at Oxford University. In 1991, after a brief career as a publisher, he began writing for Bradt Travel Guides, covering firstly hiking in east-central Europe and then backpacking and ecotourism in Latin America. He has now written seven books for Bradt and leads hiking trips in Europe's mountains.

DEDICATION

Sebastian, for you and because of you.

FEEDBACK REQUEST

Please help us to keep this book up to date and to make the next edition even better by sending any comments or suggestions to Argentina updates, Bradt Travel Guides, 23 High Street, Chalfont St Peter, Bucks SL9 9QE; e info@bradtguides.com. The author can be contacted directly on argentinaguide@yahoo.com

Reprinted October 2007, June 2008
First published July 2006

Bradt Travel Guides Ltd
23 High Street, Chalfont St Peter, Bucks SL9 9QE, England
www.bradtguides.com
Published in the USA by The Globe Pequot Press Inc, 246 Goose Lane,
PO Box 480, Guilford, Connecticut 06437-0480

British Library Cataloguing in Publication Data
A catalogue record for this book is available from the British Library

ISBN-10: 1 84162 138 2
ISBN-13: 978 1 84162 138 8

Photographs
Text: Erin McCloskey (EM), Jonathan Green (JG), Hilary Bradt (HB); South American
Pictures: Frank Nowikowski (FN), Danny Aeberhard (DA), Tony Morrison (TM); TIPS:
Andrea Pistolesi (AP), Angelo Cavalli (AC), Aris Mihich (AM), Roberto Rinaldi (RR) Glen
Allison (GA)
Front cover: Close-up of a gaucho's stirrup (Damm Fridmar/Fototeca)
Back cover: Cardon Cactus (TM/SAP), Elephant seal, Peninsula Valdés (EM)
Title page: Couple performing tango, Buenos Aires (AC/TIPS), Houses in La Boca (EM),
Glacier Upsala (HB)

Illustrations Cheryl Bozarth
Maps Alan Whitaker, Terence Crump, Steve Munns (colour country map)

Typeset from the author's disc by Wakewing, High Wycombe
Printed and bound in India by Nutech Photolithographers

PUBLISHER'S FOREWORD

The first Bradt travel guide was written in 1974 by George and Hilary Bradt on a river barge floating down a tributary of the Amazon. In the 1980s and '90s the focus shifted away from hiking to broader-based guides covering new destinations – usually the first to be published about these places. In the 21st century Bradt continues to publish such ground-breaking guides, as well as others to established holiday destinations, incorporating in-depth information on culture and natural history with the nuts and bolts of where to stay and what to see.

Bradt authors support responsible travel, and provide advice not only on minimum impact but also on how to give something back through local charities. In this way a true synergy is achieved between the traveller and local communities.

* * *

George and I spent four months in Argentina in 1974 while he recovered from hepatitis. The first-ever Bradt guide was published during that period and we made our first media appearance on Argentine television to promote it. My long acquaintance with Buenos Aires and its sophisticated citizens left a lasting impression on me and as a traveller I was enthralled by the wildlife, scenery and diversity of this huge country.

I returned as a tour leader in 1981, visiting the Falkland Islands before spending Christmas in Ushuaia. When the Falklands War broke out four months later I found my sympathy for the Argentine people at odds with the 'Gotcha!' attitude of much of Britain. Now those warm and friendly people have a stable government and steadily increasing tourism. It's well deserved.

Hilary Bradt

23 High Street, Chalfont St Peter, Bucks SL9 9QE, England
Tel: 01753 893444   Fax: 01753 892333
info@bradtguides.com   www.bradtguides.com

Contents

LIST OF MAPS

Introduction

'Diverse' is the word that springs to mind when describing a country that sprawls 2,766,890km² (from the Tropic of Capricorn to the South Pole). European architectural influences in the northwest and central regions contrast with the rugged, undeveloped terrains of the deserts and southern Patagonia. Each region is unique and merits independent exploration – indeed, one cannot visit Buenos Aires or Patagonia alone and claim to have 'seen' Argentina. The Pampas, the Alto Plano, the Mission Ruins of the subtropics, the Lake Region, the Andes, the vast Patagonian estancias, the Pacific and Antarctic coasts – all are waiting to reward those who seek them out.

Now in post-economic crisis, Argentina is focusing on new industries for a sustainable future; tourism is among the most important. Today's visitors to Argentina have a great opportunity to influence how this country will direct its growth in this sector, and ecotourism is especially valuable in supporting local markets and emphasising the importance of natural-resource conservation. Beyond the diverse terrain, other features make it attractive as a tourist destination. The Argentines are naturally kind and hospitable people making their country one of the most enjoyable in the world to visit, and the peso is stable and travel affordable.

And there's that vibrant culture. The name Argentina derives from argentum (Latin for silver). However, it is the abundance of other treasures that make Argentina truly worth admiring. Poetry, music, art and dance all echo from its plains, forests and mountain peaks, proudly proclaiming the passionate heart of this enigmatic country.

Acknowledgements

With special thanks to the Sylwan and Collin-Harguindeguy families and extended families who have shown me so much hospitality and have shared with me the charm of their Argentine heritage – often through wine, asado and song; to the Eders who have shared with me their love for the tango and, along with the Swieykowskis, a big dream and a small piece of Patagonia; and to my parents who have shared with me many things throughout my life, including the backing for the Patagonian venture, but especially their values of leading by example and making a positive influence – this has governed my life as well as my career.

Research assistance and reference maps were kindly provided by: Centros de Información Turística Argentina, Secretaría de Turismo y Cultura Argentina, Topografía y Catastro Municipalidad de Rosario, Dirección Turismo Zona Norte de Zapala e de Chos Malal, Dirección de Turismo Municipalidad de Malargüe, Secretaría de Turismo de Tucumán, Turismo Junin de los Andes, Turismo La Cumbre, Secretaría de Turismo Municipalidad de San Carlos de Bariloche, Subsecretería de Turismo Neuquén, EMTUR Mar del Plata, Centro de Informacion Turística Santa Fe, Dirección de Turismo San Antonio de Areco, Oficina de Información Norte, Secretaría de Turismo Municipalidad de San Carlos de Bariloche, the Nuequen Tourist Centre, Municipalidad de Villa Gesell

Additional thanks to all who have helped with the research and writing of this guide: Sebastian and Guingo Sylwan, Laura Collin, Federico Polesel (Hostelling International), Ernst and Tamara Eder, the Swieykowski family, Norberto Ferronato, Alex Rosato, Cheryl Bozarth, Roberto Roa (Parques Nationales Argentina), Centros de Informacion Turistica Argentina, Aerolineas Argentinas, Lucía Zone (Riders EVT Travel), Virginia Getino (Delicias Del Ibera), Carla de Castro and Anibal Parera (Fundacion ECOS/Iberá Foundation), Pablo Zelaya Huerta (Montañas Tucumanas), Jeronimo Critto (El Puesto Cabalgatas), Eduardo Veron (Hotel Guadalupe), Maria Laura Langhoff, Natalia de las Morenas (Argentina Mountain Expeditions), Choique Turismo Alternativo and Hostel Internacional Mendoza and Malargüe, Sol Mayor Cuesta Blanca, Tucumán Hostel, Yok-Wahi Hostel, Casaverde Hostel, El Gualicho Hostel, Backpackers Hostels and Tours, Patagonia Travellers' Hostel, Camino Abierto, Hostels del Glaciar, Los Cormoranes Hostel, Bodega Terrazas, Jungle Explorer, Flamenco Tours, Nunatak, Bottazzi, Michael Luongo, Gabriel Miremont (MAAM – Museo de Arqueología de Alta Montaña de Salta), Christine Fox, David Hilton, Tim Burford and to everyone who answered a question, fed me an *empanada* or offered a smile.

Sincere gratitude to all the conservation and humanitarian organisations who are doing such valuable work in Argentina.

Part One

General Information

ARGENTINA AT A GLANCE

Location Southeast section of South America, lying between 21° 40' and 55° 18' south and 53° 38' and 73° 25' west. Argentina shares borders with Chile along the western length of the country, Bolivia to the north, and Paraguay, Brazil and Uruguay to the northeast. To the east is the Atlantic Ocean.

Size 2.8 million km² (excluding the South Atlantic Islands and the Antarctic quadrant claimed as national territory).

Climate In the temperate zone of the southern hemisphere; six distinct climatic areas ranging from subtropical in the north to arid in the southeast; mild and humid in the pampas plains to sub-Antarctic in southern Patagonia. Average temperature from November to March is 23°C and from June to September 12°C.

Time Three hours behind GMT (GMT –3). Argentina does not observe daylight saving.

Electricity 220 volts, 50 hertz. Plugs are either two rounded prongs or three angled flat prongs.

Weights and measures Metric

International telephone code +54

Status Republic

Currency Peso

Population 39,537,943 (July 2005 est. CIA World Factbook); 37.9 million (2004 est. World Bank)

Population growth per year 1% (2005 est. CIA World Factbook)

Life expectancy in years at birth 74.3 (World Bank 2004); 74.5 (UNDP 2003); 75.9 (CIA World Factbook 2005)

Economy Agriculture (12% of labour force) and ranching: cattle, sheep, maize, soya, wheat, wine, cotton, sugar, tea. Mining is mainly of boron followed by tin, tungsten, cement, iron ore, gold, silver, lead, uranium, zinc. Petroleum and natural gas production falls short of domestic need.

Capital Buenos Aires

Main cities Buenos Aires, Bahía Blanca, Bariloche, Mar del Plata, Córdoba, Mendoza, Salta, Rosario, Santa Fé, La Plata, Tucumán

Language Spanish (Castellano)

Religion Roman Catholic 92% (less than 20% practising); Protestant 2%; Jewish 2%; other 4%

Flag Three horizontal stripes: white between two blue stripes. The government and military version has a yellow sun with a smiling face in the centre known as the Sun of May.

Background Information

ECOLOGY

Argentina is a large and sparsely populated country with an exceptional diversity of natural areas. Its boundaries include almost every conceivable landscape, including forests and ecosystems found nowhere else on earth. In the northeast there are virtually impenetrable jungle-like subtropical forests with hundreds of species of birds and many rare and beautiful animals such as the jaguar. The Pampa is a vast blanket of prairie that's home to numerous grassland species less conspicuous than the abundant cattle. The towering Andean mountains and the wildernesses of Patagonia reveal yet another distinct history, both cultural and natural. With deserts, lakelands, salt flats, glaciers, forests, steppes, coasts and islands, one cannot attribute to Argentina any single postcard image. It boasts the gentle climes of South America, but its southern tip is a launching point for visits to nearby Antarctica.

There are 27 national parks, many provincial parks and protected areas, plus RAMSAR (wetlands of international importance) and UNESCO (World Heritage List) sites. Three animal species have been declared national monuments: the southern Andean deer locally known as *huemel* (*Hippocamelus bisulcus*), the northern Andean deer or *taruca* (*Hippocamelus antisensis*) and the southern right whale or *ballena franca austral* (*Eubalaena australis*), and as such they cannot be hunted. Close to four million hectares have protected status, less than 1.5% of the country, as against an international guideline of at least 5%, with balanced representation of the various ecosystems. In Argentina there is adequate protection of the southern Andean and yungas forests but the coast, pampas grassland and espinal woods are underprotected. The first marine national park was only established in 2004; this is the Monte León National Park in Santa Cruz province. Península Valdés is not under National Park protection (although it is a provincial park) even though it was given World Heritage listing in 1999 and is the breeding and calving ground of the southern right whale. Owing to the unrestricted access for tourism along the Patagonian coastline, many breeding areas for sensitive migratory species have been jeopardised. The parks in general have terribly low budgets and with the increase in eco-tourism (there are now over 1.5 million visitors to the parks per year), the level of management is inadequate. Any deficiencies you may experience are reminders of the need for greater appreciation of the parks and reserves and for increased budgeting for sustainable tourism. Only a few of the national parks charge entrance fees and the others do not generate enough revenue to provide better management and reduce impact. At those that do have entrance fees, foreign tourists pay more than locals, but remember that local people also pay through their taxes for the management of the national parks and, furthermore, it is indeed their national patrimony in which we are guests.

CLIMATE AND GEOGRAPHY

Argentina's climate is classified as temperate; indeed it's the largest temperate country in South America. However, such a vast geographical space cannot be tied

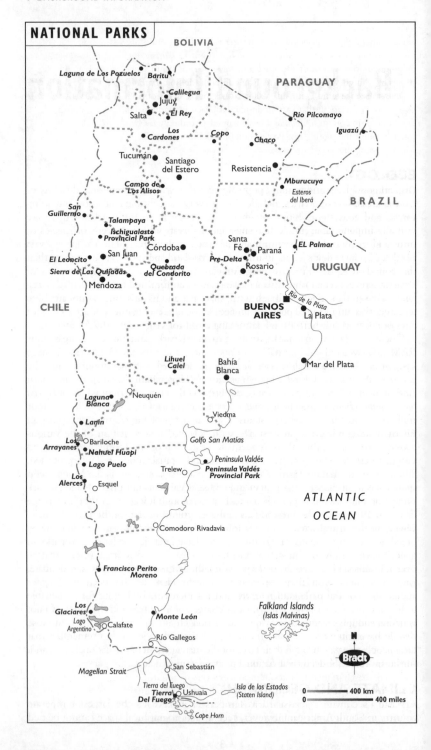

NATIONAL PARKS

down to one such precise category. The northeast of the country is the subtropical Paranaense Forest. Moving west towards the Andes the climate becomes more arid; moving south from the north-central Chaco the climate also changes from humid to dry. The gently rolling landscape begins to crumple and buckle forming the Central Sierras, surrounded by the Pampas and with wine country to the west. The windy climes of Patagonia sweep south from the Rio Colorado. At the southern tip of the country conditions are sub-Antarctic. Approximately one million km² of Antarctica are claimed by Argentina, although this is not internationally recognised; similarly, the sub-Antarctic Malvinas or Falkland Islands are claimed by Argentina but governed by Britain.

The country is divided into several geographical zones, which are followed in the organisation of this guide. These comprise the flat extensive prairies of the Pampa, the Litoral zone of the northeast (Mesopotamia and the Chaco), the Northwestern Andean region, the Cuyo and Patagonia.

Climate obviously varies with geography, from north to south in the case of temperature and from east to west in the case of humidity; the seasons, however, differ only in their variations of temperature, precipitation and duration. Argentina is in the southern hemisphere, thus the seasons occur during the opposite months from Europe and North America. Spring arrives around November; January and February mark the peak summer months and March is the end of summer when children return to school. The autumn months are April and May and winter can be perceived as early as June in the southern regions near the mountains where snow often settles and temperatures frequently drop below freezing. However, in the north winter rarely means snow – if it occurs it will not stay on the ground – but it does mean rain. The wet season here is from November to March (the wettest month in Mesopotamia is September), and the driest time of year is from May to October. The northwest is generally hot but high-altitude deserts cool off substantially in the evenings and combined with wind the perceived temperature can be close to freezing. Moving south, average temperatures fall and summers become somewhat shorter. In the far north average temperatures are in the 30s in summer and the high teens in winter, with freezing temperatures in the desert overnight. The central region is relatively warm all year, with hot summers (25–35°C) and winter temperatures always above zero. Summers are cooler and windier in Patagonia and the winters are mild, except in the far south and in the high mountains where temperatures drop below freezing. In Tierra del Fuego summer temperatures are mild, rarely reaching 20°C, with long hours of daylight.

Pampa

This temperate region hosts vast cattle ranches, or estancias, and endless horizons of grassland. The hugely fertile Pampa region is the agricultural and cultural heart of Argentina and its wealthiest region. It consists of the humid pampas or *pampa húmeda* along the eastern seaboard where there is more rainfall (including Buenos Aires and the beaches nearby) and northeast along the Paraná River, and the dry pampas or *pampa seca*, a less-populated region to the west and south supporting cattle, horses and sheep. The vast, treeless rolling pampas are part of a massive alluvial plain, the Río de la Plata basin, with six major rivers including the Paraná, the Uruguay and the Paraguay among its many tributaries. The port of Buenos Aires is on the Río de la Plata estuary, although the channels have to be constantly dredged of the large accumulation of silt. The only other topographical features of these great flatlands are the surprising upheaval of several low-lying mountain chains: the Sierras de Córdoba, de Tandil and de la Ventana. The pampas is naturally the country's most homogenous area, but with the highest density of human population in the country it has experienced the highest levels of human impact.

Litoral

Mesopotomia, one part of the Litoral zone, is a broad, flat extension of the Paraná plateau between the Paraná and Uruguay rivers, and lies only slightly above sea level. This great floodplain and delta of the Río Paraná have a mild climate and heavy rainfall year-round; this decreases as you enter the **Chaco** or Chaqueño area, the north-central region of the country and the southern sector of the Gran Chaco of Bolivia, Paraguay and Brazil. It has a humid subtropical climate in the north and is semi-humid or dry in the southwest. Precipitation averages 1.4m/year in the Mesopotamia region, and up to 2m in the region's northeastern tip, ie: it rains all year, but more heavily in summer while the far western limit of the Chaco, entering Santiago del Estero, receives 500mm per year in the north and 350mm per year in the south. Average temperatures vary between 16°C and 22°C from winter to summer, and are much warmer in the north. The wet and swampy floodplain of Mesopotamia is extremely hot in summer, when it frequently floods. The Esteros del Iberá is an area of about 37,930km² of swampland, where a nature reserve offers great wildlife viewing. Entre Rios province, the southern part of Mesopotamia, is drier grassland suitable for agriculture, most importantly raising sheep and cattle and growing animal feed. The northern province of Misiones, a small thumb of Argentina protruding into Brazil and Paraguay, is a hilly and densely forested area where the subtropical climate (the province is only just south of the Tropic of Capricorn) is hot and humid with plentiful rainfall, ideal for the cultivation of *yerba maté*, Argentina's national drink. Misiones' landscapes always impress visitors, with jungles of giant millenarian trees, tree-ferns and waterfalls such as the famous Iguazú Falls at the border of Brazil and Paraguay (one of the world's largest falls in volume and area). The north-central Chaco region, bordering Bolivia, has a warm climate, many rivers and seasonal rainfall. The vegetation graduates from jungle in the north to thorny scrub forest towards the south and grasslands and parched desert-like landscape in the west. Chaco province, the country's northernmost province, has a warm subtropical climate and many rivers and seasonal but heavy rainfall. It has a well-defined winter season, in contrast to neighbouring areas of Mesopotamia that receive even rainfall year-round. There are volcanic peaks in the extreme north and rolling forest elsewhere, draining into the Ríos Bermejo and Paraguay. The *quebracho* tree (see page 11) is typical of the forest; it is an important hardwood that is also used for firewood and to produce a resin used to treat leather. Logging is an important industry and a serious threat to these forests. The Chaco is divided into the eastern humid chaco, the western dry chaco and the mountainous (serrano) chaco. This eco-region is high in biodiversity and has the highest volume of vegetation, typically xerophilic forests with lots of shallow rivers lined by willows. Wildlife in this region differs from the humid east and the dry west, with a high diversity of aquatic, forest and subtropical species.

Northwestern Argentina

The Andean chains, or cordilleras, of northwestern Argentina boast the highest peaks in South America: Aconcagua (6,960m), the highest mountain in the western hemisphere, and Tupungato (6,550m) – see *Chapter 11*. The passes through the Andes are at a great height and are narrow, steep and dangerous. The Central Railroad crosses at an elevation of 4,475m, making it the highest standard-gauge railway in the world, until the line to Tibet opens in 2007. The northern Andes are drained by such major rivers as the Amazon, the Orinoco and the Salado. There's a dry climate with 80–200mm precipitation per year, with seasonal variation – in the north it's rainy and hot in summer, while in the south it's rainy and cool in winter and spring. The steppe vegetation consists of xerophyllic shrubs, dominantly zigofilacea trees with bare sandy soil. The forest, where there are few rivers, is dominated by algarroba, willow, maitén or arca, with many ephemeral herbs in summer.

One of South America's most unusual bio-geographic regions is the *puna*, a cold desert at an altitude of 3,500m and above. There are isolated mountains, some of volcanic origin, that reach 5,500m and are permanently snow-capped. The incessant winds make the air very dry and the altitude lowers the oxygen content. The altitude sickness caused by this thinning and drying of the air is called *puna* or *soroche*. The high pampas of the cordilleras are of special biological interest due to endemic flora and fauna adapted to this rigorous climate. The climate is cold and dry, with temperatures fluctuating greatly and frequently falling below zero at night. There's summer rain and a chance of snow year-round. Rainfall diminishes from north to south and from east to west, from about 700mm to the northeast to less than 50mm per year at the saltpans.

The area surrounding the Andes began as a colony of Peru, but today only a few miners and herders occupy this unforgiving region of volcanic peaks and salt lakes.

Cuyo

The Andes Mountains continue along the western boundary of the country and through the Cuyo region. With a comfortable climate and beautiful landscapes, this is the most densely settled region of the Andes and Andean foothills. The Andes create a rain shadow that does not permit a great amount of precipitation; however, the many rivers descending from the mountains naturally irrigate the land and create ideal conditions for agriculture. The most important agricultural sector here is the wine industry, with acres of vineyards spreading eastward from the mountains throughout the fertile valleys. Another impact of the mountains in this region is the Chinook-like wind known as *El Zonda*. This warm dry wind originates as a moisture-rich wind from the Pacific but it drops its precipitation when it hits the Andes. Its temperature and velocity increases as it passes over to the eastern side, becoming a warm dry wind by the time it reaches the eastern slopes. *El Zonda* causes a rapid rise in temperatures in the Cuyo region that in winter can create spring-like conditions and last several days.

Patagonia

This region, shared with Chile, is divided politically, geographically and climatically by the Andes, which here include some of the southern hemisphere's highest peaks. The high cordillera grabs the Pacific precipitation and throws it mostly on the Chilean side. The precipitation received on the east of the Andes diminishes towards the steppe from 4m per year to 0.8m per year, and just 150-300mm per year on the Atlantic coast. Puerto Blest has the steepest climatic gradient; within a distance of 50km it changes from temperate Validivian rainforest, with 5m per year of rainfall, to steppe, with 0.5m. Patagonia stretches 2,000km from north to south, with its northern boundary being generally accepted as the Río Colorado, at approximately 40° south. Of a total of approximately a million km², Argentina's share is about 777,000–800,000km²; this is Argentina's largest region but also its least populated. The Andes, the steppe and the Atlantic coast are the three divisions of Argentine Patagonia; and three factors influence its climate, the oceans (Pacific, Atlantic and Southern), the mountains and its relative proximity to the South Pole. Overall temperatures are mild, the summers are not too hot and the winters not too cold. For example, the average temperature in Ushuaia is 6°C and in Bariloche 8°C. However, in such a large region, this is a vast generalisation. Summer temperatures in the north average 17.4°C and can simmer for periods at 30°C or higher; and the winters are mild with little snow and temperatures rarely dropping below zero. In the south, temperatures are rarely above 25°C in summer, and in winter they are often below zero with lasting snow.

The Andean climate is temperate, with humid forests, plenty of snowfall in winter and freezing temperatures possible year-round. In the extreme south snow and ice gather on mountaintops and form the massive glaciers, the largest in the southern hemisphere.

The Patagonian steppe covers a vast mesa with scarce population. It stretches from west-central Mendoza, east of Neuquén and Río Negro, through practically all of Chubut and Santa Cruz and the northeast of Tierra del Fuego. It has large canyons cutting through the plains and high-elevation desert plateaux with great expanses of dry windswept scrub. The climate is temperate – cold and dry, with strong winds from the east, snow in the winter and frost possible all the year round.

Patagonia's coastline is jagged and rocky and therefore relatively undeveloped. Its length is even along some shores and then riddled with bays, peninsulas and capes along others. A vast continental shelf extends beyond the eastern shoreline for over 300km with relatively shallow waters (100–150m in depth) creating several small islands to peak above the sea level.

Of the region's few rivers, the most important are the Río Negro and Río Santa Cruz, born in the Andes and crossing the breadth of the plains to enter the Atlantic Ocean. Large inlets at river mouths have created mudflats, and depressions in the earth's surface have created salt lakes such as Salina Grande (at 48m below sea level) and Salina Chica on Península Valdés. Permanent freshwater sources are scarce in eastern Patagonia, in stark contrast to the lake district of Neuquén and Río Negro provinces. Most lakes in the east are created by the autumn and winter rains but dry up completely by summer from the exposure to wind and sun. There are rare freshwater springs around the Salina Grande on Península Valdés.

Meaning the 'Land of Fire', Tierra del Fuego is a mountainous archipelago at the southern tip of South America, separated from the continent by the Magellan Strait; the world's southernmost permanently inhabited territory, it belongs partly to Argentina and partly to Chile. The Argentine portion includes the eastern side of the main island (Isla Grande), Staten Island (Isla de los Estados), and many smaller islands, with Cape Horn (Isla Horno) at its southern extremity. The area of the entire archipelago is about 71,484km², with the Atlantic Ocean to the east, the Southern Ocean to the south, and the Pacific Ocean to the west. The archipelago was discovered in 1520 by Portuguese navigator Ferdinand Magellan and named for the fires seen burning along the coast, now believed to have been made by the Yahgan or Yámana people. While many zones are forested and mountainous, a great area of Tierra del Fuego is similar to the Patagonian steppe and supports an important sheep-raising industry.

GEOLOGY AND FOSSIL FINDS

Layers of sediment represent different geological eras or events. Most of Argentina's significant geological formations and strata are resultant of either glaciation or volcanic activity. Debris from the Andes (rocks, stones and sand) was carried eastward by rivers and the many great glaciers that are still advancing and retreating from the Andes today. Tumbled stones were smoothed and rounded and form an almost continuous layer of shingle, known as Tehuelche gravel, that covers the plains of Patagonia where wind erosion is also intense. Tehuelche gravel is very heterogeneous, with the hardest stones surviving the transport from the Andes, while the softer stones were worn away; thus it consists mostly of rounded fragments of granite, basalt and porphyritic rock. You can see great amounts of Tehuelche gravel along the paths and at the campsites at El Chaltén. Northern Patagonia is also an active volcanic area and recent eruptions have left areas in Neuquén province charred black, though also awash with colour from the various minerals and ores that paint the landscape red and green. Coastal Patagonia has smooth eroded sedimentary and volcanic rock and sand making up the various shorelines. The ocean causes rapid geological and morphological changes on the shoreline: tides and currents cause sedimentary rocks to break off and mould those that hold fast into smooth formations.

Buried within all these strata are petrified wood, fossil shells and even dinosaurs. Patagonia is one of the most dinosaur-rich areas of the world, with 50 species having been discovered in the past three decades in just 30 sites. The first discoveries were made in the fossil-rich coastal cliffs of Patagonia by Charles Darwin.

At the beginning of the Triassic period, some 250 million years ago, the continents were joined together into one supercontinent called Pangea (meaning 'all the earth') surrounded by the Pantalassa Ocean ('all the sea'). Eventually this landmass split into a northern continent called Laurasia and a southern continent called Gondwanaland, the latter comprising South America, Africa, Australia, New Zealand, Antarctica, Madagascar and India. South America and Australasia were in close contact 65 million years ago until the break-up of Gondwanaland, so there is a close relationship between the flora and fauna of Argentina and Australasia. It's likely that Patagonia was part of the southern landmass and separate from South America at this time. By the end of the Cretaceous period these landmasses had also divided and assumed a distribution and formation more familiar to us today; but what is now called Patagonia was a flat area, with much of the current landmass having been covered by the ocean on two separate occasions.

Palaeozoic Era (620–250 million years ago)

Some 360–250 million years ago, during the Carboniferous and Permian periods, Patagonia was subtropical. Rivers reached the Palaeo-Pacific Ocean through a deltaic system rather than from the Andes, similar to the water system of the La Plata delta today. There were rich and dense forests of which fossil remains exist today in various locations, such as near Monte León National Park and Gaiman.

Mesozoic Era (250–65 million years ago)

This was the time when the earth was host to the Kingdom of Dinosaurs. Some of the oldest and most important dinosaur fossil remains have been found in Patagonia. These include those of the Triassic dinosaurs (250–200 million years ago – a time of the appearance of the greatest number of mammal species and the first coniferous trees): *Eoraptor lunensis*, found in the Moon Valley of Ischigualasto, one of the oldest proto-dinosaurs (bipedal and the size of an average dog); *Herrerasaurus ischigualastensis*, found in La Rioja, one of the first dinosaurs; and the tiny *Mussaurus patagonicus*, found in Santa Cruz, referred to as the lizard mouse (reaching 5m in length, but under 30cm in height when newly hatched).

The Jurassic period commenced 160 million years ago, creating the great Jurassic forest and introducing the Jurassic dinosaur *Piatnitzkysaurus floresi*, found in Chubut. Flowering plants began to appear and animals began taking on characteristics that are recognisable in modern species today.

A subsequent phase, 145–65 million years ago, was the Cretaceous period when there were the most dinosaurs. The herbaceous sauropods were discovered in Neuquén: *Patagosaurus* is the earliest sauropod on record. *Amargasaurus cazaui* was found in Zapala and *Rebbachisaurus tessonei* near El Chocon. The latter is the most complete sauropod ever found in South America, similar to another in South Africa suggesting the linkage of these two continents some 100 million years ago. Another famous Argentine dinosaur is *Gigantosaurus carolinii*, the largest dinosaur ever to walk this planet. This existed some 100 million years ago and was 14m long and weighed 8 tonnes – larger than the famous *Tyrannosaurus rex*. *Epachtosaurus*, instead, was the largest plant-eater. *Carnotaurus sastrei* (King of Patagonia) was found in Chubut; the skeleton of this 85–75 million-year-old carnivore is the most complete skeleton of connected bones ever found. At the end of the Cretaceous period the Andes had not yet formed. The first buckling of the earth's crust began around 55 million years ago. The early mountains were not high, and forests formed in the warm to temperate, damp climes.

Cenozoic Era (65 million years ago to present)

This era is differentiated in part by the extinction of avian dinosaurs and the appearance of large land mammals that are responsible for it being referred to as the Age of Mammals, although this faunal group was in reality insignificant in diversity and population compared to that of fish, birds, insects and especially flowering plants. The Cenozoic Era has two main subdivisions: the Tertiary (65 million to 1.8 million years ago, comprising the Palaeogene and Neogene periods) and the Quaternary (the last 1.8 million years, comprising the Pleistocene and Holocene epochs). The Palaeogene period (65–25 million years ago) represents a period of great radiation and diversification of mammals, birds, insects and flowers (favoured by humid winds from Pacific). Patagonia, before the Andean cordillera and initial penetration of Atlantic warm waters, was subtropical but later dried and the forests were replaced by grasslands. The Neogene period (25 to 1.8 million years ago) was a time of climatic chaos. The Miocene is considered a warm epoch and saw the formation of the great grasslands of Africa and Argentina. In contrast, the Pliocene was marked by global cooling; there were glaciation events and polar plateaus formed. The cooling was accompanied by a gradual uplifting of the land and the ocean receding east across the Patagonian plains.

Ten million years ago **the Andes** rose further when the Pacific plate began to subduct the South American plate. The subsequent era of mountain formation continues today and the forces generated by this collision still trigger volcanic eruptions and earthquakes. The rising mountains caused prevailing winds from the west to dump their moisture onto the western slopes, causing the grasslands and forests to turn into deserts. The land subsided again during the Pliocene and the ocean advanced and formed a large sea known as the Patagonian Sea. The **Panamanian Isthmus** formed about three million years ago, and the migration of fauna led to the extinction of entire groups.

The Quaternary period commenced 1.8 million years ago. The Pleistocene was when the South American mega fauna appeared and animals existed such as the *Gliptodonte*, the oldest-known mammal; the *Toxodonte,* the South American hippos and rhinos; the *Smilodon*, the sabre-toothed tiger; and many other fascinating animals. The similar modern species are not descendent but migrant from the African-Asian genuses. This epoch commences with the last ice age and defines the last 10,000 years or so, during which time man made his appearance. It is sobering to note that 60 million years before the appearance of hominids, the dinosaurs were extinct, yet the lizard kings roamed the earth for 180 million years, three times the existence of man.

FLORA

Various vegetation zones exist in Argentina, including the northern subtropical forests and the Patagonian temperate rainforests. The tree line ranges from an average elevation of 3,500m at the equator to about 900m in Tierra del Fuego Argentina. Great surface areas are covered in xerophytic plants adapted to the dry and harsh conditions of the desert-like steppes of the high Andes and windblown Patagonia. The plants here are predominantly cactus, shrubs and grasses. In contrast are the wetlands of the east, rich in biodiversity of both flora and fauna. And, of course, the pampas – the great and famous grassland where the Argentine culture finds its own roots anchored and nurtured.

Northern Forests

Misiones Forest (*Selva misionera*) is an ecologically important extension of the Paraná Forest, *Selva paranaense*, whose red soil and humid subtropical climate nurture a wealth of biodiversity including over 2,000 identified species of plants – it is estimated that the province of Misiones provides the habitat for almost half of the mammals, birds, reptiles and amphibians of Argentina. The Paranaense Forest used to cover the south of Brazil, the Republic of Paraguay and, in Argentina, the entire province of Misiones, northern Corrientes and the transition area with the Chaco Region, where it is the most devastated from urban and agricultural development. There is only 10% of this forest remaining in the above-mentioned territories. Argentina possesses 45% of the Paranaense Forest, which is diminishing in area from a currently estimated 3,000,000ha, of which only 15% is protected. Brazil protects 5% of the total area and Paraguay between 13% and 20%. The largest threats to the forest are deforestation, poaching and the use of fertilisers, soil depletion from monoculture and rural poverty. The most characteristic and distinctive tree of the Paranaense Forest is the **quebracho tree** (*Schinopsis lorentzii*) of the Anacardiaceae or sumac family. Its name has come to be synonymous with a leather-tanning substance obtained from its red heartwood, which has a high level of tannin (30%). This hardwood tree is also greedily harvested for its heavy durable timber. White quebracho (*Aspidosperma quebracho blanco*) is a similar hardwood, in the dogbane family, in high demand from this forest.

The **Yungas Forest** of the northern Andes has a special ecological diversity (influenced by both arid northwestern and humid Chaco climates) ranging from forest to jungle and transitioning at high elevations to high-Andean grassland plateaux. It is similar to the *Selva misionera* of the northeast but influenced by the Chaqueño Forest. Reaching an altitude of 3,000m, it has a hot and humid climate with intense summer rains and dry winters, although with snow possible at the highest elevations. The climate varies with elevation, passing from subtropical in the foothills through Chaco-like conditions to *nuboselva* or cloud forest at higher elevations. At 2,500m the mountain forests have low tree diversity above tree line only scrub and grasses grow on the high plains.

The **Chaqueño (Chaco) Forest** has several forms, but the two most predominant are savanna (characterised by its abundant grasses) and thorn or *espinal* forest, lying between the Chaco and the Pampa, dominated by spiny trees, above all the *Prosopis* genus (algarroba, ñandubaysal, caldenar and others). Northern forests have more typically subtropical species, such as lianas, palms and caldén. The transition between these two habitat types is marked by thorny bushes and cacti with scattered quebracho trees.

Patagonian Forests

The forests of Patagonia are very diverse, influenced by (and influencing) different climatic situations. Around Lago Aluminé there are forests of 'primeval' trees such as *Araucaria araucana* (**monkey-puzzle trees**) which have existed since prehistory; in the mountains there are deciduous forests of **false beech** or *Nothofagus*; and pine forests also exist in the Andes, with edible *piñón* fruit that was an important food source for indigenous peoples crossing Andean trails. Where there were no forests on the steppe, stands of poplar trees were introduced onto many estancias years ago, and these have now reached great heights.

The most characteristic tree of Patagonia is the species of southern, or false, beech, known as **coihue** (*Nothofagus dombeyi*), which is representative of the humid perennial forest found along the border with Chile and between the west-central area of Neuquén and northern Chubut, at altitudes between 500m and 1,000m. The 40 species of this genus are found only in Australasia and in Patagonia, where there are ten species (though one is possibly a hybrid), three of which are evergreen (the coihue de Chiloé, *N. nitida*, is only in Chile, but the other two, coihue and **guindo** (*N. betuloides*), are found in Argentina). Coihue often forms single-species forests or associates with other species in more humid zones such as the Valdivian rainforest. To the north, with more precipitation and biodiversity, the coihue is dominant but mixes with the **alerce** (*Fitzroya cupressoides*). On exposed hillsides coihue can grow almost parallel to the ground as if pushed over by the persistent westerly winds; these are commonly referred to as flag trees. Yet, without the wind, its trunk grows straight and true, which along with its damp-resistant wood, makes it ideal for making furniture and also bridges, dock berths, steps, etc. This tree can reach up to 40m (in northwest Chubut) and live for 400 to 500 years; at Puerto Blest, in Nahuel Huapi National Park, a grove of coihue is referred to as The Grandfathers because they are over 600 years old.

Nothofagus species often intermingle but have preferred altitudes and ecological niches that allow for single-species stands to be seen. Argentina's **Valdivian Forest** is characterised by coihue, which is replaced in the **Magellanic Forest** by guindo. These are characterised by the large woody growths on their branches, a response to the yellow **llao-llao** fungus that favours them. Two species of llao-llao are to be found: **digüeñ** (*Cyttaria darwinii*) in the north, and *pan de indio* or **Indian bread** (*C. hariotti*) in Tierra del Fuego, the latter of which produces larger fruit (3–7cm diameter, compared to the 2–5cm of the former).

The **Valdivian Temperate Rainforest** is found in Chile and Argentina. It is the second-largest of the world's five major temperate rainforests and the only one in South America. About 70% of the Valdivian Temperate Rainforest is in Chile and about 30% just over the border in Argentina; this is just 40% of the area that existed when Europeans arrived. The forest is significant for its outstanding level of biodiversity and endemism (90% of plant species are endemic). One endemic tree that is characteristic of this forest, and fantastically unique in appearance, is the pehuén or **monkey-puzzle tree** (*Araucaria araucana*), which has been around since the time of the dinosaurs and can live for up to 3,000 years. Pure stands of monkey-puzzle trees grow in Neuquén province. Also endemic to the Valdivian Forest is the coniferous **alerce**, which can live for up to 4,000 years (second only to the bristle-cone pine) and grow to heights of 60m with a diameter of 5m. The **arrayán** (*Luma apiculata*) is a myrtle species found in the Valdivian Forest near water or humid areas. It grows very slowly, adding just 150cm in 50 years; the oldest reach almost 20m with trunks 50cm in diameter. Its slow-growing style leaves it wrinkled and twisted. Its trunk is always cool to the touch and it has distinctive red bark with white spots showing where older layers of the thin bark has peeled away. The trees spread by sending suckers along the ground to sprout up new trunks. It is found in rare groves in Parque Nacional Los Alerces and around Lake Nahuel Huapi, on Victoria Island, just west of the Llao-Llao Hotel and in the Los Arrayanes National Park (see page 301).

Magellanic Rainforest is found in the south where there is high precipitation (2.5m per year), together with peat bogs, also known as Magellanic moorland, which transitions to largely evergreen rainforest where the precipitation is approximately 0.8m per year and evergreen trees take over. The dominant species in Magellanic Rainforest are the tall **lenga** (*Nothofagus pumilio*) and **guindo** (*N. betuloides*) trees. Stands of lenga cloak the mountainsides up to 600m, while the guindo prefers the damp valleys and lakeshores. The two species mix in places such as the Río Pipo valley and many south-facing slopes.

In both the Valdivian and the Magellanic forests is another species of *Nothofagus*, *N. antarctica*, or **ñire**, found, often in a dwarf form, in the southernmost reaches of the Andes and the Tierra del Fuego archipelago. The natives here once used its wood to build their canoes.

The understorey, especially dense in Tierra del Fuego, is comprised of bushes such as **pig vine** (*Gunnera magellanica*), *Blechnum* ferns, barberis or **calafate** (*Berberis* spp.), which has edible berries with legendary properties (it's said that you will inevitably return to Patagonia if you eat them), and **chaura** or prickly heath (*Pernettya mucronata*), which has edible purple berries. In clearings are: **faschine** (*Berberis* spp.), **Magellanic currant** (*Ribes magellanica*) and notro or Chilean firebush (*Embothruim coccineum*), covered in tubular scarlet flowers in spring. Also abundant is the hemiparasitic '**mistletoe**' (*Misodendrum* spp.). Other species in this ecotone are **Andean cypress** (*Pilgerodendron uviferum*) and **canelo** or winter's bark (*Drimys winteri*), a slender evergreen tree (sacred to the Mapuche) with fragrant red bark, bright green leaves and clusters of creamy white jasmine-scented flowers. Along the shore of the Beagle Channel, canelo can take over as the dominant tree species from the coihue, which is dominant inland.

Deserts

Deserts and arid lands cover approximately 60% of the area of Argentina. Quite simplistically they can be recognised as two main types: the **Monte**, and the **steppe deserts** of Patagonia, the **Puna** and the southern **Andes**.

The **Monte** is often described as being similar to the Sonoran desert; this desert type is interesting biogeographically for lying between Neotropical and Antarctic regions. It exists in four regions of Argentina: in the northwest, the central zone, Uspallata-Calingasta and parts of Patagonia, particularly on Península Valdés; in total, it amounts to an area of 325,000km^2. It extends between the Puna and Patagonian desert steppes and the east of the Andes from Salta to Chubut. It is, of course, very warm and dry, receiving an annual maximum of about 250mm of rainfall and is covered by sand and sandy soils. Generally speaking, the vegetation is mainly of **cardón** cactus and short (40–150cm high) shrubby plants, such as **creosote bushes** (*Larrea* spp.). Hardy and resourceful animals and birds such as the armadillo, cavy, jaguar, puma, tinamou and tuco-tuco are associated with this environment. The northwestern Monte desert is the most important due to its relatively intact ecosystem, yet is without any official protected areas.

The **steppe desert of the Puna** is a cold steppe located in the high northern Andean mountains. It is related to the cold **steppe desert of Patagonia** but differentiated by its higher latitude and elevation. The **Andean steppe** borders the central Puna desert to the northeast and the two are separated from the Patagonian steppe by the rainforests along the Patagonian Andes and the eastern Monte desert.

The vegetation of the cold steppe is mainly short, stocky, hardy species of shrubs and grasses such as *Poa*, *Stipa* and *Bromus* spp. Many of the shrubs have spines as a defence against grazing herbivores. Several plants have deep rhizomes or tap roots and fleshy water-retaining leaves, while certain tiny plants mimic stones. The **cojín** (cushion plant) is probably the most representative and easily identifiable steppe plant; it can be herbaceous, semi-woody or woody but is recognised by its habit of growing pressed to the ground in dense mats, an adaptive measure to withstand extreme temperatures and winds. Sometimes other species can be growing within the mats by way of a strategy called a 'nurse-effect'. The encroaching plants reap the rewards of the cushion's ingenious form without having to trouble with evolving that way themselves. Steppe evergreens are the predominant type of shrub in this environment but there are also herbaceous and flowering varieties, which tend to remain without foliage for most of the year but when in bloom are conspicuously beautiful, attracting pollinators in the most flagrant and unabashed manner in order to take advantage of the short reproductive season. There is a high degree of endemism of plant species caused by their adaptations to survive in this demanding environment.

The **Pre-puna** is an eco-region found only in Argentina and Bolivia, occupying low mountainous areas, hill slopes and gorges from Salta and Jujuy to La Rioja and San Juan. The climate is hot and dry with summer rains and has much in common with the Monte desert with lower elevations covered in cardón cactus and hardy shrubs.

Grasslands – Pampas

Grassy prairie and grass-steppe species of Gramineae and Stipeae (*Stipa* and *Piptochaetium*) are particularly conspicuous, with perennial grasses, forbs and legumes. However, the predominant vegetation is tall thin steppe or tussock grasses, which form thick circular bunches, up to about 1.5m in diameter, with an outward radiating growth pattern. The inner, oldest grasses eventually die, creating a void in the centre of the patch and creating conspicuous rings of grass. **Pampas grass** (*Cortaderia seloana*) is a true grass of the Poaceae family. It is native to South America and also New Zealand. It is fast-growing, reaching heights of 2m and even 6m before producing tall feather-like seed heads that produce millions of seeds dispersed by the wind over great distances. It can also spread locally from rhizomes or spreading roots. It can tolerate intense sunlight and moderate drought and winter frost and can live over a decade. Shrub species do occur on the grasslands and have been observed occurring in greater numbers in recent decades; these include **chañar** (*Geoffroea decorticans*), **caldén** (*Prosopis caldenia*) and **carquejilla** (*Baccharis articulata*). Narrow and often fuzzy or hairy leaves that resist water loss are typical of grassland vegetation. In wetlands there are plants such as water lilies, cattails and other reeds. There are no trees and the fire-dependent regeneration of the grasslands prevents successional vegetation that could mature into forests. The only tree-like plant that has managed to grow on the pampas is the **ombú** (*Phytolacca dioica*), technically an evergreen shrub, although looking at a mature individual a couple of hundred years old (up to 12–15m in girth and 18m in height) you would naturally assume it to be a tree. The ombú's success on the pampas is due to its resistance to drought and fire (soft spongy wood and enlarged bases of multiple trunks that store water), cattle-grazing (its sap is poisonous, protecting it from grazing when young) and pests such as locusts. Even while the pampas have been dedicated to cattle-grazing and cleared for agriculture, the ombú were left to grow to offer limited shade for cattle and, indeed, the gaucho himself.

The humid pampas are one of the world's richest agricultural areas and for this reason have been exploited to such an extent that there are few remnants left of the original ecology, thus making the Paraná Delta and Floodplain a particularly important, interesting and complex ecological system; sections of the delta are inaccessible, creating refuges for flora and fauna. Small low-lying islands are living museums of wild and natural ecological systems, whereas more accessible lands that rise higher above water level have suffered severe degradation or modification.

The terrain is an alluvial plain of wind-transported sands or marine sediment. The climate is temperate and humid with rainfall distributed year-round and the higher temperatures moderated slightly by the river. Typical of the lower Delta are the great swamplands of rushes and floating water hyacinths, and especially the islands of dense clusters of floating aquatic plants that have consolidated and encouraged successional vegetation such as grasses to build up layer on layer. These floating islands are solid enough to carry terrestrial mammals such as marsh deer, but they feel spongy to walk upon. The larger islands actually become bowl-shaped from the weight of denser vegetation in their centres and are named *pajonales*. The particular ecological conditions of the Delta make the grass fields of the nearby pampas unusual, but instead low-level grasses of the *pajonales* develop in swampy terrain and the understorey of the forests. There are two types of forests: the diverse high and medium Delta forests; and the riparian *selva*, an intricate abundance of vines and epiphytes that reflects subtropical influences. A marginal forest of willow and river alder forms where the Delta transitions into the Chaco region.

FAUNA
Birds and mammals
Most wildlife tourism has been focused on Patagonia, for obvious reasons. There's an overview of the distinctive or important species in the *Patagonian wildlife* appendix (page 375), with some mention of similar species in the north of the country. However, there is more biodiversity in the northeastern and north-central regions of the country, especially of birdlife, comprising numerous species of songbird, colourful tropical birds, and several species of heron among the great variety of water birds. The great **harpy eagle** is the world's most powerful eagle and among the most impressive predators of the rainforest, hunting large mammals such as anteaters, howler monkeys and coatis. The male is 70cm in length and the female 90cm with a wingspan of nearly 2m. One of the most sought-after but least-seen of the northeastern birds is the **toucan**. Several birds in the subtropics, however, are difficult to see because they have potentially disappeared; **Illiger's macaw**, for instance, was last photographed in 1980. This habitat is also home to several beautiful and critically endangered mammals, such as the jaguar, anteaters, armadillos and monkeys, the latter of which are always great fun to see. **Howler monkeys** (mono carayá or aullador negro; *Alouatta caraya*) get their name from their loud vocalisations; indeed they are reputed to be the loudest land mammal in the New World, with a call that can be heard up to 5km away. It is also the largest New World monkey, reaching up to 10kg in weight; both sexes are similar in size but can be distinguished easily by colour (males are black and females are light brown). They feed mostly on leaves and occasionally fruit and maggots in the high canopy of the Chaco forest. (See page 85 for the Howler Monkey Project in La Cumbre, Córdoba.) **Caí monkeys** (*Cebus paella nigritus*) are found in the subtropical forests of Misiones, where they live in the high treetops in groups of about 20 individuals with one dominant male, feeding mainly on fruit and bromeliads but also on insects and bird eggs and chicks. They have diverse and expressive facial and vocal communications that we *Homo sapiens* love to try to decipher and anthropomorphise.

The **grey fox** (zorro gris; *Dusicyon gymnocerus*) is seen quite frequently and especially at night on country roads (throughout Argentina – see the wildlife appendix). Less common and truly a privilege to see is the **maned wolf** (aguará-guazú or lobo de crin; *Chrysocyon bradhyurus*), with its characteristic stilt-like legs.

The Chaco is important for its biodiversity, although this is for the most part unrecognised except by indigenous local peoples. For example, the giant, or **Chacoan peccary**, commonly called **tagua** (*Catagonus wagneri*), the largest and most specialised of the pig-like peccaries, was not discovered until 1974. It is endemic to the dry thorn forest of the Gran Chaco of Argentina, Bolivia and Paraguay where it lives in groups of about four individuals and feeds almost exclusively on cactus. This endangered species has been extirpated over most of its mountain range due to a combination of habitat destruction, hunting and, possibly, disease. All surviving populations are declining and becoming increasingly isolated, its best hope for survival probably being in the few protected areas within its range.

The **giant anteater** (*Myrmecophaga tridactyla*) is also highly endangered (listed as Vulnerable on the IUCN Red List), suffering from the severe habitat loss of the Chaco, like so many species in that region, but also increasingly being run over by cars or hunted for food, fur and sport. Two other anteaters are found in northern Argentina: the **southern tamandua** (*Tamandua tetradactyla*) and the **pygmy, or silky, anteater** (*Cyclopes didactylus*). The giant anteater is the world's largest anteater (1–1.2m body length, plus 45cm of snout and 65–90cm of tail, and weighing 18–39kg; in comparison the tamandua reaches only 54–88cm plus a tail of at most 60cm, and weighs a maximum of 30kg). It has a tiny mouth that only needs to open enough to allow its long tongue to pass. It has very long digits and claws which it curls under to walk on their knuckles. The tamandua defies categorisation as an anteater, tending to feed primarily on termites. The giant anteater chooses ant species without heavy jaws or chemical defences, like carpenter ants or worker termites, and can consume some 30,000 per day, yet all anteaters are wise ecologists, never cleaning out a whole nest so as not to eliminate any food source (termite and ant populations recover very quickly).

Also in the order *Xenarthra* (with anteaters and sloths), the armadillo of the Chaco is the **giant armadillo** (*Priodontes giganticus*), which can reach a length of 1.5m and weigh over 50kg. It also feeds on termites and ants and, unfortunately, has also become quite scarce for the same reasons as its other anteating relatives.

The wildlife of the Andean steppe is adapted to this rigorous climate but with a low rate of endemics; much of the wildlife, such as the **puma** and the **red fox**, can also be found in ranges that extend north or south to other regions. Sadly, one of the few endemics of the Andean steppe, the wild **chinchilla** (*Chinchilla lanigera*), is nearly extinct in the wild. The **vicuña** suffered badly from over-hunting but is now under protected status. The **guanaco** exists here in relatively sound numbers after surviving over-hunting and extreme loss of habitat elsewhere.

Many subtropical species migrate down into the Delta from the northern Misiones Forest; the Delta fauna is naturally rich in wetland species. The **carpincho** or capybara (*Hydrochaeris hydrochaerisis*) particularly noteworthy for its weight of up to 60kg, which makes it the world's largest rodent. There is also the **coipo** (*Myocaster coypus*), a local kind of beaver, whose abundance and indifference to human presence make it easy to observe. Several species of deer are found, each in its specialised habitat throughout the Litoral and into the Pampa. The one that surprises tourists by popping its head up from the foliage of the floating delta islands is the very particular **marsh deer** (ciervo del los pantanos or guazú-pucú; *Blastocerus dichotomus*). There is also the **pampas deer** (venado de las pampas or guazú-ti; *Ozotoceros bezoarticus*) and the **grey brocket deer** (Corzuela parda or guazú-birá or guazuncho; *Mazama gouazoubira*).

Reptiles and amphibians

This group of animals is not abundant in Argentina, and amphibians completely disappear in the far south of Patagonia. Naturally, the northeastern subtropical forests and wetlands more than compensate. There are two **caiman** species in the swamplands of Mesopotamia, the broad-snouted caiman or yacaré ñato or overo (*Caiman latirostris*), and the black caiman called yacaré negro (*Caiman yacare*). The **tegu lizard** (*Tupinambis* spp) can be seen in the late afternoons in Iguazú, typically in search of forbidden handouts near the cafeteria. A large group of South American lizards that spread throughout Argentina is the *Liolaemus* genus of spiny lizards. The **Austral lizard** (lagartija austral; *Liolaemus magellanicus*; 25cm), found in the south is a notable example, but there are several species (for example *L. andinus*, *L. ruibali*, *L. buergeri* and *L. fitzgeraldi*) in the northern Andean region. In addition the **Patagonian lizard** (lagartija patagónica; *Diploaemus bibrioni*; 20cm) is fairly common.

There are a few species of Geochelone **tortoises** in South America. The Argentine tortoise (tortuga terrestre; *Chelonidis donosobarrosi* or *Geochelone chilensis chilensis*), and the Chaco tortoise (*Geochelone chilensis*) are both native to Argentina and Paraguay, and despite the name do not exist in Chile. The smaller Chaco tortoise (20cm in length) is suffering from habitat loss, owing to the destruction of the Chaco Forests by slash-and-burn agriculture and overgrazing by livestock, mainly goats, and is on the IUCN Red List of Threatened Animals. In addition, an enormous threat to this animal along with many Chaco species, such as the blue-fronted parrot, is the pet trade. Although it is illegal to capture and sell or export this tortoise, it is estimated that some 75,000 Chaco tortoises are captured per year and manage to be exported all around the world, and about a third of those die within the first year of captivity. The rate of recovery of the population is very slow owing to its desperately slow reproductive rate: only one to six eggs are laid between January and March and incubation can range from 125 to over 365 days! To add to all this, unfortunately, this tortoise is also poached for its flesh.

Argentina has relatively abundant snake life. There are two vipers, the **Patagonian lancehead** (yarará ñata; *Bothrops ammodytoides*; 60cm), the southernmost snake species in the world ranging almost as far as Tierra del Fuego, and the urutu (*B. alternatus*). The Colubridae family include the **brown mussurana** (*Clelia rustica*), the **stripe-bellied watersnake** (*Liophis poecilogyrus sublineatus*) and **Dorbigny's hognose snake** (*Lystrophis dorbignyi*). Other snakes include **Bibron's whiptail** (*Cnemidophorus lacertoides*) and the **matuasto** (*Diplolaemus darwinii*), as well as coral snakes, rattlesnakes and pit-vipers. The **Valdivian snake** (culebra valdiviana; *Tachymenes peruviana*) is poisonous but not lethal and prefers to snap at the Darwin's frog rather than humans.

The **Darwin's frog** (sapito vaquero or ranita de Darwin; *Rhinoderma darwinii*) was found in the Valdivian Forest by the naturalist for whom it is named. It has a fascinating and peculiar breeding behaviour: the female lays the eggs in the typical manner but the male soon gobbles them up, not to ingest them however, but to incubate them in his vocal sac. After a few days they change into tadpoles, but he continues to carry them for 50 more days! Five to 15 froglets eventually exit from the mouth of the father, who does not eat throughout this period. There are several frog species specific to the Nothofagus Forest, Valdivian Forest or even to a single national park, such as the rana de Chalhuaco, a relict species found only in Nahual Huapi National Park. The **variegated toad** (sapito de tres rayas; *Bufo variegatus*) is fairly common, and there are several geckos, including the **Patagonian gecko** (geko patagónico; *Homonota darwinii*) and **Borelli's gecko** (*H. borellii*).

MARINE ECOSYSTEMS

Argentina's coastline is 8,397km long and mostly undeveloped, natural and rugged, yet 45% of the population lives within 100km of it. It boasts marine life that is so abundant and visible that it draws many tourists to Argentina, notably for whale-watching. Locations such as Península Valdés have worldwide acclaim as wildlife hotspots, most notably for whales and other charismatic fauna such as dolphins, elephant seals, sea lions, seals and penguins. The Tierra del Fuego and Monte León National Parks are the two coastal national parks protecting the unique flora and fauna of these ecosystems but there are 32 officially designated protected areas of various jurisdictions protecting marine or litoral areas.

Argentina has 798,373km^2 of continental shelf with significant fish stocks. The fishing industry produces an average 890,725 tons of fish per year, plus 426,985 metric tons of molluscs and crustaceans (excluding aquaculture or fish-farming). This, however, is mostly for export – the per capita annual consumption of fish is only 8kg or 2% of the total protein consumed; a greater percentage come from beef and lamb, of course. There is also a great deal of unregulated competition from foreign ships off the southern shores of Ushuaia towards Antarctica. Unlike ports further north where tourist demand has increased the supply of fish and shellfish in restaurants, Ushuaia lacks a fishermen's wharf, has one, perhaps two, fish vendors in the marina and doesn't have much seafood on the menu. The local people rarely eat it and lamb is by far the more popular dish.

The coastal and oceanic habitats of Argentina are influenced by two currents and strong tides that can reach 7m. The Brazil current, flowing south along the eastern shores of South America, is strongest off the coast of Brazil but becomes quite weak from the Tropic of Capricorn south. It then meets with the second current, the Malvinas, near the latitude of Buenos Aires. The Brazil current is pushed eastward into the Atlantic by the cold Malvinas current moving north from Patagonia. Owing to the warmer temperatures of the Brazil current, it is oxygen-poor and lacks any great abundance of plankton and fish, and therefore of seabirds or marine mammals too. The Malvinas current, however, is cold owing to the Antarctic waters it carries. Westerly winds between the southern tip of Argentina and Antarctica cause an upwelling of cold nutrient-rich waters to the surface and push them along the continental shelf of Patagonia. This is the foundation of the food chain that sustains the remarkable biodiversity of coastal Patagonia, from abundant fish and birdlife up to the magnificent large mammals such as the southern right whale and elephant seal.

HISTORY

The Argentine historian Félix Luna wrote in his *A Short History of the Argentinians* that 'to summarise Argentinean history … is a sacrilege because historical processes are always intricately interrelated. Any attempt to simplify them in a way betrays the goals of accuracy and faithfulness that must inspire the historian. But it is also true that history is by definition boundless, ungraspable, [and] untellable.' Alas, we must attempt such a folly. Mr Luna's book was 15 chapters long; here we will commit the offence of summarising the history of Argentina in these next few pages!

Human settlement in what is now Argentina dates back many thousands of years, and the groups that lived there in prehistoric times are described on pages 33–8. In this section, we will start with the arrival of the first Europeans in 1516, when a Spanish expedition led by **Juan Díaz de Solís** landed on the Río de la Plata estuary and claimed the territory for the Spanish Crown. The Ríos de la Plata and Paraná had been navigated by 1517 and the first settlement near what is today Buenos Aires was established in 1536 by **Pedro de Mendoz**a; poor knowledge of the natural resources and conflict with the Querandí people led to the abandonment of the colony. It was not until 1580 that **Juan de Garay** was able to re-found the city that would grow to become Buenos Aires. The first European to visit Patagonia was Portuguese explorer **Ferdinand Magellan**, in 1520, commissioned by the Spanish Crown.

Between 1543 and 1565 settlers from Chile crossed the Andes into the Cuyo region, founding what would become the cities of San Juan, Mendoza and San Luis. Similarly, Santa Fé and Corrientes were established by settlers from Asunción. The oldest city in Argentina is Santiago del Estero, founded by **Francisco de Aguirre** in 1553 as a dependency of Santiago de Chile, passing to the government of Tucumán in 1563. It is known as the 'Mother of Cities' because it was from here that the founding expeditions to Salta, Jujuy, Catamarca, La Rioja, Tucumán and Córdoba departed. Among the first cities to be founded were Córdoba della Nueva Andalusía (1573, by Jerónimo Luis de Cabrera) and Santa Fé (1573, by Juan de Garay). The period 1578–79 saw Franciscan missions throughout the Río de la Plata region and the first Jesuit mission was established in 1610 at San Ignacio Guazú.

The 16th and 17th centuries were largely uneventful apart from what could be considered Argentina's first war in 1680, when a Portuguese expedition landed at Colonia del Sacramento in what is now Uruguay and for trade reasons refused to leave. **José de Garro**, the governor of Buenos Aires, sought the support of Córdoba, Tucumán and La Rioja, which was swiftly provided, with the other provinces following. Additional support came from an army of Guaraní Indians sent by the Jesuit missionaries (who already disliked the Portuguese due to events in Brazil). Garro's attack was a massacre that reinforced Buenos Aires's influence and growing recognition; it was rough and young, only a hundred years old, but was able to draw on the support of older and more sophisticated cities with universities and theatres and thus the support of the country.

It was the British who next set their sights upon Argentina, and Buenos Aires in particular, seizing the territory from Spain in June 1806. *La Defensa* was the first of only a few significant events that would liberate Argentina to its autonomy. The British had noticed that the Spanish garrison or *Regimiento Fijo* (Fixed Regiment) had become somewhat defunct. What they did not perceive was the prowess of the urban militia that met their attack. The military arena had been left wide open for the *criollos*, Argentines of Spanish descent who were generally poor and eager to take a soldier's salary to defend their birthplace. The militia, led by **Santiago de Liniers**, staged an uprising and forced the British to surrender on 12 August. What was significant was that the residents (*porteños*) had organised their own defence without the aid of the colonial power and decisions were made without reference to Madrid or the viceroy. Furthermore, the events culminated in the overthrow of the Spanish viceroy, **Rafael de Sobremonte**, who had fled (under orders to place priority on protecting Spanish funds from looting) and was replaced by Liniers. A second attempt by the British in July 1807 is known as *La Reconquista*; it was led by Major-General **John Whitelock** with 10,000 soldiers. The militia, again led by Liniers, was aided by women and children bombarding the British troops with boiling water and oil from windows and balconies. The strategic error of frontal attack on a now fortified city resulted in the immediate loss of about a third of the British troops, the remainder being evacuated to Montevideo.

Independent Argentina

Meanwhile, political events back in Europe would fuel revolutionary sentiments in Buenos Aires. Napoleon's manoeuvres to bring about the fall of the Bourbon dynasty in Spain led to a revolt in Buenos Aires in May 1810 that overthrew the viceroy and replaced him with an autonomous governing body. The **May Revolution of 1810** was revolutionary simply for the massive paradigm shift that took place in the people assuming that they could choose their rulers; to crown a king was a decision previously made by God or war. Seeing that their rightful king had had his crown wrongly taken from him, the people saw no other choice but to determine their own leadership. The Spanish forces were defeated by **General Manuel Belgrano** and on 9 July 1816 a group of *criollos* met in Tucumán and proclaimed the independence of the Argentine Republic from Spain (which is why so many streets and plazas are named 9 de Julio). The decade from 1810 onwards was a great period of liberation during which Argentina not only freed itself, but also fought with Paraguay, Uruguay and Bolivia as they all broke away, and helped to liberate Chile from Spanish rule in 1817-18 when General **José de San Martín** led the Army of the Andes into Chile and defeated the Spanish, continuing to drive them from Peru by 1821.

The **Congress of Tucumán** moved to Buenos Aires and began to draw up the Constitution. Now referred to as the **Constitution of 1819**, this was never implemented due to its monarchist inclinations. There was a clear political divide between the bookish legalistic federalists and the romantic and charismatic *caudillos* (military strongmen) who called themselves the Unitarians. The latter wanted a centralised government while the federalists opposed the republican system and were in favour of a sort of direct democracy. They also rejected the proposed Constitution because it would have entrenched the wealth and power of Buenos Aires rather than sharing it with the struggling frontier provinces. In fact a federalist system was established unofficially through the *caudillo*-instigated uprising of 1820 now known as the **Battle of Cepeda**. The soldiers of the National Army, refusing to fight their countrymen, left Buenos Aires for Córdoba and thus the Congress was overthrown. The **Treaty of Pilár** was signed, establishing the federal system in Argentina. Buenos Aires was simply one of the 13 provinces of what was internationally recognised as an independent country known as the United Provinces of the River Plate (Provincias Unidas del Río de la Plata), each with an elected legislature that appointed a governor. The first president of the United Provinces of the River Plate was **Bernardino Rivadavia**, who had been active in the resistance to the British invasions and in the movement for independence in 1810 and was involved from 1811 to 1812 with creating a strong central government. This government outlawed the slave trade in 1813 (although slaves already in service at the time remained in bondage, with most, though not all, being granted their freedom by 1827); it also established the freedom of the press and organised an army.

Rivadavia had tried for years to establish a national constitution in order to achieve agrarian reform and encourage immigration. Regrettably, the *caudillos* of the interior opposed him and then the **Cisplatine War** (1825–28) with Brazil over the status of Uruguay distracted Rivadavia. The blocking of Brazilian encroachment into Uruguay was considered the last requirement for complete independence. Negotiations proved futile and war was declared, ending in Argentina and Uruguay winning their land claims while Brazil imposed a stifling trade blockade on the United Provinces of the River Plate. A peace treaty was eventually signed that established the borders of Argentina and Uruguay (Paraguay had remained neutral and was in effect ignored) and resulted in the breakdown of the viceroyalty of the River Plate, with Buenos Aires recognised as the centre of government.

Manuel Dorrego, the federal governor of Buenos Aires, was overthrown in a coup by veterans of the Brazilian wars led by **Juan Lavalle**, leading to civil war; the campaign against Lavalle was led by **Juan Manuel de Rosas**, a wealthy federalist *caudillo* and experienced soldier. He had been born on a great estancia and raised among the gauchos, leading to their support of his future campaigns. After much battling and negotiation, Rosas was able to oust Lavalle and take power. In 1829 the United Provinces of the River Plate fell and Rivadavia resigned; in his place Rosas became governor of the province of Buenos Aires, asserting the province's independence, which was opposed by the Unitarian league under General Paz. The **Federal Pact of 1831** united Buenos Aires, Santa Fé and Corrientes in a military front against the Unitarians who were soon defeated, with Paz imprisoned. The pact also covered economics and especially free trade, which had flooded the market with British imports, eliminating local crafts and draining the local currency. In a protectionist effort, customs duties were increased on wine, wheat and leather. It was proposed to abolish duties and domestic taxes on trade within the country and to distribute customs revenues throughout the country, but this was blocked by Buenos Aires.

Rosas sought virtually dictatorial powers but these were refused by the provincial council; having achieved re-election, he theatrically resigned as governor in 1832 and formed the *Sociedad Popular Restauradora* and its offshoot terror-wing the *mazorca*. In 1834 war broke out between Tucumán and Salta; Rosas urged General **Juan Facundo Quiroga**, the so-called 'Jaguar of the Plains', to establish peace and retired to the estancia where, on 20 December 1834, he wrote his famous Letter from the Hacienda de Figueroa to General Quiroga regarding his position on the government of Argentina. Quiroga was soon assassinated by agents of Rosas with the letter in his pocket, ending all hopes of constitutional agreement. This bloodstained letter is held today in the National Archives. Rosas had himself forcibly reinstated as governor in 1835, ruling by fear for the next 17 years. Red clothing and badges identified supporters of his federalist regime and opposing Unitarians who dared to wear their emblematic blue were imprisoned or executed. The '**Generation of 1837**' who opposed his dictatorship included Juan Bautista Alberdi, **Bartolomé Mitre** and **Domingo Faustino Sarmiento**, all later influential political figures.

Justo José de Urquiza also opposed Rosas' government, and when political infighting broke out within the decrepit government in 1851, he staged a rebellion with the support of exiled Unitarians and allies in Brazil (against which Rosas had recently declared war). The **Battle of Caseros** in 1852 led to the resignation of Rosas (who went into exile in England); Urquiza called elections, won by the *Porteñistas* with **Vincente López y Planes** elected governor. Urquiza, bent on implementing a national constitution, called on provincial representatives to meet in San Nicolás de los Arroyos where the **San Nicolás Agreement** was signed. This gave each province equal representation of two deputies, upsetting Buenos Aires which sought a system based on relative populations. Combined with the Treaty of Pilár, the Federal Pact and other agreements, this is referred to as the **Preamble of the Constitution**, which was signed in 1853. The provisional government that this agreement established was called a Directoire and Urquiza was elected Director, giving him control of the military and customs. In the end, Buenos Aires rejected the agreement and Vincente López y Planes resigned. In desperation, Urquiza staged a coup and took over the governorship but a popular revolt forced him out – for a moment. Soon afterwards, provincial representatives met in Santa Fé and approved the 1853 Constitution, electing Urquiza president. Buenos Aires remained outside the Constitution and was seen as an autonomous state. The rest of the country formed the Argentine Confederation of 13 provinces with a congress and executive based in Paraná.

The Argentine Republic

Efforts to bring Buenos Aires into the Confederation and finally obtain national unity led to another war and the Battle of Pavón in 1861. Urquiza's confederate forces defeated the *porteño* infantry led by **Bartolomé Mitre**, but his support had spread beyond Buenos Aires, forcing elections to be held in 1862. Mitre's Liberals won and he became first president of the new Argentine Republic, remaining in office until 1868. His term was marked by a free press, parliamentarianism and entrepreneurialism as well as the inauguration of many public institutions. Without formally having to declare itself, Buenos Aires now felt itself to be the capital of the nation and a national government set up its headquarters at the Viejo Fuerte or Old Fort, where the **Casa Rosada** is now located.

Economically, the new Constitution gave Mitre greater powers to entice foreign investment, yielding higher tariff revenue. Tariffs on rail transport from the interior were higher on finished goods; therefore, only raw materials were exported; this prevented economic diversification and development and perpetuated grievances from the interior, which objected to Buenos Aires draining the interior's resources. Santiago del Estero (already a poor region) had its agricultural base destroyed. Rebellion was on the horizon.

Meanwhile, Mitre was distracted throughout most of his term by the **War of the Triple Alliance** (1865–70) between Argentina, Brazil, Uruguay and Paraguay, which can be summarised as the genocide of the Paraguayan people, funded by the Bank of London, Baring Brothers and the Rothschild bank through loans at exorbitant interest rates that mortgaged the fate of the victorious countries. With their economy decimated, Paraguayans were flooding into Argentina in the hope of work picking cotton. Argentina and Uruguay blockaded the river mouths and imposed taxes on Paraguayans seeking to cross, and then declared war. Argentina won the war, but its main effect was to establish and strengthen the Argentine national army.

Mitre stepped down at the end of his first term, and provincial opposition to the power of Buenos Aires resulted in the election of **Domingo Faustino Sarmiento** (1868–74), former governor of San Juan. Sarmiento would have to deal with the first of the predicted revolts: for example, in 1870 **Ricardo López Jordán** sparked a revolution that led to the assassination of Urquiza in his palatial home in San José, and was quelled when Sarmiento sent the army into Entre Ríos. Aside from these bold events, Sarmiento occupied most of his term trying to establish schools; meanwhile, it was Mitre who tried to keep the peace between Buenos Aires and the rest of Argentina. By the time Sarmiento left power in 1874, Mitre's Liberal Party had split and it was the offshoot *Partido Autonomista Nacional* (National Autonomist Party or PAN) that won the elections. The new president, **Nicolás Avellaneda** of Tucumán (1874–80), immediately had to suppress a revolt led by the defeated Bartolomé Mitre. His ally, **Aldolfo Alsina**, became minister of war and in 1877 an agreement was made for him to succeed Avellaneda at the end of the latter's term. However, Alsina died that same year and was replaced by **General Julio Argentino Roca**.

Avellaneda focused on economic growth and the development of Patagonia, where much of the land went to speculators, politicians and rich landowners, instead of small settlers – a situation that continues today. In order to achieve his ambitions Avellaneda began to drive out the native communities from the area north of the Río Negro, placing Roca in charge of this expedition. Roca embraced his role and the motives of this campaign, using it to launch a presidential campaign himself. He launched the '**Conquest of the Desert**' – an unofficial yet wholehearted slaughter of the native peoples. It was an effective campaign and Roca became president in 1880; his term is often referred to as the 'Golden Years', although a small but powerful oligarchy essentially controlled the entire political system. Only adult male citizens over the age of 18 were eligible to vote; immigrants and women could not vote and so party platforms focused on the ambitions of the politically active elite and not the needs of the greater society. There were no secret ballots but rather voting was by public declaration; it was also inaccurate (there were no identity cards so people could vote repeatedly or alternatively be turned away if they were not known). Election turn-out was for obvious reasons extremely low; only about 10–20% of those eligible turned up to vote. Although presidential terms were limited to six years, Roca found often subversive and fraudulent avenues to ensure the election of his chosen successors. His PAN thus held Argentina in its clutches for an incredible three decades. Its members and leaders came from wealthy ranching families, giving the party the pseudonym of the Cattle Party.

The first national currency was put into circulation in 1881 by the Roca government, which set the value of the peso as equal to a quarter-ounce of gold. Argentina's foreign debt began to grow when the government began to rely on foreign loans to fund operating deficits and underwrite ambitious public works. Roca was succeeded by his brother-in-law, **Miguel Juárez Celman**, in 1886. Rather than stepping into Roca's shoes, he attempted to centralise his authority and broke ties with Roca loyalists. Opponents soon began to refer to his regime as the *Unicato* (one-man rule). His main platform was based upon economic development through foreign investment. In 1885 Celman abandoned the gold standard for the national currency and authorised an increase of the money supply by printing more pesos, while banks issued mortgage bonds to fund land purchases. In 1887 the government passed measures attempting to control the amount of printed currency in circulation and restrict the banks, but these proved ineffective. With this glut of currency in circulation and the lack of gold-backed currency, the economy overheated. In 1889–90 the Baring Brothers bank of London issued shares to fund public works in the city of Buenos Aires. Back in 1824 Barings had given Buenos Aires a £1 million loan, to be paid back in gold; by the beginning of the 20th century, the debt stood at £4 million. Owing to concerns over Argentina's unstable economy and rising foreign dept, there were no subscribers to Barings's current proposal, which created a panic in the financial market. Investment from Great Britain and elsewhere ceased, resulting in the so-called Baring Crisis. Exports, and thus the value of the peso, dropped and a recession hit. The crisis shook the government and stirred the other parties into action.

In 1890 a faction of the opposition *Unión Cívica* (Civic Union or UC) emerged as the most potent threat to the PAN: the *Unión Cívica Radical* (Radical Civic Union or UCR) led by **Leandro Alem**. The third major party was the *Partido Socialista* or Socialist Party, which also began as a faction of the UC, splitting in 1891 into a separate party led by none other than the tireless Mitre himself.

Trying to brush Celman's blunders under the carpet, Roca returned to the scene to maintain the PAN's control. When the UC launched a rebellion, supported by Mitre, Roca made a deal, agreeing to support Mitre's candidacy for the presidency in 1892 if Mitre agreed to preserve the PAN government in the meantime, with vice-president **Carlos Pellegrini** replacing Celman. The pact was sealed, the revolt ended and Celman resigned in August 1890. Roca and Pellegrini recovered the PAN's political position, and then broke the pact with Mitre for the 1892 elections, putting **Luis Saénz Peña** in the Casa Rosada instead.

The UCR accused the PAN regime of broad corruption and demanded free and fair elections. UCR local parties brought voters to the polls under armed protection. By 1893 the UCR had grown in strength and Alem launched a rebellion, but fear deterred many party branches from participating. The UCR presented a strong challenge to the PAN in local and regional elections in 1894–96, but PAN, with the government behind it, presented an insurmountable obstacle. Roca built alliances with the governors of the most important provinces, expanded trade incentives and filled the state's coffers with tariff revenues, which he used to reward his supporters. Alem eventually lost faith and committed suicide in 1896. His nephew, **Hipólito Yrigoyen**, assumed the leadership of the UCR, which withdrew from the tainted electoral process and urged its followers to cast blank ballots in protest, thus supporting the ideal of a democratic electoral system while also forcing a count of blank ballots to condemn the current situation. This created a swell of public support and an attempted rebellion in 1905 that resulted in the UCR being banned for a year.

Seeking a solution to the challenge of the UCR, the next elections saw **Roque Sáenz Peña**, a conservative member of the PAN but in favour of electoral reform, step up to the presidential plate for the 1910–16 term. Making a declaration of its commitment to fair process, the PAN felt confident enough to take what was the radical risk of allowing fair voting. The Sáenz Peña electoral reform law took effect in 1912, giving all Argentine-born males over 18 years of age the right to vote and also making it mandatory and by means of secret ballot. At the next election in 1916 the UCR won a sweeping victory and Yrigoyen became president.

There was massive immigration to Argentina above all in the years 1857–1916, when around six million people arrived from Europe (45% from Italy and 33% from Spain, and just 1% from Britain, although they came to dominate many industries, notably the railways); in 1914 three-quarters of the adult male population of Buenos Aires was foreign-born, and therefore without a vote.

During his time in office, Yrigoyen would have to deal with the impacts of the Great War. His government maintained neutrality despite strong economic ties to Great Britain. His government also introduced public education accessible to all including immigrants, who were also allowed to enter public service without discrimination. The ethics and ideals were strongly opposed to those of the outdated era of nepotism and elitism. The living standard of the working class rose and aside from a few remaining Socialists and minor factions the country unanimously supported the UCR. The next political split was to come from within the UCR itself, with the Anti-personalist and the Yrigoyenista movements emerging in 1924. The party's internal intellectual polemic rose to a frenetic level that led to the 1930 Revolution and – what during the UCR's peak would have been inconceivable – the breakdown of democracy.

Military rule

For the first time in Argentine history, the elected government was overthrown in a military coup. Despite the split within the UCR between Yrigoyen's supporters and opponents, Yrigoyen was elected for a second term in 1928; however, he made several economic blunders and began to be perceived as incompetent. He was also the victim of appalling slander and invasion of privacy that seems fairly normal nowadays but was atypical in his day. The public was shocked by the number of loyalists who were on the government payroll without working; but what eventually caused the greatest public alarm occurred in November 1929 when a young Anti-personalist was shot in the street in Mendoza by a Yrigoyen loyalist. Soon after there was an attempted assassination of Yrigoyen. The 1930 elections saw the loss of the Radical party's support in Buenos Aires and the rumours of a military conspiracy began to circulate.

Right-wing nationalists began to unite behind **General José Félix Uriburu**, who proceeded to lead a small convoy of troops into Buenos Aires on 6 September 1930. Yrigoyen offered to step down and allow his vice-president to take over the presidency, but Uriburu was not interested and took complete control as provisional president. For the next year, Uriburu's government attempted to deal with the economic crisis triggered by the depression throughout the Western world. It cut government spending and tried to balance the budget. Feeling confident of public approval, Uriburu offered an election in Buenos Aires. To his surprise, the Radicals still had far more support than his regime, reflecting the public's condemnation of the coup. Uriburu thus annulled the election and blocked UCR participation in future elections. At the 1931 election the conservatives saw their chance to step into the UCR's empty shoes, and campaigned as the *Partido Democrático Nacional* (National Democratic Party or PDN), combining forces with the Anti-personalist Radicals and the Independent Socialists. The shoes fit and **Agustín P Justo** became president in February 1932. There were now three parties in congress, which together formed a regime known as the Concordancia, following the same ethical approaches as Roca's government: fraud, force and corruption. Elections were rigged and the Concordancia thus maintained control of the government until 1943. The public hated Justo and routinely booed him at his public appearances – the most infamous occasion was at a Palermo horserace where he obviously reached the limits of his tolerance and saluted the hecklers with a well-known obscene gesture. Nevertheless, Justo was effective and undertook a great deal of public works, notably on the highway system. He made a good job of economic revitalisation in a depression era and pulled Argentina back into a strong global economic position, maintaining good ties with Britain. **Roberto Ortiz** was chosen as the Concordancia's candidate for the next presidential term and won the usual pretence of a democratic election. He did not complete his term owing to illness and his vice-president **Ramón S Castillo** took over the presidency.

The Rise of Peronism

When the Concordancia's next in line, **Robustiano Patrón Costa**, was readying himself for his candidacy, the Radicals had an epiphany, deciding to no longer abstain from the proceedings and proposing as their presidential candidate **General Pedro Pablo Ramírez**. As war minister he had the clout to prevent vote rigging, and thus the Radicals were able to collect their majority vote again. Castillo ordered Ramírez to withdraw his candidacy, leading to the Campo de Mayo armed uprising. In 1943, the *Grupo de Oficiales Unidos* (Group of United Officers or GOU) staged a military coup, with **General Arturo Rawson** as head of operations, supported by various colonels, one of whom was the young **Juan Domingo Perón**. President Castillo was deposed and Rawson became defacto president until the GOU installed Ramírez in June 1943. This was of course all taking place at the end of World War II and Argentina's neutrality aggravated the United States, which removed its ambassador from Buenos Aires and blocked imports of Argentine beef. Great Britain was lenient since it also respected the neutrality of Ireland and needed Argentine imports. Argentina was increasingly seen as fascist thanks to its friendly relations with Mussolini's Italy and Franco's Spain, and soon Argentina was discovered to be buying arms from Germany. Ramírez was forced out of office by the army and replaced with the war minister, **General Farrell**, in March 1944. Using United Nations membership as bait, Argentina was forced not only to break relations with the Axis powers but to actually declare war on Germany, and Japan, in the eleventh hour of the war.

Eventually, an American ambassador returned to Argentina, but not to resume diplomatic ties; Mr **Spruille Braden** was coming to deliver democracy. He campaigned throughout the country, spreading propaganda about how the USA was putting an end to totalitarianism in Europe and Asia. With much public discontent towards the government, Braden might have evangelised the country had it not been for the greater influence of trade minister Juan Perón among the working class, a stratum of society historically overlooked. Through wage increases and other benefits Perón appealed to the existing trade unions and also set up unions for previously non-unionised trades. When strikes broke out, Perón came in to mediate and favoured the unions, ensuring their solidarity with the military. When he began enforcing strong social policies such as paid and guaranteed vacations, limited working hours, and medical, pension and other social benefits, business and factory owners began to protest and sided with an opposition campaign, backed by the USA and Britain, to oust the military government. Under public pressure that threatened his government, Farrell forced Perón to resign and had him arrested and held prisoner on Isla Martín García. Perón's supporters mobilised and presented a strong challenge, in conjunction with the union leaders, the military and the followers of his celebrity mistress, Eva Mariá Duarte, or **Evita**. A demonstration outside the Casa Rosada on 17 October 1945 demanded Perón's release, and Farrell had little choice but to publicly reinstate him and call a national election to end the crisis. Naturally, Perón seized the moment and ran for president. The aforementioned Braden saw Perón's strong chance of winning and campaigned against him, which only gave Perón more publicity. The elections became 'Braden or Perón', with Perón drawing nationalist support; supporting him was akin to denouncing foreign influence. Perón won the presidency in 1946, with 54% of the vote.

For many years the dominant party would be the Justicialist Party (PJ), better known as the Peronist Party; it has been described as a conservative populist party with nationalist views on the economy and foreign policy. His government was an extension of the military dictatorship with the armed forces at its foundation. He increased military spending and the power of the military, and many officers were given government posts or positions in public institutions, such as the Central Bank, replacing the former directors. Citizens who were public in their opposition to the government were declared enemies of the state. Newspapers were censored or shut down, universities were tightly controlled and professors identified as opposed to the regime lost their jobs, as did wayward judges. Despite his totalitarian inclinations, Perón's strong labour ties and links with popular *caudillos* allowed the party to survive for decades. He gave the masses access to the political and economic benefits of industrialisation, and an industrial bourgeoisie was born, which didn't differ much from the previous ruling classes. The economy grew and became more self-sufficient in reaction to punitive tariffs imposed by the US that effectively blocked Argentine exports. However, there was no change to the land ownership system and the government didn't nationalise the US- and British-owned meat and wool plants, as it still needed foreign capital. Foreign oligopolies took over Argentine industry as the Latin American market as a whole was integrated into the multinational economy.

In 1948 the US launched the Marshall Plan, granting loans and credit to shattered European countries, partly in order to increase exports of grain and meat, Argentina's traditional strengths, from North America to Europe. Argentina's economic focus shifted from agriculture to industry, which was expanded to meet domestic needs, seeing a 43% growth by 1953. Surpluses were used to buy back foreign-owned infrastructure (such as the formerly British-owned railway system and gas company) to liberate transportation, communications, power and utilities.

Evita became Perón's wife soon after his election to the presidency and though she held no formal political title, she took full advantage of her political position and her growing celebrity status to lead the Women's Branch of the Peronist Party and generate support of its policies within sectors of the public that formerly had no voice. The standard of living of the working class, the majority of the public, rose significantly and Juan Perón and Evita won the hearts of the Argentines. Perón won re-election in 1952 but soon after Evita died of cancer. Perón's loss was both personal and strategic; Evita is to this day a phenomenon in the mystique she held over her people, being practically elevated to the status of a saint upon her death. Indeed, Perón, who was a strong Catholic and had introduced the catechism into the public school system, requested Evita be canonised. When the church refused, Perón retaliated, removing its teachings from the school curriculum and publicly denouncing it as unpatriotic. Along with aggressive and unprofessional public addresses and scandals in his personal life, this caused his supporters to lose faith and respect in him; the economy also began to slide, in part owing to his over-nationalistic and protectionist policies, now creating a significant trade deficit and inflation. In an attempted assassination, the **Plaza de Mayo** was bombed, killing 200 to 300 people; simultaneously churches were being burned. In a famously fanatical speech in the Plaza de Mayo in the aftermath of the bombings, Perón encouraged civil war. This last blunder lost him the support of the armed forces, which overthrew him in September 1955, forcing him into exile.

General **Eduardo Lonardi** led the coup, establishing a coalition government of military and civilian groups, but he was not swift enough to address the economic crisis at hand and only held power for a couple of months. Soon **General Pedro Aramburu** stepped in, acting as provisional president until 1958. He scrapped many Peronist programmes, discharged real or suspected supporters of Perón from the armed forces, and created new unions. Thousands of union leaders were arrested and they along with the Peronist Party were banned from political activity. Of course this sparked protests that culminated into a revolt led by General **Juan José Valle** in 1956. In response, Aramburu ordered the execution of 27 of the officers involved. The dictatorship next addressed the economy; the currency was devalued to cut imports and boost exports, but by 1957 this had had little effect and popular resistance was ever growing. Elections were set for 1958 and the dictatorship seemed to wish to back out of its responsibilities. With the Peronists banned from running, rumour has it that Perón strategised to support Radical Party (UCR) leader **Arturo Frondizi** in a secret pact that would legalise the Peronist Party in the future. Frondizi was elected and civilian rule returned. A new economic strategy was top of the incoming government's agenda. Tight controls on trade and finance were implemented in an attempt to redirect revenue into the development of new industries. To rally the support of the working class and Peronist supporters, Frondizi authorised massive wage increases and price freezes on consumer goods. The result was rapid inflation and a decline in industrial and rural production. The economy was on the verge of collapse when Frondizi sought the assistance of the International Monetary Fund (IMF). Economic policies had to be reversed, which meant an end to price freezes, trade and exchange controls, cuts in government spending and employment and an increase in utility and transportation rates. The IMF then granted a US$328 million loan. However, the measures taken were insufficient and, disregarding the national interest in keeping control of raw resources, Frondizi allowed US-owned Standard Oil to develop potential oil deposits in Patagonia. This was the last straw for the Peronists who orchestrated yet another revolt as Perón made public his secret pact with Frondizi. Frondizi scrambled for support but was arrested by the military, who again took charge of the government until the election of **Arturo Illia** as president in 1963.

Economic and political conditions in these years created a to and fro between military takeovers and riots and protests to regain civilian rule. Two factions appeared: those in support of constitutional rule, backed by the army and the air force (the navy remained neutral), labelled themselves *Los Azules* (The Blues) and were opposed by those in support of civilian rule, called *Los Colorados* (The Reds). The international community began to get more involved with, for example, the US threatening to suspend economic aid if a dictatorship took the helm again. By 1965 inflation was out of control, with prices for consumer goods rising at an estimated 30% per year. In 1966 the armed forces took over, dissolving congress, suspending the Constitution and the Supreme Court, banning all political parties and forcing the resignations of all elected politicians, with **Juan Carlos Onganía** as the new president. He was known to be ideologically rigid, with an admiration for Franco's regime in Spain, and viewed the military as the protector of civilian and Christian values. The economy remained a fundamental problem and his policies would only fuel further revolt. For example, a new land tax that levied higher taxes on unproductive land than on productive land was vehemently rejected by the cattle oligarchy and was never implemented. Rifts between the business community and the unions persisted. Popular protests became riots and more and more often were met by military force. Argentina appeared on the verge of anarchy and the economy in a state of chaos.

The Dirty War

By the end of the 1960s, several leftist groups had formed with dreams of political change through armed resistance and revolt. Their movement paralleled international events in Latin America such as the Cuban Revolution led by Fidel Castro and Argentine-born **Ernesto 'Che' Guevera**. The two most potent guerrilla groups in Argentina were the Montoneros and the *Ejército Revolucionario del Pueblo* (Revolutionary Army of the People or ERP). The Montoneros pursued a strategy of political kidnappings which culminated in the assassination of Pedro Aramburo in 1970, while the ERP attacked military posts. The government of course staged counterattacks, the mobilisation of the *Alianza Argentina Anticomunista* (Argentine Anticommunist Alliance or AAA) escalating the level of violence in the country. By 1975 the economy was near collapse; the peso was devalued by more than 150% against the US dollar and hyperinflation reached an estimated 1000%. A parallel unregulated economy had emerged through clandestine agreements between buyers and suppliers struggling to keep their businesses afloat. The economic and political uncertainties affected the social basis of the country as well. For example, although traditionally education was prized, in the 1970s shockingly few Argentines (just 14%) completed secondary education, and only 4% received university degrees, leading to long-term problems with an uneducated workforce.

With the escalating violence and resulting economic instability, the military sought greater control. Onganía was dismissed in 1970 and General **Alejandro Lanusse** attempted to return Argentina to civilian rule, seeing Juan Perón as the country's only possible redeemer. He approved Perón's return from exile after 15 years and the Peronist Party won the 1973 election by a great majority, despite violence that killed and injured hundreds of people. Juan Perón became president for an unprecedented third term. However, Argentina would still not be saved from its turmoil and after a single year in office and before he could effect any significant change, Perón died of a heart attack on 1 July 1974. His widow María Estela Martínez (Isabelita) succeeded him but was driven from power by another military coup. The commander-in-chief of the armed forces, **Jorge Rafael Videla**, took over the presidency in 1976 and launched the 'Process of National Reorganisation', which turned out to be the darkest era in Argentina's history. The atrocities that took place in the years 1976-83 are known as the Dirty War (*Guerra Sucia*), a state-run campaign of terrorism against real and suspected enemies of the state. Any person suspected of opposing the government was kidnapped or assassinated by the AAA. Up to 30,000 people were killed or 'disappeared'. A penal code punished writers, publishers, distributors and consumers of books considered subversive. The majority of those kidnapped and disappeared were union activists; strikes in 1977 risked not only one's job but one's life. In 1977 *las madres* (the mothers, and grandmothers) of the victims began the silent protest against the dictatorship in Plaza de Mayo. They continue to march there on Thursday afternoons to maintain public scrutiny and demand accountability for the murders.

With what had amounted to civil war, the government lost control of economic objectives. **General Leopoldo Galtieri** was president when the dictatorship finally collapsed. In an attempt to distract from the internal conflict and arouse nationalist sentiment, Galtieri shifted public attention to the border disputes with Chile and the British occupation of the **Malvinas** (Falkland) and South Georgia Islands. In 1982 the seizure of the Malvinas led to war with Great Britain, ending Argentina's previous stance of neutrality, and a swift and embarrassing defeat that proved the military's incompetence. This led to Galtieri's resignation, the collapse of the military dictatorship and the end of the Dirty War. In 2002 Galtieri (who died in 2003) and 42 other military officers were arrested and charged with the torture and killing of 22 leftist guerrilla leaders during the dictatorship.

Modern Argentina

After elections in 1983 the Radical Party resumed office under **Raúl Alfonsín**, who approved the so-called *punto final* law to block further investigations and indictments regarding the crimes of the Dirty War. This was demanded by the military as a condition of their keeping out of politics, but even so a revolt occurred at Easter 1987 to challenge his authority. Nevertheless, the lack of accountability for human rights violations plus hyperinflation caused Alfonsín's government to lose support and he called early elections. The UCR lost and the Peronist **Carlos Saúl Menem** became president. He privatised many public industries and services to try to reduce the public deficit but the process was marred by corruption, with many government cronies making huge profits; nevertheless, he was re-elected after amending the Constitution in 1995. After ten years in office (1989-99) he is remembered for his legacy of corruption, causing the currency to become hugely over-valued when he tied the Argentine peso one to one with the US dollar, and for pardoning the human rights violations of the Dirty War. He is so reviled by many Argentines that uttering his name is considered bad luck; he is often called Mendez or 'the unnameable'. Nevertheless, after some years of semi-exile in Chile, he is set on a political comeback and was elected to the Senate in October 2005.

When **Fernando de la Rua** took office in December 1999 Argentina was slipping into an even worse recession. He was perhaps Argentina's weakest president ever, with the Partido Justicialista controlling both chambers of Congress and most of the provincial governorships, as well as dominating the trade unions and judiciary. The fixed exchange rate was clearly unsustainable after the Asian and Russian crises of 1997 and 1998, and privatisation income could no longer cover profligate public spending, but it continued unchecked. The IMF stepped in to provide 13.7 billion pesos of emergency aid in January 2001 and another 8 billion pesos in August. It was not enough – in December the economy collapsed when foreign debt reached 58% of GDP, and public protests and riots (with at least 27 killed) forced de la Rua to resign. Argentina then defaulted on its foreign debt of 155 billion pesos – the largest such default in history. **Eduardo Duhalde**, leader of the non-Menemist wing of the Peronists, was named president (the country's fifth in less than three weeks, after three interim presidents had failed to establish themselves) by the Congress on 1 January 2002, and his first act was to devalue the Argentine peso. All investments and savings that were tied one to one with the US dollar were instantly converted to pesos, at a fraction of their value, triggering riots. In the hours immediately before and after the event, Argentines desperately attempted to withdraw their savings, causing a national financial crisis. Banks locked their doors and withheld funds; people were not able to access their bank accounts for days and then were only able to withdraw minimal amounts. In the end, the value of the peso was set at four to one against the American dollar and much of the savings of the middle class were effectively wiped out by this 400% reduction in value, effectively plunging millions into instant poverty. In 2002 income per head was 22% below its 1998 level, with unemployment reaching 18% (or 21% if those on an emergency welfare programme are included).

In May 2003 **Néstor Kirchner**, also a Peronist but bitterly opposed by Menem, became president by default when Menem withdrew from the runoff election when he realised he had no hope of winning. The economy has been recovering at a rate of 8% per annum since he has taken office, although of course from a very low starting-point. The IMF has been widely blamed for Argentina's woes, together with neo-colonial exploitation by inequitable global markets, but in the final analysis much of the blame lies with the Argentines themselves for consistently electing venal incompetent leaders, while better candidates give up the struggle. Thus far at least, Kirchner has proved to be a cut above his predecessors, showing integrity while also being a capable wheeler-dealer and a tough negotiator with the IMF. By September 2005 Argentina had repaid 13.5 billion pesos to the IMF; nevertheless its public debt is now US$185 billion, 143% of GDP, and too high to allow it to attract foreign investment. Corruption and tax evasion are being tackled and the courts and military have been purged of Menemite cronies; however, crime (notably kidnapping) has run wild.

Midterm congressional elections in October 2005 went very well for Kirchner and his *Frente para la Victoria* (his bloc within the PJ), giving him the legitimacy denied him by Menem's petulant walkout from the presidential election. His wife was convincingly elected to the Senate; Duhalde's wife and Menem did less well but also scraped in under Argentina's odd proportional representation system. Kirchner's supporters now dominate the Senate and are the largest bloc in the Lower House.

GOVERNMENT AND POLITICS

Argentina has been an independent country since 1816 and is now identified as a modern federal republic. The last of the periods of dictatorship that has marked Argentina's convoluted history ended in 1983, since when the country has had a democratic government. The Argentine Constitution of 1853, which established a republic under a representative and federal system, was amended in 1860, 1898, 1957 and significantly in 1994. This last amendment allows the president's re-election for a second term of four years. The executive branch is led by the President and Vice-president of the Nation, offices currently held respectively by Néstor Kirchner and Daniel Scioli (since 25 May 2003). The president is both the head of government (appointing the cabinet) and the chief of state. The president and the vice-president are both elected on the same ticket by popular vote (by citizens over 18); the next election will be held in 2007.

The legislative branch is bicameral: the Senate (composed of 72 senators, three from each of the 23 provinces plus the autonomous federal district of the city of Buenos Aires, who serve terms of two, four or six years) and the Chamber of Deputies (composed of 257 representatives elected in proportion to each district's population for four-year terms). Each province has its own senate and chamber plus a governor, following its own constitution in accordance with the National Constitution.

ECONOMY

By any standard, Argentina should be one of the wealthiest countries in South America owing to its bountiful natural resources including oil and gas, minerals, agriculture and, of course, tourism; traditionally this was the case, but government blunders and internal conflicts have caused repeated periods of economic instability.

Argentina is a large country, the eighth-largest in the world (even excluding the Falkland/Malvinas Islands and part of Antarctica) and second in South America after Brazil. Its wealth of natural resources fostered a strong trade with Europe, and Buenos Aires was one of the richest cities in South America, as is apparent in the French, Spanish and Italian architecture and extensive public transportation – in fact, Buenos Aires possessed the first subway line in South America. But the economy of Argentina is an often incomprehensible frustration. With this abundance of natural resources, its great geographic size and abundant trade partners, why has this country suffered economic crisis for so many decades?

In some ways Argentina is similar to other countries in the Americas that were exploited first by Europe and later by subversive US trade policies. Colonial exploitation of the people and natural resources weakened them from the start; then slanted trade agreements benefited the buyers or importers and short-changed the local communities. Of course, economic instability goes hand in hand with political instability, which Argentina has certainly suffered from. These sorts of patterns have left many South American countries including Argentina unable to enter the global market on equal competitive terms yet unable to opt out of it.

Argentina's foreign dept is massive. In 1990 inflation rates intended to stimulate the economy and offset debt peaked at 200% per month. Investors pulled out of the country and tax and tariff revenues dropped. In 1991 a new currency tied to the US dollar was introduced, many industries were privatised and foreign trade agreements were made to encourage exports. As was hoped, the inflation rate dropped and trade and the economy grew; however, by 1995 the unemployment rate had reached 18.4%. At the dawn of the new millennium, around 15% of the workforce was unemployed and a quarter of the population subsisted below the poverty line.

So how did the swirl of debt begin in Argentina? Economics and politics are deeply intertwined and impossible to separate. The remainder of this chapter is a historical summary that for brevity's sake must omit in-depth analysis but hopefully offers an insight into the sequence of events that have led Argentina to its current political-economic status.

Main resources

Although the name Argentina derives from *argentum* (Latin for silver), the land produces almost no silver. It does have many other natural resources, and each region has its speciality.

The Pampa With 70% of the country's population, 80% of its agricultural output and 85% of its industrial enterprises, this is the centre of Argentina's economic, political and cultural life. When the first Spanish expedition left in 1537, cows and horses that had been brought with the idea of founding a settlement were abandoned. The native population soon captured the horses and gained a mastery of horsemanship, while the pampas grasslands were ideal for sustaining cattle that soon multiplied into great wild herds called *cimarones*. It is on this stock that the ranching industry was founded in the decades between independence and the consolidation of the Argentine Republic.

In colonial times Argentina supplied draft animals and textiles to the Cerro Rico in Potosí, the world's richest silver mine. The Río de la Plata meat-packing plant was established in 1792 in the area that now lies on the border of Argentina and Paraguay. Government leasing increased and, subsequently, so did the export of dried and salted beef, hides, fats, tallow and similar non-perishable goods. When the United Provinces of the River Plate fell in 1829, the government began selling land. Juan Manuel de Rosas's dictatorship saw land grants being used to buy political allies. Soldiers were often paid not in money but in land, which was then bought by speculators. By the end of the 1840s sheep and wool accounted for over a third of trade and barbed wire started crisscrossing the prairies. Agriculture (corn, soy, wheat, wine, cotton, sugar and tea are the major products) and beef have maintained a primary importance as the basis of the Argentine economy. Technological advances such as steamships and refrigeration made trade easier, and when the first refrigerated ships began carrying exports in the 19th century, Argentina's major growth period was enhanced.

North In the northwest cotton and sugar plantations are now centuries old; in Tucumán, wealthy families controlled the available land and with high tariffs kept the sugar industry for the elite. In the northwestern valleys, cotton, sugar and tobacco production, plus sheep herding and small ranches, formed the main industries. Extractive operations such as mining and energy production are now displacing the more traditional activities. There are large reserves of oil and natural gas and the mineral riches of the Andes have not been fully exploited. Boron, tin, tungsten, cement, iron ore, gold, silver, lead, uranium and zinc are mined, and Catamarca province's copper industry, notably the Baja de la Alumbrera mine, is among the most important in the world. The northeast produces tea and the Delta region fruit. The Chaco relies on the logging of the quebracho forests as its major industry; agriculture is also important, supported by rain-fed irrigation.

Patagonia Coal mining, oilfields, agriculture, industry, large hydro-electric projects and tourism from elsewhere in Argentina and Chile established the first towns. Petroleum and natural gas are mostly for the domestic market, although production falls short of demand. Patagonia holds vast reserves of oil and coal and important mining infrastructure. Oil production dates from the discovery of deposits around Comodoro Rivadavia at the beginning of the 20th century. Sheep ranching is a major economic activity with grazing grounds supporting enormous flocks. Numerous fruit orchards and vegetable farms can be found in the valleys and farming is spreading northwest thanks to irrigation improvements. Tourism is important in the Lakes District, adventure tourism is on the rise in the far south, and abundant coastal wildlife draws eco-tourists to those areas.

Cuyo This region is famous for wine production, but is also important for mining (of copper, lead and uranium) and oil.

PEOPLE

Diverse nationalities and ethnic groups currently define the Argentine people. As with many New World countries, the demographics have changed considerably since they were 'discovered' and continue to change with the continuing migration of peoples across the globe. For brevity's sake we cannot give proper acknowledgement to all the groups that have trodden Argentine soil since the arrival some 13,000 years ago of early man, whose art and artefacts are still to be found in caves, burial sites and middens. However, it would be unjustly ethnocentric to simply speak of post-European demographics. While many ethnic groups have become extinct, they were the true people of this land before it was given the name Argentina. They are summarised below in geographical order as an overview of the native groups that once existed as well as those that have survived, before continuing with the arrival of the Europeans, their African slaves and the subsequent migrations of peoples that have continued to influence the ever-changing demographics of modern-day Argentina.

Native Peoples

By about 11,000BC hunter-gatherer cultures were moving from the north into the area of present-day Argentina and had begun settling in the Andes and along the coast by 500BC, when ceramic-making cultures emerged in the northwest (Jujuy to San Juan), with fine metalworking skills soon following. Subsequent centuries saw the growth of urban centres until 1480, when the Incas conquered the northwest and began building trade routes, roads and fortresses. However, the many groups and tribes further south remained autonomous. In 1516 the first Spaniards set foot on the coast of the Río de la Plata and the many distinct native groups throughout this vast southern expanse of South America began to disappear. The Europeans bestowed on their native hosts the typical offerings of disease, war and disruption of community. Labour recruitment was just shy of the definition of slavery, with many native men being dispersed beyond the borders of the country. Territories began shifting and certain groups became assimilated into neighbouring or advancing groups or migrated out of their former territory into that of others and thus lost their own culture and genetic identity. While in Patagonia and the dry pampas the Indians stayed independent until the second half of the 19th century, many groups disappeared owing to invasion by the Mapuche, displaced from Chile by colonial advances there. The most drastic event, however, was outright genocide by the Europeans, both accidental, through the introduction of disease, and deliberate, in the so-called Indian Wars. The native strongholds in the vast expanses of the pampas were lost in General Julio Roca's *Conquista del Desierto* (Conquest of the Desert). Roca's 1879 election campaign, when he was swept into presidency, was the climax of the Indian Wars that had lasted two decades. Whatever romantic name it was hidden under, it was quite simply an extermination campaign. Although some reject the labelling of this campaign as a genocide and claim that there was indeed a war and many Europeans were also killed, there were outright bounties placed upon the native peoples; the total native population of the pampas at that time was eliminated in that single year.

Today the native peoples fall into only a few groupings. In most of the country they are considered to be Mapuche. In the north, the Wichi remain. Both these groups are strong in number and cultural identity. Their arts and handicrafts are celebrated and recognised as definitively Argentine and the Mapuche language is being taught once again in school. What follows is strictly a limited overview of the diversity of the native communities of Argentina and describes many groups of people whose cultures no longer exist but nevertheless should not be forgotten.

Natives of Patagonia

The nomadic **Selk'nam** (also referred to as the Ona) once inhabited the whole of the Isla Grande de Tierra del Fuego, with a related group known as the **Haush** living at the southeastern tip of the island, where they endured the harshest climate in Argentina with winter temperatures dropping to −20°C accompanied by strong ocean winds. They hunted guanaco and fox for their hides, small mammals and birds for meat and gathered fruits and roots. Occasionally they could feast on a stranded whale, but they did not hunt at sea nor fish, or even collect shellfish for that matter. Nomadic hunter-gatherers, their villages of 50–100 members were always a temporary grouping of dome-shaped huts, made from tree boughs, called *chozas*. They were established where hunting was successful and taken down when the hunting dwindled, forcing them to move on to other areas in search of food. Theirs was a peaceful culture with no history of warring with neighbouring tribes, the **Yámana** (or Yahgan) and **Alacaluf** (or Kaweshkar), the two tribes of so-called 'canoe Indians'. The Yámana inhabited the coast of the Beagle Channel and the Magellanic Archipelago, while the Alacaluf were limited to the southern tip of Chile. They spent the greater part of their lives actually in their beech-bark canoes, which contributed to a physiology of strongly developed upper bodies and weak legs. A cooking fire was kept alight on board and every activity from cooking and eating to hunting to sleeping was done on the boat. A single family existed in a boat, sleeping under an onboard tent of branches and skins. The man and woman had very specific roles to keep the 'household' functioning; the man, utilising a spear, hunted or fished from the boat while the woman kept the fire burning inside the canoe – without the canoe itself becoming fuel! She also cooked and tended to the children. They hunted marine mammals such as seals, terrestrial mammals, including rodents, and birds, especially cormorants, as well as gathering shellfish. Interestingly, with such an isolated lifestyle and limited social opportunities with other members of their cultural group, the Yámanas had one of the more complex native languages of Argentina, comprising over 35,000 words. This fascinating culture has been lost as the Yámana are now extinct after being subjected to European disease and competition for resources, and embarrassingly, to a deliberate genocide fuelled by colonial prejudices. The numbers are eloquent: when the first European arrived in 1880 there were reportedly 3,000 Yámanas living on and around the island of Tierra del Fuego, yet within ten years their population was cut to a third and by 1910 there were only a hundred Yámanas left. At the time of the writing of this guide, there was one elderly Yámana woman living near Puerto Williams (in Chile) without any descendents and therefore the sole surviving Yámana; with her death the Yámana become extinct. Today the Selk'nam or Ona are the only remaining natives of Tierra del Fuego, although none are any longer pure-blood.

The **Tehuelche** (or Chonke) were the first native peoples encountered by Magellan, who was apparently impressed by their great height. They comprised various groups such as the Aónikenk (near El Calafate), Teushen, Gununa Kene and Metcharnúekenk, who all hunted guanacos and picked roots, seeds and herbs for food. The word 'Tehuelche' is also used to describe the shale-like glacier-smoothed stones found throughout this zone.

In northern Patagonia, in the region of Río Colorado and Río Negro, lived the **Puelche** and **Guénaken**, the latter reportedly reaching as far as the sierras of Tandil and Ventana and therefore often being referred to as the *Serranos* or Hill People. These two groups were nomadic hunter-gatherers subsisting on roots and seeds and hunting guanaco, ñandu and fox with bow and arrow for food and clothing. They clothed themselves in loincloths, headbands (called *vincha*) and colourful wool blankets. Their temporary homes were timber huts covered in animal skins, and their communities contained about a hundred families led by a chief or *cacique*. After the Conquest, the Mapuche were pushed into Puelche territory from further north and introduced them to horsemanship skills and the use of the spear in war.

The **Pehuenche** are the Mapuche group living in the region of Lake Nahuel Huapí. They were hunter-gatherers and made bread from the fruit of the pehuén (*Araucaria araucana*), which gave them their name and which also gave the name to the fruit 'Indian Bread'.

Natives of the Pampas

The original inhabitants of the pampas were the **Querandí**. For that reason they were also known as the Pampas Indians and the word 'pampas' was synonymous for both the region and the native peoples. Agile and strong, this deer- and rhea-hunting people were incredibly fit and overtook their prey by running it to the point of exhaustion so that they could take it down at close range with bow and arrow or with the *boleadora* (three leather ropes tied together at one end with three large stones tied to the free ends, hurled at the legs of an animal to trip it up). This was the first indigenous group met by Pedro de Mendoza's expedition in 1536 in the area of the present-day city of Buenos Aires. It was, however, the nomadic **Mapuche** who eventually displaced the Querandí from their territory when they began invading the pampas to steal horses and make contact with the Spaniards; by the mid-19th century they had overtaken the territory and frequently attacked military forts and frontier settlements to enforce their claim. Known to be the best horsemen of all the native Argentine groups, horses gave them the speed and stamina to raid and retreat and pose a considerable threat to their opponents. These surprise attacks were known as *malóns* – invasions by large groups on horseback throwing spears, screaming and capturing women. For close to 300 years the Mapuche led a violent lifestyle on the plains by stealing and plundering the larger estancias, herding the cattle over the Andes and selling them to the Spaniards on the Chilean side. Their hostility was fuelled by the frustration and anger of a displaced culture that had witnessed the death of its people from European disease and prejudice and the loss of its homeland to European greed. This hostility was met with General Roca's genocidal 'Conquest of the Desert' of 1879–83 to open up the pampas to colonisation. Roca's soldiers massacred the Mapuche, torturing and slaughtering them with no discrimination for age or gender. Those who survived also suffered the break-up of tribal units and were thus forced to work as cowhands on the large and ever-expanding estancias. Today, tens of thousands of hectares of land in Patagonia are allocated to raising sheep for meat and wool but few local people are employed. The native peoples of northern Patagonia are now homogenously referred to as Mapuche and are estimated to number approximately 200,000, living mainly on small and remote reservations in the provinces of Río Negro, Neuquén and Chubut. They are still fighting for their right to live on the lands of Patagonia but are continuously displaced by the estancia owners, many of whom are now Europeans and North Americans. It is estimated that 90% of Patagonia is private land – more so if the national parks are included.

The Mapuche are very artistic, making silver ornaments and jewellery (initially from colonial Spanish coins) that are important elements of their wardrobe and cultural expression. Perhaps influenced by contact with the

Puelche, the Mapuche were also known to dress themselves in ponchos, loincloths and the *vincha*; the women wrapped themselves in blankets of guanaco wool. The Mapuche originally came from the Arauco Valley in Chile and for that reason were named *Araucanos* by the Spaniards; *Mapuche* means people (*che*) of the earth (*mapu*) in their language, Mapudungun. They lived in simple structures made of branches with leather stretched across them; these huts were called *toldos* and the camp a *toldería*. The Mapuche culture is one of the strongest in Argentina and since 2001 Mapudungun has been taught in their community's schools in Neuquén.

Natives of Mesopotamia and the Gran Chaco

Originally from the Amazon River region, the **Guaraní** migrated into Chaco, Formosa and Misiones. The Fortín M'bororé group settled near the Iguazú Falls and two ethnic groups branched off from them – the Chiripá and the Mbyá. The common language of the Fortín M'bororé groups was Gè, which is still spoken today. There were various tribes within these groups as well but they disappeared after being pushed out of the coveted *pampa húmeda* by the Spaniards; from the south to the north of Mesopotamia, these were the Timbúe, Carcarae, Mberguae, Chanae and Mocoretae, with the Charrúa on the east side of the Río de la Plata. Not surprisingly in Mesopotamia, a region characterised by water, these were fisherfolk subsisting mainly on the river fish that they often preserved through drying or smoking. They also hunted otters, carpincho, deer and various birds, and collected honey in the forests. After the Spanish Conquest agriculture was introduced and the Guaraní learnt to grow corn, manioc, sweet potatoes, pumpkins and other vegetables. Agricultural practices made for sedentary villages that stayed in location for five or six years. They built large communal houses where several families lived together. The women spun cotton and wove fabric in simple vertical looms. The Guaraní also made ceramic vases and art objects; their artistic style was incorporated into the architecture of the missions, the ruins of which now preserve and protect various examples of their skills. When the missionaries began arriving and converted the Guaraní to Christianity at the beginning of the 16th century, the ancient native religion, which believed in a lost paradise and the creator god Tupá, was lost, being too similar to the Christian concept of heaven and its nameless omniscient god. Tupá had given the Guaraní the maté tree (*Ilex paraguayensis*), the leaves of which produce a tea favoured by the Guaraní that today is more or less the national drink of Argentina. Eventually the Jesuit principles of egalitarianism and colonial attitudes of the Spanish Crown clashed and the missions were abolished and the Jesuits expelled from Argentina in 1767.

In the Chaco there were the **Chunupí** tribes, the Vilela, Tufa and Mataguaya, as well as the Guaycurú group that was formed by the Mataco (or Wichi), Tufa and Pilegae tribes. They were nomadic hunter-gatherers and the Guaycurú group were left in relative isolation until the last century because the lands they lived in were too hostile and impenetrable to colonialists. They were never evangelised so their culture is much more intact than many other remaining native groups. The groups that did encounter the Spanish, namely the Abipona and their allies the Mocobí, resisted them violently and thus were wiped out in the 17th century. The **Wichi**, meaning 'people' in their native tongue, are from Formosa province. Today their population is approximately 80,000 inhabiting the Gran Chaco region. Theirs is one of the oldest tribes in the region. In remote times they were hunter-gatherers, hunting with bow and arrow and fishing with harpoons, collecting honey, pumpkin, prickly pear fruit and algarrobo (*Prosopis nigra*). The algarrobo stands out as significant in diet and ritual, as does the narcotic seed of the norco cebil tree (*Parapiptadenia sublime*), which was roasted and ground into a powder to be inhaled or smoked.

In modern times the Wichi have become skilled wood-carvers and knitters of unique handbags called *yicas*. They spin a special fibre from the leaves of the chaguar or caraguatá, a bromeliad that is also used for food, medicine and ritual. The fibre is died with algarrobo bark, quebracho (*Schinopsis quebracho colorado*) or palo santo (*Bulnesia sarmientoi*).

Natives of the Central Area

The **Comechingone** of Córdoba built their homes underground. They were tall in stature and the only tribe in all of Argentina with bearded men, so anthropologists believe them to have a different origin to other natives of Argentina. They were not influenced by the Incas, yet they knew how to cultivate corn, beans and pumpkin. They raised llamas and spun the wool to weave garments. They also wove grass baskets that were used as moulds to form ceramics. Their name reportedly imitates their war cry.

The **Huarpe** of Cuyo and **Olongasta** of La Rioja were settled tribes. They learnt from the Inca how to irrigate the mountain slopes and build the *pucará*, a stronghold in which to cultivate corn and quinua.

Other groups of the central region included the nomadic **Lule** and **Vilela** of Tucumán, both of which adopted the nickname Juríe, the Quechua word for ostrich, owing to their tall and thin stature. The agrarian **Tonocoté** of Santiago del Estero built round huts covered in straw. They celebrated long religious festivities that incorporated an alcoholic drink made from algarrobo fruit and corn. Finally, the **Sanavirone**, south of Santiago del Estero, lived in large houses with several families together. Their region is characterised by the giant cactus called cardón that they used as a source of wood. None of the groups of the central region exists today.

Natives of the Northwest

The history of the indigenous peoples in the northwest of Argentina (Noroeste Argentino or NOA) is significantly different from the rest of the country, having had 500 years of contact with the Inca, from whom they acquired the notions of a hierarchical society and a state dominating other groups; for this reason they adapted well to a new master upon the arrival of the Spaniards. There remains today a high degree of racial mixing and over half of the population of the northwest is considered *mestizo* (see page 39). Strong divisions between the original ethnic and tribal groups are today blurred, so although most groups no longer exist (for example, the **Quilmes**, who were eradicated), and many have abandoned traditional cultural practices, the bloodlines of many of the groups persist. In the provinces of Salta and Jujuy remain the **Kolla**, who speak Kechua (Quechua). The **Cochinoca**, divided into three groups, the Omahuaca, Tilcara and Purmamarca, occupied the famous valley called the Quebrada de Humahuaca (Ravine of Humahuaca) that links the high desert plateau or *puna* with the plains of the south. They were agrarian cultures, still greatly influenced by the Inca. They built irrigation systems and cultivation platforms, forts called *pucarás*, on which they stored their crops in silos, and also raised llamas for wool and transportation. Their houses were made of stone with mud and stone roofs; examples of these homes can still be seen in use in the region. Their woollen clothing comprised the typical Andean tunic, called an *unka*, and ponchos or blankets fastened with long woollen belts; their shoes made of llama leather were called *ojotas*. They were a very artistic and decorative people, adorning themselves in beautiful jewellery predominantly featuring lapis lazuli and malachite, and creating ceramics of red, black and white designed with animal figures. The cult of the Sun and the Moon was introduced in the mid-15th century as the Inca Empire expanded. The goddess Pachamama (Mother Earth) is of great importance as well. The **Apatama** were peaceful agrarians who kept their crops in caves. They also dressed in the distinctive Andean tunic and ponchos with geometric designs but also wore colourful wool caps, still worn today by the inhabitants of the *puna*.

The **Diaguita** and **Calchaquí** represented the most highly developed of the original cultures in Argentina. They lived in the Andean valleys of the northwest and into the central region, under the Inca domain, in complex agrarian communities cultivating corn, beans, pumpkins and quina, utilising irrigation systems, hillside platforms and water channels that are still in use today. They are responsible for the famous and mysterious dolmens and labyrinthine stone groups. They included the subgroups of the Hualfine, Pulare, Tolombone, Yuocavil and, possibly, the famous Quilmes. They made very artistic ceramics as well as producing beautiful objects from copper, brass, silver and gold.

European immigration

After the Indian Wars, different regions were settled by immigrants of different origins and cultures: Spaniards, Italians, Scots and English in the far south, Welsh in the Chubut Valley, Italians in the Río Negro Valley, Swiss and Germans in the Northern Lakes District and a few North Americans scattered throughout the country.

The main influx of immigration to Argentina was between 1860 and 1930, with great recruitment programmes to populate the pampas of Buenos Aires and the surrounding delta up into Mesopotamia, Córdoba and the northwest. Patagonia was not settled until after 1880. Three million immigrants were registered throughout Argentina by 1910. The 1914 population census shows that 30% of the residents of Buenos Aires were born abroad; 40% of the residents of Misiones were Brazilian or Paraguayan; and 70% of the population of Formosa was Paraguayan.

Afro-Argentines

Several theories, all of which cause one's eyebrows to rise, account for the virtual non-existence of black people in Argentina (only 3% of the population is non-white, including Amerindians and *mestizos*). Yet Afro-Argentines were apparently a whopping 30% of the population of Buenos Aires between 1778 and 1815. In true colonial style, the first African slaves were brought to Argentina in the 16th century by their Spanish owners and future generations were bought at a high price by way of complicated import routes via Panama and overland from Chile (trade restrictions made direct import to Buenos Aires or trade from Brazil illegal – but not uncommon). The slaves were mainly domestic servants but many were also artisans or put to work in various trades as required by the labour-short colonies. The slave trade was outlawed in 1813 but the period of emancipation was tumultuous at best. The majority of slaves were granted their freedom by 1827 though often by way of military service or paying off their purchase cost; the unfortunate ones with owners unwilling to relinquish them remained in bondage until at least 1860. It was illegal for a child to be born into slavery; however, this law could be skirted by taking pregnant slaves to Uruguay where slavery was still legal and thus categorising both mother and child as slaves upon their return to Argentina. The numbers of blacks being brought into the country did of course drop; census figures for Buenos Aires show a drastic fall from a quarter of the total population in the early 1830s to less than 2% some 50 years later. Though no longer slaves, the status of Afro-Argentines remained low with few civil rights allowed to them. Forced front-line service during the independence era, defined by incessant warfare, 'disappearances' and other violations surely decimated their numbers, and the yellow fever epidemic of 1871 and other diseases struck hard this population that was subjected to impoverishment and unsanitary living conditions.

The diminished population also probably became somewhat diluted through the mixing of races. As was the case with many of the *mestizos*, *mulatos* (partly Afro-Argentine mixed-races) sought the reclusive solitary lifestyle of the gaucho. These are among the plausible speculations for the decline but some also surmise that the black people simply made a mass exodus to Brazil. What is undeniable in old photographs and prints is the historical presence of this race that made a significant contribution in Argentina's early growth and prosperity as well as culture. The music of the tango, itself key to Argentine national identity, owes its passionate rhythms to the influence of the Afro-Argentines alongside the immigrant musicians of the early *porteño* ghetto, where the jam sessions evolved into the first tango 'orchestra'.

Mestizos

A mix of the native and European populations, this category is currently defined as 85% Caucasian with 15% black, indigenous or mixed blood. The first *mestizos* were children of one indigenous and one European parent. During the traumatic events of the Indian Wars, white women were kidnapped by the natives (it is reported that few women ever returned to their homes – possibly they were too ashamed to return to their homes, they were unable to return or they chose to remain with their captors) and the native women were raped by the European soldiers. The offspring of these unions were, of course, innocent children, yet often stigmatised by cultural prejudices. The illegitimate children of black slaves fathered by the slave owners, called *mulatos*, were treated with similar disregard. This was not always the case, but for the most part these children never fully integrated into either culture. As adults, the men often chose to live solitary lives as work-hands on the estancias. This is the origin of the gaucho culture.

The Gaucho

The first gauchos were the descendants of Spaniards and the native peoples of the pampas. Belonging to neither community, they were often outcasts and led solitary lives. They were often hired to work with livestock on the large estancias; and because they did not have families, the *estancieros* were able to pay them minimal salaries and board them in small shacks called *ranchos* on remote parts of the property. They were highly skilled horsemen, competing with one another in show-off games of skill. Their clothing was styled for horseriding: wide at the top to straddle the saddle comfortably, tight at the ankles to fit inside the high leather boots without chafing. The hat was wide for shade from the sun. The *facón* (knife) was an indispensable tool for cutting rope or spearing a piece of steak off the grill. The styles differ from region to region but the lifestyle and culture is homogenous across the prairie that seems to stretch endlessly across this expansive country.

The most famous gaucho is Martín Fierro, the eponymous immortal hero of the epic poem by José Hernandez (1834-86) that sums up the melancholy pride of this lonely archetype. It is widely regarded as the pinnacle of the *guachesque* poetry genre that evokes the rural Argentine ballads sung to the guitar, known as *payadas*.

In a grassy hollow I'll sit me down,
And sing of the days long done,
Like the ancient wind that sighing goes,
Through the prairie grass, I will sing my woes,
The hands I held and the cards I played,
And the stakes I lost and won.

I am the best of my own at home
And better than best afar
I have won in song my right of place
If any gainsay me – face to face
Let him come and better me song for song
Guitar against guitar.

It was originally published in its original Spanish in two volumes, *El Gaucho Martín Fierro* in 1872 and *La Vuelta de Martín Fierro* in 1879, and has since been translated into over 70 languages. This excerpt is from the translation rendered into English verse by Walter Owen (1884-1953).

Current demographics

Although most Argentines are of European descent, recent genetic research conducted by the University of Buenos Aires suggests that over half of the population possess at least some degree of Amerindian ancestry. With a population approaching 40 million, about 700,000 are indigenous, concentrated in the provinces of the north, northwest and south – and fewer in the central, more populous areas of the Atlantic coast and the Paraná Delta.

There was a great surge of European immigration in the late 19th and early 20th centuries, which has continued with a wave of immigrants from Syria, Lebanon and the Middle East, now amounting to about half a million, mostly in cities. The largest Jewish population in Latin America, of about a quarter of a million people, is in Argentina, with significant communities in the Once and Abasto *barrios* of Buenos Aires. In the last quarter of the 20th century Asian-Argentine immigration mirrored the trend in North America with Chinese, South Korean and Japanese arriving in Argentina, mainly settling in Buenos Aires. In recent years there has also been an increase in immigration from other Latin American countries. The Argentine population is one of the slowest growing in Latin America; the total urban population is currently estimated at around 80%, with more than a third living in the greater Buenos Aires area. The rural population is declining owing to the disparity between the standard of living of the rural and urban lifestyles. While urban Argentines have a relatively high standard of living and at least half consider themselves middle class, many rural peoples, especially in the northwest, still live in adobe huts with dirt floors and mud-and-straw roofs, without plumbing and collecting their own water from wells or streams. Realistically speaking, certain rural peoples live in such remote areas that accurate population census in Argentina is quite impossible.

CULTURE

Argentines have a deep pride and obsession with their identity, which shows itself in a fascination with their history, culture and political and sporting heroes. This is seen in the street graffiti that still shouts the names of icons long dead, such as 'Evita Forever' and 'Gardel Lives!', or vilifies political leaders in slogans such as 'Down with Menem'. The culture continues to embrace its folklore, to admire gaucho poetry and the gaucho style of singing called the *payada* (with improvised lyrics sung to traditional tunes as a challenge to other singers) and to foster a sentimental devotion to the tango song and dance. It is a passionate culture expressed not only through the boldness and drama of the tango but also through something as quiet and passive as a tree – in spring the ceibo tree blazes with a dazzling bright red flower that has been designated Argentina's national flower.

Cultural icons

As in any country, significant historical characters contribute greatly to forming and defining the societal values and cultural identity of Argentina. Early explorers, politicians, revolutionaries, sports stars, brilliant artists and musicians and other celebrities make their immortal marks on their country's profile. Most are glorified, such as **Diego Maradona** (born 1960), who is considered one of the best players in the history of soccer, but equally some are vilified, such as former president **Carlos Saúl Menem** (born 1930), who rose to international fame and then fell into infamy. In any case they remain forever a part of the nation's prides and prejudices. A comprehensive list would be lengthy if objective; however, some of the most famous Argentines who have defined their nation's identity are overviewed below.

Of course, Argentina would not be as it is today if it wasn't for the early explorers who came from the Old World to discover the New. They continue to be celebrated in legend and remembered in the names of ports and passages as well as flora and fauna of Argentina. **Ferdinand Magellan** (1480–1521) is one of the most important explorers during the founding of the land now known as Argentina. Born of a noble family in a small town near Vila Real in Trás-os-Montes, northern Portugal, Fernão de Magalhães was born to Pedro Rui de Magalhães and Alda de Mesquita, who died when he was ten years old. He went to live as a page in the royal court of King John II and Queen Eleonora in Lisbon and began studying geography and astronomy. His early explorations took him to India and Africa. Through various events and controversies Magellan renounced his nationality after falling into disfavour with King Emanuel I and losing his rank. Magellan then went into the service of the court of Spain and changed his name to Fernando de Magellanes. His transatlantic voyage began in September 1519, with a fleet of five ships under his command – the *Concepción, San Antonio, Santiago, Trinidad* and *Victoria*. They landed at Río de la Plata in January 1520, and by the end of March they had established the settlement they called Puerto San Julian (now in Santa Cruz province), and Magellan and his chronicler Pigafetta named the desolate coastline Patagonia. European law and customs fostered revolts, mutinies, banishments and executions in Puerto San Julian. Further mutinies and one wreck would leave only three of the five ships to pass through the roughly 600km-long passage that Magellan named the Estreito de Todos los Santos, or All Saints' Channel, for being discovered on All Saints' Day, 1 November 1520. Today it is called the Magellan Strait. On 28 November they sailed out of the strait and into what Magellan named Mar Pacifico (Pacific Ocean) because it seemed placid. They then sailed for months across the vast Pacific before the three ships and their surviving scurvy crew arrived in Guam and then the Philippines where Magellan was killed in the Battle of Mactan on 27 April 1521. One ship continued to complete the first circumnavigation of the world. Magellan is recognised by scholars as having made the most significant voyage in history, providing evidence to support the rumour at the time that the earth was round.

Pedro Sarmiento de Gamboa (who founded the first settlements, Nombre de Jesus and Rey Felipe, on the Strait of Misfortunes in 1584), **Sir Francis Drake** (who in 1577 discovered the Drake Passage south of Tierra del Fuego, and who used the same scaffold Magellan had used to hang his mutineers half a century before) and

Thomas Cavendish (who voyaged from England to west Africa and then Patagonia in 1586 and discovered a large harbour, Puerto Deseado, that he named after his ship, the *Desire*) were among the many explorers of this coastline, but it was not until much later that the interior of Patagonia was explored. **Robert FitzRoy** and **Charles Darwin** arrived on the *Beagle* in 1831–36 and travelled a long way up the Río Santa Cruz. In 1867 and 1873 Luis Piedrabuena, Guillermo Gardiner and Valentin Feilberg reached the lakes at the head of the Santa Cruz, and after 1876 the naturalist and surveyor **Francisco 'Perito' Moreno** visited the area several times. Disputes between Chile and Argentina over the long undefined border went on for almost a century, coming close to war at times – discussions began when both governments met in 1899 in the Straits of Magellan, and were more or less wrapped up in 1996 when the two countries finally agreed upon the position of the border in the area of the Lago del Desierto. Moreno, one of the first white men to explore these lands and discover its beauties and cultures, was one of the key persons involved in defining the border. He wanted to see Patagonia colonised and its resources utilised. He was exploring during the times of the Indian Wars but although he was sympathetic to the plight of the natives he had a European attitude that was focused on exploitation and progress, in conflict with indigenous ideals.

Heroes and bandits share podiums in Argentina where there is as much appreciation for the very good as there is for the cleverly bad! Acts of charity are praised as saintly. Those who find a way to bypass the law, however, are also deeply admired. There are many revolutionaries in Argentina's chaotic history but a few are remembered with deep respect linked to a national identity. **José de San Martín** (1778–1850) organised the forces of independence and led the invasions of Chile and Peru to secure the independence of South America. **General Manuel Belgrano** (1770–1820) holds a close second place in fame as a revolutionary leader. After rallying support for economic and trade reforms with the viceroyalty, he established a revolutionary government in 1810 in the struggle for independence. Robert Leroy Parker and Harry Longbaugh, better known as **Butch Cassidy and the Sundance Kid**, found refuge in Patagonia in the early 1900s after their infamous robbery of the American National Bank. Here their names were to change again to Santiago Ryan and Henry Place. They did not retire from their occupations as bank robbers, however, and continued to steal from banks in Rio Gallegos and Villa Mercedes. They lived for a while in the Cholila Valley where their legend is remembered with pride. Their story reportedly ends with their deaths in Bolivia. The huge fame of **Eva Perón – Evita** (1919–52) grew from humble middle-class origins. She had an early career as a radio actress but later became the key political ally of her husband, Juan Perón. After her marriage to the soon-to-be president in 1945 she became a pivotal character in rallying working-class support. She campaigned in 1947 for women's suffrage and for the rights of the poor. She died young from cancer and has remained a symbol of righteousness combined with celebrity stardom. Her fame seems not to diminish but instead to grow as she manages to combine the status of both saint and star in the eyes and hearts of her fans. Another Argentine whose fame seems to grow rather than wane, while straddling the line between seemingly opposing values as guerrilla leader and self-sacrificing human rights activist, is **Ernesto 'Che' Guevara** (1928–67). He was born in Rosario but left his homeland and comfortable upper-middle-class lifestyle at an early age to first work as a medic in leper colonies and later to devote himself to the elimination of neo-colonial poverty and labour injustices in the developing world. He fought in Castro's revolution in Cuba and became the most important Marxist/Leninist revolutionary leader in Latin America. He also fought in the Congo but was unsuccessful;

undaunted he continued to Bolivia where he was captured and killed by order of the Bolivian government (although the CIA wanted him alive). He became a cult hero and remains a symbol of anti-capitalism and defiance to imperial foreign policies in South America and elsewhere in the developing world.

An interesting phenomenon in many Catholic cultures including Argentina is a throwback to popular superstitions that go back to before the arrival of the missionaries and are still strongly held, especially by rural people. Superstitions and perceived miracles elevate particular characters to a sort of saintly status even though the Church does not recognise them. There are two good examples in Argentina. **Gaucho Antonio Gil** was a 19th-century Robin Hood whose real name (though this and even his existence are of course debated by sceptics) was Antonio Mamerto Gil Nuñez. He too 'robbed from the rich to give to the poor' and was reputedly able to predict the future, including his unjust execution, which was proclaimed as divine communication. The shrine on the site where he was hung from a tree by provincial authorities on 8 January 1875 draws tens of thousands of pilgrims on the anniversary of his death. The tree no longer stands but the shrine is an obvious landmark outside Mercedes in Corrientes, and many other shrines have cropped up all over the countryside. Although similar to shrines to the Madonna, these are usually garish red little huts or pedestals covered with red candles and artists' renditions of the gaucho. Devotees ask for small miracles and leave items such as car license plates to request protection from crashes, or wedding dresses to request a good marriage.

The other enshrined figure is **La Difunta Correa**, *difunta* meaning defunct or deceased. Legend has it that María Antonia Deolinda Correa died of thirst in the desert while following her conscript husband across the desert during the mid-19th-century civil wars. When her body was found, her baby was still alive and suckling at her breast that miraculously continued to sustain him. Shrines to La Difunta are worshipped to this day by devotees throughout the country, who leave a bottle of water in return for a wish. You will often see mountains of plastic water bottles that are more obvious landmarks than the shrine itself, which is usually a simple wooden box or cross with her name. Over half a million pilgrims visit the original site in the small town of Vallecito, San Juan, each year.

Argentina is alive with the arts and has been home to many legendary figures in music, literature and dance. The list is lengthy and includes the likes of classical pianists **Martha Argerich** (born 1941) and **Daniel Barenboim** (born 1942); tenors **José Cura** (born 1962) and **Marcelo Álvarez** (born 1963); the classical dancer and founder and director of Ballet Argentino, **Julio Bocca** (born 1967); and legendary rock musician and wild man **Charly Garcia** (born 1951). **Jorge Luis Borges** (1899–1986), poet and short-story writer, embraced most often the subjects of history and his native Buenos Aires and is seen as the father of post-modernism, but also wrote tango lyrics. Other great writers include **Julio Cortázar**, **Ernesto Sábato** and **Manuel Puig**. In the field of architecture, **Cesar Pelli** has designed Canary Wharf in London, the Carnegie Hall Tower in New York, and the Petronas Towers in Kuala Lumpur. There have also been five Argentine winners of Nobel Prizes.

Tango musicians and writers have legendary status in Argentina. The most acclaimed tango composers are **Osvaldo Pugliese** (1905–95) and **Astor Piazzolla** (1921–92). The former recorded the most famous traditional tangos, while Piazzolla went on to contemporise the music, adding elements of jazz and classical music, and is considered the most important composer of symphonic tango. Singer **Carlos Gardel** (1890–1935) found fame during the era of radio and film that established him as a symbol of the tango. He was killed in a plane crash

THE MYSTIQUE OF MARADONA
Tim Burford

To fully understand the Argentines you have to understand something of **Diego Armando Maradona** – a wonderful footballer but terribly flawed, and in ways that shed light on the psyche of the nation itself. Born on 30 October 1960 in Villa Fiorito, southern Buenos Aires, he was a soccer prodigy, making his international debut in a friendly game at just 16. He was in the initial squad for the 1978 World Cup but didn't make the final 22; however, he was the player of the competition when Argentina won the World Under-20 championships in 1979. He had scored 100 league goals by the time he was 19 and was bought by Boca Juniors for US$1 million, a record for a teenager. In 1980, when England beat Argentina 3-1 at Wembley, he dribbled through the entire defence but then shot wide. Although he failed to shine in the 1982 World Cup, partly due to limpet-like marking, he moved to Barcelona that same year for a record US$3 million. In 1984 he moved to Napoli in the first US$5 million transfer and inspired them to their first Italian league championship in 1987 and again in 1990, plus the UEFA Cup in 1989. Idolised in Naples to this day, he left an illegitimate son, Diego Maradona Jr, who is himself now a promising player for Napoli.

For the English and many others, Maradona's defining moment came in the 1986 World Cup (when fan Pedro Gatica cycled from Argentina to Mexico, found the tickets were too dear and decided to go home, but found his bike had been stolen). In the quarter-final against England, Maradona punched the ball past the England keeper Peter Shilton for a clearly illegal goal that was nevertheless allowed. Afterwards he called it *la mano de Dios* or the hand of God, but claimed to have no recollection of the circumstances. Four minutes later he scored arguably the finest goal in World Cup history, with a solo run through the entire England defence. He scored a similarly fine goal in the semi-final and in the final against West Germany he slipped free of his very close markers to give a perfect pass to Jorge Burruchaga to score the winning goal. In the 1990 World Cup Maradona played with an injury, dosed with painkillers throughout, and was again heavily marked. Argentina lost to Cameroon but still made it to the final, knocking Brazil out with a moment of magic from Maradona and fine finishing from Claudio Caniggia. In the final the Argentine players lost their tempers and lost to West Germany on a penalty.

However, in 1991 Maradona failed a cocaine test and was suspended for 15 months and committed by the Argentine courts to psychiatric treatment, picking up his career again with Sevilla in 1992. In the 1994 World Cup he scored a great goal against Greece, but looked demented as he celebrated; he was suspended again for 15 months after testing positive for ephidrine, which he variously claimed he was taking to lose weight or had been planted by the CIA in the communion host, to stop a drug-using friend of Fidel Castro from

but remains more popular than ever; there is a saying that his singing gets better and better. Current stars include singer Adriana Varela, bandoneón virtuosi Julio Pane and Rodolfo Mederos, and pianists Juan Carlos Caceres, Pablo Ziegler and Sonia Possetti. Read more about the tango below.

Music, dance and dress

For some it is the music, for some the words, but for all the **tango** is an extension of the emotion that resonates an undeniable passion. The lyrics are mournful, the

being the star of the World Cup. He returned to his beloved Boca Juniors, retiring in 1997.

In 1999 he suffered a cocaine overdose and in January 2000 a cocaine-related heart attack; he was invited by Castro for treatment in Cuba, where in September 2000 he crashed his jeep driving the wrong way along the Malecon (supposedly confused by roadworks) but claimed God had saved his life. There's no doubt that if he had stayed in Argentina he would have continued to be the victim of the army of parasites and manipulative businessmen that always surrounded him; in Cuba he was able to clean up his act to some degree. In 2003 he launched a wine label and a travelling exhibition about his career, which is due to reach Germany in time for the 2006 World Cup; in 2004 a musical about him hit the stage in Buenos Aires, and at least two films are planned, by Emir Kusturica and Marco Risi (son of the great director Dino Risi).

Visiting Italy in 2001, he had been met with a tax bill for € 30 million from his six years playing for Napoli (tax inspectors claimed they'd been unable to trace him at the time, despite his huge celebrity); in October 2005 he exhausted his legal appeals but refused to pay, claiming to have no assets in Italy. He was at the time starring in the Italian version of *Celebrity Come Dancing* (which, with his nifty footwork, he was widely tipped to win) and had been paid US$3 million, which was not taxed either.

In March 2005 he had a gastric bypass operation, and dropped in weight from a blimp-like 150kg (330lb) to 100kg (220lb) by the end of the year. In August 2005 he began a successful new career presenting a TV show called *La Noche de Diez* or the Night of Ten, referring to his shirt number in the national team (retired with him). On the opening show, together with Argentina's leading international goal-scorer Gabriel Batistes and tennis player Gabriela Abating, the star guest was Pele, the greatest soccer player ever and someone that Maradona has always been jealous of, starting a rumour in 1999 that he had had homosexual experiences. Here they made up, with Pele, whose son has drugs problems, praising Maradona for beating his addiction. He had a similarly strained relationship with Argentine team-mate Claudio Caniggia: in their playing days they used to kiss on the lips when either scored a goal, leading Caniggia's wife to accuse Maradona of being in love with her husband, and Maradona to threaten legal action; but relations later worsened, especially after injury prevented Caniggia playing in Maradona's benefit match in 2001.

Many players have been called 'the next Maradona', but in 2001 it was Andres d'Alessandro of River Plate who he hailed as 'my successor'. In the run-up to the 2006 World Cup he said, 'I see Lionel Messi as my natural heir in the side', but also saw England's Wayne Rooney as a fine player in his own mould – highly instinctual, with a low centre of gravity and a combative nature.

music straining between tragedy and ecstasy. The dancers intimately entangle themselves and yet resist one another, struggling between taboo and irreverence. Indeed, the tango was scorned as scandalous. It was born in the port ghetto of La Boca when the music of the poor Italian and Spanish immigrants blended with the primal rhythms of the Afro-Argentines. The instruments were impromptu, but most often included handmade drums and flutes, immigrant violins and perhaps a smuggled or bartered piano. The angst of the immigrant was expressed in poetry and song as most folk music rises from roots in the poor or lower classes – the music of 'the people'. The tango has evolved over the past couple of centuries since its first humble notes, first bold steps, but it has remained fiercely devoted to recognising its origins. The earliest residents of La Boca were immigrant men, and crime was fostered by the desperate economic situation of this mud-banked port where Spanish ships rarely docked. The tango was originally a dance for men, somewhat influenced by the mannerisms and foot patterns of Spanish and Italian folk dances. It was expressed in movements of bravado, and when two men danced together it was in semblance of a duel. This expression of the tango, the dance, music and songs, began to establish itself in the subculture of this community. As the port and the community grew and social establishments arose, mostly bars and brothels, women were brought into the dance, as were the taboos. Prostitutes were the first dance partners and the interaction between the man and the woman was about seduction and sex. Movements were minimal but intense. Contact was close and suggestive and every gesture and glance of the eyes, or proximity of the face, was significant. Indeed, even the request to dance was made, as is still the etiquette today, by making eye contact from a distance and wordlessly meeting together on the dance floor.

The upper class remained hostile and regarded the tango as scandalous. It was not until it made its way back to the Old World and into the Parisian dance halls that the tango was re-introduced to Buenos Aires as a sophisticated adolescent unable to refrain from expressing itself. The tango is now experiencing a renaissance and more and more tango halls are opening up not only in Buenos Aires but in many parts of the country where tango was never a part of the culture. It is a simple eight-step in its basic form but elaborated upon by variation and ornamentation (lunges, leaps, turns, kicks, etc). Those who dance the tango suffer from the same zeal as those who study classical forms of dance, art and music: one is never considered to have achieved perfection but must continuously strive for an unattainable aspiration.

Although the tango has taken the limelight of Argentine dance, in many parts of the country it is not present and the traditional **folk dance** is much more pervasive. Especially in the northwest, folk dance can be seen at weekend markets with live music and in restaurants and bars at night. One of the most popular is the *Bailecito*, which is danced with the waving of handkerchiefs. Some of the folk music, song and dance is influenced by the cultures of Peru and Bolivia, namely the *Carnavalito* dance, in the adjacent regions of Argentina; others evolved from a Creole base, such as the *Zamba*, particularly within the gaucho culture.

The traditional **musical instruments** are drums, guitars and flutes, constructed from leather, wood and animal parts. One of the most interesting and innovative variations on the common guitar is the one made from the hard armoured body of the armadillo. Wind instruments are single reeds or similar to the pan flutes.

Folk costume is similar throughout the regions, dating from the colonial period, with the women in long full skirts and shawls. The male costume involves baggy pants, high leather boots, a brimmed hat and a scarf – influenced and accessorised by a lifestyle on horseback. The gaucho attire is the most distinctive. The gaucho wears the baggy pants and high leather boots suitable for horseback riding (historically the footwear was only an ankle/shin protector and the toes were exposed to grip the small toe-stirrups of the saddle; a gaucho rarely walked and was always on his horse, therefore eliminating any need for soled footwear). His shirt is full-sleeved to shield from the sun. A vest, belt and brimmed hat are the leather accessories. Silver is the other important adornment: a *rastra* on the belt, spurs on the feet and, of course, a *facón* or *verijero* – the gaucho knife. A *facón* is as crucial as the horse to the gaucho; it is his eating utensil, work tool, hunting, or potentially defensive, weapon and undeniably a symbol of his manliness. The true hunting weapon of the gaucho, which was adopted from the native Indians, is the *boleadora* – three long rawhide ropes tied together at one end with a heavy round stone wrapped at each loose end. The *boleadora* was thrown at the legs of the prey to trip it. The gaucho saddle is surely the most comfortable saddle known to horsemanship. Obviously, if one is spending the greater part of the day atop a horse, comfort is a priority. The horse is first covered with a thin leather blanket, often made of carpincho, called a *cojinillo*, followed by a thin wool blanket then the saddle itself, which does not have the typical moulded seat of the common saddle, but has two long rolls that lie on either side of the horse's spine. Atop the saddle is a thick woolly sheepskin and finally another thin blanket.

The **poncho** is common throughout Argentina but its style and design are particular to the various regions. In the north, it is made of vicuña wool and is typically beige with rhombus patterning, symbolising the sun. This poncho design originates in Bolivia and Peru. In Catamarca province the poncho is embroidered with flowers and is strongly influenced by Spanish colonial styles and decorated with colourful fringes. The poncho of the Chaco has geometric patterns (zigzags, triangles and rhombuses), while the poncho of the Jesuit culture of the northeast has a design referred to as that of the 'thousand lines'. The Mapuche poncho has zigzags resembling steps signifying the universe divided into four regions; in the centre of the patterns are crosses related to the concept of the ascent to heaven.

Handicrafts, local goods and specialities

Wool is abundant in Argentina and not just that of sheep. Of course, the millions of sheep raised in Patagonia sustain a large wool industry, although mostly for export. In the north, however, the wool of alpaca, llama and vicuña is more common. Vicuña wool is the most expensive owing to the endangered status of this wild animal that still suffers from poaching. The wool can still be found in some stores but most conscientious merchants boycott the product and try to educate consumers not to support this industry. Ponchos, blankets, bags and sweaters are the most popular and commonly produced items; in the north the production is handmade on looms and the prices are excellent; whereas, as with most consumer goods in Patagonia, prices increase significantly as one moves south. The woollen goods in the northwest are influenced by neighbouring cultures in Peru, Bolivia and Chile; the garments made in Patagonia are a mix of native and European cultural decorations and styles.

Leather and especially rawhide leather is produced in great quantity and excellent quality. The leather industry has remained a key industry in Argentina since the first tanning and dying factories were established at the port of Buenos Aires. In the northeast, the more common leather is not from the cow but from a large rodent, the carpincho. This industry has to be closely monitored and the hunt of the animal controlled so as not to over-exploit it. However, throughout the pampas, northern Patagonia and the north-central regions of the country, where cows and cowboys are abundant, cow leather is crafted into saddles, hats, clothing, bridles and other equestrian items. Many items are also made of the pale-coloured rawhide, which is very characteristic of Argentina. The exquisite workmanship of some of these items, with elaborate embossment and silver adornment, can raise the prices substantially, but in comparison to the equivalent workmanship in North America or Europe, the prices are a steal.

Silverwork is also appreciated in decorative *matés* and *bombillas*, vital to drinking *maté*. Silver jewellery is sold everywhere from street markets to upscale jewellers; yet, despite its name, Argentina produces virtually no silver.

The mining of **precious and semi-precious stones** is a strong and active industry. The national stone is the semi-precious Rodocrosite. It is a lovely pink stone of volcanic origin that is found in Catamarca province. It has a striped structure of rose-coloured bands with light to dark tones superimposed. The bands have a fibrous structure and are separated by white or grey strata composed of a blending of various carbonates, namely calcium, magnesium, iron and a low concentration of manganese carbonate (the iron industry uses the manganese that the minerals contain). The bands are straight or wavy and the colour is most saturated and deeply hued at the heart of the stone, which influences the price along with the size and shape of the crystal (the rhombohedric, flat and perfect crystals with a length of 3–5mm are highly valued). Rodocrosite is found in volcanic shafts formed by riolite, tufa and breccia. Ornaments and other decorative objects are also made from the stone and it is growing in interest and appeal to scientists and collectors. Other popular Argentine stones are amethyst, aquamarine, topaz and various agates.

Different styles of **pottery** are found throughout Argentina, again with distinctions in styles and prices between the north and the south. The products of the north are more colourful and have a more rustic look to them owing to the techniques of sculpting, moulding and firing. The southern products are greatly influenced by European tastes (in conservative colours and designs) and are often mass-produced and much more expensive.

The northeastern regions support native groups who have preserved their cultures and sustain themselves largely by handicrafts such as **wood carving** and **weaving**. The Wichi people are especially famous for their products, which are not only beautiful but authentic, affordable, handmade, one-of-a-kind and culturally supportive and sustainable.

Practical Information

WHEN TO VISIT

The opportunities for entertainment and adventure are boundless in Argentina and there is something for everyone to enjoy. It is also a large country and unless you have copious amounts of time to see it all, you will have to make some choices that will partly be based upon season. Areas that are far apart geographically may in fact have contemporary seasons, while the places in between are definitely out of season. For example, winter is the time for snow-sports in the Patagonian Andes but not so great for visiting the coast to see wildlife or enjoy the water, while in the far north of the country, it is a good time to visit to avoid the sweltering summer temperatures. To save time you may choose to fly across the country and thus find yourself in a subtropical jungle one day and atop a glacier the next. The downside is that you will miss the landscapes and little towns in between.

Argentina's distinctly different regions offer diverse experiences at different times of the year. The northern beaches fill with foreign tourists as well as Argentines on summer vacation in December and January. This is the best time of year for the beach but not for avoiding crowds and inflated prices. Patagonia is best for coastal wildlife watching from September to November: the right whales are in their calving grounds until November, the elephant seals give birth in early September, and the penguins start nesting in September, with hatching beginning in late October. The other time to visit Patagonia is the ski season, in the southern hemisphere winter, from mid-June to October, with July being the peak season (with busier slopes and more expensive ski passes). The northeast, with its waterfalls, wetlands, jungles, subtropical wildlife, Jesuit missions and archaeological ruins, should be avoided in the rainy season, with frequent flooding around September followed by scorching temperatures in the subsequent months; however, October is one of the best times to see butterflies at Iguazú Falls. The northwest is known for stunning desert landscapes in the mineral-rich colourful mountains, cardón cactus and ancient cultural sites, high plateaux with vicuñas, a vibrantly alive culture of music and dance, crafts and cuisine; mid-summer (January–February) is extremely hot but spring and autumn are great. The beautiful central Sierras offer more stunning mountain landscapes to enjoy. The missions are scattered throughout this region, which is also popular for adventure sports such as rock climbing and paragliding. The best time of year to visit is early or late summer (mid-summer is quite hot).

SUGGESTED ITINERARIES

The following itineraries are inspired by a sense of exploration, adventure and trying to see more than the major tourist spots. There is a wealth of beauty, authenticity and uniqueness that many travellers miss due to lack of time. The country is vast, and the average tourist will see only the major points of interest. If you want more than that, the following suggestions are a starting point for planning a road trip into rural

Argentina. Although there are airports in most of the larger towns, there are not necessarily flights connecting these towns; most flights will go straight to a major hub city. The bus is the best option for travelling and seeing the countryside with the least trouble, but you will be unable to detour or to stop along the way and often be frustrated when passing rare wildlife, a great photo opportunity or some other curiosity whizzes past at 90km/h. If you do your research well (and this is a must) a road trip offers the most freedom of movement as well as the freedom to stop moving. Please, do not take off blindly with a car in rural Argentina because although a road may look significant on a map, it is often not maintained and may lack emergency assistance or even filling stations. Some roads are impassable in winter and flash snowstorms can happen at any time on Andean passes. A compromise option may be to take buses between the larger towns and rent a car to explore the surroundings, but be prepared for significant backtracking. Buses connect all the major tourist attractions and popular towns along the way with varying frequency depending upon the season. A few of the following routes are based on the main highways; it must be repeated that even a major motorway may at times turn into a gravel road. The most famous of all, Ruta 40, intersects with a couple of the other itineraries.

Following the Mystical Ruta 40

This legendary route traverses almost the entire length of Argentina, paralleling the Andes all the way from the south of Santa Cruz to Jujuy. Grandiose photographic books have been published about the magical Ruta 40, celebrating its charms and enchantments. Following it down through Patagonia will take you through many lovely villages and fascinating cities, each with a unique experience to offer: Bariloche, El Bolsón, Esquel, El Chaltén, El Calafate and many more. The Andes will be ever-present, glowing in shades of auburn in the morning and silhouetted in silvery blues at sunset, which comes quickly since this is the highest range outside Asia with 29 peaks over 6,000m. As you make your way along this route, guanacos, choiques, foxes, hares, condors, eagles and armadillos will observe your passage, and, if you are eagle-eyed, you will observe them as well.

Coastal Ruta 3

Ruta 3 starts in Buenos Aires and heads due south for the popular south-facing coastline where Mar del Plata and the neighbouring resorts are packed with *porteños* in summer. Beaches, thermal springs and wildlife watching will lure you continuously southward all the way to Penînsula Valdés. Tourist spots are rarer south of here, not because of a lack of beauty or impressive wildlife areas, but because there is a lack of infrastructure. Distances between accommodation, filling stations and places to eat increase, but so does the relative 'wildness' of the coast.

Sections of the drive have beautiful coastal views and points of interest; other sections are inland and not necessarily scenic. To see the entire coastline would require a trustworthy car, a lot of time and a sense of adventure. Inland are other fascinating places, such as petrified forests, but they require some backtracking to visit. Ruta 3 ends in Ushuaia, but connecting from Río Gallegos is complicated and you would be better off flying, which is quick and easy, and then renting a car to explore Tierra del Fuego.

Chubut Valley

This east–west valley was first settled by Welsh immigrants who landed near Puerto Madryn in 1865 and made their way slowly to the Andes, establishing towns along the way. Following Ruta 25 from Trelew you're soon in Gaiman where you can easily spend a few days exploring the river and canyon-gouged badlands and petrified forests in between teatimes. The next stretch of the route west is long and sparsely populated. It follows the Chubut River and offers detours to visit lakes and the impressive **Embalse Florentino Ameghino**. The central stretch of the valley is quite desolate, so if you are driving, make sure you are well supplied, including a spare can of fuel. Pass through the rough Patagonian grassland steppe until you reach the foothills of the Andes and the Welsh towns of Trevelin, Esquel and El Bolsón.

Northwest

This route, passing through the main towns, cities and points of interest covered in *Chapter 6*, covers one of the most stunning areas of the country, starting from the city of Tucumán and potentially heading due north all the way to the Bolivian border. There are many national parks along the way and various excursions and side trips that will each distract you for a day or two. There is less need to have a car in the northwest as many tour companies focus on this area with frequent and well-organised trips. Car rental may save you some money but most of the roads are gravel, dusty and hot and may cause engine problems. If you are exploring by car, take precautions and drive slowly.

The Rivers Paraná and Uruguay

This route is circular with the chance to start and finish in Buenos Aires. While travellers with limited time will fly directly to the spectacular Iguazú Falls, the entirety of Mesopotamia, which is encircled by these two major rivers, is well worth exploring. The following itinerary takes a clockwise route: following the Paraná River north from Buenos Aires, call in at El Tigre if you have not already been here on a day trip, then take Ruta 9 to Rosario. There are many little towns to see between Buenos Aires and Rosario, and Rosario itself deserves a couple of days. Cross the bridge from Rosario to Victoria (from Santa Fé province to Entre Ríos province), where you can again spend a day. Continue north to visit the Pre-Delta National Park and the twin cities of Paraná and Santa Fé on opposite banks of the river, connected by a tunnel. Staying on the east bank, take Ruta 12 to Corrientes, with prime river-fishing and wetland birdwatching opportunities along the way. Just east, in the middle of Corrientes province, are another national park, Mburucuya, the must-see wetlands of Esteros del Iberá and the town of Mercedes, which you can visit on the return leg of this circular itinerary. Without a car your options are limited, and the town of Corrientes has bus connection to Mercedes whereas the more conveniently placed Posadas does not. The bus schedules to visit the park and the wetlands are also quite inconvenient. Posadas has little to offer beyond the river, though it's a good stopover point. Head north from Posadas on Ruta 12 to explore the mission ruins, the mining town of Wanda and eventually reach Puerto Iguazú. Get an early morning start and go to the falls; one or two days here are sufficient (which is why the falls are a popular option for visitors with limited time who can quickly fly up from Buenos Aires). The itinerary now heads south on Ruta 14 for the return section of the loop, offering different scenery as well as some interesting detours such as Moconá Falls, which are worth seeing though overshadowed by Iguazú. Continuing south along the Uruguay River you will pass through the thermal region and can visit a number of pools: Parque Thermal Chajari, the spas in the towns of Federación, Concordia and Colon and the Termas Villa Elisa, where there you can also see the San José Palace, once General Urquiza's home. Along the route through the thermal region is El Palmar National Park, a unique wetland park where the last stands of yatay palms are protected. The next town on the route, famous at Mardi Gras when the town celebrates in full carnival style, is Gualeguaychu. Finally Ruta 14 crosses back over the Paraná River and rejoins Ruta 9 to return to Buenos Aires.

Central

This region is one of the easiest to explore independently. You will probably fly into Córdoba and spend a couple of days seeing this city, one of the oldest in the country. Afterwards, rent a car and explore the missions, the Central Sierras, the lakes and national parks. Córdoba, surrounded by sites of interest on all sides, may act as the hub of a wheel which you pass through repeatedly. Driving from here to Mendoza will reward you with fine scenery, and if you can afford the time and a bit of backtracking, head first towards San Luis on Ruta 20, visit some of the hot springs, then head northwest up to San Juan on Ruta 147, taking the time to visit the Sierra de las Quijadas National Park. From San Juan to Mendoza on Ruta 40 is a brilliant section of the wine country to explore.

TOUR OPERATORS
In the UK

Andean Trails The Clockhouse, Bonnington Mill Business Centre, 72 Newhaven Rd, Edinburgh EH6 5QG; ↘ 0131 467 7086; e info@andeantrails.co.uk; www.andeantrails.co.uk. A specialist adventure tour operator, offering challenging activity and adventure holidays in Patagonia, trekking in FitzRoy or Torres del Paine National Park, skiing or snow-shoeing on the South-Patagonian Ice Cap, as well as climbing, mountaineering, mountain biking, rafting or sea-kayaking throughout the Andes.

Audley Travel Willlows Gate, Stratton Audley, Oxon OX27 9AU; ↘ 01869 276 222; e mail@audleytravel.com; www.audleytravel.com

Discover the World 29 Nork Way, Banstead, Surrey SM7 1PB; ↘ 01737 218 800; e enquiries@discovertheworld.co.uk; www.discover-the-world.co.uk

Explore Nelson House, 55 Victoria Rd, Farnborough, Hants GU14 7PA; ↘: 0870 333 4001; f 01252 391110; e info@explore.co.uk; US office: Adventure Center, 1311 63rd St, Suite 200, Emeryville, CA 94608; ↘ 800 227 8747; e ex@adventurecenter.com; www.exploreworldwide.com. An adventure and cultural travel company with over 20 years' experience; with small groups of like-minded people, they aim to get 'further and closer', do things the local way as much as possible, respect the local culture and invest in responsible tourism.

Guerba Wessex House, 40 Station Rd, Westbury BA13 3JN; ↘ 01373 826611, 828303; e info@guerba.co.uk; www.guerba.com. This agency has focused on adventure travel for over two decades, guiding people to Africa, Asia, South America and Europe. Their Andean trekking and tours to Tierra del Fuego focus on helping local communities through sustainable tourism efforts.

High Places Globe Centre, Penistone Rd, Sheffield S6 3AE; ↘ 0114 275 7500; e treks@highplaces.co.uk; www.highplaces.co.uk

Sunvil Latin America Sunvil House, Upper Sq, Old Isleworth, Middx TW7 7BJ; ↘ 020 8758 4774; e latinamerica@sunvil.co.uk; www.sunvil.co.uk

Trailfinders One of the UK's leading independent travel companies with individual tailor-made itineraries in Argentina and worldwide. They offer discounted airfares, hotels, tours, cruises and vehicle rental. Offices are throughout the UK, Ireland and Australia, with four offices in London; consult their website (*www.trailfinders.com*) or ↘ 0845 058 5858.

In North America

Abercrombie & Kent 1520 Kensington Rd, Suite 212, Oak Brook, IL 60523-2156, USA; ↘ 630 954 2944, toll-free 800 554 7016; www.abercrombiekent.com. This luxury travel agency began with African safaris back in the 1960s. They offer escorted or independent

agency began with African safaris back in the 1960s. They offer escorted or independent packages, with Argentine tours focusing on Patagonia and the northeast, in conjunction with Chile and Brazil.

ATAC Patagonia Tours PO Box 5498, Incline Village, NV 89450, USA; ✆ +1 530 448 14818; e info@adventure-tours-south.com; www.adventure-tours-south.com. Small-group adventure packages to Patagonia, including rafting, horseriding, fly-fishing, kayaking, mountain biking, skiing and hiking.

All Mountain Vacations 555 Dayton St, Suite A, Edmonds, WA 98020, USA; ✆ 800 838 8142, 425 697 5013; e sales@all-mountain.com; www.all-mountain.com.Ski trips to Las Leñas, Chapelco near San Martín and Cerro Catedral near Bariloche, together with sightseeing opportunities; tours can be extended to other sites of interest such as Iguazú or Buenos Aires, not for skiing obviously.

Amazon Adventures 2711 Market Garden, Austin, TX 78745, USA; ✆ 512 443 5393, toll-free 800 232 5658; e jmc12@amazonadventures.com; www.amazonadventures.com/argentina.A wide variety of tours throughout the country including Buenos Aires, Iguazú Falls, Food and Wine Tours in Mendoza, various destinations in Patagonia including the Lakes District, the glaciers, Península Valdés and Tierra del Fuego, and hard-to-reach areas such as the Valley of the Moon, Tilcara and the Salinas in the far northwest.

Argentina Discover 1601 NW 97th, Miami, FL 33012-5216, USA; ✆ 305 716 9216, toll-free 866 369 8046; e contact@latindiscover.com; www.argentinadiscover.com; also in the UK (✆ 800 169 8163) and in Australia (✆ 800 127410). Customised tours to Buenos Aires, Iguazú and Patagonia.

Blue Parallel Maryland, USA; ✆ +1 301 960 4449; ✆ toll-free 800 256 5307; e info@blueparallel.com; www.blueparallel.com. Luxury tours focusing on World Heritage Sites. Cultural experiences, gourmet food and wine and first-class lodgings are part of the package.

Gap Adventures 19 Charlotte St, Toronto, Ontario M5V 2H5, Canada; ✆ 0870 999 0144; toll-free 800 708 7761 (North America), 0870 080 1756 (UK); www.gapadventures.com. Up to 40 tours throughout Argentina.

Grand Circle Travel 347 Congress St, Boston, MA 02210-1230, USA; ✆ 617 350 7500, toll-free 800 959 0405; e reservations@gct.com; www.gct.com. A tour of the Lakes District of Argentina and Chile. This agency also has experience catering to senior citizens.

LaTour 233 Park Av South, New York, NY 10003, USA; ✆ 800 223 7460; www.isram.com/latournew. Tours to Buenos Aires, Iguazú and Bariloche and other South American destinations.

Lost World Adventures 217E Davis St, Decatur, GA 30030, USA; ✆ 0800 011 2592; e info@lostworld.com; www.lostworld.com. Scenic tours and activities include birdwatching, hiking, snorkelling, and rafting. Accommodation ranges from luxury hotels, comfortable haciendas and full-service resorts to basic lodges. Cultural and eco-tours are led by bilingual local guides with extensive knowledge of the flora, fauna and culture.

Patagonia Travel Adventures 50 Franklin St, 4th Floor, Boston, MA 02110, USA; ✆ 617 738 4700; www.realadventures.com. Though a US company, tours are organised and led by local Patagonian people in the land they know best, so that you can have an unforgettable adventure.

Postales del Plata c/o Rivers to Reefs Excursions, 1505 L Av, La Grande, OR 97850, USA; ✆ 541 963 7878, toll-free 866 963 7870 (US); +54 261 429 6210 (Mendoza); e info@postalesdelplata.com; www.postalesdelplata.com. Tours to Argentina's Andes region, particularly to Mendoza for wine tours, as well as Salta and the Andean northwest and skiing at Las Lenas.

Travel Wizard 100 Smith Ranch Road, Suite 110, San Rafael, CA 94903, USA; ✆ 415 446 5252, toll-free 800 330 8820; e concierge@travelwizard.com; www.travelwizard.com. Tours of Buenos Aires and Patagonia, and Paraná River cruises.

International offices

Hostelling International Calle Florida 835 3? Piso Of 319B, CP 1005, Ciudad de Buenos Aires; ☎ +54 11 4511 8712/23; e hiargentina@hostels.org.ar; www.hostels.org.ar

Mix Travel Viajes y Turismo Gay Maipu 971 5C, Buenos Aires; ☎ +54 11 4312 3410; e mixtravel@davostours.com; www.mixtravel.com.Gay and lesbian travel agency featuring trips to the pampas, beaches, rainforests, tango clubs, glaciers and cordilleras of Argentina, as well as various tours in South and Central America.

South American Travel Tours to Buenos Aires, the Lakes District, Patagonia, Iguazú, Salta and Mendoza, with tours around South America and custom service available. Contact is through the website: www.south-america-travel-cruises.com.

4Star Argentina Tours and Travel Vacations Discover Buenos Aires tango, Mendoza wine, Patagonia, Iguazu Falls and the Andes, on 4- and 5-star guided custom tours. Offices are in the US, Europe, Mexico and Rio de Janeiro; contact through www.4starargentina.com.

Turar This local operator offers a variety of cultural tours of cities such as Buenos Aires, Mar del Plata, Córdoba and Bariloche as well as to scenic areas including Iguazú and the Andes. They are also a member of the International Gay & Lesbian Travel Association. Bartolomé Mitre 559, Piso 4, Buenos Aires; ☎ +54 11 4103 3100; f 11 4103 3111; e turar@turar.com; www.turar.com.

Zelayaoutdoors Tucumàn; ☎ 4354982; m 156093336; e info@zelayaoutdoors.com; www.zelayaoutdoors.com. For adventure, nature and 'spirit' travel in Argentina and several South American countries.

There are a few good link pages listing tour agencies working in Argentina. Try **InfoHub Argentina**, www.infohub.com/TRAVEL/SIT/sit_pages/Argentina.html. Listed here are independent tour operators in Argentina, with itineraries and prices.

Specialist tours

Fishing tours can be planned with **John Eustice & Associates Ltd** (*1445 SW 84th Av, Portland, OR 97225, USA;* ☎ *503 297 2468, toll-free 800 288 0886;* e *johne@johneustice.com, www.johneustice.com*) focusing on the best spots in Patagonia, Tierra del Fuego and Esteros del Iberá.

Excellent **golf** courses are found throughout the country and many are mentioned in the guide; in addition, **Classic Golf Tours** (*3045 South Parker Rd, Suite 201, Aurora, CO 80012, USA;* ☎ *303 751 7200, toll-free 800 359 7200;* e *golfdreams@classicgolftours.com, www.classicgolftours.com*) offers golfing experiences at the prime resorts in Patagonia as well as neighbouring Chile and Brazil.

Whale-watching specialists are **Out Of The Blue** (*Brookfield House, 38 St Paul St, Chippenham SN15 1LJ, UK;* ☎ *+(44) (0)1249 449533/47;* e *outoftheblue@wdcs.org*).

Birdwatching is unbelievably rewarding, with a vast and easily viewed diversity of avian species that reflects the country's various habitat types. For the best local advice and tours contact **Aves Patagonia** (*San Martín de los Andes;* ☎ *+54 02972 422022;* e *info@avespatagonia.com.ar; www.avespatagonia.com.ar*).

Wildlife and birdwatching tour operators

UK

Naturetrek Cheriton Mill, Cheriton, Alresford, Hants SO24 0NG; ☎ 01962 733051; e info@naturetrek.co.uk; www.naturetrek.co.uk

Ornitholidays 29 Straight Mile, Romsey, Hants SO51 9BB; ☎ 01794 519445; e ornitholidays@compuserve.com; www.ornitholidays.co.uk

Travelling Naturalist PO Box 3141, Dorchester, Dorset DT1 2XD; ☎ 01305 267994; e jamie@naturalist.co.uk; www.naturalist.co.uk

Wildlife Worldwide Chameleon Hse, 162 Selsdon Rd, South Croydon CR2 6PJ; ☎ 020 8667 9158; e sales@wildlifeworldwide.com; www.wildlifeworldwide.com

North America
Birdtreks 216 Spring Lane, Peach Bottom, PA 17563; ☎ 717 548 3303;
e info@birdtreks.com
Eagle-Eye Tours 9744 84 Av, Edmonton, Alberta T6E 2E9, Canada; ☎ 780 435 1824, toll-free 800 373 5678; e travel@eagle-eye.com; www.eagle-eye.com
Victor Emanuel Nature Tours 2525 Wallingwood Drive, Suite 1003, Austin TX 78746;
☎ 512 328 5221; toll-free 800 328 8368; e info@ventbird.com; www.ventbird.com

VISAS AND EMBASSIES
A valid passport is necessary for all tourists entering Argentina. A tourist visa is required of some nationals, but not of EU or North American citizens. Upon arrival in Argentina you will be given a tourist card which must be handed in when leaving the country; if you have lost it, you will be fined.

Argentine embassies abroad
Australia John McEwen House, Level 2, 7 National Circuit, Barton, ACT 2600. Postal address: PO Box 4835, Kingston ACT 2604; ☎ (612) 6273 9111; e info@argentina.org.au
Canada 81 Metcalfe St, Suite 700, Ottawa, Ontario K1P 6K7; ☎ (613) 236 2351;
e embargentina@argentina-canada.net
United Kingdom 65 Brook St, London W1K 4AH; ☎ (020) 7318 1300; www.argentine-embassy.uk.org
United States 1600 New Hampshire Av, NW, Washington DC 20009; ☎ (202) 238 6400;
f 332 3171; www.embassyofargentina-usa.org

Foreign embassies in Buenos Aires
Australia Villanueva 1400; ☎ 4779 3599/6580; open Mon–Fri 08.30-11.00.
Canada Tagle 2828; ☎ 4808 1000/3032; open Mon–Thu 08.45-11.30.
United Kingdom Dr Luis Agote 2412; ☎ 4808 2200; open Mon–Thu 08.45–17.30
(Jan/Feb to 14.30), Fri 08.45–14.00.
United States Av Colombia 4300; ☎ 5777 4533/34, 4774 7611; open Mon–Fri 09.00-17.30.

TOURIST INFORMATION
Information for visitors is available abroad mainly through embassies and consulates, which do not have a great deal of free material to hand out:

UK 27 Three Kings Yard, London W1Y 1FL; ☎ 020 7318 1340; f 7318 1349.
USA 5505 Wilshire Boulevard, Suite 210, Los Angeles CA 90036; ☎ 213 930 0681; f 934 0076; 2655 Le Jeune Rd, P I Suite F, Coral Gables, FL 33134; ☎ 305 442 1366; f 441 7092; 12 West 56th St, New York, NY 10019; ☎ 212 603 0443; f 315 5545. It's also well worth looking at www.turismo.gov.ar and www.welcomeargentina.com; www.cybermapa.com.ar is a slightly clunky mapping site.

For postal enquiries, the Secretaría de Turismo de la Nación is at Suipacha 1111 Piso 21, 1368 Buenos Aires; their visitor centre is at Avenida Santa Fé 883; ☎ 4312 2232, toll-free 0800 555 0016. They also have offices at the capital's two airports (daily 08.00-20.00), Retiro bus terminal, and half a dozen other locations (see page 95). The country's provinces all maintain a Casa de Provincia in the capital, each keen to persuade you to visit that province before any other.

Buenos Aires Av Callao 237; ☎ 4373 2636
Catamarca Av Córdoba 2080; ☎ 4374 6891/4
Córdoba Av Callao 332; ☎ 4372 8859, 4373 4277
Corrientes San Martín 333 Piso 4; ☎ 4394 7390

Chaco Av Callao 322; ℡ 4372 0961
Chubut Sarmiento 1172; ℡ 4382 8126
Entre Ríos Suipacha 844; ℡ 4328 2284
Formosa Yrigoyen 1429; ℡ 4381 2037
Jujuy Av Santa Fé 967; ℡ 4393 6096
La Pampa Suipacha 346; ℡ 4326 0511
La Rioja Av Callao 745; ℡ 4813 3417
Mendoza Av Callao 445; ℡ 4371 0835
Misiones Av Santa Fé 989; ℡ 4393 1812
Neuquén Perón 685; ℡ 4311 9440
Río Negro Tucumán 1916; ℡ 4371 5599
Salta Av Sáenz Peña 933, Piso 5; ℡ 4326 2456/7, 4326 1314
San Juan Sarmiento 1251; ℡ 4328 5580, 4382 9241
San Luis Azcuénaga 1087; ℡ 4822 0426
Santa Cruz 25 de Mayo 277, Piso 1; ℡ 4334 3692, 4342 7756, 4343 8478
Santa Fé Montevideo 373, Piso 2; ℡ 4375 4570/3, 5811 4327
Santiago del Estero Florida 274; ℡ 4326 3733, 4326 9418
Tierra del Fuego Sarmiento 745; ℡ 4322 7324
Tucumán Suipacha 140; ℡ 4322 0010, 4322 0564

Finally, for longer stays and off-the-beaten-track tourism, it's well worth joining the **South American Explorers**, who have recently opened a clubhouse in Buenos Aires (*Jerónimo Salguero 553;* ℡ *911 4861 7571;* e *baclub@saexplorers.org, argentina@saexplorers.org; or see www.saexplorers.org; open Mon–Thu 10.00–18.00 and Fri–Sat 13.00–17.00).* To visit them take the B-Line subway to Medrano, walk half a block to Salguero, then turn right; the club is situated on the left-hand side of the street. They will provide maps, guidebooks, information packs, and a wealth of networking opportunities, as well as social and educational activities. For more information on Patagonia, members can contact Eric in Bariloche (*patagonia@saexplorers.org*).

GETTING THERE AND AWAY

An unprecedented surge in tourism has been brought about by the devaluation of the Argentine peso in 2001, climbing by about 40% the subsequent year and continuing to rise since then. Tourism has become one of the most important economic activities in the country. Tourists keen to take advantage of the weak Argentine peso are welcomed by those businesses, organisations and institutions that cater to visitors to the country. Argentina is relatively easy to get around but expect certain inconveniences at times, such as late buses or lax business hours (this varies region to region and with the size of the city or town). In poorer areas you may not find convenient transport connections or strict adherence to opening hours. For the most part, Argentina, even after the economic crash, has a higher standard of service than other South American countries. This is largely due to the strong history of tourism and cosmopolitan attitudes in Buenos Aires and the enormous increase in eco-tourism in Patagonia. I use the term eco-tourism loosely, since it seems to be used for a normal style of tourism offering wildlife watching and wilderness settings; it rarely, however, implies any environmental impact awareness such as innovative waste disposal, energy conservation or minimal water use. You will have to take it upon yourself to be as low impact as you can and make polite suggestions to hotels and restaurants as to what you would like to see in the future. In relation to transportation, oil and gas are big business in Patagonia and fuel prices are low compared to North

America and Europe, and the only way to move freely to remote areas is with a car. Buses provide frequent service to almost any decent-sized town, but if you want to move beyond the towns you will need your own wheels. Argentina is a big country and to cover larger distances you may need to take bus rides of over 24 hours (sample distances: Buenos Aires to Ushuaia, 3,200km; Salta to Ushuaia, 4,700km). Thus you may want to consider using both flights and buses for an efficient use of your time.

Airlines and flights to Argentina

Book international flights at least a month in advance for the best fares. If you intend to take at least two domestic flights in Argentina during your trip, you would be wise to purchase a *Visit Argentina* **airpass** from Aerolíneas Argentinas, typically sold as two internal flight coupons per international flight. Domestic flights are reasonably priced but the airpass gives discounts of up to 50% (with lower discounts if it is not bought in conjunction with an international ticket). Airpasses must be booked in advance and purchased in the traveller's country of residence (not in Argentina). All coupons must be fully paid for together with the international ticket; the first flight must be booked then, while the remaining coupons may be booked at any time with rebooking permitted (usually at a cost of about US$20) but not rerouting. The entire journey must be completed within the validity of the international ticket. Stopovers are not permitted. Discounts are available only for children under the age of two years.

Round-the-World tickets are an option for visiting several continents without having to purchase return flights for each destination, but rather continuing around the globe. For example, you can fly out of Europe into North America, onwards to South America and then visit Asia on your way back home. This is not necessarily an economical or inexpensive option but is flexible and convenient.

If you're visiting both Chile and Argentina, the Buenos Aires–Santiago route sees around ten flights per day, and there are connections from Punta Arenas and Puerto Montt to towns in Argentinean Patagonia. You can also take buses although not all are direct and may require more than one change, with layovers and border checks.

If you wish to fly straight to Patagonia and bypass Buenos Aires, it may be more convenient and less expensive to fly to Santiago de Chile and then to Bariloche, which has a small but well-serviced airport for flights across the border as well as throughout the country. Similarly, heading to the northeast to visit Iguazú and the Mesopotamia region, you may consider flying into Brazil, but this country requires visas (except for Europeans and a few others), which may dissuade you.

Airlines flying into Buenos Aires

Argentine airlines have limited international routes, but many major airlines, representing all three main alliances, fly into Buenos Aires. These airline alliances allow passengers with one airline to reach Argentina on code-shared flights operated by their partners.

Star Alliance Air Canada, Air New Zealand, ANA-All Nippon Airways, Asiana Airlines, Austrian Airlines, BMI British Midland, LOT Polish Airlines, Lufthansa, SAS-Scandinavian Airlines, Singapore Airlines, South African Airways, Spanair, TAP Portugal, Thai Airways, United Airlines, US Airways and Varig Brazilian Airlines.
SkyTeam AeroMexico, Air France-KLM, Alitalia, Continental Airlines, CSA Czech Airlines, Delta, Korean Air and Northwest Airlines.
OneWorld LAN, American Airlines, British Airways, Iberia, Cathay Pacific, Finnair, Aer Lingus and Qantas.

THE ORIGINS OF ARGENTINA'S AIRLINES

Air services in Argentina were first developed to carry mail around the immense expanses of Patagonia. The first pilots were mostly French, including Antoine de Saint-Exupéry, who arrived in 1929, and drew on his experiences to write *Vol de Nuit*. Another of them, Leonardo Servetti, remembers the dreadful weather conditions: 'Winds were of a speed that almost stopped the plane and blew it backwards. I remember that in order to land we had to nose-dive at full power and stick the plane to the soil. We had to fly close to sea level so the ice would melt on the wings. On the other hand, the snow blurred the windshield and we had to lean out of the window to see. Then our goggles blurred and when we took them off we had tears which froze on our faces.'

Argentina's very first airline was Aeroposta Argentina, formed in 1928 to carry mail and passengers to the far reaches of Patagonia. It remained the only Argentine airline until 1946 when several airlines hit the skies in that year. ALFA (Aviacion del Litoral Fluvial) and FAMA (Flota Aerea Mercante Argentina) offered passenger flights to Europe, and Zonda (Zonas Oeste y Norte de Aerolíneas Argentinas) flew between Buenos Aires and Salta. The inefficiency of the partially state-owned airlines made a merger necessary and **Aerolíneas Argentinas**, the country's flag-carrier ever since, was formed in 1949. The Argentine Air Force had also created its own airline **LADE** (Lineas Aéreas del Estado) in a separate merger of LASO (Lineas Aereas Suroeste) and LANE (Lineas Aereas Nor-Este), and it was the only airline not to join the merger that formed Aerolíneas Argentinas. LADE began flying between Buenos Aires and Bariloche at holiday times during the war and has effectively continued this and other limited season/destination services to this day. It has routes that are not typically offered by the commercial airlines but require either booking far in advance or taking a gamble for a standby place.

The first international flight of the fledgling Aerolíneas Argentinas in May 1950 was from Buenos Aires to New York (taking 21 hours in a DC-6). Five years later a new law opened the industry to competition, countered by the introduction of the Comet IV jetliner in 1959.

Austral was founded in 1971 also by way of a merger, this time of two airlines established in the 1950s: ACATA (Austral Compania Argentina de Transportes Aereos) and ALA (Aerotransportes Litoral Argentino). Austral was saved from

Airline offices

Aerolíneas Argentinas (still using the name **Austral** for some internal charter services) Buenos Aires offices (Mon–Fri 09.00–19.00, Sat 09.00–13.00): Perú 2 (↘ 4320 2000); Cabildo 2900 (↘ 4783 2507, 4784 9870/2); Av LN Alem 1134 (↘ 4130 3625/6). Central Service local rate ↘ 0810 222 VOLAR (86527); e informes@aerolineas.com.ar, www.aerolineas.com.ar. From Miami, New York (with Chicago and Los Angeles planned), Mexico City, Madrid and Rome to Buenos Aires, plus the widest range of internal services. **LADE** Perú 710; ↘ 5129 9000, 0810 810 LADE (5233); e informes@lade.com.ar (limited domestic flights only).
LAN Cerrito 866 at Paraguay; ↘ 4378 2200, local rate 0810 999 9526 (press 8 for English); www.lan.com. Via Santiago de Chile to Buenos Aires, Mendoza or Córdoba with LAN Chile, and from Miami (↘ 1866 435 9526, 305 670 9999) to Buenos Aires and internal services with LAN Argentina.
AeroMexico Reconquista 737, Piso 3, office F, Capital Federal; ↘ 5238 1200; e aeromexico@cmsgsa.com.ar. From Mexico City (↘ 4312 1200) via Santiago de Chile.

bankruptcy by Aerolíneas in 1980 and both were privatised in 1990; by 1995 the Spanish airline Iberia owned 83% of it but in 1997 had to hand some of its shares back to the airline staff and the Argentine government. American Airlines also purchased shares in the airline. However, management failures, first under Iberia, then American Airlines and finally SEPI (Sociedad Estatal de Participaciones Industriales), a Spanish state-owned holding company, led to the airline accumulating more than $1.2 billion in debt. By October 2001 Aerolíneas was bankrupt, most of its international flights were grounded and with consumer trust gone, passengers stopped flying. Antonio Mata and a group of investors from Barcelona's Grupo Marsans took over from SEPI and resuscitated the airline through cost cutting, bringing maintenance work in-house, and, after 9/11, negotiating discounts on any remaining debts with suffering suppliers and manufacturers in the industry.

Southern Winds, founded in 1996, was Aerolíneas Argentinas' main competitor, operating as a discount airline with no-frills service but low ticket prices. It had just launched international flights to Madrid and Miami when a drug-trafficking scandal hit it in September 2004. Unaccompanied baggage arrived in Madrid with 60kg of cocaine in it, and investigations showed that Southern Winds and Ezeiza airport personnel were involved. The airline lost a government subsidy of over US$1 million and soon ceased operations. LAN, the main Chilean airline and by far the most efficient and profitable in South America, offered to absorb both Southern Winds and the state-owned LAFSA (Líneas Aéreas Federales SA, formed in 2003 when Dinar, LAPA and Aerovip went bust); Argentine trade unions protested against handing the local market over to foreign ownership, despite this being the only realistic way of saving the jobs. Eventually the Argentine government broke its habit of creating new amalgamations whenever airlines failed, and **LAN Argentina** was created in 2005, flying from Buenos Aires to Córdoba, Rosario, Mendoza and Bariloche, soon followed by Neuquén, Puerto Iguazú, Comodoro Rivadavia, Río Gallegos and Miami. Other LAN companies also fly from Ezeiza to Santiago (up to eight times daily), Lima, Quito and Guayaquil, and from Santiago to Rosario and Mendoza (daily) and Córdoba and Bariloche (twice weekly). Interestingly, Aerolíneas Argentinas, in order to make use of its surplus planes, has set up subsidiaries in Chile and other nearby countries.

AeroSur Av Santa Fé 851, Piso 1; ☏ 5031 2808; www.aerosur.com. From Santa Cruz, Bolivia (☏ (3) 336 7400).

Air Canada Av Córdoba 656; ☏ 4327 3640/41; www.aircanada.com. From Toronto (☏ 1888 247 2262).

Air Europa Av Santa Fé 962, Piso 1; ☏/f 4327 1700; e info.argentina@air-europa.com, www.aireuropa.com. From Madrid (☏ 902 401501).

AirFrance San Martín 344, Piso 23; ☏ 4317 4700, toll-free 0800 666 1379; www.airfrance.com/ar. From Paris (☏ 0820 820820) via Santiago de Chile.

Alitalia Suipacha 111, Piso 28; ☏ 4310 9990, 0810 777 2548; www.alitalia.com.ar. From Rome (☏ 062222).

American Airlines Santa Fé 881, Pueyrredón 1997, Av del Libertador 5038; ☏ 4318 1111; www.aa.com. From Miami, New York or Dallas (☏ 1800 433 7300).

Avianca Carlos Pellegrini 1163, Piso 4; ☏ 4326 9556, 4394 5990; e info@avianca.com.ar. From Bogotá (☏ 243 1613).

British Airways Av del Libertador 498, Piso 13; ☏ 4320 6600, toll-free 0800 666 1459;

www.ba.com. From London (✆ 0870 850 9850).
Continental Airways c/o Copa Airlines (below). From Houston (✆ 1800 231 0856).
Copa Airlines Carlos Pellegrini 989, Piso 2; ✆ 4132 3532, 0810 222 2672;
www.copaair.com. From New York (✆ 1800 359 2672) via Panamá (✆ 507 217 2672).
Cubana Sarmiento 552, Piso 11; ✆ 4326 5291–3; e ventas@cubanadeaviacion.com.ar,
cubana@velocom.com.ar, www.cubanadeaviacion.com.ar. From Havana (✆ 537 834 4446;
e informacion.cliente@cubana.avianet.cu).
Delta Airlines Av Santa Fé 887; ✆ 5238 1200; e delta@cmsgsa.com.ar, www.delta.com.
From Atlanta (✆ 404 765 5000, toll-free 1800 241 4141) via Santiago or São Paulo.
Iberia Carlos Pellegrini 1163, Piso 1 and 3; ✆ 4131 1000/1, toll-free 0800 444 1024;
e iberia.ar@iberia.com, www.iberia.com. From Madrid or Barcelona (✆ 902 400500) to
Buenos Aires, Mendoza or Córdoba.
KLM San Martín 344, Piso 23; ✆ 4326 8422, 0800 222 2600;
e reservations.argentina@klm.com, www.klm.com. From Amsterdam (✆ 020 474 7747) via
São Paulo.
LAB Carlos Pellegrini 137/141, Piso 2; ✆ 4323 1900; e ventaslab@labairlines.com,
www.labairlines.com. From Miami and Washington (✆ 1800 327 7407) via Santa Cruz,
Bolivia (✆ 800 103001).
Lufthansa M T de Alvear 590, Piso 6; ✆ 4319 0600; www.lufthansa.com. From Frankfurt
(✆ 0810 583 8426) via Santiago.
Mexicana Av Córdoba 755, Piso 1; ✆ 4000 6300; e reservas@mexicana.com.ar,
ventas@mexicana.com.ar. From the USA (✆ 1800 531 7921) via Mexico City (✆ 5448 1038).
Pluna Florida 1, Piso B; ✆ 4329 9211, 4342 4420; e info@ar.pluna.aero,
www.pluna.aero/argentina. From Montevideo, Uruguay (✆ 604 4080).
Qantas Av Córdoba 673, Piso 13; ✆ 4114 5800; e qantasbue@qantas.com.au;
www.qantasargentina.com. From Sydney (✆ 131313) and Auckland (✆ 0800 808 767) via
Santiago.
South African Airlines Carlos Pellegrini 1141, Piso 5; ✆ 5556 6666;
e argentina@flysaabue.com.ar, www.flysaa.com. From Johannesburg (✆ 0869 359722) via
São Paulo.
TACA Carlos Pellegrini 1275; ✆ 4325 8222; www.taca.com. From the USA (✆ 1800 400
8222) via Lima, Peru (✆ 01 8001 8222).
TAM Cerrito 1030; ✆ 0810 333 3333; e reservas.bue@tam.com.br; www.tam.com.ar.
From the USA via São Paulo, Brazil (✆ 400 2570, 0800 570 5700); also TAM Mercosur
from Asunción, Paraguay (✆ 21 646000).
Varig Av Córdoba 972, Piso 3; ✆ 4329 9211; www.varig.com.ar. From Rio de Janeiro or
São Paulo (✆ 4003 7000).

HEALTH
By Tim Burford and Dr Felicity Nicholson
General health
Argentina has modern medical facilities and excellent doctors. No vaccinations are
required, but make sure you're up to date with your diphtheria and tetanus injections.
Hepatitis A vaccine (e.g. Havrix Monodose, Avaxim) and typhoid vaccine may be
recommended for some visits, especially if visiting poorer areas or for long stays,
Yellow fever and polio have now been eradicated in Argentina, and malaria will only
be a problem in the extreme north of Argentina if you plan to go into the jungles.
Have your teeth checked, carry your prescription (or write it in an email message
saved to yourself) if you wear glasses, and be sure to take out medical insurance.
Many drugs, available only on prescription in the UK and US, are sold over the
counter in South America, and they are often cheaper, so do not worry about
replacing your basic medical supplies there. You are, however, advised to check

expiry dates, and to take your own first-aid kit, in particular some sterilized needles. In Britain you can buy specially designed Sterile Equipment Packs from the Medical Advisory Service for Travellers Abroad.

Malaria prevention
There is a risk of malaria only in the far north of Argentina. It's crucial to avoid being bitten by mosquitoes, and you should take chloroquine pills, starting a week or so before reaching affected areas. Consult with the doctor as to which type of anti-malarial would be suitable and remember to specify if you plan on doing any diving since certain anti-malarial drugs will prevent you from participating in this activity. Telephone the Malaria Reference Laboratory in London for the latest advice; tel: 0891 600 350, or in the USA the Center for Disease Control in Atlanta; tel: 404 332 4559.

Innoculations
Hepatitis A is common throughout the continent, so vacccination is recommended; two shots at least 6 months apart give you twenty years of immunity. Cholera is not a great problem at the moment but *ceviche* (uncooked shellfish) should be avoided.

Common medical problems
Many of the ailments that beset travellers are caused by poor toilet practice, eating contaminated food and drinking unclean water, so you can do much to avoid illness by taking a few simple precautions: wash your hands after using the toilet (to remove other people's germs, not your own), don't eat raw vegetables, salads or fruit you haven't peeled yourself; boil water or purify it with chlorine (Sterotabs, Puritabs or Halozone) or better still with iodine (which kills amoebae). Compact water purifiers are now available, to filter out and kill amoebae, viruses and bacteria. Tea and coffee are usually made with hot rather than boiling water, and ice is also unsafe. But don't spoil your trip by never eating in wayside restaurants or from street stalls. Just be cautious at first while your system adjusts, and don't eat food that's been sitting around cooling.

Diarrhoea
Although Argentina is a good deal more hygienic than some of its northern neighbours, you have to face the fact that almost everyone comes down with diarrhoea somewhere in South America. 'Traveller's trots' is usually caused by the enterotoxic forms of the bacteria *Escherischia coli*, which everyone has naturally in their intestines. The problem is that each area has its own strain of *E. coli*, and alien strains cause inflammation of the intestine and diarrhoea. On a long trip you'll acquire a nice collection of the local E. coli in your gut and be troubled no more, but the first few weeks can be tough. Everyone has a favourite remedy, but most people agree that it's best to let nature take its course rather than rushing off to the pharmacy for antibiotics at the first signs of *turista*. It is far better to rest and drink plenty of tea, *manzanilla* (camomile tea) or *maté de coca* (coca tea – only in the far north) without milk. Don't eat any greasy or fatty food for 24 hours, then for a few days stick to a bland diet with plenty of mashed potatoes or rice and bananas. Avoid alcohol, fatty and spicy foods, and milk products and take plenty of fluids. Replace the lost salts and minerals by sipping a solution of half a teaspoon of salt and four teaspoons of sugar or honey in a litre of water; if possible add baking soda (half a teaspoon) and potassium chloride (a quarter teaspoon), or a little orange or lemon juice. You can buy or make up some 'electrolyte replacement' formula before leaving home.

There will be times when you'll want to block the symptoms of diarrhoea: before

LONG-HAUL FLIGHTS, CLOTS AND DVT
Dr Jane Wilson-Howarth

Long-haul air travel increases the risk of deep vein thrombosis. Although recent research has suggested that many of us develop clots when immobilised, most resolve without us ever having been aware of them. In certain susceptible individuals, though, large clots form and these can break away and lodge in the lungs. This is dangerous but happens in a tiny minority of passengers.

Studies have shown that flights of over five-and-a-half-hours are significant, and that people who take lots of shorter flights over a short space of time form clots. People at highest risk are:

- Those who have had a clot before – unless they are now taking warfarin
- People over 80 years of age
- Anyone who has recently undergone a major operation or surgery for varicose veins
- Someone who has had a hip or knee replacement in the last three months
- Cancer sufferers
- Those who have ever had a stroke
- People with heart disease
- Those with a close blood relative who has had a clot

Those with a slightly increased risk:

- People over 40
- Women who are pregnant or have had a baby in the last couple of weeks
- People taking female hormones or other oestrogen therapy
- Heavy smokers
- Those who have very severe varicose veins
- The very obese
- People who are very tall (over 6ft/1.8m) or short (under 5ft/1.5m)

setting off on a long bus ride, for instance, or when camping in heavy rain. Probably the best 'chemical cork' is loperamide (Diocalm or Imodium), but acetaminophen (Paracetamol or Lomotil) is an effective codeine-based blocker and painkiller.

Dysentery

If you have diarrhoea with a fever, bad gut cramps and blood in your stool, you may have bacterial (bacillary) dysentery. Amoebic dysentery is similar but starts more gradually, and the diarrhoea is persistent but not dramatic. Get your stool analysed and take the result to a doctor, who will probably prescribe a week's course of Flagyl (metronidazole or tinidazole) for amoebic dysentery, or an antibiotic such as ciprofloxacin for the bacterial variety.

Fever

If you develop a fever for any reason, you should rest and take aspirin or paracetamol/Tylenol. You should also bring with you a supply of antibiotics, such as ciprofloxacin or tetracycline, in case you are struck by some more serious infection in a hopelessly inconvenient place. If this happens, take antibiotics as instructed on the packet and see a doctor within four days. For gut infections, taking ciprofloxacin for three days should suffice, but otherwise you should finish the course (usually seven days).

A deep vein thrombosis (DVT) is a blood clot that forms in the deep leg veins. This is very different from irritating but harmless superficial phlebitis. DVT causes swelling and redness of one leg, usually with heat and pain in one calf and sometimes the thigh. A DVT is only dangerous if a clot breaks away and travels to the lungs (pulmonary embolus). Symptoms of a pulmonary embolus (PE) include chest pain that is worse on breathing in deeply, shortness of breath, and sometimes coughing up small amounts of blood. The symptoms commonly start three to ten days after a long flight. Anyone who thinks that they might have a DVT needs to see a doctor immediately who will arrange a scan. Warfarin tablets (to thin the blood) are then taken for at least six months.

Prevention of DVT
Several conditions make the problem more likely. Immobility is the key, and factors like reduced oxygen in cabin air and dehydration may also contribute. To reduce the risk of thrombosis on a long journey:

- Exercise before and after the flight
- Keep mobile before and during the flight; move around every couple of hours
- During the flight drink plenty of water or juices
- Avoid taking sleeping pills and excessive tea, coffee and alcohol
- Perform exercises that mimic walking and tense the calf muscles
- Consider wearing flight socks or support stockings (see www.legshealth.com)
- Taking a meal of oily fish (mackerel, trout, salmon, sardines, etc) in the 24 hours before departure reduces blood clotability and thus DVT risk
- The jury is still out on whether it is worth taking an aspirin before flying, but this can be discussed with your GP.

If you think you are at increased risk of a clot, ask your doctor if it is safe to travel.

Hanta fever (or hantavirus pulmonary syndrome) crossed from Argentina to Chile in 1995 and caused a degree of panic; for a while campsites were even kept clean; in 2000 it reached the Santiago Metropolitan Region. The fever is carried by a virus which has been common for some time in the USA, where it has a fatality rate of over 40%. The symptoms are flu-like fever, muscle pains, headache and fainting, followed by breathing difficulties. Hanta fever is not responsive to drugs so treatment, even in hospital, is 'supportive', controlling symptoms until the body fights off the infections. The virus is transmitted mainly by the long-tailed mouse (ratón colilargo; *Oligoryzomys longicaudatus*), which is about 10cm long with a tail of the same length. Don't touch food that's been chewed or defecated on by a rodent, and don't leave food where this might happen.

Injury
If you plan on hiking in remote areas and you're not familiar with backcountry and/or mountain first aid, carry a booklet on the subject, and pack an appropriate medical kit. If there are only two of you and one has an accident, the other should stay with the injured one and wait for help to arrive. The temptation is to rush for help, but being injured, worried and alone could have a disastrous effect on the patient. So, except for the rare cases when you know the trails are little used, wait for someone to come along, and keep the injured

SUNGLASSES AND SUNBURN
With thanks to Dr Bob Vinton

Depletion of the ozone layer, coupled with dry, unpolluted air, has led to increased levels of ultraviolet radiation in southern Argentina, causing sunburn and increasing the risk of cataracts and skin cancer. A broad-brimmed hat reduces eye damage to a certain extent, but sunglasses should also be used, especially at altitude or when light is reflected off water or snow. Together they can cut UV exposure by 95%; buy sunglasses which block 95–100% of UVB rays and at least 60% of UVA rays. The ability to absorb UV radiation is not determined by lens colour or darkness, although they should be dark enough for you not to see your eyes in a mirror. Grey and green lenses distort colours least; brown-amber improves contrast in haze or fog, but cause other colour distortions. Polarized lenses reduce reflected glare off glass and water, but have no UV protection. The best sunglasses are large, curved to fit the face and with opaque or UV-blocking side-shields.

Remember that even on hazy or cloudy days you can still receive 70-80% of a clear day's radiation. Prevent sunburn by using sunscreens, which come in two main kinds. Reflectors such as zinc oxide and titanium oxide reflect and scatter UV wavelengths; because they are thick and messy, they are used only in high-risk areas such as the nose and lips. Absorber sunscreens, such as PABA (para-aminobenzoic acid), cinnamates, benzophenones and parsol, absorb UV waves.

Soak mild to moderate sunburn in cold water, give ice massages and take painkillers if needed. Solarcaine and other anaesthetic creams may cause allergic reactions. Severe sunburn with blisters should receive medical treatment. It leads to rough, sagging skin with liver spots, wrinkles and increased skin-cancer risks; these effects are cumulative, irreversible and begin at an early age. By the time wrinkles appear, the damage is done. To avoid any of the above, take preventative action all the time.

person warm and comfortable. In general, don't hike when you're tired, and don't take risks.

Heat-related problems
It takes up to two weeks for the body to adjust to hot weather, but you can help by drinking lots of water, avoiding alcohol and taking extra salt in your diet. Avoid being in the sun during the hottest part of the day. If in the mountains, remember that dehydration occurs faster at altitude, and can be brought on even by travelling in air-conditioned buses or on the windswept back of a pick-up truck.

Mountain health
Altitude sickness (*soroche*) is more likely to affect you on the altiplano of Peru or Bolivia than in Chile or Argentina. However, you are almost certain to feel the effects of altitude if you climb Aconcagua, and may do so if you visit northwest Argentina, where villages you may be visiting are situated above 2,400m. Most people will need to do little more than rest for an hour or two for the usual symptoms of thumping heart and gasping breath to pass; however, some will experience other symptoms including headaches, fatigue, dizziness, loss of appetite and nausea (similar to a hangover). Take plenty of fluids and carbohydrates (up to

70% of your diet), and perhaps aspirin or paracetamol, and if it fails to clear up overnight, consider descending at least 500m and then returning in shorter stages. If there is no time for this, you could take acetazolamide (Diamox) for five days, starting two or three days before the ascent.

Two dangerous varieties of altitude sickness – cerebral oedema and pulmonary oedema – cause a rapid collapse with coughing, frothing and blue lips; the only solution is immediate and rapid descent. The key symptom of both types is a loss of coordination, accompanied in the case of cerebral oedema by illogical thought processes, loss of interest in events and surroundings, and even hallucinations, and in pulmonary oedema (water in the lungs) by a dry cough, breathlessness and a rapid heartbeat.

Hypothermia

Sometimes referred to as exposure, this is a simple but effective killer. Simply put, it means the body loses heat faster than it can produce it. If hiking high mountains where the weather is unpredictable, the combination of wet and cold can be lethal, with mountain winds chilling you even if the air temperature is well above freezing; fatigue is also often a contributory factor. Symptoms include lethargy, shivering (initially only), numbness (especially of fingers and toes), staggering, slurred speech and irrational perceptions and behaviour. The loss of rationality is particularly dangerous as it means the sufferer often fails to recognize his condition and to take necessary measures. Further exercise is exhausting and soon results in worse hypothermia. As soon as possible get the victim out of the wind and into dry warm clothing or a sleeping bag, and give high-energy food and warm, non-alcoholic drinks. If the situation becomes serious, climb into the sleeping bag too and use your naked body as a radiator.

It is extremely unlikely that long-distance hikers will succumb to hypothermia because they carry their weather protection with them. Inadequately equipped day hikers are in more danger, so if you're going above 2,000m or so, be sure to carry a good sleeping bag (keeping it dry), a light sweater or fleece jacket, and, most importantly, a thoroughly waterproof jacket and trousers. There are various ways of keeping warm without relying on heavy or expensive clothing: wear a hat to prevent heat loss from your head, and make sure your collar fits snugly, or use a scarf. Turn back if the weather looks threatening, and get under cover before becoming soaked.

Travel clinics and health information

A full list of current travel clinic websites worldwide is available from the International Society of Travel Medicine on www.istm.org. For other journey preparation information, consult www.tripprep.com. Information about various medications may be found on www.emedicine.com.

UK

Berkeley Travel Clinic 32 Berkeley St, London W1J 8EL (near Green Park tube station); ℄ 020 7629 6233

British Airways Travel Clinic and Immunisation Service 213 Piccadilly, London W1J 9HQ; ℄ 0845 600 2236; www.ba.com/travelclinics. Walk-in service (no appointment necessary) Mon, Tue, Wed, Fri 08.45–18.15, Thu 08.45–20.00, Sat 09.30–17.00. As well as providing inoculations and malaria prevention, they sell a variety of health-related goods.

Cambridge Travel Clinic 48a Mill Rd, Cambridge CB1 2AS; ℄ 01223 367362; e enquiries@cambridgetravelclinic.co.uk; www.cambridgetravelclinic.co.uk. Open Tue–Fri 12.00–19.00, Sat 10.00–16.00.

SUGGESTED MEDICAL KIT
- Elastoplast (Band-aids)
- butterfly closures
- micropore tape
- bandages
- tubular bandages
- Melolin dressings
- Vaseline (for cracked heels and ticks)
- 'moleskin' (for blisters)
- antifungal foot powder
- scissors
- safety pins
- tweezers
- earplugs
- sterile hypodermic needles
- drugs
- malaria pills
- aspirin or paracetamol/Tylenol (for fever and toothache)
- a more powerful painkiller/anti-inflammatory such as ibuprofen (Nurofen/Advil)
- diarrhoea medicine (Diocalm, Imodium)
- antihistamine tablets such as terfenadine (Seldane)
- antibiotics (ciprofloxacin, tetracycline, ampicillin)
- antiseptic and wipes
- travel sickness pills

Edinburgh Travel Clinic Regional Infectious Diseases Unit, Ward 41 OPD, Western General Hospital, Crewe Rd South, Edinburgh EH4 2UX; ℡ 0131 537 2822; www.link.med.ed.ac.uk/ridu. Travel helpline (0906 589 0380) open weekdays 09.00–12.00. Provides inoculations and antimalarial prophylaxis and advises on travel-related health risks.
Fleet Street Travel Clinic 29 Fleet St, London EC4Y 1AA; ℡ 020 7353 5678; www.fleetstreetclinic.com. Vaccinations, travel products and latest advice.
Hospital for Tropical Diseases Travel Clinic Mortimer Market Building, Capper St (off Tottenham Ct Rd), London WC1E 6AU; ℡ 020 7388 9600; www.thehtd.org. Offers consultations and advice, and is able to provide all necessary drugs and vaccines for travellers. Runs a healthline (0906 133 7733) for country-specific information and health hazards. Also stocks nets, water purification equipment and personal protection measures.
Interhealth Worldwide Partnership House, 157 Waterloo Rd, London SE1 8US; ℡ 020 7902 9000; www.interhealth.org.uk. Competitively priced, one-stop travel health service. All profits go to their affiliated company, InterHealth, which provides health care for overseas workers on Christian projects.
MASTA (Medical Advisory Service for Travellers Abroad) London School of Hygiene and Tropical Medicine, Keppel St, London WC1 7HT; ℡ 0906 550 1402; www.masta.org. Individually tailored health briefs available for a fee, with up-to-date information on how to stay healthy, inoculations and what to bring. There are currently 30 MASTA pre-travel clinics in Britain. Call 0870 241 6843 or check online for the nearest. Clinics also sell malaria prophylaxis memory cards, treatment kits, bednets, net treatment kits.
NHS travel website www.fitfortravel.scot.nhs.uk. Provides country-by-country advice on immunisation and malaria, plus details of recent developments, and a list of relevant health organisations.

Nomad Travel Store/Clinic 3–4 Wellington Terrace, Turnpike Lane, London N8 0PX; ℡ 020 8889 7014; travel-health line (office hours only) 0906 863 3414; e sales@nomadtravel.co.uk; www.nomadtravel.co.uk. Also at 40 Bernard St, London WC1N 1LJ; ℡ 020 7833 4114; 52 Grosvenor Gardens, London SW1W 0AG; ℡ 020 7823 5823; and 43 Queens Rd, Bristol BS8 1QH; ℡ 0117 922 6567. For health advice, equipment such as mosquito nets and other anti-bug devices, and an excellent range of adventure travel gear.

Trailfinders Travel Clinic 194 Kensington High St, London W8 7RG; ℡ 020 7938 3999; www.trailfinders.com/clinic.htm

Travelpharm The Travelpharm website, www.travelpharm.com, offers up-to-date guidance on travel-related health and has a range of medications available through their online mini-pharmacy.

Irish republic

Tropical Medical Bureau Grafton Street Medical Centre, Grafton Buildings, 34 Grafton St, Dublin 2; ℡ 1 671 9200; www.tmb.ie. A useful website specific to tropical destinations. Also check website for other bureaux locations throughout Ireland.

USA

Centers for Disease Control 1600 Clifton Rd, Atlanta, GA 30333; ℡ 800 311 3435; travellers' health hotline 888 232 3299; www.cdc.gov/travel. The central source of travel information in the USA. The invaluable Health Information for International Travel, published annually, is available from the Division of Quarantine at this address.

Connaught Laboratories PO Box 187, Swiftwater, PA 18370; ℡ 800 822 2463. They will send a free list of specialist tropical-medicine physicians in your state.

IAMAT (International Association for Medical Assistance to Travelers) 1623 Military Rd, 279, Niagara Falls, NY14304-1745; ℡ 716 754 4883; e info@iamat.org; www.iamat.org. A non-profit organisation that provides lists of English-speaking doctors abroad.

International Medicine Center 920 Frostwood Drive, Suite 670, Houston, TX 77024; ℡ 713 550 2000; www.traveldoc.com

Canada

IAMAT Suite 1, 1287 St Clair Av W, Toronto, Ontario M6E 1B8; ℡ 416 652 0137; www.iamat.org

TMVC (Travel Doctors Group) Sulphur Springs Rd, Ancaster, Ontario; ℡ 905 648 1112; www.tmvc-group.com

Australia, New Zealand, Singapore

TMVC Tel: 1300 65 88 44; www.tmvc.com.au. 31 clinics in Australia, New Zealand and Singapore including:

Auckland Canterbury Arcade, 170 Queen St, Auckland; ℡ 9 373 3531

Brisbane 6th floor, 247 Adelaide St, Brisbane, QLD 4000; ℡ 7 3221 9066

Melbourne 393 Little Bourke St, 2nd floor, Melbourne, VIC 3000; ℡ 3 9602 5788

Sydney Dymocks Bldg, 7th floor, 428 George St, Sydney, NSW 2000; ℡ 2 9221 7133

IAMAT PO Box 5049, Christchurch 5, New Zealand; www.iamat.org

South Africa and Namibia

SAA-Netcare Travel Clinics P Bag X34, Benmore 2010; www.travelclinic.co.za. Clinics throughout South Africa.

TMVC 113 D F Malan Drive, Roosevelt Park, Johannesburg; ℡ 011 888 7488; www.tmvc.com.au. Consult website for details of 9 other clinics in South Africa and Namibia.

Switzerland

IAMAT 57 Chemin des Voirets, 1212 Grand Lancy, Geneva; www.iamat.org

Note Travellers to remote regions of Argentina with extremely limited access to modern Western medical care will naturally have their own health concerns at the forefront. The health of tribal and poor rural peoples should also be considered: do not bring disease into these communities; even colds can kill (see *Appendix 3*).

SAFETY

There is little casual crime in Argentina, but you should take sensible precautions, especially in cities. Avoid looking like a wealthy tourist. If you can avoid bringing any jewellery or similar valuables you can free your mind of the worry of losing it; otherwise, keep it to a minimum and wear it with discretion. If you carry a bag in addition to your pack, don't put it down and do not keep valuables in it: not only can it be snatched, but it can be picked, slit or slashed open. The same applies to hip pouches, belt bags and the like. Items dangling on a cord such as compact cameras can be easily snipped and stolen. Having spoken to tourists who visited Argentina some 20 years ago, it is apparent that crime and tourist safety were far more of a problem then. Larger cities are much more cosmopolitan today, with standards of conduct similar to any other major centre in North America or Europe – there is always a chance of being pickpocketed or basically 'ripped off' in Buenos Aires as in New York, and by the same token, there is every likelihood that you will encounter no problems whatsoever and be treated with fairness and courtesy. In smaller towns where there is considerable poverty, a tourist who flaunts valuables may become a target of theft but usually the local people would rather share their meal with you than rob you of your funds to buy your own. A fellow traveller missed his bus while at a coffee stop and had his baggage arrive at his destination several hours before him; he caught a later bus and arrived in a very poor town where many people had no shoes and found his conspicuously North American backpack sitting unattended in the bus station under no apparent threat of pilfering. In summary, simply use common sense; don't be a complete idealist and leave your personal belongings lying about, but do not ruin your trip by being paranoid about security either.

It would be wise to make a photocopy of your passport and other important documents, such as insurance forms, air tickets, travellers' cheques, etc, to carry and store separately from the originals. Keep the numbers of your travellers' cheques, passport, credit cards and air tickets separate from other valuables (with the emergency telephone numbers for lost credit cards), so that if they are lost you can replace them more easily. In addition, send this list as an email to yourself, taking care to use some sort of code. You could also choose to leave photocopies of important documents such as your plane ticket and passport at home with a friend or family member.

To carry reserve cash and travellers' cheques (as well as passport and air tickets), discreet money belts, neck pouches or secret inside pockets are smart. If your passport is too bulky to carry comfortably and safely, keep handy some other form of identification, such as a driving licence, or photocopies of the key pages of your passport. Divide your money and travellers' cheques between at least two different places, in your baggage and on your body, and keep your everyday cash separate from your concealed stash.

When visiting places where you don't have any accommodation you will want to find a safe place to leave unwanted baggage. If you are leaving a hotel, they will most likely store it for you free of charge or for a minimal fee until later in the day, or even overnight if you are going on an excursion. Hostels are especially helpful in this way. Therefore, be sure you can lock your bags and make sure that the storage facility is also locked. If it is not locked storage or if other people have unsupervised access, you might also consider having the means to lock your bag to an immoveable object (a bike lock would work).

Insurance for baggage and medical costs must be purchased prior to departure from your home country, from travel agencies or through insurance companies. The various policies can cover you for loss and/or theft of your personal belongings and for medical costs incurred while travelling. Certain policies also cover trip cancellation and/or interruption, accidents, permanent injury and death.

Sexual harassment

Argentina is a safe country to travel in for women and it is tolerant of homosexuality. Use common sense and do not take risks that you wouldn't take at home or in any city environment: don't walk alone in shady, unlit, deserted streets; be aware of which areas have higher crime rates; don't accept car lifts or social invitations from strangers; be aware of your body language, etc. This said, don't be paranoid either. Argentine men are very forward and gregarious. Beautiful women are appreciated and will receive whistles, catcalls and comments; these are generally tasteful though not always. A woman can respond to polite attention with a smile but is best to ignore the rude and avoid further interaction. Both male and female homosexuality is not only tolerated but in cities such as Buenos Aires, openly expressed. Gay pride is celebrated and there are ever-increasing numbers of gay-friendly bars and dance clubs, including *milongas* (tango clubs). Rural areas of Argentina, however, are more staunchly Catholic and conservative; sexuality (of all kinds) is a subject that is viewed and expressed with discretion, and overtly sexual behaviour and dress is offensive.

WHAT TO TAKE

Before packing for your trip to Argentina, be sure to check your airline's baggage allowance. From North America most airlines permit two checked bags, each with a 20kg weight limit, but from Europe they may well allow only one, of 20kg or 23kg. Domestic flights in Argentina also have a 40kg per person weight limit. Airlines usually allow one carry-on bag; in any case you'll probably want a daypack to comfortably carry personal or purchased items. When carrying a daypack in busy areas such as markets, it is good practice to wear it on your front rather than your back to stop thieves getting at it. Most basic supplies can be purchased at pharmacies and convenience stores in most cities if you either forget something or prefer to buy it after arrival. Business hours are typically Monday to Friday 09.00–19.00; shops also open on Saturdays and, particularly outside major centres, most close from 13.00 to 16.00.

Clothing

Packing lightly will save you hassles at the airport, save your back when on the move and give you space to add the items you may buy along the way. Innovative travel garments such as convertible trousers (with zippers that allow them to become shorts) and wick-away and wrinkle-free fabrics that dry in hours and can be stuffed into luggage and still look tidy when pulled out again are convenient articles to pack. Clothing requirements will vary according to where you are going, the time of year and what activities you will be involved in. Remember that in the southern hemisphere summer is from December to February and winter June to August. The seasons vary with latitude but, generally speaking, winter is not very cold, especially in the north, with rare snow, and summers are warm in the south and hot in the north. Of course, the mountains and Tierra del Fuego are the coldest part of the country and experience the greatest snowfall. The north is very hot, but the humidity and altitude create different climates from east to west: the northeast is subtropical and humid whereas the northwest is dry desert and, although very hot in the daytime, gets significantly colder at night. In the north, summer is actually not the best time of year to visit because it marks the wet season, from November to March (a bit earlier in Mesopotamia, where September is best avoided), while the driest period is May to October. So, when selecting your wardrobe, consider these climates. Bring hats and shoes that will be warm or cool and will protect you against sunburn or rain, depending on where you will be travelling. Dressing in layers is a strategy that allows you to adapt to temperatures and conditions as they change through the day. Rather than a lined windbreak which may be too warm, bring a waterproof windbreak and wear a sweater or fleece underneath if additional warmth is required.

City wear in Argentina is generally smart and in larger cities fashions follow US and European trends. As Argentina is by and large a Catholic country, scanty clothing may offend and to visit churches you should cover shoulders and knees, remove hats and, in general, dress discreetly. Of course, in cosmopolitan cities such as Buenos Aires, fashion is more liberal – the dress for a night of tango is elegant and even provocative.

Throughout most of your travels, even if staying on estancias, your dress can be casual. You may want to have a few dressier items for dining or dancing, but overall, keep your wardrobe simple, casual and comfortable.

Accessories and personal supplies

Footwear that is comfortable and practical is vital. Uncomfortable feet equate to an uncomfortable trip. However, footwear can take up an excessive amount of space, so do limit the number of pairs you take. You will need a sturdy and comfortable pair of walking/hiking shoes that are suitable for the climate (ie: hiking sandals in the northeast but heavy hiking boots in the mountains). You may want to pack a pair of dress shoes to dress up for dinner, the theatre or going tango dancing.

The electrical supply is 220 volts. The sockets are particular, typically with angled square prongs, and you would be wise to carry a travel adaptor that has universal settings. Accommodation may have unreliable or inconvenient electrical sockets. A battery-operated travel alarm clock or a watch or mobile phone with an alarm function may come in handy if you will not always be staying in hotels with wake-up service, or if you'll be getting off long-haul buses in the early hours. It's essential to carry toilet paper or tissue because many public facilities will not have paper available. (Also note that in some rural areas where plumbing is basic, toilet paper is not flushed but discarded in a waste bin beside the toilet.) Some public toilets are maintained by individuals who will either sell you toilet paper or expect a small tip, usually about 0.50 pesos. It is always a good idea to have small change as many poor people make a living by providing small services.

Additional useful items may include a sewing kit, safety pins and a penknife or Swiss-Army knife (when flying, do not pack sharp objects such as knives or scissors in your carry-on luggage as they will be confiscated). 'Zip-loc'-style plastic bags are also handy for keeping damp items separate, or for keeping paper and the like dry.

If you expect to do hand laundry while travelling, you should bring concentrated travel soap (biodegradable soaps will avoid adding to the phosphates and other pollutants going down Argentina's drains, especially in ecologically sensitive areas or poor communities lacking adequate (or any) water treatment infrastructure), a universal bath plug (also if you prefer bathing to showering), clothes pegs, a scrubbing brush and a laundry bag for dirty clothing.

Certain products seem to be found anywhere in the world, such as aspirin (which can even be purchased by the tablet in obscure convenience stores and kiosks), but this is not always the case and the choice of first aid, pharmaceuticals and feminine hygiene products outside the larger cities may be unfamiliar and even archaic. If you have any brand loyalty, you would be best to bring it from home.

Finally, please remember to 'Bring it Back'. Even though you may be staying in larger urban areas, keep in mind how much waste you produce while visiting any country. You may be in areas with limited or non-existent waste disposal facilities. Try to dispose of extraneous packaging before it goes into your luggage. If recycling is not possible where you are staying, take items such as empty plastic bottles back home to dispose of them properly. If you find your bags too full at the end of your trip, many travellers to poor areas of northern Argentina or the inner cities have found grateful recipients for items such as clothing and shoes (see *Appendix Giving Back*). In sum, do your best to be a low-impact and a high-benefit visitor.

Backpacking and camping
Taken from the Bradt Hiking Guide to Argentina and Chile *by Tim Burford, an excellent accompaniment to this guide if you plan on doing some hiking and camping during part of your trip.*

To carry your gear you need a backpack or rucksack – above all make sure you have a padded hip belt, preferably with a so-called 'internal frame'. This is less likely to be caught on jungle creepers, and is handier for travelling on trucks and buses. No rucksack is ever totally waterproof, so you should keep clothes and other important items in plastic bags. Ideally you should carry 50% of your load on the hips – any more and you slip out of your shoulder straps, even with a chest strap. Nowadays there are also likely to be straps to adjust the balance of the load for uphill or downhill work, away from the body going uphill, and closer to the body downhill.

A hiking pole is invaluable: for establishing a rhythm on level ground, for extra security and confidence downhill, crossing scree, bogs and log bridges, for leverage uphill, for fending off dogs and wet or spiky foliage, for digging toilet holes, and of course essentially for playing noughts and crosses in the sand.

You're also likely to need a tent – don't wait until you get there to buy one. It'll need to be waterproof, and as light as possible – no more than 2.5kg for a two-person tent. Make sure it can take a pounding from those Patagonian winds; it's worth spending a bit more to be sure you have a tent which will last. In the north ventilation will be a problem, but elsewhere condensation is more of an issue: most tents are made of permeable nylon which allows moisture to escape. A cotton inner tent, under a separate flysheet, is more effective against condensation, but is heavier. Light tents (such as those made by Doite and Cacique) can be bought cheaply enough in Buenos Aires, but they're not of high quality; in some places you'll find tents for hire, but these tend to be ancient and leaky.

Some sort of insulation and protection from the cold, hard ground is essential; closed-cell 'ensolite' foam mats are the most efficient, providing good insulation and tolerable comfort even when less than a centimetre thick. The most comfortable mat of all, though, is the combination of air-mattress and foam-pad made by Thermarest, available in three-quarters or full length.

Rather than a conventional flashlight, use a head torch, which frees your hands and is ideal for cave exploration and for putting up your tent after dark. Remember a spare bulb; alternatives are a candle-holder or a camping gas-fuelled lantern.

See more on camping, page 76.

MONEY
The local currency is the Argentine peso, which comes in 2, 5, 10, 20, 50 and 100 peso notes and 1, 5, 10, 25 and 50 centavos coins. From 1991 until 2002 the peso

was tied to the US dollar at parity (one to one); the peso was then floated and became the primary currency and therefore is quoted (with US$ used occasionally by establishments that cater almost exclusively to American tourists or are shy of quoting in an unstable currency). You will never receive American dollars from a bank machine and will not necessarily get a fair exchange rate if you try to use American money in shops. Be aware that the prices quoted in this guide may change and should be treated as estimates and not as promises.

For day-to-day cash, it's best to use an ATM (cash machine), allowing you to keep your cash in your home account, where it might even earn interest. ATMs can be found at most banks, as well as at modern bus stations and supermarkets. There are two systems: Cirrus, linked to Mastercard and Plus, linked to Visa. Both the issuing bank and Visa or Mastercard take a fee of 1–2%, still cheaper than buying cash or travellers' cheques at home. You can also draw cash from ATMs on your credit card, but you will pay a high interest rate. In Argentina there's often a surcharge on credit card purchases and businesses experience very slow payment by the credit card companies, making them reluctant to accept a credit card. The real advantages are in being able to get cash at any time, without queues, with English instructions, and in small quantities. Still in 2005 the maximum daily withdrawal remained excessively low, approximately 500 pesos. Personal cheques are of course useless and travellers' cheques can only be cashed in banks, but you may choose to have them as a security reserve and spend them only at the end of the trip. Remember that you will not be charged commission if you cash them at the issuing company's offices (Thomas Cook, American Express, etc) but otherwise you will pay a minimum of 2% (either declared as a commission or hidden in the exchange rate), as well as the 1–1.5% paid when you bought the cheques. Travellers' cheques are not known to be the most economical option.

Avoid having money sent to you through a bank if at all possible. During the crisis Argentines were not able to receive cash wires from abroad because the banks were withholding the funds, offering criminal exchange rates and basically mishandling credit – it was of course an economic collapse. Since then, there has been little trust in sending money through a bank and although you may not have any problem it is not recommended unless absolutely necessary. Plan this in advance with your bank, which will have a partner bank in Argentina. Citibank and Western Union are present in Argentina, while LBSA (Lloyds Bank South America) is part of Britain's Lloyds-TSB.

Banks are open Monday to Friday, 10.00–15.00.

Owing to the low buying power of the peso and the need to rebuild the economy, many services have two-tiered prices: foreigners pay more than Argentines for such things as transportation, flights, entry to museums, parks and nature reserves, etc. One must try not to begrudge this system and see the many reasons that justify it. Tourism is a way to generate funds that local people cannot afford with their deflated peso. Certain fees that tourists pay reflect the cost prior to the crash of the peso (in other words, more closely tied to the American dollar as it was pre-crisis), whereas Argentines pay the current peso value. If it were not this way, budgets for institutions such as parks and museums would either be critically low or services would become elitist with Argentines unable to afford to travel or visit places of interest within their own country (it is already almost impossible for many Argentines to travel abroad with their weak currency).

Out of the 23 national parks, 11 charge an admission fee (12 pesos for all except Los Glaciares, which is 20 pesos, and Iguazú, which is 30 pesos). Some tourists complain when they realise that they have to pay park admission fees while

Argentines do not. It must be pointed out that the citizens of Argentina do pay through their taxes and that the parks belong to the people of Argentina and that tourists are guests. Think of your park admission fee as a way of giving back something for the privilege of being invited to visit these special areas.

GETTING AROUND
By air
Most cities have airports with daily connections to Buenos Aires, although not necessarily any direct flights to geographically closer cities; often you will have to go via the hub of Buenos Aires and backtrack. There are frequent flights between Buenos Aires and major cities such as Córdoba, Bariloche and Mendoza. Córdoba is becoming more of a hub with direct flights to popular destinations such as Salta and Iguazú; flights from Ushuaia in particular may call at cities such as El Calafate or Trelew, owing to its isolation and tourist demand.

As mentioned above, it may be better to buy an airpass for internal travel; both Aerolíneas Argentinas and LAN Argentina try to restrict foreigners to their more expensive (and flexible) fares, but if you book online claiming to be resident in Argentina and request airport pick-up of tickets (or e-tickets), or use an Argentine-based travel agency, it's possible to get around this. Two useful agencies are ArgentinaGo (*Tucumán 1427, Oficina 201;* ◊ *011 4372 7268; USA 786 245 0513;* e *mayra@argentinago.com, reservas@argentinago.com*) and Asatej (*Florida 835, Oficina 320;* ◊ *4114 7595, 0810 777 2728;* e *informes@asatej.com.ar, info@asatej.com.ar*).

By bus
Buses are the most popular and economical mode of long-distance travel in Argentina and the quality of the major operators and their vehicles are comparable to those in North America (particularly Mexico), and better than many in Europe. The trip from Buenos Aires to Bariloche, for example, costs about US$70, about two-thirds of the airfare, but takes 22 hours. Regular buses are called 'pullmans' and almost all have reclining seats, toilets, videos or music and drink service; they are fitted with alarms that sound when they go over the speed limit of 90km/h. For not much more money you can have a lot more comfort with a level of service referred to as *semicama, cama, supercama* or *first class presidencial*. The higher the price, the larger your seat and the further it reclines. These seats fold down almost into a bed allowing a comfortable night's sleep, and also saving on accommodation costs. Be aware when requesting departure times that the next available bus may not be the most comfortable, so you should ask specifically for the departures of the quality of bus you prefer. In January and February, the main holiday period, buses may be booked up weeks in advance. Conversely, at low season times there is a lot of competition, so you should always ask for a student discount or a *promoción*, which close to departure time may be as much as a third off. Buses may not run on backroads or to national parks in winter.

Your baggage should be loaded for you and when you reclaim it, a tip of a peso or two is expected. You will usually be given a baggage tag in order to reclaim your belongings. Likewise a control tab may be torn off your travel ticket when you get off. It's best to sit on the right, not so much to keep an eye on your baggage as to avoid being dazzled by oncoming headlights.

By trains
A cheap and civilised way to travel, though rarely possible beyond the commuter lines and tourist trips, is by train. Argentina has an extensive railway system, but unfortunately it is largely defunct. In 1993 the federal government withdrew

funding for the railways, leaving it to provinces to decide on subsidies. As a result there is limited passenger service in Buenos Aires province (with certain routes that are actually recommended for visiting the small towns outside Buenos Aires city, such as the Tren de la Costa to Tigre) and far more limited service elsewhere. The extreme sparsity of settlements in the vast pampas of the south meant that railways were never an economic proposition there, except for a few special lines such as that from the Río Turbío coal mines to the sea, and the Viejo Expreso Patagónico to Esquel, *La Trochita*, made famous through Paul Theroux's *The Old Patagonian Express*. Nostalgia for the old trains is what has saved the last few lines now catering mostly to sightseers: *La Trochita*, as well as the *Tren a las Nubes* (Train to the Clouds) in Salta, *Tren de las Sierras* in the Central Sierras and *Tren del Fin del Mundo* in Tierra del Fuego. Indeed a journey by these trains is a beautiful way to see the passing scenery.

Hitchhiking

If you have got time to spare, hitchhiking (*hacer el dedo/viajar a dedo*) will more than repay the effort. On the main roads of Argentina there is plenty of traffic, particularly in the summer months, and hitchhiking is common and accepted. However, on the backroads of Patagonia and Tierra del Fuego it's recommended only for the very patient. Argentines are very helpful and generous people and are likely to go out of their way to give you a lift.

Car rental

Although much more expensive than taking buses, the freedom of movement a car gives is often necessary to get where you want to go efficiently, especially in Patagonia. That said, the distances are great and many roads are in poor condition, with service stations few and far between. The roads in Argentina are reputedly dangerous, and signs marking one-way streets are often discreet with just a small arrow on a wall. In the extreme reaches of the country, that is in the far northwest, the depths of the central pampas or in remote areas of Patagonia, a car may not be a wise idea at all. The best option may be to use the bus for longer journeys and rent a car for a day or two to make short excursions in areas that buses reach rarely or not at all. For example, take the bus to the Lakes District from Mendoza or Córdoba (or Buenos Aires, although there are frequent and affordable flights for this journey) and then hire a car to tour around the scenic areas and small towns throughout the area. You may prefer to hire a pick-up (*camioneta*) if you are intending to spend a lot of time on unsurfaced (*ripio*) backroads. There are car rental companies in every major city or town, often with offices at the airports and bus stations, and international companies such as Avis and Hertz are both commonly found.

In order to drive in Argentina you will need an International Driving Permit, available at a low cost from your home automobile association. If you plan to take the car into a bordering country, be prepared for a lot of additional expense and bureaucracy.

Automóvil Club Argentino (*Av del Libertador 1850;* \ *011 4802 6061 or 4802 7071; www.aca.org.ar*) has excellent road maps and services. You can see the logo at service stations throughout the country, with local maps available and someone to offer directions, advice or assistance.

Large amounts of money are being spent on surfacing roads and building bridges, such as that across the Río Uruguay to Brazil. There are tolls to use the *autopistas* (freeways), but they are usually only a couple of dollars. For example, the short drive from Victoria to Rosario costs 9 pesos.

REMEMBER THAT...
- A vehicle going uphill has priority over a vehicle going down.
- On slippery roads, accelerate or decelerate gradually.
- If you are driving on snowy roads during a storm, keep calm. If stuck, do not leave the vehicle unless you see a house close by. Stay with the car and you will be helped.
- Carry an emergency kit: blanket, matches, heat-producing candles, flares, water, booster cables, and a reflective warning triangle to show a stopped vehicle at night.
- If driving on gravel roads, do not rely on your tyres, even if they are new, and do not underestimate bends. Do not slam on the brakes or pump them but apply slow even pressure. Slowing down is the most effective precaution.

Cycling and motorcycling

Cycling is increasing in popularity in scenic areas such as the Lakes District, where distances between sites of interest are short and the scenery along the way spectacular. Hiring a bike is also a good idea for sightseeing within towns (beware of heavy traffic in larger cities) or for getting out of town to camp or visit a nearby winery. There are many unsurfaced roads, so a mountain bike may be a better choice than a road bike. These can be rented by the day, but otherwise you should bring your own. Southern Patagonia is too windy for cycle-touring, as a rule.

With the fame of the book and recent movie *Motorcycle Diaries* about Che Guevara's travels by motorbike in Argentina in the 1950s, this romantic mode of travel has become more popular. There are motorbike rental companies in the major cities, both north and south; useful websites include www.argentinamotoadventure.com or www.motocare.com.ar. Motorcycling is a great way to travel the countryside, though you should take care. Wear a helmet even though it is still acceptable to ride motorbikes without them.

Travel by sea

Cruises to the Antarctic Peninsula are very popular, nearly all departing from Ushuaia. If your teeth are already chattering at the thought of Antarctica, consider that summer also occurs in this part of the world when temperatures range from –6°C to 6°C, with a possibility of their soaring all the way to a balmy 10°C. The various island groups have microclimates of their own with particularities of precipitation, winds and intense sun; make sure that your tour agency explains what weather to expect and check the forecasts prior to your trip. Also be sure to check whether or not you are responsible for expedition clothing and equipment, such as parkas, binoculars, etc.

Other cruises, typically from Rio de Janeiro to Valparaíso, call at Buenos Aires and Puerto Madryn; this route is dominated by the Norwegian cruise line Princess and Celebrity.

The **International Association of Antarctica Tour Operators** www.iaato.org. Operates occasional voyages to Antarctica and has included larger vessels (up to 960 passengers), some of which conduct sightseeing cruises only without landings.
Abercrombie & Kent www.abercrombiekent.com. Has 3 different cruises, the basic Antarctic Peninsula cruise and 2 others that include the Falkland/Malvinas and South Georgia Islands. Cruises are for 14 days, costing US$5,000 and up. They are located in the USA (see overleaf).

Andean Trails www.andeantrails.co.uk. Organises Antarctic cruises on the Argentine and Antarctic peninsulas, South Shetland Islands, Falkland/Malvinas Islands and South Georgia. Cruises last 2–3 weeks, and rates start at £3,275 per person depending on cabin category. They are located in the UK (see below).

Argentina Discover www.antarcticadiscover.com. Organises cruises from 11 to 19 days, ranging in price from US$4,900 to US$7,300. Tours have various itineraries and may travel to Cape Horn, across the Drake Passage, to the South Shetland, Southern Orkney and Falkland/Malvinas Islands and the Antarctic Peninsula. They are located in the USA (see page 53).

Cruceros Australis Carlos Pellegrini 989, Piso 6, Buenos Aires; ↘ +54 11 4325 8400; www.australis.com; Av El Bosque Norte 0440, Piso 11, Santiago de Chile; ↘ 2/442 3110; 4014 Chase Av, Suite 202, Miami Beach, FL 33140, USA; ↘ 305 695 9618, toll-free 877 678 3772. Has 2 luxury cruises a week between Ushuaia and Punta Arenas (3 to 4 nights in each direction, Oct–Apr) with stops at Cape Horn, Glaciar Pia, Isla Magdalena, Puerto Williams, Bahía Ainsworth and Glaciar Marinelli, and excursions in rigid inflatable boats to view elephant seal, penguin and cormorant colonies. Rates start at US$490 per person per night.

Cruise Norway 5 Camp Av, Merrick, NY 11566, USA; ↘ 516 546 8711, toll-free 800 334 6544; e info@cruisenorway.com; www.cruisenorway.com. Sails from Puerto Montt via Chile's Patagonian Channels and the Antarctic Peninsula to Ushuaia; a simple ship but a very interesting route.

Discovery World Cruises 800 SE 10th Av, Suite 205, Fort Lauderdale, FL 33316, USA; ↘ 954 761 7878, 866 623 2689; e info@mvdiscovery.com; 15 Young St, London W8 5EH, UK; ↘ 020 7795 4900; e info@discoverycruisesuk.com; www.discoveryworldcruises.com.

Gap Adventures www.gapadventures.com. Have various cruises to Antarctica and the southern islands from Tierra del Fuego. Trips cost approximately US$2,800–6,300 for 10–21 days. They are located in Canada.

Grand Circle Travel www.gct.com. Has a 15-day Antarctica package, with 10 days on the cruise plus time in Buenos Aires and Ushuaia; it can be extended to see other parts of the country. It costs from US$5,700 including flights from/to the United States. They are located in the USA.

Lost World Adventures www.lostworldadventures.com. Tour the shorelines of Antarctica in ice-strengthened ships allowing close navigation of the glaciers and opportunities to board Zodiac boats. Cruises take in the Antarctic Peninsula as well as the Polar Circle, Falkland/Malvinas and South Georgia Islands depending upon duration of package; from 11 to 19 days, starting from US$4,220 to US$8,000 and up. They are located in the USA.

Noble Caledonia 2 Chester Close, London SW1X 7BE, UK; ↘ 020 7752 0000; e info@noble-caledonia.co.uk; www.noble-caledonia.co.uk. Offer Valparaíso–Buenos Aires cruises, costing from £2,395 for 17 nights, and Falklands/Antarctic cruises.

Norwegian Cruise Line 1 Derry St, London W8 5NN, UK; ↘ 0845 658 8010; 7665 Corporate Center Dr, Miami FL 33126, USA; ↘ 305 436 4000, toll-free 800 327 7030; www.ncl.com. Offers cruises from Valparaíso to Buenos Aires via the Falklands/Malvinas (14 nights from £1,168).

Travel Wizard www.travelwizard.com. Organises cruises to Antarctica, Tierra del Fuego and the Falkland/Malvinas Islands. 2-week trips cost about US$7,000. They are located in the USA.

ACCOMMODATION
Camping
Argentine campsites often offer two options: you can either pitch your own tent or stay in a small rustic cabin, usually supplying your own sheets. Municipal campsites may provide no facilities beyond an outhouse. The cheapest form of

accommodation available (5–20 pesos per site), these are only available in summer. In high season you would be wise to call ahead if possible to reserve a cabin and check what is provided (there may or may not be electricity, hot water, bedding, etc). You are not permitted to pitch a tent outside designated campsites; most land is either private, in which case you must ask permission from the owner if you want to camp, or within a park. Fires are usually not permitted (camping stoves are fine) and campsites will usually have small grills available.

Hostels

Hostels offer cheap accommodation with no frills and may or may not offer breakfast or bedding. They often have dormitory bunks, shared rooms and private rooms, with prices increasing respectively (starting from 20 pesos, but rates can be double this in high season or in more expensive regions, such as Patagonia). Because of their low rates these are great places to meet budget long-haul travellers, to either team up for excursions or share travel experiences and advice. Hostels typically have readily available information on transportation and local activities. Some hostels are small and independent while others are part of an association. Hostelling International Argentina is the country's largest hostel chain, part of an international association that maintains particular standards within its member hostels and a website giving all their contact details (*www.hostels.org.ar or www.hihostels.com*); beware of other groups in Argentina that mimic the name and logo of HI (note that in El Calafate, one of these has a kiosk in the airport arrivals area); some of these copycats may well have good hostels but their dishonest approach deserves scrutiny. You can buy a membership card in any HI hostel in the world but it is cheaper in Argentina than in Europe or North America. Membership gives you discounts on accommodation as well as on excursions, shopping and travel (several bus companies give a 10% discount off ticket prices for HI members). Hostelling International Argentina is continuously adding members to its association, now approaching 100 hostels throughout Argentina, and hopes to provide bus services between hostels in neighbouring cities. The convenience of the large association is that the hostels are in contact with each other and can help you to book HI hostels elsewhere on your itinerary.

Bed & breakfast, guesthouses, hospedajes

The B&B is a fairly new concept in Argentina; more common is the guesthouse, or hospedaje, which is not very different. They are like small hotels, usually only half a dozen rooms, with breakfast served in a communal dining room. Staying in a guesthouse is like staying in somebody's home. Your room is private and usually you can lock it; the bathroom is typically shared and there is communal space throughout the house, such as a living room, kitchen, dining room, patios, etc. Single and double rooms average about 25–50 pesos per person.

Hotels

Hotels in Argentina are graded on a star system but the standards are lower than in the US and Europe. A five-star hotel may not necessarily be very luxurious, especially in smaller cities. On the other hand, a two-star hotel is humble but quaint and clean. A better way of interpreting the quality of a hotel is not by how many stars but by what it charges. A basic hotel will average 50 pesos for a double whereas a deluxe hotel can run into the hundreds. The presidential suites at the Alvear Palace in Buenos Aires, indeed, run into the thousands. Many hotels do not list their prices on their websites because they fluctuate with demand and the rate of the US dollar was so unstable for a long time. You can expect at least a 20% variation between high and low season, and at peak seasons rates often double. In low season you can try to haggle, especially if the rates are not posted and you suspect that you are being quoted a 'foreigner's' rate. It would be unfair to state that tourists get overcharged since most proprietors are very honest, but it does happen, so follow your instincts when a quote is not being provided in a quick and straightforward manner.

Estancias and lodges

Staying at an estancia or at a fishing lodge, typically for a week or just a weekend, is a real 'getaway' for those wanting an escape into a country or wilderness setting to experience nature and culture. Most ranches struggle to make a living on agriculture alone and have moved their business activities towards cultural tourism, although it would be naïve to believe that Argentine estancias have all moved beyond the colonial decadence of wealthy landowners exploiting poor workers and gauchos. They are still true working cattle ranches on the vast rolling plains of the pampas or sheep ranches in the rough wilds of Patagonia, with the large estancia houses either converted or with annexes built to accommodate guests coming here to see authentic Argentina (though with gauchos in traditional clothing providing some fake nostalgia) and thus provide new lifeblood to a bygone era. Guests can watch the day-to-day activities or actually participate in certain activities such as sheep-shearing or feeding livestock; outings to explore the surroundings and sites of interest are often programmed. Prices start at around US$100 per person per night for full board (with traditional to gourmet menu options) and typically the rates of Patagonian estancias are double those in the pampas. Nevertheless these places are not necessarily overly fancy or formal; in fact, they are typically elegantly rustic, beautiful but natural and traditional, and guests are expected to dress casually and practically for the setting, dressing up for dinner only if it suits your style.

In the Lakes District and the wetlands of northeast Mesopotamia, fishing and wilderness lodges offer stunning settings for escapes into nature. They range in style from rustic to luxury and can be set close to other amenities or deep in the wilds and far off the beaten track. Your meals will usually be provided, possibly basic local fare or fabulously gourmet, with a chef preparing regional meals. Successful fishermen can have their catch cooked for dinner. Lodges may have rigid programmes to keep you busy sightseeing or fishing (fishing equipment is generally provided), or may cater to their guests' pace and have guides for hire for whenever it is convenient or allow you to explore certain areas on your own. Your intentions and therefore any potential restrictions to your plans should be discussed between you and the lodge prior to your booking and arrival.

EATING AND DRINKING

Subtle differences and regional specialities are found in Argentine cuisine. Patagonian lamb, trout in the Lakes District or river fish in the northeast cannot be beaten in other parts of the country. These local treats are mentioned in the relevant sections of the guide. To discuss in a general sense what the traditional Argentine menu is, we can imagine a day of dining pleasure. Between dawn and late morning your day would probably commence at a neighbourhood café. With time, this café would recognise your loyalty and know your particular taste in coffee, which can be drunk *con leche* (with milk) or without, and accompanied by a couple of *medialunas* or *fattorias* (the local terms for croissants, often filled with jam or chocolate or other sweet options). Other variations on the coffee theme are *cafecito* (short and strong), *café cortado* (short with milk), *café lagrima* (hot milk with a teardrop of espresso), *café doble* (double shot) or *cappuccino* (espresso with steamed milk). There is also a lovely form of hot chocolate called a *submarino*, which is hot milk with a bar of chocolate to melt in it. Though tourists are excused with varying degrees of exasperation, it would not be generally considered acceptable to have milk in your coffee following any other meal than breakfast, especially a meal that includes meat, which is usually the case.

Maté, a strong bitter tea, can be drunk at any time but can be prepared in different ways according to the time of day. For example, it can be had with hot milk or even with coffee in the morning, or with sugar or fruit to make it sweeter or more flavourful. In its pure form, however, it can be drunk all day long and many Argentines can be seen carrying around their hot-water thermos and *maté* with *bombilla* (a cup made of a hollowed gourd with a silver straw) much as a coffee mug is carried about by many North Americans. Hot water dispensers are often conveniently and considerately set up in public areas either as a free service or with a minimal fee to allow people to refill their thermos or top up their *maté*. Obviously the whole business of sucking warm feel-good juice from a breast-shaped vessel is highly suspect, and Argentines generally see drinking *maté* as a perfectly normal alternative to doing some work.

One o'clock is the start of the lunch hour, a loose term since it can last up to two or three hours, siesta time included. Do not expect stores or services to be available to you between one and four o'clock unless you are in the tourist centre of a larger city. Lunch is often the largest meal of the day and most restaurants offer *asado* (see below) and a salad buffet. The most famous and undoubtedly traditional Argentine cuisine is grilled meat. Argentine meat is world-acclaimed. The animals are free-range and breed naturally (the breeds include the Holando Argentina, Aberdeen Angus, Charolais, Shorthorns and Herefords). The expansive pastures of the pampas offer grazing that is rich and natural resulting in meat that is flavourful and clean (no herbicides, pesticides, growth hormones, etc). The same can be said for Patagonian lamb, which is also free-range.

In ordering your meat dishes, getting some basic terminology straight is your first priority. Laid out on a *parrilla* or grill, a *parrillada* is a spread of meats that will include almost every imaginable part of the cow as well as a few chunks of pig, mutton or chicken thrown in for good measure. *Asado* is the style of cooking and/ or often the kind of cut (eg: *asado de tira*). The *asador* is the man (it is very unusual and against tradition for a woman to work the *parrilla*) who grills the meat and prides himself on his skill at keeping the coals at the perfect red-hot degree without the flame ever licking at the meat (tubes are set to carry the fat away so it doesn't fall into the fire and flare up). Lamb is typically grilled whole and splayed *al asador* (on the cross). *Asado* should be served with spicy *chimichurri* sauce and salad.

The following are some typical main dishes:

bife de chorizo	New York strip or sirloin steak
bife de lomo	beef tenderloin or fillet mignon
chinchulines	intestines
choripán	bread roll with sausage inside
chorizos	beef or pork or mixed sausages
mollejas	thyroid gland or sweet bread
matambre	marinated flank steak rolled up with vegetables
matambrito	pig's flank
morcillas	blood sausage
provoleta	grilled cheese appetiser
riñoncitos	kidney
salchichas	sausages
tripa gorda	large intestine

Apart from *asado*, Italian influences are the most common, such as pizza and pasta, most commonly *ñoci* (ie: *gnocchi*), *tallarines* (plain noodles), *ravioli*, *cappeletis* (*ravioli* of a different shape, looking more like *empanadas* – see below), *sorrentinos* (larger *ravioli*) and *milanesa* (veal grilled in breadcrumbs). Stews are also popular, including *carbonada*, made with oxtail, potatoes, carrots, corn and various meats, or a stomach stew called *mondongo*. *Churrasco* is another form of barbecue. *Pescados y mariscos* are fish and seafood. In northern Argentina, *empanadas* are standard fare. These baked or fried savoury pastries are most commonly stuffed with beef mixed with egg, olives, herbs and spices, or cheese and onion, creamed corn and ham. Any dish with the term *choclo* means 'stuffed'. *Tamales* and *humitas* are wonderful northern specialties; *tamales* are corn and meat wrapped in a corn leaf and steam cooked, and *humitas* are very similar but lack the meat. *Locro* is a popular *sopa* (soup) dish in the north made from meat, tripe, sausage, corn, potato and bean; *puchero* is a thick soup made with chickpeas, corn and meat. *Cazuela* (*de ternera, de cerdo* or *de gallina*) is a hotpot of stew made of veal, pork or chicken. Fruit pies may be offered as a dessert but usually a coffee (*cortado*, without milk) would be the cap on your meal.

Sweets are abundant a few hours later, at teatime. In the Chubut Valley, owing to the strong Welsh influence, teatime is taken much more seriously and includes breads and jams, cheese, cakes, pies and cookies. Elsewhere, more typically between five and seven o'clock, a simple cup of tea and an *alfajor* (biscuit filled with *dulce de leche* and covered in chocolate or icing sugar) would be in order. *Dulce de leche* is a sweet gooey caramel-like spread and a staple of any Argentine diet. There is also *dulce de batata*, a sweet potato preserve; *dulce de zapallo*, sweet pumpkin preserve; and *dulce de membrillo*, quince jelly. *Churro* is a deep-fried pastry stick that may be filled with *dulce de leche* or chocolate. Chocolate is another famous Argentine delight mainly produced in the Lakes District. One cannot miss the large chocolate shops lined up on the main street of Bariloche. Many of the chocolates and truffles are made with other Argentine sweets such as *dulce de leche*. *Ambrosia* is a wonderful dessert similar to zabaglione made with egg yolks, milk and sugar.

In the early evening before dinner (which offers the same options as lunchtime, but is eaten much later than in many other countries – perhaps as late as 22.00) you might fit in a happy hour, when your drink is accompanied with *picadas* – finger foods, often cold cuts (*fiambres*), olives, goat cheese (*queso de cabra*) and fresh cheese (*quesillo*) among other delicacies. The most common drinks enjoyed in Argentina are wine, cider and beer; hard spirits are less common. Argentine wine, grown in the Cuyo region (see *Chapter 7*), is becoming more refined and internationally recognised; Merlot and Cabernet go especially well with steak.

If you are able to indulge in two full Argentine meals as well as breakfast, tea and a happy hour, you will definitely be well fed, will probably need to participate in the tradition of siesta and are hopefully not expecting to partake in any strenuous tourist activity such as climbing Mt Aconcagua!

If dining in a restaurant, **tipping** is becoming more institutionalised, and especially in areas with higher levels of tourism it is expected, at a rate of 10 or 15%. Elsewhere, for bar service tipping is not expected, but if you have been served at your table, the spare change from your bill is typically left as a tip, and an additional peso or two per person is appreciated as a gesture of thanks.

PUBLIC HOLIDAYS

1 January	Año Nuevo (New Year's Day)
February/March (date varies, ending on Shrove Tuesday)	Carnival

February/March (date varies)	Wine Harvest Festival
March/April (date varies)	Viernes Santo (Good Friday) and Pascua (Easter)
2 April (holiday observed on closest Monday)	Día de las Malvinas (Veterans' Day and tribute to the fallen in the Malvinas War)
1 May	Día del Trabajador (Labour Day)
8 May	Día del Virgén de Luján
25 May	Revolución de Mayo (anniversary of the first independent Argentine government, in 1810)
June (third Monday of the month)	Día de la Bandera (National Flag Day)
9 July	Día de la Independencia (anniversary of the proclamation of independence in 1816)
17 August	Día de San Martín (anniversary of the death of General José de San Martín)
12 October	Día de la Raza (Columbus Day)
10 November	Día de la Tradición (Day of Traditional Culture)
8 December	Día de la Concepción Inmaculada (Day of the Immaculate Conception)
25 December	Navidad (Christmas Day)

PHOTOGRAPHY

Generally speaking, camera equipment is more expensive in Argentina than in North America and Europe. Bring all the supplies that you will need. Bring extra camera batteries (these expire much faster at higher altitudes).

For those who have not yet leapt into the realm of digital photography, many brands of 35mm colour print film at 200 ASA are available throughout the country, as are 24-hour developers. Faster speeds and black and white film are rarer. Slide film is expensive and hard to come by, especially outside Buenos Aires, and if found will only be available at 200 ASA, usually made by Acta. Kodak film is also available, but Fuji is very rare.

Be aware that taking photographs of military and communications installations as well as airports and sensitive border areas is forbidden.

For photographic tips, see box overleaf.

COMMUNICATIONS
Telephones

The international dialling code from abroad is +54. Payphones take tokens (cospeles) or magnetic cards (tarjetas telefónicas) purchased at cigarette kiosks. There are different cospeles for local and long-distance calls and each provides a couple of minutes of time. Locutorios or telephone centres are abundant in most cities and towns and can be used for local or long-distance calls. These often also offer internet access, and there are many internet cafés in almost every city and town in the country. Only if you are going well off the beaten track will you possibly find a lack of technology, but in this case you are probably trying to escape the high-tech lifestyle anyway.

The two telephone companies in Argentina are Telecom (in Buenos Aires on San Martín 650; www.telecom.com.ar) and Telefónica (in Buenos Aires on Av Corrientes 707; www.telefonica.com.ar), both open 24 hours per day. Numbers beginning 0800 are free while those beginning 0810 are charged at local rates.

PHOTOGRAPHIC TIPS
Ariadne Van Zandbergen
Equipment
Although with some thought and an eye for composition you can take reasonable photos with a 'point-and-shoot' camera, you need an SLR camera if you are at all serious about photography. Modern SLRs tend to be very clever, with automatic programmes for almost every possible situation, but remember that these programmes are limited in the sense that the camera cannot think, but only make calculations. Every starting amateur photographer should read a photographic manual for beginners and get to grips with such basics as the relationship between aperture and shutter speed.

Always buy the best lens you can afford. The lens determines the quality of your photo more than the camera body. Fixed fast lenses are ideal, but very costly. Zoom lenses are easier to change composition without changing lenses the whole time. If you carry only one lens, a 28–70mm (digital 17–55mm) or similar zoom should be ideal. For a second lens, a lightweight 80–200mm or 70–300mm (digital 55–200mm) or similar will be excellent for candid shots and varying your composition. Wildlife photography will be very frustrating if you don't have at least a 300mm lens. For a small loss of quality, tele-converters are a cheap and compact way to increase magnification: a 300 lens with a 1.4x converter becomes 420mm, and with a 2x it becomes 600mm. Note, however, that 1.4x and 2x tele-converters reduce the speed of your lens by 1.4 and 2 stops respectively.

For photography from a vehicle, a solid beanbag, which you can make yourself very cheaply, will be necessary to avoid blurred images, and is more useful than a tripod. A clamp with a tripod head screwed on to it can be attached to the vehicle as well. Modern dedicated flash units are easy to use; aside from the obvious need to flash when you photograph at night, you can improve a lot of photos in difficult 'high contrast' or very dull light with some fill-in flash. It pays to have a proper flash unit as opposed to a built-in camera flash.

Digital/film
Digital photography is now the preference of most amateur and professional photographers, with the resolution of digital cameras improving the whole time. For ordinary prints a 6 megapixel camera is fine. For better results and the possibility to enlarge images and for professional reproduction, higher resolution is available up to 16 megapixels.

Memory space is important. The number of pictures you can fit on a memory card depends on the quality you choose. Calculate in advance how many pictures you can fit on a card and either take enough cards to last for your trip, or take a storage drive on to which you can download the content. A laptop gives the advantage that you can see your pictures properly at the end of each day and edit and delete rejects, but a storage device is lighter and less bulky. These drives come in different capacities up to 80GB.

Most **mobile phones** in Argentina operate on an AMPS or NAMPS analogue system. However, Compania de Comunicaciones Personales del Interior also operates a TDMA digital system. Check with your operator at home to see if a partnership in Argentina exists. Calling an Argentine mobile number requires the

Bear in mind that digital camera batteries, computers and other storage devices need charging, so make sure you have all the chargers, cables and converters with you. Most hotels have charging points, but do enquire about this in advance. When camping you might have to rely on charging from the car battery; a spare battery is invaluable.

If you are shooting film, 100 to 200 ISO print film and 50 to 100 ISO slide film are ideal. Low ISO film is slow but fine grained and gives the best colour saturation, but will need more light, so support in the form of a tripod or monopod is important. You can also bring a few 'fast' 400 ISO films for low-light situations where a tripod or flash is no option.

Dust and heat

Dust and heat are often a problem. Keep your equipment in a sealed bag, stow films in an airtight container (eg: a small cooler bag) and avoid exposing equipment and film to the sun. Digital cameras are prone to collecting dust particles on the sensor which results in spots on the image. The dirt mostly enters the camera when changing lenses, so be careful when doing this. To some extent photos can be 'cleaned' up afterwards in Photoshop, but this is time-consuming. You can have your camera sensor professionally cleaned, or you can do this yourself with special brushes and swabs made for the purpose, but note that touching the sensor might cause damage and should only be done with the greatest care.

Light

The most striking outdoor photographs are often taken during the hour or two of 'golden light' after dawn and before sunset. Shooting in low light may enforce the use of very low shutter speeds, in which case a tripod will be required to avoid camera shake.

With careful handling, side lighting and back lighting can produce stunning effects, especially in soft light and at sunrise or sunset. Generally, however, it is best to shoot with the sun behind you. When photographing animals or people in the harsh midday sun, images taken in light but even shade are likely to be more effective than those taken in direct sunlight or patchy shade, since the latter conditions create too much contrast.

Protocol

In some countries, it is unacceptable to photograph local people without permission, and many people will refuse to pose or will ask for a donation. In such circumstances, don't try to sneak photographs as you might get yourself into trouble. Even the most willing subject will often pose stiffly when a camera is pointed at them; relax them by making a joke, and take a few shots in quick succession to improve the odds of capturing a natural pose.

Ariadne Van Zandbergen is a professional travel and wildlife photographer specialising in Africa. She runs The Africa Image Library. For photo requests, visit www.africaimagelibrary.co.za or contact her on ariadne@hixnet.co.za.

prefix '15' before the area code (15 + area code + subscriber number); however, calling from abroad to an Argentine mobile number requires the prefix '9' before the area code (without the '15' prefix, ie: +54 + 9 + area code + subscriber number).

Direct access numbers

While in Argentina, you can call direct access numbers to providers in your home country to get better long-distance rates. You can also obtain a prepaid overseas phonecard from your long-distance carrier.

AT&T Direct 0800 555 4288 (Telecom), 0800 222 1288 (Telefónica)
BT Direct 0800 555 4401 (Telecom), 0800 666 4400 (Telefónica)
MCI WorldPhone 0800 555 1002 (Telecom), 0800 222 6249 (Telefónica)
Sprint 0800 555 1003 (Telecom), 0800 222 1003 (Telefónica)

Postal services

The post office in Argentina is called Correo Argentino (see www.correoargentino.com.ar for office locations, postcodes, etc). A standard letter from Argentina to Europe or North America costs 4 pesos and takes, on average, two weeks to arrive in Europe and one to two weeks to reach North America. However, sometimes letters take much longer. From personal experience, one letter was posted in Puerto Madryn on 22 November and arrived in Europe on 18 February! Postal offices are open Monday to Friday 08.00–18.00, Saturday 08.00–13.00.

Courier service

FedEx Argentina www.fedex.com/ar_english

GIVING SOMETHING BACK

Organisations working for humanitarian, ecological and environmental rights and protection

Amazon Society

This organisation has an active volunteer programme in the Chaco region of northern Argentina working to protect the habitat of the blue-fronted parrot, a parrot struggling to survive the pressures of illegal nest-poaching of tens of thousands of these birds per year (this peaked at 263,000 in the mid-80s) for the pet trade. The society has several projects but is collaborating with the Blue-fronted Amazon Breeding Ecology Project of the Universidad de Buenos Aires, Argentina (Universidad Nacional de La Plata, Argentina) to protect this beautiful bird. The project is remotely located but you can plan to spend a field season as a volunteer; donations can always be made remotely.
www.amazonasociety.org/

Centre for the Implementation of Public Policies Promoting Equity and Growth (CIPPEC)

CIPPEC is a private, non-profit, non-governmental organisation working to promote equality and growth for a more just, democratic and efficient state in Argentina and to improve the quality of life for all Argentine citizens. CIPPEC aims to make public institutions stronger, to make opportunities equal for everyone and to better the social situation for all Argentinians. Volunteers can work on a range of projects. Volunteers will work for four hours a day.
Avenida Callao 25, Piso 1, C1022AAA Buenos Aires, Argentina; ℡ *011 4384 9009;* f *4371 1221; email vweyrauch@cippec.org; www.cippec.org*

Centro de Investigación y Extensión Forestal Andino Patagónico (CIEFAP)

The research centre is an educational institute focused on the conservation of the Andean Patagonian forests, sustainable forest practices, environmental protection

and the promotion of eco-tourism in the region. It runs a public library that is open 08.00–14.00 where you can meet with a consultant, peruse the research and literature or subscribe to the organisation.
Ruta 259, km4, CC14 9200 Esquel, Chubut Argentina; ✆ *02945 453 948, 450 175;* e *info@ciefap.cyt.edu.ar; www.ciefap.org.ar*

Centro de Ecologie Aplicada del Neuquén (CEAN)
This group of experts is dedicated to researching and protecting the aquatic and terrestrial fauna of the province of Neuquén, in collaboration with conservation bodies and projects throughout the country. They seek ways to diversify beyond the crude exploitation of natural resources in the province.
Ruta Provincial 61, km 7, Valle San Cabao, CC 7, Junín de los Andes, 8371 Neuquén; ✆ *02972 491427; www.neuquen.gov.ar/org/cean/*

Centro de Reeducación del Mono Aullador Negro (Reintroduction and Rehabilitation Centre of the Black Howler Monkey)
The centre is in a beautiful location surrounded by forest that is the adopted home of howler monkeys brought here or born here after being displaced from their natural habitat in northeast Argentina. The aim is to re-introduce rehabilitated monkeys that were captured for the pet trade or their offspring back to their native forests. The centre also takes in wildlife that has been abandoned by zoos or circuses, such as capuchin monkeys as well as cougars and lions that are unable to be re-introduced owing to them being de-clawed or de-toothed in attempts to domesticate them. The director, Alejandra Juarez, and her staff will happily show you around the facility and would greatly appreciate any donations you can offer. They also take volunteers. The centre is located 80km outside of Córdoba in Tiu Mayu, outside the town of La Cumbre, about 9km from the locally famous Estancia Rosario biscuit factory.
Paraje Tiu Mayu, 5178 La Cumbre, Córdoba; e *refugiodelcaraya@yahoo.com.ar, carayaproject@yahoo.com.ar; www.refugiodelcaraya.com.ar*

Ecology and Conservation of Andean Huemul Deer
The project objectives are to estimate population size and to determine the reproductive status, social behaviour, food habits, genetic diversity and degree of genetic isolation between the northern and southern populations. During the summer months, members of the public can apply to join the project for two weeks to help with field research (see www.greenvolunteers.org for more information).
e *JoAnne Smith-Flueck at flueck@cab.cnea.edu.ar*

Fundación Patagonia Natura (FPN)
Founded as a non-governmental, non-profit organisation in 1989, FPN has since been working to protect and conserve the flora and fauna, eco-systems and environment of Patagonia. It runs programmes involve public education, working with private sector and government institutions, research, local community development, environmental impact mitigation, violations watchdog and wildlife rescue and/or rehabilitation. It has a healthy and active volunteer programme. With the support of the Wildlife Conservation Society in the US the foundation runs the Punta Flecha Observatory (*www.puntaflecha.org.ar*).
Marcos A Zar 760 (or Casilla de Correo 160), Puerto Madryn, 9120 Chubut Argentina; ✆ *02965 451 920, 427 023;* e *pnatural@patagonianatural.org; www.patagonianatural.org/*

NOTES FOR DISABLED TRAVELLERS
Gordon Rattray

Although disabled travellers are not yet able to tango with ease from Tierra del Fuego to Iguazú, Argentina can boast a developing accessible-tourism industry. There has been disabled rights legislation here since 1982, and in 2002 the first Acts were passed to make tourist facilities accessible by law. This certainly doesn't mean that every hotel has rooms with roll-in showers, but main tourist centres and public buildings often have access by means of ramps or lifts. This is a sure sign that travel for all is becoming a priority.

Accommodation As with everywhere, the more you pay, the higher the standard of service you can expect to receive. Argentina has a range of lodgings available, from international hotels with fully adapted facilities, to backpacker hostels where budget rather than bubble bath is the priority. That's not to say that the disabled budget traveller is not catered for. With some research and effort, and maybe some improvisation, it will be possible to find what you need at an affordable price.

Transport By air Good disability services are to be expected from airlines, and all international airports reportedly have accessible toilets. However, travellers on domestic flights to smaller airfields will find fewer provisions. Here, entering and exiting the aircraft may be a manhandling affair rather than with a narrow aisle chair, and staff will not be as highly trained.

By rail Some buses and trains in Buenos Aires are fully accessible, but this is not yet standard countrywide.

By road In regular taxis, drivers will normally be happy to help with transfers, but it is worth remembering that they are not experienced in this skill. Therefore, you must always not only give a good explanation in advance of what is necessary, but stay in control of the transfer as it proceeds. Only in the larger cities is it possible

Fundacion Vida Silvestre Argentina
This foundation is one of the most important conservation organisations in the country, having been working for the past 25 years, with the dedication of over 150 volunteers, establishing numerous private refuges, parks and reserves. This entity is associated with and financially supported by the Worldwide Fund for Nature (WWF) in Argentina, holding joint campaigns and arranging global actions. You can become a member, make a donation, volunteer or request information on the environmental issues and initiatives in Argentina.
Defensa 251, Piso 6 K 1065 Buenos Aires, Argentina; ☎ *011 4343 4086;* f *011 4331 3631*
Programa Marino (Marine Programme) Av Córdoba 2920, Piso 4 B 7600 Mar del Plata, Argentina; ☎ *0223 494 1877*
Programa Selva Paranaense (Atlantic Forest) Av Córdoba 464, 3370 Puerto Iguazú, Misiones, Argentina; ☎ *03757 422370*
www.vidasilvestre.org.ar

Help Argentina
This non-profit organisation collaborates with other non-profit and social development organisations with the intent to strengthen the social sector in its

to find wheelchair accessible taxis. In Buenos Aires, try Transpdisc (+54 911 4993 9883; e info@transpdisc.com.ar; www.transpdisc.com.ar).

Personal assistance Travellers can arrange a personal assistant through Decthird travel (see below).

Health Doctors will know about 'everyday' illnesses, but you must understand and be able to explain your own particular medical requirements. Hospitals and pharmacies may not carry the medication you need, so try to take this with you. It is advisable to pack medication in your hand luggage during flights.

Security It is worthwhile remembering that as a disabled person, you are more vulnerable. Stay aware of who is around you and where your possessions are, especially during car transfers and similar. These activities can draw a crowd, and the confusion creates easy pickings for an opportunist thief.

Activities Some national parks cater extremely well for disabled visitors. Iguazú, for instance, has ramped access to tourist buildings and accessible footbridges, and the 'green train of the jungle' (which takes you to various viewpoints) has recently been made wheelchair accessible. Peninsula Valdes, Arrayanes, Nahuel Huapi, Tierra del Fuego and Los Glaciares national parks all have some degree of access and improvements are evident all the time. For the more adventurous traveller, there is even tutored skiing for disabled people, with equipment hire available, at Bariloche and at San Martín de los Andes.

Specialist travel companies
Decthird +54 911 4182/5469; e marcelo@decthird.com; www.decthird.com
Amapi Expeditions +56 9 9179365; e organisation@amapiexpeditions.com; www.amapiexpeditions.com

entirety. It mainly works in the field with beneficiary organisations, conducting surveys, delivering supplies, etc. Volunteers and donations are always appreciated. Its website lists events, has an organisational directory, a virtual library and a newsletter.
Av de Mayo 1370, Piso 16, 1085, Buenos Aires; *011 4381 4049*
1220 Park Avenue, suite 12A, New York, NY 10128
e *Info@HelpArgentina.org; www.HelpArgentina.org*

Kairos onlus
This Italian-based non-profit humanitarian organisation has three distinct projects in Argentina. A programme to bring clothing and basic medical supplies to the children of a school with a high level of poverty as well as a bakery to provide daily bread is making a difference in Escuela no. 107 Hernández, in a suburb of the city of La Plata, 50km from Buenos Aires. Kairos also works in the Fortin Mbororè indigenous community in Puerto Iguazú, Misiones, constructing a large outdoor traditional adobe oven, donating medical supplies, clothing and educational materials, drilling a fresh-water well and building and running a school. Finally, a paediatric hospital in Mendoza receives support and donations through Kairos. If

pick-up can be arranged in Buenos Aires or the aforementioned cities where the projects are running. The main point of administrative contact, however, is in Italy. *Kairos Onlus, Centro Studi Clinici sul Disagio Social, Viale Gran Sasso 10, Milano;* ❭ *+39 (02) 2951 4153;* e *kairos.onlus@tiscali.it; www.kairosonlus.it*

Red Yaguarete
This non-governmental, non-profit organisation is working to protect Argentina's largest cat, the jaguar, and its habitat. It works through local and public education, diffusion of information, sustainable development projects, scientific research and participation with other groups in various sectors.
www.jaguares.com.ar, www.redyaguarete.com.ar

Wilderness Conservation Society in Argentina
This international conservation organisation works in Argentina to protect wildlife and wilderness in coastal, marine, steppe and Andean environments in Patagonia. One of its more important programmes working to protect coastal and marine ecology is the Patagonian Coastal Zone Management Plan, funded by the United Nations Development Programme (UNDP) and the Global Environmental Facility (GEF). On the Patagonian steppe it is studying endangered species and protecting them through conservation interventions for the protection of their habitat.
WCS Southern Cone, J A Roca 1882 (9120), Puerto Madryn, Chubut, Argentina; ❭ *02965 474 524;* e *conosur@wcs.org; www.wcs.org/international/latinamerica/180640*

Organización ProFauna
Avenida Corrientes 1145, 4° piso, dpto. 47, Buenos Aires 1043; ❭f *0054 11 4 382 9557;* e *profaunaconservacion@yahoo.com.ar; www.profauna.org.ar*

Futafriends
This US organisation works directly in Chile to protect the Futaleufu River from damming, and the resultant effects upon the ecology and the communities which live alongside the river in Argentina. For those concerned about the conservation of this important river system, for both recreational and community welfare.
❭ *+1 970 527 3986 or +1 970 921 3809;* e *info@futafriends; www.futafriends.org*

Conservación Patagonica
Dedicated to the protection and restoration of wildland ecosystems and biodiversity in Patagonia, Conservación Patagonica aims to preserve intact ecosystems by acquiring and protecting privately owned wildlands and returning them to the public domain for permanent protection in the form of national parks or reserves. Over 155,000 acres and 25 miles of coastline were protected by the creation of Monte León National Park, after Estancia Monte León was purchased in 2001. They are now working towards the transfer of the Estancia El Rincón lands to enlarge Perito Moreno National Park, as well as establishing a park around Valle Chacabuco. You can spend a volunteer holiday from two weeks to three months on restoration projects in the field. This organisation collaborates with Vida Silvestre and the Patagonian Land Trust.
Conservación Patagonica, Building 1062, Ft. Cronkhite, Sausalito CA 94965; ❭ *415 229 9339;* f *415 229 9340;* e *info@conservationpatagonica.org; www.conservacionpatagonica.org, www.patagonialandtrust.org*

For volunteer and internship opportunities in Argentina, see: www.greenvolunteers.org as well as www.internabroad.com/Argentina.cfm

Part Two

The Guide

90

Buenos Aires

Area code 011

Different expectations and preconceptions of South America
set many visitors up for a surprise when first arriving in
Buenos Aires. Whether flying directly in without having seen
other parts of Argentina or arriving by land across the vast
emptiness of the interior, the big city never gives a dull first
impression. Beautiful European architecture stands among
the bland North-American-style high-rise buildings, garish
neon lights and advertising billboards. The energy of big-city
traffic and gridlock and the large and long-established metro
system imply prosperity (although evidence of extreme
poverty is also inescapable). The city effortlessly blends South
American colour, rhythm and spice with European elegance,
style and sophistication and North American economic and
commercial ambitions, all the while maintaining a culture, a
language, folklore, music and dance that is purely Argentine, and distinctly *porteño*.

The city is referred to as the Capital Federal or sometimes the *Ciudad Autónoma
de Buenos Aires* or Autonomous City of BA, and has a population of over three
million; the metropolitan area of Gran Buenos Aires, also known as the *Gran Aldea*
(great village), includes the Capital Federal and surrounding districts, or *partidos*,
and reaches a population of 13 million. Around 1910 Buenos Aires became the first
South American city to reach a population of one million; its inhabitants came to
be referred to as *porteños* or port residents, a great mix of Italian, Spanish, British,
Jewish, Afro-Argentine, German and Portuguese immigrants. It is a unique city
within Argentina and the people even have a characteristic accent that differs from
the rest of the country.

HISTORY

Buenos Aires was actually founded twice, some say even three times. The first was
in 1536, by Pedro de Mendoza, leading one of the first Spanish expeditions to
Argentina. He arrived at a large estuary that had been previously claimed by Juan
Díaz de Solís in 1516 on the first, and unfortunately fatal, expedition to Argentina,
sailing down from Brazil in search of a southern passage to the Pacific. This second
voyage followed the fall of the Inca Empire in 1532; the King of Spain, Carlos I,
sent Mendoza's group to counter Portuguese advances in the territory. The group
was able to settle on the southwestern bank of the estuary, and the settlement was
soon named *Nuestra Señora Santa María del Buen Aire*. However, the native
Americans who were long established in the area did not perceive their lands as
available for settlement. Their warriors, who had already become skilled
horsemen, launched repeated attacks upon the settlement and any exploration
parties it attempted to send out. Shortage of food and supplies led Mendoza to

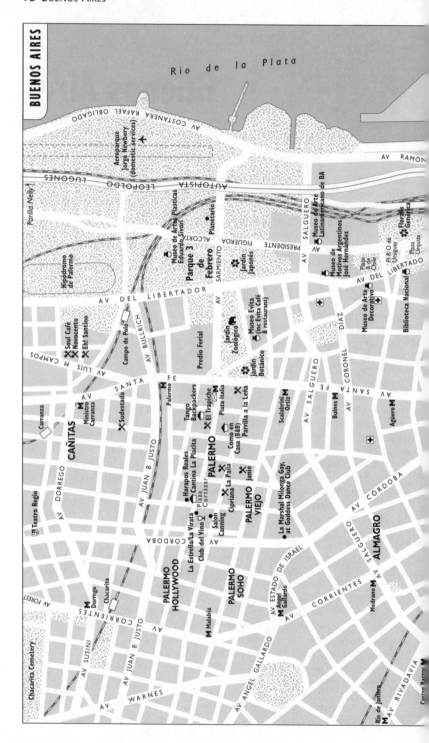

BUENOS AIRES

Río de la Plata

AV COSTANERA RAFAEL OBLIGADO

Aeroparque
Jorge Newbery
(domestic services)

AUTOPISTA LEOPOLDO LUGONES

AV RAMÓN

Parrilla Nelly

Museo de Arte Plásticas
Eduardo Sívori

ALCORTA

Planetario

Museo de Arte
Latinoamericano de BA

Floralis
Genérica

Plaza
Urquiza

Hipódromo
de Palermo

Parque 3
de Febrero

SARMIENTO

FIGUEROA

PRESIDENTE

Jardín
Japonés

Museo de
Motivos Argentinos
José Hernández

AV SALGUERO

Plaza
R de Chile

P R O de
Uruguay

AV DEL LIBERTADOR

AV DEL LIBERTADOR

AV

Museo de Arte
Decorativo

Biblioteca Nacional

DÍAZ

AV BULLRICH

Campo de Polo

Soul Café
Novocento
El Santino

Predio Ferial

Jardín
Zoológico

Museo Evita
(inc Evita Café
& restaurant)

Jardín
Botánico

AV SALGUERO

AV CORONEL

AV LUIS M CAMPOS

SANTA

FE

Sudestada

CAÑITAS

Carranza

Ministro
Carranza

Palermo

Tango
Backpackers

El Trapiche

Plaza Italia

Como en
Casa (B&B)

Parrilla a la Leña

Scalabrini
Ortiz

Bulnes

Agüero

AV SANTA FE

AV

AV DORREGO

AV JUAN B JUSTO

Harapos Reales

Cantina La Plácita

Plaza
Cortázar

La Pulla

Janio

Cipriana

PALERMO
VIEJO

La Marshal Milonga Gay,
at Goddess Dance Club

AV CÓRDOBA

AV FOREST

Teatro Regio

Chacarita

Dorrego

La Estrella/La Virata

Club del Vino

Salón
Canning

AV CÓRDOBA

AV CORRIENTES

PALERMO
HOLLYWOOD

PALERMO
SOHO

Malabia

AV JUAN B JUSTO

AV SUSINI

CORRIENTES

Chacarita Cemetery

AV ESTADO DE ISRAEL

Ángel
Gallardo

CORRIENTES

ALMAGRO

SALGUERO

Medrano

AV JUAN B JUSTO

AV WARNES

AV ÁNGEL GALLARDO

Río de Janeiro

AV RIVADAVIA

Castro Barros

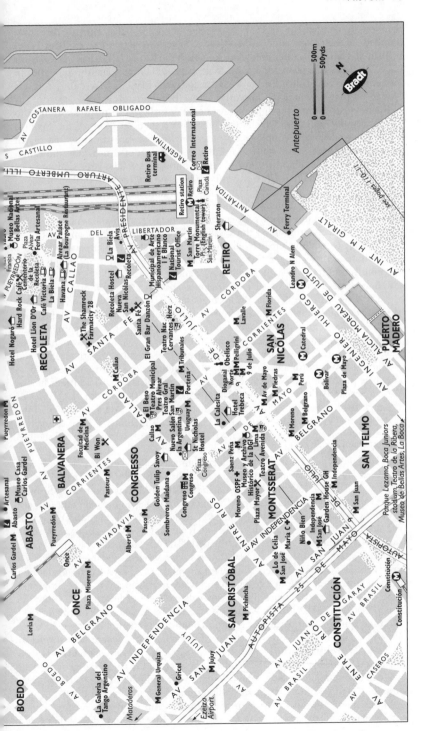

abandon the settlement in 1537. It was not until 1580 that Buenos Aires was founded for the second time at the 'River of Silver' (*Río de la Plata*, or River Plate) by Juan de Garay. His intention was to establish the Río de la Plata as a gateway for trade. Rudimentary plans for a town took shape with streets laid out in a grid. In the centre was established the Plaza Mayor, today the Plaza de Mayo, and a fort was erected on the site where the Executive Office Building now stands.

Buenos Aires was subordinate to Asunción, which was in turn subordinate to the viceroyalty of Lima, which was subordinate then to Madrid, the Spanish capital; it would take a couple of centuries for Buenos Aires to grow and match Lima's level of power and status. Meanwhile, it was cut off from communication with Spain owing to colonial and mercantile bureaucracy. The large trading fleets from Spain would stop in Cuba and at Portobello on the Isthmus of Panamá, send their goods by mule across the isthmus to the Pacific and load them onto fresh ships for Callao, near Lima. This route was relatively safe from attack but very lengthy and costly and Buenos Aires was quite neglected. Buenos Aires was only permitted to receive registered ships, sailing only every year or so, and up to five years could pass without a registered ship arriving from Spain. The *porteños* in those days suffered greatly under this system; culturally they could not adapt to the Querandí's hunting-and-gathering lifestyle, and it was inevitable that bootlegging would become a means of survival. Against Spanish authorisation, the *porteños* began trading with the British and Portuguese vessels that passed; and what they had to trade was leather. Cattle and horses abandoned by the Mendoza expedition had by this time grown into semi-wild herds that populated the pampas. The leather was too crude to trade with Spain, but it was acceptable for contraband trade. It was during these early days of pioneering the pampas that the leather and beef industry was born, and so was born the famous *gaucho* or Argentine cowboy. The increase in commercial activity, smuggling and the slave trade caused Buenos Aires to expand. By 1776 its population exceeded 25,000; Spain had come to recognise the importance of Buenos Aires and in that year made it the capital of the newly created Viceroyalty of the River Plate, which included the wealthy silver region of Potosí (in present-day Bolivia). In 1778 the Atlantic ports were allowed to trade freely, giving a big boost to the city's growth.

In 1800 the British Empire began implementing its colonial expansion policies and the Río de la Plata was in its sights as a potential British base for trade. The first attack on Buenos Aires in 1806, led by Commander Beresford, was opposed by Spanish troops led by Santiago de Liniers from Montevideo (taking command in the absence of Viceroy Rafael de Sobremonte, who had fled at the onset of the attack), together with an urban militia of Spanish civilians, Creole *patricios* and peasant *gauchos*. The battle was short and the British force surrendered and was interned in Luján. A second ill-advised attack in July 1807 by 10,000 men under Major-General John Whitelock was repelled by the heroic defence of the urban militia, aided by women and children using such tactics as pouring boiling oil and water from windows and rooftops and firing cannons from balconies (in particular the balcony of Defensa 372, now the Museo Nacional del Grabado). Whitelock's headstrong frontal attack on the fortified city resulted in the immediate loss of almost a third of his men. He accepted a truce offered by Liniers and was evacuated to Montevideo, from where he returned to Britain to face court martial. These battles are known as *La Reconquista* and *La Defensa* and were remarkable because the residents themselves, the *porteños*, organised their own defence without the aid of the colonial power and with decisions being made without reference to Madrid or intervention from the viceroy.

Meanwhile in Europe, Napoleon had crossed Spain to invade Portugal (allied with Britain) with the assistance of Charles IV; Charles was forced to abdicate and was replaced on the throne by Ferdinand. Napoleon forcibly re-established Charles as king, in order for Charles to then yield it to Napoleon, who then put his brother Joseph on the Spanish throne. This created anti-French sentiment in Buenos Aires leading to the execution of Liniers solely on the basis of his French name. On 25 May 1810 the citizens of Buenos Aires revolted and disposed of Viceroy Sobremonte for he was seen as a coward and not capable of protecting the River Plate. The May Revolution of 1810 replaced him with an autonomous governing body.

On 9 July 1816, absolute independence of Argentina from the King of Spain was granted. Buenos Aires itself had reached a population of over 300,000, and recognisable neighbourhoods, *barrios*, had been established. Some consider the city to have had a third founding with mass immigration in the late 19th century. A century later, Buenos Aires' population had grown eightfold and the city was modern and cosmopolitan. The first subway line (the first in Latin America) opened in 1911, and the city's first skyscraper, the Barolo Building, appeared in 1920. By 1950, Buenos Aires was one of the largest cities in the world.

GETTING THERE
By air
Most major European, North American and Australasian airlines have regular flights into Buenos Aires, as well as most South American countries. Sometimes flying into a neighbouring country, such as Chile or Uruguay, may prove to be more economical. The national flag-carrier is Aerolíneas Argentinas.

Aerolíneas Argentinas offices (*Mon–Fri 09.00–19.00, Sat 09.00–13.00*): Perú 2 (❧ *4320 2000*); Cabildo 2900 (❧ *4783 2507, 4784 9870/2*); Avenida L N Alem 1134 (❧ *4130 3625/6*). Central Service local-rate number 0810 2228 6527 (*09.30–17.00*); e informes@aerolineas.com.ar. Lineas Aéreas del Estado (LADE) (*Perú 710;* ❧ *5129 9000 or 0810 810 5233;* e *informes@lade.com.ar*) has flights once or twice a week from various minor domestic destinations.

LAN has international flights from other South American countries and Europe via Santiago to Buenos Aires and other major Argentine cities. Their offices are located at Cerrito 866 on the corner of Paraguay (❧ *4378 2200, local-rate: 0810 999 9526*). LAN Argentina has domestic flights from Buenos Aires to major Argentine cities; they share the same offices (❧ *4378 2222; local-rate 0810 999 9256; free: 0800 2222 424*). Other airline offices are mostly on or near Carlos Pellegrini in Retiro.

Airports
Aeropuerto Internacional Ministro Pistarini is the country's main international airport, commonly known as **Ezeiza** (code EZE), Autopista General Ricchieri km33.5; ❧ 4480 0235 or 5480 2500. It is 22km from the Capital Federal, a 45-minute bus or taxi ride from the city.

Although normally included in the ticket price, there is a departure tax from Ezeiza of US$20. Upon arrival and departure from the airport, have cash on hand because the bank machines (of which there are only two) are often out of service.

Aeroparque Jorge Newbery (code AEP) is the domestic airport, within the city limits on the riverside Avenida Rafael Obligado, Palermo. It mainly serves flights within Argentina, but does receive some flights from neighbouring countries.

See below for details of bus services from both airports.

By bus
Retiro's Estación Terminal de Omnibuses is the main bus station in Buenos Aires. It is located at Avenida Antárdida and Avenida Ramos Mejía 1860 (❧ *4310 0700;*

www.tebasa.com.ar). It is within walking distance of Subte Línea C, at the Retiro train station. There are over 170 bus companies serving destinations throughout Argentina and in neighbouring countries. On the first floor of the building are the information office, lost and found and taxi information. There is a tourist office open 07.30–13.00. The ticket offices are on the second floor; the companies are grouped according to the regions of the country that they serve. Advance reservations are wise during summer and holiday periods. Ticket prices vary according to quality of bus: regular *pullman* reclining seats, spacious *servicio diferencial* seats, partially reclining *semicama*, fully reclining beds called *cama*, plus *supercama* and first/executive class.

By train

There is no international rail service to or from Buenos Aires and there are only a few long-distance domestic services. Apart from the Buenos Aires suburban network, the rail system in Argentina is very limited, with many lines out of use. There's a weekly (Fridays 19.30) passenger train from Buenos Aires (Retiro) to Santa Fé via Zárate, Lima, Baradero, San Pedro, Ramallo, San Nicolás, Arrollo Seco, Rosario, San Lorenzo and Santo Tomé; and two trains a week from Retiro to Rosario and Tucumán (*Trenes de Buenos Aires (TBA)*; ✆ 4317 4400; *www.tbanet.com.ar*). Journeys are slower by train than by bus and have restricted schedules; however the current government is committed to modernising the railways and expanding passenger services, for instance to Posadas and Bariloche.

There are also a few historical lines that continue to run for nostalgia and are therefore more of a tourist attraction than practical transportation; these include the *Tren a las Nubes*, in Salta, and the Old Patagonian Express, *La Trochita*.

By car

Entering Argentina by car is not recommended. Crossing borders from neighbouring countries may be bureaucratically problematic (specific insurance and paperwork will be required). If you are flying into a city in Argentina other than Buenos Aires, you can easily hire a car. Driving into Buenos Aires is quite straightforward.

By boat

Ferries run across the river from Buenos Aires and El Tigre to the city of Montevideo and the towns of Colonia del Sacramento, Carmelo and Nueva Palmira in Uruguay (see page 121).

GETTING AROUND
Metro/subway (subte)

Buenos Aires has a five-line underground system (known as the Subte – short for Subterráneo) that accesses most tourist areas. It operates from 05.00 to 22.00 (Sun 08.00–22.00), and the fare is 0.70 pesos (a multi-trip pass is also available).

In 2001 Buenos Aires city council approved plans for additional metro lines totalling 22km. The new Line H will open between Plaza Once and Caseros at the end of 2006 and will eventually form an orbital line running for 11 km from Retiro through Recoleta and south to Nueva Pompeya, including interchanges with all other Subte lines. Later, Line F will run from Plaza Italia (on Line D) to Constitución, with 13 stations; Line G from Retiro to CID Campeador (11 stations roughly parallel to Line B); and Line I from Plaza Italia to Emilio Mitre (on line E), with 10 stations. Meanwhile, Line A will be extended from Primera Junta to Avenida Nazca and Lina B from Los Incas to Villa Urquiza, both by 2008. Line E will eventually be extended from Bolívar to Retiro. Note that there are stations

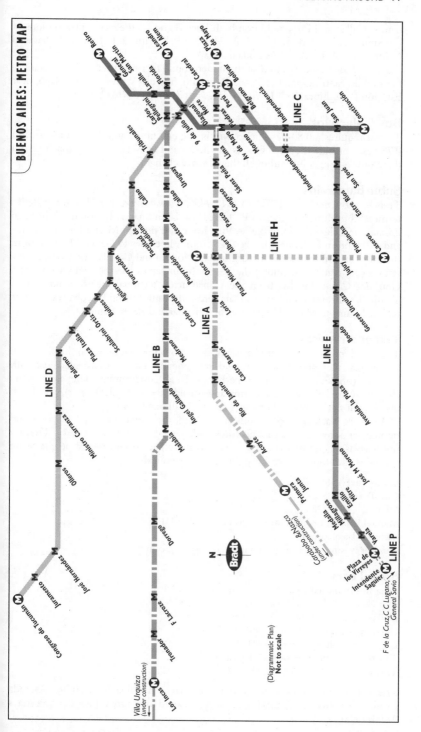

BUENOS AIRES: METRO MAP

(Diagrammatic Plan)
Not to scale

named Callao and Pueyrredón on both lines B and D; the city-centre stations of Catedral, Perú and Bolivar are linked, as are Pellegrini, 9 de Julio and Diagonal Norte, and also Lima and Avenida de Mayo.

Flor de Buenos Aires is a tour of the underground focusing on the 1930s ceramic-tile murals. Starting point at Pasaje Roverano, 500 block, Avenida de Mayo, near Estación Perú, Línea A (❱ *15 4049 3337; tours daily 14.00–16.00; 3 pesos*).

Bus (colectivo)

Transit requires a 0.80-peso ticket within the city limits and a minimum fare of 0.75 pesos outside the city. Tickets can be bought from an onboard machine but these only accept coins (although they do give change).

Suburban trains

Trenes de Buenos Aires (TBA; ❱ *4317 4400; www.tbanet.com.ar*). From the Retiro terminal the Mitre line goes to El Tigre, José León Suarez, Bartolomé Mitre and Zárate; the Belgrano Norte line to Villa Rosa; and the San Martín line to Caseros and Pilár. From Federico Lacroze the Urquiza line goes to General Lemos; from the Once station the Sarmiento line serves Moreno and Castelar. From the Alsina station (not reached by Subte) the Belgrano Sur serves Marinos del Crucero and González Catán. Finally, from the Constitución terminal the Roca line serves Temperley, Ezeiza, Glew and La Plata. From the same station Ferrobaires operates regional trains to Mar del Plata, Tandil, Pinamar and Bahía Blanca.

Taxi and remises

Taxis and *remises* offer similar services but *remises* (radio taxis) have several advantages: they are private cars and are generally newer, more spacious, with seatbelts (unlike most taxis) and perhaps even air conditioning. They are usually cheaper (especially for longer trips and outside the Federal District), and often quote a flat rate. Any hotel or restaurant will call one for you.

Taxis are black and yellow and everywhere; the meter starts at 1.12 pesos and tipping is not required (although you should round up to the next peso). They do not have as a good reputation as *remises* as there have been cases of people being robbed while stopped at traffic lights; just lock your door.

Radio Taxi ❱ 4860 0707
City Taxi ❱ 4585 5544
Mi Taxi ❱ 4931 1200
Manuel Tienda León Remise Av Santa Fé 790; ❱ 4315 5115, 0810 888 5366; www.tiendaleon.com.ar
Remises Naon ❱ 4545 6500; e remisesnaon@sinectis.com.ar

Rental cars

Ansa International Paraguay 866, Retiro; ❱ 4311 0220
Avis Cerrito 1527, Retiro; ❱ 4378 9640
Dollar Marcelo T de Alvear 523, Retiro; ❱ 4315 8800
Hertz Paraguay 1122, Retiro; ❱ 4816 8001
Localiza Maipú 924, Retiro; ❱ 4315 8334
Tauro Posadas 1590, Recoleta; ❱ 4807 1002
Thrifty Av L N Alem 699; ❱ 4315 0777

The Microcentro (between Avenida de Mayo, Avenida 9 de Julio, Avenida Córdoba and Avenida Alem) is – in theory – closed to private vehicles on weekdays 07.00–19.00.

From the airports

To reach the city centre from either airport there are public buses, shuttle buses, metered taxis and flat-rate radio taxis (*remises*). Public buses, or *colectivos*, are the cheapest option, but more practical from the Aeroparque than from Ezeiza as the latter take circuitous routes. Shuttle buses are more expensive than *colectivos* but more direct. They have stops at offices near Plaza San Martín and will also take you to your hotel. If you are flying into one airport and out of the other with Aerolíneas Argentinas they'll provide a free transfer.

A shuttle service from Ezeiza (also known as Ministro Pistarini) to the city and to the Aeroparque is provided by Manuel Tienda León (✆ *0810 888 5366; www.tiendaleon.com.ar*) for 26 pesos (47 pesos return). Public bus 86-A (*Aeropuerto*) takes up to two hours to reach the centre for US$0.50; there is also a *Servicio Diferencial* bus that is more comfortable and faster, for US$2. You can also take bus 502 to the suburb of Ezeiza and then an all-stops train to Constitución station, taking an hour at most (1 peso). Be aware, though, that the security situation at Ezeiza train station is not great. Note, too, that Ezeiza train station does not directly connect with Ezeiza airport.

Shuttle buses

From Ezeiza Transfer Express (*Edificio Kavanagh, Florida 1045;* ✆ *4314 1999 or 0800 555 0224*) has 20 shuttles per day, US$3.50, 06.30–20.45 (from the centre; first departure from Ezeiza at 07.15). Manuel Tienda León (*Av Santa Fé 790;* ✆ *4315 5115 or 0810 888 5366; www.tiendaleon.com.ar*) has a departure every 30 minutes, costing 26 pesos one way.

From the Aeroparque (bus stop on Avenida Costanera Rafael Obligado, 0.80 pesos (US$0.25) ticket) to:

Retiro, the Microcentro, Plaza de Mayo, Puerto Madero and La Boca – No 33
Plaza Italia, Av las Heras, Av Callao and Plaza del Congreso – No 37-C (Ciudad Universitaria)
Retiro, Plaza San Martín and Plaza Constitución – No 45
Plaza Italia and Av Las Heras – No 160-C or 160-D

Manuel Tienda León provides a shuttle service from the Aeroparque to the centre for 9 pesos. Transfer Express has nine shuttles per day (08.50–21.10; US$1.40).

Taxis and remises

For a group of three or four people going to or from the airport, the cost will be equal to the total cost of the shuttle (bear in mind trunk space however if your group has a lot of bags). There are several companies in both terminals at Ezeiza; the following prices include all tax and tolls and are flat rates to the centre regardless of address.

City Car 45 pesos from the airport to the centre, credit cards not accepted; www.citycar.com.ar
Manuel Tienda León 54 pesos, credit cards accepted.
Taxi Ezeiza 43 pesos, with a discount to 35 pesos for the return, www.taxiezeiza.com.
Transfer Express 54 pesos, credit cards accepted; ✆ 0800 444 4872;
e reservas@transferexpress.com.ar
VIP Car 49 pesos; if paying by credit card 59 pesos.

ORIENTATION

A good starting point, and the most popular point of interest for tourists, is the Plaza de Mayo and the Microcentro, from where you can head towards the Río de

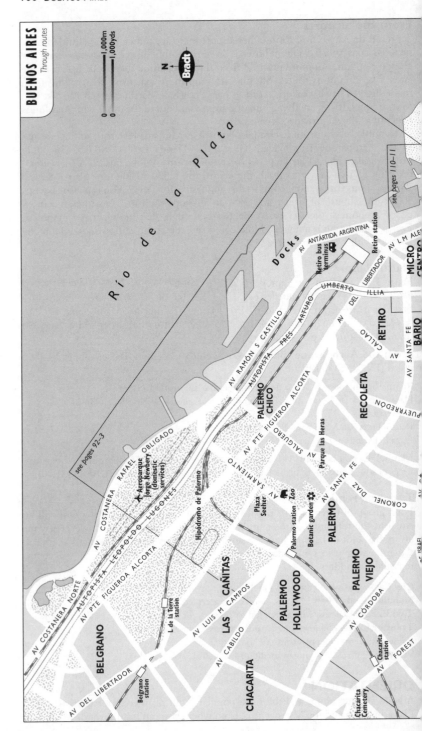

BUENOS AIRES
Through routes

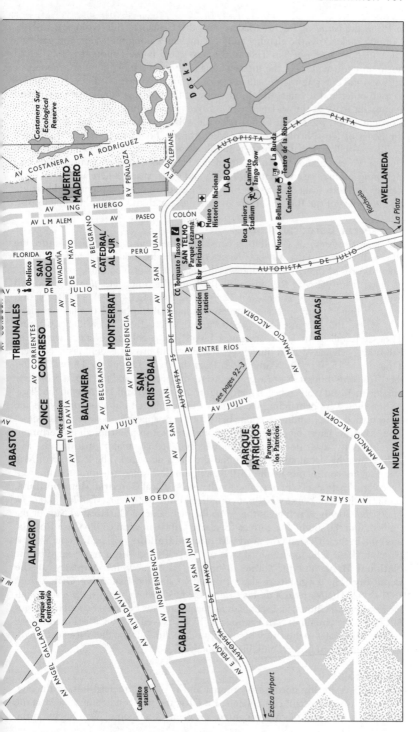

la Plata, the *barrio* of Puerto Madero and the Costanera Sur ecological reserve. Coming back across the channel and heading south along the water, you will pass the bohemian *barrio* of San Telmo; the next *barrio* is the famous La Boca. Head north and you will meet the intersections of the three most popular avenues for business and entertainment: Santa Fé, Córdoba and Corrientes. These run parallel to each other and if you turn left onto one of them or any parallel street you will eventually arrive at the 16-lane frenzy of Avenida 9 de Julio. At the junction with Corrientes, you will see the 67.5m-tall white Obelisco. Avenida 9 de Julio separates the *barrio* of San Nicolás from the Microcentro. Following Avenida 9 de Julio north you will arrive at the upper-middle-class *barrio* of Retiro, which leads into Buenos Aires' grandest *barrio*, Recoleta. Palermo follows, leading you into charming suburbs resplendent with parks and green space. There are a total of 48 neighbourhoods (called *barrios*) in Buenos Aires; most of those mentioned here are on the shores of the Río de la Plata and are those with most appeal for the tourist.

Monserrat/Catedral al Sur

Although the *barrio* of Caballito is considered the city's geographical centre, the **Plaza de Mayo**, in the barrio of Monserrat, is the location of the re-founding of Buenos Aires in 1580 by Garay and was the locus of Spanish colonial power. It takes its name from the May Revolution in 1810, and the original *cabildo* (city council) from 1764 still stands (*open Tue–Fri 12.30–19.00, Sun 15.00–19.00*). The Revolution was only one of many spectacular events that have taken place in this famous plaza. It is where the Peronist party was born and where Evita received her acclaim. Thousands rallied here for or against pivotal socio-political events such as the Falklands/Malvinas War. A quieter yet still powerful protest is demonstrated every Thursday at 15.30 by the Madres de la Plaza de Mayo. During the Dirty War after the 1976 coup thousands of Argentines were 'disappeared' and the mothers of these missing men and women began marching around the **Pyramid of May** in the Plaza. At first they were demanding the return of their children but after some years the focus turned to demanding accountability for the disappeared, now presumed dead. The Madres have received international recognition although government accountability has not been acknowledged. Most major institutions and architectural/historical edifices surround the Plaza de Mayo. The Pyramid of May was raised to commemorate the 1810 Revolution; few other structures remain from the colonial period, except of course for the Neoclassical **Catedral Metropolitana**, begun in the 18th century but not completed until 1827 (*tours Mon–Fri 13.00, Sat 11.30, Sun 10.00*), which gives this *barrio* the nickname of **Catedral al Sur**, or the Cathedral in the south. The former Executive Office, now called the **Casa Rosada**, was built in the 1870s, and the nearby **Municipal Building** was built, as the Victoria Hotel, in 1902. The monumental style of the 1930s and '40s is represented by the **National Bank** and the former Mortgage Bank, now the **Ministry of the Economy**. The **Legislature** dates from 1930 and the **Executive Office** from 1891–1902. The **Manzana de las Luces** (the block where in 1616 the Jesuits built the San Ignacio Church and school, now the prestigious National School of Buenos Aires) and the church of **San Francisco** (1730), as well as the **Café Tortoni** (one of the leading cafés of the city, where celebrities, politicians and dignitaries gathered), are the other main historic buildings of note.

San Nicolás

This *barrio* is directly north of Monserrat and is the commercial hub of the city. There are two important components: **La City**, the small and compact area of the financial district, and the **Microcentro**, the capital's version of Wall Street on the boundary of San Nicolás and Retiro. At the time of the economic collapse of 2001–02 many of the financial institutions were defaced with graffiti from angry depositors. A lot of the damage has been repaired but there are still some banks whose metal doors show dents and scrapes and there are always guards on duty. Three important edifices of this *barrio* are the **Correo Central** (Central Post Office, 1928), the **Bolsa de Comercio de Buenos Aires** (Stock Exchange, 1916) and the **Banco Central de la República Argentina** (Central Bank, 1876). Several museums in San Nicolás are dedicated to the history of the economy and banking. Avenida 9 de Julio separates the Microcentro from the rest of the *barrio*; to the west is the **Palacio de Justicia** or **Tribunales** (Law Courts, 1904), the colloquial name now also defining the surrounding area. At 09.53 every Monday morning members of the Jewish community gather to observe a moment of silence for the 18 July 1994 bombing of the Asociación Mutualista Israelita-Argentina (AMIA) and the judicial inaction that followed. They have been doing so since 1994 and recently others have joined to protest against the judicial decisions that allowed the unpopular banking restrictions. This is a popular shopping and theatre district with the **Teatro Colón** (1908) at Libertad 621, and **Calle Florida**, running north from Rivadavia and crossing Avenida Córdoba into the *barrio* of Retiro. **Avenida Corrientes**, 'the street that never sleeps', is the city's traditional nightlife strip, although less trendy than Puerto Madero and Palermo, and is popular for its theatres and bookstores. The famous **Obelisco** is on Avenida Corrientes at the intersection with Avenida 9 de Julio. It was erected in 1936 to commemorate the 400-year anniversary of Pedro de Mendoza's original settlement on the banks of the Río de la Plata. You used to be able to climb its 206 steps to the top, but recently the entry door has been locked.

San Telmo

This *barrio* is historically famous for the civilian defences on the streets of the Santo Domingo block during the British invasions of *La Defensa* (1806) and *La Reconquista* (1807). On Calle Defensa the residents poured boiling oil and water from the rooftops onto the British troops. Cannons were fired from the house at Defensa 372. The tomb of Marmiel Belgrano is in the mausoleum of the **Santo Domingo Church**.

San Telmo had a prestigious beginning in 1735 as a wealthy hamlet on the outskirts of the city where aristrocratic families built large houses and mansions. Yellow fever outbreaks caused by poor sanitation in the late 19th century resulted in the evacuation of the families who could afford it to move to uncontaminated areas. The old houses were converted into tenements or *conventillos* where immigrants would rent rooms. By the first half of the 20th century these buildings were in a terrible state of disrepair. It was only in the 1970s that restoration work began to preserve the historic architecture of this quarter of the city, now a bohemian *barrio* of artists and musicians with cobblestone streets, tango bars, antique shops, the flea market at Plaza Dorrego and the Feria de San Telmo (corner of Defensa and Carlos Calvo) every Sunday from 10.00 to 17.00. It is the place to find antiques and collectables. The side streets are closed to traffic and the lively market ambiance is enhanced with the colour, sights and sounds of artists, tango dancers and musicians. The plaza was declared a site of National Historical Interest because it was where the people gathered to hear the Declaration of Independence from Spain. It is the second-oldest square in the city (after Plaza de Mayo). Two impressive churches stand out: the **Church of our Lady of Belén and San Pedro González Telmo** (1734–1918) and the Russian Orthodox **Church of the Holy Trinity** (completed in 1904 in 17th-century Muscovite style).

Lezama Park was the ranch of the Lezama family until the area was bought by the government and turned into a public park. During the 17th century, the area was characterised by warehouses and slave cabins.

San Telmo has some examples of the *casas chorizo* (sausage houses) built in the 1850s. These long narrow buildings are similar to the Roman *domus* built to fit land plots that were only 11m wide. The house of the Ezeiza family at Defensa 1179 is one such. At some point many became tenements housing over 30 families. At Defensa 755 you can enter **El Zanjón de Granados**, a series of arched tunnels below the *conventillos*, where a stream once flowed and a trove of 18th-century relics was found. The former Eva Perón Foundation, now the Engineering College, exemplifies 1930s architecture, and the former home of the artists Raquel Forner and Alfredo Bigatti at Bethlem 443 is now the Forner-Bigatti Foundation, with a selection of their work on show.

La Boca

This working-class district and artists' colony has never been prosperous, but it is the most characteristic, iconic and historically rich *barrio* of the city, where you can watch tango shows in the street and see artists displaying their works. Named for the *boca* or mouth of the Río Riachuelo, it is the original port built up by the French Basques, followed by Italian and Spanish immigrants. It is the birthplace of the tango and is famous for the **Caminito** (the artists' walk named after a famous tango ballad) and the old corrugated metal and wood houses painted bright yellow, red, green and blue. Apparently it was the creativity and foresight of the painter **Benito Quinquela Martín** (see the Museo de Bella Artes here exhibiting his paintings of the area when it was the main port for immigration and trade) who instigated the painting of the houses to bring some colour and beauty to the area. In contrast, the colour of the harbour water is nothing short of foul. The port was and still is filthy! Several highly polluting industries, such as leather-tanning, dump their various chemicals into the water and the resulting stew of industrial waste and petroleum, rusting offshore vessels and dredgers, sickens the poor Riachuelo. A massive transporter bridge crosses the river, which is lined by meat-packing plants and warehouses. There is a strong sense of community in La Boca, home to the **Boca Juniors** soccer team, the former club of icon Diego Maradona. In the stadium at Brandsen 805, fans should visit the **Museo de la Pasión Boquense** (Museum of Boca Passion; *open daily 10.00–18.00, except when there's a home game; admission 8 pesos, stadium tour 8 pesos, combined 13 pesos*).

Puerto Madero

This is the city's newest *barrio* (1994). The port itself has existed since 1880 when it was established as the new port upstream from the dirty old one at San Telmo. The design of the port however did not allow for the growth and demand of the city and by 1910 it was already too small to cope. The current port to the north was then built and Puerto Madero was abandoned. An urban renewal project initiated in the 1990s has reconceived the old port as a promenade with apartments, offices, hotels, restaurants and a university campus. The striking Puente de la Mujer is by famed Spanish architect Santiago Calatrava. The Costanera Sur is a long pedestrian waterside boulevard opposite which is the **Reserva Ecológica de la Costanera Sur**, a 250ha wildlife reserve (☏ *4315 1320*). Most easily entered at Avenida Tristán Achaval Rodríguez 1550, it is open to the public daily, April to October 08.00–18.00, November to March 08.00–19.00. Guided tours are available on weekends and holidays 09.30 and 17.30.

Retiro

This upper-middle-class residential *barrio* is more familiar to the tourist as the location of all the major transport interchanges; the Retiro bus terminal and railway stations and the ferries are all located here. Outside the bus and railway station are numerous bars and kiosks selling grilled sandwiches and other fast foods. The central plaza of the *barrio* is **Plaza San Martín**, in which stands the **Torre a los Ingleses** or English Tower, ie: a replica of Big Ben (St Stephen's Tower) in London; deliberately placed opposite it is a memorial to those killed in the 1982 Falklands/Malvinas war. Other buildings of interest around the plaza include the **Basilica del Santísimo Sacramento** and the **Kavanagh building** where Jorge Luis Borges once lived (*the Borges Cultural Centre, located in the Galerías Pacífico, is open Mon–Sat 10.00–20.00*). At Santa Fé 690, the offices of the **National Parks Administration** are in one of the oldest buildings in the area dating from 1880. The **Galerías Pacífico** is an architectural landmark from the late 19th century by the architect Levacher, inspired by the Galleria Vittorio Emmanuelle II in Milan. It once housed the National Museum of Fine Art but was restructured in 1910 and today is a busy shopping centre between Avenidas Córdoba, San Martín, Florida and Viamonte. Following Avenida Alvear you'll see the elegant old homes that are now the **French and Brazilian embassies**, the **Jockey Club** and the **Alzaga Unzue Palace**. Continue along Avenida Alvear to the **Alvear Palace Hotel** and the *barrio* of Recoleta.

Recoleta

This *barrio* is the most expensive area in the city but also the most popular for dining, shopping and nightlife. The famous **Cementerio de la Recoleta** (*daily 07.00–18.00*) is worth touring to see the European-style above-ground tombs that make it feel like walking through a small city neighbourhood. Many important government figures and elite families are buried here. You have to be somebody special to have your final resting place in these haughty haunts; it was considered scandalous for Evita to be buried here since she was from a common family. Many agencies offer guided tours, many in English. The **Iglesia de Nuestra Señora del Pilar** is a national historical monument, a Baroque-style colonial church consecrated in 1732. Outside the cemetery a sprawling crafts fair is held in **Plaza Intendente Alvear** every Sunday. The **Recoleta Cultural Centre** at Junín 1930 (*Tue–Fri 14.00–21.00, weekends & hols 10.00–21.00*) houses exhibitions, theatrical productions, an auditorium and an interactive science museum. Next door is the **Buenos Aires Design** shopping mall. Beyond this focus of Recoleta are many parks, the **National Library** (*Agüero 250; ☏ 4806 97642; open Mon–Sat 08.00–21.00, Sun 11.00–19.00*) and important museums such as the **National Museum of Fine Art** and the **National Museum of Decorative Arts** (see details under *Museums*). Barrio Norte is not an official *barrio* but the upscale northern half of Recoleta. *Paseaperros*, professional dog-walkers, can be seen in Recoleta and onwards to Palermo walking over a dozen dogs at once.

Palermo

This expansive *barrio*, largely comprising wooded parks and artificial lakes, was once the estate of dictator Juan Manuel de Rosas. It is a middle-upper-class district, with fine dining and wild nightlife on offer. The **Rosedal** (Rose Garden), **Planetario Galileo Galilei**, **Campo de Polo** (polo grounds), **Hipódromo Argentino** (racetrack) and **Japanese Gardens** are located in this *barrio*, the city's largest. Palermo has recognised subdivisions, including **Palermo Chico** between Avenida del Libertador and the river (many embassies are located in this area), and

Palermo Viejo across Avenida Santa Fé, a residential and nightlife zone that further subdivides into **Palermo Soho** and **Palermo Hollywood**. A newly popular zone near the hippodrome is **Las Cañitas** where there are many good restaurants. In the Armenian area just south of Palermo Viejo you can find pitta and hummus diners. **Plaza Serrano**, also known as Plazoleta Cortázar, is a fun nightlife area. The streets around it contain the city's 'best' bars and restaurants, especially popular on Friday and Saturday nights. By day it is also pleasant to sit outside one of the cafés in this plaza and enjoy a cappuccino. In Plaza Naciones Unidas (Figueroa Alcorta and Austria) you cannot overlook the enormous **Floralis Genérica** installed in 2002; designed by architect Eduardo Catalano it is made of metal from Lockheed Martin aircraft and its 20m petals open in the day and close at night. At the far end of the *barrio* is the **Parque 3 de Febrero**, a vital green lung for a city that has almost no public open spaces (other than its cemeteries).

Belgrano

Belgrano had a moment in history as Argentina's capital and for that reason now considers itself a republic. In reality it is a middle-to-upper-class residential suburb; Avenida Cabildo is a busy street full of neon signs, shops and restaurants but elsewhere there are quiet plazas and little-visited museums, such as the **Museo Histórico Sarmiento** (*Av Juramento 2180;* ☏ *4782 2354; www.museoarmiento.gov.ar; Tue–Fri & Sun 14.00–19.00, admission 1 peso, free Thu*) and the **Museo de Arte Español Enrique Larreta** (*Av Juramento 2291;* ☏ *4784 4040; Mon/Tue, Fri–Sun & hols 15.00–19.00, admission 1 peso*).

Balvanera

This *barrio* subdivides into several neighbourhoods, including Congreso (Legislature), which overlaps Monserrat *barrio*, Once (the largely Jewish garment district) and the Abasto (where a new statue marks the home of tango legend Carlos Gardel in Pasaje Gardel).

Mataderos

This *barrio* is on the far side of the city from the main centre but has recently become one of the unmissable highlights of a weekend in Buenos Aires, thanks to its large Sunday market, the *Feria de Mataderos*, with a musical stage hosting a long afternoon of performances by various Argentine singers and traditional folk musicians. The locals are up dancing and singing and clapping and it is hard not to jump up and join them. This is also the place to eat *empanadas, humitas, tamales* and other Argentine specialties. One of the true highlights is seeing all the gauchos in traditional clothing milling about dancing and chatting. *Mataderos* means 'slaughterhouses', and this is where gauchos traditionally brought herds of cattle from the pampas on their final journey. Nowadays many of them come with their horses to compete in the traditional gaucho games and sports that are held on the main street, offering them the chance to show their horseriding skills. One sport in particular is the *carrera de sortijas*, which involves a small metal ring hanging from a tall crossbar at a few hundred meters from a starting line. One by one the men take a run at the target at a full gallop on their beautifully saddled horses and attempt to spear the ring with a tiny stick. The *Museo Criollo de los Corrales* (or gaucho museum) at Avenida de los Corrales 6476 is worth visiting (*only open Sun noon–18.30*).

To reach Mataeros, take subway line E to the end at Plaza de los Virreyes, then take bus 103 and ask the driver to tell you when to get off for the market (other buses that arrive from elsewhere in the city are the 36, 55, 63, 80, 92, 97, 117, 126,

141, 155, 180 and 185). Walk about six blocks from where you are dropped off to the entrance of the market at Lisandro de la Torre and Avenida de los Corrales.

PRACTICALITIES
Tourist information
The national **tourist office** is at Santa Fé 883, with additional branches at the airports (✆ *0800 50016, 4312 2232; open Mon–Fri 09.00–17.00*). The municipal office is located at Pellegrini 217 (✆ *4372 3612; www.buenosaires.gov.ar; open daily 10.00–18.00*). The government's secretary of tourism has several local tourist information centre kiosks set up throughout the city:

Florida Florida 100; Mon–Fri 09.00–18.00, Sat & hols 10.00–15.00.
San Telmo Defensa 1250; Sat & Sun 11.00–19.00.
Puerto Madero Alicia Moreau de Justo 200, Dique 4, Grua 8; Mon–Fri 11.00–20.00, Sat & Sun 10.00–20.00.
Retiro bus terminal Av Antártida Argentina (office 83); Mon–Sat 10.00–18.00.
Recoleta Av Quintana 596; Mon–Fri 10.30–18.30, Sat & Sun 10.00–19.00.
Abasto Av Corrientes 3200 (Abasto shopping centre); daily 11.00–21.00.
Parada Liniers Av General Paz 10,868; daily 08.00–24.00.

There is also a telephone information service (✆ *4313 0187; Mon–Sat 07.30–18.00, Sun 11.00–18.00*), plus a new multi-lingual free phone number for the Tourist Police (✆ *0800 999 5000*), in addition to a 24-hour helpline for victims of crime (✆ *101*). Provincial tourist offices, Casas de Provincia, are located throughout the city, and offer information on regional destinations.

City tours
One-day tours are suitable for a quick stopover in the city. **Free guided tours** of the city are offered through the government undersecretary of tourism (✆ *4114 5791; Mon–Fri 10.00–16.00*). Some of the creative approaches to the city tours on offer are thematic, such as the Carlos Gardel and the Evita tours that take in the relevant sites and buildings.

Free tours with **Cicerones de Buenos Aires** (✆ *4330 0800; e cicerones@cicerones.org.ar; www.cicerones.org.ar*) are run by a group of dedicated local volunteers. The visits are organised in small groups of up to six people and typically last two or three hours but vary with guide and visitor. You may choose the places to visit that may or may not be included in traditional tours.

Argentina Diferente (*Tucumán 540, second level of '13';* ✆ *4328 7426; www.argentinadiferente.com*) organise tours of three or four-and-a-half hours (30 pesos or 45 pesos respectively), highlighting the main *barrios* of the city and including a light lunch or afternoon snack. Daily at 10.00 and 14.00 (subject to change). Walking tours are also arranged.

Buenos Aires Urban Biking (*Moliere 2801;* ✆ *4568 4321;* m *15 5165 9343; e info@urbanbiking.com; www.urbanbiking.com*) offer tours to the main *barrios* of the city and to El Tigre as well as night tours. Trips are from three to six-and-a-half hours in length, depending on the tour, and include lunch.

Banking
There are many banks throughout the city with ATMs that accept Cirrus, Plus, MasterCard, Visa, Maestro cards, etc. Travellers' cheques are not commonly accepted in shops or hotels and you will probably have to cash them at a bank or travel agency. Banks are open Monday to Friday 10.00–15.00. Do not exchange money with people on the street offering better exchange rates – most are frauds.

Credit cards (Visa, MasterCard, American Express and Diners Club) are usually accepted (although rarely outside larger cities) but you may be subject to a 15–20% surcharge. In general, daily purchases are in cash but large payments are safest with a credit card. If you have to carry around large amounts of currency, separate it into different pockets and clothing items. Eves (*Tucumán 702;* ☎ *4585 5544*) changes money and travellers' cheques.

Health and emergencies
There are many hospitals in the city. One in Recoleta is at Avenida General Las Heras 2670 and another in Palermo at Cerviño 3356. There are a few centrally located 24-hour pharmacies:

Porteña Corrientes 1499; ☎ 4371 3244
Farmacity 20 Florida 474; ☎ 4322 7777
Maria C Independencia 1460
Moreno OSPF Moreno 1550; ☎ 4346 5758
Nueva San Nicolás Santa Fé 1299; ☎ 4811 4152
Farmacity 28 Santa Fé 1740; ☎ 4816 0212

In case of emergency dial 107, for the police dial 101, and for fire 100. Recently the North American emergency dispatch number of 911 has been activated. The tourist police commission is located at Corrientes 436 (☎ *4346 5748 or 0800 999 5000 for assistance in English, Italian, French, Portuguese and Ukrainian*).

Post and communications
The central post office is at Sarmiento 151 (☎ *4316 3000; Mon–Fri 08.00–20.00, Sat 09.00–13.00*), in an impressive beaux-arts building by architect Norberto Maillart and inspired by New York City's main post office. The Public Works Ministry modified the original designs to include a Francophile mansard. Heavy parcels, over 2kg, for international destinations are best sent from the Correo Internacional, Antártida Argentina near the Retiro bus terminal (☎ *4316 1777; open Mon–Fri 10.00–17.00*).

WHERE TO STAY
High-end hotels
Alvear Palace Hotel Av Alvear 1891 (Recoleta); ☎ 4808 2100; e info@alvearpalace.com, www.alvearpalace.com. Aside from lavishing flowers and fruit baskets around your room, services include such luxuries as complimentary pressing of 2 garments upon arrival. Rated by international travel magazines as the best hotel in South America, guests have included many heads of state and royals, including Charles, Prince of Wales, and celebrities such as Antonio Banderas, Isabel Allende and Oliver Stone. Rates from US$440 per night, and the Royal Suite costs US$3,700.
Sheraton Buenos Aires Hotel Plaza San Martín 1225, overlooking the river; ☎ 4318 9000; f 4318 9346. 24 storeys high and with the largest spa in the city, and rates from US$145 for a standard dbl, US$190 for a suite.
Golden Tulip Savoy Hotel Av Callao 181 (Microcentro); ☎ 4370 8000; f 4370 8080; e info@hotel-savoy.com.ar. This upscale hotel's rates start at US$130 plus tax (21%).
Faena Hotel & Universe Martha Salotti 445 (Puerto Madero), ☎ 4010 9000; www.faenahotelanduniverse.com. This glamorous boutique hotel designed by Philippe Starck opened in 2004. In a re-invented dockside warehouse, it is a sort of updated version of the Hotel de Inmigrantes, once a dosshouse where new arrivals were given free bed and board for 5 days. Rates from 300 pesos plus tax for a sgl (including b/fast, transfers, wireless internet access and local phone calls). The 'Universe' refers to the restaurant, shops, spa and other leisure facilities open to all.

Mid range

Tango Guesthouse Estados Unidos 780 (San Telmo); ↘ 4361 6817;
e lina@tangoguesthouse.com.ar. 8 rooms, patio for tango dancing, dance lessons, airport
transfer. Rates 60–150 pesos depending on style of room. B/fast included.
Como en Casa B&B Gurruchaga 2155 (Palermo Viejo); ↘ 4831 0517;
e info@bandb.com.ar; www.bandb.com.ar. B&B is a new concept in Buenos Aires but is
becoming popular. Rates from US$30 for a dbl, with b/fast.
Hotel Tribeca Bartolomé Mitre 1265; ↘ 4372 5444; e info@hoteltribeca.com.ar. Located
only 4 blocks from the towering oblisk, you will have little excuse not to find your way back
to your well-landmarked hotel after touring the city. This clean and elegant 4-star hotel is
US$50 for a sgl, US$60 for a dbl, US$73 for a triple. Tax (21%) is not included but b/fast is.
Hotel Lion d'Or Pacheco de Melo 2019; ↘f 4803 8992; www.hotel-liondor.com.ar. Safe,
fairly clean, and inexpensive as well as reminiscent of the 1920s. Sgls 39 pesos, dbls 53–69
pesos, triples 78–93 pesos (ranges for remodelled rooms).
Hotel Nogaró Diagonal Roca 562; ↘ 4331 0091; e reservas@nogarobue.com.ar. Flat rate
for a sgl or dbl is 97 pesos, but this fluctuates slightly in high and low periods.

Budget

Garden House Guesthouse San Juan 1271 (San Telmo); ↘ 4304 1824:
e gardenhouseba@yahoo.com, www.gardenhouseba.com.ar. There is a feel-at-home
environment with kitchen facilities, an entertainment room (TV, stereo, movies, etc) and
laundry. Maps, guidebooks, bikes to rent and advice for exploring the city are provided and
special activities are arranged, such as *asados* and tango, Spanish or cooking lessons. There
are 6 rooms sharing 2 bathrooms. Room for 8 people 18 pesos per person, for 6 people 21
pesos, sgl 36 pesos, dbl 54 pesos, suite 60 pesos.
Hotel Omega Paraguay 2991; ↘ 4962 5431; e hotelomega@arnet.com.ar. Dbl rooms with
good private bathrooms, cable TV and minimal b/fast cost just 45 pesos (sgl 35 pesos).

There are several **hostels** in Buenos Aires that are members of Hostelling
International. They all come recommended for their high standards.

The Recoleta Hostel Libertad 1216; ↘ 4812 4419; e info@trhostel.com.ar,
www.trhostel.com.ar. Conveniently located within walking distance of the bus terminal
and railway station, cinemas, pubs, shopping areas and tourist attractions. Dorms or dbl
rooms, lockers, TV, cooking facilities, internet and fax and laundry service. Friendly staff
and atmosphere. Dorm beds cost US$8 and dbls from US$17.
Tango Backpackers Thames 2212; ↘ 4776 6871; e reservas@hostels.org.ar;
www.tangobp.com. In a great location for access to the Subte and the lively Palermo
neighbourhood, this hostel has a great top-storey patio with a café and *asado* area. There is a
TV room and free internet. The private rooms are comfortable and quiet. Dorm beds 18
pesos, sgls 30 pesos, dbls 50 pesos (with private bath 70 pesos).
St Nicholas Hostel Bartolomé Mitre 1691; ↘ 4373 8841; f 4371 4364;
e reservas@hostels.org.ar, info@snhostel.com. Dorms for 18 pesos per person.
Milhouse Hostel Hipólito Yrigoyen 959; ↘ 4345 9604, 4343 5038;
e reservas@hostels.org.ar, info@milhousehostel.com. Dorms 20 pesos, sgls with private
bath 64 pesos, dbls with private bath 68 pesos. Quite a party place for younger travellers;
best to book ahead in season.
Mandinga Hostel Cochabamba 514, San Telmo; ↘ 4361 2255;
e info@mandingahostel.com. A very clean, friendly and cheap hostel between the centre
and La Boca, with a large common room and kitchen. Prices from 15 pesos for a dorm bed
or 50 pesos for a dbl with ensuite bathroom.

If you're staying for more than a month (and especially if there are several of you),
it can be well worth renting an apartment for about US$100–150 per week (plus a

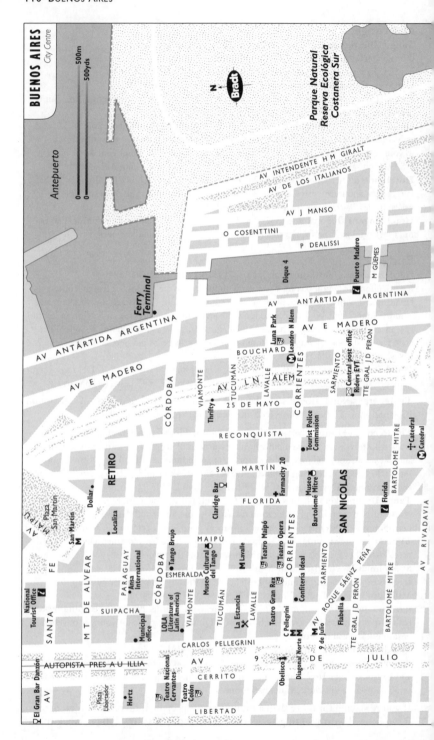

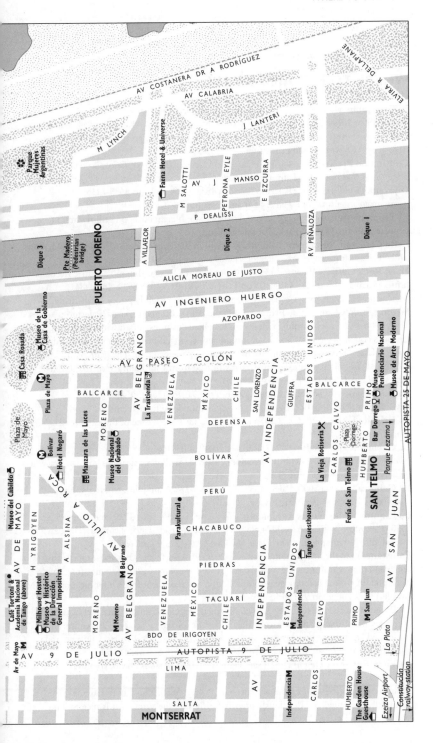

US$25 service fee). Recommended agencies include ByT (↘ *4821 6057/75; www.bytargentina.com*) and My Space (↘ *4793 3496;* m *5852 8509;* e *info@myspaceba.com; www.myspaceba.com*).

WHERE TO EAT AND DRINK
Restaurants
Bi Won Junín 548 (Once); ↘ 4372 1146. A good Korean restaurant.
Cabaña Las Lilas Alicia M. de Justo 516 (Puerto Madero); ↘ 4313 1336, 4343 6404. Possibly the best steak in Argentina, at a price. Great wine list, great service. Try to get a table at the rear, overlooking the water.
Cantina La Placita Borges 1636, Plaza Julio Cortázar (Palermo Viejo); ↘ 4832 6444. A place to eat traditional food among the locals.
Cipriana Honduras 4780 (Palermo Soho) ↘ 4833 1389; mob: 15 5633 7235; e cipriana@argentina.com. Gallery bar and restaurant.
El Trapiche Paraguay 5099, Palermo; ↘ 4772 7343. Neighbourhood grill restaurant, popular with families and packed at the weekends.
Evita Café and Restaurant Lafinur 2988 (within the Evita museum); ↘ 4807 9433, 4809 3168. The sugar packages are collector's items for the die-hard Evita fan.
Hard Rock Café Av Pueyrredón 2501 (Buenos Aires Design shopping centre, Recoleta)
Janio Malabia 1805 at Costa Rica (Plaza Palermo Viejo); ↘ 4833 6540, 4833 4841; www.janiorestaurant.com. Casual yet sophisticated with a slightly pricey Asian-fusion menu.
Jardín Japonés Parque 3 de Febrero, Av Figueroa Alcorta and Casares (Palermo); ↘ 4804 9141, 4804 4922; www.jardinjapones.com. Excellent sushi restaurant within the tranquil Japanese botanical gardens. Special events are also arranged such as art expositions and music, classes in bonsai, origami, martial arts and Sumie painting. The gardens are lovely with ponds full of enormous goldfish that will feed from your hand. *Open 10.00–18.00 daily, admission US$1 (free for retirees weekdays).*
La Bourgogne Alvear Palace Hotel, Av Alvear 1891 (Recoleta); ↘ 4808 2100; www.alvearpalace.com/1024/ingles/r_bourgogne.htm. Fine French cuisine.
La Brigada Estados Unidos 465 (San Telmo); ↘ 4361 5557. One of the city's least touristified *parrillas*.
La Cabaña Rodríguez Peña 1967, Recoleta; ↘ 4814 0001; www.lacabanabuenosaires.com.ar. Provides a barcode with your steak, so you can 'trace' its owner and his past diet – the place for a rib-eye steak.
La Cabrera Cabrera 5099, Palermo Viejo;↘ 4831 7002. A hip joint, where the black-puddings, ribs and sausages are divine.
La Esquina de las Flores Av Córdoba 1575; ↘ 4813 3630, 4811 4729; and Gurruchaga 1630 (Palermo); ↘ 4832 8528, 4224 5000; e info@esquinadelasflores.com.ar. The best macrobiotic restaurants in town. *Open Mon–Sat 09.00–21.00 (cash only).*
La Estancia Lavalle 941 (Tribunales); ↘ 4326 0330, 4326 0025, 4393 9504. Open daily for lunch and dinner featuring the typical *asado* as well as *chinchulines* (crispy intestines) and black pudding; often offering tango and folkloric entertainment too. Other locations at Lavalle 1149, Tucumán 952 and Suipacha 580.
La Paila Costa Rica 4848; ↘ 4833 3599. Northern Argentine cuisine and handicrafts such as textiles and native ceramics, local wines and *matés* for sale, a library of Argentine short stories and legends, archaeology and guidebooks, a gallery of local artists' paintings and photographs and live folk music. *Open Tue–Sat from 17.30, Sun from 12.30.*
La Vieja Rotiseria Defensa 963 (San Telmo); ↘ 4362 5660. A cheap, friendly steakhouse.
Maleva Serrano 1598 at Honduras (Palermo); ↘ 4831 3850. This bar-restaurant serves beautifully presented and deliciously prepared dishes. In the summer it is nice to dine outside near the plaza.

Pan y Teatro Muñiz and Las Casas; ☎ 4924 6920. A personal favourite recommended by a local tango dancer.

Parrilla a la Leña Av Santa Fé 3954; ☎ 4832 4449, 4831 8015. Serve a good steak and house red at the 'Wood-fired Grill'. The waiters create an ambiance, albeit for the tourists, by wearing a bit of gaucho costume.

Patagonia Sur Rocha 801 (La Boca); ☎ 4303 5917. Run by Francis Mallmann, who also has acclaimed restaurants in Mendoza and the Hamptons, this offers the finest nouvelle Patagonian fare (lamb, above all) in Buenos Aires.

Plaza Mayor Venezuela 1399 (Monserrat); ☎ 4383 3802. Try the *sidra* (apple cider) and the best Christmas bread to be found; this restaurant features Argentine grill while the same owner also features pasta, at **Campo di Fiore** across the street.

Parrilla Nelly J B Alberdi and Río de la Plata; ☎ 4794 4466. Out of central Buenos Aires, at Puerto de Olivos, with a great view overlooking the port.

Santa Fé 1234 Santa Fé 1234 (Recoleta); ☎ 4811 2356, 4813 2769. This restaurant-pizzeria has a simple menu.

Te Mature Ramirez Locally regarded as serving the best food in BA, with branches throughout the city. Aphrodisiac dishes a speciality!

Several trendy restaurants are receiving good reviews in the Cañitas area of Palermo such as **Eh! Santino** (*Báez 196;* ☎ *4779 9060*) for pasta; **La Corte** (*Arevalo 2977;* ☎ *4775 0999*) with vegetarian and fish options; **Novecento**, (*Báez 193;* ☎ *4778 1900*) for Argentine-Mediterranean-Asian; **Soul Café** (*Báez 246;* ☎ *4778 3115*); **Sudestada** (*Guatemala 5602;* ☎ *4776 3777*) with a southeast Asian menu; and **El Trapiche** (*Paraguay 5099;* ☎ *4772 7343*), a mid-market steakhouse.

Cafés and pubs

Café Victoria Roberto M Oritz 1865 (Recoleta); ☎ 4804 0016, 4806 0383.

La Biela Quintana 596 off Plaza Intendente Alvear (Recoleta); ☎ 4804 0449. An old café from 1850. It has a large patio that is a favoured spot to pass an afternoon under the shade of the enormous rubber tree. It is overpriced due to its location.

Havana Av Quintana 558; ☎ 4807 6891. This location is in Palermo, but there are several throughout the city where you can stop for a coffee and a famous Cuban *alfajor* (*dulche de leche* cookie).

The Shamrock Rodriguez Peña 1220 at Arenales; ☎ 4812 3584; www.theshamrockbar.com. Popular hangout with the backpacking crowd. Diverse program of live music and special events. *Open Mon–Fri from 18.00, Sat & Sun from 20.00.*

Claridge Bar Tucumán 535 (Recoleta); ☎ 4314 7700. A classic hotel bar.

El Gran Bar Danzón Libertador 1161; ☎ 4811 1108. A hip wine bar-restaurant with great cocktails.

Two old and popular bars in San Telmo are the **Bar Dorrego** (*Humberto Primo and Defensa*), a traditional 1920s tavern; and **Bar Británico** (*Brasil 399, opposite Parque Lezama;* ☎ *4300 6894*), a famous yet unpretentious bar that has remained popular since 1928.

MUSEUMS

Museo Histórico Nacional Defensa 1600 (in Parque Lezama, San Telmo); ☎ 4307 1182. *Open Tue–Fri 11.00–19.00, Sat 15.00–18.00, Sun 14.00–18.00; admission 2 pesos.*

Museo de la Casa de Gobierno Hipólito Yrigoyen 219; ☎ 4344 3802. Attached to the Casa Rosada; tours of the Casa Rosada in English, Fri at 17.00 (reserve in advance or arrive early). *Open Mon–Fri 10.00–18.00, Sun 14.00–18.00; admission free.*

Museo del Cabildo Bolívar 65; ☎ 4334 1782. The story of the City Hall, and thus of the city. *Open Tue–Fri 12.30–19.00, Sun 15.00–19.00; admission 2 pesos.*

Museo Evita Lafinur; ☏ *Lafinur* 2988, 4807 9433, 4809 3168;
e institutoevaperon@museoevita.org. Uncritical, nay adulatory, and pure kitsch, but one of
the few museums with information in English. *Open Tue–Sun 14.00–19.30.*

Museo Bartolomé Mitre San Martín 336; ☏ 4394 8240. Memorabilia of the modernising
1860s president. *Open Mon–Fri 13.00–18.00, Sun 14.00–18.00; admission 2 pesos.*

Museo Nacional de Bellas Artes Av del Libertador 1473 (Recoleta); ☏ 4803 0802.
Argentine artists of the 19th and 20th centuries as well as works by the European masters
including Renoir, Monet and van Gogh. *Open Tue–Fri 12.30–19.30, Sat & Sun 09.30–19.30;
admission free.*

Museo de Arte Decorativo Av del Libertador 1902 (Recoleta); ☏ 4802 6606, 4801 8248;
www.mnad.org. Both permanent and temporary exhibitions on various themes, such as
collections of one-of-a-kind *matés*, housed in the spectacular Palacio Errázuriz, built in 1911
by French architect René Sergent (who never came to Argentina). *Open Tue–Sat
14.00–19.00; admission 2 pesos, Tue free.*

Museo de Arte Moderno Av San Juan 350 (San Telmo); ☏ 4361 1121. There's also a
branch in the **Teatro General San Martín** at Corrientes 1530 (San Nicolás), a municipal
arts complex that also puts on theatre, dance, art films and photography shows. *Open
Tue–Fri 10.00–20.00, w/ends & hols 11.00–20.00; closed Feb; admission 2 pesos; Wed free. Guided
tours Tue–Sun 17.00.*

Museo Nacional del Grabado Defensa 372 (San Telmo); ☏ 4345 5300. Engravings and
prints. *Open Sun–Fri 14.00–18.00; admission US$2.*

Museo de Bella Artes de La Boca Pedro de Mendoza 1835 (La Boca); ☏ 4301 1080.
Home and studio of painter Benito Quinquela Martín, now exhibiting his work along with
other important Argentine artists of the early 20th century. *Open Tue–Sun 10.00–18.00;
admission 1 peso.*

Museo de Motivos Argentinos José Hernández Av del Libertador 2373; ☏ 4802 7294.
A fine show of traditional Argentine arts and crafts. *Open Mon–Fri 13.00–19.00, Sat & Sun
15.00–19.00; admission 2 pesos.*

Museo de Arte Latinoamericano de Buenos Aires Av Figueroa Alcorta 3415
(Palermo); ☏ 4808 6505; www.malba.org.ar. Opened in 2001, this lovely airy gallery houses
one of the world's finest collections of Latin American art. *Open Wed–Mon 12.00–20.00;
admission 7 pesos, Wed free.*

Museo Municipal de Arte Hispanoamericano Isaac Fernández Blanco Suipacha
1422; ☏ 4327 0272. More Latin American art. *Open Tue–Sun 14.00–19.00; admission 2 pesos,
Thu free.*

Museo de Artes Plasticas Eduardo Sívori Av Infanta Isabel 555; ☏ 4772 5628;
www.museosivori.org.ar. Modern art. *Open Tue–Sun 12.00–18.00, admission 1 Arg peso, free
Wed.*

Museo Penitenciario Nacional Humberto Primo 378 (San Telmo); ☏ 4362 0099. Once
a former Jesuit convent, then a women's prison, this is now a museum of imprisonment.
Open Tue & Fri 14.00–19.00, Sat & Sun 12.00–19.00; admission US$1.

Museo y Archivo Histórico de la Dirección General Impositiva Av de Mayo 1317,
5th floor; ☏ 4384 0282. The history of taxation. *Open Mon-Fri 11.00–19.00; admission free.*

**Archivo y Museo Histórico del Banco de la Provincia de Buenos Aires Dr Arturo
Jaúretche** Sarmiento 362; ☏ 4331 1775. The history of banking. *Open Mon–Fri
10.00–18.00; admission free.*

ENTERTAINMENT AND NIGHTLIFE
Tango
Tango is omnipresent in the city of its birth. Not only are there tango radio stations
(with dub tango and electro-tango as well as the classics), there's the *Solo Tango* 24-hour
cable TV channel, websites such as www.tangocity.com, www.clubdetango.com.ar,

www.milongaytango.com.ar and www.tangodata.com.ar, the free monthly magazine *El Tanguata* (available at most *milongas*) listing dances and shows, and even a new tango hotel. At the **Mansión Dandi Royal** (↘ *4361 3537, www.dandiroyal.com.ar; from US$150*), there are non-stop classes amid the brash *belle époque* furnishings. The **Festival Buenos Aires Tango**, with lots of free concerts and displays, is held annually in the last week of February and the first of March (*www.festivaldetango.gov.ar*).

The new **Museo Mundial del Tango** (*Rivadavia 830, Centro*) is a good museum (in Spanish only) recounting the history of tango from its seedy origins to its current worldwide respectability. There are two museums dedicated to the superstar of tango, the **Museo Casa Carlos Gardel**, at his home (*Jean Jaures 735, Abasto;* ↘ *4516 0943*) and the **Museo de Carlos Gardel** in the Casa del Teatro (*Av Santa Fé 1243, Barrio Norte;* ↘ *4813 5906*). The **Museo Cultural del Tango** (*Maipú 666;* ↘ *4326 5445;* e *museotango@fibertel.com.ar*) has a restaurant and bar where they put on dinner shows and offer lessons. The **Confitería Ideal** (*Suipacha 384;* ↘ *5265 8069 or 15 4526 7580*) holds drop-in lessons on Wednesdays from 15.30 to 20.00. Opened in 1912, the Ideal is one of the most famous and historic locales on the tango scene and most city tours include it. The two-storey building has ceilings over 6m high, dark wood-panelled walls, marble floors and Art-Deco chandeliers. It has a crumbling decadence in which you can enjoy a coffee or a meal, and the lessons are held on the second floor. **Café Tortoni** (*Av de Mayo 829, Centro;* ↘ *4342 4328*) is another of these old gems, patronised by celebrities since 1858, with live tango most weekends. At the **Academía Nacional de Tango** (*Av de Mayo 833;* ↘ *4345 6968*), above the Café Tortoni in the Palacio Carlos Gardel, students can receive a Bachelor of Arts in Tango after three years of study; lessons, both theoretical and practical, are also offered to tourists with less than three years available (*18.00–21.00*).

Shows

Dinner-and-tango extravaganzas are strictly for foreign tourists at up to US$50 a pop, but the standards are high and it may be preferable to waiting till after midnight for even a hint of action.

Bar Sur Estados Unidos 299, San Telmo; ↘ 4362 6086; www.bar-sur.com.ar. More intimate than most tango shows.
Caminito Tango Show Del Valle Iverlucea 1151, La Boca; ↘ 4301 1520. Lunch and dinner tango shows.
El Viejo Almacén Av Independencia 313, San Telmo; ↘ 4307 7388; www.viejoalmacen.com. A lively enjoyable show in a historic venue (with or without dinner).
La Esquina Carlos Gardel Pasaje Carlos Gardel 3200, Abasto; ↘ 4867 6363; www.esquinacarlosgardel.com.ar. The all-Argentine experience: great steaks, rich wine and flawless dancing!
La Rueda Magallanes 584, La Boca; ↘ 4303 8702; e larueda_resto@hotmail.com. Restaurant, café and wine bar with tango shows.
Piazzolla Tango Galería Güemes, Florida 165, Centro; ↘ 3338 2646; www.piazzollatango.com. Slick (and pricey) new show, as well as a museum honouring the re-inventor of tango in the late 20th century.

Milongas

Milonga is the name of a style of tango as well as the word used to describe the social occasion of going tango dancing. These popular events (as opposed to the tourist tango dinner shows) are held at various clubs around the city on different nights of the week. Most will offer lessons in the late afternoon or early evening and then the *milonga* will start at 22.00 at the earliest. Lessons generally cost less than 10 pesos and you can stay for the *milonga* for no additional charge. Some of the most popular and famous *milongas* in the city are held at:

Salon Canning Av R Scalabrini Ortiz 1331; ℡ 4342 4794 (Mon, Fri, Sat, Sun)
Bar de Roberto Bulnes at Perón, Almagro. Dingy neighbourhood venue, with musicians playing after midnight Thu–Sat.
Centro Cultural Torquato Tasso Defensa 1575, San Telmo; ℡ 4307 6506; www.tangotasso.com, www.tangodata.com.ar. Restaurant-*milonga* with both modern and traditional shows; classes offered every evening with various instructors.
Club del Vino Cabrera 4737, Palermo Viejo; ℡ 4833 0050. 1940s veteran Horacio Salgan's quintet on Fri nights, octogenarian *tangueros* on Sat nights.
Club Sunderland Lugones 3161; ℡ 4541 9776, 4605 8234 (Sat)
Confitería Ideal Suipacha 384; ℡ 5265 8069 or 15 4526 7580 (nightly)
El Beso Riobamba 416; ℡ 4953 2794 (Tue)
Gricel La Rioja 1180, San Cristóbal; ℡ 4957 7157 (Fri, Sat, Sun)
La Catedral Sarmiento 4006, Almagro; ℡ 15 5325 1630. Industrial-hip warehouse (most nights).
La Calesita Commodoro Rivadavia 1350; ℡ 4792 0585 (Wed, Fri, Sat in the summer only because it is open air)
La Estrella/La Virata Armenia 1366, Palermo; ℡ 4774 6357 (Wed, Fri, Sat)
La Galeria del Tango Argentino Boedo 722; ℡ 4584 6311, 4957 1829, 4175 8747 (Sat)
La Marshal Milonga Gay Goddess Dance Club, Av Córdoba 4185; ℡ 5406 9784 (Wed 22.00, lessons from 20.30)
Lo de Celia Humberto Primo 1783, Piso 1; ℡ 4371 1030 (Mon)
Niño Bien Humberto Primo 1462; ℡ 15 4496 3053, 4413 1562 (Thu, Sun)
Nuevo Salón La Argentina Mitre 1759; ℡ 4371 6767 (Fri, Sat, Sun)
Parakultural Perú 571; ℡ 4302 8682 (Fri, Sun)
Sin Rumbo J P Tamborini 6157; ℡ 4574 0972 (Wed, Fri, Sat)
Viejo Correo Av Díaz Vélez 4820; ℡ 4958 0364 (Mon, Thu, Sat, Sun)

There are several tango **shoemakers** in the city and if you have the time to wait, they will custom-make your shoes starting with a traced outline of your foot. **Flabella** (*Suipacha 263;* ℡ *4322 6036; www.flabella.com*) is one of the most reputable, with an excellent selection and high quality. **Susana Villaroel Artesanal** (*Anchorena 537;* ℡ *4865 3713 or 4864 2111; www.shoes-susanaartesanal.com*) is employed by many professional dance companies. **Candela Zapatos de Tango** (℡ *15 5806 8853;* e *perajuffe@tutopia.com*) is another option for men and women.

Tango **Brujo** (*Esmeralda 754, Centro;* ℡ *4325 8264;* e *info@tangobrujo.com.ar, www.tangobrujo.com.ar; open Mon–Sat 10.00–20.00*) sells tango accessories, hats, gifts, music, videos, books and jewellery. **Zival** (*Av Callao 395;* ℡ *4371 7500*) is the best source of tango and folk music recordings.

Dance clubs
Buenos Aires is known as a clubbing destination and the scene is ever-changing. Lately, popular clubs include **Pacha**, Avenida Rafael Obligao and Pampa (Costanera Norte, Belgrano); ℡ 4788 4280, which has a monthly Cream night – nothing starts till 02.00, then they dance till lunchtime. Also try **Big One** (*Palacio Alsina near Plaza de Mayo*).

Cinemas and theatres
The cinema district is along the Lavalle pedestrian mall (crossing Florida and one block north of Corrientes). Unfortunately, competition with large multiplexes has

closed down many of the traditional cinemas, which have subsequently been converted into bingo halls, video arcades or evangelical churches. Avenida Corrientes is the hub of the theatre and musicals zone where finding a taxi is next to impossible around midnight when all the shows let out.

Teatro Colón Libertad 651; ↘ 4378 7132; f 4378 7133; www.teatrocolon.org.ar. The inaugural performance was Verdi's opera *Aida* in 1908. This is the most famous theatre of the city and an unmistakable landmark of Italian Renaissance design. Ballet, opera and symphony concerts are staged here. Guided tours are available by appointment.

Teatro Nacional Cervantes Av Córdoba 1155; ↘ 4815 8883. From 1921 the theatre has been one of the city's most impressive and important, staging productions by Argentine and Hispanic playwrights; the National Theatre Museum (1961) illustrating the history of *criollo* theatre is also here.

Teatro Gran Rex Av Corrientes 857; ↘ 4322 8000; f 4322 8001. By the same architect as the Oblisko, Alberto Prebisch.

Teatro Opera Av Corrientes 860; ↘ 4326 1335. A classical venue that stages ballets and musicals.

Teatro Maipo Esmeralda 443; ↘ 4322 4882; f 4322 4883. This theatre had its glory days in the early 1900s (Carlos Gardel performed here in 1917).

Teatro General San Martín Av Corrientes 1530; ↘ 4372 2247; www.teatrosanmartin.com.ar. Complex of three modern halls including ballet and theatre in the round.

Teatro Municipal Presidente Alvear Av Corrientes 1659; ↘ 4373 4245. Inaugurated in 1942 and named for the former president and his wife, the opera singer Regina Pacini. It is now a municipal playhouse.

Teatro de la Ribera Av Pedro de Mendoza 1821, La Boca; ↘ 4302 9042. This theatre was funded by Argentine painter of La Boca, Benito Quinquela Martín; his works are also on display here.

Teatro Regio Av Córdoba 6056; ↘ 4772 3350. A Spanish Baroque-inspired theatre from 1929.

Teatro Avenida Av de Mayo 1212; ↘ 4381 0662. Often has Hispanic singers and musicians on the programme.

La Trastienda Balcarce 460; ↘ 4342 7650. Alternative theatre and music shows.

Luna Park Bouchard 465; ↘ 4311 5100. In 1932 the old Pacific Railway station was converted into a sports venue. Today it is used to stage large musical productions.

SPORTS

The two rival football (*fútbol*) teams of the city are Boca Juniors (*www.bocajuniors.com.ar*) and River Plate (*www.carp.org.ar*). If you take a ticket in the cheap seats, go with a group and keep a low profile – these games are rowdy. Matches between these rival teams often witness high numbers of casualties, on and off the field. When Argentina hosted the World Cup in 1978, Argentine poet/author Jorge Luis Borges was quoted as saying 'football is a calamity' (he hated tango too). These two teams are legendary, as is their ancient animosity. They have less than affectionate names for each other: River are the *gallinas* (chickens) and Juniors are the *bosteros* (*bosta* means 'horse dung' and is a slur on the name of the smelly La Boca port, the team's home turf). There is an economic division between the two teams as well: both clubs formed in La Boca but in 1938 River Plate moved to the affluent uptown area of Palermo, became the team followed by the higher society and have since been coined *los millionarios*; Boca Juniors was formed in 1905 by mostly poor Italian immigrants and has remained 'the people's' team. Soccer legend Diego Maradona played for Bocas.

A more civilised sport to observe is a polo match. *Pato* is a traditional gaucho game that got its name from using a dead duck instead of a ball – a ball is used nowadays.

Asociacion Argentina de Polo www.aapolo.com
Federación Argentina de Pato www.fedpato.com.ar
Argentina Travel Sports Tres Arroyos 3379, Los Polvorines; ✎ 4660 5719, 15 5144 5365; e info@atsports.com.ar, www.atsports.com.ar. This agency organises tours to see or partake in sporting events.
Riders 25 de Mayo 267, office 417; ✎f 5031 3068; e info@riders-trips.com.ar; www.riders-trips.com.ar. Run by the enthusiastic and bilingual Lucia Zone, this agency is creative and resourceful, up-to-date on current travel deals and focused on discovering the best adventure and sport activities throughout the country.

SHOPPING

The Florida pedestrian mall in the Centro and Avenida Santa Fé in Retiro are the two main shopping strips. Designer shops are mainly within the Retiro-Recoleta area. **Galerías Pacíficos** on Florida and Córdoba is a three-storey shopping centre packed with shops. One of the main shopping centres for home design is **Buenos Aires Design**, in Recoleta near the cemetery and outdoor market (*Av Pueyrredón 2501;* ✎ *5777 6000;* f *5777 6150; open Mon–Sat 10.00–21.00, Sun & hols 12.00–21.00*). Another shopping mall is **Patio Bullrich** at Posadas 1250.

LOLA (Literature of Latin America; *Viamonte 976, 2nd floor;* ✎ *4322 3920; www.lola-online.com; open Mon–Fri 12.00–18.30*) is a small bookshop with an excellent selection of natural history books.

Harapos Reales (*Pasaje Santa Rosa 4901, Palermo;* ✎ *4834 6363;* e *info@haraposreales.com.ar or haraposreales@fibertel.com.ar; also in Bariloche – see page 121*) sells beautiful handmade one-off garments that are works of art. Items are made from 100% natural and local textiles including silk, cotton, wool, fur and leather and are knit by local women. Argentine celebrities, painters, theatre directors and actresses have purchased Harapos pieces, but the most famous was the Queen of Spain who now owns two of their wraps. In 2004, five HR pieces were designed in honour of Salvador Dalí and exhibited in his centenary exhibition at Buenos Aires' Centro Cultural Borges.

To find the best selection of Argentine hats, go to **Sombreros Maidana** (*Av Rivadavia 1923;* ✎ *4953 2257*). For an extra 10 pesos you also get a hat box!

There are several **markets** in the city: San Telmo is famous for antiques. Every Sunday the **Feria de San Telmo** brings vendors to Plaza Dorrego to sell their pricey wares. The entire area is full of antiques and collectables and a knowledgeable shopper will discover overlooked treasures. A naïve shopper will have to rely on luck or merely shop for pleasure and personal taste. In the same *barrio*, also on Sundays, the sprawling **Feria Parque Lezama crafts fair** is held in the park and along Defensa. The most popular is the **Feria Plaza Intendente Alvear** in Recoleta, northeast of the cemetery, 09.00–19.00 at weekends.

The colourful artists' walk, **Feria del Caminito**, in La Boca is a daily affair. There is also the nearby **Feria Artesanal Plazoleta Vuelta de Rocha** off Avenida Pedro de Mendoza at weekends.

The **Feria de Mataderos** on Sundays cannot be missed for its gaucho music and entertainment, food stalls and great shopping with rows of kiosks selling handmade wool, silver, wood and leatherware. A few artisans engrave silver *matés* – you can have your name engraved while you watch.

SPECIAL EVENTS

February Carnaval or Mardi Gras with the usual parades and festivities.

March In late March the Exposición de Caballos Criollos is a show of Argentine horse breeds at the Predio Ferial on Av Sarmiento in Palermo (Subte Plaza Italia). Asociación Criadores de Caballos Criollos, Larrea 670; ✆ 4961 2305.

April Motor racing at the Autódromo Municipal Oscar Gálvez.

May Feria de Galerías de Arte with art from around the world.

24 June Día de la Muerte de Carlos Gardel. Tango events and pilgrimage to his tomb at Chacarita Cemetery (where he always has a fresh carnation in his buttonhole and a cigarette between his fingers).

Late July Exposición de Ganadería, Agricultura e Industria Internacional (the country's leading agricultural show) also at the Predio Ferial in Palermo.

November Maratón Internacional de la Argentina, 15,000 runners.

11 December Día del Tango in commemoration of Gardel's birthday.

EXCURSIONS OUTSIDE BUENOS AIRES
Estancias

La Sofia Polo Ranch Pilar, Ruta 25 (55km from the city); ✆ 15 5061 2134; e lasofiapolo@yahoo.com.ar. Come to learn or play polo, drink *maté*, have an *asado* and enjoy the countryside.

Estancia Santa Maria General Las Heras; ✆ 4772 0571, 15 5374 1747; e info@estanciasantamaria.com.ar, www.estanciasantamaria.com.ar. Spend a day at the estancia (founded in 1882) riding horses or taking a carriage tour through the pampas, learn polo or the national sport of *pato* created by the gauchos, and of course have a typical *asado* (barbecue) for lunch.

El Tigre and Río Paraná Delta

An easy, popular and characteristic excursion from the city is to El Tigre (32km north of Buenos Aires) jumping-off point for the Paraná delta, which offers a deliciously cool retreat from the city's summertime heat. The Autopista del Sol motorway goes north to El Tigre; follow the signs for Acceso Norte and Ramal Tigre. Although bus no. 60 from Constitución station will take you to El Tigre, it takes well over an hour and for once the train, from the Retiro station, is more efficient. At Bartolomé Mitre cross to the linked Maipú station and take the *Tren de la Costa* (every 20 minutes) to the last stop on the line, Delta. Leaving the station, to your right is a fairground, and to your left the river and the Estación Fluvial or port ticket office, where you'll find the tourist office (*Mitre 305;* ✆ *4512 4497;* e *turismo@tigre.gov.ar; daily 09.00–17.00; also at the railway station, open only Fri–Sun 09.00–17.00*). From here there are frequent boats into the Delta, both *lanchas taxis*, which take you where you want, and *lanchas colectivas*, which operate fixed routes (see *www.xcolectivo.com.ar/barco/index.html*); you can stay on board for the whole circuit of about three hours, if you wish. The main *lancha colectiva* operators are La Interisleña (✆ *4731 0261*), Jilguero (✆ *4749 0987*) and Líneas Delta Argentino (✆ *4749 0537*). A ferry to the Tres Bocas, operated by La Interisleña, leaves at 13.30 and 16.30 (*roughly hourly on weekend afternoons*). Day trips to Isla Martín García (where Perón was detained) are operated by Cacciola (*Lavalle 520;* ✆ *4731 0931;* e *info@cacciolaviajes.com*) on Tuesdays, Thursdays, Saturdays and Sundays.

There is a lot of infrastructure in El Tigre to accommodate the tourism that sustains the economy here. The following are just two recommendations for a high- and a low-end option. **La Pascuala Delta Lodge** (*Arroyo Las Cañas, Delta del Río Paraná;* ✆ *4728 1253/1395; www.lapascuala.com*) is a luxury lodge with lovely bungalows, a restaurant and terraces and patios onto the waters. The rate is

US$150 for a single, US$250 for a double (at weekends US$210 and US$350). **Hostería Cruz Alta** (*Río Paraná de las Palmas km56; office at the Estación Fluvial stand 14;* \ *4728 2786 or 15 5470 4994*) has rooms with private bath and breakfast starting at 40 pesos per night (weekends 80 pesos), plus a garden gazebo and restaurant. Photographic safaris through the islands of the Paraná Delta can be arranged with **La Canoa** (\ *4728 1638; www.la-canoa.com.ar*); trekking and fishing and bed-and-breakfast are available. For horse-trekking excursions contact **Pioneros** (\ *4814 5070;* e *info@pioneros.com.ar, www.pioneros.com.ar*).

La Plata

La Plata is a small city 56km (1 hour) east of Buenos Aires by motorway and railway. There is a bus from Retiro station every 20 minutes, 24 hours a day, with Costera Metropolitana (\ *4310 0700*), arriving at La Plata bus terminal, which is probably the most attractive bus terminal in all of Argentina. There is an upper level with a gallery and bar where live jazz or other performances are held on Friday and Saturday nights. However, to visit the city centre you should get off the bus at Plaza Italia instead of heading all the way to the terminal. There are also regular trains from Estación Constitución (at Avenida Brasil and Lima), taking little more than an hour.

La Plata is a lovely clean city, which comes as a surprise after seeing the shanty town along the plastic- and litter-clogged river before entering the city proper. On a large-scale map La Plata looks like a checkerboard of parks and plazas. Plaza San Martín is the most central, where you will see the Government House, the Cultural Centre and the tourist information office. Avenida 7 and the pedestrianised Avenidas 51 and 53 cross the plaza; walking about half a dozen blocks in either direction on any one of them will bring you to another plaza. Heading southwest you will arrive at the great Plaza Moreno whose gardens and fountains spread between the Municipal Palace and the cathedral. **La Catedral de la Inmaculada Concepción** has a lift (*until 19.00; 3 pesos*) up one of the towers to give a close-up view of the cathedral architecture and the plaza. Back at Plaza San Martín, heading in the opposite direction, northeast, will bring you to Plaza Rivadavia, behind which is the vast **Paseo del Bosque**. Bus 214 will bring you to the park from Plaza Italia. This expansive and beautiful city park holds the racetrack, a small lake and waterfall with an open-air amphitheatre, a zoo, a sports club, the **astronomical observatory** (\ *0221 423 6593; open Mon–Fri 09.00–16.00*) and the famous Museo de Ciencias Naturales.

The **Museo de Ciencias Naturales** (Museum of Natural Sciences) (*Paseo del Bosque s/n;* \ *0221 425 7744, 425 9161 or 425 9638;* e *servguia@museo.fcnym.unip.edu.ar; open Tue–Sun 10.00–18.00; admission 3 pesos*) represents the life's work of explorer and naturalist Francisco 'Perito' Moreno and has developed to be probably the most important natural history museum in the country. Zoological, geological, palaeontological and anthropological collections fill the many rooms. A good few hours could well be spent at this museum. If the museum has inspired you to want to do some wildlife viewing in situ, there are the nearby **Punta Lara Nature Reserve** (12km north, bus 275 from La Plata) or the **Costero del Sur Biosphere Reserve** near the town of Magdalena, 100km south of La Plata.

La Plata has some fine architecture to enjoy while walking around the centre. If you are with small children, this tour may include a visit to the **Republica de los Niños** (\ *0221 484 1409 or 484 1206; open daily 10.00–18.00; admission 2 pesos, free for children under 12*), though whether or not the Disney-inspired children's park falls into this category is open to debate. This little city covers 53ha with castles and palaces and has a kiddie train to ride. There are restaurants as well.

The Fundacion Vida Silvestre's reserve at **Bahía Samborombón**, placed on the RAMSAR list of Wetlands of International Importance (one of 13 in Argentina) in 1997, is located on the Río de la Plata estuary and covers 243,965ha, over a third of which is aquatic habitat. It represents one of the last natural remnants of the once expansive pampas vegetation before cattle grazing was introduced and is home to the severely threatened Pampas deer (*Ozotoceros bezoarticus celer*). There is limited infrastructure, including interpretation centres in the FVSA Campos de Tuyú Wildlife Reserve and in the Punta Rasa Biological Station.

Visiting Uruguay

Regular ferries across the Río de la Plata are operated by Buquebus from their terminal at Avenida Antártida Argentina 821, at the north end of Puerto Madero (↘ *4316 6500/50;* f *4316 6423;* e *atclientes@buquebus.com; www.buquebus.com*). The ticket office is open Mon to Fri 09.00–19.00, Sat 09.00–12.00, and there is another at Patio Bullrich, Avenida del Libertador 750, in Retiro. Their ships take under three hours to the Puerto Fluvial, Rambla 25 de Agosto, in Uruguay's capital Montevideo, but it may be more enjoyable to take the catamaran (twice daily) to Colonia del Sacramento (a UNESCO World Heritage Site, under an hour from Buenos Aires). From here there are bus connections to Montevideo, and Buquebus also provide through tickets by either route to Punta del Este, the beach resort where many *porteños* have second homes. Buquebus charges from 89 pesos for the catamaran to Colonia, 106 pesos with the connection to Montevideo, or 155 pesos for the direct ship to Montevideo. Ferries can also be taken from El Tigre, with Cacciola leaving daily at 08.30 and 16.30 to Carmelo (with bus connection to Montevideo), and Líneas Delta daily at 07.45, plus 17.00 on Fridays to Nueva Palmira (with bus connection to Colonia).

Buses from Retiro terminal in Buenos Aires depart daily at 23.30 with General Belgrano (↘ *4315 6522 or 4315 1226*), at 21.30 with Cauvi (↘ *4314 6999 or 4314 4930*), and 10.00, 22.00 and 22.30 with Carrera (↘ *4313 1700*), costing about 70 pesos. Buses arrive at the Tres Cruces terminal in Montevideo, at Bulevar Artigas and Avenida Italia (↘ *0598 401 8998; www.trescruces.com.uy*) after roughly nine hours.

Visas are not required from most nationalities visiting Uruguay for less than 90 days. The consulate in Buenos Aires (*Av Las Heras 1907;* ↘ *807 3044/5;* e *conuruarg@embajadadeluruguay.com.ar*) can help if you are in doubt about your status. The Uruguayan peso is slightly stronger than the Argentine; US dollars are accepted.

harapos reales

tejido sin tiempo.

The Pampas

Pampa comes from a Quechua word loosely meaning 'flatland' and for the most part this area is just that. Both geographical and ecological definitions of the pampa are unclear, even contentious. This vast flat prairie of typical grasses has two divisions: wet *pampa húmida* around the Paraná Delta and the Atlantic coast, and dry *pampa seca* further west. **La Pampa** province, which is indeed mostly flat grasslands with far more cows than people, is the heart of the pampas, which ecologically speaking must surely cross over the border into what is normally considered Patagonia. **Córdoba** province contains areas of pampas but is far from flat; it is instead characterised by the dynamic and hilly Central Sierras; **Santa Fé** province is a fascinating blend of *pampa húmida* and *seca* but its relationship with the Paraná River and its saturated wetlands further north often lead this province to be included in the Litoral region. **Buenos Aires** province has both humid and dry pampas areas as well as riparian, Paraná Delta and coastal influences. All this said, these four provinces comprise the central region of the country, once a seemingly endless pampas prairie that gave birth to the cowboy culture that so strongly personifies Argentina as a whole. Buenos Aires, Córdoba and Santa Fé were the nucleus of Spanish colonisation and are today the most populated and industrialised provinces.

Buenos Aires Province

Buenos Aires province is home to a third of the country's population and thus is its political powerhouse. It is the most culturally and geographically diverse with the old and cosmopolitan city of Buenos Aires (see previous chapter), coastal cities such as Mar del Plata and gaucho towns such as San Antonio de Areco. While people born in the city of Buenos Aires are called *porteños*, those born in the province of Buenos Aires are *bonaerenses*.

MAR DEL PLATA
Area code 0223
Known as *La Perla del Atlántico* (Pearl of the Atlantic), this elite beach resort of the 1930s remains the favourite holiday spot for the *porteños* who come in droves for the holidays. With just over half a million residents (many retired), the population of Mar del Plata surges in the summer, filling with tourists and vacationers. The temperatures are gentler than in Buenos Aires, averaging 22°C, and there are 47km of beach.

Patricio Peralta Ramos founded Mar del Plata proper in 1874 and developed its commercial, industrial and holiday potential. With the railway's arrival in 1886,

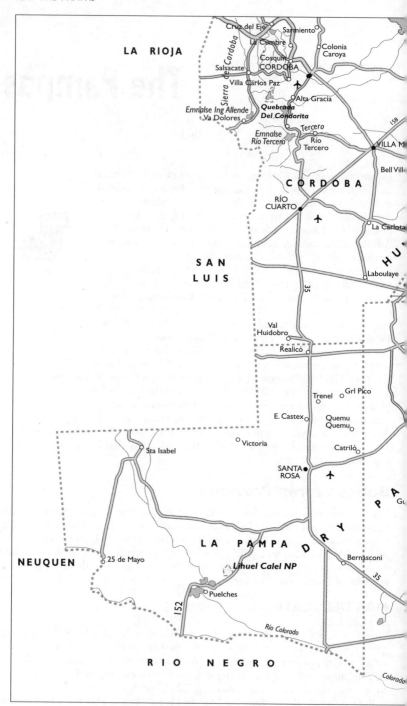

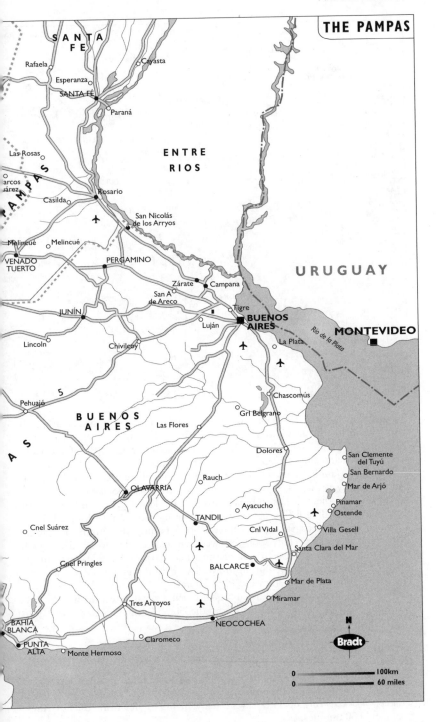

THE PAMPAS

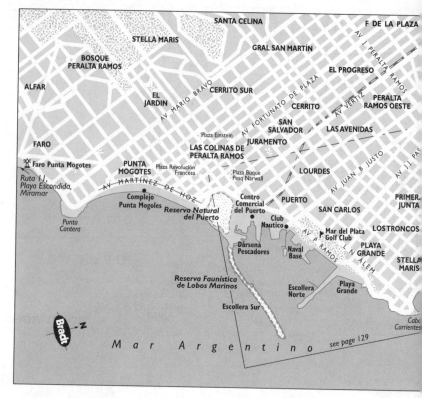

Mar del Plata was transformed from colonial town to a modern urban centre, with many Italian and Spanish immigrants moving in. In 1907 it was declared a city, in 1923 the port was established (fishing in fact accounts for 30% of the city's economic activity) and in 1938 Ruta 2 was inaugurated.

Aristocratic families started building summer homes here back in the late 1920s and would stay at the seaside from November until *Semana Santa* (Easter). They started building their chalets and mansions near the Hotel Bristol and spent their days at the Playa Bristol. The *barrio* between here and Torreón del Monje became known as Los Troncos. Perhaps for the celebrity-spotting, the citizens of Mar del Plata, mostly working class, soon followed suit and decided to lay their beach towels right alongside Playa Bristol, naming their territory Playa Popular. In the finest tradition of snobbery, a group from Playa Bristol then moved south of the city and established Playa Chica and Playa Grande.

There is a wonderful century-at-a-glance sense of architecture in this city; however, many of the old residences from the '50s, '60s and '70s were torn down to put up skyscrapers.

Getting there
By air
The Brigadier Don Bartolomé de la Colina airport is 10km north at km396 on Autovia 2 (✆ 478 5811). Aerolíneas Argentinas/Austral (*Moreno 2442;* ✆ 496 0101; e *llledo@infovia.com.ar*) operates several daily flights to and from Buenos Aires, taking only 50 minutes.

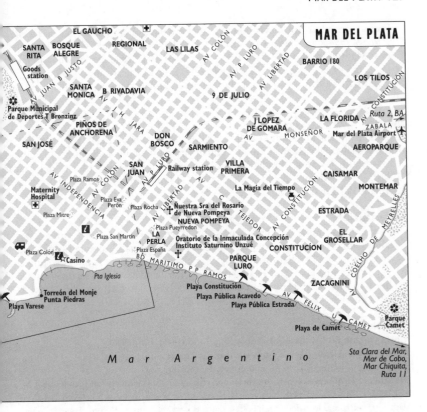

LADE (*Rambla Casino, Local 5;* ☎ *493 8220;* f *493 8211;* e *mardel@lade.com.ar*) has flights from Buenos Aires to Mar del Plata on Tuesdays and Thursdays, continuing to Bahía Blanca, Necochea, Puerto Madryn, Trelew, Bariloche, El Bolsón, Esquel, El Calafate and Río Gallegos.

A taxi to the centre will cost about 14 pesos (40 minutes), or bus no. 542 will take you to Plaza Colón for 1 peso. Hertz (☎ *478 7324;* e *reservas@milletrentacar.com.ar; www.milletrentacar.com.ar*) and Avis (☎ *470 2100;* e *avismardelplata@infovia.com.ar; www.avis.com*) rental car agencies are both at the terminal.

By train
Three trains a day (and a fourth on Fridays) run from the Constitución terminal in Buenos Aires to Mar del Plata taking five and a half hours (a bit more than the bus) to reach the Estación Ferrocarril Ferrobaires (*Av Luro 4500,* ☎ *475 6076, free 0800 222 8736*). Fares start at 22 pesos.

By bus
From Buenos Aires, approximately one bus per hour travels direct to Mar del Plata (5 hours) arriving at the centrally located Estación Terminal de Omnibus (*Alberti 1602;* ☎ *451 5406*). The main companies are Empresa Argentina (☎ *011 4000 5252 in Buenos Aires; 451 0666 in Mar del Plata*), Chevallier (☎ *011 4000 5255 in Buenos Aires; 451 8447 in Mar del Plata*), PlusMar (☎ *011 4312 9925*) and Flecha Bus (☎ *011 4000 5200*). Fares range from 30 pesos for a *pullman* to 42 pesos for a *cama* or 46 pesos for a *supercama*.

From Comodoro Rivadavia, Don Otto/Líder Patagónico (*main office in Trelew* ☎ *02965 423943; in Mar del Plata 491 9951*) has daily service via Trelew and Puerto Madryn to Mar del Plata. From Neuquén, Via Bariloche (*in Mar del Plata* ☎ *451 2555 or in Neuquén* ☎ *02299 442 7054*), leaves at around 20.30, passing through Bahía Blanca, Necochea and Miramar, and arriving in Mar del Plata at 10.00.

By car

Arriving from Buenos Aires (4 hours; 404km from Buenos Aires), take Autovia 2; from Necochea take Ruta 88. Ruta 11 stitches each little town to the next along the coast – south towards Miramar (53km) or north towards Santa Clara del Mar (19km), Mar Chiquita (35km), Villa Gesell (113km), Pinamar (134km) and San Clemente del Tuyú (238km).

Orientation

From the bus terminal Las Heras brings you in five blocks to the sea, with to your left the green park of Plaza Colón facing the concrete Plaza Almirante Brown, and beyond them the Playa Bristol and Playa Popular. To your right is the Torreón del Monje, with a small port tucked into the rocky headland beyond. The main coastal highway is Boulevard Marítimo Patricio Peralta Ramos, which becomes Avenida Martinez de Hoz to the south (buses 541 or 221).

Where to stay

Costa Galana Bd Marítimo P P Ramos 5725; ☎ 486 0000; f 486 2020; e reservas@hotelcostagalana.com; www.hotelcostagalana.com. Rooms start at 250 pesos in low season; from mid-Dec to the end of Feb they are 300 pesos and up.

Hermitage Hotel Av Colón 1679 with second entrance at Bd Marítimo P P Ramos 2757; ☎ 451 9081; f 451 7235; e reservas@hermitagehotel.com.ar; www.hermitagehotel.com.ar. Large, with 350 rooms, and luxurious, with both 4-star and 5-star categories of room. The restaurant has a diverse menu without exaggerated prices. The 4-star rooms are unavailable in low season, but otherwise start at 220 pesos. The 5-star room rates range from 195 pesos (low season) to 300 pesos (high season) and if they have an ocean view, 250 pesos (low) to 350 pesos (high).

Sheraton Mar del Plata Hotel Alem 4221; ☎ 499 9000; f 499 9009; e informes@mardel.sheraton.com.ar; www.sheraton.com. Rates start at US$70 per person in low season, US$126 in high (Dec–Feb).

Hotel Presidente Corrientes 1516; ☎ 491 1060; f 491 1183; e reservas@hahoteles.com; www.presidentehotel.com.ar. Room service, valet parking and use of a nearby gym are some of the services offered at this centrally located hotel. Rates are 94–107 pesos in low season; 119–139 pesos in high season.

Hotel Guerrero Diagonal Juan B Alberdi 2288; ☎/f 495 8851, 491 1417; e info@hotelguerrero.com.ar; www.hotelguerrero.com.ar. Room service, internet, use of a gym and pool and other services provided. Standard dbls start at 60 pesos in low season, 100 pesos for an ocean view. In high season, dbls start at 150 pesos; parking is 2 pesos per day.

Boulevard Hotel Corrientes 1965; ☎ 492 2069; e hotelboulevard@gruopvalles.com.ar; www.boulevardhotel.com.ar. Basic accommodation a few blocks from the sea. Dbls cost 30 pesos per person in high season dropping to 16 per person in low, including b/fast.

Hotel Niza Santiago del Estero 1843; ☎ 495 1695. A tiny hotel with clean rooms managed by a couple of sweet elderly ladies. Rates start at 15 pesos but double in high season.

Hotel Baloo Las Heras 2459; ☎/f 492 5229, 493 6625; e baloohotel@hotmail.com. This is just one of the many low-end hotels along this main street near the bus terminal, convenient for arriving late or leaving early but not the nicest part of town. Sgls 20 pesos, dbls 40 pesos, triples 60 pesos, etc.

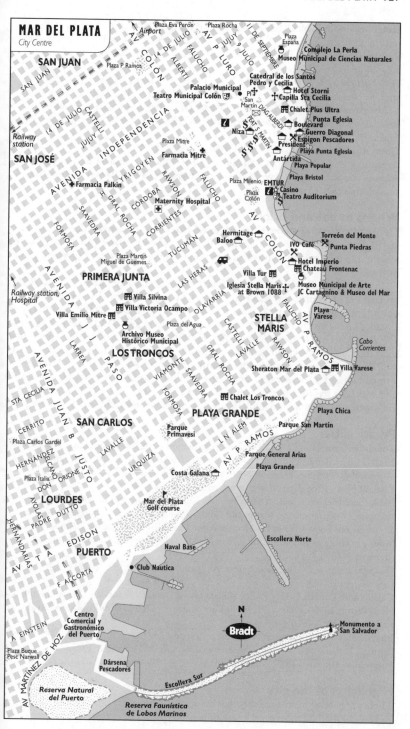

MAR DEL PLATA
City Centre

Bradt

N

Hotel Imperio Av Colón 1186; ✆f 486 3993, 451 2029. Well located for several of the museums and the aquarium. There is a restaurant and b/fast is included. Parking is available for 10 pesos per day. Sgls start at 50 pesos, dbls 65 pesos; in high season expect to pay 100–150 pesos for a dbl.

Hotel Storni 11 de Septiembre 2642; ✆ 496 1460; e hotelstorni@yahoo.com.ar. Named after the poet Alfonsina Storni who drowned herself here in 1938, this pretty stone 1920s building overlooks the sea. The main road is a bit busy, but the location is excellent for strolls down the beachwall or heading into the centre. Sgls start at 30 pesos, dbls 60 pesos, triples 90 pesos, with b/fast.

Hotel Antártida Av Luro 2156; ✆ 491 5450, 491 5454; f 491 2411; e resantar@lacapitalnet.com.ar; www.diba.org.ar. This hotel, restaurant and *confitería* holds *milongas*, jazz and live music events. Dbls with American b/fast 68/106 pesos in low/high season; triples 84/122 pesos.

Where to eat and drink

Centro Comercial y Gastronómico del Puerto, on Avenida Martínez de Hoz starting at Avenida 12 de Octubre, is an area with many different types of restaurants that specialise in fish and seafood, where you can find specialties such as paella.

In the centre, **Espigón Pescadores** (*Bd Marítimo and Av Luro;* ✆f *493 1713*) specialises, of course, in seafood. You won't have any trouble identifying this restaurant with the enormous neon Quilmes beer sign above it, visible from a great distance on the beach. Its location overlooking the sea is great. **IVO Café** (*Bd Marítimo P P Ramos 3027 and corner of Güemes;* ✆ *486 3160*) is an elegant café with a spectacular view through its bay windows or from the patio on to the sea – it has great desserts as well. In the landmark **Torreón del Monje** (*Paseo Jesús de Galíndes s/n;* ✆ *451 9467*) is a restaurant and cafeteria with a simple menu of pizza, sandwiches, breakfast or coffee and sweets. It has a great terrace over the beach. The Torreón del Monje dates from 1904 when it was built by a homesick Señor del Monje from Arabia.

Practicalities

Tourist information EMTUR, Tourist Information Centre, Bd Marítimo P P Ramos 2270, Local 51 Rambla, Edificio Casino; ✆ 495 1777; open daily 08.00–20.00. Ente Municipal de Turismo, Belgrano 2740; ✆ 494 4140; open Mon–Fri 08.00–15.00.

Central post office (Correo Argentino) Av Luro 2460; ✆ 494 1060.

Bank machines are found on Santa Fé at Av Colón, Belgrano and Rivadavia; at the Shopping Los Gallegos; San Martín and Córdoba; Buenos Aires and Moreno; Brown at Tucumán and Buenos Aires; Las Heras at Albertí and Gascón; and at the Casino Central.

Money exchanges Jonestur Cambio, San Martín 2574; ✆ 494 5218; and La Moneta, Rivadavia 2615; ✆ 494 0535.

Hospital Interzonal General de Agudos, Av Juan B Justo Calle 168; ✆ 477 0030, 477 0262 (emergency dial 107).

Casino and Tourist Safety Police (Subcomisaria Casino y Seguridad Turistica) Rambla Hotel Provincial, Local 56; ✆ 492 0027. There's also the **Delegación Policia Federal**, Sarmiento 2551; ✆ 451 7909, 451 6425.

Pharmacies include Farmacia Mitre (open 24 hours), Av Colón at San Luís; ✆ 494 1232; Farmacia Palkin (open 24 hours), Av Independencia 3503; ✆ 472 9266; Farmacia Pueyrredón, Rivadavia 2587; ✆ 0800 333 3334.

Highlights of the city

There are several tourist circuits that are recommended by the city tourism board and emphasised on most tourist brochures and maps. For example, the Paseo Zona

Norte is a walk from Plaza España down Boulevard Marítimo Patricio Peralta Ramos along the shore all the way to Parque Camet, a large green space for picnics and recreation. The Peatonal Rambla goes in the opposite direction, taking you from the Hotel Provincial opposite Plaza Colón towards the Torreón del Monje. The Güemes vehicular tour passes through the old elite *barrio* of Los Troncos and Calle Alem. The Punta Mogotes and Playas del Sur tour follows the beaches south from the Torreón del Monje to the commercial port, at the long pier at the far end of the beach.

The centre is packed with highlights. There is a section of beaches, **Playa Bristol** and **Playa Popular**, and behind them the Casino and tourist office, the large **Plaza Almirante Brown** with the two symbols of the city, the large statues of sea lions set at the corners of the plaza watching over the sea like sentinels, the Hotel Provincial and across the street, Plaza Colón. You can walk the beachfront from Plaza Colón to Plaza España, then loop back to walk up the two diagonal streets, Alberdi and Pueyrredón; from Plaza San Martín that intersects the two, you can take the pedestrianised Calle San Martín. In Plaza San Martín is the **Catedral de los Santos Pedro y Cecilia**, which was the central landmark of the original city plan. It has French, Italian, Norman and neo-colonial features and was declared a National Historic Monument in 1985. The **Palacio Municipal** (City Hall), Hipólito Yrigoyen 1627, was inaugurated in 1938, although construction had begun in 1890.

From the early 20th century the houses of the elite include **Villa Silvina** (at Quintana 1949, now a private school), which was the property of writers (and intimates of Borges) Silvina Ocampo and Adolfo Bioy Casares; **Villa Victoria Ocampo**, the English-style residence of Silvina's sister, writer Victoria Ocampo (1851 Matheu Street, now a cultural centre); **Villa Emilio Mitre**, built in 1930 (Lamadrid 3870, now the municipal history museum); and **Chalet Los Troncos** (3440 Urquiza Street), a wooden house built in 1938 after which the neighbourhood was named. The fantastically haunted-looking **Chateau Frontenac** at Alvear and Bolivar sits abandoned and for sale, awaiting someone to return it to its former glory. **Villa Unzué de Casares** (1930) at Jujuy 77 is now the Instituto Saturnino Unzué and also the location of the Oratorio de la Inmaculada Concepción. Other villas worth seeing are **Villa Tur**, Güemes 2342; **Villa Varese**, Alem and La Costa; and **Chalet Plus Ultra**, Santiago del Estero 1228.

Chapels and churches of note include the **Capilla Santa Cecilia**, Córdoba 1338; **Nuestra Señora del Rosario de Nueva Pompeya**, Avenida Libertad and Olazabal; and **Iglesia Stella Maris** at Brown 1088, near the Torre Tanque at Falucho 993. The **Torre Tanque** is a beautiful stone water tower (built in 1943) that you can climb for a view over the city (*Mon–Fri 07.00–13.30; free*).

Museums

Museo Histórico Municipal Roberto T Barili Lamadrid 3870; ℣f 495 1200. This history museum houses a collection of old photographs and paraphernalia from the early days of the city. *Open Mon–Fri 09.00–16.00, Sat & Sun 14.00–16.00; admission 2 pesos.*
Museo Municipal de Ciencias Naturales Lorenzo Scaglia Av Libertad 3099, Plaza España; ℣f 473 8791. An aquarium and museum holding live, fossilised and 'stuffed' specimens of practically every living creature that has walked, crawled, slithered, swum or simply existed in this region. Geological, botanical and palaeontological collections are also housed here. *Open Mon–Fri 08.30–16.30, Sat & Sun 15.00–20.00; admission 2 pesos.*
Museo Municipal de Arte Juan Carlos Cartagnino Av Colón 1189 at Alvear; ℣f 451 9461. Almost 500 works of art by national and local artists (a collection started in the 1920s)

housed in the former **Villa Ortíz Basualdo** (1909), an example of a summer house of the elite crowd in the city's heyday. *Open Mon–Fri 14.00–19.00; admission 2 pesos, free on Tue and Wed.*

Museo del Mar Av Colón 1114; ❨ 451 9779, 451 3553; e informes@museodelmar.com. An eclectic centre with wall-sized aquariums and a large collection of seashells, as well as an art and culture programme featuring music and cinema events. The Gloria Maris café has a great ambiance that makes you feel as if you are sipping your coffee inside a sea cave – 2 levels of aquarium encircle the sitting area which itself encircles a rocky tidal pool full of small marine organisms. *Open daily 08.00–02.00 in high season (Dec–Feb), cutting back to Mon–Thu 08.00–21.00, Fri & Sat 08.00 –24.00, Sun 09.00–21.00 the rest of the year; admission 5 pesos, students and pensioners 3 pesos.*

Though not exactly a museum, there's a sort of exhibition of antiques and curiosities at **La Magia del Tiempo** (*Av Constitución 5850;* ❨ *481 1110*). In the same building, directly above the Torreón del Monje, is a restaurant and *parrilla*. Free admission.

Entertainment and nightlife

The beach of Mar del Plata is not only for enjoying the sunshine; 20km of promenade call out for moonlit walks and are lined with plenty of restaurants and bars with ocean views. *Confiterías* and discos keep you dancing late into the night and in the summer there are beach parties. Casinos are popular social centres in Argentina, and Mar del Plata boasts a large one, the **Casino Central**, located beside Plaza Almirante Brown at Boulevard Marítimo P P Ramos 2242 (❨ *495 7011; open Sun–Thu 16.00–04.30, Fri, Sat and holidays to 05.00*). The casino features 565 slot machines and 138 gaming tables. The dress code is casual but shorts or T-shirts are not allowed.

The **Teatro Auditorium**, at Boulevard Marítimo P P Ramos 2280 on the east side of Plaza Almirante Brown (*tel 493 7786;* e *auditorium@copetel.com.ar; www.auditorium.com.ar*), has a diverse programme of classical and contemporary dance, music and theatre. Another important theatre is the **Teatro Municipal Colón** (*Yrigoyen 1665;* ❨ *499 6210 or 494 8571;* e *teatrocolon@mardelplata.gov.ar*).

Shopping

Avenida del Pullóver is a lengthy stretch of stores selling clothing at bargain prices. **Paseo de Compras Güemes** is the upscale shopping zone along Güemes with elegant shops selling fashion, furniture and decorative objects.

The **Centro Comercial del Puerto** is along Avenida Martínez de Hoz close to the tourist dock at the main port. At the nearby fishing port, the **Banquina de Pescadores**, a small commercial area, has also developed, selling local products and fresh fish, with several bars and restaurants too.

There are often markets and street vendors along the pedestrian streets such as **Peatonal San Martín**; and frequent summer markets including **Diagonal de los Artesanos**, weekends and holidays, 15.00–20.00; Diagonal Pueyrredón at San Martín and Rivadavia; ❨ 495 2428; all the bus lines pass here. There is an **Antique Fair**, weekends and holidays, 11.00–18.00; Plaza Rocha, XX de Septiembre at Avenida Luro and San Martín (bus 511/2 or 541); ❨ 495 2428. The **Artisan Exhibition and Market** runs Sunday and Thursday 10.00–19.00, Friday and Saturday 10.00–20.00, holidays 10.00–22.00, at the Rambla Edificio Casino, Locales 45-47, Boulevard Marítimo P P Ramos and Moreno; all the bus lines pass here. The **Artists and Artisans Walk** is on weekends and holidays, 14.00–18.00; Diagonal Pueyrredón at Rivadavia and Belgrano; ❨ 495 2428; all the bus lines pass here.

Special events

Fiesta Nacional del Mar is the ocean festival held in January, at the height of the summer season. Beach parties and seafood are a main focus of entertainment.

Semana Fallera Valenciana, held in March, coincides with this same festival in the Spanish region of Valencia. Parades, events, shows, fireworks and gastronomy that culminate in the final event – the ritual burning of a large cardboard and paper monument made in honour of the festival.

The **Festival Internacional de Cine,** also held in March, fills the city with artists, producers, directors and movie stars.

Activities
Nature reserves

Reserva Natural del Puerto is a green space directly off the southern jetty of the fishing port; the **Reserva Faunística de Lobos Marinos** is home to a large colony of sea lions directly on the southern jetty. You can walk along the jetty and see hundreds of sea lions at fairly close quarters – and smell them too! This colony is almost completely male, with a reported population of 800 individuals, who return here every year after mating off the coast of Uruguay. This unusual colony was declared a Natural Monument of Mar del Plata in 1994.

La Serranita Natural Resort (*Ruta 226 km24.5, Barrio Colina Verdes – bus 717 from the centre;* ✆ *463 0003 – and care of Guido 1009;* ✆ *474 4520 or* ✆/f *492 2966*) is a tourist resort where you can book excursions for trekking, rock climbing and abseiling, Monday to Friday 10.00–13.00 and 17.00–21.00, Saturday 10.00–13.00, for 40 pesos per person (including equipment); mountain biking, archery, swimming and trekking, 30 pesos per person. Entrance to the resort is included with the activities, otherwise general entrance is 4 pesos (3 pesos for minors); the resort is open daily 07.00–20.00. There is also a trekking club that meets every first and third Saturday and Sunday 09.00–18.00 (confirm with the resort).

Laguna and Sierra de los Padres (*Av Luro – Ruta 226, km16.5 – 15 minutes by car from centre or bus 717*). In around 1747, the Jesuits made their way to the southern pampas to try to evangelise the native populations living there. The name of the Laguna de los Padres commemorates their brief stay here; it's now a good site for birdwatching. The Jesuits were shortly thereafter forced out of Argentina and it would be another century before any development took place in this area. An attempt was made by Portuguese investors who established El Puerto de Laguna de los Padres with a pier and a *saladero*, a salting factory for preserving meat and fish. The economics did not work in their favour and they sold out to Patricio Peralta Ramos, the city founder, in the 1860s. On the same property, the **José Hernández Museum** (*Ruta 226 km14, Laguna de los Padres;* ✆ *463 1394*) is a museum of gaucho, native and missionary culture and integration, with a replica of the mission of Reducción del Pilár. Activities to enjoy in the area include **horseriding** with El Cobijo Cabalgatas (2½ hours for 35 pesos), daily depending upon the weather (✆ *463 0309, 15 684 8139*); or a game of golf (see below). Bus 717 will drop you about 600m from the entrance.

Sports and recreation activities

Within the city, the **Mar del Plata Golf Club** has two courses: a Scottish links-style course of 18 holes along the beach in front of the naval base and the Yacht Club, between Playa Grande, the Escollera Norte and Avenida Juan B Justo, at Aristóbulo de Valle 3940; and a new American-style parkland course, also 18 holes, 4km away at Avenida Mario Bravo and Triunvirato (✆ *486 2221*). You can also play at the 18-hole Sierra de los Padres golf course (✆ *463 0062*), where there is a clubhouse with swimming pool.

There are a few companies offering **sea-fishing** excursions. Rates are around 70–90 pesos for an outing, with equipment to rent for 20 pesos if needed. Mako III (*Av Luro and Bd Marítimo;* ✆ *493 5338;* e *mako580@hotmail.com*) offers day excursions on a luxury boat. Leo Pesca Embarcado run trips through the Club de Motonáutica, daily at 09.00 and 15.00, for 120 pesos all inclusive. Fortuna II (✆ *480 1648*) leaves the Banquina de Pescadores at the main port at 07.00 and returns at 14.00. All excursions are subject to cancellation due to adverse weather. Fishing licences should be obtained from the Dirección de Fiscalización Pesquera (*Mitre 2853*), or at sport fishing stores and boat hire companies.

Bicicletería Madrid (*Yrigoyen 2249 and Plaza Mitre;* ✆ *494 1932*) has **bike rentals** from half an hour (4 pesos) to a full day (18 pesos).

Horseriding is available at the Campo del Mar ranch (✆ *460 5448*) and on the beach, weekends and holidays only. The ranch is located on the Costanera on Presidente Illía, about 11km from the Rotonda del Faro at the Los Lobos beach, Calle 17. You can take a Rápido del Sud bus from the main terminal, which will drop you 600m from the ranch. Half an hour riding for 5 pesos, one hour for 8 pesos.

Paragliding with Arcángel Parapente & Paramotor (✆ *463 1167, 15 680 0689*). No experience necessary, weather permitting, 50 pesos per person.

Boat excursions on the *Crucero Anamora* (✆ *489 0310;* ✆f *484 0103; 14 pesos, under-tens 10 pesos*) depart at 11.30 and 16.00 from Dársena 'B' of the main port, and tour the harbour for a little over an hour on weekends and holidays. Buses 221, 511 and 581 pass the port.

Nearby cities

The nearby city of **Necochea** (area code 02262) has the beauty and benefit of being both a riverside and a seaside town. Alongside the Río Quequén as it passes through the town and into the Atlantic are the Rowing Club, the Yacht Club and the Club del Valle. There are tennis courts and places to rent paddle boats, kayaks and fishing gear. At the mouth of the river is Puerto Quequén and on either side are the beaches. Following Avenida 2 on the west side of the port you will find the **tourist office** (*Av 79;* ✆ *425983*) followed by the local casino and then the Parque Miguel Lillo, the former estancia of the Díaz family with over 650ha of green space: trees, flowers, grassy picnic areas, a pond with ducks and swans, etc. Within the park are two museums: the **Historical Museum**, which contains objects and information on the Díaz family and the founding of the city; and the **Natural History Museum**, interpreting the natural history, evolution and ecology of the sea. Continuing along the beach you discover the many rocky enclaves called Las Grutas. Small tidal pools fill with marine life such as anemones and starfish, and the larger ones are great for swimming in as the sun warms their waters. On the far east side of the port is the 33m-tall **Quequén Lighthouse** where you can climb the 163 stairs to its main platform. There are daily buses from the terminal, near the river on Avenida 58, to Mar del Plata, Buenos Aires, Bahía Blanca and Neuquén. There are plenty of hotels, restaurants, shops and camping options.

Tandil (area code 02293) is a pretty and laid-back inland town, popular with backpackers for its many trekking, bicycling and rock climbing options in the scenic Sierras de Tandil. Its most famous attraction is a large round boulder perched precariously atop a cliff. At Easter a group of pilgrims comes to visit Calvario hill, which resembles the hill at Golgotha where Christ was crucified. There are several daily buses to Buenos Aires (331km) and Mar del Plata (169km) from the terminal at Avenida Buzón 650 (✆ *432092*). The railway station (*Av Machado and Colón;* ✆ *423002*) has one arrival from Buenos Aires on Friday nights, returning to Buenos Aires on Sunday night. Tickets cost (according to class) 16/24 pesos for adults, 8/14 pesos for minors. The **tourist office** is located at Avenida Espora 1120 (✆ *432225;* e *tandilturismo@infovia.com.ar; open Mon–Sat 08.00–20.00, Sun 09.00–13.00*). The post office, **Correo Argentino**, is at 9 de Julio 455 (✆ *424860*); the **Hospital Municipal** at Paz 1406 (✆ *422010/4; in emergency dial 107*). There are many banks throughout the centre with bank machines. A **money exchange** is Jonestur, San Martín 698 (✆ *434838*). Two museums worth visiting are the **Museo Municipal de Bellas Artes de Tandil** (*Chacabuco 353;* ✆ *432067; open Tue–Fri 08.30–12.30, 17.00–21.00; Sat & Sun 17.00–21.00*) and the **Museo Tradicionalista Fuerte Independencia** (*4 de Abril 845;* ✆ *424025; open 16.00–20.00 except Mon*).

VILLA GESELL
Area code 02255
The beach here is wide and backed with *balnearios*, and the main street is packed with shops, bars and restaurants. Outside the summer months, however, Villa Gesell seems a ghost town with not enough resident population to support the level of business infrastructure. A few places stay open year-round, but for the most part the doors close when the crowds leave. All the establishments along the beach are totally shut out of season and the boardwalk covered with blown sand. If you are looking for a quiet walk on the beach, this is the time to come. By mid-December Villa Gesell (pronounced Bizha Hesell) completely transforms itself: the beaches are full and the town is alive with activity.

Getting there
By air
Aeroclub Villa Gesell (✆ *458600, 454657*) has flights to Buenos Aires on Fridays and Sundays, although this service is much more limited in low season. This airport is located off Ruta 11 turning west (away from the sea) at the farthest northeast junction, Camino de los Pioneros.

By bus
Villa Gesell has a regular bus service to and from Retiro terminal in Buenos Aires, at approximately 45 pesos for a five-hour journey.

Alberino ✆ 454090; in Buenos Aires 011 4576 7940
Plaza ✆ 472000; in BA 011 4315 1225, 4312 9328
PlusMar ✆ 475580; in BA 011 4315 3494, 4315 6085
El Rapido Argentino (✆ 476344; in BA 011 4314 7999
Río de la Plata ✆ 476058, 462224; in BA 011 4313 3616, 4313 3602
Santa Fé ✆ 476639; in BA 011 4312 9006, 4312 3877

From the main terminal in Mar del Plata, El Rapido leaves for Villa Gesell at 07.00, 12.30, 15.00, 17.30, 20.30 and 22.00, taking two hours (8 pesos). In high season, tourist information is available at the terminal in Villa Gesell, but in low season there is practically no information at all. To get to the centre of town, which is 40 blocks north, exit the front of the station and to your right there will be a path down to the main street directly opposite a *colectivo* stop; all buses should go to the centre, but check with the driver when you board. To be specific about your drop-off point, the main street is Avenida 3 and the central blocks of town are between 101 and 110.

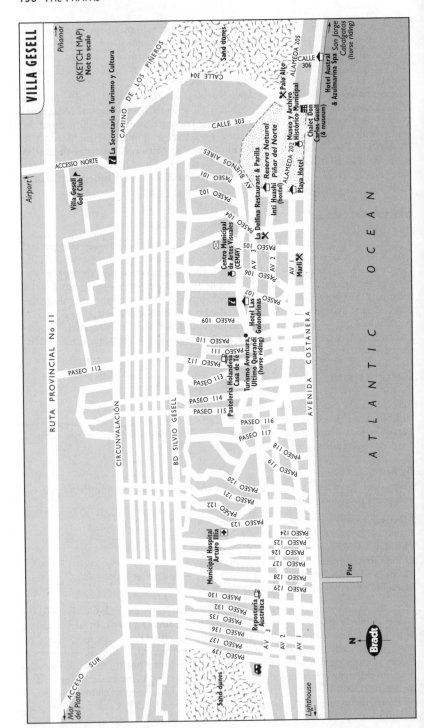

VILLA GESELL

(SKETCH MAP)
Not to scale

By car
From Mar del Plata take Ruta 11 northeast for 105km. If coming from Buenos Aires, head south on Ruta 2 and at Las Armas take Ruta Provincial 74 east towards Pinamar, from where Ruta 11 leads south to Villa Gesell.

Orientation
Villa Gesell is set out in a simple grid. The avenues parallel the sea – the shoreline itself is Avenida Costanera, the first avenue inland is Avenida 1. The main one is Avenida 3, where you will find most shops, restaurants and services. Bisecting the avenues are *paseos* (many unpaved); the central core is between Paseo 101 and 110. Paseo 100 becomes Avenida Buenos Aires leading away from the sea and connecting to the Camino de los Pioneros, the far northeast boundary of the town and the road to the golf course, Ruta 11 and the airport.

Where to stay
There are hundreds of hotels of various levels, but only a fraction of these stay open year-round. Full listings are available at the tourist information office or www.gesell.com.ar. The following suggestions stay open all year.

Hotel Austral and the Azulmarina Spa Calle 306 on the beach; ✆ 458050, 450545; www.haustral.com.ar. The cost of a room varies with season and demand, but dbls generally are 200 pesos and up, with American b/fast included. They do not accept credit cards or travellers' cheques – cash only. Prices include use of the spa, pool, gym, volleyball and bicycles.

Hotel Las Golondrinas Av 3 no. 864 between paseos 108 and 109; ✆ 468112, 460950; e lasgolondrinasgesell@yahoo.com. High-season rates for a dbl are 120–140 pesos, triple 130–180 pesos; low-season rates drop to 60 pesos for a dbl, 90 pesos for a triple. There are also quadruples and suites available.

Playa Hotel Alameda 201 and Av Buenos Aires; ✆ 458027. A 2-star hotel and one of the oldest in town; 76 pesos for a dbl with b/fast.

Guesthouses (*hospedajes*) charge around 40 pesos in high season. **Inti Huashi**, in the Reserva Forestal Pinar del Norte to the north of town (*Alameda 202 no. 82, Av Buenos Aires;* ✆ *468365*), is popular with backpackers but is not always open in low season – call ahead to confirm.

Where to eat and drink
La Delfina Restaurant and Parrilla Paseo 104 and Av 2; ✆ 465863. A wood-fired *parrilla*, fresh fish and excellent prices. Traditional cuisine recommended by the locals.
Marli Costanera and Paseo 105; ✆ 466769. This seafood restaurant comes highly recommended and is on the beach, but it can only be enjoyed in high season.
Palo Alto Alameda 205 and Calle 304; ✆ 454428. This is a cute little restaurant secluded in the forest.

There are several teahouses in Villa Gesell, several of which have proprietors of European descent who enjoy sharing the sweets and specialities of their heritage. For example, **Pasteleria Holandesa Casa de Té** (*Av 6 and Paseo 111;* ✆ *452488*) and **Repostería Austríaca** (*Av 4 and Paseo 129;* ✆ *466631*).

Practicalities
You have various **tourist offices** to choose from in Villa Gesell. Besides the one at the bus station, which is open only during the high holiday season (05.00–13.00 and 17.00–01.00), there is the **Central Tourist Office**, next to the town hall at

Avenida 3 No. 820 between Paseos 108 and 109 (✎ *462201 or 462782;* e *turismo@gesell.com.ar; open Mon–Fri 08.15–midnight*). In addition, information can be obtained through **La Secretaria de Turismo y Cultura**, Camino de los Pioneros 1921 (Bd Los Pinos and Buenos Aires); info@villagesell.gov.ar; www.villagesell.gov.ar; open 05.00–13:00 and 17:00–01:00.

The **post office** is located on Avenida 5 between Paseos 105 and 106 (✎ *462695*). Banks include: **Banco de la Provincia de Buenos Aires** (*Av 3 No. 751;* ✎ *462644, 462238*); **Banco de la Nación Argentina** (*Av 3 No. 906;* ✎ *462562, 463562*); **Banco Río de la Plata** (*Av 3 between Paseos 102 and 104;* ✎ *465450, 465540*). A money exchange is Fénis SA, Avenida 3 No 813 (✎ *462399, 463581*).

The **Hospital Municipal Arturo Illía** is at Avenida 8 and Calle 123 (✎ *462618*).

Besides the many shops along Avenida 3, there are also a few artist and artisan **markets** during the summer weekends.

Highlights

The oldest landmark is the **Faro Querandí**, a lighthouse dating back to 1922, surrounded by sand dunes that are part of a protected area established in 1999, 30km south of Villa Gesell.

La Reserva Forestal Pinar del Norte is something of a misnomer. The forest is truly lovely, and merits praise for creating a natural area that holds fresh water, establishes a stronghold of permanent ground in contrast to the shifting landscape of the surrounding sand dunes, and is responsible for the establishment of the town. It is however, completely unnatural. It is a plantation forest of various species that would not have occurred without the deliberate efforts of man – actually one man, Carlos Gesell. Nonetheless, it has existed here since the 1930s and offers habitats to many species of birds. The natural vegetation of the surrounding coastal desert is much subtler than a forest and does not immediately impress. The tenacious tiny plants that manage to exist on this challenging terrain are actually very sensitive and fragile and have captured the attention of botanists and ecologists who are now working to protect them and their ecosystem. Ethics and ecology aside, the forest is a wonderful place to cool off from the summer heat and it has great little walks with sculptures and a *matera*, a little shelter under which a group can sit and share a *maté*.

One of the highlights of Villa Gesell is the **Chalet Don Carlos Gesell**, (*Alameda 201 and Calle 303;* ✎ *450530; open daily in summer 10.00–12.30, 17.30–22.30, in winter 13.30–19.30*). Don Carlos lived here from 1952 until his death in 1979; it's now a cultural centre. The **museum** is at the same address (*in fact 70m away;* ✎ *468624;* e *museo@gesell.com.ar*) but with different hours, in summer daily 09.00–13.00, 16.00–21.00, winter 14.00–21.00, admission 1 peso. It houses a large quantity of photographs, documents and objects relating to the lives of Carlos Gesell and his father Silvio, who established this town and planted this forest. When they first came to this area there was nothing but beach and sand dunes. They bought 1,648ha and began planting a pine forest with the long-term intention of making wooden furniture. Carlos built the house quite close to the sea in 1931, and until the forest matured there was no blocking the wind and the house was often swept over by the sand dunes. The house had no electricity and the wooden walls were insulated with newspaper. There was a door in each wall so that when one was blocked by a sand-drift the others could still be used. By 1943 there was a railway, a road from Ruta Provincial 11 and the first hotels, the Playa, the Parque and the Gaviota pension, began taking in tourists – Villa Gesell was on its way to being established as a town.

Also worth a visit is **CEMAV**, the Centro Municipal de Artes Visuales, in the Galería Futura at Avenida 3 and Paseo 106 (✆ *466439;* e *cultura@gesell.com.ar*), which houses temporary art shows.

Activities
The main **tour agencies** in town are in two neighbouring cabins on Avenida 3 between Paseos 110 and 111, Plaza Carlos Idaho Gesell: **Turismo Aventura** (✆ *463 118;* e *turismoyaventurasgesell@yahoo.com.ar*) and **El Ultimo Querandí** (✆ *468989;* e *querandi@gesell.com.ar*), who take excursions onto the sand dunes with 4x4s.

You can go horseriding with **San Jorge Cabalgatas** (*Calle 313 and Alameda 201;* ✆ *454464*). Outings are possible any day of the week at 18.00, or, if the weather is not too hot, 15.00 with a reservation.

The nine-hole golf course of the **Villa Gesell Golf Club** is on Camino de los Pioneros 2463, right before the junction for Ruta 11 (✆ *458249*).

PINAMAR
Area code 02254
The same buses that serve Villa Gesell continue 22km further to the terminal of Pinamar at Jason 2250 (✆ *403500*). There is also a train service to the station at Ruta 74 km4 (✆ *497973*), although there are only two trains a week from Buenos Aires, on Wednesdays and Fridays. Pinamar is a small town but it caters to such a large influx of vacationers in the summer that it has over 140 hotels and 160 restaurants. There are discos, cinemas and theatres, art galleries, two casinos, three golf courses, a polo field, several tennis courts and many excursion and sporting companies. Southwest of Pinamar proper are three other popular beach areas: **Cariló** right at the southern end of Pinamar, where there are many shops, small malls, cafés and restaurants; **Valeria del Mar**, which is a quieter and less developed area; and **Ostende**, an early Belgian settlement where there are still the remains of waterfront boardwalks. The **Secretary of Tourism** office is at Avenida Bunge 654 (✆ *491680/1;* e *unestilodevida@telpin.com.ar; www.pinamarturismo.com.ar; open Mon–Sat 08.00–20.00, Sun 10.00–18.00*).

Where to stay and eat
Hotel del Bosque Av Bunge and Jupiter; reservations in Buenos Aires, ✆ 011 4394 9605, 800 999 5137; f 011 4394 9599; e maresur@maresur.com. A hotel and health club with dbls from 182/350 pesos (low/high season).
Playas Hotel Av Bunge 250 at La Sirena; ✆ 482236; f 482226; e playashotelreservas@pinamarsa.com.ar. High-season rates 100–140 pesos sgl, 150–190 pesos dbl, including b/fast.
Hostería Bora Bora Del Ruyu 441; ✆ 482394, 480164. The restaurant specialises in *picadas de fiambres* (finger food), cheeses, salami and typical dishes.

SAN ANTONIO DE ARECO
Area code 02326
The toll-bridge of San Antonio de Areco, a symbolic town of the pampas with honest small-town appeal, marked the entry to the vast interior of the country, abode of the gaucho. Nowadays it hosts the country's biggest gaucho festival culminating on the Día de la Tradición on 10 November. Shops and artisans specialise in braided rawhide items, fine leatherwork, silver and woodwork. Your appetite for a good *asado* with local wine followed by homemade *alfajor* will be authentically satisfied. It's a small town, quickly explored, allowing you to easily

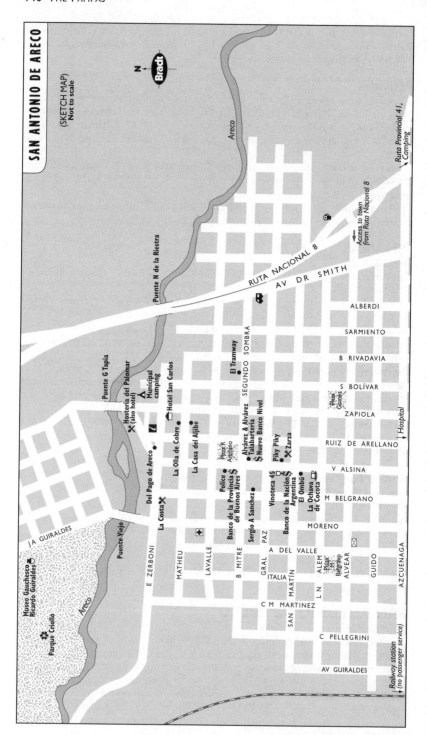

SAN ANTONIO DE ARECO
(SKETCH MAP)
Not to scale

shop 'downtown', walk the woods by the river and go horseriding all in one day, with all these activities available within a few blocks of each other.

Getting there
By bus
A couple of hours by bus from Retiro terminal in Buenos Aires will bring you to San Antonio de Areco, where buses stop on the main highway, Avenida Smith. Chevallier have their own terminal at Smith and Gral. Paz (⟍ 453904) has a service almost every hour for 19 pesos. Pullman General Belgrano, at Smith and Segundo Sombra (⟍ 454059), has a couple of departures per day for 12 pesos.

By car
San Antonio de Areco is 110km northwest of Buenos Aires, right on Ruta National 8.

Orientation
Arriving by bus you will find yourself at the roadside bus stop surrounded by cow pastures, but a five-minute walk will lead you right into the central Plaza Arellano. This has a gazebo in the centre piping in classical and folk music, giving an almost surreal feel to the quiet rose gardens during midday siesta when there is barely a soul to be seen. To the left, Avenida Alsina is the main shopping strip, with most services and a few cafés; in the opposite direction Ruiz de Arellano will take you to the river, the famous bridge, the tourist office, the museum and some nice restaurants.

Where to stay
Hotel San Carlos Zerboni and Zapiola; ⟍ 453106, 453619; e info@hotel-sancarlos.com.ar. There is a pool and free use of bicycles. Sgls are 35 pesos but prices sometimes go up at w/ends.

Camping Recreativo La Segunda Ruta 8, km110 then Ruta 41 towards Baradero for 13km; ⟍ 498068 , in Buenos Aires 011 4799 1106; e laufrise@ba.net; www.crlasegunda.com.ar. A day at the camp with b/fast and activities costs 38 pesos per person (19 pesos for under-12s); a day plus a night in various forms of accommodation from a 'country wagon' to a cabin or in the *hostería*, 55–125 pesos. You can also come here just for lunch or dinner for about 15 pesos.

Estancia El Ombú de Areco Ruta 31, cuartel VI, Villa Lía, San Antonio de Areco; ⟍ 492080; m 15 682 598; reservations ⟍ 11 4710 2795; e reservas@estanciaelombu.com. A 300ha working ranch raising Herefords and Aberdeens. Located 20km from San Antonia de Areco, it offers a rustic ranch setting with horseback riding or carriage rides and special folkloric events to entertain you. Rates are seasonal and subject to change but are estimated at US$45 per person for a day visit; the overnight rate for single occupancy is US$120 per person; dbl occupancy is US$90 per person. Children under 11 are half price. Prices include full board, soft drinks, wines and spirits, and all activities (except special folklore musical and gaucho events, for which you must request more information). Transfers to and from the centre of Buenos Aires or either airport is available from around US$50–60.

Where to eat and drink
La Costa Belgrano and Zerboni. Has been recommended by travellers as the best restaurant in town.

Hostería del Palomar Güiraldes and Arellano; ⟍ 452012. A wonderful couple of hours can be spent here on a sunny afternoon under the shade of an umbrella by the river enjoying *asado* and a bottle of Malbec.

Vinoteca 45 Alsina 297; ✆ 456296. A wine bar and speciality shop where you can enjoy a glass of wine accompanied by a plate of cheese and other typical delicacies.
La Ochava de Cocota Alsina and Alem; ✆ 452176. Located on an old corner of the town in a building over 100 years old. It is open for coffee and *medialunas* as well as *empanadas* and house specialities throughout the day. W/ends often come with live music by local performers.
Zarza San Martín 361; ✆ 453948. Describes itself as serving a classic modern cuisine.

Practicalities

In the summer there is often a kiosk providing **tourist information** in the plaza. Heading towards the river you will find the main office, the **Dirección de Turismo de San Antonio de Areco**, at Zerboni and Arellano, Parque San Martín (✆ 453165; e *direcciondeturismo@areconet.com.ar, www.arecotur.com.ar; open Mon–Fri 08.30–14.00, Sat 10.00–20.00, Sun & hols 10.00–17.00*). There are many old photos on the walls of the old town and buildings and the staff are very helpful.

The **post office** is at Correo Argentino on Aristovulo del Valle and Alvear, and *locutorios* for telephone and internet are found along Avenida Alsina, Avenida Alvear and Avenida del Valle. Banks are mostly on Alsina: **Banco de la Nación Argentina** (at San Martín); **Banco de la Provincia de Buenos Aires** (at Mitre); and **Nuevo Banco Bisel** (no. 167). The **hospital** is on Lavalle and Moreno (✆ 452759, 452391, 452345), and the **police station** on Alsina between Lavalle and Mitre (✆ 452113).

Museums

Parque Criollo and **Museo Gauchesco Ricardo Güiraldes** (Museum of the Gaucho; ✆ 455839, 455990 or 456202; e *museoguiraldes@areconet.com.ar; open Wed–Mon 11.00–17.00; admission 2 pesos*) is a short walk up Calle Ricardo Güiraldes past the old pink bridge (1857). This wonderful museum creatively interprets the gaucho culture and lifestyle. The first section is in a building over 150 years old; here an installation of objects and mannequins re-creates *La Pulperia* (a multi-purpose general store, post office, bar, restaurant and more). There is a flourmill from 1848, a horse shed with carts and other typical objects and a simple country house. The museum is within an estancia with wonderful exhibits, most impressive of which are the silver equestrian tack and ornamentation and the gaucho literature collection including that of Señor Güiraldes, after whom the museum is named. The author of the famous gaucho novel *Don Segundo Sombra* (1926), he is buried in the local cemetery. Latticework, intricate cast-iron gates and colonial architectural details enhance the overall setting.

Shopping

In the heart of the pampas and home of the gaucho, San Antonio de Areco is the place to come to buy horse equipment, leather, typical Argentine objects and traditional clothing. The gaucho get-up includes the *rastra*, a broad belt laden with silver and gold chains and charms, the *facón*, a large knife that serves as tool, weapon and cutlery, plus equally ornamented stirrups, bridles, *maté* gourds and *bombillas* or *maté* straws. The art is confident in its kitschy vulgarity and thus achieves a sort of beauty.

El Ombú Alsina and corner of San Martín. Sells all traditional Argentine crafts and objects, silver, leather and wool items and horsemanship equipment.
Talabartería y Taller Alsina and Gral Paz; ✆ 15 5177 4898; e ssanchez@areconet.com.ar; www.sanantoniopolo.com. Sergio A Sanchez has a workshop here where he produces beautiful silver objects. Polo equipment is also sold here.

El Tramway Segundo Sombra 411; ↘ 455561. An antique shop with a collection of the most diverse oddities; almost like a museum and a great place for treasure hunters.

Alvárez & Alvárez Talabartería Alsina and Mitre; ↘ 15 651935; e alvarezmm@hotmail.com. Sells traditional Argentine objects.

La Casa del Aljibe Matheu 375; ↘ 452407. A nice little shop with handmade pieces and traditional items.

La Olla de Cobre Matheu 433; ↘ 453105. Some of the street signs in town can be misleading; Matheu, for example, used to be Speroni and some of the old signs still hang. However, the frequent crowd outside this sweetshop will be the best indication that you have found it.

Del Pago de Areco Bd Zerboni 280; ↘ 454751; e delpago@areconet.com.ar. Makes superb homemade *dulce de leche* as well as excellent *alfahores* and preserves.

Piky Piky Alsina 287; ↘ 453659. Music of most genres, but especially traditional tango and folk music. You will likely also find titles and artists that are ghosts in their home countries.

Day trips and excursions

There are a couple of even smaller gaucho towns nearby that you may choose to visit. **Duggan**, just outside San Antonio de Areco at km128 on Ruta 8, has about 800 inhabitants. The Capilla San Juan Bautista and the old railway station are the main historic buildings, but the whole town seems historic. A convenient bus (5 pesos) leaves from San Antonio de Areco on weekdays at 12.10 or 13.30 to return at 16.30 or 18.15. **Villa Lia** is another option, reached by buses (2 pesos) from San Antonio de Areco at 07.30 or 11.30, returning at 15.00 or 17.00 on weekdays.

Santa Fé Province

Santa Fé was one of the first colonial expansions beyond Buenos Aires province. Colonisation projects began in the 1850s well past the identified native territories. Immigrants, mainly Italian, German and Swiss, were encouraged to settle on small sheep farms and pioneer the land. By 1875 there were about 60 agricultural colonies, with a focus on cereal cultivation, which grew to 400 by 1900. The River Paraná was a vital transportation link south and soon the economy of Santa Fé was to boom thanks to grain exports, still key to the province's economy. Over 4 million tons of grain pass through the port every three months, but this may increase by 50%, and there is an even more substantial boom in soya production, so that up to US$4bn may soon have to be invested in docks and other infrastructure.

ROSARIO
Area code 0341

Not often on the tourist track, Rosario, 320km from Buenos Aires, is a beautiful old city of over a million people, with much to offer. The Río Paraná is the lifeline of the city, providing a transportation conduit, a fishing industry, summer tourism, water-based activities, a major port for export and import of agricultural products, a water source for various admittedly dirty industries such as pulp mills, and an astounding 490 million litres per day of drinking water for its residents. Beautiful colonial architecture graces the centre and old villas are strung along the tree-lined Boulevard Oroña. Still within the heart of the pampas, Rosario holds onto its gaucho traditions but also throws great river fish such as a *boca* or *dorado* right next to the steaks grilling on the *parrilla*.

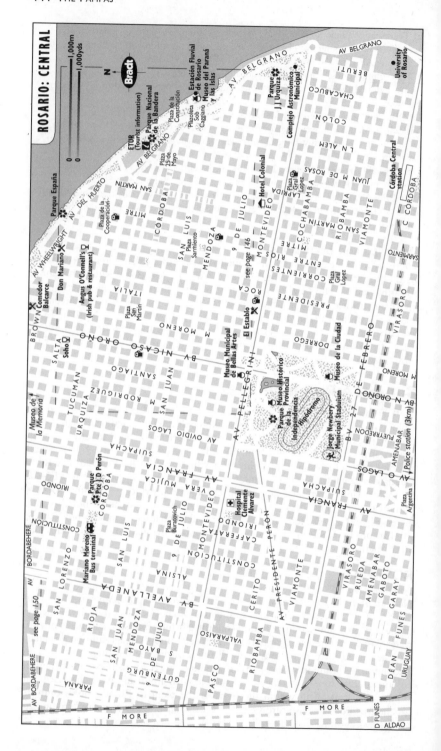

ROSARIO: CENTRAL

Getting there

By air

The Aeropuerto Rosario Fisherton (✆ *456 7997*) is 8km west of the centre; taxis to the city cost about 15 pesos. Rosario is not conveniently serviced and many flights actually have to transfer through Santa Fé city.

Schedules change frequently, but in general Aerolíneas Argentinas/Austral (*Santa Fé 1412;* ✆ *424 9332;* f *424 9292;* e *rosgte@aerolineas.com.ar; open Mon–Fri 08.30–19.30, Sat 08.30–12.30*) operates two flights per day, Monday to Friday, from Buenos Aires Aeroparque (only one at weekends).

LAN Chile (*San Lorenzo 1116;* ✆ *424 8205, 0810 999 9526;* f *424 2828;* e *mirtadiap@lanchileros.com.ar*) has flights between Rosario and Santiago via Córdoba on Monday, Wednesday, Friday and Sunday.

By bus

The Mariano Moreno bus terminal is at Cafferata 702, on the corner of Santa Fé (✆ *437 3030 or 437 2384;* e *informes@terminalrosario.com.ar; www.terminalrosario.com.ar*). This architectural landmark was the original provincial railway station of Santa Fé; founded in 1927, it was converted into a bus terminal in 1950.

Public transport to the centre is by *colectivo* 115. Bus tickets cost 0.75 pesos and can be bought in prepaid *tarjetas* (1.50 pesos, 3 pesos and 6 pesos). Rosario does not have a subway system, but the extensive bus system has about 60 different routes.

Several bus companies connect with Retiro terminal in Buenos Aires, for 25–30 pesos; the most frequent schedule is offered by El Rosarino Rutamar (✆ *425 2523, in Buenos Aires 011 432 8728*) or Nueva Chevallier (✆ *438 6700, in Buenos Aires 011 4000 5255*). Between Rosario and Santa Fé there are seven or eight buses per day (13.50 pesos) with Nuevo Rápido San José (✆ *439 8493*). There are as many with Tata Rapido (✆ *439 0901*). Mercobus (✆ *438 0038*) connects Córdoba and Rosario overnight (7 hours) for 25 pesos.

By train

Trains between Buenos Aires and Rosario are infrequent, usually leaving Retiro station on Monday and Friday evenings, reaching Rosario Norte five and a half hours later (fares from 11 pesos). There are plans to build a high-speed train to reduce travelling time to 1.5 hours. Work is scheduled to begin in 2007. The trains continue to Córdoba, Tucumán and Santiago del Estero on Mondays and Santa Fé on Fridays. The Estación Rosario Norte is on Avenida del Valle at Avenida Ovidio Lagos (✆ *430 7272 or 426 3713*).

By car

Ruta 9 connects Rosario and Buenos Aires as well as Rosario and Córdoba. Santa Fé and Rosario are connected by Ruta 11. The Rosario–Victoria bridge was completed in 2003 and has become a landmark of the city. The bridge connects Rosario to the town of Victoria and the province of Entre Rios. Previously it was necessary to drive through Santa Fé or Buenos Aires provinces to cross the river. Now it's a mere 40 minutes' drive to Victoria, with a toll of 9 pesos that you only have to pay once if you return on the same day.

Car rental is available through Hertz-Millet (*Rioja 573;* ✆ *424 2408*).

Orientation

Arriving from the airport you will probably drive into the centre by way of Avenida Eva Perón, which is the extension of Ruta 9 to Córdoba. Before crossing the Avenida de Circunvalación 25 de Mayo (the large motorway that rings the city in a

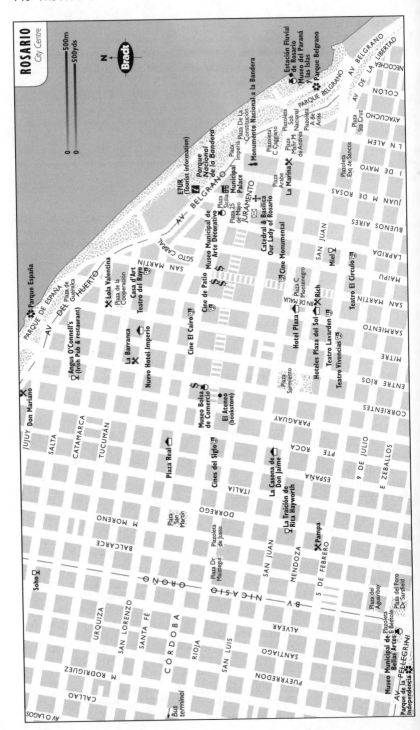

ROSARIO
City Centre

0 ____ 500m
0 ____ 500yds

N

Bradt

wide loop from Avenida Belgrano all the way to the Nuestra Señora del Rosario bridge at the north end of the city), you will see to your left the Golf Club of Rosario and soon after to your right the Jockey Club, which is a private club for various sports. At the far end of the Jockey Club's property there is a traffic circle to the north of which is the prestigious Fisherton residential area where you can see beautiful old villas with stunning gardens. Continuing into the city, after crossing Boulevard Avellaneda Avenida Eva Perón changes its name to Avenida Córdoba, passes several parks and eventually leads directly into the heart of the city.

Avenida Belgrano runs along the lovely riverfront of Rosario, an expansive green zone with a pedestrian/cycling track, wide grassy boulevards and viewpoints over the river and its delta. There are a few bars and restaurants and the tourism offices, as well as museums and residences on the far side of the avenue. The centre point of the city is at the mid-point of this riverfront, conspicuously demarcated by the 78m-high Monumento Nacional a la Bandera (National Flag Monument).

Where to stay

Hoteles Plaza del Sol San Juan 1055; ↖ 421 9899; e gerencia@hotelesplaza.com. Rates start at 179 pesos for a sgl or dbl, 219 pesos for a suite. A second location opens in November for the high season, **Hotel Plaza** (*Barón de Maua 26;* ↖ *421 6446*) with junior suites for 99 pesos, sgls/dbls 109 pesos and suites from 199 pesos.
Plaza Real Santa Fé 1632; ↖ 440 8800. From 155 pesos for a sgl, 175 pesos for a dbl, with other options all the way up to 750 pesos for the presidential suite.
Nuevo Hotel Imperio Urquiza 1234; ↖ 448 0091; e contacto@hotelimperio.com.ar. Sgls 76 pesos, dbls 92 pesos, b/fast included.
Hotel Mayoral Av Alberdi 1142; ↖ 438 0694; e informes@hotelmayoral.com.ar. Sgls for 64 pesos, dbls for 86 pesos and triples for 106 pesos.
Hotel Colonial Maipú 1543; ↖ 421 9041, 421 7453. Nothing fancy, but affordable at 45 pesos for a sgl, 60 pesos for a dbl, b/fast included.
La Casona de Don Jaime Presidente Roca 1051; ↖ 527 9964; e lacasonadedonjaime@yahoo.com.ar; www.youthhostelrosario.com.ar. A simple youth hostel charging 18 pesos per person in a dorm.

Where to eat and drink
Restaurants

El Establo Av Pellegrini 1775; ↖ 454 1777, 481 5900, 15 500 0630; e el_establo@ciudad.com.ar. The main feature is the *parrilla*. Customer parking at Italia 1737 (between Cochabamba and Av Pellegrini).
Los Pipos Restaurant Av de las Americas 3685; ↖ 435 0566. Affiliated to Lola Valentina (below) and offering similar menu items.
Pampa Moreno 1206; ↖ 449 4303. For *parrilladas*.
Comedor Balcarce Brown 2093; ↖ 425 6765. Great pasta, every type imaginable, also with great prices.
La Barranca Urquiza and Corrientes; ↖f 423 5741. For traditional *parrilla*.
Rich San Juan between San Martín and Sarmiento. Serves fish but also *yacaré*, a member of the crocodile family; this is an old establishment that has maintained its traditions.

For fish dinners in the centre:

La Marina Rioja and corner of 1 de Mayo; no telephone. This characteristic old restaurant has a cantina with great fish.
La Cabaña del Pescador Rondeau 1180; ↖ 455 7931. The house speciality is the grilled fish *parrilla*.
Lola Valentina Mitre 302; ↖ 423 5234. Pasta, river fish and also meat *parrilla*.

For fish, most importantly surubi, dorado, pacu and boga, dinners by the river near the north port

Escauriza Bajada Escauriza and Paseo Rivereño (La Florida); ❧ 454 1777, 15 500 0630. *Parrilla* specialising in local fish. Reputed to be one of the best fish restaurants in town.

Don Mariano Paraguay and Barrancas del Río (entrance for Pte Roca); ❧ 425 0048, 15 549 2375. *Parrilla*, pasta and fish. Spartan in style but inexpensive with excellent preparation of the river fish.

Puerto Sauce Av Lisandro de la Torre and el Río (Baiagorria); ❧ 471 4395; e puertosauce@uolsinectis.com.ar. This suburban restaurant offers great fish and river views.

Cafés and bars

Angus O'Connell's Irish Pub and Restaurant Paraguay 212; ❧ 440 0512; www.oconnell.com.ar. This traditional Irish-style pub serves typical Argentine sandwiches called *Carlitos* (named after the beloved tango singer Carlos Gardel) and other fare. Microbrews are a highlight. There are several other good pubs within this area.

Miel La Prida 1159; ❧ 440 0057. A lovely teahouse and restaurant near the opera house. *Open Tue–Sat from 16.00.*

Soho Salta 2298; ❧ 480 7421. Wine bar and restaurant.

La Traición de Rita Hayworth Dorrego 1170; ❧ 448 0993. This restaurant/bar/pub often stages small cabaret-style plays and performances.

The riverfront, from the flag monument north to Av Roca, has recently been spruced up and pedestrianised, lining the river with great bars and restaurants. A great place for a stroll or meeting friends, especially on warm summer nights.

Practicalities

Tourist information is available from ETUR at Avenida Belgrano and Buenos Aires, by the river near the flag monument (❧ 480 2230/1; f 480 2237; e info@rosarioturismo.com; www.rosarioturismo.com). A second office is located in the main bus terminal. There are many banks in the centre with ATMs. The **post office** (Correo Argentino) is at Córdoba 721, and the **Hospital Clemente Alvarez** at Rueda 1110 (❧ 480 2111).

Highlights

Most city tours begin at the **Monumento Nacional a la Bandera** at Santa Fé 581 (❧ 480 2238). This anything but subtle monument is an exaggeratedly demonstrative display of patriotism even by Argentine standards. However, it holds its space by being set before the great expanse of the Paraná Delta, drawing the attention of the traffic that would otherwise race past on Avenida Belgrano, and announcing that here is indeed the city centre. The monument was designed by architect-engineer Angél Guido and inaugurated on 20 June 1957 in celebration of the Argentina flag that was created in Rosario in 1812 by General Manuel Belgrano; in recognition of this, Rosario is also colloquially named *Cuna de la Bandera* (the cradle of the flag). An enormous example of the flag waves loftily at the front of the monument, which is made up of three components: the tower (which claims to hold the tomb of General Belgrano), the Patio Cívico, an expansive open area in the mid-section of the structure that is laid out before a series of deeply sloped steps, the Pasaje 'Juramento', that lead up to the Propileo, a sort of pantheon of columns, torches and a perpetual flame. When you arrive at the top of the steps you will be rewarded with a lovely view of the plaza and beyond it the river. Events such as concerts are often staged here with the patio as the stage and the audience on the steps. Also within the monument is a flag museum that preserves the original flag (❧ 480 2238 or 480 2239; open Mon 14.00–18.00, Tue–Sun 9.00–13.00, 14.00–17.00, admission 1 peso).

Behind the monument is a fountain with illuminated waters and statues by Lola Mora. Continue walking up and away from the river and you will arrive at the main central plaza – 25 de Mayo, in the centre of which is the **Independence Monument** by sculptor Alejandro Biggi, inaugurated in 1883. Surrounding the plaza are impressive buildings such as the **Municipal Palace** (1891–96), the **Uranja Building** (or Council of Engineers, 1925), **Museo Municipal de Arte Decorativo 'Firme y Odilo Estévez'**, the **Snowball Building** (1906–08) and the **Palace of the Post and Telegraph Company** (1934–48), which were all once family homes. The **Cathedral of Our Lady of Rosario** was founded in 1731 and raised to the status of cathedral in 1934 (after modifications in 1925 when the Alcove of the Virgin and entrance portico were added, the façade modified and towers replaced with small domes) and then minor basilica in 1966.

One way to see the city and take in most of the gorgeous European-style architecture is to take a tour of the theatres and old family homes. Most are in the centre but several are scattered across the city. The affluence and importance of the city of Rosario is apparent in the old family houses and historic buildings. Many incredible homes of wealthy families are now public offices; the **Banco de Santa Fé, Banco Nación, Banco Municipal** and the **Bolsa de Comercio** are found one after the other while walking up Avenida Córdoba. Make sure to look up and see the beautiful cupolas that adorn the corners of some of these buildings. A dedication to Rosarino Ernesto 'Che' Guevara is in Plaza de la Cooperción.

Parks

Parks stretch all along the riverfront creating a long green band of public recreational space. Begin with **Parque J J de Urquiza**, south of downtown, next to the Barrio Martín, which is currently the most expensive *barrio* in the city, with many tall new buildings being erected for a view of the river.

Parque Belgrano continues where Urquiza leaves off. Here the Estación Fluvial is located for boats to the islands (see below). Next comes the **Parque Nacional a la Bandera and monument**, to the north of which is **Parque de España**, between Sarmiento, Wheelwright, España and the river, where an enormous old onbu tree and the College of Parque de España are located. Several tunnels were built in this area originally for trains; they were eventually abandoned and became infamous locales for contraband trade. Today they are simply streets with blindingly bright lights surely putting an end to any shady dealings. Certain extensions of the tunnels reach the college where they are used for temporary art exhibitions; there is also a theatre at the college.

Parque Independencia lies between Avenida Pellegrini, Boulevard 27 de Febrero, Moreno and Avenida Ovidio Lagos. There are museums, sports clubs and the horseracing track within this lovely large park. An area called **El Rosedal** is full of rosebushes and other flowers and Spanish tiled gazebos to sit in. A small artificial lake creates a picturesque scene of paddleboats and swans and at night the romantic setting is enhanced by dancing fountains and lights, the **Fuente de Aguas Danzantes** (\ *480 2720; open Thu, Fri & Sun 18.30–21.30, Sat & hols 18.30–22.15, except rainy days*). The **Jardín de los Niños** (children's park) is also in Parque Independencia (\ *480 2611; open Wed–Fri 08.30–12.00, 14.00–17.30, w/ends 13.30–19.00; admission 1 peso*). The Exposición Rural is an annual event with agricultural machinery, produce and livestock. The soccer stadium is also here, home of the Newells Old Boys Club, one of the city's two rival soccer teams (Rosario Central being the other). Further north up the river is **Parque Alem**, between Avenida de los Trabajadores, the Arroyo Ludueña and the Paraná. Several yacht clubs are located here with views over the river of the islands; there is also a public swimming pool.

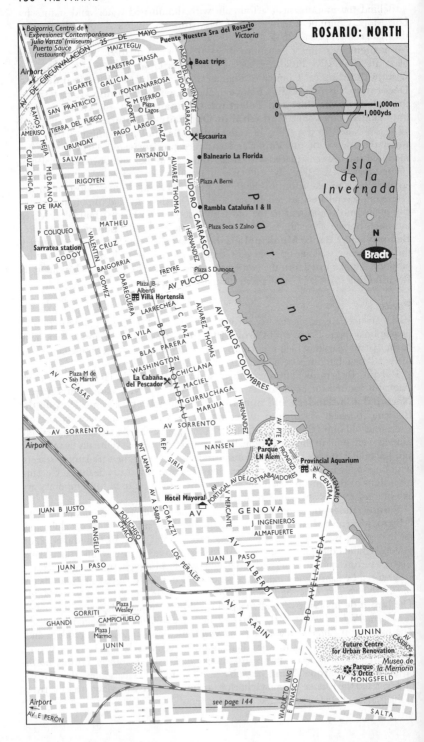

Baigorria, Centro de
Expresiones Contemporáneas
'Julio Vanzo' (museum)
Puerto Sauce
(restaurant)

DE MAYO
MAIZTEGUI
Puente Nuestra Sra del Rosario
Victoria

Airport

AV DE CIRCUNVALACIÓN

25

MAESTRO MASSA

UGARTE   GALICIA

SAN PRATRICIO   P FONTANARROSA

TIERRA DEL FUEGO   M FIERRO   Plaza
LAPORTE   O Lagos

URUNDAY   PAGO LARGO

SALVAT

IRIGOYEN

REP DE IRAK

MATHEU

P COLIQUEO

VALENTIN   CRUZ
Sarratea station

GODOY

BAIGORRIA

GOMEZ

DARREGUEIRA

FREYRE

Plaza JB   AV PUCCIO
Alberdi

Villa Hortensia

LARRECHEA

DR VILA

BLAS PARERA

WASHINGTON
La Cabaña   OCHICLANA
del Pescador   MACIEL

GURRUCHAGA

MARUIA

AV
C   Plaza M de
CASAS   San Martín

AV SORRENTO   AV SORRENTO

Airport   NANSEN

Parque
LN Alem

Provincial Aquarium
AV CENTENARIO

Hotel Mayoral   GENOVA

JUAN B JUSTO   J INGENIEROS
ALMAFUERTE

JUAN J PASO   JUAN J PASO

GORRITI   Plaza J
Wesley

GHANDI   CAMPICHUELO

Plaza J
Marmo

JUNIN

JUNIN

Future Centre
for Urban Renovation

Museo de
la Memoria

Parque
S Ortiz

Airport
AV E PERÓN

see page 144

SALTA

Isla
de la
Invernada

N
Bradt

Paraná

Boat trips

Escauriza

Balneario La Florida

Plaza A Berni

Rambla Cataluña I & II

Plaza Seca S Zalno

Plaza S Dumont

AV EUDORO CARRASCO

ALVAREZ THOMAS

MAZA

J HERNANDEZ

AV CARLOS COLOMBRES

C PAZ

J HERNANDEZ

AV PTE A FRONDIZI
AV DE LOS TRABAJADORES

AV PORTUGAL
V MERCANTE

AV A SABIN

BD AVELLANEDA

AV A SABIN

AV MONGSFELD

0   1,000m
0   1,000yds

Entre Rios 480 is the former home of the Guevara family where young Ernesto, or 'Che', was born. The house is inconspicuous and lacks the usual plaques and tributes often bestowed upon former dwellings of important historical personas. Two hundred metres away is a small park, the Plaza de la Comunidad, at Tucumán and Mitre, with a mural of the late Che.

Pedestrian areas and scenic streets
The tree-lined Boulevard Oroña is resplendent with old French villas and green gardens and parks. Many universities and institutions are housed in some of the larger villas and estates. The pedestrianised streets Córdoba (between Paraguay and Laprida), Paseo del Siglo (between Paraguay and España) and San Martín (between Santa Fé and Mendoza) are lined with shops, bars and cafés.

Museums
Museo del Bolsa de Comercio Corrientes and Córdoba; ℄ 421 3471, 421 3478, int 2121. Museum of the stock exchange. *Open Mon–Fri 10.00–16.30; free admission.*
Museo Histórico Provincial Dr Julio Marc Parque Independencia; ℄ 472 1457. The heritage of the pre-Hispanic and colonial eras. *Open Tue–Fri 09.00–17.00, Sat & hols 14.30–17.30, Sun 10.00–13.00; free admission.*
Museo Municipal de Bellas Artes Juan B Castagnino Av Pellegrini and Bd Oroño; ℄ 480 2542, 480 2543. This building dating from 1937 houses a collection of more than 1,600 works of art, paintings and sculpture by Argentine artists including Prilidiano Pueyrredón, Antonio Berni, Eduardo Schiavoni and Benito Quinquela Martín. *Open Mon–Sat 14.00–20.00, Sun 13.00–19.00; admission 1 peso.*
Museo de la Ciudad Bd Oroño 2350, Parque Independencia; ℄ 480 8665. The city's history museum. *Open Tue–Fri 09.00–12.00, w/ends 15.00–19.00; free admission.*
Museo Municipal de Arte Decorativo Firma y Odilo Estévez Santa Fé 748; ℄ 480 2547. Inaugurated in 1968 to hold a collection of art corresponding to the different cultures who came here since the colonial times. *Open Thu–Sun 16.00–20.00; free admission.*
Museo del Paraná y las Islas Estación Fluvial de Rosario, Av Belgrano and Rioja; ℄ 440 0751, 437 1953, 15 504 6116. Interprets the importance of the river and the surrounding floodplain to the city and displays paintings of Raúl Domínquez (known as the painter of the river). *Open Wed–Sun 15.00–18.30; admission 1 peso.*
Complejo Astronómico Municipal Montevideo and Av Belgrano, Parque Urquiza; ℄ 480 2533, 480 2554. An observatory, planetarium and museum of experimental sciences. **Observatorio 'Victorio Capolongo'** is open for stargazing Wed–Fri 20.30–22.00, w/ends 20.00–22.00; free admission. **Planetario Luis Cándido Carballo** is open w/ends 17.00–18.00; admission 2 pesos. **Museo Experimental de Ciencias.** This science museum suffered a serious fire in 2003 and lost most of its extensive collection. The museum is being rebuilt with a re-opening date yet to be fixed.
Acuario Provincial de Rosario Paseo Ribereño and Cordiviola; ℄ 472 4695. *Open Mon–Fri 08.00–13.00, 14.00–18.00, Sat & Sun 15.00–18.00.*
Villa Hortensia – Centro Municipal Distrito Norte Warnes 1917; ℄ 480 6822. A 19th-century Italian Renaissance-style villa. *Open Mon–Fri 08.00–18.00, Sat & Sun 15.00–18.00.*
Museo de la Memoria in the Rosario Norte railway station, ℄ 480 4511. A memorial to those lost both in the Holocaust and in Argentina's Dirty War. *Open Mon–Fri 08.00–20.00, Sun 10.00–18.00.*

Entertainment and nightlife
There are a few cinemas in the city, but the Cine El Cairo (*Santa Fé 1120;* ℄ *421 9180*) is almost a historic building as well, a classic theatre from years back adding old-fashioned ambiance to your movie. Modern cinemas include Cine

Monumental (*San Martín 999;* ☎ *421 6289*), Cines del Siglo (*Córdoba and Roca;* ☎ *425 0761*) and Cine del Patio (*Sarmiento 778*).

Casa d'Arte Teatro del Rayo San Martín 473; ☎ 421 3980. A small theatre staging mostly independent plays.

Teatro El Círculo Laprida 1235 and Mendoza; ☎ 448 3784; f 424 5349; e info@teatroelcirculo.com.ar. This old opera house was recently given a major restoration to show off the splendour of its frescoed ceiling, its gilt balconies and crystal chandeliers. In the basement is a collection of religious art and statues.

In addition there are two other theatres in the city for live performances, the **Teatro Lavarden** (*Mendoza and Sarmiento;* ☎ *472 1462*) and **Teatro Vivencias** (*Mendoza 1173;* ☎ *424 2539*).

The *Cartelera* section of *Rosario/12*, the local daily newspaper, has the fullest entertainment listings; tickets for many events can be bought at the Ateneo bookstore (*Córdoba 1473*).

Shopping

Aside from the busy shopping area of the pedestrianised Avenida Córdoba, there are several markets in the city.

Centro Artesanal Parque Alem An old textile factory that has been restored and converted into a large shopping mall. *Open 15.30–19.30 w/ends and national hols.*

Feria del Boulevard Bd Oroño and Wheelwright. An outdoor craft market with 120 stands. *Open winter (Apr–Nov) Sat 14.00–20.00, Sun & hols 10.00–20.00; summer (Dec–Mar) w/ends & hols 17.00–22.00.*

Mercado Retro 'La Huella' In front of the Rosario Norte railway station; ☎ 421 8147. Antiques. *Open Sun 10.00–18.00.*

Feria de Artesanías del Boulevard Bd Oroño and Av Rivadavia. *Open Sat 14.00–20.00, Sun 10.00–20.00.*

Mercado de Pulgas Av Belgrano and Buenos Aires. Flea market and craft fair. *Open w/ends 14.00–20.00.*

Artesanos Plaza Sarmiento Entre Ríos between San Luis and San Juan. *Open Thu–Sat 10.00–18.00.*

Centro Artesanal Pichincha Callao and Brown. *Open w/ends and hols 10.00–18.00.*

Daytrips and excursions
Visiting the islands

Across the river from Rosario are thousands of river islands created by the countless streams that wind through this vast wetland area. There are many little lakes for fishing and the birdlife is astounding. In the spring you will see great storks nesting and preparing for their own special deliveries. This birdwatching paradise is painted with the flashy pinks of the flocks of flamingoes and foraging spoonbill. The diversity of birds is so great that you will start to feel your binoculars are glued to your eyes! Contrasting with all this water are the grasslands – this area is still considered the pampas. It is oddly surreal to stare out at a typical scene of a gaucho on horseback amid a field of heifers and watch a fisherman paddle into the frame on his little boat as he navigates the many streams that pass through these fields.

A few lakes offer good fishing, such as El Perro and Chata and on **Isla Charigue**. For enjoying the beach, **Isla Invernada**, **Isla Ensenada** and **Isla Espinillo** are the most popular. There are bars, restaurants and accommodation on these islands, and on Isla Ensenada there are places to camp and fish such as at El Holandes (☎ *15 641 5880*) or cabins and a restaurant run by Isla Deseada (☎ *455*

7945). Cabins are also rented at Bavañas del Frances (✎ *530 9832*) on the far side of the island, where there is also a restaurant, along the Paraná Viejo. Puerto Pirata is a restaurant and recreation park on one of the furthest north islands reachable for a day trip. The restaurant specialises in river fish and *asado*, and there is plenty of beach for sun-bathing or walking and parkland to explore. Camping is available as well as windsurfing lessons (✎ *453 4994, 15 505 8338, 15 693 3464*).

There are two ports for boats to the islands of Rosario: the main one is the Estación Fluvial, Avenida Belgrano and Rioja, in front of the National Flag Monument, from where boats mainly cross to the Banco San Andres where there are beaches and a bar and at night a great view of the skyline of the city; the other one is Embarcadero Costa Alta, just south of the Rosario–Victoria bridge, at the Rambla Cataluña and Playa Florida, for boats to the northern islands.

Boat tour companies

Barco Ciudad de Rosario ✎ 449 8688. For tours of the nearby islands. From the Estación Fluvial. *W/ends & hols14.30–17.00; 6 pesos, under-10s 1 peso.*

El Biguá Pedro Tuella 952; ✎ 438 0625, 439 9336; e rrppnautico@arnet.com.ar; www.cnauticoavellaneda.com.ar. Half-day, full-day or 2-day excursions along the river cost 30 pesos, 50 pesos and 85 pesos, including meals and accommodation as relevant; accommodation only at the hostel on Isla La Invernada is 20 pesos per person.

A main attraction of the Río Paraná river is the beach area where the crowds of Rosarinos come to beat the summer heat. **La Costanera Sur** and **Norte** run for 15km from Park Urquiza to Embarcadero and La Costa Alta. While the Costanera Sur is active year-round, the Norte is most popular in the summer months with public beaches and bars on the **Rambla Cataluña**. The most popular municipal public beach is **Playa Florida,** but you must pay 2 pesos to enter. Across the street, several fish vendors sell fish fresh from the boats. The most important fish are *dorado, boca* and *pejerrey*. In this part of Argentina the *asado*, or grill, will often include fish – butterflied and salted and laid on the flame they are delicious.

Baigorria

North of the city is one of Rosario's riverside suburban *barrios*, Baigorria. It is becoming an upmarket dormitory community of the city where many people have weekend and summer homes. Yet much of the community is an extremely poor sort of shanty town (*villa miseria*) with makeshift houses situated on the riverbanks. Within the community proper is a mix of homes of dispersed economic classes; 50-year-old tin-roofed cinderblock houses neighbour modern upper-middle-class houses with swimming pools or humble boxy houses. The people living along the riverbank are mostly fisher folk and just a short way upstream is a pulp and paper mill that notoriously dumps effluent and toxins into the river, a pollution problem that those further upstream can turn a blind eye towards but the people living along the river bear the brunt of.

Being representative of many *barrios* outside Rosario where poverty is definitely an issue, it is worth seeing, but come by car. There is little public transport and at night safety may be an issue. Coming in the late afternoon to see the area and the port then visiting a riverside restaurant for a fine fish dinner would be the way to experience this *barrio*, which is not a tourist area as such. From the centre you take the motorway to the Costanera Norte, passing the Rambla Cataluña, then under the bridge and inland to Avenida San Martín and Baigorria. Turn right on Lisandro de la Torre to arrive at the port, from where you can see the city centre and the Rosario-Victoria bridge.

Agriculture is an important industry in the province and Rosario is a major grain port. The colourful grain silos, formerly known as Silos Davis, are landmarks along the motorway leading from the city towards Baigorria and have been converted into the **Museo de Arte Contemporáneo Rosario** (on Bd Oraño at the river). Enjoy the art, giftshop, excellent river and city views and the riverside restaurant and bar. *Open Thu–Tue, 16.00–20.00, free.*

Victoria

A day trip across the river to the town of **Victoria** is possible by car (follow the Rosario–Victoria motorway across the bridge) or bus. You will leave the pampas and enter the province of Entre Ríos in Mesopotamia. See page 179 for more details.

SANTA FÉ

Area code 0342

Although the capital city of its province, Santa Fé is not a demonstrative city; however, it has a lovely riverfront with the pedestrianised Avenida Leandro Alem running its length lined by old-style street lamps that make for an elegant evening stroll but is also popular for walking, jogging and cycling.

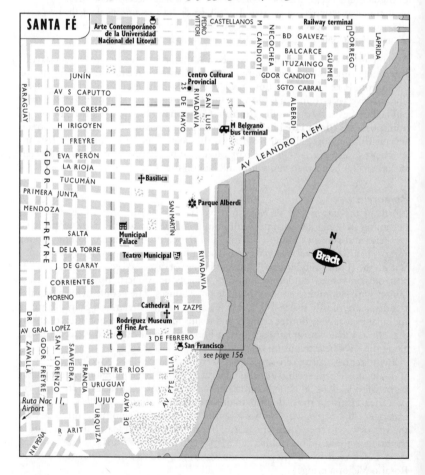

Getting there
By air
Aerolíneas Argentinas (*25 de Mayo 2287;* ✆ *452 5959, 452 7251;* e *sfngte@aerolineas.com.ar; open Mon–Fri 08.30–12.00, 16.00–19.30, Sat 08.30–12.00*) has flights most days from Buenos Aires, arriving at the Aeródromo Sauce Viejo, 15km south (✆ *499 5064, 499 5061*); *remises* provide transport to and from the city.

By bus
The Manuel Belgrano bus terminal is at Belgrano 2910 at Hipólito Irigoyen. The commuter bus that passes through the tunnel between Santa Fé and Paraná (2.60 pesos) runs every 20–60 minutes around the clock, operated by Empresa de Transito Fluviales del Litoral (*in Santa Fé, Boletería 26,* ✆ *455 4132; in Paraná: Belgrano 59;* ✆ *423 0342 or at Boletería 14;* ✆ *431 3689*).

From Rosario there are frequent departures with Tata Rapido (✆ *0341 439 5461*) and Nuevo Rápido San José (✆ *0341 439 8493*). Travel time is two hours, cost 13.50 pesos.

By train
An overnight train travels from Buenos Aires (specifically Retiro train station) and Rosario to Santa Fé on Friday, returning on Sunday. The journey takes about ten and a half hours and costs about 20 pesos.

By car
From Buenos Aires take Ruta 9 to Rosario, then Ruta 11 to Santa Fé (continuing north to Resistencia). Ruta 19 leads west to Córdoba. Santa Fé and Paraná are connected by Ruta 168, passing under the river by the Uranga–Sylvestre Begnis tunnel.

Orientation
Heading three blocks south from the railway station will take you to the end of the Santa Fé port. From here you can follow the pedestrianised riverside Avenida Leandro Alem. Alternatively, turning west away from the river you will come to Avenida San Martín, a popular pedestrianised street leading south to the main Plaza 25 de Mayo.

Where to stay
Holiday Inn San Jerónimo 2779; ✆ 410 1200; e info@holidaystafe.com.ar. The best hotel in town. 120 pesos for a dbl.
Hotel Conquistador 25 de Mayo 2676; ✆ 455 1195. Sgls 69–79 pesos, dbls 79–89 pesos.
Gran Hotel España 25 de Mayo 2647; ✆ 400 8834; e linverde@gigared.com. Sgls 40–57 pesos, dbls for 59–69 pesos.
Hotel Castelar 25 de Mayo 2349; ✆ 456 0999; e castelarhotel@arnet.com.ar. Sgls start at 42 pesos, dbls at 57 pesos.
Hotel Gran Carlitos Irigoyen Freyre 2336; ✆ 453 1541. Sgls 26 pesos, dbls 30 pesos.
Hotel Niza Rivadavia 2755; ✆ 452 2047. Sgls 22 pesos, dbls 32 pesos.

Where to eat and drink
Grilled fish is the speciality at the riverside restaurant **El Quincho de Chiquito**, at Alte Brown 7100 at Obispo Principe (✆ *460 2608*). This is well north of the centre near the very weird monument to Carlos Monzón – take bus No. 16. Both the food and the prices are popular. In the centre are **El Brigadier** (*San Martín 1670;* ✆ *458 01607*) and **España** (*San Martín 2644;* ✆ *400 8834*).

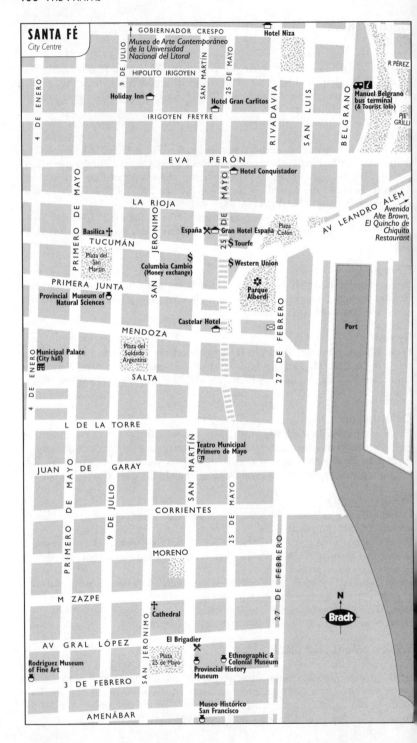

SANTA FÉ
City Centre

GOBERNADOR CRESPO

Hotel Niza

Museo de Arte Contemporáneo de la Universidad Nacional del Litoral

9 DE JULIO

HIPOLITO IRIGOYEN

SAN MARTÍN

25 DE MAYO

R PÉREZ

4 DE ENERO

Holiday Inn

Hotel Gran Carlitos

RIVADAVIA

SAN LUIS

BELGRANO

Manuel Belgrano bus terminal (& Tourist Info)

PJE GRILLI

IRIGOYEN FREYRE

EVA PERÓN

PRIMERO DE MAYO

MAYO

Hotel Conquistador

LA RIOJA

25 DE MAYO

AV LEANDRO ALEM

Avenida Alte Brown, El Quincho de Chiquito Restaurant

Basilica †

TUCUMÁN

SAN JERÓNIMO

España

Gran Hotel España

Plaza Colón

Plaza del San Martín

$ Tourfe

Columbia Cambio (Money exchange)

$ Western Union

PRIMERA JUNTA

Provincial Museum of Natural Sciences

Parque Alberdi

Castelar Hotel

MENDOZA

27 DE FEBRERO

Port

4 DE ENERO

Municipal Palace (City hall)

Plaza del Soldado Argentina

SALTA

L DE LA TORRE

Teatro Municipal Primero de Mayo

SAN MARTÍN

JUAN DE GARAY

PRIMERO DE MAYO

9 DE JULIO

SAN MAYO

CORRIENTES

25 DE MAYO

MORENO

27 DE FEBRERO

M ZAZPE

Cathedral †

SAN JERÓNIMO

N

Bradt

AV GRAL LÓPEZ

El Brigadier

Rodriguez Museum of Fine Art

Plaza 25 de Mayo

Provincial History Museum

Ethnographic & Colonial Museum

3 DE FEBRERO

Museo Histórico San Francisco

AMENÁBAR

Practicalities

There is a one-person show at the tiny **tourist information** desk in the bus terminal, with extremely limited information available and nothing in English. There are two government websites that offer some assistance: www.santafeciudad.gov.ar and www.turismo.santafe.gov.ar.

The **Hospital Provincial** is at José Maria Cullen, Irigoyen Freyre (✆ 457 3350, 457 3359; *emergencies* ✆ 107, 455 4634, 457 3359). For **police** ✆ 452 9984.

There are banking and money exchange facilities at **Columbia Cambio** (*San Martín 2275;* ✆ 456 5802 or 456 5668); **Tourfe** (*San Martín 2550;* ✆ 455 0157/8); or **Western Union** (*San Martín 2500/2600*).

The **post office** is at Avenida 27 de Febrero 2331 and there are several internet cafés on the 2500 and 2900 blocks of Avenida San Martín.

The pedestrian strip of San Martín and the Shopping Estación Recoleta on Rivadavia and Gelabert are the two main **shopping** areas.

Museums

Museo de Arte Contemporáneo de la Universidad Nacional del Litoral 9 de Julio 2154; ✆ 457 1182/3. Contemporary art in rotating shows. *Open Tue–Fri 09.00–13.00, w/ends 16.00–20.00; free admission.*

Museo Rodríguez de Bellas Artes 4 de Enero 1510; ✆ 457 3577. The city's main art gallery. *Open Tue–Fri 08.00–12.00, 16.00–20.00, Sat & Sun 16.00–20.00.*

Museo Provincial de Ciencias Naturales Florentino Ameghino Primera Junta 2859; ✆ 457 3730. Natural history, especially the birds of the region. *Open Mon–Wed 08.00–12.00, 14.00–20.00, Sat 16.00–19.00; free admission.*

Museo Histórico San Francisco Amenábar 2557; ✆ 459 3303. The museum is within the San Francisco Convent and contains historical documents, antique objects, artwork, silver items, colonial furniture, weapons, coins and other elements that recall the history of Santa Fé. *Open Mon–Fri 08.00–12.00, 16.00–18.30, Sat 08.00–12.00, 16.00–18.00, Sun 09.30–12.00, 16.00–18.00.*

Museo Histórico Provincial Gen. Estanislao López San Martín 1490; ✆ 459 3760. This museum is housed in a 17th-century building and is filled with antiques and historical objects. *Open Tue–Fri 08.00–12.00, 16.00–19.00, Sat & Sun 16.00–18.00.*

Museo Etnográfico y Colonial Juan de Garay 25 de Mayo 1470; ✆ 457 3550. A collection of items related to the founding of the city. *Open Tue–Fri 08.30–12.00, 15.30–19.00, Sat & Sun 16.00–18.30.*

Córdoba Province

Landlocked in the absolute centre of the country, Córdoba province makes up for its isolation by having everything of interest within its boundaries. The large capital city of Córdoba is an important historical centre full of secular and religious colonial architecture; missionaries established most of the surrounding towns. Far from the Andes, Córdoba instead has its own independent mountains, the Central Sierras. Juxtaposed against the homogenous flat-as-a-pancake pampas where barely a hiccup of a hill exists, the Central Sierras showboat onto the empty stage and appear as if they were tossed up by the landscape in a burst of architectural inspiration. There are three mountain chains: the Sierras Chica in the east, Sierras Grande in the centre, and the Sierra del Pocho, which becomes the Sierra de Guasapampa, in the west. The highest peak is Champaquí (2,884m), which is a national monument of 12,000ha. Wildlife in the province is abundant, with pampas and montane habitats home to a wide array of species, such as burrowing owls, rheas, maras and guanaco in the grasslands and condors at their most eastern range in the sierras.

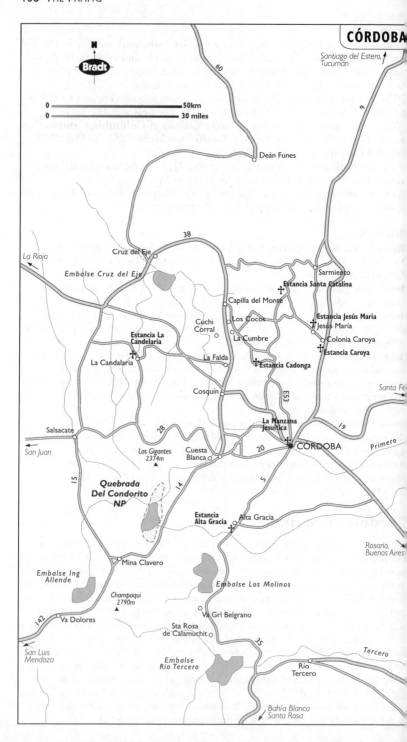

ÓRDOBA

a code 0351

unded in 1573 by Jerónimo Luis de Cabrera, Córdoba was soon settled by Jesuit ssionaries who made it and the surrounding towns the ecclesiastical heart of the intry, establishing monasteries and universities for the study of art, literature l religion. The Nueva Córdoba adjacent to Parque Sarmiento was once the r's aristocratic neighbourhood, as can be seen from the neoclassical architecture Palacio Ferrerya, built in 1900. Since the Universidad Nacional de Córdoba was iblished here, the *barrio* has remained one of the most interesting of Córdoba for blend of antiquity and youth. Today there are many modern buildings for dent housing that also line the streets; but with this compromise has come a re youthful and energetic atmosphere, complete with internet cafés, pizzerias l bars.

etting there

air

rdoba International Airport is 11km north on Camino a Pajas Blancas (✆ 475 2, 475 0874, 475 0877).

Aerolíneas Argentinas (*Colón 520;* ✆ *410 7676, 0810 2228 6527; orqte@aerolineas.com.ar*) flies from Buenos Aires to Córdoba on Monday, ursday and Sunday, and also connects Córdoba with several other major cities vith Mendoza daily, Salta on Monday, Wednesday and Thursday; Jujuy on esday, Friday and Sunday; Tucumán on Sunday, Monday, Wednesday and day; and Iguazú on Thursday and Sunday.

LAN Argentina (*Figueroa Alcorta 206 at Colón;* ✆ *425 3030, toll-free 0800 222 2424*) ves Córdoba from Buenos Aires three times a day Monday to Friday and once Saturday and Sunday. Its parent LAN Chile has flights from Santiago daily and hts from Rosario on Monday, Wednesday, Friday and Sunday.

Public bus A5 leaves from the parking lot and goes downtown (0.80 peso token). ere is also a shuttle service with Transfer Express (✆ *475 9199/9201; ransfercba@datafull.com*), and taxis charge approximately 9 pesos to take you vntown. Hertz (✆ *475 0581 or 475 0587;* e *hertzcordoba@arnet.com.ar; w.milletrentacar.com.ar*) and Avis (✆ *475 0815 or 475 0785;* e *cordoba@avis.com.ar; w.avis.com*) car rental agencies are both located at the airport.

bus

e main bus terminal is at Boulevard Perón 380 (✆ *434 1692/94; w.terminalcordoba.com*) at one corner of Parque Sarmiento. Approximately 25 bus npanies have daily services to Córdoba from Buenos Aires with various levels service: a basic service costs 44 pesos; a *semicama* bus costs 45 pesos; *supercama* 55 os; and first class 70 pesos.

Mercobus Plus Ultra (✆ *427 2727*) connects Córdoba and Rosario overnight hours) for 25 pesos. From Mendoza buses to Córdoba are run by San Juan r del Plata (✆ *422 1951*), TAC (✆ *423 7666*) and Expreso Uspallata (✆ *425 6*), costing about 35 pesos for a regular seat or 45 pesos for *semicama*. Service ween Córdoba and Bariloche is offered by TUS (✆ *429 9510*) in a first-class t for 118.50 pesos or with TAC in a *semicama* for 110 pesos. The trip takes just der 24 hours.

car

rdoba is centrally located and can therefore be reached from almost every part he country. The Circunvalación is a motorway that encircles the entire city. All

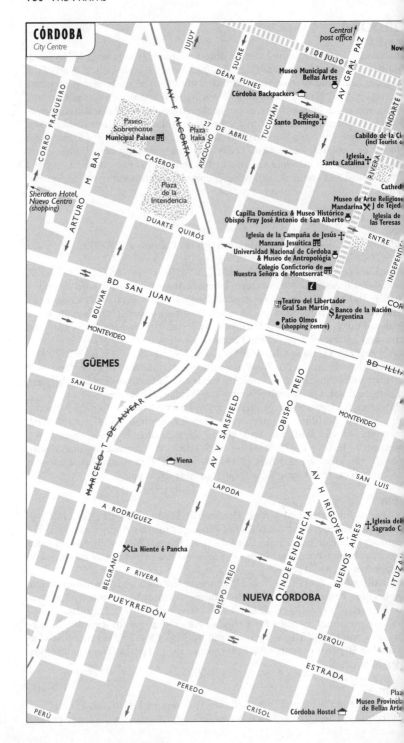

CÓRDOBA
City Centre

Central post office

9 DE JULIO

Nov

JUJUY

SUCRE

DÉAN FUNES

Museo Municipal de
Bellas Artes

AV F ALCORTA

AV GRAL PAZ

INDARTE

Córdoba Backpackers

TUCUMÁN

27 DE ABRIL

Eglesia
Santo Domingo

CORRO FRAGUEIRO

Paseo
Sobremonte
Municipal Palace

Plaza
Italia

AXACUCHO

Cabildo de la Ci
(incl Tourist o

CASEROS

Iglesia
Santa Catalina

RIVERA

M BAS

Plaza
de la
Intendencia

Cathed

Sheraton Hotel,
Nuevo Centro
(shopping)

Museo de Arte Religios
Mandarina J de Tejed

ARTURO M BAS

DUARTE QUIRÓS

Capilla Doméstica & Museo Histórico
Obispo Fray José Antonio de San Alberto

Iglesia de
las Teresas

ENTRE

Iglesia de la Campaña de Jesús
Manzana Jesuítica
Universidad Nacional de Córdoba
& Museo de Antropológia
Colegio Confictorio de
Nuestra Señora de Montserrat

INDEPENDE

BD SAN JUAN

BOLIVAR

Teatro del Libertador
Gral San Martín
Patio Olmos
(shopping centre)

Banco de la Nación
Argentina

COR

MONTEVIDEO

GÜEMES

BD ILLI

SAN LUIS

MARCELO T DE ALVEAR

AV V SARSFIELD

OBISPO TREJO

MONTEVIDEO

Viena

LAPODA

AV H IRIGOYEN

SAN LUIS

A RODRÍGUEZ

INDEPENDENCIA

BUENOS AIRES

Iglesia del
Sagrado C

ITUZA

BELGRANO

La Niente é Pancha

F RIVERA

OBISPO TREJO

PUEYRREDÓN

NUEVA CÓRDOBA

DERQUI

ESTRADA

PEREDO

Plaz
Museo Provincia
de Bellas Arte

PERÚ

CRISOL

Córdoba Hostel

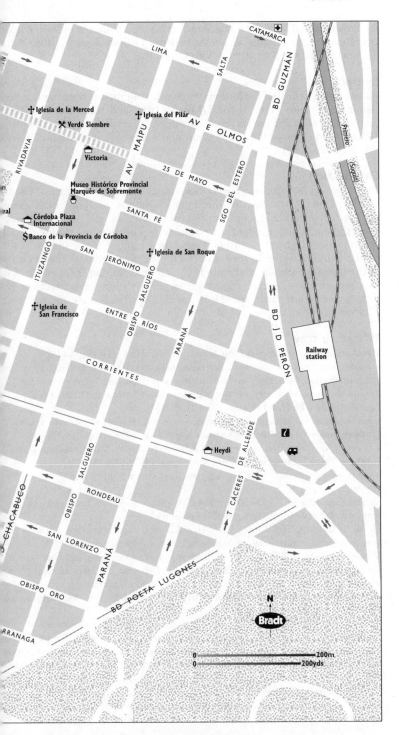

the Provincial and National routes therefore intersect with it in order to enter ‖ city: Ruta 9 from Rosario/Buenos Aires, Ruta 19 from Santa Fé, Ruta 9 fro Tucumán/Salta, and Ruta 20 from Villa Carlos Paz.

By train

An overnight train leaves Córdoba on Sunday afternoon, reaching the Ret station in Buenos Aires about 14 hours later, and returning on Mond evenings. Seats cost from 25 pesos and sleeper compartments (for two peop 150 pesos. In Córdoba the station is just north of the bus terminal on Bouleva Perón (↘ 426 3565).

Orientation

The city is set on a grid and is easy to navigate. The historic centre of Córdo is Plaza San Martín, where the Iglesia Catedral becomes magnificen silhouetted at sunset. Facing the cathedral, Avenida San Martín extends your right and Independencia to your left. The avenues running para‖ behind the cathedral, Obispo Trejo (becoming Rivera Indarte to t right/north) and Sarsfield (becoming General Paz), are the addresses for m‖ of the historic buildings and churches. Heading south on Independencia a‖ turning left on to Avenida Irigoyen, you will arrive in a few blocks at Pla España and Parque Sarmiento. Note that almost all streets are one way, exc‖ Illia/San Juan (see map).

Where to stay

Hotel and Spa Santa Cecilia I José Ingenieros 299, Villa Carlos Paz; ↘ 421258; e info@hotelsantacecilia.com; www.hotelsantacecilia.com. If you are suffering a few ache and pains from all the trekking in the mountains or perhaps from too much trekking through the streets of the city, you may want to consider a stay at this hotel with a spa. **Sheraton Córdoba Hotel** Duarte Quiros 1300; ↘ 526 9000; e reservas@sheratoncordoba.com; www.sheraton.com/cordoba. Dbl rooms from US$11‖ **Holiday Inn** Fray Luis Beltrán and Manuel Cardeñosa; ↘ 477 9100; e reservas@holidayinncba.com.ar; www.holidayinncba.com.ar. Dbl rooms from US$80. **Córdoba Plaza Internacional Hotel** San Jerónimo 137; ↘ 426 8900/99; e reservas@corplaza.com; www.corplaza.com. Rates start at 125 pesos sgl, 150 pesos dbl plus tax. **Cristal** Entre Ríos 58; ↘f 535 5000; e hoteles@arnet.com.ar; www.hotelcristal.com.ar. Rates start at 80 pesos sgl, 92 pesos dbl, 102 pesos triple. **Heydi** Bd Illia 619; ↘f 421 8906, 423 3544, 422 2219; e info@hotelheydi.com.ar; www.hotelheydi.com.ar. Rates are 64 pesos sgl, 79 pesos dbl, 95 pesos triple. **Victoria** 25 de Mayo 240; ↘ 421 0198, 429 0898; e hotelvictoria@hotmail.com; www.granhotelvictoria.net. Rates start at 40 pesos sgl, 60 pesos dbl, 80 pesos triple. **Viena** Laprida 235; ↘ 463 9814, 460 0909; e hotelviena@ciudad.com.ar; www.hotelviena.com.ar. Standard rooms start at 44 pesos sgl, 56 pesos dbl, 76 pesos triple including b/fast. Superior rooms are slightly pricier. **Estancia Los Potreros** ↘f 03548 452121; m 0 3548 (15) 566628; e info@ride-americas.com; www.ride-americas.com. Set in a nature reserve at the top of the Córdoba hills. The estancia dates from 1574, a time when the area focused on breeding mules that were the beasts of burden working the silver mines in Peru. Today, however, the British-style estancia raises Paso Peruano horses and Aberdeen-Angus cattle. Horseriding is a principal activity at the estancia, for fun around the ranch or for organised overnight trips. The cost to stay at the estancia is about 600 pesos per person (US$230) with a 3-night minimum stay, which includes full board, activities and transfers.

ostelling International runs two clean, reputable hostels in Córdoba where there is
ways a good gathering of backpackers and adventure travellers with staff willing and
le to provide excursions or information to take advantage of the many activities in
e province. At **Córdoba Hostel** (*Ituzaingó 1070;* ↘ *468 7359;*
info@cordobahostel.com.ar, reservas@hostels.org.ar; www.cordobahostel.com) dorms cost
1 pesos and rooms with private bath cost 35 pesos for two, 52 pesos for four and 60
esos for six people. At **Córdoba Backpackers** (*Deán Funes 285;* ↘ *15 515 4989 or
22 0293;* e *cbhostel@arnet.com.ar, cbhostel@hotmail.com; www.cordobabackpackers.com.ar*)
orms cost 11 pesos; doubles cost 32 pesos with bathroom, 28 pesos without; and a
ur-person room with bathroom costs 12 pesos per person.

Where to eat and drink

Mandarina Obispo Trejo 171; ↘ 424 0795; e mandarinabar@uol.com.ar. If you need to
ve your system a rest from Argentine steak, there are plenty of vegetarian meals and
licious dishes that are a fusion of Asian and traditional cuisine. On w/ends there is often
guitarist or other live music. The dessert with the enticing translated name of 'Flaming
udin' is enthusiastically recommended.
erde Siempre 9 de Julio 36; ↘ 421 8820. A vegetarian restaurant that also serves vegan
shes and has a buffet salad bar.
a Nienta é Pancha Belgrano 783; ↘ 469 0229, 471 3248, 468 1920. Serves regional
órdobesa cuisine.

the Güemes neighbourhood near Avenida Belgrano and the antique shops and
arket (see Shopping) there are many good restaurants, and in Nueva Córdoba
ere are many cafés, bars and restaurants.

Practicalities

or such a large city, the **tourist office** in the historic Cabildo de la Ciudad, near
laza San Martín at Rosario de Santa Fé 39 (\/f *433 2749;* e *munturis@cordoba.gov.ar*),
a bit short on information. The staff are extremely helpful but lacking the glossy
aps, restaurant and hotel lists and other city details that would be expected. There's
other office at the Patio Olmos shopping centre three blocks away on Corrientes
d a third in the railway station. An alternative is to check out the Casa de Córdoba
Buenos Aires, where the helpful staff speak English,
The central **post office**, Correo Central, is on Avenida Carlo Paz at Avenida
olón. The **Banco de la Provincia de Cófo de Arecordoba** is at San Jerónimo
6 (↘ *420 7200, 420 7407*), and the **Banco de la Nación Argentina** has several
cations, many along 25 de Mayo, as well as at Obispo Trejo 385 between San
an and Duarte Quirós and at the airport.
Gay and Lesbian Travel (*General Paz 120, Piso 3, Oficina H;* \/f *422 0316;*
156 288130; e *info@gayandlesbiantravel.com.ar*) is a group of bilingual travel agents
fering trustworthy recommendations for accommodation, dining, entertainment
d excursions.

Highlights

uided city tours on a double-decker London bus run daily from Plaza San Martín
front of the cathedral (↘ *424 7999, 421 8012*).
What characterises Córdoba are the many beautiful churches. The Iglesia
atedral in Plaza San Martín looms dramatically overhead but it is difficult to get
clear view of the building from any point in the narrow plaza. Construction
gan in 1577 and proceeded slowly, under first the Jesuits and then the
anciscans, after the Jesuits were ousted from the country in 1767. The building
therefore a mix of architectural styles with a Neo-Baroque interior.

The 17th-century Carmelite church **Iglesia de las Teresas** is dow Independencia just off Plaza San Martín and next door to it, at No. 122, is the **Muse de Arte Religioso Juan de Tejeda** (*Wed–Sat 09.30–12.30; admission 1 peso*).

The **Manzana Jesuítica** or Jesuit Block starts with the **Iglesia de I Compañia de Jesús**. The Manzana is the actual block of buildings whos construction began in 1608. The first was the **Colegio Máximo** (1610), whic later became the first university in Argentine territory, the **Universida Nacional de Córdoba**. The **Colegio Confictorio de Nuestra Señora d Monserrat** was built in 1687 but rebuilt in 1782 after the expulsion of th Compañia. The **Noviciado** dates to approximately 1710. The church of I Companie and the **Capilla Doméstica** chapel were built in 1644 and 1671 in th Baroque style of the colonial era in Argentina. After the expulsion of the Jesui the Manzana was taken over by the Franciscans until 1853 when the universi and college were taken over by the state. *Open Tue–Sun 09.00–13.00, 17.00–20.0(tickets 3 pesos. Tours with bilingual guides 10.00, 11.00, 17.00, 18.00;* ❭ *433 207. e museo_historicounc@yahoo.com.ar.*

The **Museo Histórico Obispo Fray José Antonio de San Alberto**, facin the Capilla Doméstica at Caseros 124 (*Tue–Fri 08.30–12.30, Sat 9.30–12.3(admission 2 pesos*) has a standard display of religious art and also covers the Jesuit activities as educators and missionaries.

Other museums

Botanical Gardens Yunyent 5491; ❭ 433 7327, 433 7326. *Free admission.*
Centro de Arte Contemporáneo Complejo Ferial Córdoba. *Open Tue–Sun 16.00–21.0(free admission.*
Museo de Antropología de la UNC Hipólito Irigoyen 174. *Open Mon–Sat 10.00–13.00, 16.00–19.00.*
Museo del Banco de la Provincia y Archivo Histórico San Jerónimo 166. *Open daily; free admission.*
Museo Histórico Provincial Marqués de Sobremonte Rosario de Santa Fé and Ituzaingo. *Open Mon–Fri 08.30–14.30.*
Museo Municipal de Bellas Artes Genaro Pérez Av General Paz 33. *Open Tue–Sun 09.00–21.00; free admission.*
Museo Provincial de Bellas Artes Emilio Caraffa Av Leopoldo Lugones 411 at Deodoro Roca. This modern-art museum is housed in a neoclassical building typical of th neighbourhood. *Open Tue–Sun 13.00–19.00; free admission.*
Museo Universitario de Tecnología Aeroespacial Av Fuerza Aerea 5500. *Open daily 08.00–14.00; guided tours Tue–Thu 09.00–12.00.*

Entertainment

Teatro del Libertador General San Martín Sarsfield 365. The oldest theatre in Argentina and arguably one of the most beautiful, it was inaugurated in April 1891 and in 1991 was declared a National Historical Monument.
Teatro Real San Jerónimo 66; ❭ 434 1150/1. *Ticket office open Mon–Fri 09.00–13.00, 16.00–20.00.*

Shopping

There are many street markets in Córdoba at weekends and holidays, from 18.00 ❭ 23.00. One of the most popular is the **Feria de las Antiguedades, Reciclados Curiosidades**, Pasaje Revol and Belgrano, also Friday. Avenida Belgrano is full ❬ antique shops to explore during regular shopping hours. Off Belgrano is Rodrígu(where another large and popular market, the **Paseo de las Artes**, is a labyrinth ❬

vendors selling jewellery, leather, art and various handmade pieces. It also opens on Friday evening. The **Feria de Flores y Plantas** (plants and flowers market) is at Patio del Paseo, Paseo de las Artes, also at Belgrano 770. Other art and craft markets are at Paseo de los Niños, Centro Cultural Manuel de Falla, and the **Feria Artesenal del Parque Las Heras**, on Boulevard Las Heras, between Lavalleja and Sáenz Peña (also Friday evening). On a sweet last note, the **Feria Artesanal de Savores y Dulzuras** is found on Laprida at the corner of Cañada.

Patio Olmos Shopping Centre (*Bd San Juan at corner of Sarsfield*) is an indoor shopping centre located on the site of the ancient Olmos College; the façade of the building is the only original feature. Tax-free shopping, restaurants and a cinema are all under this roof.

Day trips and excursions
Tren de las Sierras
This tourist train (also known as the *Trencito Serrano* or Little Train of the Hills; ✆ *0351 482 2252*) runs from the Rodríguez del Busto station in Alto Verde *barrio*, 12km west of the city, into the Valle de la Punilla, passing the San Roque dam, Cosquín, La Cumbre, Cruz Grande and Los Cocos and stopping for almost four hours at Capilla del Monte. This excursion runs on Saturday (and perhaps Sunday). The Punilla valley lies between the Sierras Chicas, where Cerro Uritorco (1,979m) and the Pan de Azucar (sugar-loaf mountain, 1,250m) stand out, and the Sierras Grandes, with the Los Gigantes massif (2,374m).

Estancias
Back in the 17th century Córdoba was the capital of the Jesuit Province of Paraguay, which included the territories of Paraguay, Brazil, Uruguay, Bolivia and Argentina. Strong social and economic connections made this area one of the most important religious centres in South America. In 1599 the Jesuits began establishing spectacular estancias with incredible churches. The estancias of Caroya, Jesús María, Santa Catalina, La Candelaria and Alta Gracia were important rural centres and collaborated economically, and can still be visited by car. The founding establishment of 1608, the **Manzana Jesuítica**, is in Córdoba city (see under *Highlights*). Leaving the city, most estancias are found to the north along Ruta Provincial 9.

Estancia Caroya (1616; ✆ *03525 426701*) was the first in the progression of rural estancias in the area. Many early immigrants were housed here. The estancia is a national and provincial historic monument. It has a wide central yard, a chapel, a *perchel* and a *tajamar* or conduit. From here head north on Ruta Provincial 9 towards Colonia Caroya for 48km.

Estancia Jesús María (1618; ✆ *03525 420126;* e *mjn-jm@arnet.com.ar*) was an important wine-making estancia. Elaborately designed in Spanish style, there is a church, residence, *bodega*, mill and *tajamar*.

Estancia Santa Catalina (1622; ✆ *03525 421600;* e *javico@onenet.com.ar*) is the biggest of the Jesuit estancias and was very important economically, with thousands of head of cattle and sheep, and a high level of skill in textile-making. It also had two mills and a *tajamar* that supplied fresh groundwater from several kilometres away. It was declared a National Historical Monument in 1941. The architecture is in the colonial Baroque style adapted from central Europe. Take a secondary road for 20km from Jesús María to reach this rural estancia.

Returning south you'll reach the E53; at the town of Manzano you can take a detour to see **Candonga** and the Jesuit Chapel from 1730. The word *candonga* is an ancient Castilian word for 'loaded old mule', in reference to the hardworking animal that helped pioneer these lands. The chapel was declared a National

Historical Monument in 1941. From the next town, Salsipuedes ('Get Out If You Can'), head west to La Falda and continue onwards to the next Jesuit estancia.

Estancia La Candelaria (1687) is situated in the middle of the vast Sierra plains; take Ruta 38 and at La Falda turn onto a secondary road to the estancia. It has several interesting features in addition to the chapel; there are many ruins in the area as well as the former horse corrals, mill and *tajamar*. It is a unique structure, midway between a fort and a sanctuary.

Last estancia on the itinerary, but one of the most important, is **Estancia Alta Gracia** (1643; ↘ *03547 421303*: e *info@museoliniers.org.ar; www.museoliniers.org.ar*). It was one of the most prosperous of the estancias and its main objective was to support the Colegio Máximo in Córdoba city. In 1810 it became the residence of Viceroy Santiago Liniers and ten years later was bought by José Manuel Solares, who in his will delineated the lands to form the village. The family maintained the ownership of the buildings until 1969 when the national government expropriated them and turned them into a museum, officially opened in 1977. Alta Gracia was also home to Ché Guevara between the ages of four and 20 (1932–48), and having been totally ignored under the junta and for many years after, his birthday on 14 June is now celebrated. From Alta Gracia take the Ruta Provincial 5 northeast for 36km to return to Córdoba.

The towns along Ruta 38
Many wonderful little towns of the Central Sierras lie in a row along Ruta Provincial 38, just northwest of Córdoba city. **Villa Carlos Paz** is actually quite a large and bustling dormitory community of Córdoba. It is popular in the summer for days at the lake. It also acts as a gateway city for the other little towns of Cuesta Blanca, Cosquín, La Falda, La Cumbre and Cruz del Eje. These towns are simpler, quainter and definitely quieter places to stay, and the mountains and the region's excellent outdoor activities are right outside your front door, rather than having to navigate your way out of the big city.

Cuesta Blanca
Allowing you to get into the countryside, which is the real attraction of the area, **Sol Mayor** (*Los Molles s/n;* ↘ *03541 495748;* e *solmayorcuestablanca@yahoo.com.ar*) is a hidden treasure. You have to have faith as you follow the long, winding and bumpy road leading to the hostel. You will see signs with the Hostelling International symbol urging you onwards – keep going! On a hilltop overlooking river valleys and trees full of parrots, José and Roxane run a lovely hostel and cabins surrounded by their organic herb and vegetable gardens that supply the ingredients for their excellent home-cooked menus (which cater very well to vegetarians). The trekking and outdoor activity possibilities are numerous, but just relaxing by the shallow, swimmable river is heavenly. You may even happen across the friendly resident hermit who rejected the city life of Córdoba in the late '90s, set up a lean-to by the river and never left! Dorm beds start at 14 pesos; a double room is 42 pesos; and the cabins sleep two to six people for 60–75 pesos.

La Posada del Qenti (*Ruta 14, km14.5, Icho Cruz;* ☎ *03541 495715;* e *qenticho@dcc.com.ar; www.qenti.com*) is a spa and health centre which will pamper you with its service and the setting. There is also a diet-conscious restaurant. Standard, mountain view and jacuzzi rooms. Further along Ruta 14, at km101, is **La Posta del Qenti** (☎ *03544 426450;* e *laposta@qenti.com, laposta@vdikires.com.ar*) where you will find lodgings starting at 190 pesos single, 260 pesos double, with numerous excursion and outdoor recreation packages.

Cruz del Eje

Cruz del Eje is along the *Ruta del Olivo* and you will recognise this as soon as you drive into town on Ruta 38 and see the kids selling containers of olives on the street. If you are an olive fan, do not hesitate to buy a jar; they are cheap, home-prepared and delicious! Turn south off Ruta 38 onto Avenida Sarmiento to take a scenic detour to the Dique de Cruz del Eje. You will first enter the main plaza of Nuestra Señora del Carmen, dominated by the unexpectedly large basilica. Continuing down the road into the river valley, you will arrive at a lovely park with picnic areas. The damming of the river has tamed the volume and speed of the water, creating a sort of lagoon that is a bird haven. You can have a picnic of olives and pickled *pejerrey* fish and watch the numerous herons, cormorants and ducks in the river. Continue along this road as it winds uphill to the dam and viewing platform.

LA CUMBRE

Area code 03548

Traditions here somewhat reflect those of the English immigrants who arrived with the railway and founded the city. It has always had a strong focus on nature, hiking and exploring the hillsides, and this appreciation of nature continues with its many hikes, drives, viewpoints and adventure excursions available. The quaint town is relaxing and pretty, with little cafés surrounding the main square.

Getting there

By air

There is a small Aero Club La Cumbre (*Camino Presidente Juan Domingo Perón s/n;* ↘ *452544*), but there is no service to the major cities. The closest airport is in Córdoba city, from where a *remise* will cost around 75 pesos. Local taxis are available from Yerba Buena (↘ *452222*).

The Aerolíneas Argentinas office in town is at Belgrano 337 (↘ *451025, 0810 2228 6527;* e *gradellaar@arnet.com.ar*).

By bus

The bus terminal is at Juan José Valle and Ruznak (↘ *452400, 452442, 451955*). From the Retiro station in Buenos Aires there are many daily connections with different schedules and services, and fares ranging between 48 pesos and 85 pesos:

Empresa El Práctico ↘ 452442; in Buenos Aires ↘ 011 4312 9551/52
Empresa General Urquiza/Sierras de Córdoba Tel: 452400; in Buenos Aires ↘ 011 4313 2771
Empresa Merco Bus ↘ 452135; in Buenos Aires ↘ 011 4576 7900.

From La Rioja there are three buses per day charging 18 pesos. From San Juan there are two buses per day, for 25 pesos. From Córdoba city there are four bus companies with various departures between 14.00 and 24.00, for 7 pesos.

Empresa Ciudad de Córdoba ↘ 452442; in Córdoba ↘ 0351 428 2811
Empresa El Serra ↘ 452949; in Córdoba ↘ 0351 426 0036
Empresa La Calera ↘ 452300; in Córdoba ↘ 0351 461 841/42
Empresa Transierras ↘ 451955; in Córdoba ↘ 0351 424 3810, 424 3030

By car

La Cumbre is on Ruta 38 between Villa Carlos Paz to the south and Cruz del Eje to the north. It is 94km northwest of Córdoba city. You can leave Ruta 38 between La Cumbre and the little town of San Estefán and take the more scenic

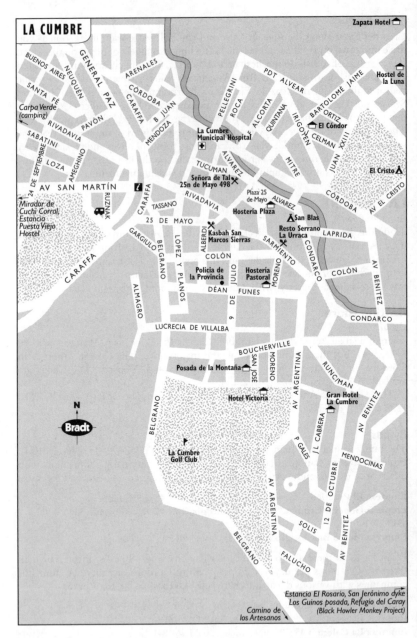

secondary road through Los Cocos, Cruz Chica and Cruz Grande. All along this route are lovely residences, little hotels and B&Bs, small parks and amusement parks and access to footpaths and hiking trails. Alternatively, leaving Córdoba you can take Ruta 9 to Jesús María and then head west to La Cumbre. There is a 'hippy' quality to the area with artists' shops, lavender farms and lots of surrounding nature.

Orientation

The river that divides the town makes finding addresses a bit tricky. The central Plaza 25 de Mayo is on the west bank of the river, with the main streets Alvárez Condarco, Sarmiento and 25 de Mayo leading off it.

Where to stay

Many hotels close in low season, so call ahead for reservations; on the other hand, rates may be lower than usual in those that remain open.

Gran Hotel La Cumbre Posadas s/n; ☎ 451550, 452316;
e info@granhotellacumbre.com.ar; www.granhotellacumbre.com.ar. This 1950s alpine-inspired hotel has a bar, swimming pool and lovely views of the surrounding hills. Dbls start at 135 pesos.

Hostería Pastoral Mariano Moreno 480 on the corner of Déan Funes; ☎ 452787;
e hosteriapastoral@arnet.com.ar; www.hosteriapastoral.com.ar. This *hostería*, surrounded by parks and gardens, has a good restaurant and a swimming pool and is located only 4 blocks from the golf course. Rates start at 110 pesos for a dbl with b/fast.

Hotel Victoria Posadas 254; ☎ 451412; e victoria@agora.com.ar; www.hotelvictoria.com.ar. The building dates back to 1929 and the current hotel has a swimming pool, bar and a restaurant where they take great pride in their food. Rates start at 110 pesos with b/fast.

Zapata Hotel Camino Provincial a Los Cocos, Cruz Grande; ☎ 492058;
e hotelzapata@punillanet.com.ar; www.zapatahotel.com.ar. This rural setting affords access to outdoor pursuits, such as trekking and horseriding. The swimming pool and beautiful scenery make staying at the hotel equally satisfying. Rates start at 76 pesos with b/fast.

El Cóndor Bartolomé Jaime and the corner of Juárez Celman s/n; ☎ 452870; e el_condor_2001@hotmail.com. 50 pesos for a dbl with b/fast.

Hostería Plaza Vásquez Cuesta 538; ☎ 451252; e hosteriaplaza@punillanet.com.ar; www.hosteriaplaza.com.ar. A simple and comfortable setting close to the centre. Rates start at 40/50 pesos for a sgl, 60/70 pesos for a dbl.

Posada de la Montaña 9 de Julio 753; ☎ 451867; e delamontania@arnet.com.ar; www.posadadelamontania.com.ar. Common areas to relax in as well as a swimming pool. With b/fast a sgl is 30/35 pesos, a dbl 45/50 pesos.

Hostel de la Luna Monseñor Pablo Cabrera s/n, Cruz Chica; ☎ 451877;
e informes@delaluna.com.ar; www.delaluna.com.ar. Standard suites are 69/79 pesos with b/fast. The restaurant offers a set menu at 18 pesos per person.

Camping

Several camping options are available: **Carpa Verde** (*Paraje Balata, 4km from the centre off Ruta 38;* ☎ *15 566847;* e *carpaverde@yahoo.com.ar*), **El Cristo** (*Monseñor Pablo Cabrera s/n;* ☎ *452545, 15 636648*) or **San Blas** (*near the river on Sigfrido Scherzer s/n;* ☎ *451886*).

Where to eat

Resto Serrano La Urraca Sarmiento 19. Traditional dishes using only local products and ingredients.

Kasbah San Marcos Sierras Sarmiento 218; ☎ 452865. This fusion restaurant combines Chinese and Indian ingredients and uses organic vegetables to create exotic dishes from Asia in the middle of the pampas.

Señora de Tal 25 de Mayo 498, facing the plaza; ☎ 15 631683. *Parrilla* and pasta.

Practicalities

The **tourist office** is at Avenida Caraffa 300 (☎ *452966;* e *info@lacumbre.gov.ar; www.lacumbre.gov.ar*). The **Hospital Municipal** is off

López at Planes 74 (↘ *451100; in emergency dial 107*); and the **Policia de la Provincia** are at Déan Funes 335 (↘ *456641; in emergency dial 101*).

Activities

At the southeast end of either Avenida Argentina or Benítez you can find the head of the **Camino de los Artesanos**, a road to visit the dozen or more *casas taller,* or workshops of artisans, such as silversmiths and leatherworkers.

La Cumbre Golf Club (*Belgrano s/n;* ↘ *451170, 452283; www.lacumbregolf.com.ar*) is very proud of its 18-hole golf course; services include caddies, instructors and a putting green; there is also a pool and tennis courts.

Mirador de Cuchi Corral, 8km west, is on an 18th-century estancia that was declared a National Historic Monument in 1994, but is more famous for being one of the best locations in the country to practice paragliding (hosting national championships and the 1999 World Cup). You can arrange an instructor and try it for yourself for about 100 pesos.

Paragliding can also be arranged through the **Aero Club La Cumbre** (↘ *452544; Fechu;* ↘ *15 574566;* e *parapentefechu@yahoo.com.ar*) or **El Viejo Piquete** (↘ *15 635948;* e *elviejopiquete@yahoo.com.ar*). Mountain-bike rentals are available through **Rent-a-Bike** (↘ *451575, 15 637451*).

Excursions

Leaving town on Ruta E66 you can drive to the San Jerónimo dam, passing the **Los Guindos** *posada* and restaurant (*Camino al Dique San Jerónimo s/n;* ↘ *451235;* e *los_guindos@hotmail.com*), 5km from town; you can come to eat or choose to stay. Reservations are requested.

One of the most famous sweets factories in the region is that of **Estancia El Rosario** (*Ruta E66;* ↘ *451257 or 452913*). You can come here any day of the week and take a tour of the factory that makes *dulce de leche, alfajores* and other cookies, preserves and condiments. It is 4km from La Cumbre and set on a big beautiful estancia dating from 1924 overlooking hills and valleys. Open daily 08.00–19.00; entrance and tour are free.

Further up the long and winding road through this stunning landscape you will arrive at one of the most interesting, if slightly displaced, attractions of the area – the **Refugio del Carayá** (the Black Howler Monkey Project). A group of conservationists have set up a grassroots initiative to rehabilitate howler monkeys that have been victims of the illegal pet trade and either abandoned by or confiscated from their previous owners. The project currently has over 50 monkeys living in eight social groups, most of which are free-swinging in the trees. This is not the natural habitat of this species; they come from the northern forests of the Chaco, which is seriously threatened by deforestation. The aim is to re-introduce them into their wild habitat, as they are an endangered species, but this is difficult to achieve due to several factors: most of the adult monkeys are no longer self-sufficient, either because they've come to rely on humans to feed them or because they are physically disabled; baby howlers are not weaned for several years, at which time they are as domesticated as their parent; entire social groups must be re-introduced together which adds to the complications; and captive monkeys can introduce disease into wild populations. You can visit this project and see the monkeys climbing in the trees all around you, as well as several orphaned babies. There are also four pumas and a lion that have been rescued from zoos or circuses; neutered, de-clawed and missing teeth, they are also unable to return to the wild. The government has no programme to help them, so they are rescued by the monkey project – which, by the way, receives

QUEBRADA DEL CONDORITO NATIONAL PARK

The 40,000ha Parque Nacional Quebrada del Condorito and the 145,000ha buffer zone of the Reserva Provincial Pampa de Achala were created to protect the headwaters feeding the various dams in the vicinity. High landscape and geomorphologic value are the attractions of this park. The Pampa de Achala is a high pampas rolling across the Sierras Grandes at elevations between 1,900 and 2,300m. Impressive gorges, or *quebradas*, include the Yatán, Batán, del Sur and Corralejo and the namesake of the park, El Condorito, from above which you can look into the canyon and observe the great Andean condors riding the thermals. These birds are apparently an isolated eastern population that is now protected by the park but had often been persecuted by cattle ranchers. It is a rare opportunity to watch the condor from above or at eye level! There is a high level of endemism in the park, with several birds recognised as distinct subspecies, as well as two batrachians, a green lizard and a striped snake, and a race of the red fox, all of which are restricted to Achala. Though difficult to place in the accepted biomes of Argentina, these rolling upland grasslands with occasional patches of *Polylepis* forest and sections of rocky sierra without vegetation are included in the Mountain Chaco district despite the similarities of this zone to Andean uplands.

In prehistoric times the Pampa de Achala was occupied by groups of hunter-gatherers who have left a cultural heritage of artefacts and rock paintings in the rock shelters they once occupied. Frequent finds in the soft bedrock of arrowheads and mortars indicate that the area was a hunting-ground, most probably of the guanaco that was so abundant here. When the arrival of the Spaniards displaced many of the indigenous groups in the area of present-day Buenos Aires province, the Comechingones came to the Pampa de Achala undoubtedly as a refuge from persecution. By the end of the 19th-century waves of colonisers arrived and established estancias. Today, presumed descendants of these first Europeans now merit the name *Achalenses* or 'del alto'. Small landowners, somewhat dispersed in the area, live in family groups in simple rustic houses. Isolated from the market economy and modern technology, they maintain a social structure within their own strict sense of values and beliefs. They live off the land and local materials, producing handicrafts such as pottery, primitive weaving and practical leatherwork.

no government aid. A small donation is requested to visit and further donations are gratefully received. From La Cumbre you can get here by taxi in 20 minutes for about 12 pesos. If you are able to plan ahead, you can take an alternative vacation and volunteer here.

The **Estancia Puesto Viejo Hostel** (\f *423809;* e *info@estanciapuestoviejo.com; www.estanciapuestoviejo.com*) takes a bit of effort to reach, but will really give you the feeling of getting out into the countryside. This horse ranch is located in a beautiful setting of rivers and waterfalls with great areas for riding and trekking. You can reach the road to the ranch from La Cumbre, 24km past Cuchi Corral (approximately one hour by car); or from the opposite direction, from Cruz del Eje taking the exit off Ruta Provincial 38 for San Marcos Sierra and continuing for about 26km. There will be a sign indicating the turn-off to Puesto Viejo, a further 2–3km. If without a car, you can arrange to be picked up in La Falda. This hostel is a member of Hostelling International and charges 20 pesos (25 pesos non-members) in a four-person dorm; 35 pesos (42.50 pesos) in a double, with breakfast included. Various packages including full board and excursions are available, from 100 pesos per person.

Quebrada del Condorito National Park is a young park in the National Park designations; it is interesting as it protects the unique ecology of the high pampas and a fabulous series of outstanding natural gorges. It is reached by Ruta 14, also known as the route of the *Altas Cumbres* or High Peaks, between Villa Carlos Paz and Mina Clavero, about 100km from Córdoba. There is little to no infrastructure here; the entrance is about half way along this route.

La Pampa Province
Area code 02954

The most popular reason to visit the agricultural province of La Pampa is to see the Lihue Calel National Park. Santa Rosa de al Pampa is a small but adequate base.

SANTA ROSA

Santa Rosa is the capital city of the province of La Pampa and one could say that it is in the middle of nowhere. Founded in 1892, it began to grow in 1894 when it was reached by the railway, and by 1897 there was a population of 1,000. The city is one of the most isolated in the country, which keeps it small, quiet and humble. This is not a city on the tourist trail, but for this reason it may be more attractive to those in search of an authentic Argentine city that is relatively uninfluenced by foreigners or for that matter by its own neighbouring countrymen. Luro Park nature reserve, with a lakeside area, low mountains and sand dunes (*medanos*), 35km from Santa Rosa, is worth visiting. To reach it by car, take Ruta 35 south and then Ruta 143 followed by Ruta 152.

Getting there
By air
Aerolíneas Argentinas flies three times a week (Mon, Wed and Fri) from Buenos Aires to Santa Rosa airport, 4.5km from the city on Ruta 35, km330 (☏ *434490*). There is no public transport to or from the airport; a taxi costs about 5 pesos.

By bus
The Santa Rosa bus terminal is at Luro 365 (☏ *422952*); the main companies are Andesmar (☏ *495142*), Albus (☏ *431841*), Chevallier (☏ *426981*) and Via Bariloche (☏ *423354*).

By car
Considering how central Santa Rosa is on the map, you can approach from several directions. Ruta 5 leads from Buenos Aires in the east; Ruta 35 comes from Córdoba in the north, continuing south to Bahía Blanca. From Mendoza and San Rafael in the west, take Ruta 188 and then Ruta 35 heading south.

Lihue Calel National Park
Most travellers come to Santa Rosa to visit the Lihue Calel National Park, 220km from Santa Rosa on Ruta 152, which meets Ruta 35 120km southwest of the city. The nearest town to the park is Puelches, 35km away. At the park there is rough camping with toilets near the administration (☏ *02952 436595 or 432639;* e *lihuecalel@apn.gov.ar or informes@apn.gov.ar*).

LIHUE CALEL NATIONAL PARK

The park was designated in 1977 with a surface area of 9,901ha, but that last hectare is not enough – the park aims to expand north to include the special habitat of the Levalle saltpan that is thus far unprotected and whose flora and fauna species are rare or missing from the park. Lihue Calel was named by the indigenous peoples 'mountain of life' for the outcrop of humid hills that reach 589m in an otherwise arid and flat landscape. The freshwater reserves captured by the hills sustain a rich flora of ferns, epiphytes, and colourful lichen of yellow, orange and black. Surrounding the hills, the climate of La Pampa is temperate but semi-arid, with just 100–200mm per year of rainfall; but the water is retained and impermeable areas receive seasonal (winter) streams that filter into the sandy soils around. The characteristic flora consists of creosote bushes, patches of caldén trees, *Prosopis* spp, some endemic daisies and plenty of cacti. Burrowing animals are typical of this zone where there is little other protection from the sun. Examples are the maras, fox, ferrets, tuco-tuco and the plains vizcacha; red lizards (*Tupinambis tegu*) over a metre in length live in vacated *vizcacheras* (vizcacha burrows). The birds that you can expect to spot include the tinamou and various raptors. The yellow cardinal is a rare treat but pressure from the illegal pet trade threatens its numbers. When the caldén fruits ripen, another spectacle is the large noisy flocks of barranqueros (burrowing parrots) in search of the seeds.

This eruption of hills jutting out of the immense surrounding flatlands was a natural oasis for human occupation and the archaeological evidence of prehistoric human inhabitation of this area was a fundamental reason for designating the park. The Valley of Paintings retains 2,000-year-old rock art, and burial and ritual sites have been identified. Hunter-gatherers did well here with freshwater reserves from the hills and rich flora and fauna including seeds, berries (caldén and chañar), guanaco, rhea and armadillo. The rocky areas provided materials for tools and the minerals offered pigments for their art, which is characteristically geometrical with red and black pigments dominant. More recently, in the 19th century Tehuelche and Araucanian Indians came to inhabit the pampas after their displacement from Buenos Aires province and the mountains. Chief Namuncurá was the last chief of the Pampean Confederation of Indian Tribes until his surrender in 1885; the Quebrada de Namuncurá (Namuncurá Gorge) and the hiking trail in the park are named after him. Stone houses are left here from the colonial period and General Roca's 'Campaign of the Desert'. The colonialists that came to this area survived by agriculture and mining for copper in the hills.

Hiking in the hills is not difficult if you stay on the gentle northern slopes of the range; the southern sides are much more abrupt. Most day-hikes start from the camping grounds. The Huitru and Namuncura trails ascend the Hill of the Scientific Society to see characteristic flora and fauna, and there is an easy ascent to a panoramic viewpoint. The Valley of Paintings trail (600m) passes through the area used in ancient times by the indigenous peoples and finishes at the rock paintings.

174

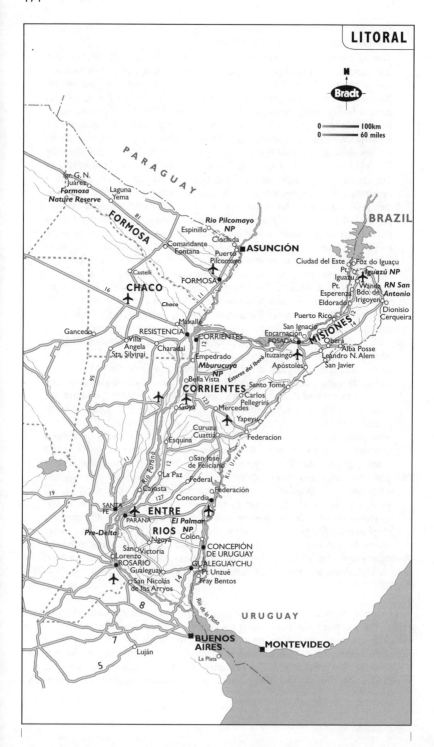

Litoral

The northeast of Argentina is referred to as the Litoral zone, the humid riparian and wetland area encompassing the Paraná delta. The east side of the river is Mesopotamia, comprising the provinces of Entre Ríos, Corrientes and the thumb of Misiones, between Paraguay and Brazil. Mesopotamia is geographically separated from the rest of the country by the Río Paraná extending from Paraguay to the Río de la Plata and the Atlantic. On the west side of the Paraná is the Gran Chaco (the provinces of Chaco and Formosa), sparsely populated and with little infrastructure to date for tourism, but with fantastically expansive territory of 'wilderness', several national parks, an enormous amount of wildlife and traditionally subsisting indigenous communities.

Entre Ríos Province

Entre Ríos province is the southern section of the Mesopotamia, which also means 'between the rivers'. On a map it looks as if it is hanging in a river hammock, with the Ríos Paraná and Uruguay reaching down the east and west flanks of the province and linking together at the confluence with the Río de la Plata. Tributaries and streams are blue veins across the face of the landscape, making fishing and water-based activities attractive to tourists. All along the eastern border of the province is a thermal zone with 'thermal cities' that have developed several wonderful spas that are more like large city parks full of hot tubs where folk walk about in their bathrobes and slippers.

PARANÁ
Area code 0343
Paraná is the capital city of Entre Ríos province but it is one of the quieter and less conspicuous of the country's provincial capitals and a younger and quieter sister city to Santa Fé right across the river (which dates from the early 1500s). Paraná, however, has a prettier layout of hills and plazas and a great riverfront with a wide boulevard for strolling, cycling and jogging. Of course, the river is the source of the many great fish that will appear on your plate in the local restaurants.

Getting there
By *air*
LADE (*25 de Junio 135;* ✆ *423 5704;* e *parana@lade.com.ar*) has two flights from Buenos Aires on Monday at 9.15 and 12.50. There is a more frequent service to Santa Fé, across the river.

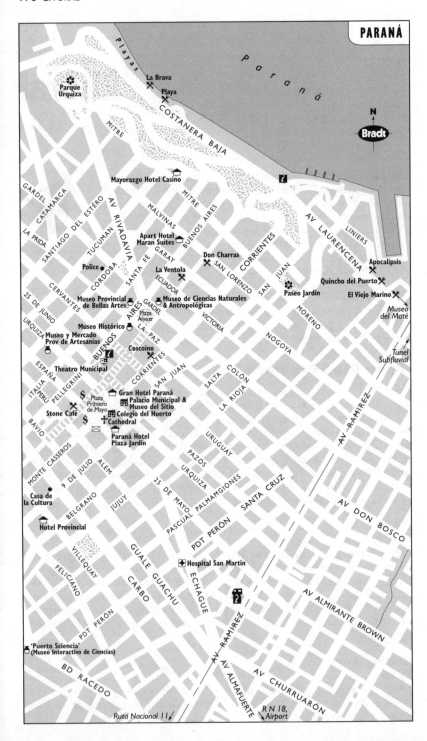

PARANÁ

Paraná

Playas

Parque Urquiza

La Brava

Playa

COSTANERA BAJA

N

Bradt

GARDEL

CATAMARCA

LA PRIDA

MITRE

SANTIAGO DEL ESTERO

AV RIVADAVIA

TUCUMAN

MALVINAS

MITRE

BUENOS AIRES

Mayorazgo Hotel Casino

AV LAURENCENA

LINIERS

CERVANTES

CORDOBA

SANTA FE

GARAY

Apart Hotel
Maran Suites

CORRIENTES

Apocalipsis

Police

La Ventola

Don Charras

SAN LORENZO

SAN JUAN

Quincho del Puerto

25 DE JUNIO

ECUADOR

Museo Provincial
de Bellas Artes

BUENOS AIRES

GARDEL

Museo de Ciencias Naturales
& Antropológicas

Paseo Jardín

El Viejo Marino

URQUIZA

Plaza
Alvear

LA PAZ

VICTORIA

MORENO

Museo
del Maté

Museo Histórico

Museo y Mercado
Prov de Artesanias

NOGOYA

Tunel
Subfluvial

ESPAÑA

Coscoino

CORRIENTES

SAN JUAN

COLON

ITALIA

PERÚ PELLEGRINI

SALTA

LA RIOJA

Theatro Municipal

Stone Café

Plaza
Primero
de Mayo

Gran Hotel Paraná

Palacio Municipal &
Museo del Sitio

AV RAMIREZ

BAVIO

Colegio del Huerto

Cathedral

URUGUAY

Paraná Hotel
Plaza Jardín

PAZOS

MONTE CASEROS

9 DE JULIO

ALEM

25 DE MAYO

URQUIZA

PASCUAL PALMAMGIONES

SANTA CRUZ

AV DON BOSCO

Casa de
la Cultura

BELGRANO

JUJUY

PDT PERÓN

Hotel Provincial

VILLEGUAY

GUALE GUACHU

Hospital San Martín

AV ALMIRANTE BROWN

FELICIANO

CARBO

ECHAGUE

'Puerto Sciencia'
(Museo Interactivo de Ciencias)

BD RACEDO

PDT PERÓN

AV RAMIREZ

AV ALMAFUERTE

AV CHURRUARÓN

Ruta Nacional 11

RN 18,
Airport

The airport is 10km east of the city at Salvador Caputo s/n (✆ *426 1658/72, 426 0850*). Bus no. 4 (1 peso) connects the airport to the bus terminal and downtown. No taxi service is available at the airport; if you are not lucky enough to find one arriving at the airport with another passenger to drop off, call Radio Taxi (✆ *424 5555*) or Telerradio (✆ *424 6565, 424 0000, 424 6000*) for a taxi to come from the centre. There are several *remise* companies as well: Litoral Remises (*Almafuerte 570;* ✆ *439 0490*), Remis Alem (*Alem 165;* ✆ *431 1111*), Remises Ciudad Paisaje (*Alem 487;* ✆ *423 2100*), Remises Colón (*Colón 369;* ✆ *423 3338*), San Cayetano Remises (*Buenos Aires 551;* ✆ *422 2200*), Sol Remises (*Moreno 82;* ✆ *422 0220*), Uruguay Remises (*Uruguay 652;* ✆ *423 4223*).

Avis car rental is at the airport in the main hall (✆ *436 5555; www.avis.com.ar*).

By bus
The bus terminal is at Avenida Ramírez 2300. The bus between Santa Fé and Paraná via the tunnel under the Río Paraná runs every 20–60 minutes around the clock (3 peso). The ticket office in Paraná is at Boletería 14 (✆ *431 3689*); also at Belgrano 59 (✆ *423 0342*). In Santa Fé buy tickets at Boletería 26 (✆ *0342 455 4132*).

There are buses from Buenos Aires every few hours; the journey takes seven and a half hours and costs about 40 pesos. The bus from Concordia costs 21 pesos (an additional 3.50 pesos from Federación); from these towns and from Mercedes services are very limited, typically once a day. There is a daily service with TAC connecting Corrientes with Paraná in just over eight hours for 36 pesos. There is also one bus per day with Mercobus Plus Ultra from Posadas (11 hours; 58 pesos) and this company also has a daily service from Puerto Iguazú (28 hours; 77 pesos).

By car
The Tunel Subfluvial, inaugurated in 1969, is a 3km-long crossing beneath the Río Paraná, connecting to Ruta 19 west to Córdoba and Ruta 11 north to Resistencia and south to Rosario and on to Buenos Aires (377km). Ruta 12 leads northeast to Corrientes and Misiones; to head directly east to the thermal region along the Uruguayan border, take Ruta 18. Distances between cities in Entre Ríos are long. Take advantage of service stations when you see them and carry an extra petrol can.

Orientation
The central plaza around which are found most of the main historic buildings is Plaza de Mayo; from here the pedestrianised José San Martín leads north past Plaza Alvear to Parque Urquiza on the riverfront. Note that streets change their names on either side of José San Martín.

Where to stay
Mayorazgo Hotel Casino Echeveria and Miranda; ✆ 423 0333; e reservas@mayorazgohotel.com. A 5-star hotel with swimming pool, restaurant and many services. Sgls start at 90 pesos, dbls at 135 pesos, triples at 170 pesos.
Gran Hotel Paraná Urquiza 976; ✆ 422 3900; f 422 3979; e reservasgranhotel@ hotelsparana.com.ar. Sgls range from 60 pesos to 110 pesos, dbls 84–140 pesos, triples 112–195 pesos.
Paraná Hotel Plaza Jardin 9 de Julio 60; ✆ 423 1700, 423 0764, 0810 444 6835; f 422 3205; e infoph@hotelesparana.com.ar; www.hotelesparana.com.ar. Simple rooms with colour TV, AC, bar and room service. Sgls 48 pesos, dbls 68 pesos, triples 92 pesos.
Hotel Provincial Villaguay 162; ✆ 423 5619; e hotelprovincialer@hotmail.com. Basic rooms with private bath and AC. Sgls 40 pesos, dbls 55 pesos, triples 75 pesos inc b/fast.
Apart Hotel Maran Suites Buenos Aires and Malvinas; ✆ 423 5444;

e reserves@maran.com.ar; www.maran.com.ar. Rooms with cable TV, AC and kitchenettes. Sgls 90 pesos, dbls 120 pesos, triples 140 pesos, with continental b/fast.

Where to eat and drink

Apocalipsis Laurencena 200 (at Liniers); ☎ 422 6708. Specialises in regional fish such as *surubí, boga, pacú* and *dorado*, grilled meats and pastas.

El Viejo Marino Laurencena 341 (Plaza de las Provincias); ☎ 432 9767. River fish, seafood and homemade pasta; tango and folkloric shows are often held.

Playa Costanera Baja; ☎ 421 8699. Located on the beachfront of the Río Paraná, the excellent view is complemented by a menu of river fish (*boga, dorado* and *surubí*) as well as ocean fish (salmon, trout and *pejerrey*). *Empanadas, parrilla* and homemade pasta are other options.

Quincho del Puerto Laurencena 350; ☎ 423 2045. *Pacú, dorado, boga, surubí* and *armado* are on the menu as well as *parrilla* and pasta. *Open for lunch and dinner, Tue–Sun.*

Don Charras San Martín and San Lorenzo; ☎ 422 5972 or Av Uranga 1127; ☎ 433 1760. Estancia-style setting with meat or vegetable *parrilla*.

Le Montmartre Urquiza 792; ☎ 402 4785, 15 512 0785; e le-montmartre@mixmail.com. A French restaurant, if you need a break from Argentine food. *Open Tue–Fri for dinner, Sat also for lunch and Sun only for lunch.*

La Brava Costanera Baja (Paraná Rowing Club); ☎ 423 5338. Offers international and fusion dishes as well as traditional Argentine dishes.

Coscoino Corrientes 373; ☎ 422 4120. Offers pasta and traditional fare at low prices.

La Ventola San Martín 630; ☎ 432 0319. Irish pub and restaurant open for b/fast, lunch, happy hour and dinner.

Stone Café San Martín and 25 de Mayo; ☎ 422 2923. The café in this characteristic old building has patios overlooking Plaza 1 de Mayo. The café hosts parties, shows and other events and has a simple menu of pasta, pizza and sandwiches, such as *lomitos* – try the *completo*, with hot steak, cold ham, tomato and fried egg, cheese and lettuce on a sesame-seed bun.

Practicalities

The **Secretaria de Turismo** is at Buenos Aires 132 (☎ *420 1661/62, 423 0183, 0800 555 9575;* e *informes@turismoenparana.com*). There are two other offices, one at San Martín 637 and one in Parque Urquiza at Laurencena and Juan de San Martín (☎ *420 1837*). There is also tourist information in the bus terminal (☎ *420 1862*).

The **post office** is on the corner of 25 de Mayo and Monte Caseros on Plaza 1 de Mayo.

The **Hospital San Martín** is at Presidente Perón (☎ *423 4545*).

There are many **banks:**

Almafuerte Coop Urquiza 1078; ☎ 423 0344
Banca Nazionale del Lavoro Urquiza and Buenos Aires; ☎ 423 0145
Banco Francés San Martín 763; ☎ 423 0215
Banco Nación San Martín and España; ☎ 431 3646
Banco Río Pellegrini 29; ☎ 422 5951
BERSA Monte Caseros and 25 de Mayo; ☎ 420 1400
Bisel Monte Caseros 173; ☎ 423 0124
Hipotecario Nacional Urquiza 1092; ☎ 431 4697

Highlights

Plaza 1 de Mayo is the main plaza of interest. Here you can see the neo-Byzantine architecture of the **Cathedral**, a National Historic Monument (1883) on the site of the first parish church of 'la Bajada del Paraná', built in 1730. You can also see the post office, once the house of General Urquiza, president from 1854 to 1860.

Behind the cathedral is the **Colegio del Huerto**, which also had a former life as the senate house when Paraná was capital of the Argentine Confederation. The **Municipal City Hall** (Palacio) (1890), in Italian-French style, is on Corrientes.

Plaza Alvear is a short distance north from Plaza 1 de Mayo along the pedestrianised José de San Martín. The church of **San Miguel** (1822) is here, and a few blocks west on Córdoba is the **Government House** (1884–90).

The **Teatro Municipal 3 de Febrero** (*25 de Junio 60;* ✆ *431 0562*) does not stage elaborate works but the Baroque frescoes on the ceilings (1908) are a show in themselves.

The riverfront **Parque Urquiza** is the popular area for swimming or lying on the municipal beach by day or for strolling by night. On the coast are numerous fishing spots for several fish species, especially the *amarillo, boga, mandubé, armado* and *patí*, but there is also the possibility of catching *dorado, surubí* and rays. The tourist board has details of fishing licences and special events such as sailing regattas (✆ *0800 555 9575; www.turismoenparana.com*). The Club de Pescadores y Nautico Paraná (Paraná Fishing and Boating Club) is on J M Estrada s/n (✆ *422 2400*).

Museums

Museo Histórico Martiniano Leguizamón Buenos Aires 286 and Laprida; ✆ 420 7860. *Open Tue–Fri 07.30–12.30, 15.00–19.30, Sat 09.00–12.00, 16.00–19.00, Sun 9.00–12.00; admission 1 peso.*

Museo Provincial de Bellas Artes Dr P E Martínez Buenos Aires 355; ✆ 420 7868. *Open Tue–Fri 09.00–12.00, 16.00–21.00, Sat 10.30–12.30, 17.30–20.00, Sun 10.30–12.30; free admission.*

Museo de Ciencias Naturales y Antropológicas Dr. Antonio Serrano Carlos Gardel 62; ✆ 431 2635. *Open Tue–Fri 07.30–12.30, 14.00–19.00, Sat 08.30–12.30, 15.00–19.00, Sun 09.00–12.00.*

Casa de la Cultura, Carbó and 9 de Julio; ✆ 422 4493. *Open Mon–Sat 09.00–12.00, 16.00–20.00.*

Museo y Mercado Provincial de Artesanías de Entre Ríos Urquiza 1239; ✆ 420 8891. *Open Tue–Fri 08.00–12.00, 17.00–20.0; Sat 10.00–12.00, 18.00–20.00, Sun 10.00–12.00; free admission.* Local cradfts on display and for sale.

Museo Interactivo de Ciencias 'Puerto Ciencia' Bd Racedo and P Palma; ✆ 497 5077
Museo de la Ciudad 'César B Pérez Colman' Buenos Aires 234; ✆ 420 1697
Museo del Maté Antonio Crespo 159; ✆ 403 0244
Museo del Sitio Urquiza and Corrientes (Palacio Municipal); ✆ 420 1674

VICTORIA

Area code 03436

An easy day trip from Rosario, many *rosarinos* spend weekends and holidays in this quiet town, but Victoria has many appealing qualities for tourists from further afield as well. Being on the Riacho Victoria, fishing and camping are popular. The streams and swamps that join with the nearby Paraná River system mean that fishing is as important to the area as the cattle industry. A drive into the surrounding countryside shows a peculiar blend of the gaucho's pampas with the fisherman's wetlands. But perhaps a more obvious presence in Victoria are the monasteries and churches where monks make special liquors, sweets, honey and preserves from the fruits, flowers and berries of the countryside, as well as tonics, lotions and natural medicines.

Victoria is sometimes referred to as *La Ciudad de la Sieta Colinas* (the city of the seven hills); set on a hill, it stands out in the landscape from a distance as you approach from Rosario. In the old district, the Barrio Quinto Cuartel, you can see

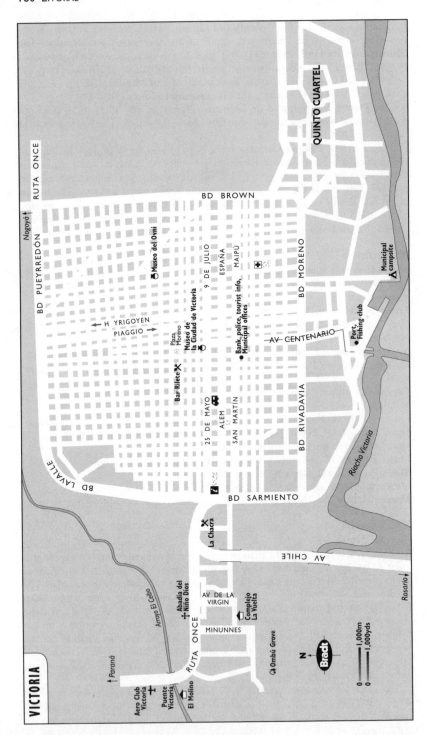

VICTORIA

examples of the original Spanish architecture. The other significant part of town is the big fishing port where you can see hundreds of fishermen, seemingly the entire town population, casting lines from the pier.

Getting there
By bus
There are half a dozen or so buses per day between Victoria and Rosario with Basa Costera Criolla, taking an hour and 15 minutes (8 pesos). The bus terminal is on Alem at Junín, two blocks from the main Plaza Libertad.

By car
Victoria is on Ruta 11 south of Paraná, but is more easily reached from Rosario in 40 minutes by the Rosario–Victoria bridge, opened in 2003. There is a 9 peso toll, which you only pay once if you return by midnight the same day.

Orientation
Arriving from Rosario you will come to a T-junction, where you should turn right for the town centre, laid out in the usual grid north of the Riacho Victoria. Turning left will take you to the Abadia del Niño Dios church, the ombú grove and campsites.

Where to stay
El Molino Ruta 11, km112.5; ✆ 421200; f 421623; e elmolinosa@ar.inter.net; www.complejoelmolino.com.ar. Camping, cabins and a *hostería* are available at this converted farmhouse. Here you can stay submerged in nature yet have at your disposal a football and recreation area, a swimming pool to cool off in and an excellent *parrilla* in the backyard. Cabins cost 15 pesos per person or 50 pesos dbl, without b/fast; apts are the same price but inc b/fast. The *hostería* charges 10 pesos per person or 30 pesos for a matrimonial suite, with b/fast.
Complejo La Vuelta Ruta 11, km114; ✆/f 424240 or in Buenos Aires 011 4918 8011; www.la-vuelta.com.ar. Fully equipped cabins for rent for 45 pesos for 3 people, 60 pesos for 6, or 70 pesos for 7.

Where to eat and drink
El Molino (above) prepares an excellent afternoon *asado* behind the *hostería* with picnic tables alongside the park and river. There is also an indoor restaurant.
La Chacra Ruta 11, km114, after the turn-off from the Victoria–Rosario viaduct heading into Victoria centre; ✆ 426073. *Parrilla* and fish specialities. *Open daily for lunch and dinner.*
Bar Rilete Sarmiento 478; ✆ 425937; e barriletevictoria@hotmail.com

Practicalities
The **Municipal Tourism Office** is at 25 de Mayo and Boulevard Sarmiento (✆/f 421885; e munivictoria@ciudad.com.ar; www.victoriaturismo.com.ar, www.victoriaglobal.com.ar).

The **hospital** is on the blocks between Avenida Rondeau, López, Chacabuco and Sánchez. The **police station** and the **bank** are both strategically housed within the Centro Civico on San Martín and Sarmiento.

Highlights
The **Museo de la Ciudad de Victoria** (*Av Congreso 593;* ✆ *421606; open Tue–Sun 16.00–20.00, Sat 10.00–12.00*) uses artefacts, furniture, historic objects, artworks and other items to interpret the history of the city.

One of Victoria's most bizarre attractions is the **Museo del Ovni** (*San Miguel and Rondeau;* ✆ *15 579514;* e *ssimondini@hotmail.com.ar; www.visionovni.com.ar; suggested* *donation 1 peso*) or 'the museum of non-identified flying objects', which turns out to be a one-room 'centre of investigation' of extraterrestrial occurrences, mostly in the form of livestock mutilation which reportedly occurs with alarming frequency in this region. You will find here various objects ranging from cult collectors' items to fragments of spaceships that have theoretically crashed in the vicinity to photographs of sightings as well as gruesome specimens such as a sheep's eyeball.

At the **Abadía del Niño Dios** (*Ruta 11, km112,* ℡ *423171,* e *monacal@ ciudad.com.ar, abadiadelninodios@ciudad.com.ar; www.abadiadelninodios.com.ar*) the *sanitería* sells products to cure anything that ails you. Continuing a little further up the road away from the city centre you will see a little road veering to the left with a sign to the **Monte de los Ombúes**, a large and ancient forest of the lovely ombú (*Phytolacca dioica*) trees.

In July, the **Fiesta Provincial del Amarillo** is a festival in celebration of fishing.

CONCORDIA
Area code 0345
This small town is the largest in the thermal region on the eastern side of the province. It is situated between two tempting tourist destinations: the thermal park of Federación and El Palmar National Park. It is also the easiest gateway city to the town of Mercedes, jumping-off point for the fantastic Esteros del Iberá nature reserve. Concordia does however have a few highlights of its own, including thermal spas. The citrus industry is important to the local economy and you can find several grocers selling fresh fruit, especially oranges and lemons.

Getting there
By bus
From the bus terminal on Boulevard San Lorenzo (at Av Justo) it's a dozen blocks to the central Plaza 25 de Mayo, but only a cheap taxi ride.

Flecha, San José and Zenit bus companies connect Concordia with Paraná, charging 21 pesos for the four- to five-hour journey, and also go to Federación for 3.50 pesos. Buenos Aires and Concordia are linked by Nuevo Rápido San José (℡ *422 0599; in Buenos Aires 011 4312 0365/7*) approximately eight times per day in each direction. They also have three or four services per day from Federación, Paraná and Santa Fé.

By car
Stretching the north–south length of Entre Ríos is Ruta 14. Driving direct from Buenos Aires, take Ruta 9 then Ruta 14 into Entre Ríos, continuing north into Corrientes province; from Paraná and locations to the east take Ruta 18.

Orientation and practicalities
Plaza 25 de Mayo is the town's central plaza, site of the tourist office, the Catedral San Antonio and the police station. East–west street names change on either side of the plaza.

The **Secretary of Tourism** is at Urquiza 636 (℡ *421 2137, 422 5408 or 421 3905;* f *421 1393;* e *turismo@concordia.com.ar; www.concordiaturistica.com.ar*). The tour agency **EmContur** (*1 de Mayo 126;* ℡ *421 9051;* e *emcontur@concordia.com.ar*) is also very helpful.

Where to stay
Hotel Salto Grande Urquiza 581; ℡ 421 0034; e info@hotelsaltogrande.net; www.hotelsaltogrande.net. In the centre of Concordia, this 4-star hotel is only a 15-min

CONCORDIA

Avenida Perón ↑

↑ Complejo Terma 'Vertiente de la Concordia', Airport

BD SAN LORENZO "O"

RAWSON

(SKETCH MAP)
Not to scale

TUCUMÁN

BALCARSE

ESPEJO

PIROVANO

LINIERS

LAS HERAS **N**

COLDAROLI

Bradt

AVELLANEDA

ASUNCIÓN

SANTO CABRAL

MONTEVIDEO

Palacio Museo
Arruabarrena

RAMÍREZ

3 DE FEBRERO

Plaza
Urquiza

SAAVEDRA

ESTRADA

GÜEMES

SAN JUAN

SALTA

RIVADAVIA

Ruta Nac 14
North & South

ENTRE RÍOS

VELEZ SARSFIELD

CORRIENTES

From R N 14
North & South

URDINARRAIN

URQUIZA

PELLEGRINI

H YINGOYEN

LA RIOJA

CATAMARCA

D P GARAT

SARMIENTO

SAN LUIS

A   DEL   VALLE

ALBERDI

25 DE MAYO

Municipalidad ●

SAN MARTÍN

MITRE

Catedral San Antonio ✝
Secretary of Tourism
Museo de Artes Visuales

Plaza
25 de
Mayo

● Police
ENCOMTUR

B DE IRIGOYEN

PRIMERO DE MAYO →

Hotel
Salto Grande

QUINTANA

BUENOS AIRES

Hotel
Concordia

ALEM

R S PEÑA

ANDRADE

CARRIEGO

S M DE ORO

Hospital
Félipe Heras ↓

ESPINO

Museo de
Antropología ↓

drive to the thermal baths and the beaches of Lago de Salto Grande. Rooms have TV, AC and telephone, and there's a b/fast buffet, restaurant, bar, room service, swimming pool, covered parking, convention halls and banqueting rooms. Standard sgls are 126 pesos, dbls 146 pesos and triples 183 pesos, with b/fast; suites are also available.

Hotel Concordia La Rioja 518; ❧ 421 6869; e hotel@artcon.com.ar. Clean and quiet accommodation close to the centre; private rooms with bathroom cost 30 pesos per person.

Highlights

The **Cathedral of St Anthony of Padua**, founded in 1833, was rebuilt in 1899 and now has a neo-Romanesque façade with rather Germanic bell-towers.

In a 25ha park with groves of eucalyptus and pine trees are five thermal pools, two of which are covered, ranging from 38 to 43°C. **Complejo Terma 'Vertiente de la Concordia'** is an oasis with massage and beauty treatments, picnic and walking areas in the forest and a restaurant.

In February, the **Fiesta Nacional de la Boga** takes place in celebration of this river fish and the sport of catching it.

Museums

Palacio Museo Arruabarrena Ramírez and Entre Ríos, facing Plaza Urquiza. A historical museum of the region housed in a beautiful French-style mansion, built in 1919. *Open Mon 07.00–13.00, Tue–Fri 07.00–19.00, Sat & Sun 16.00–19.00.*

Museo de Artes Visuales Urquiza 636, facing Plaza 25 de Mayo. Local and regional art. *Open Tue–Sun 08.00–13.00, 15.00–20.00.*

Museo de Antropología Av Robinson s/n; ❧ 421 3149. In the former railway station, this displays archaeological items, fossils and handicrafts, among other diverse objects. *Open Mon–Fri 08.00–12.00, 15.00–21.00 in summer, 08.00–18.00 in winter.*

Day-trips and excursions

The **Parque Nacional El Palmar** is 53km south of Concordia on the way to Colón and Buenos Aires; by car is the easiest way to visit the park. Otherwise, take Jovi Bus or Nuevo Expreso from Concordia. There is a limited service: the recommended departure is at 08.00 (the next leaves at midday). You'll be dropped off an hour and 20 minutes later beside Ruta 14 (which is the western border of the park), from where you have to walk 12km to the park gate (so travel light, wear good hiking shoes and carry water). The last bus back passes the drop-off point on the highway at about 19.15 and you will have to flag it down; so there's quite a risk of missing the bus and having to hitchhike back to town. Camping is permitted in the park at the campground, where there are bathrooms and a store. The nearby Visitor Centre has information on the flora, fauna and history of the park. Park admission is 12 pesos.

FEDERACIÓN

Area code 03456

Federación is the 'thermal city' where the hot springs offer a relaxing and luxurious way to pass part of your day. This town began, like so many in Argentina, with one family settling and starting to farm. In 1777, Don Juan de San Martín founded the Estancia Mandisoví. At this time the political boundaries of Argentina were still in dispute. Entre Ríos was part of Paraguay until General Belgrano's Campaign of Paraguay in 1810 and the province's subsequent incorporation into Argentina.

Getting there

Federación is 79km north of Concordia, via Ruta 14. Buses leave Concordia at 08.00, 09.00, 12.00, 12.30, 18.30, 19.00, 19.50 and 22.00, arriving at Federación's

above left **Magellanic woodpecker,** *Campephilus magellanicus*, **on coihue tree** (DA/SAP)
top right **Mixed** *Pieridae* **butterflies, Iguazú** (EM) page 203
above right **Black-and-white tegu lizard,** *Tupinambis teguixin*, **Iguazú Falls** (EM) page 203
below **Three-banded armadillo,** *Tolypuetes matacus* (TM/SAP) page 378

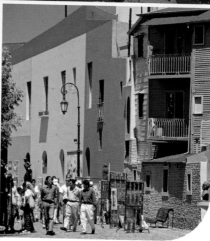

top **Ushuaia, Tierra del Fuego** (AC/TIPS) page 363
above left **Fonda restaurant, Mataderos, Buenos Aires** (DA/SAP) page 112
above right **Brightly coloured houses, La Boca, Buenos Aires** (GA/TIPS) page 91
below **Av 9 de Julio, Buenos Aires** (FN/SAP) page 103

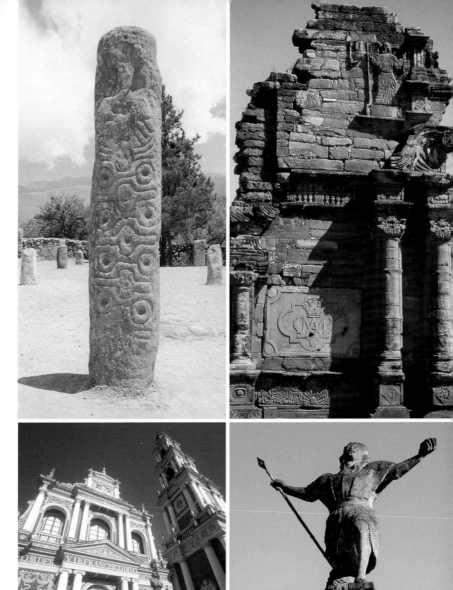

opposite page **Mountaineers on glacier, Mount Tronador**
(AM/TIPS) page 312

top **Vineyards of Mendoza, with the Andes in the background**
(EM) page 252

centre **Lake Nahuel Huapi, near San Carlos de Bariloche**
(FN/SAP) page 302

right **Amethyst at Wanda mines, Misiones Province**
(EM) page 206

opposite page **Plains of northern Patagonia** (AM/TIPS) page 273

top **Gauchos on Saints' Day, Santa Barbara, Jujuy Province** (DA/SAP) page 80

centre **Typical grill, _asado_, San Carlos de Bariloche** (AM/TIPS) page 78

right **Elderly man of the high desert, San Antonio de los Cobres** (EM)

next page **Aguja Pollone, Parque Nacional Los Glaciares** (DA/SAP) page 322

EL PALMAR NATIONAL PARK

Approximately 8,500ha were set aside in 1966 to create El Palmar National Park and preserve the last remaining groves of yatay palm (*Syagrus yatay*) which still dominate the park interspersed with grassland and small woods. The tall palms are striking as they are all more or less the same age, extensive cattle grazing having prevented any regeneration for at least two centuries. At the lower levels younger trees are finally making a comeback, interspersed with grasses and flowering plants. However, there are problems with introduced species such as the European wild boar that digs up and eats the palm seeds. Another invasive tree, introduced from Asia, is the chinaberry (*Melia azadarech*), competing with the native flora, among which is an endemic petunia.

There are tracts of gallery forest of myrtles and laurels, more typical of the rainforests along the banks of the Río Uruguay, where acacias also grow. Three species of woodpecker, the golden-breasted and white woodpeckers and the field flicker, live among the palms. The rufous cacholote builds great nests of sticks and reeds along the river. Rheas and tinamous live in the grassland, where great numbers of monk parakeets make enormous communal nests. The rare crab-eating fox also relies on this habitat. In the summer large tegu lizards lie in the sun outside the burrows that they take over from the plains vizcachas. The park is significant in terms of human as well as natural history. In the 1700s the Portuguese encouraged settlement in this area and a lime quarry was developed on the banks of the Río Uruguay, traces of which remain at the Calera de Barquín, within the park on the road to the beach. Far older are the artefacts left by ancient hunter-gatherers, dating back almost 1,000 years, that have been discovered at sites in the park.

bus terminal, on Las Violetas and Entre Ríos, an hour later. There is a limited bus service from other destinations such as Mercedes.

Where to stay

Hostería Salto Grande, Concepción del Uruguay 551; ℸ 481554; e hosteriasaltogrande@yahoo.com.ar. This lovely little B&B is located right by the lake and within walking distance of the bus terminal and the spa. Rooms cost 60–80 pesos per person depending upon size of room and whether or not b/fast is taken.

Practicalities

The **tourist office** is at Avenida San Martín and Las Hortensias (ℸ *481586;* e *securismo-fed@bitbyte.com.ar; www.03456federacion.com.ar*). The **post office** is at Las Hortensias and Inmaculada Concepción. The **police station** is at San Martín and Las Azaleas (ℸ *481222*). The **Banco Nación** is at San Martín 208.

Highlights
La Posta de Mandisoví

This spa is Mesopotamia's leading thermal park (ℸ *482022;* e *infos@spamandisovi.com.ar; www.spamandisovi.com.ar; admission 5 pesos*). Its nine pools cover 9ha beside the lake and attempt to fit gracefully into their natural environment with a few boardwalks and bridges to lookout areas onto the lake and

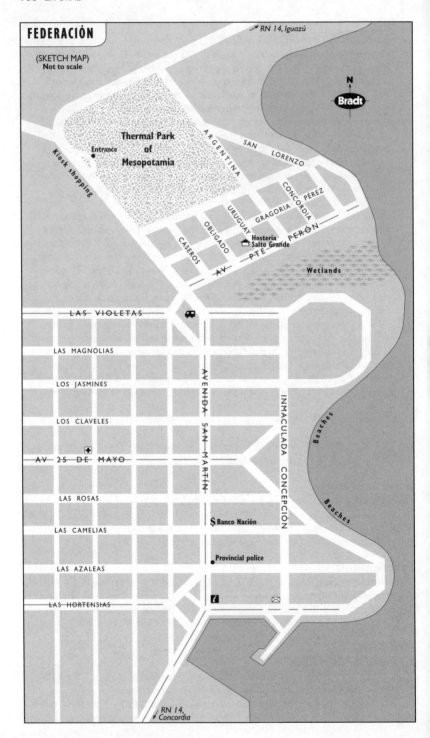

FEDERACIÓN

(SKETCH MAP)
Not to scale

RN 14, Iguazú

Bradt

Thermal Park
of
Mesopotamia

Entrance

Kiosk shopping

ARGENTINA

SAN LORENZO

CONCORDIA

PÉREZ

URUGUAY

GRAGORIA

CASEROS

OBLIGADO

Hostería
Salto Grande

AV PTE PERÓN

Wetlands

LAS VIOLETAS

LAS MAGNOLIAS

LOS JASMINES

AVENIDA SAN MARTÍN

INMACULADA CONCEPCIÓN

Beaches

LOS CLAVELES

AV 25 DE MAYO

LAS ROSAS

LAS CAMELIAS

$ Banco Nación

Provincial police

Beaches

LAS AZALEAS

LAS HORTENSIAS

i

✉

RN 14,
Concordia

surrounding area. There are several open-air pools, ranging in heat from about 37 to 41°C, connected by paths. The warmest pool is covered, and there's also a recreation pool that has cooler temperatures and deeper waters to actually swim in (the rest of the pools being simply for soaking in). There is also a spa centre for massage, facials, mud therapies, etc. Opposite the spa is a string of shops and kiosks selling craftwork and souvenirs.

Boat excursions
Departures from the port are at 10.00 and 16.00 daily; 7.50 pesos per person (free for those under ten). Fishing excursions cost 20 pesos per hour.

Pre-Delta National Park
This national park was established in 1992 and has been declared part of the Delta Natural Heritage Site by UNESCO. It is a small park of only 2,458ha but of great importance for protecting the species that rely on the wetland habitat of the Paraná Delta, including mammals such as the capybara and the Paraná otter, caymans and other reptiles, and many birds including the kingfisher, which is so prolific that it has become the symbol of the park. The park is reached by Ruta 11 from north of Paraná city to Diamante, followed by a dirt road to La Axotea and La Jaula, just outside the park. In order to visit, a boat excursion must be arranged with the park administration (*Hipólito Irigoyen 396, Diamante, Entre Ríos;* ✆ *034 3498 3535;* e *predelta@apn.gov.ar*).

Corrientes Province
The greater part of this province is covered by wetlands, which are one of the most impressive areas of the country for eco-tourism and wildlife photographic safaris. The Guaraní culture infiltrates through the folklore, music and craftwork that have become signatures of the province. The arrival of missionaries from the east, and the presence of the Río Paraná, a major transport axis, along the northern frontier of the province, led the Spaniards to secure this province at an early stage, and the capital city of Corrientes is one of the oldest colonial cities in the country. In the south-central part of the province, a strong gaucho culture holds to tradition with ease.

CORRIENTES
Area code 03783
The historic architecture and overall beauty of Corrientes impress almost all visitors. The French- and Italian-influenced architecture of Plaza 25 de Mayo and the older colonial buildings are always noteworthy. The Costanera is a popular boulevard where townspeople stroll by the river in the evenings, and the high percentage of indigenous people in the community means that wonderful handicrafts are available in the markets. As well as being an important junction city between Iguazú and Salta, Corrientes is itself worthy of a visit. If you are only passing through, however, spending some time at least in the central plaza is preferable to waiting for your connection in the bus terminal.

Getting there
By air
The airport is 10km east on Ruta 12, reached by bus no. 8. There are daily flights from Buenos Aires at 08.30 (except Sun at 11.15) with Aerolíneas Argentinas (*Junín 1301;* ✆ *428678;* f *342 5731;* e *cnggte@aerolineas.com.ar; open Mon–Fri 08.00–12.30, 16.30–20.00, Sat 08.30–12.30*).

By bus

The terminal at Avenida Maipú 2700 (☎ *446533*) is reached from Buenos Aires (Retiro) by the following companies, taking about 14 hours for the 927km:

El Pulqui ☎ 011 4312 4311, 4313 7177. Daily at 15.30 and 19.30; 58 pesos.
ERSA ☎ 011 4314 4042/3. Daily at 19.00; 50 pesos.
La Nueva Chevallier ☎ 011 4000 5255. Daily at 19.55.
Flecha Bus ☎ 011 4111 5211, 4313 2781. Daily at 19.30.
San José ☎ 011 4313 3762. Daily at 19.20, 20.40 and 21.15.

From Resistencia there are departures every 15 minutes with ERSA and TAC; 45 minutes, 3 pesos.

By car

From Paraná/Santa Fé Ruta 12 leads to Corrientes. From Resistencia it's 20km on Ruta 16.

Orientation

Both the local and long-distance bus terminals are on Avenida Costanera and a couple of blocks from the main Plaza 25 de Mayo. The city is laid out on a simple grid that is easy to navigate.

Where to stay

Hotel Guaraní Mendoza 970; ☎ 423090, 433800; e hguarani@spacio.com.ar. One of the best in the city.
Hotel Orly San Juan 861; ☎ 427248; f 420280; e hotelorly@arnet.com.ar.
Hospedaje Robert La Rioja 415. Budget accommodation that's popular with backpackers.

Where to eat

The popular **Mercado Central** is always recommended for cheap and fresh food. It's on the pedestrianised central strip of Avenida Junín, along which are plenty of restaurants and cafés.

Practicalities

The **tourist office** is located at Plaza 25 de Mayo 1330, the **post office** at San Juan and San Martín and several banks with ATMs along 9 de Julio.

The **Hospital Escuela** is at Rivadavia 1250 (*in emergency* ☎ *107*). There are many pharmacies in the city, such as **Catedral** (*Junín 1492;* ☎ *429347/8*).

Highlights

Many buildings remain from the colonial period, after the city's founding in 1588. Mainly focused around religious structures, a tour of the city should include the **Convento de San Francisco** and the **Museo Franciscano** (*Mendoza 450*), and on this same block the **Monumento a la Gloria y Murales Histórico**, a long series of murals recounting the history of Corrientes, the **Santuario de la Cruz del Milagro** in Plaza La Cruz, and of course the **Cathedral** (Sanctuary of the Cross of the Miracle, with a wooden cross that protected the colonial city from native attacks on the altar), at Bolivar and San Lorenzo.

The **Museo Histórico de Corrientes** (*9 de Julio 1044*) and the **Museo de Bellas Artes Dr Juan Ramón Vidal** (*San Juan 634*) are two of the more interesting museums, and both are free.

The city's carnival, usually at the end of February, is known as one of the largest and liveliest in the region.

Mburucuyá National Park

The former estancia of Dr Troels M. Pedersen, in the northwest of the province, was donated to form a national park in 1997. Owing to its vast area of 15,060ha, it holds a great degree of biodiversity within three biomes: chaco, espinal and Paranáense rainforest. Many of the animal species it protects are endangered, such as the maned wolf, the Paraná otter, howler monkeys and the yacaré negro and yacaré overo (black and broad-nosed caimans). The original estancia house is now the park headquarters, and there are basic camping facilities in the park. The park is 150km from Corrientes city, between the towns of Palma Grande and Mburucuyá on Ruta 84.

MERCEDES

Area code 03773

The quiet little town of Mercedes is the most practical stopping point to access the Esteros del Iberá natural reserve. Surrounded by the pampas and economically sustained by agriculture, you can walk to the edge of town and see fields of cattle and gauchos on horseback. Just before the lunch hour, when the heat of the day is just starting to maximize, you can find these men in Plaza 25 de Mayo, off San Martín street, having returned from working the fields since dawn. By lunchtime the plaza is deserted until the heat has tapered and the siestas have ended.

Getting there

By bus

The bus terminal is at San Martín and J A Ferreyra, six blocks down San Martín from Plaza 25 de Mayo. Direct buses leave Buenos Aires at 21.00 daily (arriving in Mercedes at 06.00) with Flecha Bus (✆ 4315 2718; *www.flechabus.com.ar*) and twice a day with San José (✆ 4313 3762). There is one bus per day from Paraná with Flecha Bus (taking 9 hours) and daily connections from Concordia and Federación (approximately 4½ hours). There is no direct connection with Iguazú, but there are eight services per day to Corrientes with Expreso Ortiz, Santa Lucia and Nuevo Expreso (several leaving between 02.30 and 03.30; taking 3 hours); from Corrientes to Iguazú, Expreso Singer has a departure at 22.00 and Expreso Río Uruguay at 23.45, taking eight hours. These also pass through Posadas.

By car

Driving from Buenos Aires you should take Ruta 9 to Zárate and turn right on Ruta 12 to cross two bridges over the Río Paraná and enter the province of Entre Ríos (paying a toll of 4.20 pesos). Continue on Ruta 14 from Ceibas, passing through Concordia and Federación and continuing north into Corrientes province, and you will reach Mercedes after a total of 739km.

Orientation

The bus terminal is on the edge of town at San Martín and J A Ferreyra. Six blocks straight down Avenida San Martín is the centre, where Plaza 25 de Mayo is surrounded by Sarmiento, Chacabuco, Pujol and San Martín.

Where to stay

Delicias del Iverá Hostel Dr Rivas 688; ✆ 422 508/423 167;
e deliciasdelibera@yahoo.com.ar; www.hostels.org.ar. This hostel is the most highly recommended accommodation in town. Private and shared rooms. Free shuttle from bus terminal. *Dorm 13 pesos (15 pesos non-members); sgl 22 pesos (25 pesos); dbl 33 pesos (36 pesos); dbl with private bath 38 pesos (46 pesos); quadruple 72 pesos (86 pesos). B/fast 5–6 pesos (8 pesos); full American b/fast 10 pesos (12 pesos).*

Hotel Plaza San Martín and Chacabuco; ↘ 420 013. Directly on the Plaza 25 de Mayo, this is a historic hotel for this small town.

Where to eat and drink
At **Delicias del Iberá Hostel** (*Pujol 1162*) a breakfast buffet or American-style breakfast is available in the morning for 5–12 pesos; the dinner menu changes daily and is very good quality, at around 10 pesos for a meal. Two other recommended restaurants are **El Quincho** (*San Martín 1240;* ↘ *420314*) and **Chirolá** (*Pujol and Sarmiento, no telephone*); a meal at either costs about 15 pesos.

You can eat inexpensively on Friday, Saturday and Sunday at the town **casino**, on Avenida Belgrano off Plaza San Martín (the french fries have a great reputation). On Avenida Chacabuco you will find **Pizza Libre Restaurant** and **Cremolati Ice Cream Parlor**.

Practicalities
Although there is **tourist information** at the bus terminal, you will be hard pressed to receive any information from them. What you will likely encounter is a Spanish speaking woman in a practically empty room who will not have even a map to offer you. If you want to know about the town and excursions to the Esteros del Iberá natural reserve, go to the **Delicias del Iverá Hostel** (*Pujol 1162;* ↘ *422 508; 15 493 985*), that functions as a hotel, restaurant and tourist information. The owner, Virginia, has maps, brochures and bus schedules and is extremely helpful and knowledgeable about all the excursions, transportation and activities in the area.

For additional information on the Esteros del Iberá natural reserve, a small book called *Vida y Color* (15 pesos), makes an excellent guidebook for the flora and fauna – especially birds – that you will see in the reserve, or pick up a two-page pamphlet (2 pesos) from the tourist centre in Colonia Pellegrini. The money is put into an account that will be used for works to better Colonia Pellegrini. These works will be decided by Fundacion Iberá and the townspeople of Pellegrini. This is very important for Colonia Pellegrini and its conservation. The first 1,000 pesos raised will go into the first project. Contact Fundacion Ecos (*www.ecosibera.org*) or FUNAFU (e *info@funafu.org, www.naturalezaparaelfuturo.org*) for more information.

The **Hospital Las Mercedes** is on Avenida Juan Roman Lacour 1057 (↘ *420 031 or 429 975*), and a health clinic (sanitario) is on Avenida San Martín off Alvear. Farmacy Kairuz is on Avenida Sarmiento, between Avenidas San Martín and Pujol.

There are two banks with ATMs: **Banco de la Nación Argentina**, San Martín and Rivadavia, and **Banco de Corrientes**, San Martín and Pedro Ferre. The **post office** is at San Martín and Rivadavia. There are a few internet cafés: **Cyber de Manu** on Plaza San Martín; **Winners**, San Martín 833; and another on the 900 block of Juan Pujol.

Shopping and local specialities
Chac Cucros (*San Martín 853;* ↘ *420341*) is a great shop for leather products, especially if you own a horse and are looking for things such as saddles and bridles, as well as typical products such as *matés*, *bombillas* and *porta-matés*. They have many items made from capybara, the large rodent that you may see if you visit the parks; this has been extensively exploited for its unusual hide, soft and with a pock-marked appearance. A few other shops sell leather and regional products, such as **Talabarteria El Nandu**, on the plaza on the corner of Pujol and Chacabuco; **Manos Correntinas**, on the corner of San Martín and Sargento Cabral (400 block); and **Casenave Cueros**, on Avenida Pellegrini.

MERCEDES (SKETCH MAP) Not to scale

N Bradt

Manos Correntinos

SAN LORENZO — SAN LORENZO

SARGENTO CABRAL — SARGENTO CABRAL

GENERAL PAZ — GENERAL PAZ

BATALLA DE SALTA — BATALLA DE SALTA

B MITRE — B MITRE

Hotel Plaza
Pizza Libre Restaurant & Cremolati ice cream parlor
Talabartería El Nandú

Iglesia Nuestra Señora de la Merced

CHACABUCO — CHACABUCO

Police station

Plaza 25 de Mayo

SARMIENTO — SARMIENTO

Chac Cueros
Farmacy Kairuz
Chirolá

BELGRANO — BELGRANO

Banco de la Nación Argentina
Town casino

RIVADAVIA — RIVADAVIA

Banco de Corrientes
Delicias del Iverá Hostel (incl restaurant & tourist information)

Hospital Las Mercedes

PEDRO FERRÉ — PEDRO FERRÉ

Sanitario (health clinic)

DR RIVAS ESPAÑA ALVEAR

El Quincho

SAN MARTÍN JUAN PUJOL P MARTÍNEZ F L BELTRAN M F MANTILLA JUAN RAMÓN LACOUR M CARRUEGA

ALVEAR

J M GÓMEZ — J M GÓMEZ

Casenave Cueros
Bus terminal

Excursions to Esteros del Iberá and Colonia Carlos Pellegrini

Go to the Delicias del Iberá Hostel in Mercedes and ask Virginia for all information on tours to the park. She has several packages available with all transportation and guiding arrangements in place. The hostel package includes two nights' accommodation in a hostel or *hospedaje*, meals (three breakfasts, one lunch, one dinner), bus tickets and guided excursions for 180 pesos per person (300 pesos for two). Other packages are available with accommodation at the *posadas* (lodges) and restaurant meals. Because of the limited public transport to the park, booking through the hostel is the most efficient approach. Activities in the park include a two-hour boat tour, a walking tour with hired guide, rented canoes or kayaks, trips on horseback or in 4x4 vehicles, fishing, birdwatching (350 species) and wildlife viewing.

About 800km from Buenos Aires, this stunning park is most easily reached from Mercedes, the only town that has a bus connection to the reserve; the only other option is to hire a *remise*, but this is much more expensive (for example, a *remise* to Posadas costs about 270 pesos, shared by a maximum of four passengers). A bus leaves Mercedes for the park at 11.30 or 12.00 – there is no tight scheduling here – Monday to Saturday only. Day trips of a sort are possible but the bus schedule is very inconvenient, arriving at the reserve around 15.00 and having to catch the bus back to Mercedes at 04.00 the next morning. At the Mercedes bus terminal Rayobus (✆ *420184*) and Empresa Itatí II (✆ *421722*) sell tickets (12 pesos) and confirm schedules for transport to the park.

RESERVA NATURAL ESTEROS DEL IBERÁ

Several hours on a boat through the swamps, full of carpincho and amazing birdlife, with an experienced guide is the highlight experience in the reserve. The guides are local people who once subsisted by hunting for food and animal products to sell, and have now been employed by the reserve to use their wildlife expertise for the benefit of conservation. This wise initiative has multiple benefits: the wildlife and navigational expertise of these former hunters is preserved, tourists are rewarded with knowledgeable guides who are able to track and point out the animals that novices would have difficulty finding, the animals are no longer threatened, the reserve authorities can document the wildlife inventory and ecological history, and finally the guides themselves are provided with a stable income and have pride in their work. Among the most hunted animals, still at risk outside the park, is the carpincho or capybara (*Hydrochaeris hydrochaeris*). This herbivore, the largest member of the rodent family, lives in the wetlands in communities of 30–40 individuals with a dominant male. Breeding occurs twice in the summer, the males fighting among themselves over the females. Litters are of four to eight young, which stay with their mother for several months. The carpincho is hunted for meat, oils (reputedly with curative properties for asthma), and leather, which is soft with a dotted texture and often has scars from fighting; it is used for clothing, bags, belts, boots, moccasins and the like.

Hiking in the adjacent forest will allow you to see howler monkeys, vultures and butterflies and be impressed by the colours of the bromeliads and bright orange fungus. In all the reserve protects over 300 species of birds and many endangered reptiles, amphibians and mammals. Established in 1983, it covers an area of 13,000km² (including over 60 lagoons), and only the area around Colonia Carlos Pellegrini is accessible to tourists.

The bus is a rickety old *colectivo* that makes its way down the bumpy dirt road in the heat of the midday sun with no air conditioning and without enough speed to get a good breeze through the windows. It makes its way through the countryside, stopping anywhere that passengers request, until it arrives at Colonia Carlos Pellegrini three hours later. Most of the passengers are local people making trips to town for supplies or to catch a bus from the main terminal. During the trip you may be seated next to a chicken or a rabbit. Through the window you will see gauchos on horseback, rheas, armadillos and crested caracaras.

If you have the option of driving to the park, make sure you have a full tank before leaving either Mercedes, Posadas or Corrientes, and carry a spare can for your return trip. Leaving Mercedes, take Avenida San Martín towards Ruta 123, then Ruta Provincial 40 for roughly 120km to the reserve. The dirt road is in fair condition until the last few kilometres, where you will have to drive slowly to avoid the many potholes. You will enter the village of Colonia Carlos Pellegrini after crossing a bridge of noisy wooden slats.

Accommodation is available in Colonia Carlos Pellegrini, base for all visitors to the park. One option is a basic hostel or *hospedaje* costing about 30 pesos per person per night; the other is a lodge or *posada* that will cost close to 200 pesos per person per night. This village is very small and there is little infrastructure; there are no fixed phone lines so you may wait up to a week for replies to emails. Meals will be available at your accommodation, or your host will direct you to the closest neighbour who runs a kitchen.

Posada de la Laguna Calle Agurá s/n; ✆f 499413; m (0377) 15 629827;
e posadadelalaguna@ibera.net, info@posadadelalaguna.com; www.posadadelalaguna.com.
Transfers can be arranged from Mercedes, Corrientes or Posadas. Tours of the wetlands and interpretative centre, photographic excursions, birdwatching, trekking, canoeing or carriage rides in the pampas.

Posada Aguapè ✆f 499412 or in Buenos Aires 011 4742 3015;
e aguape@interserve.com.ar, aguape@fibertel.com.ar. This beautiful lodge is surrounded by the nature and wildlife of the reserve. Transfers can be arranged from Mercedes, Corrientes or Posadas. A basic dbl starts at 160 pesos.

Irupé Lodge Yacare and Ysipo; ✆ 15 402193, 15 400661; www.irupelodge.com.ar. This is a rustic wood-frame lodge giving you a 'safari' feeling. A dbl room with FB (meals and 1 boat excursion) costs 120–160 pesos per person, varying according to style of room and time of year (Easter is very busy, Dec and Jan very quiet).

Rancho Ypa Sapukai ✆ 420155, 15 629536; e ypasapukai@ibera.net;
www.ypasapukai.com.ar. Rooms cost 30 pesos inc b/fast. Excursions are available for 25 pesos per person.

Rancho Inambu Hostel Calles 2 and 28; ✆ 0221 491 6751 or in Buenos Aires 011 471 4431; e ranchoinambu@yahoo.com.ar. Rooms cost 30 pesos.

Activities

Take advantage of a boat tour with one of the excellent and knowledgeable guides – feel free to tip them for their skill at finding the incredible species hidden in the swamps for your viewing and photographing pleasure and for sharing with you their great knowledge of the ecology.

An alternative to the excursions in the swamps is a 'Day at the Ranch', a full day of horseriding, starting at 09.00 with saddling up and learning the rules, followed by lunch at the beautiful ranch house, after-lunch ride in the forest and back to the ranch for late-afternoon tea. This costs 100 pesos per person including transport from the Delicias del Iberá Hostel in Mercedes.

You can also take horseriding excursions with the naturalist and birding guide José Martín, whose tours include a two-and-a-half-hour ride through the palm forest and marshland (25 pesos per person), a half-day trip (65 pesos per person with lunch) or full-day trip (85 pesos per person) through Cambá Trapo marshlands or a one-hour ride through the village (20 pesos per person). Again, book through the hostel.

While staying in Colonia Carlos Pellegrini you can arrange a two-hour carriage ride for 20 pesos per person or a wildlife night tour safari-style in a car, two hours for 25 pesos per person (❧ 15 402876).

Misiones Province

Misiones features two main highlights, the awesome Iguazú waterfalls on the border with Brazil, and the Jesuit ruins throughout the province, most notably the largest at San Ignacio Miní. The name of the province comes from the missionary colonies that grew to great size and power in this area before they were exiled from the country. Of additional interest is the mining of precious and semi-precious stones, such as in the small town of Wanda. The province is technically subtropical, but being practically atop the Tropic of Capricorn the difference will not be felt. It is a zone of fast-flowing rivers that spill over several waterfalls, and lush green jungle growing from brick-red dirt which provides habitat for monkeys, reptiles, coatis, jaguars and colourful tropical birds.

POSADAS
Area code 03752
Although an important gateway city for buses to the mission ruins, Iguazú Falls and cities to the west, Posadas does not offer much for tourists.

Getting there
By air
The Aeropuerto Internacional Libertador General San Martín is 10km southwest of the city centre at km1336.5 of Ruta 12 (❧ 451699, 451104, 457413). Public bus no. 28 (0.70 pesos) connects the airport to the centre, the bus terminal, the riverside road and the port. *Remise* service is provided by Libertador Gral San Martín (❧ 15 691049, 15 508291), and car rental by Millet-Hertz (❧ 422415) and Avis (❧ 596660), also at the airport.

Aerolíneas Argentinas has flights from Buenos Aires (Aeroparque) early every morning but Sunday and every evening but Saturday. The Aerolíneas Argentinas offices are at Ayacucho 1728 between San Martín and Bolivar (❧ 438069, 422036; f 435544; e pssventas@aerolineas.com.ar; open Mon–Fri 08.00–12.00, 16.00–20.00, Sat 08.00–12.00).

By bus
The bus terminal is on Ruta 12 at Santa Catalina, about 3km southwest of the centre (❧ 454888). From Buenos Aires the journey takes 13 hours and costs 77–105 pesos, depending on level of service. Expreso Singer (❧ 011 4313 3927, 4313 2355) has several departures between 19.30 and 22.00; Crucero del Norte (❧ 011 4315 1652, 4315 0478) departs daily at 18.00, 20.00 and 22.45; San Cristobal (❧ 011 4313 2387, 4312 5902) departs daily at 19.30; and Empresa Río Uruguay (❧ 011 4312 0828, 4315 1223) departs at 20.00. There are a few connections per day to Iguazú (5 hours; 24 pesos) with Empresa Benjamín Horianski (❧ 426254), Empresa Sol del Norte (❧ 03758 422471) or Expreso del Valle (❧ 03743 420487).

Heading west across the country, Horianski has one service per day to Salta (leaving Posadas at 13.00), but this bus is unreliable and often breaks down. There's a more frequent service to Tucumán (50–68 pesos), the higher fares usually indicating either fewer stops or a more comfortable seat – bear in mind that is a long-haul overnight journey (approximately 17 hours). A better route to Salta is via Corrientes, which has frequent connections with Posadas or Iguazú.

By car

Posadas is on Ruta 12 exactly 310km from both Corrientes and Puerto Iguazú. In order to move west or south you will have to go through the city of Corrientes. Northeast of Posadas Ruta 14 also leads to Puerto Iguazú through the centre of the province, connecting with roads to Uruguay and south all the way to the Río de la Plata, north of Buenos Aires (1,310km).

Orientation

Downtown Posadas is considered to be the area bordered by Avenidas Guacurarí, RS Peña, Mitre and Corrientes. The central Plaza 9 de Julio seems to also be a

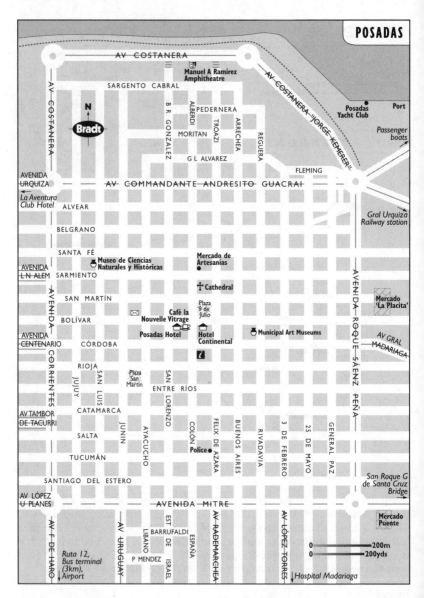

homeless camp; after strolling past the craft kiosks around its periphery and visiting the cathedral there won't be much to keep you. Downtown provides services such as banks and internet and has a few museums, but is not highly entertaining. The attractions are along the river and in the surrounding parks. From the Plaza 9 de Julio, walk north down Avenida Colón, which changes its name to Alberdi on the north side of the wide Avenida Comandante Andresito Guacurarí, to arrive at the riverside Costanera, where there is a large pedestrianised area with a jogging and cycling path, a beach area, the yacht club and a port with restaurant and bar service.

Practicalities
Tourist information is available at Colón 1985 (✆ *447539/40 or 0800 555 0297;* e *turismo@misiones.gov.ar; www.misiones.gov.ar*). The **post office** is at Bolivar and Ayacucho (✆ *436544*). The **police station** is at Félix de Azara and Tucumán (✆ *447662*). The **Hospital Madariaga** is at Avenida López Torres 1177 (✆ *447787*). A nice market is the **Mercado de Artesanías** at Sarmiento 317 (✆ *425427; open 08.00–12.00, 16.00–20.00*). Off the central plaza, **Café la Nouvelle Vitrage** (*Bolivar 1899;* ✆ *429619*) has a diverse menu, including full breakfasts, with decent prices.

Where to stay
Posadas Hotel Bolivar 1949; ✆ 440888; f 430294; e hotelposadas@arnet.com.ar; www.hotelposadas.com.ar. Centrally located with a gym and a coffee shop, standard rooms cost 70 pesos sgl, 90 pesos dbl, 110 pesos triple and 130 pesos for a suite (25 pesos more for a superior room).
Hotel Continental Bolivar 1879; ✆ 440990; f 435302; e hotel@hoteleramisiones.com.ar; www.hoteleramisiones.com.ar. This large hotel with restaurant is located in the centre of the city; sgls cost 55 pesos, dbls 78–95 pesos, triples 100–115 pesos, and suites 140 pesos.
La Aventura Club Hotel Av Urquiza and Av Zapiola; ✆ 465555; f 463593; e aventuraclub@hotmail.com; www.laaventuracentroturistico.com. The hostel, a Hostelling International affiliate, is a bit out of town (5 pesos by taxi from the centre), but is an excellent choice for price and setting. In a large forested area by the river, it is extremely quiet in the off-season, but in the summer becomes a lively resort with a swimming pool, tennis courts, outdoor pub and restaurant (open in high season only or for special functions) and plenty of open space. Cabins for 4 people cost 70–107 pesos; dorms (with thin walls) sleep 4 for 10–15 pesos per person. Prices vary depending on the length of stay, time of year and whether b/fast is included.

Museums
Museo de Ciencias Naturales y Históricas San Luis 384; ✆ 425569. This boasts one of the country's best natural-history displays, with a serpentarium, aviary and large aquarium. *Open Mon–Fri 07.00–12.00, 14.00–19.00.*
Museo Arqueológico y Histórico 'Andrés Guacurarí' General Paz 1865; ✆ 447373. *Open Tue–Fri 08.00–12.00, 14.00–19.00, w/ends & hols 09.00–12.00, 15.00–19.00.*

There are a few art museums in the city:

Museo Municipal de Bellas Artes 'Lucas Braulio Areco' Rivadavia 1846; ✆ 449074
Museo de Arte 'Juan Yaparí' Sarmiento 317; ✆ 447375/6
Museo Municipal de Artes 'Palacio del Maté' Rivadavia near Bolivar; ✆ 428139. *Open Mon–Fri 08.00–12.00, 16.00–22.00.*

SAN IGNACIO MINÍ
Area code 03752
An hour by bus from Posadas (63km east on Ruta 12) is one of the most important ruined missions: San Ignacio is a large archaeological site where between 1609 and 1818 the Jesuits established one of the most significant and unique social, cultural and religious centres of South American history. Three other missions are in the area: Santa Ana, Nuestra Señora de Loreto and Santa María La Mayor. A ticket covering all four missions costs 12 pesos (*6 pesos for those under 12, 2.50 pesos for those over 65*) and lasts for 15 days. Without a car, you will have to rise to the challenge of taking the local buses that are cheap but not very frequent. Santa Ana and Loreto are respectively 30 and 45 minutes from San Ignacio; to continue to Santa María, a couple of hours away, requires a full-day excursion.

SAN IGNACIO MINÍ

AVENIDA PARAGUAY →

Cataratas del Iguazú →

BRASIL

ALBERDI

ROCA

AZCUENAGA

AVENIDA MORENO

Ruta Nacional 12

GME MEDINA

MITRE

J J LANUSSI

AVENIDA SARMIENTO

BELGRANO

INDEPENDENCÍA

IRIGOYEN

R Z PEÑA

Ruta Nacional 12

PELLEGRINI

ALCORIA

URQUIZA

SANTO CABRAL

LAVALLE

SAN MARTÍN

RIVADAVIA

AVENIDA BOLÍVAR

GÜEMES

ALVEAR

URUGUAY

AVENIDA BOLÍVAR

AVENIDA QUIROGA

Museum

Hospedaje
El Descanso

Almacén de
Arte y Sanías
(craft shop)

Ruins of San Ignacio

Police

La Aldea Pizzeria

Hotel San Ignacio

Church

Municipalidad

Plaza

N

Bradt

200m
200yds

0
0

Casa H Quiroga,
Playa del Sol →

Teyu Cuare Ozununu,
Bain La Boca →

Loreto & Santa Ana (ruinas),
Posadas →

YERBA MATE

Yerba *maté* (*Ilex paraquariensis*) is a bitter tea-like herb, high in caffeine, that is drunk from a dried and hollowed gourd, also called a *maté*, which is often decorated with elaborately engraved silver bands and trimmings. The *maté* is steeped loose in hot water, and an elegant silver straw or *bombilla* with a small sieve at the bottom is used for sipping. It is of great cultural and symbolic importance, and there is a language and ceremony of *maté*, just as with tango. When a group of people drinks *maté* together, only one gourd with a single straw is prepared by the tea master, '*el sebador*', who passes it to each member of the group. When a person is passed the gourd he or she sips it until the liquid is finished and the satisfying sound of air passing through the straw is heard. The gourd is returned to the tea master who refills the hot water for each turn. To indicate that you do not want to be passed the *maté* again you must return it with a 'thank you'; otherwise the *maté* can continue circling indefinitely, with fresh leaves added as necessary. *Maté* may also be brewed and drunk just as a regular tea; in this manner it is called *maté cocido*. Kids drink *maté* with sugar and/or milk, while *maté de leche con cascarita de naranja* has hot milk and orange peels added.

This drink was popular with the native peoples of Argentina as well as those of Uruguay and Chile. In Misiones, the Jesuits tried to ban *maté* as an addictive substance, but they soon realised that it had health- and energy-giving properties and not only permitted the drinking of *maté*, but started its cultivation. *Maté* became a major crop in Misiones, but after the Jesuits were expelled from the colonies and the Franciscan monks took over religious dominance, the crops were somewhat abandoned. However demand for the drink grew throughout the country and by 1876 the State of Corrientes regulated the crops and the industry was born there. The red fertile earth and regular rainfall in the region are ideal for growing yerba *maté*, and approximately 180,000ha in Misiones and 21,000ha in Corrientes are dedicated to its cultivation. Plants are set perpendicular to the slope to limit soil erosion, and hedgerows are used for protection from wind. The tea is no longer collected by hand but harvested mechanically. The fame of this tea has crossed Argentina's borders and it is now an export product, mainly to the United States and certain countries in Europe.

Buses stop to drop off and pick up passengers on the highway at the entrance to the town of San Ignacio, where there is a small information building with bus schedules. Buses from Puerto Iguazú or Wanda cost 15–20 pesos; from Posadas 4 pesos. It's a couple of kilometres from the bus drop-off to the centre of town or the ruins; there are local taxis, but they usually wait in the main plaza.

The Interpretive Centre Ruinas de San Ignacio, near the entrance to the ruins (↘ *470186; open daily 07.00–19.00*), has displays and installations interpreting the culture and mission lifestyle. Within the ruins, near the exit, is a small museum housing artefacts. There is a nightly hour-long light and music show, starting, more or less, at 19.30 or 20.00. It costs 5 pesos (*free for the disabled and those under 6*).

San Ignacio Miní was founded in 1610 and moved to the present site in 1695, growing to a population of 3,300; it remains the best preserved of all the missions, with a central square, church, priest's house, cemetery and over 200 dwellings still in a fair state. The church, 74m long, was an outstanding example of the 'Guaraní Baroque' style, with floral bas-reliefs carved into the red sandstone.

By the time of their destruction and extinction, the greater mission comprised 30 towns within Brazil, Paraguay and Argentina. Half of these were in Argentina, with 11 in the territory of Misiones. The Jesuits were expelled from the area in 1767 and the missions themselves raided and destroyed by Portuguese and Paraguayan invasions between 1816 and 1819. A remarkable civilisation that had prospered for a couple of hundred years was thus destroyed in three. The social organisation and economic structure are considered unprecedented in the world. The missions' structure and stability empowered them to deal with sanitary issues and avoid devastation from plagues, to deter military attack and to maintain a completely self-sustaining agricultural economy with advanced skills and trades that provided a high quality of life for all who lived there. For these reasons San Ignacio Miní reached a population of 28,714 inhabitants after its first hundred years. By 1732 the population had reached 141,182. This seeming utopia caused discomfort to the political powers colonising the surrounding countries, and is the reason for the expulsions and attacks. The missions, lost in the jungle, were rediscovered in 1897 but restoration did not begin until the 1940s; in 1984 the best were placed on UNESCO's World Heritage List.

Nuestra Señora de Loreto was founded in 1632 and moved in 1686 to the present site, 3km off Ruta 12 about 10km back towards Posadas; although now in a particularly bad state, it is on the World Heritage List.

Santa Ana is 40km from Posadas along Ruta 12 (and 700m from the highway) in the Sierra del Tapé; it was first founded in 1633, but due to attacks by bandits it was abandoned and then re-established in 1660. The church, cemetery, dwellings and workshops can still be seen.

Santa María La Mayor, founded in 1636, is 150km from Posadas on Ruta Provincial 2, between San Javier and Concepción de la Sierra; the walls of the priests' dwelling, school and workshops can still be seen.

Practicalities
Almacén de Arte y Sanías on Avenida Moreno is a great little store selling one-of-a-kind handmade items of jewellery, handbags and *maté* gourds. It is opposite the kiosks lining the edge of the ruins.

Where to stay and eat
Hotel San Ignacio Sarmiento and San Martín; ☏ 470422. 25 pesos for a sgl; 50 pesos dbl. B/fast is not included but there is a restaurant serving 3 meals a day adjacent to the lobby.
Hospedaje El Descanso Pellegrini 270; ☏ 470 207. Among several cheap accommodation options on this street.
La Aldea Pizzeria on Rivadavia adjacent to the ruins; ☏ 470567. Offers simple and tasty food.

There are also cheaper *hospedajes*, and camping by a lake 5km south.

PUERTO IGUAZÚ
Area code 03757
This town exists to service tourists visiting the falls. There are several restaurants, shops and places to stay, but you will spend most of your time in the national park.

Getting there
By air
The Aeropuerto Internacional Iguazú (☏ *421996*) is located on Ruta Provincial 101, 6km from the Iguazú Falls National Park and 21km from downtown Puerto

Iguazú. There is a shuttle service available for 8 pesos (✆ *422962, 421140;* e *blancafit@arnet.com.ar*). There are also taxis (✆ *420008*) and *remises* (✆ *421503*) charging about 30 pesos. Hertz (✆ *423362*) and Avis (✆ *424125*) offer car rental at the airport.

Aerolíneas Argentinas (*Victoria Aguirre 295;* ✆ *420168;* f *420786;* e *igrgte@aerolineas.com.ar; open Mon–Fri 08.00–13.00, 15.00–20.00, Sat 08.00–13.00*) has four flights a day (four on Sunday) from Buenos Aires, taking one hour and 45 minutes, and LAN Argentina (*Perito Moreno 184;* ✆ *420390;* f *420214*) has two a day. There are also direct flights from Córdoba (also 1 hour 45 mins) with Aerolíneas on Thursdays and Sundays.

By bus

The large bus terminal is at Avenida Córdoba and Misiones (✆ *423006*). Buses from Buenos Aires Retiro station cost 95–125 pesos for a 30-hour journey that requires some stamina. You would be well advised to pay the extra few pesos for the comfort of a *supercama*. Espreso Singer (✆ *011 4313 3927, 4313 2355*) has departures from the capital at 13.30 or 19.00; Crucero del Norte (✆ *011 4315 1652, 4315 0478*) has four or five departures per day starting from 14.30; Expreso Tigre Iguazú (✆ *011 4313 3915, 4313 7158*) has departures at 15.00 and 20.00 (plus 18.00 Tuesday, Friday, Sunday); and Via Bariloche (✆ *011 4315 4456*) departs daily at 18.50.

Buses run frequently from Corrientes and Resistencia, as well as from Posadas (5 hours; 24 pesos). Flecha Bus and Andesmar offer *supercama* service between Salta and Iguazú, taking about 24 hours and costing 150 pesos; there are cheaper options with worse seats and schedules.

By car

Driving from Buenos Aires you should take Ruta 9 to Zárate and turn right onto Ruta 12 to cross two bridges over the Río Paraná and enter the province of Entre Ríos (paying a toll of 4.20 pesos). Continue on Ruta 14 from Ceibas, passing through Concordia and Federación and continuing north through Corrientes province to enter Misiones. At Aristóbulo del Valle turn left to take Ruta Provincial 7 for 40km to Jardín América, from where you should pick up Ruta 12 again, past Wanda and all the way to Puerto Iguazú. You will have driven a total of 1,392km and have spent roughly 300 pesos on fuel. Ruta 14 continues through the centre of the province all the way to the junction of Ruta 101, to continue north to Iguazú and south to Río de la Plata. This is a long journey and you would be well advised to consult a road atlas to determine your most suitable course and pay attention to distances between service stations. Ruta 12 also leads north from Posadas passing through the mission area.

Orientation

The city centre is Plaza San Martín, around which are most municipal offices such as the tourist and post offices. North of the plaza are the Río Iguazú and the port. The main traffic artery is Avenida Victoria Aguirre, heading southeast from Plaza San Martín out of the city and towards the airport, the falls and the junction with Ruta 12.

Where to stay

There are two high-end hotels in Puerto Iguazú (as well as the Sheraton in the national park – see below).

Hotel Cataratas Ruta 12, km4; ✆ *421100;* f *421909;* e reserves@hotelcataratas.com; www.hotelcataratas.com. Has a swimming pool, recreation facilities, a gym and many services; sgls and dbls start at 230 pesos and 250 pesos in low season.

Iguazú Grand Hotel Resort and Casino Ruta 12, km1640; ↘ 498050; f 490060; e reservas@casinoiguazu.com; www.casinoiguazu.com. If you have been lucky at the slots you can afford the 2,575 pesos for the presidential suite; otherwise, you will have to rough it in a standard at 554 pesos.

Hostería Los Helechos Paulino Amarante 76; ☎f 420338; e info@hosterialoshelechos.com.ar; www.hosterialoshelechos.com.ar. Rates start at 40 pesos for a sgl; 50 pesos for a dbl.

There are two well-run hostels affiliated to Hostelling International, which have communal spaces, kitchen and internet access. **Iguazú Falls Hostel** (*Guaraní 70; ↘ 421295; e info@hosteliguazufalls.com*) has very basic dorms and plenty of showers – though often in need of a bit of maintenance. Dorms start at 15 pesos for HI members (18 pesos for non-members), and doubles with private bath start at 45 pesos. A similar place is the **Sumaj Hostel** (*Andresito 145; ↘ 420995; e info@sumajhostel.com.ar*) where doubles with shared bath start at 30 pesos.

Where to eat and drink

Real Panificadora Av Córdoba and Guaraní; ↘ 420213. Has wonderfully delicious *facturas* (croissants made with chocolate, ricotta, nuts or other sweets) as well as cakes and savoury items.

La Rueda One of the fancier restaurants along Av Córdoba, with a good selection of Argentine wines. There are also casual *parrillas* and informal restaurants along the same street.

Practicalities

Tourist information is available at Avenida Victoria Aguirre 396 (↘ 420800, 0800 555 0297; e turismo@misiones.gov.ar, infoiguazu@iguazunet.com). The **Iguazú National Park office** is at Avenida

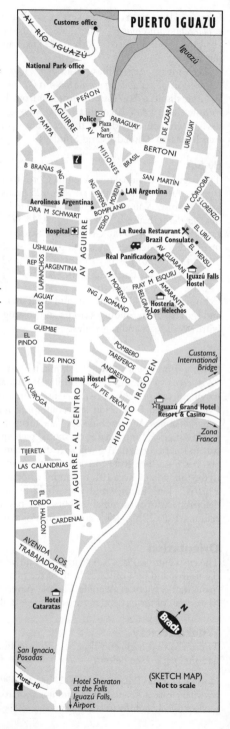

PUERTO IGUAZÚ
Customs office
AV RÍO IGUAZÚ
Iguazú
National Park office
AV PEÑON
AV AGUIRRE
LA PAMPA
Police
Plaza San Martín
Paraguay
F DE AZARA
URUGUAY
MISIONES
BERTONI
B BRAÑAS
ING UMA
ING EPPENS
BRASIL
SAN MARTÍN
AV CÓRDOBA
S LORENZO
DRA M SCHWART
MORENO
LAN Argentina
Aerolíneas Argentinas
BOMPLAND
PEDRO MORENO
EL URU
Hospital
Hospital
La Rueda Restaurant
Brazil Consulate
EL MENSU
USHUAIA
Real Panificadora
AV GUARANI
REP ARGENTINA
LOS LAPANCHOS
M MORENO
J P ESQUIU
Iguazú Falls Hostel
AGUAY
ING J ROMANO
FRAY M ESQUIU
BELGRANO
AMARANTE
Hostería Los Helechos
GUEMBE
EL PINDO
POMBERO
TAREFEROS
Customs, International Bridge
LOS PINOS
H QUIROGA
ANDRESITO
HIPOLITO IRIGOYEN
Sumaj Hostel
AV PTE PERÓN
AV AGUIRRE - AL CENTRO
Iguazú Grand Hotel Resort & Casino
Zona Franca
TIJERETA
LAS CALANDRIAS
EL TORDO
HALCON
CARDENAL
AVENIDA LOS TRABAJADORES
Hotel Cataratas
N
Bradt
San Ignacio, Posadas
Ruta 10
Hotel Sheraton at the Falls
Iguazú Falls,
Airport
(SKETCH MAP)
Not to scale

Victoria Aguirre 66 (✆ *420180, 420722, 420382;* e *iguazu@apn.gov.ar*), a few blocks north of Plaza San Martín near the port and **customs office** (✆ *420219*).

Many essential services are located on Plaza San Martín, including the **post office** (✆ *420371*) and **police station** (✆ *420016*). The **hospital** is at Avenida Victoria Aguirre and Schwart (✆ *420288*).

Parque Nacional Iguazú

The park hours are 09.00–18.00 in autumn and winter; 08.00–19.00 in spring and summer. Buses operated by El Práctico run between Puerto Iguazú and the park every 45 minutes between 07.15 and 19.15 (7 pesos). Entering the park you'll have to pay a fee of 30 pesos (*15 pesos for children of 6–12; there's a raft of discounts for local residents*). If you want to enter the next day too (advisable if you want to do all the hikes), ask for the *sello* of your ticket to get a 50% discount next day. You will find an information desk here (as well as at the Centro Operativo near the Cataratas Station; ✆ *420180 to report problems*); the *Iberá retá* visitor centre, with an interpretative hall with wall panels, photos, specimens and installations to provide information about jungle ecology and the history of human occupation in the area; shops selling film and souvenirs; and the La Selva restaurant, a pizzeria and fast- food outlet. There is another fast-food restaurant on the lower circuit.

Give yourself at least one full day to take in this incredible natural wonder. The falls cover a large area of park. You will spend a lot of time walking on boardwalks over the rivers and tributaries to the falls and taking in the beauties of the forest as you approach the falls themselves. Although the falls are just south of the Tropic of Capricorn, and thus technically sub-tropical, it feels truly tropical – in the summer it will be very hot and humid so dress appropriately and carry water. The best time of year to visit from the point of view of temperature and rain/water levels is spring or autumn.

The falls are shared with Brazil, from where you view the panorama of the falls rather that walk among them as on the Argentine side. In order to visit the Brazilian side of the falls, North Americans and Australasians (but not most Europeans) must in theory organise a visa, which requires photos, 48 hours for processing and approximately 130 pesos (US citizens must pay a US$100 reciprocity fee). This can be organised in Iguazú at Avenida Córdoba 264 (✆ *421348*) or in Buenos Aires at Pellegrini 1363, near 9 de Julio (✆ *011 4515 6500*). In practice it's unlikely to be a problem for day-trippers, most of whom don't even have to get out of their buses or taxis at the border, but be sure to get properly stamped back into Argentina. It's best to visit the Brazilian side early in the morning (you'll only need a couple of hours). It's also better to sleep on the Argentine side if you have a choice. Sightseeing helicopters often fly along the Brazilian side, although this practice is being restricted owing to the significant environmental damage they cause.

One of the beautiful aspects of Iguazú Falls is that development of the park has been kept fairly minimal, funnelling the thousands of visitors each day along the boardwalks and on the little train. Visitors are able to enter and walk through this incredible environment with minimal impact by staying on the boardwalks and not traipsing through the jungle, thus sparing the delicate flora and keeping a respectful distance from wildlife. The upper and lower falls each have a walkway with the occasional interpretative sign introducing a species of plant or animal. A small train, the Tren Ecológico or 'green train of the jungle', departs from the Central Station every half hour, taking ten minutes to the Cataratas and 20 to the Garganta Station; this is included in your park entry fee.

IGUAZÚ NATIONAL PARK

Alvar Nuñez Cabeza de Vaca, the second governor of Río de la Plata, presumed that he was the first to discover the falls on his voyage from Santa Catarina to Asunción in 1541, and named them the Santa María Falls. The Guaraní indigenous people, however, were here much earlier and had already named them *Iguazú* 'Great Water'. The Garganta del Diablo (Devil's Throat) swallows 1,700m³ of water per second with an unquenchable thirst, and still more water from the enormous floodplain spills over hundreds of smaller cascades. The 67,620ha surrounding the Iguazú Falls were given National Park status in 1934 and designated a UNESCO World Heritage Site in 1984. The natural wonder of the falls and the high biodiversity of the subtropical rainforest (2m of precipitation on average per year) make it one of the most valuable and beautiful parks in the country; yet that recognition came almost too late. The subtropical Paranáense rainforest that once covered a great area of Brazil, Paraguay and Argentina has been reduced to 6% of its original area. The forest around the falls is successional, or in the early stages of re-growth, having been cleared many years ago. Orange trees can be found close to the falls, where early foresters dropped pips from the fruit they brought for their lunch – oranges are not native to the Americas. Old-growth jungle is characterised by a full canopy of tall trees blocking the sun and thus leaving the understorey quite bare.

Of the more than 1,000 bird species in Argentina (South America has one of the highest diversities of birdlife on the planet) around 450 have been recorded in Iguazú, making it Argentina's richest hotspot of biodiversity. The great dusky swift, the park's emblematic species, can be seen flying over the falls and in the mists, roosting and nesting on the cliff faces beside and even behind the falls. Toucans are elusive, but can be seen at dawn and dusk. Bright green birds such as blue-winged parrotlets and green-headed tanagers are often overlooked hiding in the jungle foliage, but are stunning to see. One of the more interesting behaviourally is the red-rumped cacique. More often heard before seen, their rowdy chatter will draw attention upwards to large colonies of hanging nests in a single tree. Iguazú in springtime is a wonderful spectacle with over 200 species of butterfly, enchanting clouds of *mariposas* converging en masse and filling the jungle with moving colour. Eighty mammal species, including caí monkeys (*Cebus paella nigritus*) and the elusive jaguar, are known to inhabit the jungle. Coatis (members of the raccoon family) are an obvious presence, easily habituated to human presence by scrounging for food scraps.

Perhaps the most ominous forest creature is the mythical river snake or Boi. The Guaraní tell the legend of the giant snake that dwelt in the Río Iguazú, appeased by their ancestors with the sacrifice of a village maiden. One chief, Tarobá, loved the next intended victim, Naipi, so ran away with her into the forest to save her. Boi was so furious that it broke the riverbed with an angry twist of its back, causing the lovers to fall into its lair and thus creating the falls. Boi turned Tarobá into the trees that canopy the upper falls and Naipi's hair became the waterfalls. Boi lives in Devil's Throat, preventing the lovers from meeting; but when the sun shines at a sympathetic angle it creates a rainbow to link the couple, if only for a few minutes.

From the Central Station there are several walking routes, great for seeing birds: the Senderos Verde, Macuco and Garganta. The Macuco trail is a 6km round trip through secondary rainforest to the Arrechea waterfall, easily done at the start or end of your day in the park. The other two are alternatives to the Ecological Train. To reach the trailheads you can either take a short and easy walk through the forest along the Sendero Verde, which is green and cool and quiet, or ride on the Ecological Train, often packed with people and noisy, although you will probably use it to return at the end of the day. Either way, you arrive at the main Cataratas Station, where it's best to start by walking the boardwalk trails and perhaps visiting Isla San Martín, and to leave the Garganta del Diablo for last – it is the most spectacular and the afternoon sun will be in your favour rather than in your eyes.

The main areas of the park are: the upper circuit, which is 700m of boardwalk along the upper Río Iguazú; the lower circuit, 1.4km of boardwalk, most of which is wheelchair-accessible and in the shade of the forest with fantastic wildlife (take a clockwise tour); and Isla San Martín, below the falls, reached by a free boat (weather and water level permitting) at the bottom of the lower circuit. A fair level of physical fitness is needed to hike on the island.

Take the train from the Cataratas Station to the Garganta Station to walk the 2.2km (round trip) of boardwalk over the expansive floodplain of the river behind the falls. You can see the old boardwalk that was washed away in a flood. The Garganta del Diablo or Devil's Throat is the most dramatic of the falls, 85m of thundering spray. The last train back from Garganta Station leaves 30 minutes prior to the closing of the park; if you miss it you will have to walk the Garganta trail back to the park gates.

You may opt to stay at the **Sheraton Hotel at the Falls**, located right in the park (\ *491800;* f *491848;* e *reservas@iguazu.sheraton.com.ar; www.sheraton.com*). The five-star status, swimming pool and restaurant are secondary to the remarkable location; some of the rooms have views of the Devil's Throat Falls. Singles start at 200 pesos in low season.

A **bird rehabilitation centre** is located 1km before the entrance and the information centre. Sick and injured birds from the area are nursed back to health here for re-introduction to the wild.

Iguazú Jungle Explorer (*information kiosks throughout the park; www.iguazujunglexplorer.com*) offers excellent guided tours of the falls. Their Green Passport package offers an excursion by safari-style jeep, or *movitruck*, into the jungle with a guide who interprets a bit of the ecology of the forest; 3km of navigating the upper Iguazú delta on an inflatable raft; and a thrilling boat ride into the mists and deluges of the falls (expect to get very wet) to see the falls from in front. If you were considering obtaining a visa and crossing to the Brazilian side of the falls to obtain this view, this tour package might be much more convenient and surely more fun. This tour costs 80 pesos; portions of this package and other excursions are optional. You can take the boat ride to the falls alone for 30 pesos, but it's over before you know it.

For three nights during the full moon of every month, the park stays open till midnight, with moonlight excursions to the Devil's Throat. Check the calendar and enquire with the park administration.

Jungle Safaris (70 pesos) are given by **Explorador Expediciones** (*in the Sheraton Hotel;* \ *491800 ext 511, or 421922 or 421632;* e *explorador.expediciones@ rainforestevt.com.ar; www.rainforestevt.com.ar*) at 10.00 and 16.00 (four hours) to learn about ecology, how to identify animal tracks and recognise the sounds of the jungle. Part of the tour is in jeeps and part hiking the trails. Water, binoculars, wildlife identification guides, insect repellent and raincoats are provided.

Wanda

A short day trip by bus (40 minutes; 5 pesos) from Puerto Iguazú is the precious-stone mining town of Wanda. Wanda itself is a bit lacklustre, and it may be worth taking a package tour from Iguazú direct to the mines to avoid waiting for a *colectivo* (1.60 pesos) to take you to the mines and back to the terminal in town. The facilities at the mine site include a snack bar, a few kiosks selling *maté* and other souvenirs, and the main store where you can buy jewellery, polished stones and craftwork made of the various precious and semi-precious stones of Argentina. Part of the mine is now allocated to short interpretative tours (4 pesos). Amethyst and agate are the main stones found in this seam. To offer a bit of trivia: there are 111 recognised colours of agate, five of which are found in Argentina (clear blue, yellow, pink, white, black); and in 20 tons of rock, 1kg of precious stones is found on average (the commercial value of amethyst is US$20 per kg). Silica and manganese create the colour of amethyst, which is considered to be a stone with special properties and energies. On the tour into the mine, you will be told to hold your hand over an open seam of amethyst and make a wish. These beliefs go back far into human history: six thousand years ago the Greeks put amethyst into wine to influence the positive energy; it is considered a protective stone and is deemed the international stone of peace – the Pope wears an amethyst ring. The more valuable aquamarine (worth US$50/kg) is found mostly in Córdoba. The Inca rose (Rosita) is a similar stone and is found in Catamarca.

THE GRAN CHACO

The Gran Chaco is a large and sparsely populated region which includes the provinces of Chaco, Formosa, Santiago del Estero and the northern part of Santa Fé. Chaco and Formosa are often classed within the Litoral zone owing to their proximity in distance as well as their ecological connections to the subtropical Paranáense rainforest of Misiones, Brazil and Paraguay. The city of Santiago del Estero is discussed in *Chapter 6* (*Northwestern Argentina*) owing to its proximity to the province of Tucumán.

Chaco Province

This province is frequently passed through by long-distance travellers between the northeastern and northwestern corners of the country. Its cities are small and the capital is no exception. Though not easily accessible by public transport, the province holds great reserves of cultural and natural history. There are two national parks and vast areas of forest that are home to many wonderful wild species, often prized on various black markets, which, coupled with serious deforestation problems, causes species such as the jaguar to struggle to survive.

RESISTENCIA

Area code 03722

The hot and sweaty capital of Chaco province is a useful staging post between Iguazú and Salta; founded in the 18th century as a Jesuit mission, it was soon abandoned and then refounded by colonists from southern Italy in 1878.

Getting there

By air

The Aeropuerto Internacional Resistencia (✆ *446009, 425317, 420233*) is 6km west of the city centre, and 14km from the city of Corrientes, at km1003.5 of Ruta 11.

Aerolíneas Argentinas/Austral (*J B Justo 184;* ❭ *445550–3;* f *446802;* e *resgte@aerolineas.com.ar; open Mon–Fri 08.00–12.30, 16.30–20.00, Sat 08.00–12.30*) fly from Buenos Aires (Aeroparque) twice daily Monday to Saturday (and also 16.00 on Sunday), and also once daily to the El Pucú airport in Formosa.

By bus

Resistencia's bus terminal is on Avenida MacLean at Malvinas (❭ *461098*). A couple of long-haul bus companies connect Buenos Aires with Resistencia daily;

GRAN CHACO NATIONAL PARKS AND RESERVES

Chaco National Park, 1954; 15,000ha; in the eastern Chaco, 130km northwest of Resistencia. This forest is referred to as the 'impenetrable *chaqueño*', with dry (see page 7) chaco transitioning at the Río Negro to riparian forest. Owls, howler monkeys, many wetland birds and an abundance of frogs and toads are all heard in the chaco wilderness. Take Ruta 16 from Resistencia, turn north onto Ruta 9 to Colonia Elisa, then it's 15km to Capitán Solari (reached by buses from Resistencia) and 6km further to the park. There is camping with fire pits, tables, drinking water and electricity.

Río Pilcomayo National Park, 1951; 47,754ha; humid eastern Chaco, in northeastern Formosa province, along the Pilcomayo River and the Paraguayan border. In the summer this park, a RAMSAR wetland reserve, is a series of marshes, lakes, floodplains and flooded grasslands, but it dries out almost completely in winter. The caranday tree (*Copernica alba*) or white palm grows to 14m high and is an important habitat for species such as the black-hooded parakeet and the monk parakeet, which build large communal nests. The pale-crested woodpecker can be heard hammering at the trunks of these palms and the free-tailed bulldog bat roosts in the hanging dead fronds. The maned wolf or *aguará-guazú* lives in the park, as well as capuchin, howler and night monkeys. Laguna Blanca is the largest body of open water (800ha) and is home to two species of caiman, the water boa and capybara. Take Ruta 11 to Clorinda, Ruta 86 to Naick Neck, and 4km of dirt road to Laguna Blanca for camping and bathroom facilities and the ranger station.

Colonia Benítez National Reserve, 1990; 7ha; 20km from the city of Resistencia. Botanist Augusto Schultz set aside this small reserve to preserve a sample of chaco woodland. He created comprehensive flora inventories and published a list of these plants. Take Ruta 11 across the Río Tragadero and turn east to Colonia Benítez agricultural station. Note: public access is restricted and permission and a permit must be obtained prior to visiting.

Formosa National Reserve, 1968; 10,000ha; dry chaco, in western Formosa province on the north bank of the Río Teuco (or Bermejo). The nearest town is Inginiero Juárez, 65km north of the western edge of the reserve. The park protects the endangered *palo santo*, an aromatic hardwood, and the highly endangered giant anteater. Blue-fronted parakeets are found here and are also threatened by poaching of chicks for the pet trade. Capybara and a species of fishing bat can also be seen. Take Ruta 81 to Inginiero Juárez, then head south along Ruta 39 to the reserve and a camping area (with bathrooms).

they travel through the night (13–18 hours depending upon the service), so paying the extra for a *supercama* (78 pesos) will give a more comfortable journey than a basic seat (50 pesos). From the capital's Retiro terminal, Flecha Bus (✆ *011 4315 2781, 4000 5200*) has several departures every night and occasionally at midday; ERSA (✆ *4314 4042/3*) leaves daily at 19.00; San Cristobal (✆ *4313 2387, 4312 5902*) at 19.45; El Norte (✆ *4315 1102*) daily at 20.00 and 20.45; and El Cometa (✆ *4313 7872*) at 20.30. In addition, there are services with Expreso Gualeguaychu (✆ *4311 1032, 4314 1599*), El Pulqui (✆ *4312 4311, 4313 7177*) and Empresa Silvia (✆ *4312 4110*).

By car

From Buenos Aires, take Ruta 9 then Ruta 11 (via Santa Fé) to Resistencia, continuing north to Formosa and the Paraguayan border. Ruta 89 connects Resistencia to Santiago del Estero and Ruta 12 leads through Corrientes and Posadas up to Iguazú.

Practicalities

There are several tourist offices in town. The **Municipal Tourist Office** is on Plaza 25 de Mayo (✆ *458216*) and the **Provincial Tourist Office** at Santa Fé 178 (✆ *423547, 438880*), as well as a **tourism office** at the bus terminal, at Avenida MacLean and Malvinas (✆ *468311*). The **post office** is on Plaza 25 de Mayo at Avenida Yrigoyen.

In case of emergency, the **Hospital Julio C Perrando** is at Avenida 9 de Julio 1101 (✆ *442399, 425944, 425050*) and the **Policia Federal** at Colón 234 (✆ *422053 or 429129*). Banks include the **Nación Argentina** (*Av 9 de Julio 101;* ✆ *447722*), **Nuevo Banco del Chaco** (*Güemes 102;* ✆ *447400*) and **Citibank** (*Av 9 de Julio 146;* ✆ *437900, 434162, 448409, 433595*). The **El Dorado Money Exchange** is at J M Paz 50 (✆ *435680*).

Northwestern Argentina

Often referred to as Noroeste Argentino (NOA) or as the Northern Andean region of Argentina, this region comprises the provinces of Jujuy, Salta, Tucumán, Santiago del Estero, Catamarca and La Rioja. There are three identifiable eco-geographical zones. The first is the most obvious and attractive to tourists with its colourful mineral-rich *quebradas,* the arid high *precordillera,* or foothills, of the Andes with *cardón* cactus-filled valleys. Possibly the next in fame is the cold, high-altitude desert plateau called the *puna,* in the far northwestern corner of the province of Jujuy. Lastly the *yungas* are dense, mossy, jungle-like subtropical forests that run from Bolivia through Jujuy,Salta and Tucumán to Catamarca, covering the humid mountainous area on the eastern sides of the Eastern Andes range and the sub-Andean Sierras.

This is a region with a rich diversity of climate and topography, with the green valleys of the *yungas,* the desert of the *puna* and the gorges of the *quebradas* of the subtropical east. The silhouette of the horizon seems to be drawn with the wave of a conductor's baton; high crests and deep valleys accented against high *puna* flatlands and smooth extensive *salinas.* In the northeast, clay and stone houses built into the ground seem historic sites but are still used by the rural people. The Quebrada de Humahuaca is a UNESCO World Heritage Site; it is a long corridor with small villages and pre-Inca archaeology set amid mountains that range in altitude from 1,260m to over 6,000m.

Jujuy Province

Jujuy is a tiny, quiet and relatively poor province in the seemingly forgotten northwestern corner of the country. It has a border of 312km with Bolivia, with which it shares its indigenous cultural heritage, to the north, and another of 139km with Chile to the west.

SAN SALVADOR DE JUJUY
Area code 0388
Owing to its location, historically Jujuy was an important frontier town and had to have the strength to hold its ground against pressure from political interests and cultural influences from every direction. Illustrating this point, the city was 'founded' repeatedly, two early attempts being razed to the ground. Between 1575 and 1577 it was named 'Ciudad de Nieva de Gregorio de Castañeda' and shortly thereafter 'San Francisco de la Nueva Provincia de Alava de Pedro de Zárate'. Military force finally prevailed and in 1593 the town was founded again by Juan

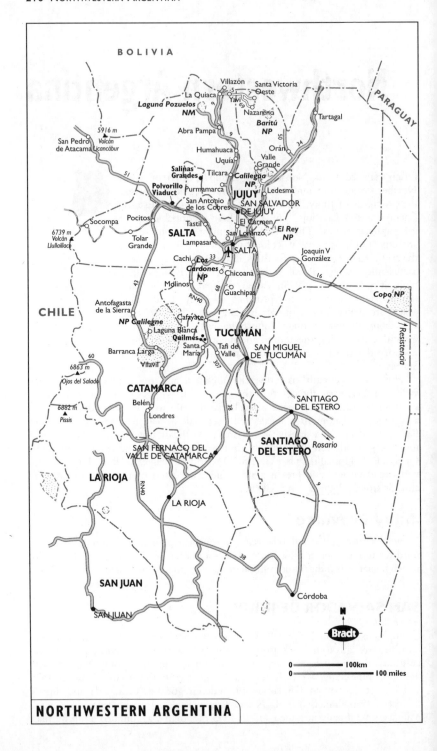

Ramírez de Velazco, who vaingloriously named it San Salvador de Velazco. This is considered the city's founding date, although the name changed again some years later to San Salvador de Jujuy.

Getting there
By air
The Gobernador Horacio Guzman airport (✆ *491 1109*) is 30km southeast of the city. Aerolíneas Argentinas/Austral (*Belgrano 1053, local 6;* ✆ *422 7198 or 422 2575;* f *422 3897;* e *jujgte@aerolineas.com.ar; open Mon–Fri 08.30–12.30, 16.30–20.30, Sat 08.30–12.30*) offers one flight per day from Buenos Aires, taking approximately two hours. On Tuesday and Friday the flight calls first at Córdoba.

Car rental is available at the airport with Localiza (✆ *491 2734 or 0800 999 2999; www.localiza.com.ar*) and Argus (✆ *490 6173;* e *info@arguscarhire.com*); or in the centre with Avis, Belgrano 1060 (✆ *491 1501;* f *431 1184*).

By bus
The bus terminal is at Dorrego 356 at the corner of Iguazú (✆ *422 1373–5*). The journey from Buenos Aires to Jujuy takes almost 23 hours and costs approximately 100 pesos; Almirante Brown (✆ *011 4314 8050*), La Veloz del Norte (✆ *4315 0800, 4314 8090*) and El Rápido (✆ *4314 7999, 4314 8722*) have daily services. Balut (*Jujuy* ✆ *423 1947, 422 2134; Salta* ✆ *0387 432 0608*) or La Veloz del Norte (✆ *423 2366*) have buses between Salta and Jujuy every hour between 05.30 and midnight; the journey takes two and a quarter hours and the fare is 7 pesos.

By car
Ruta 9 north from Salta is 115km of paved highway through fabulous mountain and forest scenery. If driving at night, however, Ruta 34 is more direct and secure.

Orientation
Jujuy is a small city but one that is becoming more familiar with the increasing numbers of tourists coming to explore the far northern reaches of Argentina. The city's main square is Plaza Belgrano, which of course has several historic architectural sights such as the cathedral, as well as a few shops, cafés and hotels. The city centre sits in the fork of two rivers: the Río Grande to the north, and the Río Xibi Xibi, which cuts through the city to the south before joining the Río Grande. While most of what you will want to find or see will be on the same side as Plaza Belgrano, the bus terminal is three blocks south of the Xibi Xibi on Dorrego, at Avenida Iguazú.

Where to stay
Hotel Altos de la Viña Pasquini López 50; ✆ 426 1666, 426 2626; e lavina@imagine.com.ar; www.altosdelavinahotel.com.ar. This 4-star hotel is AC and has a pool and gym. B/fast is included in the rates, which are 102/135 pesos for sgls, 126/165 pesos for dbls (low/high season).
Hotel International Jujuy Belgrano 501; ✆ 423 1599. Rates start at 70 pesos sgl, 90 pesos dbl, 130 pesos suite per person in low season.
Hotel Inti Punku San Antonio 659, Alto Gorriti; ✆ 422 6846; e intipun@imagine.com.ar; www.hotelintipunku.com.ar. This affordable hotel is near the bus station but in a relatively quiet neighbourhood; 30 pesos sgl, 50 pesos dbl, 65 pesos triple, b/fast with regional products included.
Jujuy Hostel Yok Wahi Lamadrid 168; ✆ 422 9608; e info@yokwahi.com.ar, reservas@yokwahi.com.ar. The staff are very helpful with tourist information and planning excursions. Sgls 12 pesos, dbls with private bath 32 pesos; also dorms.

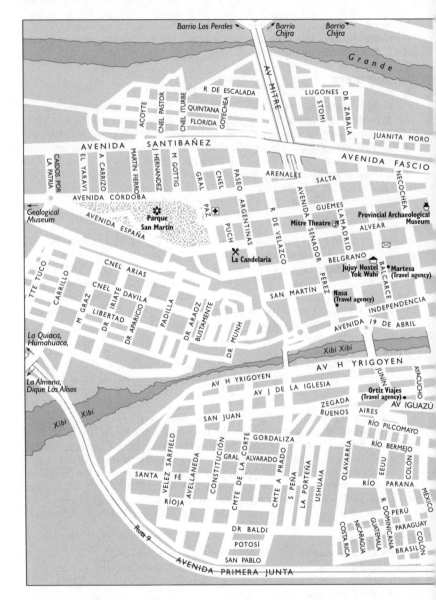

Where to eat and drink

La Candelaria Alvear 1346; 🕿 15 686 2637. Reportedly the best *parrilla* in town.
Confitería La Royal Belgrano 766; 🕿 422 6202. Serves b/fast and has pavement tables for watching life in the plaza.

Practicalities

The main **tourist office** is at Gorriti 295 (🕿 *422 1326;* e *turismo@jujuy.gov.ar*). There is also a tourist information kiosk at the bus terminal.

The **Hospital San Roque** is on San Martín at the corner of Gorriti (🕿 *422*

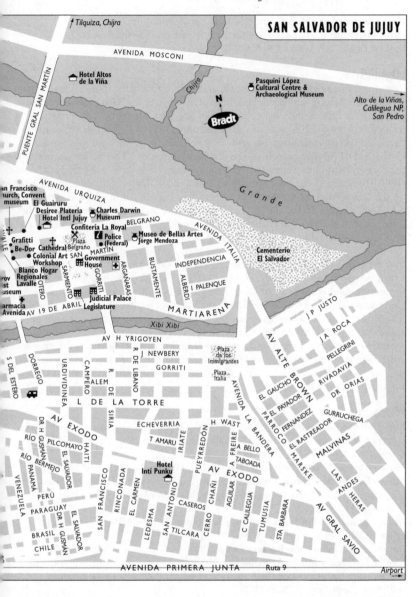

SAN SALVADOR DE JUJUY

1302/3). There are many pharmacies; one in the centre is **Farmacia Avenida** (*Lavalle 76–80;* ☏ *422 2515, 422 6113*). The **police** can be reached on ☏ 429 1901 or 423 7710.

The **post office** is at Independencia and Lamadrid and there are several **banks** along Avenida Alvear and Avenida Belgrano between Lamadrid and Necochea.

Travel agencies
Grafitti Belgrano 601; ☏ 423 4033; e grafittitour@arnet.com.ar
Martesa Balcarce 208; ☏ 422 9181, 423 1056; e martesatours@cootepal.com.ar

Nasa Senador Pérez 154; ☎ 422 3938, 423 3117; e nasatmo@arnet.com.ar
Ortíz Viajes Alem 917; ☎ 424 0728, 423 3565; e ortizviajes@hotmail.com
Be-Dor Lavalle 295; ☎ 402 0239, 424 0241; e be-dor@imagine.com.ar

Highlights

Palm-treed Plaza Belgrano is historically and architecturally the most interesting part of the city. Among the main buildings of interest is the **Government House** (1907–21), a French-style palace that holds the first Argentine flag, presented to the people from the balconies of the neighbouring Town Council (1812), now the provincial police headquarters, and then blessed by Canónigo Gorriti in the **Cathedral** (1761–65), which is also on Plaza Belgrano. The statues in front of the Government House are somewhat controversial: they were made by Lola Mora (1866–1936), one of the most prestigious artists and sculptors of the country, in 1906 for the inauguration of the National Congress in Buenos Aires. The two groups are 'Freedom, Trade and Two Lions' and 'Peace, Justice and a Masculine Figure'. They were considered somewhat daring and inappropriate for the National Congress and were removed and donated to the province of Jujuy in 1915.

Following Avenida Belgrano from the plaza, at the corner of Lavalle you will find the **San Francisco church and convent** (1927) and the **Museo Histórico Franciscano Jujuy** (*open daily 08.00–12.00, 17.00–20.30*), both worth a visit. The museum houses colonial art of the Cuzco school as well as Franciscan religious art. Continuing down Avenida Belgrano, the Mitre Theatre (1901) is a gorgeous historical relic at the corner of Lamadrid. Concerts, ballets and other performances are on the programme at www.teatromitre.jujuy.gov.ar.

Market kiosks and vendors are often set up on Plaza Belgrano and facing the bus terminal. Some stores in town that have artisans at work include El Guairuru (*Belgrano 615*), Blanco Hogar (*Lavalle 261*), Desiree Platería (*Belgrano 592*) and Regionales Lavalle (*Lavalle 268*).

Museums

Museo Arqueológico Provincial Lavalle 434; ☎ 422 1343. In the museum's 6 exhibition rooms are collections of artefacts and mummies from the various ancient cultures of this region. *Open Mon–Fri 08.00–13.00, 15.00–21.00.*
Museo Carlos Darwin Gorriti 363. Anthropological and archaeological collections.
Museo Lavalle de Historia Provincial Lavalle 252. General Juan Lavalle was killed in this old house in 1841 after failing to overthrow Roas. *Open Mon–Fri 08.00–20.00, Sat 09.00–13.00, 15.00–21.00.*
Museo de Bellas Artes Jorge Mendoza San Martín 230; ☎ 423 2109. *Open Mon–Fri 09.00–12.30, 17.00–21.00, w/ends 09.00–13.00.*
Arte Colonial Fundación Recrear Otero 220. *Guided tours 10.00–13.00, 18.00–21.00.*
Centro Cultural y Museo Arqueológico Pasquini López Victor Hugo 45; ☎ 426 2569. The museum has archaeological, ethnographical, botanical and other natural history collections. *Open Mon–Fri 09.00–18.00.*
Museo de Mineralogia Av Bolivia 1661. *Open Mon–Fri 09.00–13.00, 15.00–20.00.*

Day trips and excursions

Quebrada de Humahuaca

Added to UNESCO's World Heritage List in 2003, the Quebrada de Humahuaca is a corridor of small villages, with many traces of prehistoric hunter-gatherer communities, pre-Incan and Incan archaeology, set amid mountains up to 6,000m in altitude. The Circuito de la Quebrada is fairly well serviced by local buses, but having a car will give you the most freedom to move at your own pace and stop at all the villages. From Jujuy's bus terminal the El Quicequeño bus line has ten departures per day to Humahuaca (2½ hours, 126km); there are 15 departures to Tilcara (2 hours, 84km); and four to Purmamarca (1½ hours, 65km). There are several other bus companies, such as PanAmericano de Jujuy and Linea La Quiaca, giving a departure to Humahuaca every half hour or so on average. The cost of a ticket to Humahuaca, the furthest north, is only about 7 pesos; connections between intermediate towns obviously cost less, for example just 3 pesos from Tilcara to Humahuaca, and taking a *remise* between some of these towns is also not expensive. For example, between Tilcara and Purmamarca you can be charged up to 15 pesos, although these negotiations are very open and locals probably pay less than that. Of course, you can also arrange tours from Jujuy or Salta. All of the little villages have something special to offer if you have the time to explore. A well-paced day trip will take in the most important towns, primarily Purmamarca, Tilcara and Humahuaca; but there are several other interesting places strung along this road.

Purmamarca

Most of the towns are directly on Ruta 9, but to reach Purmamarca you must take a 3km detour east at the well-marked intersection about 60km from the capital. The town was declared a National Historic Monument in 1941. Beside the Church of Santa Rosa (dating back to 1648 but rebuilt in 1778) is a vetch or algararrobo tree believed to be about 500 years old. The town has not changed a whole lot in that time, however.

The Seven Colours Hill is a stunning backdrop to the town and the reason most tourists come to visit. The best time to see it is in the morning, as the sun is behind it in the afternoon, glaring into your eyes, silhouetting the hill and dulling all the colours. The sedimentary mineral layers are coloured blue, green, ochre, red, pink and purple. Iron oxide creates the tan, maroon and many of the green colours in the mountains in this region; turquoise-green indicates the presence of copper sulphate; violet indicates manganese. The subtle browns and beiges are high in clay content and borax will soften them to pastel colours.

The main plaza has a permanent craft market. On its east side are some good restaurants, while a nice hotel is not far to the south; buses stop here, and the convenience store on the corner can tell you the schedules, although you have to buy tickets on board. Up the street from the north side of the plaza, walking towards the Seven Colours Hill, is an inconspicuous little diner, where the señora cooks traditional dishes such as *tamales* and *humitas*. Also just off the main plaza is a very nice hotel, **La Posta de Purmamarca** (*Rivadavia s/n;* ✆ *490 8040;* e *postadepurmamarca@yahoo.com.ar*), which has quaint and simple rooms with private baths (*doubles 50 pesos, triples 80 pesos, quadruples 90 pesos*); it also has a good restaurant. **Los Morteros** (*Salta s/n;* ✆ *490 8063*) is a restaurant and tea house that would be a good choice for a more elegant evening dinner – it played a major role in creating the currently trendy *nuevo cocina de altura* or modern Andean cuisine, with llama meat, frost-dried potatoes, quiñoa and corn. Rather grander, and a kilometre from the village, is **El Manantial del Silencio** (✆ *490 8080;* e *silencio@arnet.com.ar, www.hotelmanantial.com.ar*), also specialising in *nuevo cocina de altura*. Meals cost from US$15 upwards, and rooms are available, starting at US$105.

Tilcara

Tilcara is probably the most popular of the little towns along this route. It is in a valley giving it more shelter from the winds and also making it warmer, which may be a good or a bad thing depending on the time of year. If town-hopping along the Quebrada, the central Plaza Prado should be your target, full of kiosks where locals sell woollen, wooden, ceramic and leather products, some handmade and some manufactured. In low season it is quaint and quiet, in high season it is buzzing with activity. If you take the time to wander through the streets the town will reveal itself to you with many little craft shops, galleries, cafés and restaurants with inner gardens, and you will see the non-tourist-oriented society going about its normal activities. Important archaeological excavations are under way at the Pucará de Tilcara, the old fortress a kilometre from the centre.

For accommodation, try the **Hotel de Turismo Tilcara** (*Belgrano 590;* ℣f *495 5720, 495 5002*), which has a restaurant and has rooms with private bath and breakfast, at 48 pesos single, 65 pesos double or 80 pesos triple. **Los Molles** (*Belgrano 155;* ℩ *495 5410*) is a backpackers' hostel whose owner is a fine chef who fled Buenos Aires and makes the best *empanadas* for miles around.

Museo Regional de Pintura José Antonio Terry Rivadavia 459; ℣f 495 5005. Named for the Argentine painter who lived and painted in Tilcara from 1910 to 1953. His works are exhibited here along with other painters from the region. *Open Tue–Sat 09.00–19.00, Sun & hols 09.00–12.00, 14.00–18.00.*

Museo Arqueológico Dr Eduardo Casanova Belgrano 445; ℩ 495 5006. In collaboration with the University of Buenos Aires, this museum has a very good collection of artefacts of the region. Tickets (2 pesos) also cover the excavations at Pucará de Tilcara. *Open 09.00–13.00, 15.00–18.00, closed Tue.*

Museo Ernesto Soto Avendaño Belgrano near Rivadavia; ℩ 495 5354. Exhibiting sculptures by this Humahuacan artist. Tickets also cover the nearby archaeological site. *Open 09.00–13.00, 15.00–18.00, closed Mon and Tue; admission 2 pesos, free Thu.*

Museo Irureta de Bellas Artes Belgrano and Bolivar; ℩ 495 5124. Contemporary art exhibit inc works by the sculptor Hugo Irureta. *Open 10.00–13.00, 15.00–18.00, closed Mon; admission free.*

MEC Artesanías Belgrano 351; ℩ 15 404 0168. A shop selling beautiful craftwork and colonial-style art typical of the Andes.

Humahuaca
Area code 03877

Arriving at the bus terminal you will likely be bombarded by people selling homemade sandwiches and other snacks. To find your way into town, make your way to the back of the terminal, walking away from the motorway (in high season you can probably follow the crowd). You will wander a few blocks down cobbled streets of adobe houses and eventually be tempted to turn right, which will bring you to busier and busier streets until you arrive at the main plaza, absolutely full of kiosks selling every imaginable souvenir or craftware. This town survives largely on tourism so don't expect to walk past any of these merchants unnoticed. Also inescapable is the overly ostentatious Monumento a la Independencia (1950), a wedding cake-style set of stairs topped with a statue, by Tilcara sculptor Ernesto Soto Avendaño, of a native Indian with arm raised skyward in celebration of freedom. This exaggerated monument has received much scrutiny for its inappropriate size and statement in this small indigenous community; nevertheless, the view from the top over the town to the terracotta mountains behind is worth the climb. Back at the foot of the monument, south of the plaza, is the 17th-century Iglesia de la Candelaria y San Antonio. This church has also triumphed over hardships, having been damaged by earthquakes and then enduring over ten years of restoration work from 1926. The paintings by Cuzco-schooled Marcos Sapaca date from the 18th century and the bell towers were raised in 1880.

There are also some fine Cuzco School paintings in the tiny church of **Uquía**, a few kilometres south, as well as a German-run hotel, the **Hostal de Uquía** (✆ *490508*).

The post office is at Jujuy 399, where there is the Telecentro communications centre (07.00–23.30), where you can make long-distance calls or send faxes. There is a bank machine on Jujuy between Córdoba and Santiago.

Posada el Sol – Hostal de Humahuaca (*Medalla Milagrosa s/n;* ✆ *421466;* e *elposada@imagine.com.ar*) is a simple rustic-style hostel that has dorms for 11 pesos and doubles for 28 pesos.

The **Humahuaca Colonial Restaurant** (*Tucumán 16;* ✆ *421178*) specialises in regional cuisine – *empanadas, tamales, humitas* and *locro*. **El Rosedal** (*Buenos Aires 175*) also has good regional dishes.

Calilegua National Park

Head east from San Salvador de Jujuy to San Pedro, then take Ruta 34 north towards Bolivia. After crossing the Río San Lorenzo at Libertador San Martín (also known as Ledesma) it's 5km to the village of Calilegua and the park office. Before

CALILEGUA NATIONAL PARK

In 1979 76,320ha of the eastern slopes and deeply eroded canyons of the Calilegua range in eastern Jujuy province were put under national park protection, becoming the largest park in northwestern Argentina. There's a great variety of vegetation due to the elevation range, from 500m to the highest points of Cerro Hermoso and Cerro Amarillo at some 3,000m. Three biomes are recognised: high mountain pasture, *yungas* cloud forest (550–1,600m) and, above these, alder, podocarp and chaco woods transitioning to montane forest on the lower slopes.

Deforestation on the lower slopes of the Andes, where the soil is very sandy and unstable, had led to erosion and serious landslides that had dammed streams and threatened farmland and villages in the valleys. The park now protects not only the forest but also the streams flowing from the Andes into the agricultural valleys, most importantly the Río San Lorenzo. The high-elevation area of *yungas* cloud forest remained unexploited and relatively pristine owing to its dense foliage and difficult terrain making timber extraction too difficult.

Four hundred species of bird are found in the park, including toucans, motmots, ant-shrikes, hummingbirds, king vultures and several endemic species such as the red-faced guan. There are also two endemic frogs: one has beautiful orange, yellow and black colouring and the other has marsupial-like breeding habits. The red agouti, honey-bear, tuco tuco, ferret and puma are other park faunal species. The tapir and Paraná otter are also found at lower levels, and *yaguareté* (like a smaller jaguar) up higher. Nectar-feeding bats pollinate the flowers by night. The uplands are home to the taruca, or northern huemul deer (huemul andino; *Hippocamelus antisensis*), which was declared a Natural Monument in 1996. This short stocky deer is geographically isolated from the southern populations and is recognised as a separate subspecies. Its population is scattered throughout the high mountain peaks which are unprotected, but within the Calilegua, Campo de los Alisos and Los Cardones national parks and even as far east as Iguazú it finds protected habitat.

the village and immediately north of the bridge, a dirt road heads north towards the mountains. After 9km you'll reach the ranger station at the Aguas Negras stream, from where Ruta Provincial 83 travels 23km through the park, rising to elevations of 1,700m and ending at Valle Grande. Another ranger station at Mesada de las Colmenas is about halfway along this route and has a campsite with bathrooms and several walking trails to different points of interest.

Salta Province

Salta province, long overlooked by mass tourism, is becoming increasingly popular with tourists who realise the appeal of its unarguably stunning but desolate landscape. Rural people live traditional lifestyles seemingly unchanged for centuries and scratch out an existence on the dry desert soil. Driving the endless dirt roads such as the one that follows the route of the famous *Tren a las Nubes* (Train to the Clouds), you begin to believe that it is the dust clouds that are being referred to. Your vehicle may never be the same and will likely require a full wash, engine, interior and all – as will you. People living in this area walk incredible distances to their work or their schools and they too have a not-so-fine layer of grey dust covering them. They will gladly accept a ride from you, as you are surely a rare sight on these roads. If the dust doesn't affect you, the altitude might. San Antonio de los Cobres sits at 3,774m. Salta has a raw beauty indeed and travelling its outback will reveal incredible scenery, tenacious rural farms, great herds of vicuña and several national parks.

SALTA
Area code 0387

Travelling throughout the northwest of the country gives a feeling of isolation and simplicity. Many of the towns on the map turn out to be no more than a collection of a few houses. The long-established towns are slow-paced and quiet, allowing for reflection on the ways of the past more than scrutiny of the hectic transgressions of modern society. However, when you arrive in Salta you are back in the big city. Almost. Salta is a large and bustling commercial centre but with a strong attachment to its music, dance, folklore, art and cuisine, and full of wonderful architecture from its long colonial history. The first Spanish incursion into what is now Argentina came in 1536 when Diego de Almagro arrived from Peru; the area soon bcame important as a source of food and mules for the huge silver mines of Potosí in present-day Bolivia. By the late 17th century an estimated 20,000 mules and 40,000 cattle were being sent north from Salta every year.

Getting there
By air

The Aeropuerto Internacional Martín Miguel de Güemes (✆ *424 3155*) is on Ruta 51, 6km south of the city centre. There is no public bus to the airport, but there is a shuttle service at 5 pesos per person or *remise* for 12 pesos. Car rental is available at the airport through Avis (✆ *424 2289*) or Millet-Hertz (✆ *424 0113 or 424 4102*).

Aerolíneas Argentinas/Austral (*Caseros 475;* ✆ *431 1331;* f *431 1454;* e *slaventas@aerolineas.com.ar; open Mon–Fri 08.30–13.00, 16.30–20.30, Sat 09.00–13.00*) has up to four flights per day from Buenos Aires, with some flights connecting through Córdoba.

LAN Argentina (*Alberdi 53, Galaria Baccaro;* ✆ *431 8982*) also plans flights from Buenos Aires. Its parent company LAN flies to Salta from Iquique in Chile on Saturdays.

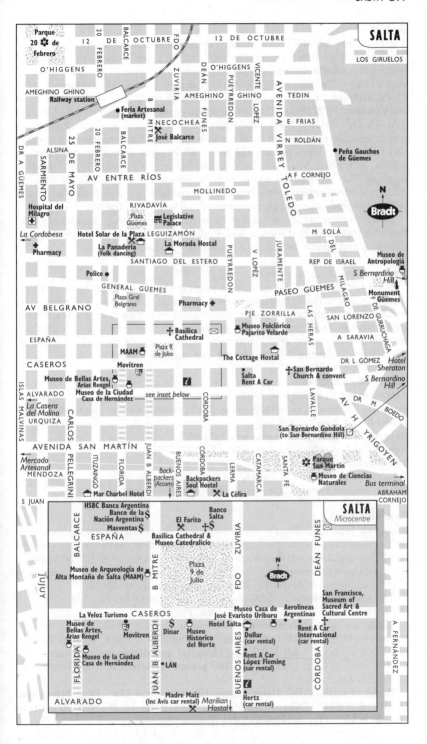

By bus

The bus terminal is at Salvador Mazza, 9 de Julio and Coronel Suárez. About half a dozen buses leave Buenos Aires daily for Salta; the journey takes approximately 20 hours and costs 100–135 pesos, depending on level of service. The main companies are La Nueva Chevallier (↘ 011 4000 5255), departing from Retiro station at 14.00, 15.45, 20.00 and 20.30; La Veloz del Norte (↘ 4315 0800) with a departure at 13.20 and four between 21.00 and 22.00; Almirante Brown (↘ 4314 8050) at 16.00 daily; and TAC (↘ 4312 7012) at 19.00 daily. There are daily connections from almost every major Argentine city as well as small nearby towns: from Córdoba there is a morning and two evening buses per day (12 hours; 50–70 pesos depending upon level of service) with either Mercobus, La Veloz del Norte or Chevallier. From Mendoza there are daily services (19 hours) with Andesmar for 90 pesos. Flecha Bus and Andesmar offer *supercama* service between Salta and Iguazú, taking about 24 hours and costing 150 pesos; there are cheaper options with worse seats and schedules.

In season there are also services to the oasis of San Pedro de Atacama in Chile; these are operated by Géminis and Pullman Bus, leaving Salta on Tuesday, Thursday and Sunday and taking 12 hours (66–75 pesos).

By car

Driving to Salta from the south is a pleasure. From Cafayate Ruta 68 passes through the remarkable landscapes of the Quebrada de Cafayate. The vibrant red rock formations and sand dunes are stunning and every turn in the road (126km of paved road in excellent condition) bestows upon you ever more breathtaking views. The only caution would be to keep at least one eye on the road while driving these curves and being distracted by the awesome landscapes.

Car rental companies

Avis Alvarado 537; ↘ 431 1184
Hertz Buenos Aires 88, Local 14 Shopping; ↘ 421 1144 (also at the airport, see above)
Dollar Buenos Aires 1; ↘ 421 2069
Rent A Car International Caseros 489; ↘ 431 0875
Rent A Car López Fleming Buenos Aires 33; ↘ 421 2333
Salta Rent A Car Caseros 225; ↘ 421 2069
Sudamerics Buenos Aires 88, Local 6/7; ↘ 422 7359, 15 500 0773;
e sudamerics@argentina.com; www.sudamerics.todowebsalta.com.ar

Practicalities

Plaza 9 de Julio is the most important square in the city. The cathedral is here as well as museums, shops, travel agencies, communication centres, restaurants and bars. The central Avenida Caseros runs east–west across the south side of the plaza; the north–south streets change their names on either side of it. The bus terminal is at the south end of Avenida H Yrigoyen, near Parque San Martín.

The **tourist office** is at the Gobernación de Turismo, Buenos Aires 93 (↘ 431 0721, 431 0956). The **post office** is at Deán Funes 170.

There are many **pharmacies** throughout the city, with central ones at Sarmiento 402 (↘ 421 3813) and Deán Funes 208 (↘ 421 3962). There is also one at the bus terminal (↘ 421 1201). The **Hospital del Milagro** is at Sarmiento 557 (↘ 431 7400, 421 5595, 431 7420). The **police station** is at Gral Güemes 726 (↘ 421 2519, 422 2286).

Banks include **HSBC Banco Argentina** (*Bartolomé Mitre 143*); **Masventas** (*España 610–614*); **Dinar** (*Caseros 576*); **Banco de la Nación Argentina** (*Bartolomé Mitre 151*) and **Banco Salta** (*España 550*).

Gustavo and his wife at the **Las Rejas Hostal** (*General Guemes 569;* ☏ *421 5971;* e *metropolitannoa@hotmail.com*) are able to book tours and car hire, and have lots of good advice about travelling in the surrounding area. **Ferro Turismo** (*Buenos Aires 191;* ☏ *431 5314*) offer an enjoyable trip to San Antonio de Los Cobres, following the route of the train by bus. It is a much cheaper alternative to the train itself (which only runs on Saturdays).

Where to stay
Hotel Sheraton Av Ejército del Norte 330; ☏ 432 3000; f 432 3001;
e reservas.salta@sheraton.com.ar, www.sheraton.com/salta. Opened only in 2005, in a quiet district just below Cerro San Bernardo, with rooms (with great views to the Cordilleras) starting at US$135.
Hotel Solar de la Plaza Juan M Leguizamón 669; ☏/f 431 5111 (reservations in Buenos Aires 011 4700 1417, 4700 1615); e reservassolar@salnet.com.ar; www.solardelaplaza.com.ar. This high-end hotel is in a colonial building, formerly the family home of the Patrón Costa family. It has many lovely salons and outdoor terraces, a spa and a restaurant. Standard rooms cost 260 pesos, sgl or dbl, with city view or 280 pesos with a view of the plaza; superior rooms cost 300 pesos and suites 385 pesos, all inc b/fast.
Hotel Salta Buenos Aires 1; ☏ 431 0740; f 431 1918; e reservas@hotelsalta.com. An elegant hotel with an exceptional spa. Rates start at 100 pesos for a standard sgl, 135 pesos for a dbl, with buffet b/fast included.
Mar Charbel Hotel Ituzaingo 404; ☏ 422 1002; e hotelmarcharbel@hotmail.com. Comfortable rooms with private baths. Sgl 42 pesos, dbl 84 pesos, triple 104 pesos, inc b/fast.

Hostels
Two Hostelling International hostels organise events between the two locations and also run a very good excursion company called Active Argentina (*Zuvuria 982;* ☏ *431 1868;* e *argentina@active-argentina.com; www.active-argentina.com*) – see below. There is always somebody available to answer your questions or offer tourist advice and the atmosphere is very social. **Backpackers** (*Buenos Aires 930;* ☏ *423 5910;* e *hostelsalta@backpackerssalta.com.ar*) is where more of the social occasions such as *asados* are held. **Backpackers Soul Hostel** (*San Juan 413;* ☏/f *431 8944; reservas@hostels.org.ar*) is quieter with a very nice rooftop patio on which to enjoy a *maté*. Rates at both locations are 13 pesos for a dorm bed, 38 pesos for double rooms with or without private bath, 45 pesos for a triple, 60 pesos for a quadruple.

La Morada Hostal Zuviria 417; ☏ 421 9400; e hostallamorada@hotmail.com. This hostel has laundry service, a fully equipped kitchen, internet and social areas such as the large terrace for *asado* or sunbathing. Rates per person are 11 pesos in a dorm, 20 pesos in a sgl room, 14 pesos in a twin, 15 pesos in a dbl, or 12 pesos in a triple.
Las Rejas Hostal General Guemes 569; ☏ 421 5971. This hostel is in a good location and has an integral travel agency, with English-speaking staff. B/fast costs extra. Recommended.
Marilian Hostal Buenos Aires 160; ☏ 437 0531. This hostel is conveniently located 2 blocks off Plaza 9 de Julio, although this may not appeal if you are interested in a quiet night. Rates start at 15 pesos per person with b/fast.
The Cottage Hostal Juramento 54; ☏ 421 3668; e hostalthecottage@hotmail.com. Close to the main plaza and 5 blocks from the bus station. Dorm beds 10 pesos with b/fast.

Where to eat and drink
Food in Salta has a strong indigenous flavour, with *humitas*, *tamales* and *locro* (all corn-based dishes) popular, as well as *empanadas*. The best and most authentic are sold on the street – *empanadas* served by a woman from a cardboard box in the

middle of Plaza Güemes may not be within everybody's comfort zone, but she has probably just made them fresh in her own kitchen, so if you want delicious authenticity at a fraction of restaurant prices, buy your *empanadas* from her. Alternatively, you will find great *empanadas* at **El Farito** (*Plaza 9 de Julio, diagonally opposite the Hotel Colonial*) and at **El Corredor del Empanada** (*Caseros 117*). **El Solar del Convento** (*Caseros 444;* ✆ *421 5124*) and the more touristy **Doña Salta** (*Córdoba 46;* ✆ *432 1921*) also have excellent local fare.

A great little wine bar is **La Cordobesa** (*Leguizamón 1502;* ✆f *422 2794, 421 7281*). The walls are covered by bottles from throughout Argentina; the friendly owner will help select the best to suit your tastes and wash down the tasty spread of olives, cheeses and salamis he puts together.

Vegetarian meals can be found at **Madre Maíz** (*Alvarado 508;* ✆ *432 9425; Mon–Fri 12.00–15.00, 20.00–23.00, Sat 12.00–15.00*), which also specialises in macrobiotic cuisine and will cater to special dietary requests.

La Céfira (*Córdoba 481;* ✆ *421 4922*) serves excellent homemade pasta.

Peña Gauchos de Güemes (*Av Uruguay 750;* ✆ *421 7007/73*) is housed in a building which is a reconstruction of the historical Posta de Yatasto where in 1814 Colonel José de San Martín met General Manuel Belgrano to organise the Alto Perú Army; and where Colonel Martín Miguel de Güemes subsequently stayed. The house is decorated in gaucho style and traditional dinners are accompanied by folk dancing.

José Balcarce (*Mitre at Necochea;* ✆ *421 1628; open Mon–Sat from 21.00*) is the leading exponent of *nuevo cocína de altura*, the re-invented indigenous cuisine (with maize, quiñoa and other altiplano ingredients) that is suddenly very fashionable.

Highlights

San Bernardo Hill, at 1,454m (174m above the city), can be reached by car by taking Avenida Ciudad de Asunción to Via Crucis, but there is a gondola or *teleférico* from Parque San Martín (*every two minutes 09.00–19.30; 8 pesos return*). There are beautiful gardens and walkways that pass little ponds with waterfalls. The view at night over the city is great.

Basilica Cathedral (*España 537*), built in 1858, holds the Señor del Milagro and the Virgen del Milagro chapels. To its rear at Belgrano 587, the **Museo Catedralicio** (✆ *431 8206*) is open Monday–Friday 10.30–12.30, 16.30–18.30, Sat 10.30–12.30; admission 0.50 pesos.

San Francisco Church (*Caseros and Córdoba*) is the Basilica Menor (status below cathedral), built in 1796. Its elaborate terracotta, white and yellow façade and ornate designs make it one of the most impressive and memorable pieces of architecture in the city. There is also the **San Francisco Museum of Sacred Art** (*Córdoba 33;* ✆ *431 0830; open Mon–Fri 09.00–21.00*) displaying religious art, furniture and ornamentation. The **Centro Cultural San Francisco** (*Córdoba and Deán Funes*) is open Monday–Friday 09.30–12.30, 17.00–19:30, Sunday and holidays 09.00–12:00, 18.00–19.30.

San Bernardo Church and Convent (*Caseros and Santa Fé*) is only open for daily mass at 06.30 (08.00 and 10.30 on Sunday) in the church. The original hermitage dates from 1582 and the church from the late 16th century, reconstructed and added to several times.

Museums

Museo Histórico del Norte Caseros 549; ✆ 421 5340. The *cabildo*, or former Town Council, was begun in 1626 and took over a century to finish. It was remodelled several times and was in use until the end of the 19th century. Restored in 1942, it is considered the best-preserved *cabildo* in Argentina. It contains archaeological materials, cultural objects and historical interpretation. *Open Tue–Fri 09.30–13.30, 15.30–20.30, Sat 09.30–13.30, 16.30–20.00, Sun 09.30–13.00; admission 2 pesos.*

Museo Casa de José Evaristo Uriburu Caseros 417; ↘ 421 5340. Built in 1773, this is considered one of the oldest houses in Salta. It has been home to generals and presidents but today is a museum of the viceroyalty of Salta. *Open Tue–Sat 09.00–13.30, Sun 09.30–13.00.*

MAC Museo de Arte Contemporáneo Zuviría 90; ↘ 437 0498. A spacious gallery with both permanent and temporary exhibitions of contemporary Argentine art. *Open Tue–Fri 09.00–13.00, 16.30–20.30, w/ends 10.30–13.00, 17.00–21.00.*

MAAM – Museo de Arqueología de Alta Montaña (Museum of Archaeology of the High Mountains) Mitre 77; ↘f 437 0499; e info@maam.org.ar. This new and beautifully designed museum (the full-sized metal *cardón* cacti in the lobby are especially noteworthy) has collections of artefacts from the high mountain cultures of Salta as well as installations and displays of mountaineering technology, which draw striking comparisons to the ancient cultures and their impressive stamina. The most famous and intriguing attractions of this museum, however, are the children of Llullaillaco, the almost perfectly preserved mummies of 3 young children who were sacrificed to their gods 5 centuries ago. Their tomb was found at 6,730m on Llullaillaco volcano in 1999 by high-altitude archaeologists. However, as a video explains, the native community finds this display sacrilegious and feels that the children, who are thought to be not dead, but sleeping, should be returned to their mountaintop resting place. *Open Tue–Sun & hols 09.00–13.00, 16.00–21.00; admission 10 pesos, children and seniors free; Wed free.*

Casa de la Cultura Caseros 460; ↘ 421 5763. The main floor houses a photo exhibition and special events are held regularly.

Museo de Antropología de Salta Juan M Leguizamón Ejército del Norte and Polo Sur; ↘ 422 2960, 431 1229. Archaeological and ethnographical objects of the region are displayed from the Santa Maria, Incan, Wichi, Chané, Ava and other cultures and ethnic groups. *Open Mon–Fri 08.00–18.00, Sat 09.00–13.00, 15.00–18.00; admission 1 peso, children free.*

Museo de la Ciudad Casa de Hernández Florida 97, off Alvarado; ↘ 437 3352. Furniture and architectural elements from 18th- and 19th-century homes that had been demolished were saved and given a new home in this museum. *Open Mon–Fri 09.00–13.00, 15.00–21.00, Sat 09.00–13.00.*

Museo de Bellas Artes Arias Rengel Florida 20; ↘ 421 4714. Art from the colonial period as well as contemporary regional art. *Open Mon–Sat 09.00–13.00, 16.00–20.00.*

Museo Folclórico Pajarito Velarde Pueyrredón 106. Colonial house showing paintings, furniture and musical instruments, plus mementoes of tango singer Carlos Gardel and racing champion Juan Manuel Fangio. *Open Tue–Fri 08.00–12.30, 17.00–20.00, Sat 10.00–13.00; admission 1 peso.*

Museo de Ciencias Naturales Mendoza 2; ↘ 431 8086. *Open Tue–Sun 15.30–19.30.*

Entertainment and nightlife

The wonderful **Cine Victoria** on Plaza 9 de Julio, built in 1945, has a very large screen and old wooden seats. When *The Motorcycle Diaries* was shown here, the setting was perfect for this movie showing scenes of northwestern Argentina in the early '50s, during the formative years of the Argentine revolutionary Ernesto 'Che' Guevera.

The area of **Balcarce**, around the railway station, was once a place for local people to meet after work for a *milonga* or dance, but fell into disregard and decay; it has recently been reborn and is one of the most popular *barrios* for restaurants, bars, discos and dance clubs. The bars and clubs do not charge admission so you can hop from one to the next in search of the music style that you prefer, which can range from current top-of-the-charts pop to Colombian *cumbia*. There are also *peñas folklóricos*, restaurants with professional folk singers, musicians and dancers, at weekends and more often in summer. The most famous are **La Panadería** (*Balcarce 475;* ☎ *421 9609*), **La Vieja Estación** (*Balcarce 885;* ☎ *421 7727*) and **La Casona del Molino** (*Luis Burela 1 at Caseros;* ☎ *434 2835*); the music starts at about 21.00 and can go on all night. The diners never hesitate to get up and accompany the singers – it seems that everybody knows the lyrics to all the traditional songs, such as the slow sad *zamba* and the yodelling *baguala*, and everybody knows how to dance the *chacarera*. The energy and cultural pride make a strong impression on most tourists.

Shopping

Salta is a shopper's paradise for regional handicrafts such as woven goods, ponchos, ceramics, woodwork and leather- and silverware, etc. The **Feria Artesanal** market is held on weekend afternoons on Balcarce near the railway station. The **Mercado Artesanal** is a large and popular handicraft market at San Martín 2555 (☎ *434 2808*); Plaza Güemes also has a small craft market.

There is an excellent and cheap English bookshop – **Libereria San Francisco** (*Caseros 350;* ☎ *431 8456*) – which stocks all the classics.

Day trips and excursions

Salta is something of a hub for tour agencies covering the northwest region:

Backpackers Tours Buenos Aires 930; ☎ 423 5910; e hostelsalta@backpackerssalta.com
Cafayate Viajes y Turismo Buenos Aires 224; ☎ 401 2106, 15 683 9432;
e cafayateviajesturismo@hotmail.com
Altiplano Excursions Galería Buenos Aires, Local 1A, Buenos Aires 68; ☎ 422 2394;
e laltiplano@yahoo.com.ar; www.kitebuggy-andino.com.ar. One of their special features is a kite-buggy on the salt lakes (from 150 pesos per person).
Active Argentina Zuvuria 982; ☎ 431 1868; e argentina@active-argentina.com;
www.active-argentina.com. Associated with the HI hostels in town, this agency caters to budget backpackers.
MoviTrack, Safaris & Turismo Buenos Aires 28; ☎ 431 6749; f 431 5301;
e movitrack@movitrack.com.ar. A fancy office, glossy advertising and a very good reputation; therefore, the prices are higher.

San Lorenzo

The village of San Lorenzo is a dormitory community above Salta where many residents live on elegant properties with space for pools, horse paddocks and gardens and still enjoy all the amenities of the nearby city, just 15 minutes' drive away. For the tourist, this short drive is entertaining for gawking at the incredible villas but it is also an alternative to staying in the centre. Leave Salta to the west following Avenida Entre Rios, which becomes a motorway directly to San Lorenzo. Entering the town, turn right onto Avenida San Martín then left onto Avenida Juan Carlos Dávalos, which leads into the small centre where you'll find the extremely helpful tourist office (*Dávalos 960;* ☎ *492 1757;* e *info@turismosanlorenzo.com*), the church, a few shops and a police station. Continuing through the town to La Quebrada de San Lorenzo you'll come to a picnic area. Back on Avenida San Martín, rather than turning into the town proper, continue north and the avenue becomes the Camino a Lesser y Vaqueros, a stretch of villas, estancias and guesthouses. **Residencia de Campo Arnaga** (☎ *492 1478*) is a traditional guesthouse, costing 120–140 pesos, with a pool and restaurant. **Eaton Place**, at Avenida San Martín 2457 (☎ *492 1347*), is a beautiful bed-and-breakfast with an excellent reputation;

doubles are in the 50–80 pesos range. A budget option, for around 15 pesos per night, is **El Tatata** (*Dávalos 1598;* \ *492 1139;* e *hostal@eltatata.arg.net.ar*).

For a drink, there is a nice café, **El Refugío**, on Dávalos at Alberdi, and a tea house, **Don Sanca**, at Dávalos 1450 (\ *492 1580*); restaurants include **El Duende de la Quebrada** (*Dávalos 2309;* \ *15 685 8687*); **Restaurante lo de Andrés**, on Dávalos at Gorriti (\ *492 1600*); and **Pizzeria Dionicio**, on San Martín at Hernández (\ *492 1650*). **El Castillo** (*Dávalos 1985;* \ *492 1052*) is a bar and restaurant which also offers accommodation (120–180 pesos); it is a late 19th-century Italian-style *castello*, the former summer home of Italian immigrant Luigi Bartoletti. The particularly interesting wrought-iron fence is made from Remington rifle barrels used in the War of the Triple Alliance.

You can also reach San Lorenzo by taxi or *remise* (around 8 pesos), or by a bus that picks up passengers on Entre Rios – this costs just 1 peso but is very infrequent.

Many activities in the area can be arranged through the tourism office and excursion agency, **Turismo San Lorenzo EVT** (*Dávalos 960;* \ *492 1757, 15 684 0400;* e *info@turismosanlorenzo.com*). You can explore the area by quadbike, horseback, bicycle or on your own two feet. Four-wheel-drive excursions to the Quebrada de Areaga cost 55 pesos for one person or 90 pesos for two for an hour; to the Potrero Grande 90/120 pesos for two hours; or to the Puerta del Cielo 150/220 pesos for one hour. A three-hour horseback excursion to Las Lomas costs 45 pesos per person and the seven-hour excursion to Potrero Grande costs 95 pesos. There is also a two- to three-day excursion on horseback to the Puerta del Cielo, which costs 345–460 pesos per person with a minimum of two people participating.

You can go by bicycle to the Quebrada de Areaga (2 hours, 35 pesos), Potrero Grande (3 hours, 45 pesos) or Puerta del Cielo (7 hours, 95 pesos). A guide can be hired for treks to the Quebrada de San Lorenzo (3 hours, 35 pesos), Los Cajones in the Quebrada (7 hours, 70 pesos) or Puerta del Cielo (2 days, 285 pesos; enquire about the equipment needed).

Tren a las Nubes

The 'Train to the Clouds' is a well-publicised tourist operation and one of the best ways to see Argentina's desolate *puna* or *altiplano*. From 2007, when the railway to Lhasa (Tibet) opens, this will be only the fourth-highest railway in the world, reaching an altitude of 4,475m at the Chorrillos pass. It is a remarkable feat of engineering, using hairpin bends, loops, 21 tunnels and 13 viaducts to tackle the 3,000m climb to La Polvorilla, where the tourist train turns around, at an altitude of 4,186m, 217km from Salta. The metre-gauge line, built only in 1921–48 by Richard Fontaine Maury to service borax mines, continues via Chorrillos to Socompa in Chile, across the salt lakes of Salar Pocitos and Salar de Arizaro, the third-largest in the world.

A hard-working diesel engine pulls, and on certain sections pushes, the eight first-class carriages with a maximum capacity of 500 souls up to the clouds, a scenic journey from the fertile Valle de Lema into the hostile *puna*. The colours of the hills and the diversity of the landscape keep passengers hopping from one side of the train to the other to capture the views. It is possible to catch sight of vicuña, and in spring yellow acacia and red ciebo flowers bring even more colour to the scenery. The giant *cardón* cactus is also common, with large white flowers in spring. The bridge at La Polvorilla is the highlight of the trip for many, but if you are afraid of heights, do not look out of the window here. The viaduct is little more than a 224m-long pair of iron rails 63m above the gorge.

From the Belgrano railway station at Balcarce and Ameghino (✆ *431 0999*), the train departs at 06.00 and returns at 22.00, having covered 434km at roughly 32km/h. It has an erratic schedule, only making the trip on certain days each month and only from April to November. Tickets cost 189 pesos. The altitude affects people differently but headaches and dizziness are not uncommon forms of *soroche*; there is first aid on the train to help any sufferers. From January to March there may be a shorter journey of just 262km, known as the *Tren del Sol*, running from Salta to Diego de Almagro.

In July 2005 the train service was suspended when over 400 passengers were abandoned after the train broke down at over 4,000m; due to a history of under-investment the operators lost their concession, but it's expected that the service will start again in 2006, perhaps run by a foreign concession.

Two companies provide information and bookings for the trains in Salta:

La Veloz del Norte Turismo Caseros 400; ✆ 431 1010; f 431 1114; also in Buenos Aires: Esmeralda 320, 4th floor; ✆ 011 4326 0126; f 4326 0852; e info@lavelozturismo.com.ar
Movitren Caseros 431; ✆ 431 4984/6; f 431 6174; also in Buenos Aires: Esmeralda 1008; ✆ 011 4311 8871, 4311 2012/9

In addition MoviTrack (see above) operates its Safari a las Nubes (for 266 pesos) in a road-railer truck that runs along the railway to Polvorillo and San Antonio de los Cobres but also continues by road to the salt lakes and Purmamarca.

Alternatively you may choose to drive Ruta 51, following the route of the train, but although it's a faster trip the rough and dusty road is very hard on car engines. There are no service stations until the town of **San Antonio de los Cobres**, 165km from Salta, where the train also pauses (and buses also come here, taking four hours from Salta). The nearby salt mine of the same name is a vast white desert where the refraction of light over the salt surface creates waves in the air, as over a hot road – a mirage typical in deserts. San Antonio de los Cobres, at 3,774m, is a desolate and unattractive town, existing as a base for copper and salt mines rather than for any aesthetic appreciation of the area. Arriving by car, you will descend into the valley that holds the tiny town of mainly government houses, and one of the first things to catch your attention will probably be the 1950s Coca Cola billboard with a girl holding a coke, commenting on its great taste. Ironically, it's the town itself that you'll taste – the wind blows mercilessly, blasting sand and dust in your eyes and up your nose and covering you in a layer of gritty chalky powder. There is a small restaurant, the Hostería de Las Nubes, in what could be considered the centre; children with cracked red windburnt cheeks are stationed outside ready to pounce on arriving tourists and sell them trinkets and crafts. Begging is a problem with children in these poor communities – it is better to purchase something from them rather than make donations. Some of the local people, including the children, are excellent weavers and you may have the opportunity to buy items made from untreated, undyed llama wool. This is the last town before the border crossing into Chile and has a customs office and gendarmerie post.

Las Salinas

Along Ruta 40 west of San Antonio de los Cobres are the 100km-wide salt flats, partially in Jujuy province. A highlight is Tres Morros, with an ancient cemetery at the first hill and ruins of a mine at the second. The impressions of the light quality and colours enhanced by the clear dry air are quite memorable.

Rafting

Norte Rafting (*Ruta 47km 34 Cabra Corral;* ✆ *424 8474 or 15 683 0555;* e *info@norterafting.com; www.norterafting.com*) offers two-hour guided tours on the

Juramento River to see dinosaur tracks and algae fossils for 65 pesos per person in high season.

Salta Rafting (*Buenos Aires 88, Local 13 in Galería Salta;* ❧ *421 4114 or 401 0301, 15 402 2876;* e *info@saltarafting.com; www.saltarafting.com*) has overnight river excursions (165 pesos), kayak lessons (three days for 280 pesos), rafting day trips (60 pesos for 2 hours on the river) at both white water and floating paces, full-moon rafting (70 pesos) as well as camping, horseriding and abseiling. Transportation costs to river/trail heads are 25 pesos per person and family rates are available for certain activities.

Salta's many national parks
El Rey National Park and the thermal baths of Rosario de la Frontera
The characteristic feature of this 44,162ha park in the middle of Salta province is the natural amphitheatre created by the encircling mountains from which descend several streams that merge to form the Río Popayán – an important resource for agriculture in the surrounding region. The park was named for a farm given by the Spanish Crown to Colonel Fernandez Cornejo; in the 18th century the Finca del Rey was an eastern outpost of the territory administered by the Viceroy of Peru. In recent history, the farm was expropriated and turned into a park and in 1948 designated the Parque Nacional El Rey. The park protects the forest that transitions from hill chaco (with species such as *horco quebracho*) upwards to the yungas forests with epiphytes, orchids, bromeliads and ferns. Myrtle cloudforests take over at about 800m, followed by alder and pine from 1,500m. At still higher elevations are *Polylepis* (*queñoa*) trees and the upland grasslands. The diversity of flora and fauna through these transitions includes walnut and large cedar trees, lianas and orchids and giant cactus depending on elevation. Colourful birds live in the subtropical forests, and coots, jacanas and many duck species are common at pond and wetland areas; condors and certain falcons nest on cliffs at higher altitudes. There are rattlesnakes, cross snakes and coral snakes, and the waters are rich with dorado and other fish species. Important mammal species in the park include the puma, jaguar, fox, tapir (the largest land mammal in South America), coati, biting bat, monkeys and two species of brocket deer, as well as two peccaries, the collared and the white-lipped.

The native human presence in the park was that of farmers in the lowlands. Archaeological studies of their ceramics (grey and orange in colour with animal shapes forming the handles) and polished stone axes draw cultural similarities with the Candelaria and San Francisco groups.

Although in Salta province (about 175km from Salta city), the hot springs of Rosario de la Frontera are most easily reached from San Salvador de Jujuy. *Colectivo* no. 14 leaves from Calle Dorrego, near the bus terminal, hourly from 06.30 to 20.30. You can arrive by car on Routes 9, 5 and 20, the last of which washes out in the rainy season (November to March – the best time to visit the park is between April and October). The thermal waters of the baths have reputed medicinal powers. At the centre is the spa, hotel and restaurant **Hotel Termas de Reyes** (*Ruta Provincial 4, km19;* ❧ *0388 492 2522;* e *info@termasdereyes.com; www.termasdereyes.com*). Singles cost 157 pesos, doubles 180 pesos, and doubles with a view 210 pesos; breakfast is included. One of its big attractions is supposedly that Evita stayed here, in Room 100. There is free camping nearby – it is very rustic but there are public baths and an outdoor swimming pool at the hotel. Hiking in the area is excellent.

El Baritú National Park
This park is reached by taking Ruta 50 from Orán (properly San Ramón de la Nueva Orán) to Aguas Blancas, from where the unpaved Ruta Provincial 19 runs 34km to

the park's southern border. Created in 1974 to preserve over 72,400ha of *nuboselva* (cloud rainforest), this is a relatively pristine forest thanks to the difficulty of penetrating it for timber extraction owing to the dense foliage on a steep terrain. It is part of the *yungas*, with tree species that further south remain stunted but here reach full development because of the hot and humid climate. An interesting tree-like fern, the *maroma*, germinates on another tree, living its first years epiphytically while its roots grow toward the ground. Once firmly rooted it wraps itself around the host tree and eventually kills it. The park shelters threatened animals like the jaguar, the ocelot (*Leopardus pardalis*) and the otter (*Lontra longicaudis*). There are many rivers, the most important of which are the Lipeo in the north, and the Porongal and Pescado, emptying into the Río Bermejo, which forms the northeast boundary of the park.

Los Cardones National Park
To reach this park, southwest of Salta, take Ruta 33, which also goes to Cachi. The park is devoid of services so be sure to bring water and all other supplies. The park administration is at the town of Payogasta, on Avenida San Martín 4415 (✆ *0386 849 1066*).

In 1996, 65,000ha of dry uplands full of *cardón* (also called teasel or candalabra cactus; *Trichocereus pascana*) were designated a national park. A rich cultural legacy includes the legend that these cacti are indigenous sentries watching over their native lands; it is fitting that national park status should now protect them and their land. Cut and dried, the 'wood' was used both by the aboriginals and later on by the *criollos* for construction. Because there are no other trees in this region, it was badly over-exploited. This classic desert cactus, with its 'hands-up' posture, can live 250–300 years and reach 3m in height. A cactus of 1m is generally taken to be a century old but their age can be gauged by counting growth rings, much the same as a woody tree except that the rings are visible on the main column of the plant. They are able to withstand the harsh climate and can grow at altitudes as high as 3,400m, well above the level of tolerance for most flora species. The edible fruit is called *pascana*.

The three biomes within the park are mountain, high Andean plateau, and the *puna* with dry uplands and deep valleys (2,700–5,000m). It is an arid climate, dry and warm with an average 11°C in winter with lows slightly below zero, and an average 18°C in the summer with highs of 30°C; there is very little precipitation to speak of (maximum 200mm, only in summer ie: Nov–Mar).

Surviving the harsh climate, several endemic birds are found here such as the puna hawk and two species of tinamou: the ornate tinamou and the puna tinamou. Endangered species such as the vicuña and a northern subspecies of huemul deer live in this park. In spring the valleys are filled with yellow pompom-shaped acacia flowers and the red blossoms of the ciebo, matching the colours of the surrounding hillsides.

CAFAYATE
Area code 03868
An important city in the Calchaquí Valley circuit, this is also a favoured tourist destination for its vineyards and wineries and excellent shopping for crafts and local products. The main plaza, dominated by the huge cathedral of Nuestra Señora del Rosario, has wonderful shops, such as the Mercado Artesanal, selling textiles and other products, and a good ice-cream parlour.

Getting there
There are two routes linking Cafayate and Salta (see more under *Excursions*, page 230): Ruta 68 along the Guachipas Valley and Ruta 40 along the Calchaquí Valley,

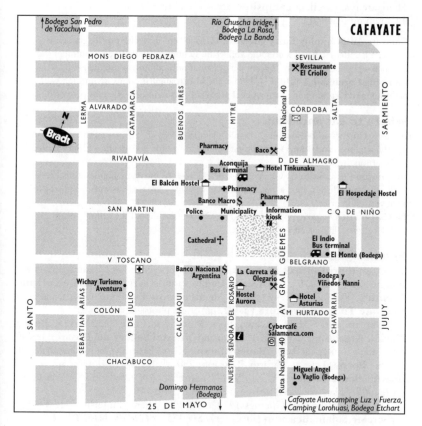

continuing south from Cafayate into the province of Tucumán. **El Indio** (℡ *421002*) has a terminal at Belgrano 34, with daily services to Salta; and **Aconquija** (℡ *421052*) has a terminal at Mitre and Rivadavia, and a daily bus to Tucumán for 24 pesos.

Where to stay

Luxury accommodation is coming to Cafayate, or at least its outskirts, with the opening of the **Patios de Cafayate** (part of Starwood's The Luxury Collection) at the junction of Ruta 40 and Ruta 68 (℡ *421201*) and the **Viñas de Cafayate** resort on the Camino al Divisadero (*Ruta Provincial S21;* ℡ *15 509 6681*).

Hotel Asturias Güemes 154; ℡ 421328; f 421040; e asturias@infonoa.com.ar. A very well-presented, clean and cool hotel near the main plaza with garden, swimming pool and restaurant. Sgls 40 pesos, dbls 70 pesos, triples 100 pesos (all inc b/fast), with prices 10 pesos higher in Jan–Feb, winter vacation and other important hols.

Hotel Tinkunaku Diego de Almagro 12; ℡/f 421148. A pleasant hotel with a swimming pool; sgls cost 30 pesos, dbls 60 pesos, triples 90 pesos.

El Balcón Hostel Pasaje 20 de Febrero 110; ℡/f 421739. Dorm 12 pesos, dbl with private bath 30 pesos, inc b/fast.

El Hospedaje Hostel Salta 13; ℡ 421680; e reservea@hostels.org.ar. A colonial-style house with a cute internal patio, near the plaza. Dorms 10 pesos, dbl with private bath 24 pesos.

Hostel Aurora Nuestra Señora del Rosario 73; ℡ 421342. A hostel with shared rooms and bathrooms and communal kitchen, in a good location facing the church.

There are two excellent **campsites** facing each other at the southern entrance to the town on Ruta 40:

Cafayate Autocamping Luz y Fuerza ☏ 421568. Tent sites with private grills; hot showers; laundry facilities; soccer and volleyball; swimming pool. Open in summer only; 2.50 pesos per person per day, 2 pesos per person if only coming to use the pool.
Camping Lorohuasi ☏ 421051, 421133. Cute little triangular cabins, swimming pool, bathrooms and a restaurant. Tent space 2 pesos per person; cabins 20 pesos per person.

Where to eat and drink

Baco Av Güemes and Rivadavia; ☏ 15 402 8366, 15 509 7177. This restaurant is open all day (b/fast, lunch and dinner) and all year. They have a little bodega and a gallery approach to the art on the walls.
Restaurante El Criollo Av Güemes 254; ☏/f 422093. As the name implies, this serves traditional local dishes, such as *tamales*, *humitas*, *locro* and *empanadas*, as well as a good *parrilla*, all at very good prices.
La Carreta de Olegario Av Güemes 20; ☏ 421004. Grandest of the central restaurants, with local specialities such as *cabrito* (goat).

Practicalities

There are **tourist offices** in a kiosk in the main plaza and at Nuestra Señora del Rosario 132 (☏ *421470*). They recommend two tourist agencies: **Wichay Turismo Aventura** (*9 de Julio 64;* ☏ *421333*) highlights mountain trekking options, and **G-S Cafayate Turismo Aventura** (☏ *421266*) offers photographic hikes.

There are a few banks in town, open Monday to Friday 09.00–14.00. **Banco Nación Argentina**, at Vicario Toscano and **Nuestra Señora del Rosario**, has an ATM and a money exchange. **Banco Macro**, at San Martín and Mitre, has an ATM.

The **hospital** is at Vicario Toscano 280 (☏ *421094*). There are a few **pharmacies**: at Rivadavia 37 (☏ *421214*); Mitre 24 (☏ *421299*); and San Martín 36 (☏ *421008*). The provincial **police** are at San Martín 145 (☏ *421111*).

The **post office** is at Güemes 197 (☏ *421097*). There is internet access at the **Cybercafé Salamanca.com** (*Av Güemes Sur 155;* ☏ *421470, 421558*).

Wineries

There are about a dozen wineries in Cafayate, and the surrounding landscape is full of vineyards and bodegas, several along the main Ruta 40. The world's highest vineyards are here, at over 3,000m (close to 10,000ft). Many use the Torrontés grape, producing sweetish white wines that delight fans of Alsace wines; others include Cabernet, Malbec, Syrah, Tannat, Barbera and Bonarda. The following lists just a few places that you can contact for wine tastings or tours of their bodegas.

Bodega La Rosa (Michel Torino) Ruta 68 Norte at Ruta 40; ☏ 421139
Bodega Etchart Ruta 40 km1047; ☏ 421529, 421310
Bodega y Viñedos Nanni Silverio Chavarría 151; ☏/f 421252
Miguel Angel Lo Vaglio Gral. Güemes 238; ☏ 421203
Bodega San Pedro de Yacochuya Finca Yacochuya; ☏ 421233
El Monte Belgrano 34/48; ☏/f 421002
Domingo Hermanos Rosario and 25 de Mayo; ☏ 421225

Excursions

The Guachipas Valley offers a spectacular three- to four-hour drive along Ruta 68, which seems deliberately to wind and twist to create an effect somewhat like drawing back a curtain from a masterpiece of art. Each bend in the road reveals yet another spectacular view of the multi-coloured hills and red-earth landscape, and the weirdly-shaped rocks that seem like modern sculptures. A second route takes you along the Calchaquí Valley through little colonial towns rich in Hispanic architecture, food, arts and craft. **Cachi**, 157km from Salta, is one of the most popular of these, with large old houses on narrow streets, a handsome colonial plaza, a church with roof beams and confessional of *cardón* (cactus) wood, and an interesting anthropological museum.

Heading south, it's an hour to the ruins of **Quilmes** (see page 234).

Tucumán Province

Driving into Tucumán from the province of Salta, the landscape changes from arid desert and *cardón*-covered rocky ground to the lush and humid climes of San Miguel de Tucumán. The province is referred to colloquially as the 'Garden of the Republic' and is also frequently described as an oasis for being a tiny humid green zone surrounded by large provinces largely composed of desert.

Tucumán is the smallest province ($22,524km^2$), yet the most densely populated. During the Spanish Conquest it was the meeting point of commercial expansion and defence between Río de la Plata and Alto Perú. Commercial savvy and industrialisation remained fundamental to this province's success. Sugar-cane plantations were its first industry, today producing over 60% of Argentina's sugar in 15 factories or *ingenios,* still seen puffing away throughout the valley. The second most important industry is citrus-growing; Tucumán is the world's leading producer of lemons. Tobacco, potatoes, grains, especially soya, beans, corn and wheat, as well as strawberries, avocadoes and cranberries are also intensively farmed. All this bountiful production is possible due to a unique climate and topography. Being so close to the Tropic of Capricorn, the region is considered subtropical but has a marked dry season with no rain for most of the year – heavy rains from January to March account for almost all the annual average of 242mm of rain.

A mossy forest known as *yungas*, occupying part of the mountain range, is one of the most threatened eco-systems on earth. There are 80,000ha of this forest in Tucumán with high biodiversity especially of epiphytic plants.

There are seven microclimates in the province, five of which are in the mountains. Approximately 60% of the area is flatland (10–12°C in winter; 22–35°C in summer), while the western mountain zone (with an average of 18°C and a minimum of 6°C in January; an average of 5°C and a minimum of 0°C in July) has its highest point in the snow-capped mountains such as El Aconquija (5,550m) in the Sierra Nevado range. Two other ranges are Las Sierras del Cojón/Quilmes and the Calchaquíes Mountains; the Choromoros, Tafí and Calchaquí valleys run longitudinally between them.

TAFÍ DEL VALLE
Area code 03867
This tiny town offers innumberable attractions for tourists. Avenida Perón is a haven for souvenir shopping and sampling the area's excellent farmhouse cheeses, some seasoned with red peppers. The surrounding countryside is stunning and beckons you to come hiking, mountain biking, horseriding or exploring archaeological ruins. Called *Taktillaktu* in the Calchaquí language, it derives from the native word *taktillakta* meaning 'a village with a splendid gate'.

Getting there
The town is halfway to Cafayate from Tucumán on Ruta Provincial 307, which takes a winding and climbing route; atop one of the passes is a sculpture of the Tafí Indian and the condor representing the strength of nature. The bus terminal is on

Avenida Critto, Tafi's main east–west street, and has an ATM and public telephone. There are daily connections to Tucumán (approximately eight daily on an erratic schedule; six on Sunday; 10 pesos) or north to Cafayate and Salta with Aconquija, which also serves Amaicha del Valle, Quilmes, Colalao and Cafayate.

Where to stay

Hostería La Guadalupe La Costa 650; ↘ (0381) 15 643 5127, 15 642 1264. A hotel in the countryside that is wonderful for stargazing on the patio by night and is located next to a ranch that organises horseback excursions by day (see below). The hotel's exterior is whitewashed adobe and the interior is decorated with Frida Kahlo-inspired murals. The rooms are simple but with locally made furniture with hand-woven bedspreads and cushions. Rates 60 pesos sgl, 70 pesos dbl, 90 pesos triple with b/fast.

Lunahuana Av Critto 540; ↘f 421330, 421360; e info@lunahuana.com.ar; www.luanahuana.com.ar. Sgls 198 pesos, dbls 254 pesos, triples 310 pesos, 4/5 people 352/285 pesos.

La Rosada Av Belgrano 322; ↘f 421323, 421146; e miguel-torres@sinectis.com.ar. Sgls 60 pesos, dbls 70 pesos, triples 85 pesos.

La Cumbre Hostel Av Perón 120; ↘ 421768; e lacumbrehostel@uolsinectis.com.ar. Conveniently priced and located, it also runs excursions and offers tourist information. Sgl 13 pesos, dbl 25 pesos.

Nearby estancias include **Los Cuartos** (*Av Critto and Av Juan Calchaqui;* ↘ *15 587 4230*), where you can stay at the bed-and-breakfast (*50 pesos single, 60 pesos double, 70 pesos triple; reserve a day in advance*), or just visit for a creole tea, a traditional lunch (15 pesos per person, including a short tour of the estancia), or a full-day walking or horseriding excursion with lunch (*55 pesos per person*); **Las Tacanas** (*Av Perón 372;* ↘ *421821/2;* e *lastacanas@hotmail.com*), a former Jesuit estancia in town; and **Las Carreras** (*Ruta Provincial 325 km13;* ↘ *421473, 15 500 2373;* e *info@estancialascarreras.com*).

Where to eat

There are several restaurants on Avenida Perón, but the best are slightly outside the centre:

El Pabellon At km60 on Ruta 307; ↘ 15 607 185, 15 401 8500. A humble little restaurant with fantastic traditional cooking – authenticity emphasised by the *parrilla* and the clay oven fired up at the side of the building. The *locro* soup here is excellent.

Hostería La Guadalupe La Costa 650; ↘ 0381 15 643 5127, 15 406 4292. The restaurant enhances your already excellent meal with regional music and views of the valley (see more above).

La Quebradita At km62 on Ruta 307; ↘ 421126. An inconspicuous little café with a view of the valley. Makes homemade cakes and cookies that are far too good to miss; the best are the various *alfajores*, but the decadent cakes oozing with *dulce de leche* are also wonderful.

Activities

For more information, the **tourist office** is on Peatonal Los Faroles (↘ *421 009*). Horseriding on the hillsides around Tafi is highly recommended. An expert outfitter and horseman, with the somehow appropriate name of Jerónimo, has short excursions (for riders at every level of experience) up into the hills near his ranch and round the nearby archaeological sites as well as two-and six-hour excursions (rates US$10–24) to Cerro Mala Mala, Cerro Muñoz and Cumbre del Nuñorco. **Señor Jerónimo Critto's ranch** on the outskirts of the town (*Av Lola Mora, La Costa 1;* ↘ *421 457;* m *0381 15 409 5900;* e *jjcritto@hotmail.com*) is beautiful with adobe (mud and straw) huts that have been artistically designed into tack sheds, haylofts and the most gorgeous outhouse (with plumbing) that I have ever seen. For overnight horse riding excursions as well as other outdoor activities contact **Montanas Tucumanas** (*Av Peron y Gobernador Critto, local 5;* \ *15 609 3336;* e *montanastucumanas@argentina.com; www.montanastucumanas.com*). The best months for this activity are April to June and September to November, but all excursions are subject to cancellation due to adverse weather.

Excursions

The little town of **Simoca**, 53km southwest of Tafí, has a colourful *Feria Sabatina* every Saturday where traditional wares and regional gastronomic treats are sold. Music and dance are presented on an open-air stage and gauchos are on parade. Sulkies or two-wheeled carts pulled by a donkey or horse are a common sight here.

To the north of Tafí, Ruta 307 climbs through high mountain passes and past tiny rural schools and rustic farms. At the Abra del Infiernillo (3,040m), through which the Spanish conquistadores came from the north, there is usually a local family selling souvenirs and also some hand-knitted items.

The greatest archaeological interest is in the menhirs (a Celtic word meaning standing stones) at the **Reserva Arqueológica de los Menhires** in El Mollar. This group of stone monoliths, raised in various locations by the Tafí culture (400BC–AD900), is engraved with ceremonial symbols, including overlapping human faces, snakes and felines, and phallic and fertility symbols. This was one of the first sedentary cultures in northwestern Argentina, raising maize, potato, quinoa and beans, and hunting llama, guanaco, rodents, deer, birds and armadillos. Their houses were made of stone and were circular. These rings can be found throughout this area; there are some examples at the horse ranch in Tafí (see above). In the La Angostura (or Tafí I) stage of the culture (to AD450), the menhirs represented ancestors, clans or lineages of social groups. In the Carapunco (Tafí II) stage (AD450–900), a change in concept saw ceremonies performed at a domestic level; the menhirs were inside dwellings and were seen as bringing fertility, nourishment, permanence and home comforts.

The **Museo de Mitos y Leyendas** (Museum of Myths and Legends) at km58 of Ruta 307 (\ *0381 15 640 8500;* e *casaduende@yahoo.com; admission 3 pesos*) is really an art gallery and small library with art and figurines describing the mythology of the region. The main figures are Pujllay, the deity of autumn harvest, folksongs and happiness; Madre Tierra, Mother Earth, who ripens fruit, fertilises fields, raises animals and protects travellers through her tears; Yastay, a sort of white-bearded Old Man Winter or flute-playing elf, the protecting father of the mountain animals; and Ñusta, the princess of spring and fertility and sower of seeds. A creative and artistic adobe hut is a gift shop.

At the entrance to the town of **Amaicha del Valle** there is a tourist complex with a filling station, convenience store, a restaurant, highly recommended for traditional dishes at a good price, and accommodation in a cabin for 20 pesos or a dorm for 15 pesos (\ *03892 421140*). There is also accommodation at Altos de Amaicha Posada Boutique (*Ruta 307, km 117;* \ *03892 421 429, 421 430;* e *info@altosdeamaicha.com.ar; www.altosdeamaicha.com.ar*). Nearby is the **Pachamama Museum** (*Ruta 307, km165;* \ *03892 421075, 421004;* e *complejopachamama@cosama.com.ar*) with designs and figures of the Santamaría culture (from AD850). In Amaicha del Valle, the ancestral festival of Pachamama (Mother Earth) is celebrated in the summer when the gods of the Kolla nation (Mother Earth and the sun) are honoured.

Also along this route is a mining museum describing the important minerals and stones found in this region where 50kg of gold and 400kg of silver are extracted per year. The Capillatas mine yields gold, silver, copper, lead, molybdenum, zinc, iron, manganese and rodochrosite, while the Rumi Tuka mine (10km^2 in area) yields topaz, quartz and other minerals.

The Quilmes people were a warlike tribe dating back to at least AD1000; they resisted the Incas and endured 130 years of Spanish colonisation. The **Ruinas de Quilmes** or Diaguita ruins, 5km west of Ruta 40 an hour (46km) south of Cafayate, are the remains of their large urban centre that housed up to 5,000 people. The labyrinthine complex (admission 2 pesos) rises up a hillside, which you can climb to the top of, where once only their chief resided. From here you have a view of the entire valley and the impressive stone wall that reaches out of sight to either end of the complex. The Quilmes culture was destroyed in 1667 when the Spaniards expelled them from their territory and forced them to walk 1,500km across the desert to Buenos Aires, a destination which none of them reached (although a renowned brewery and a suburb are named after them). It may come as a surprise to learn that the ruins of Quilmes, one of the great archaeological and cultural treasures of the province and the country, were privately owned by the late Hectór Edwardo Cruz, an architect and weaver of traditional textiles. There is a small museum of sorts but the main function of the building is to sell imitation souvenirs and other regional gifts. There are no interpretative materials in English except for books and brochures that you can purchase. Give yourself a couple of hours to explore the ruins — wear proper sun protection and carry water. The restaurant is very nice, although a bit overpriced, and comfortably cool to escape the intense heat of the sun. Accommodation is available at the **Parador Ruinas de Quilmes** (✆ *03892 421075, 421004;* e *complejopachamama@cosama.com.ar*), costing 72 pesos for singles, 97 pesos for doubles, 127 pesos for triples and 159 pesos for quadruples, all with breakfast.

SAN MIGUEL DE TUCUMÁN
Area code 0381
This city was first founded in 1565 south of its current location in a place called Ibatin on the Tejar River, now Publo Viejo (Old Town). The second founding happened 120 years later on the present site, and it is now northern Argentina's largest city, with more than half a million residents. The nation's freedom was born here, at *La Ciudadela* (citadel) where General Manuel Belgrano defeated the Spanish in 1812. A group of *criollos*, known as the Congress of Tucumán, met in a house now known as the Casa Histórica and proclaimed the independence of the Argentine Republic from Spain on 9 July 1816 (this is why so many streets and plazas are named 9 de Julio). The city's buildings and gardens are beautiful, and the passing sulkies add to the charm. The word *sulky* means 'muy solitario' or very lonely and aptly describes the two-wheel carts pulled by a mule or horse that are still in common use and seen even in the midst of city traffic.

Getting there
By air
It is a two-hour flight from Buenos Aires to Benjamin Matienzo International Airport (✆ *426 4906, 426 5072*) 10km east of Tucumán. With Aerolineas Argentinas (*9 de Julio 110;* ✆ *431 1030;* f *431 1419;* e *tucgte@aerolineas.com.ar; open Mon–Fri 8.30–13.00, 17.00–20.30, Sat 9.00–13.00*) there are at least two daily flights to and from Buenos Aires, as well as flights on Monday, Wednesday, Friday and Sunday between Tucumán and Córdoba. LAN Argentina (*Marcos Paz 194;* ✆ *421 1410 or 422 3897;* e *gabrielogas@arnet.com.ar*) also has daily flights to and from Buenos Aires.

Public bus line 121 (1 peso) connects the airport with the bus terminal and downtown. Transfer Express (✆ 426 7945) also offers transport to and from the airport for 10 pesos (by *remise*) or 3.50 pesos (by a shuttle); either service will take you to or pick you up from your hotel. Avis (✆ 426 7777) and Hertz (✆ 426 4112; e ractucuman@yahoo.com.ar) car-rental agencies are at the airport.

By bus
The bus terminal is at Avenida Brígido Terán 250, at the Shopping del Jardín (✆ 430 4696, 422 2221). Numerous buses throughout the day link Buenos Aires to San Miguel de Tucumán. The journey takes 16 hours and costs about 75–110 pesos depending upon level of service. The most frequent services from the Retiro terminal are with Flecha Bus (✆ 011 4000 5200, 4315 2781) at various hours; as well as La Nueva Chevallier (✆ 4000 5255) daily at 09.15 and 15.45; General Urquiza/Sierra de Córdoba (✆ 4000 5222, 4000 5252) daily at 17.50; Transfer Lines (✆ 4314 4030, 4311 9873) daily at 20.00; and La Veloz del Norte (✆ 4315 0800, 4314 8090) on Thursday and Friday at 20.00. Tucumán is also well connected to the surrounding cities.

By train
From October 2005 a weekly train runs from Buenos Aires, Rosario and La Banda (Santiago del Estero) to Tucumán, leaving on Monday at 18.00 and reaching Tucumán at 20.00 the next day.

By car
It's 1,193km by road from Buenos Aires, taking Ruta 9 to Rosario then Ruta 34 to Santiago del Estero and Ruta 9 through Córdoba. The provincial capitals north and south are reached by Ruta 9 and Ruta 38.

Car-rental agencies in the city include: Dollar Rentacar (*Congreso 89;* ✆ 430 4625); Localiza (*San Juan 959;* ✆ 421 4100); Móvil Renta (*San Lorenzo 370;* ✆ 421 8635); and All Rent A Car (*Av Soldati 380;* ✆ 421 1372).

Orientation
Many of the city's more important institutions and offices surround the central Plaza Independencia. At the northwest corner of the plaza is the church of San Francisco and across Avenida San Martín is the Government House. Along San Martín the Jockey Club, the former Hotel Plaza and the Federación Económica stand out for their architecture. On the opposite corner of the plaza is the cathedral, with the tourism office next door. The north side of the city, near Plaza Urquiza, is a popular area with bars and cafés. To the east side is the large Parque 9 de Julio with lawn tennis, rose gardens, fountains, lakes, horseracing track and ample green space. The bus terminal is on the edge of the park on Avenida Brígido Terán. The main artery of the city is Avenida 24 de Septiembre, linking Plaza Independencia and the park. All the north–south streets change their names on either side of Avenida 24 de Septiembre. Also running east–west is Avenida Sarmiento at the northern edge of the microcentre; it changes its name to Avenida Gobernador del Campo beyond the park as it continues east towards the airport.

Where to stay
Grand Hotel del Tucumán Av Soldati 380; ✆ 450 2250; e ghotel@arnet.com.ar. The city's high-end 5-star hotel, it faces Parque 9 de Julio 6 blocks from downtown. Sgls cost 110 pesos, dbls 130 pesos and standard suites 220 pesos, with b/fast and parking included.
Hotel del Sol Laprida 35; ✆/f 431 1755; e reservas@hoteldelsol.com.ar. A very nice hotel just off Plaza Independencia. Sgls 90 pesos, dbls 120 pesos, triples 160 pesos, suite 190 pesos.

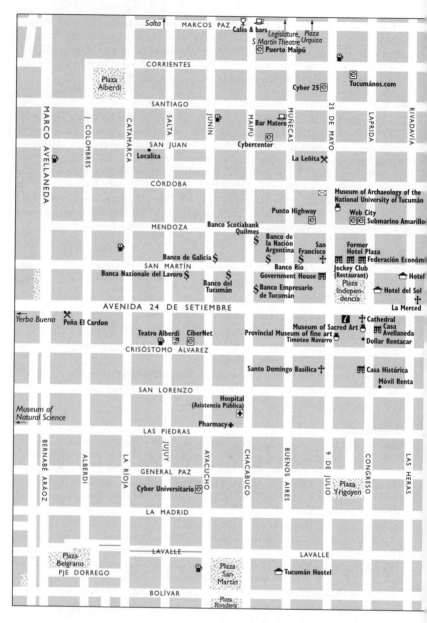

Hotel República Rivadavia 71; 431 0481; e hotelrepublica@leonalperovich.com.ar. A block from Plaza Independencia, this hotel is conveniently located for the main attractions of the centre. Sgls 70 pesos, dbls 90 pesos, triples 120 pesos.

Hotel Mediterráneo 24 de Septiembre 364; 431 0025; info@hotelmediterraneo.com.ar. Located in the historic centre 5 blocks from the bus terminal, this simple hotel has a swimming pool and b/fast included in its services. Sgl 40 pesos, dbl 80 pesos, triples 95 pesos.

Tucumán Hostel Buenos Aires 669; 420 1584; e info@tucumanhostel.com. This

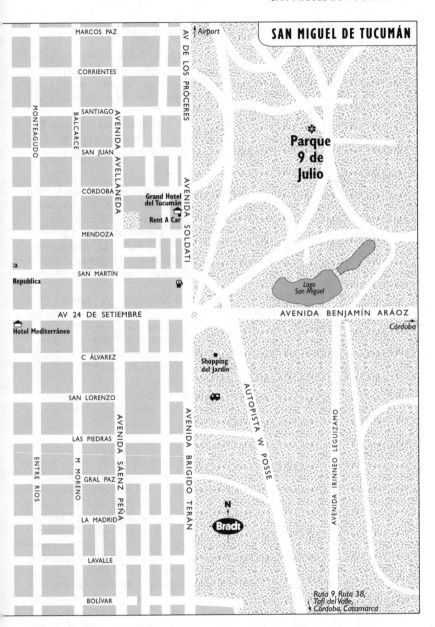

SAN MIGUEL DE TUCUMÁN

Parque 9 de Julio

Lago San Miguel

Shopping del Jardin

Hotel Mediterráneo

Grand Hotel del Tucumán

Rent A Car

Republica

Ruta 9, Ruta 38, Tafí del Valle, Córdoba, Catamarca

friendly and laid-back hostel, affiliated to Hostelling International, has a communal kitchen and lots of shared areas for relaxing, inc a back garden for summer *asado*. Dorm beds cost 11 pesos and dbls 28 pesos per person (2 pesos per person extra for non-members).

Where to eat and drink

The most popular area for bars and restaurants is north of the centre, and Plaza de Almas has a lively pub scene. Around Plaza Independencia, the **Jockey Club** (*San*

Martín 451; ℳ *421 3946*) is a beautiful old building with a restaurant on the first floor, offering a lunch buffet and a dinner menu.

Dinner is accompanied by live folk music at **Peña El Cardón** (*24 de Septiembre 1199*). This restaurant is also reputed to have the best *empanadas* in the country, having won a national competition to prove it. A good Argentine steak can be found at **La Leñita** (*25 de Mayo 377;* ℳ *422 0855, 422 9196*), where there are often folk musicians performing at night.

You can have a traditional Argentine breakfast with a well-made *maté* at **Bar Matero** (*Muñecas 491;* ℳ *431 2569*). This bar-café incorporates the **Arte Primitivo** gallery and shop, with handmade wooden objects and ceramics.

Practicalities

The **Secretaria de Turismo de Tucumán** is at 24 de Septiembre 484 (ℳ *430 3644;* e *info@turismoentucuman.gov.ar*). The **post office** is on 25 de Mayo between Córdoba and Mendoza (ℳ *422 0943*). There are several internet cafés, and more are springing up all the time. A few to mention include: **Puerto Maipú** (*Maipú 664*), **Tucumanos.com** (*Corrientes 447*), **Cybercenter** (*San Juan 612*), **Submarino Amarillo** (*Mendoza 400*), **Web City** (*Mendoza 486*), **Punto Highway** (*Mendoza 534*), **Cyber25** (*25 de Mayo 566*), **CiberNet** (*Crisóstomo Alvarez 830*) and **Cyber Universitario** (*Ayacucho 407*).

There are also plenty of banks, such as **Banca Nazionale del Lavoro** (*San Martín 879*), **Banco del Tucumán** (*San Marín 721*), **Banco Empresario de Tucumán** (*Maipu 32*), **Banco de la Nación Argentina** (*San Martín 690*), **Banco de Galicia** (*San Martín 766*), **Banco Rio** (*San Martín 590*) and **Banco Scotiabank Quilmes** (*Maipu 162*). Banks are open Monday to Friday 08.30–13.30; currency-exchange counters open Monday to Friday 08.30–13.30 and 16.30–20.00; some are open Saturday mornings.

Public assistance is at the **hospital** (Asistencia Pública) at Chacabuco 239 (ℳ *421 6307*). There is also a **pharmacy** (although there are many throughout the city) at Chacabuco 243 (ℳ *422 2824*).

Highlights

A quick tour round the centre will allow you to see the most significant buildings, notably religious edifices, and above all the Neoclassical **cathedral**, built in the years 1846–56; the **Museum of Sacred Art** is also housed here (*Av Congresso 47;* ℳ *421 2707*). The church of **San Francisco** (*25 de Mayo 110*) was built by the Jesuits in 1885 and later taken over by the Franciscans; its museum (ℳ *421 1333*) is open daily 08.30–12.00 and 16.30–20.30. The **Basilica of Santo Domingo**, consecrated in 1884, is located at 9 de Julio 164 (ℳ *422 8805*), and opening hours are 07.00–12.00 and 16.00–20.30. The church of **La Merced** (*Av 24 de Septiembre 253*) has Spanish influences in its design and was inaugurated in 1950.

The **Ex-Hotel Plaza** (*San Martín 400*) dates from 1932, when it was the most prestigious hotel in the city; its architecture is influenced by the Viennese *Jugendstil* style. **The Jockey Club** (*San Martín 447*) was built in 1939, and the El Circulo social club met here. The Bourbon French architecture has been preserved, as has the beautiful old escalator. The first floor functions as a restaurant. Step inside the internal garden of the **Federación Económica** (*San Martín 427;* ℳ *421 1854*) and see the beautiful Spanish tiling and stained glass dating from the house's remodelling by Dr Ricardo Frías in 1924. Since 1954 it has been used as a public office.

The **Casa de Gobierno** (*25 de Mayo and San Martín*) is usually heavily guarded but you can enter and request a guided tour. The Salón Blanco is where many important treaties and documents are signed. Unusually, the ceiling (1916) is covered with ornately painted canvases, rather than having been painted upon directly. The painter, José Vila Prades, cleverly combined religious elements such as cherubs with Argentine wildlife. The elaborate sweeping scenes of naked ethereal people riding white horses, walking through thistles and thorns and carrying laurel leaves all relate to the struggles for independence. Other imagery includes the harvest, the book of Argentine history, war and liberty, and music and art. The balcony overlooks the plaza, but you are not allowed to step out onto it for security reasons. The entire building has marble, crystal chandeliers and furniture brought over from France.

In the **Casa Histórica** (*Congreso 151;* ✎ *431 0826; open Mon–Fri 09.00–13.00, 16.00–18.00, mornings only at w/ends*) Argentina's declaration of independence from Spain was signed on 9 July 1816. The document itself is not on display for security as well as conservation reasons, but if staff are not too busy and are feeling friendly you may be allowed to view it. The colonial house is a museum with portraits of the signatories and other paraphernalia.

The **Casa Avellaneda** was built in 1836 by Governor José Manuel Silva and was home to him and his family, including his grandson President Nicolás Avellaneda. It is now a museum housing thousands of items that describe the history of Tucumán.

The city's three main **theatres** are the Teatro San Martín, the Teatro Alberdi (1912, restored from 1978). and the cultural centre of Universidad Nacional de Tucumán, home to the symphony orchestra.

Concentrated in the centre, **shops** are open 08.00–12.30 and 16.30–20.30 Monday to Friday and morning only (though this is changing to all day) on Saturday. There is a large shopping centre, Shopping del Jardín, at the bus terminal.

Museums

Provincial Museum of Fine Art 'Timoteo Navarro' 9 de Julio 44; ✎ 422 7300. A collection of paintings, sculptures and other fine art from the 18th and 19th centuries. *Open Tue–Fri 9.00–13.00, 16.30–20.30, w/ends 15.30–20.30.*

Museum of Archaeology of the National University of Tucumán 25 de Mayo 265; ✎ 423 3962. The collections and exhibits focus on technology and culture, with interactive experiments on learning. *Open Mon–Fri 08.00–12.00, 16.00–20.00; admission 1 peso.*

Pedagogical Museum of Natural Science Miguel Lillo 251; ✎ 423 0056. Two exhibits in this large building focus on biology and geology, while the outdoor botanical garden blossoms with the flora of the Tucumán forest. *Open daily 08.30–13.30, 14.30–18.00; free admission.*

Day trips and excursions

The most highly recommended outfitter for trekking, climbing, horseback riding and overnight expeditions is **Montañas Tucumanas** (*Av San Lorenzo 418;* ✎ *15 609 3336;* e *montanastucumanas@argentina.com; www.montanastucumanas.com*). Contact Pablo Zelaya Huerta, a professional guide with great enthusiasm for and expertise on the backcountry of this area (see also page 233).

Yerba Buena is a large garden suburb of the city. There are beautiful houses with spacious lush gardens, plenty of parks, and popular bars and restaurants along Avenida Aconquija. You could stay overnight at the **Hostel Aconquija** (*Av Aconquija 2530;* ✎ *425 6901;* e *info@aconquijahostel.com.ar*), where singles cost 35/42 pesos without/with private bath, doubles 52/68 pesos; dorm beds are 18/22 pesos. Buses to Yerba Buena (Lines 118 and 100) run along San Lorenzo and Santiago every 30 minutes and cost between 1 peso and 1.30 pesos. Three times a day line 118 continues to **San Javier**, just a bit further up the road, costing 3.50 pesos. An option for accommodation here is the **Hostería Imanay** (*Calle 3;* ✎ *492 9029, 423*

6744; reservas@imanay.com.ar) where doubles cost 70 pesos, triples 100 pesos and suites 130 pesos, all with breakfast.

Villa Nougués, 24km from San Miguel de Tucumán atop the Sierra del Aconquija, gives incredible views of the valleys and the somewhat ostentatious 18th-century European-style villas plopped on the rolling hilltops. To get there you need a car as there isn't any public bus service. From the south of the city, Avenida Roca becomes Ruta 38, leading to the village of Ohuanta, from where 2km of winding paved road followed by 14km of winding unpaved road lead up the mountains to the Chapel of Villa Nougués. Alternatively, drive up from the district of Yerba Buena by Avenida Maté de Luna, continuing on Avenida Aconquija then Avenida Solano Vera, and then turn left onto the winding mountain road already described. The drive from the city and into these hills will take you through sugar and citrus fields, and when you have reached a vantage point on the hills you can see the different shades of green representing the different crops (sugar cane is light green and lemons are dark green) and the plumes of smoke coming from the sugar factories.

Throughout this area are wonderful places for many outdoor sports (hiking, biking, paragliding, rock climbing, etc). You may choose to stay at **Villa Lolette Hotel Resort** (*400m to the left of the Chapel of Villa Nougués;* \ *422 1515;* e *info@vila-lolette.com.ar*); doubles cost 180 pesos with breakfast. It is a lovely hotel and there is also a restaurant featuring traditional Argentine dishes. The **Hostería Villa Nougués** (\ *0381 431 0048 or 435 5863;* e *info@villa-nougues.com.ar*) is a 19th-century villa with accommodation for US$65 per night, breakfast included, and restaurant.

Continuing along Rutas 340 and 341 you will make a large loop back to the city, passing through the **Bosque de la Memoria** at the University of Tucumán where all the trees were planted in memory of the lives lost during the Subversion of Tucumán (1975–83). You can also stop to walk at the feet of the third-largest **statue of Christ** in Latin America (28m; the tallest is in Rio de Janeiro and the second-tallest in Mendoza) atop a hill overlooking the agriculturally rich Valle la Salla. Along this circuit are many little villages selling local products, such as the famous cheeses of the region. **El Siambon** is a monastery where Benedictine monks sell honey, preserves, baked goods and other treats.

Campo de los Alisos National Park

At the southern end of the Sierra del Aconquija, the first range of mountains west of the great chaco-pampean lowlands, some 10,000ha were designated as national park in 1995 to protect an area of montane habitat, from 800m to the peak of Cerro de la Bolsa, the highest in the park at 5,200m. The borders of the park are the rivers Las Pavas and Jaya, meeting at its eastern corner, and the border of Tucumán and Catamarca provinces to the west. Alder, podocarp and walnut are typical trees of the montane forest, with flowers such as lilies and lupins until altitude permits the growth only of low and tenacious cushion plants. Of great archaeological importance are the Incan ruins at the Ciudadcita or Pueblo Viejo (4,300m), dating from c1480.

To get to the park, take route 38 south from the city of Tucumán to Concepción (80km) then go west for 28km through Alpachiri to the border of the national park at La Jaya. The roads are unpaved and in poor condition. There are no services in this park.

Santiago del Estero Province

Not often on the tourist track, Santiago del Estero province is one of the country's most traditional areas. It's mostly pampa, with some variety added to the geography by a few mountain ranges, the Guasayán and Mogotes Mountains to the west and the Ambargasta and Sumampa Hills, part of the Pampean Range, to the south. Large salt flats cover great areas of the province as well, extending into the neighbouring provinces. The vegetation is classified as semi-arid chaco, dominated by quebracho trees and cactus. It is a hot, dry region and the siesta here is taken very seriously. The greatest draw for tourism is the Termas de Río Hondo.

SANTIAGO DEL ESTERO
Area code 0385
Santiago del Estero is actually the oldest city in Argentina, founded in 1553 by Francisco de Aguirre. A bishopric from 1570 and provincial capital from 1577, it was the base for Spanish expansion in the northwest, and is still the commercial centre of the Chaco region.

Getting there
By air
The Aeropuerto Santiago del Estero is 6km northwest of the city on Avenida Madre de Ciudades (↘ 434 3654). There are daily flights with Aerolíneas Argentinas/Austral (*24 de Septiembre 547;* ↘ *422 4335/7;* f *422 4333;* e *sdegte@aerolineas.com.ar; open Mon–Fri 08.30–13.00, 17.00–20.30, Sat 09.00–13.00*) from Buenos Aires, often via Córdoba. No public transport is available from the airport but there are taxis, charging about 5 pesos to the centre.

By bus
Almirante Brown, El Rápido, San Cristóbal, TAC, Transfer Line, La Union, Nueva Chevallier and Mercobus are the main companies linking Buenos Aires and Santiago del Estero. The journey takes 12–14 hours and most departures leave the Retiro terminal in the early evening, arriving in Santiago del Estero the following morning; tickets cost 60–105 pesos depending on level of comfort and service.

By train
Since October 2005 a weekly train runs from Buenos Aires and Rosario to Tucumán, leaving on Monday at 18.00 and reaching the station of La Banda, 4km from Santiago del Estero, at 16.00 the next day.

By car
From Buenos Aires (1,039km) take Ruta 9 to Rosario then Ruta 34 to Santiago del Estero. From Tucumán and Córdoba take Ruta 9, and from Catamarca Ruta 6.

Practicalities
For both food and accommodation go to the **Hotel and Restaurant Carlos V** (*Independencia 110;* ↘ *424 0303;* e *reservas@carlosvsantiago.com.ar*) where doubles cost 130 pesos.

The **tourist office** is at the Subsecretaría de Turismo de la Provincia de Santiago del Estero (*Plaza Libertad 417;* ↘ *421 4243;* f *421 3253;* e *turismosgo1@arnet.com.ar*).

Highlights
The **cathedral**, on Plaza Libertad at 24 de Septiembre, is the fifth built on this seemingly cursed site. The first cathedral, and the first in Argentina, was built in 1591 and destroyed in 1611; a second one was started then but caught fire in 1615.

A third one was inaugurated in 1617 but continuous floods led to its collapse into the river in 1677. The fourth was inaugurated in 1686 but was partially destroyed by an earthquake in 1816. The present building was inaugurated in 1877. Fifth time lucky! It was declared a National Historic Monument in 1953 and made a Minor Cathedral Basilica in 1971.

The Franciscans founded the **Convento de San Francisco** (*Avellaneda and Av Roca*), also one of the first monasteries in the country, which houses a religious art museum and the cloister cell of San Francisco Solano, who was here in 1593. The **church of Santo Domingo** has one of the two existing tracings of the Holy Shroud of Turin.

Museums

Museo Arqueológico Avellaneda 355; ☏ 421 1380. The museum covers palaeontology, the natural sciences and ethnography, as well as archaeology. *Open Mon–Fri 08.00–13.00, 15.00–20.00, w/ends 09.30–12.00.*

Museo Histórico Urquiza 354; ☏ 421 2893. Founded by Orestes de Lullo in 1941 and since declared a Historic National Monument, it preserves portraits, documents, military paraphernalia and other items pertaining to the history of the province. *Open Mon–Fri 07.00–13.00, 14.00–20.00.*

Museo de Bellas Artes Av Belgrano 1554; ☏ 421 1839. An excellent collection by many of the important contemporary Argentine artists. *Open Mon–Fri 08.00–13.00, 15.00–20.00, w/ends 09.30–12.00.*

Day trips and excursions

The hot springs of the **Termas de Río Hondo** are in the town of the same name, 65km west of Santiago del Estero by Ruta 9, reached by bus with Nueva Chevallier (☏ 03858 422104). **Tourist information** is at the Dirección Provincial de Turismo (*J B Alberdi 245;* ☏ *03858 421571;* e *secturriohondo@argentina.com; www.termasderiohondo.com*). In addition there is the **Ente Municipal de Turismo** (*Caseros 268;* ☏ *421969;* e *entur-riohondo@ciudad.com.ar or entur-riohondo@argentina.com*).

All the hotels have thermal waters in their swimming pools and bathrooms. One recommended hotel is **Inti Punku** (Puerta del Sol), Juan Felipe Ibarra s/n, on the road west to the Río Hondo dam (☏ *02966 15 630 553;* e *elhuayra@yahoo.com.ar*).

Catamarca Province

Some of the highest mountains in the Andes are found in Alta Catamarca. Monte Pissis (6,882m) is the highest inactive volcano in the world and the second-highest peak in the Americas; Ojos del Salado (6,864m) is the third-highest mountain in the Americas and the highest active volcano in the world. On Llullaillaco (6,739m) the famous mummies were found in the 1990s that now sleep in Salta's MAAM museum (see page 223). Tres Cruces, Incahuasi and Los Nacimientos are all over 6,000m. The Atacama Puna is a high unpopulated desert. The landscapes are fascinatingly stunning, with diverse colour and texture, adobe huts and small desert cemeteries.

SAN FERNANDO DEL VALLE DE CATAMARCA
Area code 03833
Founded in 1683, the capital of the province of Catamarca is usually known by the same name, meaning 'small town'. It's a pleasant and little-visited city, with some fine public buildings dating from the late 19th century.

Getting there
By air
The Aeropuerto Felipe Varela is 22km south in the district of Los Puestos, on Ruta Provincial 33 (☎ 453683–4). There's a daily flight from Buenos Aires with Aerolíneas Argentinas/Austral (*Sarmiento 589;* ☎ *424450/60;* f *431000;* e *ctcgte@aerolineas.com.ar; open Mon–Fri 08.00–13.00, 17.00–21.00, Sat 08.30–13.00*). A taxi to the centre will cost about 18 pesos.

By bus
The bus terminal is at Avenida Güemes 820. TAC (☎ *451232*) has a daily service overnight from Buenos Aires (14½ hours) with a *semicama* for 80 pesos. There is a cheaper option at 66 pesos but with regular seats. El Rápido (☎ *453787*) has one morning and one evening service to La Rioja, Mendoza and San Juan for 10–12 pesos. Other bus companies serving various cities include: Plus Ultra (☎ *451040*); Chevallier-La Estrella (☎ *430921*); Sierras de Córdoba-Urquiza (☎ *434980)*; Flecha Bus (☎ *456 523*); and AndesMar (☎ *423777*).

By car
The city is over 1,100km northwest of Buenos Aires; take Ruta 9 to Rosario then Ruta 34 to Santiago del Estero and Ruta 64 to Catamarca.

Where to stay
Amerian Catamarca Park Hotel República 347; ☎ 425444; e reservas@amerian.com. Sgls 115 pesos, dbls 150 pesos, triples 180 pesos, with b/fast, gym and swimming pool.
Hotel Casino Catamarca Pasaje César Carman s/n; ☎/f 432928, 430891; e infocentral@hotelcasinocatamarca.com. This is one of the most popular hotels for business travel and, of course, gamblers. There is entertainment, night and day, though not for every traveller's tastes. Sgls 50 pesos, dbls 63 pesos, triples 75 pesos.
Inti Huasi República 299; ☎ 426715; e intihuasi@hotmail.com. Sgls 51 pesos, dbls 70 pesos, triples 80 pesos. Another mid-range option that should prove to be a bit quieter.
Plaza Hotel Rivadavia 258; ☎ 426558. A *residencial* centrally located on a pedestrianised street; sgls 15 pesos, dbls 24 pesos, triples 30 pesos.
Hospedaje del Peregrino San Martín 490; ☎ 431203; f 431201. This budget option charges 6 pesos for a bed without bedding or 8 pesos with bedding.

Municipal **camping** is available (5 pesos per site) 5km west of the city off Ruta Provincial 4; *colectivo* 101 leaves from the San Francisco Convent at Esquiú and Rivadavia. There are a swimming pool, showers and electricity.

Where to eat and drink
Salsa Criolla Parrilla República 546; ☎ 433584. Salad bar and *asado* lunch specials are very good quality; it seems to cater to tourists, which makes the prices a little high.

Practicalities
The **Secretaria de Turismo** (*General Roca 1;* ☎ *437743; turismocatamarca@ cedeconet.com.ar*) has information on the city and surrounding area.

Alta Catamarca (☎ *430333;* f *430339;* e *info@altacatamarca.com; www.altacatamarca.com*) is a tour company that organises mountaineering expeditions, trekking, 4x4 trips and nature and cultural tours into the mountains and the high *puna* plateau.

There are a couple of **banks** off Plaza 25 de Mayo. The **post office** is a couple of blocks east on San Martín.

The **Hospital San Juan Bautista** is at Avenida Illia 150 (☎ *437655*), and there's

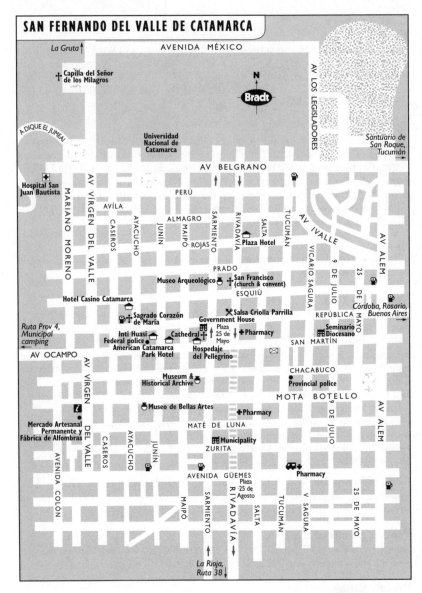

SAN FERNANDO DEL VALLE DE CATAMARCA

also an **Emergency Medical Centre** (*Luis Herrera 255;* ℡ *107*). There are several **pharmacies**, including one at the bus terminal (*Av Güemes 820;* ℡ *439112*), and others by the cathedral (*Rivadavia 626;* ℡ *437342*) and in the centre (*Rivadavia 970;* ℡ *423913*). The federal **police** are located at San Martín 244 (℡ *422917, 430409*); the provincial police are at Tucumán 836 (*emergency* ℡ *101*).

Highlights

The main pedestrianised street, Rivadavia, is on the east side of the central Plaza 25 de Mayo, off which is one important historical building – the **Government**

House (1859). Most of the architecturally significant buildings, however, are churches. The **Catedral Basílica Nuestra Señora del Valle** (1859) is the showpiece of Plaza 25 de Mayo, with beautiful stained glass; one of its nice features is that its steps lead directly onto the plaza and do not require you to cross a street to reach the cathedral. Other important structures, mostly dating from the late 1800s, include the **Capilla del Señor de los Milagros** (Choya), Avenida Virgin del Valle; the **Santuario de San Roque**, Avenida Puente Castillo; the **Iglesia Sagrado Corazón de María**, República 100; the Neoclassical **San Francisco Church and Convent**, on Esquiú at Rivadavia; and the **Seminario Diocesano**, San Martín 900.

Museums
Museo Archeológico 'Adán Quiroga' Sarmiento 450. Collections of artefacts dating from thousands of years ago and to colonial times. *Open Mon–Fri 07.00–13.00, 14.30–20.30, w/ends 08.30–12.30, 15.30–18.30; admission 1 peso.*
Museo y Archivo Histórico Chacabuco 425. A bit short on interpretation but there are plenty of pictures of provincial governors and personal effects. *Open Mon–Fri 08.00–12.00, 15.00—19.00; free admission.*
Museo de Bellas Artes 'Laureano Brizuela' Speck Botello 239. Named for the local painter whose works are displayed here, together with other influential Argentine painters. *Open Mon–Fri 07.00–13.00, 15.00–21.00; free admission.*

You may also wish to visit the ruins of **El Pueblo Perdido de la Quebrada** 7km west of the city. These are the remains of 4th- and 5th-century adobe houses built by the Aguada culture which also left beautiful ceramics and other artefacts.

Shopping
The **Mercado Artesanal Permanente y Fábrica de Alfombras** (*Virgen del Valle 945*) is a permanent market of handicrafts, including textiles, jewellery and musical instruments. Other temporary markets spring up in the various plazas at weekends. Shops around Plaza 25 de Mayo specialise in local foodstuffs such as olives and olive oil, cheeses, jams and meringues.

La Rioja Province

Area code 03822
Here you are entering the country's prime wine-producing region, and La Rioja holds its own by growing the Spanish Torrontés grape, which produces a fruity white wine. Most of the region is technically scrubland and desert with dry steppes of scraggy thorn bushes and gleaming white desiccated cow bones. The province's most infamous son is former president Carlos Saúl Menem, elected as its senator in 2005.

LA RIOJA
At the foot of the Sierra de Velasco, the provincial capital of La Rioja was founded in 1592. Many colonial buildings were destroyed by an earthquake in 1894 and the city was totally rebuilt.

Getting there
By air
The Aeropuerto La Rioja, Ruta Provincial 5 (❧ *461919, 439211*) is surrounded by spectacular views of the Velasco Mountains. A taxi from the airport to the centre

costs around 8 pesos. Aerolíneas Argentinas (*Belgrano 63;* ❧ *426307;* f *426385;* e *irjgte@aerolineas.com.ar; open Mon–Fri 08.00–13.00, 17.30–20.30, Sat 08.30–12.30*) has a direct flight from Buenos Aires daily except on Tuesdays.

By bus
La Nueva Chevallier (❧ *422723*) has departures from Buenos Aires at 14.15, 15.15 and 18.50 daily; TAC (*in Buenos Aires* ❧ *011 4312 7012*) leaves every night at 20.00 and 20.30; and General Urquiza (❧ *436272*) departs every night at 20.00. La Rioja's bus terminal is at España and Artigas (❧ *435453*).

By car
Driving to La Rioja from Buenos Aires, pass through Córdoba and continue an additional 400km on Ruta 38, which also links to the Andean Ruta 40.

Winner Rent a Car Los Granaderos 33; ❧ 431318

Where to stay
Naindo Park Hotel San Nicolás de Bari 475 at J V Gonzalez; ❧ 470700; www.naindoparkhotel.com. The city's 5-star option, with sgls at 133 pesos and dbls at 140 pesos.
Plaza Hotel San Nicolás de Bari and 9 de Julio; ❧ 425215. Located in the centre of the city, in front of the principal plaza, this hotel has laundry service, rooms with minibars and room service, and an outdoor swimming pool. Sgls cost 99 pesos, dbls 114 pesos and triples 138 pesos, all with buffet b/fast.
Hotel de Turismo La Rioja Av Perón and Quiroga; ❧f 422005. This hotel has many services, inc a large pool area, restaurant, bar, buffet b/fast and a 24-hour snack bar. Rooms with balconies are 55 pesos sgl, 65 pesos dbl, 75 pesos triple.
Gran Hotel Embajador San Martín 250; ❧ 438580; e reservas@granhotelembajador.com.ar. Friendly staff and good coffee and *medialunas* for b/fast. Sgls 35 pesos, dbls 50 pesos, triples 65 pesos.
Residencia Florida 8 de Diciembre 524; ❧ 426563. The town's budget option, with sgls at 15 pesos, dbls at 30 pesos and triples at 35 pesos.

Where to eat and drink
La Vasija P B Luna 87; ❧ 433505. This bar takes advantage of the excellent local wines.
La Vieja Casona Rivadavia 427; ❧ 425996. Regional food.
La Querencia Av Perón 1200; ❧ 430939. Regional food.
El Corral Av Facundo Quiroga and Rivadavia; ❧ 15 686155, 15 540175. Country-style cooking.

For meat, **Rotisería Sabor City** (*Rivadavia and Davila*) or **Rotisería Facundo** (*Av Perón 735*).

Practicalities
The **tourist office** is at Avenida Perón 715 (❧ *427103*); for the region, go to the general office at P B Luna 345 (*for information on Talampaya National Park,* ❧ *03825 470356*). The **Banco de la Nación Argentina** is at P B Luna 699 (❧ *439230*). For medical assistance, call the **Hospital P Plaza** (❧ *427814*); for the **police** ❧ *425374*.

Highlights
Paseo San Ignacio is an attractive little plaza, a reproduction of the original colonial square. It has a few little bars with pavement tables and is full of flowers

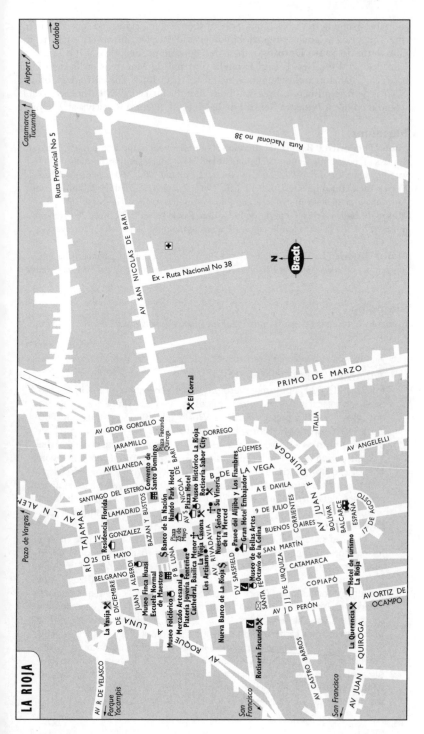

and vines hanging from balconies. Several shops selling crafts and speciality items ring the plaza. Certain original buildings did survive, however, such as the **Convento de Santo Domingo**, the oldest convent in Argentina, at P B Luna and Lamadrid; and the Neoclassical **Escuela Normal de Maestros** on Pelagio Luna between Catamarca and Belgrano, which dates from 1884. The **cathedral**, on San Nicolás de Bári at Buenos Aires, was built after the quake in 1899. Another notable religious edifice is **Nuestra Señora de la Merced**, Avenida Rivadavia at 9 de Julio.

Museums

Museo Folklorico P B Luna 811. In colonial houses rebuilt in the 19th century, there are displays of indigenous ceramics, religious art and *criollo* housekeeping, farming and weaving. *Open Tue–Fri 09.00–13.00, 16.00–20.00, w/ends 09.00–12.00; admission 1.50 pesos.*

Museo Inca Huasi J. Bautista Alberdi 650. The archaeology and culture of northwestern Argentina over 10,000 years, as well as colonial religious art. *Open Tue–Sat 09.00–12.00.*

Museo de Bellas Artes 'Octavio de la Colina' Pasaje Diaguita 75. Since 2001 this art museum has also become a cultural centre where symphony, ballet and theatre events are held. *Open 08.00–13.00, 15.00–21.00.*

Museo Histórico La Rioja, Adolfo Dávila 79. A display of military paraphernalia and mementoes of *caudillos* such as Facindo Quiroga, Felipe Varela and Angel Peãloza. *Admission 1 peso.*

Shopping

Mercado Artesanal Pelagio B Luna 782. This market has silverware, ceramics and other regional crafts for sale.

TALAMPAYA NATIONAL PARK

In 1975, 215,000ha of forest were put under protection, primarily for the palaeontological and archaeological finds in the area. These are significant enough to be awarded UNESCO's World Heritage Site status in 2000 along with the neighbouring Ischigualasto Provincial Park in San Juan province. Both parks have abundant fossils, giving a complete record of the Triassic period (245–208 million years ago). *Lagosuchus talampayensis* was one of the first dinosaurs to evolve, 250 million years ago. *Paloecheris talampayensis* is a turtle that appeared here 210 million years ago. Human presence dates from between AD120 and 1180. Caves used as shelters, storage and burial sites have been explored and figurines and petroglyphs have been discovered.

The red sandstone canyon of the Talampaya River is favoured habitat for condors, peregrine falcons and other raptors that roost and perch on the 150m-high cliffs and soar on the thermals above the canyon. Erosion from wind and water shapes the easily transformable sandstone into wondrous formations. There are desert-like areas, called *huayquerías*, where only small fleshy leaved plants grow. Otherwise, the vegetation is sparse, with low, almost leafless, branches with green stems similar to that of broom that are capable of photosynthesis without much water loss. This water-saving trick is also performed by another plant called *brea*, which flowers profusely in spring with many bright yellow flowers. Many species of cactus, including tall candelabra types, grow in the park. Of the various wild animals within the park, the mountain viscacha (*Lagidium viscacia*) and the endemic fairy armadillo (*Chlamyphorus truncatus*) are most notable.

Les Artisans Av Rivadavia 633; ℸ 435174. Regional crafts and traditional items such as handcrafted *matés*.

Su Vinería Av Rivadavia 477; **Platería Joyería Fonteñez** Alberdi 458 and San Nicolás de Bari 681; and **Paseo del Aljibe** San Martín 211, are all recognised and reputable producers and vendors of regional products, crafts, speciality foods, wines, *matés* and other items.

Los Fiambres San Martín 211; ℸ 435074. Sell speciality foods as well as wines from their extensive bodega.

Talampaya National Park

This park is some 215km south of the city by Ruta 38 to Patquia, then west on Ruta 150 to Ruta 26, joining the localities of Villa Unión and Baldecitos near the border with San Juan province, which crosses the park. A sideroad leads 14km to the entrance where you can get information and orientation, as well as paying the 12 pesos admission charge.

The park is new and has limited infrastructure. At the information office there is a toilet and refreshments. From here, two-hour tours in 4x4s are organised to the canyon; private vehicles may not enter the park. Permission from the park ranger must be given to access the Ciudad Perdida (Lost City) and see the unusual rock formations, 60km from the information office. Tours cost 40 pesos and up, depending on the number of people and length of excursion. Dress appropriately to visit this park: the days are very hot and the evenings cold. It does not rain often but if it does it does so with force.

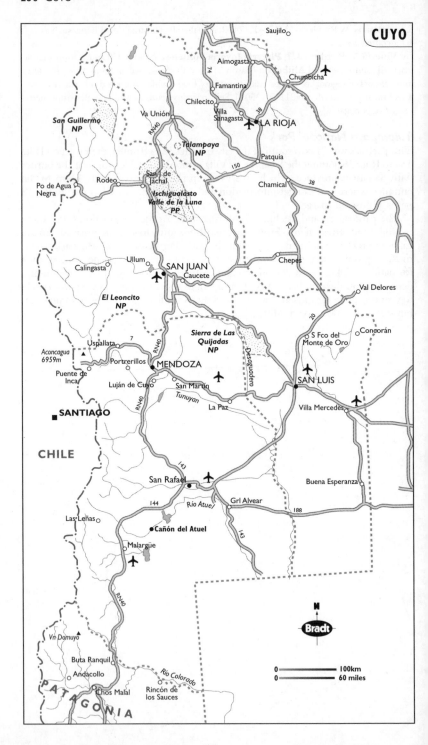

CUYO

Saujilo

Aimogasta

74

Famantina

Chumbicha

Chilecito

Villa
Sanagasta

28

LA RIOJA

San Guillermo
NP

Va Unión

RN40

Talampaya
NP

Patquía

150

Po de Agua
Negra

Rodeo

San J de
Jáchal

Chamical

38

Ischigualasto
Valle de la Luna
PP

79

Ullum

Calingasta

SAN JUAN

Chepes

Caucete

El Leoncito
NP

Val Delores

20

Sierra de Las
Quijadas
NP

S Fco del
Monte de Oro

Concorán

Uspallata

7

RN40

Aconcagua
6959m

Portrerillos

MENDOZA

Desaguadero

SAN LUIS

Puente de
Inca

Luján de Cuyo

San Martín

Tunuyán

La Paz

Villa Mercedes

SANTIAGO

RN40

CHILE

143

San Rafael

Buena Esperanza

144

Río Atuel

Grl Alvear

188

Las Leñas

Cañón del Atuel

143

Malargüe

RN40

N

Bradt

Vn Domuyo

Buta Ranquil

Andacollo

Río Colorado

0 ————— 100km

0 ————— 60 miles

Chos Malal

Rincón de
los Sauces

PATAGONIA

Cuyo

World-class vineyards and the highest and most magnificent mountains in the Andean cordillera define this region of Argentina. The word *cuyum* is indigenous and means 'sandy earth', which is apt – this region, despite its fruitful bounty, is a desert, receiving very little precipitation (about 250mm per year, mainly between December and February), and is irrigated by snowmelt streams from the Andes.

The provinces of San Juan, Mendoza and San Luis that make up the region of Cuyo produce the country's best and most prestigious wines. The best time of year to visit is February to March when the summer is ending and the wine harvest is beginning. Owing to the high economic importance of the wine industry, the highway borders between provinces have serious biological controls in place. In an area where apples are a form of contraband, ensuring that you are not transporting fruit (and possible pests or diseases) is more important than the status of your passport. Crossing from San Luis province into Mendoza, my travelling companion and I had to eat half a dozen apples under military guard at the side of the road or throw away our precious food ration. It was bizarre and a bit unnerving to be munching away under such scrutiny, but their caution is justified. After proving that you are not transporting fruit, you will be required to drive through a pesticide spray – remember to close your windows and air vents!

Mendoza Province

Mendoza is a very diverse province and very attractive to tourists. The large and energetic city of Mendoza is one of the most popular Argentine cities to visit, with plenty of entertainment, shopping, gastronomic and sightseeing options. Ideally sited at the foot of the Andes, this city is the gateway to a paradise for outdoor enthusiasts. World-class skiing is found at the Las Leñas resort, near Malargüe, rafting and hiking are popular along the Río Atuel near San Rafael, and mountain climbers head above all for Mount Aconcagua, which at 6,962m is the highest mountain in the Americas, within Aconcagua Provincial Park. After all the sporting challenges have been met, there are wineries and thermal spas as a reward.

MENDOZA
Area code 0261
Being set in the foothills of the Andes and surrounded by vineyards would be publicity enough for the capital city of Mendoza, but there is so much more. By day, it is a great city to walk around, with plentiful trees and flowers in the streets

ARGENTINE WINES

In the past ten years Argentina has become one of the recognised 'New World' wine producers and is giving some competition to the longer established industries in the USA, Australia, New Zealand, South Africa and Chile. Ancient vines had been brought from Europe in the mid-1800s and wine-makers concentrated on producing high volumes but with low quality and thus no export market. Modernisation in recent decades began to see better production of the noble French varieties Cabernet Sauvignon, Syrah, Merlot and Pinot Noir and Italian Bonarda among the reds, and Chardonnay, Semillon and Sauvignon Blanc as well as the German Riesling and French Viognier among the whites. Most interesting was the realisation that the Malbec grape, from the south of France, adapted to the Argentine soil better than it had to its *tierra madre*, its mother soil; Argentine Malbec is not only among the world's best Malbecs but is seen as the national wine, being perfectly matched to steak. Similarly, the Tempranillo grape, of Spanish origin, is not common elsewhere in the world but in Argentina is third in importance (in terms of area planted), following the Bonarda and Malbec varieties. The emblematic white is the Torrontés, grown only in the Iberian Peninsula and in Argentina (including Salta province), where it too has done better than in Europe; it generally gives a light wine but with strong muscat-like aromas.

Argentina's wine-making region stretches for 2,400km along the Andean foothills from Salta to Río Negro. The most important region is Cuyo and above all the province of Mendoza, where wine-producing regions are divided into zones according to climate, elevation and soil. The Upper Río Mendoza Zone is situated at 800–1,100m and is where the Malbec grape prospers and where most of the noble varieties have adapted. The Northern Zone is suitable for the fruity whites and young reds, while the most productive is the Eastern Zone; they are both set at 600–700m. The Uco Valley is at 800–1,400m, making it a colder zone producing wines with good acidity. San Rafael, at 450–800m, has its own Denomination of Origin. Finally, at 600m in San Juan province, the Tulum Valley has a dry and warm climate with alluvial sands and permeable clayish soils that produce a great variety of grapes, notably Syrah/Shiraz. At altitudes of 1,000m or more the grapes stay on the vine for 150 days, as against just 100 in France, giving the wines more fruit, freshness and complexity and less tannin.

and numerous plazas with markets and street musicians. By night there are theatres and nightclubs to enjoy as well as restaurants with pavement tables where in summer you can sit and watch the passers-by. The centre of Mendoza is largely pedestrianised with attractive streets lined with poplars, elm and sycamore (all planted by the city and none of which are native to Argentina) and irrigation channels called *acequias*. Although Mendoza is an old city, founded in 1561, much of its historic architecture has been lost in earthquakes. The most devastating of these was in 1861 when the city was almost completely destroyed and some 10,000 people were killed. The city was rebuilt with mainly ground-hugging single-storey buildings. The most serious quake in recent times was in 1985 when there were few fatalities but tens of thousands lost their homes.

Getting there
By air
Aeropuerto Internacional Mendoza is at Ruta 40 north (✆ *520 6000*). There are four flights per day (only 3 at weekends; 50 minutes) from Buenos Aires Aeroparque to Mendoza with Aerolíneas Argentinas; and two per day with LAN Argentina. Aerolíneas Argentinas (*Paseo Sarmiento 82;* ✆ *420 4100;* f *420 4139;* e *mdzadmin@aerolineas.com.ar; open Mon–Fri 09.00–20.00, Sat 09.00–12.30*) also has a daily connection between Córdoba and Mendoza (1 hour). LAN (*España 1012;* ✆f *425 7900, 0810 999 9526; LAN Argentina free 0800 222 2424*) flies from Santiago de Chile to Mendoza twice daily (1½ hours).

The airport is located 7km north of the city and a taxi fare will be about 10 pesos. There is a shuttle service that is cheaper. The most economical means of transport, however, is public bus 60 (sub-route 63 or 68, specifying *Aeropuerto*; 1.20 pesos); this runs hourly along Avenida Alameda to the centre at Plaza Independencia.

Car rental is available at the airport with Hertz (✆ *448 2327, 488 4392*) and Avis (✆ *447 0150;* e *mendozaapt@avis.com.ar*).

By bus
The bus terminal is at Videla and 25 de Mayo, near the end of Avenida Zapata where it meets Ruta 40 (✆ *431 3001/5000*).

There are over 15 services per day between Buenos Aires and Mendoza, with various companies and levels of service. It has been suggested that TAC (✆ *431 1039*) offers the poorest service; better companies include Andesmar (✆ *420 4836*), Chevallier (✆ *431 3900*), El Rápido (✆ *432 4456*), Expreso Uspallata (✆ *431 3303*), Central Argentino (✆ *431 3112*) and CATA (✆ *431 0782*).

A ticket costs 72–160 pesos, depending on the level of service, for the 14-hour journey. There are three daily departures to Neuquén with TAC, El Rápido and Andesmar; the 12-hour journey costs 55 pesos. Travelling north to San Juan takes only two and a half hours, 10–14 pesos, with many companies including TAC, Del Sur y Media Agua (✆ *431 2570*), San Juan Mar Del Plata (✆ *431 2840*) and Andesmar. From San Rafael there are buses every two hours with Vientos del Sur (✆ *431 4050*) and Expreso Uspallata (✆ *431 3303*); five of these each day start from Malargüe. Andesmar also go daily to Mendoza, taking 19 hours (104 pesos for *semi-cama*).

There are plentiful international buses (about two dozen departures a day) to **Santiago**, taking about six hours (US$15–20), as well as *taxis colectivos* (shared minibuses), taking about five hours (US$20–25).

By car
Ruta 7 is the most direct road between Buenos Aires and Mendoza, passing through San Luis. You will drive almost 1,100km with great distances between service points. Make sure that your vehicle has all the appropriate emergency equipment, including a spare tyre and extra fuel.

Orientation
Plaza Independencia is the central plaza where tourists and *mendocinos* can enjoy open-air concerts and markets. Often described as looking on a map like the five-spot side of a die, the city has four smaller plazas all two blocks from the central plaza and four blocks from each other. They are diplomatically named Italia, España, Chile and San Martín, making a perfect square of the microcentre's boundary. They are all lovely but Plaza España is particularly noteworthy – it was built in the 1940s to re-create an Andalusian square with fountains and beautiful Spanish tilework.

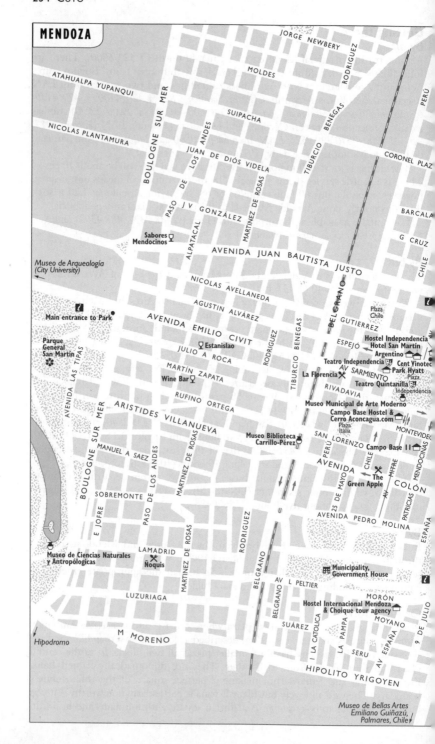

MENDOZA

JORGE NEWBERY

ATAHUALPA YUPANQUI

MOLDES

NICOLAS PLANTAMURA

BOULOGNE SUR MER

SUIPACHA

RODRIGUEZ

BENEGAS

PERÚ

JUAN DE DIÓS VIDELA

PASO DE LOS ANDES

TIBURCIO

CORONEL PLAZ

PASO J V GONZÁLEZ

MARTINEZ DE ROSAS

BARCALA

ALPATACAL

G CRUZ

Sabores Mendocinos

AVENIDA JUAN BAUTISTA JUSTO

CHILE

Museo de Arqueología (City University)

NICOLAS AVELLANEDA

AGUSTIN ALVÁREZ

BELGRANO

Plaza Chile

Main entrance to Park

AVENIDA EMILIO CIVIT

GUTIERREZ

Parque General San Martín

JULIO A ROCA

RODRIGUEZ

BENEGAS

ESPEJO

Hostel Independencia
Hotel San Martín
Argentino

TIBURCIO

AV SARMIENTO

Teatro Independencia
La Florencia

Cent Yinotec
Park Hyatt

Estanislao

MARTÍN ZAPATA

AVENIDA LAS TIPAS

Wine Bar

RIVADAVIA

Plaza Independencia

Teatro Quintanilla

RUFINO ORTEGA

Museo Municipal de Arte Moderno
Campo Base Hostel &
Cerro Aconcagua.com

ARISTIDES VILLANUEVA

BOULOGNE SUR MER

MANUEL A SAEZ

MARTINEZ DE ROSAS

Museo Biblioteca
Carrillo-Pérez

SAN LORENZO

PERÚ

Plaza Italia

Campo Base II

MONTEVIDEC

E JOFRE

SOBREMONTE

PASO DE LOS ANDES

CHILE

AVENIDA

MENDOCINAS

AVENIDA

25 DE MAYO

The
Green Apple

COLÓN

MFRE

Museo de Ciencias Naturales
y Antropológicas

LAMADRID

MARTINEZ DE ROSAS

AVENIDA PEDRO MOLINA

PATRICIAS

ESPAÑA

Ñoquis

RODRIGUEZ

LUZURIAGA

BELGRANO

Municipality,
Government House

Hipodromo

M MORENO

BELGRANO

AV L PELTIER

MORÓN

Hostel Internacional Mendoza
& Choique tour agency

MOYANO

9 DE JULIO

SUÁREZ

I LA CATÓLICA

LA PAMPA

SERU

AV ESPAÑA

HIPOLITO YRIGOYEN

Museo de Bellas Artes
Emiliano Guiñazú,
Palmares, Chile

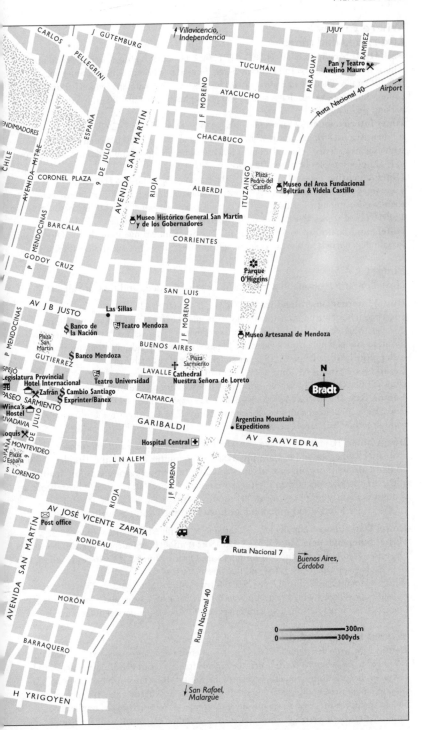

Where to stay
Luxury and mid range
Park Hyatt Mendoza Chile 1124; ☎ 441 1234; f 441 1235; e phm-reservas@hyattintl.com. This is the city's best hotel and its only 5-star, housed in a beautiful 19th-century villa with a colonial façade. There is a restaurant (with wine tower), bar, café, spa (with Thai massage), casino, shops and bodega. Rates start at 480 pesos plus tax for a dbl; b/fast, use of the spa and parking are included.
Hotel Internacional Av Sarmiento 720; ☎ 425 5600, 425 5606; f 429 8777; e hinternacional@lanet.com.ar; www.hinternacional.com.ar. This is a large 4-star hotel with excellent service. There is a buffet b/fast, a swimming pool and parking. Sgls 99 pesos, dbls 121 pesos; triples or suites 176 pesos.
Hotel Argentino Espejo 455; ☎/f 405 6300; e info@argentino-hotel.com; www.argentino-hotel.com. On Plaza Independencia with pool, restaurant, internet and room service among other facilites, this is rated as a 3-star hotel. Sgls 115/130 pesos, dbls 130/150 pesos, triples 160/180 pesos (low/high season), taxes and b/fast included.
Hotel San Martín Espejo 435; ☎/f 438 0677; e hotelsanmartin@hotmail.com. Directly off Plaza Independencia, in a great location. Sgls 68 pesos, dbls 89 pesos, triples 108 pesos.

Budget
Hostelling International has three affiliates in Mendoza and they are all excellent:
Hostel Internacional Mendoza España 343; ☎ 424 0018, 424 843; e reservas@hostelmendoza.net, www.hostelmendoza.net. Owned and run by fellow travellers who are very helpful with planning activities. There is a very nice common area for meals and planning trips. Dorms are 13 pesos per person, sgls, dbls and quadruples all with private bath are 23 pesos, 38 pesos and 52 pesos; b/fast included.
Campo Base Hostel Av Mitre 946; ☎ 429 0707; e info@campo-base.com.ar. Dorms 10 pesos per person, sgl 28 pesos or quadruple 40 pesos with private baths.
Campo Base II Patricias Mendocinas 876; ☎ 429 0775, 438 0818. Dorms 11 pesos, dbl 32 pesos, triple 36 pesos, quadruple 48 pesos with private baths; rooms for 4 or 6 people without private bath are 44 pesos and 66 pesos.

Both Campo Base hostels have abundant communal space and encourage a festive ambiance, whether it be planning *asados* or hanging around the fireplace. They consult and help organise excursions and adventure programmes. Book in advance at these hostels, especially in high season; email all three at: reservas@hostels.org.ar. Rates are slightly higher without HI membership.

There are a few good independent hostels in the centre as well:

Hostel Damajuana Centrally located, and one of the nicest *hostals* in Mendoza.
Hostel Independencia Mitre 1237; ☎ 423 1806; e info@hotelindependencia.com.ar. Organises excursions and offers Spanish lessons. Dorms 17 pesos; dbls 46 pesos and triples 60 pesos have private baths. B/fast and free internet access.
Winca's Hostel Sarmiento 717; ☎ 425 3804; www.windashostel.com.ar. This is a very well-presented hostel with a swimming pool, *asado*, Spanish lessons and a great location. Dorms 18 pesos per person, dbls with private bath 25 pesos per person; b/fast included.

Where to eat and drink
Zafrán Sarmiento 765; ☎ 429 4200, 429 9009. A great meal can be enjoyed outside on the pavement tables where you can watch the crowds milling about Plaza Independencia. This restaurant has an exquisite menu, especially the meat dishes. They also have a speciality shop selling preserves, oils, pasta and other foodstuffs, and there's a sizeable high-quality bodega to choose the wine to accompany your dinner or to purchase for another occasion.
La Florencia Sarmiento and Perú; ☎ 429 1564. A central restaurant with great steaks.

Montecatini General Paz 370; ↘ 440 1097. Excellent pasta and other dishes.
Ñoquis 9 de Julio 987 (↘ *423 8854*) or Lamadrid 500 (↘ *428 5865*). Quick bites or takeaways, as well as homemade pasta, are available in these small barstool cafés; the *empanadas* are very good and the pasta can be bought fresh for cooking at your hostel on one of those communal evenings with other travellers.
Pan y Teatro Avelino Maure 1297, Mermejo; ↘ 445 1196. After its success in Buenos Aires, this restaurant's second location has been well received in Mendoza.
The Green Apple Colón 458; ↘ 429 9444. A break from the meat – it is considered the best vegetarian restaurant in town.

Wine bars

It's only fitting to point out a few wine bars in town that have a selection of regional wines: **Estanislao** (*Emilio Civit 554;* ↘ *425 5960*); **Sabores Mendocinos** (*Juan B Justo and Paso de los Andes;* ↘ *423 1762*); and (named to leave no doubts) **Wine Bar** (*Martín Zapata 504;* ↘ *422 9324*).

Entertainment and nightlife

You can practise your tango moves at the *milongas* held every Wednesday from 23.00 and Friday from midnight at **Las Sillas** (*San Juan 1436;* ↘ *429 7742*).

The **Fiesta Nacional de la Vendimia** (National Wine Harvest Festival), held on the first weekend of March in the Parque San Martín, will give you the opportunity to take part in the harvest and wine-making.

The main **theatres** in Mendoza (*www.teatro.mendoza.edu.ar*) are **Teatro Mendoza** (*San Juan 1427;* ↘ *429 7279, 425 3744*), **Teatro Independencia** (*Espero and Chile;* ↘ *429 3555, 438 0644*), **Teatro Quintanilla** (*Plaza Independencia;* ↘ *429 3555, 423 2310*) and **Teatro Universidad** (*Lavalle 77;* ↘ *429 7279*).

A great free monthly publication called *The Grapevine* has up-to-date listings on what there is to see and do in and around Mendoza. It is found in many hotels, hostels and bars in the centre.

Shopping

The best shops are along Avenida San Martín (as well as cafés such as Bonafide, famous for its *medialunas*) and on Avenida Las Heras (known for leatherware). There are a few good markets in the city. For food and clothing, the **Central Market** is on Avenida Las Heras. There are stalls in Plaza Independencia every afternoon and all day on Sunday; many sell jewellery, while some people simply lay out blankets on the ground to showcase their handicrafts. At weekends (Friday to Sunday) there is also a market in Plaza España and an antique market in Plaza Pellegrini. The **Mercado Artesanal** (craft market) at San Martín 1133 is open every day but Sunday.

If you don't have the time to take a tour to a winery, **Central Vinoteca** (*Mitre 1201 on the corner of Espejo;* ↘ *459 0658;* e *centralvinoteca@yahoo.com.ar*) is conveniently in the centre and has a selection of excellent wines from the region. The staff are very helpful in providing information on the wines and the producers.

Practicalities

Tourist information is available at the various Centros de Información Turística: 9 de Julio (↘ *449 5185*), Avenida San Martín and Garibaldi (↘ *420 1333*) and Avenida Las Heras and Mitre (↘ *429 6298*). The **hospital** is on José F Moreno and Alem (↘ *428 0000 for emergencies*).The **post office** is on San Martín and Colón. **Banco Mendoza** (*Gutiérrez and San Martín*) and **Banco de la Nación** (*Necochea and 9 de Julio*) are centrally located. There is also money exchange at **Cambio Santiago** (*San Martín 1199*) and **Exprinter/Banex** (*opposite at no. 1198*).

Highlights

A city bus tour (*daily 09.30–12.30, 14.30–17.30*) tours the microcentre, passes the sites of interest and travels to the Parque General San Martín. Tickets are 10 pesos (*5 pesos for under 12 years and free for under 5 years of age*). The ticket is good for the day so you can jump on and off the bus at the various stops (Microcentro, Area Fundacional, Acuario Municipal, Avenida Las Heras and Cerro de la Gloria).

On the main plaza are the **Legislatura Provincial** (1889) and **Teatro Independencia** (1925), a couple of the grander buildings erected after the great 1861 earthquake. The **Parque General San Martín**, a monument to the general and his liberation of Argentina, Chile and Peru from Spain, is a large park with over 50,000 trees; a climb up the **Cerro de la Gloria** gives a great view of the valley on clear days. There are also various museums in the park (see below). You can get to the park by taking bus 110 from Plaza Independencia or Plaza España or walk a long dozen blocks east.

Museums

Museo Municipal de Arte Moderno Plaza Independencia; ☏ 425 7279. *Mendocinos* and Argentines of note have their works displayed here. *Open Mon–Sat 09.00–13.00, 16.00–21.00; free admission.*

Museo del Area Fundacional Beltrán and Videla Castillo, in Plaza Pedro del Castillo; ☏ 425 6927. On the site of the city's oldest structures (1562), this historical museum also covers independence from Spain in 1861, and has archaeological finds from the ruins of the Basilica San Francisco. *Open daily 08.00–14.00; free admission.*

Museo Artesanal de Mendoza Ituzaingó 1420; ☏ 425 1393. An exhibition of *Mendocino* craft and handiwork with items also for sale. *Open Mon–Sun 09.00–13.00, 15.30–20.00; free admission.*

Museo de Bellas Artes 'Emiliano Guiñazu' San Martín 3651, Mayor Drummond, Luján de Cuyo, south on Ruta 40; ☏ 496 0224. The century-old former estate and summer home of Emiliano Guiñazú, surrounded by beautiful gardens, is filled with the murals and collections of art by Fernando Fader (1882–1935) and other important *Mendocino* artists of that period. *Open Tue–Fri 09.00–18.30, w/ends 15.00–19.30, Mar–Oct.*

Museo Biblioteca Carrillo-Pérez Belgrano 721; ☏ 424 8443. A historical library and museum. *Open Mon–Sat 16.00–22.00; free admission.*

Museo Histórico General San Martín – Museo de los Gobernadores Remedios Escalada de San Martín 1843; ☏ 425 7947. This museum conserves documents and personal items of General San Martín as well as military arms and uniforms, photographs and folkloric objects. *Open daily 09.00–12.00; free admission.*

Museo de Ciencias Naturales y Antropológicas 'Juan Cornelio Moyano' Av de Circunvalación Arq. Thais and Av de las Tipas, in Parque San Martín; ☏ 428 7666. An extensive natural-history collection, as well as exhibits on mineralogy, palaeontology, anthropology, ethnology, archaeology and zoology. There is also a bookstore. *Open Tue–Fri 09.00–12.00 and 14.00–18.00, w/ends 15.00–19.00; admission 1 peso.*

Museo de Ciencias Naturales Domingo Sarmiento Also in Parque San Martín on Av San Francisco de Asís; ☏ 444 1966. *Open Mon–Fri 08.00–12.30, 13.30–18.00; free admission.*

Museo de Arqueología In the City University, Faculty of Philosophy; ☏ 423 0915. Artefacts from the Cuyo region as well as the northeast and Patagonia. *Open 09.00–13.00; free admission.*

Day trips and excursions
Aconcagua Provincial Park

Aconcagua is the highest summit in the Americas at 6,962m and the highest outside the Himalayas. Its present height is the result of the continuing tectonic lifting of the Andean range. The first recorded ascent of Cerro Aconcagua was by

Mathias Zurbriggen, from Switzerland, on 14 January 1897, although it's likely that Araucanian and Aymara people reached the summit centuries earlier. Although Aconcagua is considered an easy climb, you must be in good physical condition, have the right equipment, good weather and the appropriate time to allow for acclimatisation (two to three weeks is suggested). There have been 110 recorded deaths on the Stone Sentinel (from the Quechua term *Ackon Cahuac*, though some affirm the name is of Araucanian origin from *Aconca-Hue*, a Mapuche name for the river). Yet as more people attempt the summit (7,000 in 2003) the frequency of deaths increases: over 60 in the past hundred years, but 10 in 1998 alone, not to mention serious injuries from falls or frostbite.

A permit is required to enter the park. This must be obtained from the Ministry of Tourism (*Av San Martín 1143;* ❧ *261 4202800;* f *261 4202243; email: subturismo@mendoza.gov.ar; www.turismo.gov.ar*).

The cost to enter the park varies with route, number of days and season. If you are a foreigner or non-Argentine resident climbing in the high season (15 Dec–31 Jan), it will cost US$330; US$500 climbing to Plaza Guanacos; US$60 for a long trek of seven days; US$40 for a short trek of three days (trekking visitors may stay at the base camps). In mid-season (1–14 Dec and 1–20 Feb) the costs are US$220/400/50/30; in low season (15–30 Nov and 21 Feb–15 Mar) US$110/400/50/30.

Children under the age of 14 may not enter the park. They may walk up to Durazno Gorge (3,100m) only. Argentine minors between 14 and 21 years of age may enter the park with the legal authorisation of both parents, certificated by a notary public or a legally qualified authority.

In the off-season (31 March–14 November) there are restrictions on entering the park. Climbers must present an affidavit assuming personal responsibility for all risks and any cost of rescue or medical assistance that may be incurred; upon the discretion of the park directors, they may have to present a technical equipment list, in addition to a valid insurance policy, a CV of climbing experience and qualifications and a medical certificate of health.

Expreso Uspallata (❧ *431 3303, 438 1092*) has three departures per day (06.00, 07.00, 10.00) from Mendoza, taking two and a half hours (20 pesos). The bus will drop you on Ruta 7 177km from Mendoza, at the turning to Laguna Los Horcones, a mile from the road, from where it's a three-hour hike to the Confluencia base camp. You can also stop at the village of Puente del Inca, 174km from Mendoza, where there are hot springs and snack bars, and you can stay at the pricey **Hostería del Inca** (❧ *0261 438 0480, 02624 420266*) or the **Refugio La Vieja Estación** (❧ *155 696036*). Puente del Inca is the place for climbers to hire mules to carry their supplies to base camp.

Routes

The South Face (conquered by a French team in 1954) is the most difficult and dangerous route (base camp at Plaza Francia, 5km north of Los Horcones). The Polish Glacier Route is long and scenic, and of medium difficulty (via the Refugio Las Leñas to the Plaza Argentina base camp). The park information office where you buy your permit will have all the route descriptions and advice available. The Normal (northwest) Route ascends the west side. Not a technically difficult climb, it is the weather and altitude that offer the challenges. The base camp is at Plaza de Mulas (4,200m), at the head of the Horcones Valley. This is the busiest camp with a doctor based here throughout the year, and even a makeshift pub. The mules can climb to this height so there are more supplies, or luxuries, available, at a price. The **Hotel Plaza de Mulas** (❧ *0261 425 7065*) could possibly be the highest hotel in the world; its luxury prices are definitely in keeping with the high theme.

Equipment and clothing

Dress in layers: a synthetic, moisture-repelling innermost layer, a synthetic insulating second layer and a waterproof third layer. Synthetic materials are recommended over cotton and wool for warmth and weight. You should also have three layers on your hands: polypropylene inner gloves then fleece then outer mitts. Socks should also be synthetic (polypropylene, thermostat, coolmax, etc.) inside light comfortable shoes or boots to keep feet dry, comfortable and warm. Plastic boots such as Koflach are a must for summiting. Up to 30% of our body heat is lost through our heads so a warm hat is necessary and a balaclava mask will further retain heat as well as protect from the sun. Crampons and ice axes are usually necessary and hiking poles are energy saving (make sure that they are not too long so that hands stay below a 90° angle to the body to maintain circulation; then lengthen them for the downhill leg). Ropes and screws may be necessary, depending upon which route you take. Tents must be wind-resistant, with heat-sealed stitching, a skirt and lightweight aluminium poles. Spikes or pegs will likely not enter the hard earth so don't bother carrying them and use heavy rocks to weigh down your tent.

The park recommends the following equipment list:

- goretex (or similar breathable material) coat
- down coat
- polartec fleece or windproof jacket
- goretex (or similar) waterproof pants
- polartec fleece pants
- polypropylene undershirt
- polypropylene underwear
- polypropylene interior gloves or first skin
- polartec fleece gloves
- goretex (or similar) mittens or gloves
- balaclava (ski mask)
- polypropylene interior socks
- warm socks such as thermostat
- trekking boots for the approach climb
- double boots eg: Koflach
- sunglasses (plus reserve pair)
- kitchen elements
- personal hygiene elements
- stove (gas or benzene)
- high mountain tent
- telescopic hiking poles
- ice axe
- crampons
- gaiters
- supergaiters and bootcovers
- thermos for hot water
- multi-function utility knife
- sunblock (minimum SPF 15)
- sunhat

Outfitters

Argentina Mountain Expeditions Lavalle 606 (Guaymallén); ✆ 431 8356/15 525 6400; e info@argentinamountain.com; www.argentinamountain.com or www.lagunadeldiamante.com. Specialists on expeditions (climbing, horseriding, wine tours, cultural) and non-conventional programmes at natural reserves and national parks.

Cerro Aconcagua.com Expediciones y Servicios Av Mitre 946; ⟩ 425 5511; www.cerroaconcagua.com. Excursions are organised through the Campo Base hostels.

Choique Turismo Alternativo at the Hostel International Mendoza, Av España 343; ⟍f 424 0018; e reservas@hostelmendoza.net. Trekking excursions to Plaza Francia (370 pesos) and Plaza de Mulas (1,100 pesos), and a full ascent of Cerro Aconcagua along the normal route for 17 days (US$1,450 with 3 people), as well as horseriding, rafting and other activities.

Fernando Grajales Aconcagua Expeditions ⟍f 428 3157, 15 500 7718; e expediciones@grajales.net, www.grajales.net. The longest-established outfitter on Aconcagua, matching mules to climbers since 1976; now with a full range of services.

Inka Expeditions J B Justo 345; ⟩ 425 0871. Aconcagua climbing expeditions for climbers of all levels.

After climbing Aconcagua you can treat yourself to a well-deserved soak and spa at **Termas Cacheuta** (⟩ *02624 490 152–3*). It is found 38km from the city by taking Ruta 40 south to the intersection of Ruta Provincial 82 heading west to km38. It takes 45 minutes by bus; Expreso Uspallata (⟩ *431 3303, 438 1092*) connects five times per day (7 pesos). Admission Monday to Saturday is 8 pesos, Sunday and holidays 10 pesos (*5 pesos for under ten and over 65 years of age every day*). There are outdoor and covered thermal pools as well as a regular swimming pool. Nine thermal pools range from 18° to 36°C. There are picnic areas and an informal buffet restaurant.

The Wine Route

The province of Mendoza is the traditional heart of the viticulture industry, of which hundreds of wineries nestled in the foothills of the Andes could, and indeed do, have entire guidebooks written about them alone. To tour to those that are close to the city of Mendoza, a good starting-point would be **Bodega Terrazas de los Andes** (*Thames and Cochabamba, Perdriel Mendoza, on Ruta Provincial 15, km22 to Thames;* ⟩ *488 0057 or 011 4410 6001;* e *visitor@terrazasdelosandes.com.ar*), owned by the Moët Hennessy-Chandon Estates group. They have studied the advantages of various elevations and have found that Syrah gives its best fruit at 800m, in the Cruz de Piedra terraces; Cabernet Sauvignon at 980m, in the Perdriel terraces; Malbec at 1,067m, in the Vistalba terraces; and Chardonnay at 1,200m, in the Tupungato Valley. The Spanish-style winery dates to 1898 and in November 2005 a new six-room guesthouse opened allowing you to stay at the bodega and enjoy the wine and vineyard tours, the restaurant and the stunning scenery of the vineyards backdropped by the Andes. Rates for a double room are 210 pesos, single 180 pesos, breakfast included, plus 60 pesos for dinner, with Terrazas wines of course.

Tours are available Monday to Friday at 10.00, 12.00 and 15.00 by advance booking. The tour of the winery with a small tasting is free, while tastings of the top and reserve wines cost 20 pesos. A full-day complete tour of the vineyards in both Vistalba and Tupungato, the winery and a full tasting with lunch is 600 pesos per person, for four people.

Bodegas Chandon (*Ruta 40, km29, Agrelo;* ⟩ *490 9900 or 490 9968;* e *visitorcenter@chandon.com.ar*), founded by the famed French house in the late 1950s, produces excellent sparkling wines. Free tours are offered in high season (Feb, Mar, July) at 09.30, 11.00, 12.30, 14.30 and 16.00 Monday to Friday, 09.30, 11.00 and 12.30 Saturdays, or the rest of the year 10.30, 12.00, 14.30 and 16.00 Monday to Friday, and on Saturday and holidays by advance booking on weekdays with a minimum of 20 people per group. Various tastings with lunch with advance booking start at 28 pesos.

The origins of the **Bodega Catena Zapata** (*Calle Cobos s/n, Luján de Cuyo;* ℡ *490 0214–6; www.catenawines.com*) date back to 1902; a fantastic new winery, styled like a Mayan pyramid, opened in 2001. The Malbec is superb. A big company focusing more on the export market than on passing tourists, it does nevertheless offer free tours Monday to Friday 10.00–18.00 (reservation required); however, tastings have to be paid for.

Luján de Cuyo, to the south of the city, is also where you will find the Vistalba Valley and **Leoncio Arizu, Luigi Bosca's Wines** (*Av San Martín 2044;* ℡ *498 0437;* e *bodega@leoncioarizu.com.ar*). Leoncio Arizu settled in Mendoza in 1890 and founded the winery in 1901. Vistalba, La Puntilla, Carrodilla and El Paraíso are the four vineyards belonging to Leoncio Arizu.

Bodegas y Viñedos López is the producer of Monchenont, Casona López, Château Vieux, Rincón Famoso, López, Traful and Vasco Viejo. It is located at Ozamis 375, General Gutiérrez, Maipú, which is east of Mendoza city (℡ *497 2406, 481 1091;* f *497 3610;* e *lopezmza@bodegaslopez.com.ar; www.bodegaslopez.com.ar*). Various tasting arrangements are in place, all requiring advanced booking. The basic 20-minute visit to the vineyard and one-hour visit to the bodega are both free. Special tastings are 25 pesos per person, maximum four people; a Guided Vertical Tasting is 50 pesos, maximum four people. Special lunches and dinners can be arranged and wine-tasting courses are offered.

Finca Flichman, also in Maipú, has been established since 1873. Now it is a modern winery making fine wines largely for export, culminating in the rich, strong Dedicado. They are at Munives 800, Barrancas, Maipú (℡ *497 2039/45;* e *marketing@flichman.com.ar*); booking is required for tours, held Wednesday to Sunday 10.00–12.00, 13.00–17.00.

Bodegas Salentein, located at 1,200m in the Alto Valle de Uco, Emilio Civit 778, Los Arboles (℡ *0261 423 8514;* e *salenteintourism.com; www.bodegasalentein.com*) is a spectacular new winery, built in 1999 with US$50m of Franco-Dutch investment, which produces Malbec, Merlot, Cabernet Sauvignon, Sauvignon Blanc, Chardonnay and Tempranillo. The Posada Salentein offers full-board accommodation, single 275/330 pesos, double 225/270 pesos (low/high season), with trekking, riding and fishing on offer. Day visit 50 pesos.

Familia Zuccardi winery (*Ruta Provincial 33, km7.5, Maipú;* ℡ *441 0000; email info@familiazuccardi.com*), founded in 1968, has the same owners as Santa Julia and Finca Beltrán. Zuccardi wines are fantastic value, and include organic varieties.

Bodega Escorihuela (*Belgrano 898 and Alvear, Godoy Cruz, Mendoza;* ℡ *0261 424 2282, 424 2744*). This historic winery, dating from 1884, has the largest French-oak barrel in the province, plus a good wine museum and one of Argentina's finest eateries, **Francis Mallmann's Restaurant 1884** (*Belgrano 1188;* ℡ *424 6298*).

Bodega La Rural (*Montecaseros 2625, Coquimbito, Maipú;* ℡ *0261 497 2013*) makes the excellent Rutini and Trumpeter wines and runs a Museo del Vino.

Chateau d'Ancón (*San José, Tupungato, southwest of Mendoza;* ℡ *0262 248 8245*) is a 1933 estancia and bodega in the little town at the foot of Cerro Tupungato, a 6,5500m volcano. Double rooms at the estancia cost 320 pesos.

SAN RAFAEL AND THE CAÑÓN DEL ATUEL
Area code 02627
San Rafael is the service centre of southern Mendoza province, a region dominated by irrigated agriculture and winemaking. It's also a good base for tourism in the Andes, including skiing and rafting.

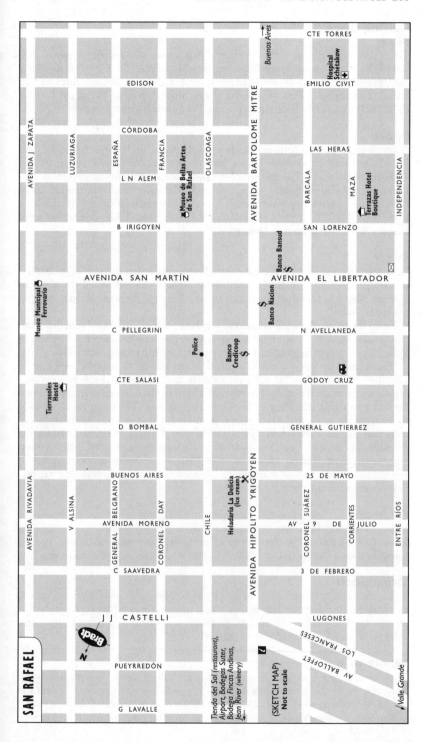

SAN RAFAEL

CTE TORRES

Buenos Aires

Hospital Schetakow

EMILIO CIVIT

EDISON

AVENIDA J ZAPATA

LUZURIAGA

ESPAÑA

CÓRDOBA

FRANCIA

L N ALEM

OLASCOAGA

Museo de Bellas Artes de San Rafael

AVENIDA BARTOLOME MITRE

LAS HERAS

BARCALA

MAZA

INDEPENDENCIA

Terrazas Hotel Boutique

B IRIGOYEN

SAN LORENZO

Banco Bansud

Museo Municipal Ferroviario

AVENIDA SAN MARTÍN

AVENIDA EL LIBERTADOR

Banco Nación

C PELLEGRINI

N AVELLANEDA

Police

Banco Credicoop

CTE SALASI

GODOY CRUZ

Tierrasoles Hostel

D BOMBAL

GENERAL GUTIERREZ

AVENIDA RIVADAVIA

V ALSINA

GENERAL BELGRANO

CORONEL DAY

BUENOS AIRES

CHILE

AVENIDA HIPOLITO YRIGOYEN

Heladaría La Delicia (ice cream)

25 DE MAYO

CORONEL SUÁREZ

AV 9 DE JULIO

CORRIENTES

ENTRE RÍOS

AVENIDA MORENO

C SAAVEDRA

3 DE FEBRERO

J J CASTELLI

LUGONES

Bradt

N

PUEYRREDÓN

Tienda del Sol (restaurant, Airport, Bodegas Suter, Bodega Fincas Andinas, Jean River (winery)

AV BALLOFFET

LOS FRANCESES

(SKETCH MAP) Not to scale

G LAVALLE

Valle Grande

Getting there
By air
There are daily flights with Aerolíneas Argentinas (*Av Hipólito Yrigoyen 395;* ☏ *438808;* e *aerolineasafa@infovia.com.ar; open Mon–Fri 09.00–13.00, 16.30–20.30, Sat 09.00–13.00*) from the Aeroparque Jorge Newbery in Buenos Aires to San Rafael. The airport is 7km west of the city on Ruta Provincial 143 in Las Paredes (☏ *427103*). A taxi fare from the airport to downtown is about 7 pesos.

By bus
A few bus companies connect Retiro bus terminal in Buenos Aires and San Rafael's terminal on Coronel Suárez just off Avenida Avellaneda, taking around 13 hours via Ruta 7. The fare is 72–85 pesos, depending on service level. San Rafael is located between Mendoza and Malargüe with numerous daily connections to both (approximately 3 hours and 10 pesos in either direction). La Estrella (☏ *422079*), Expreso Uspallata (☏ *423169*) and TAC (☏ *424236*) serve Buenos Aires, Mendoza and Malargüe.

By car
Ruta 188 is the most direct route between Buenos Aires and this part of the Andes. It starts from Ruta 7 in Junín; after about 700km you will reach the town of General Alvear in Mendoza province and take Ruta 143 for an additional 90km to reach San Rafael.

From the south, Ruta 151 connects from Neuquén to Ruta 143. From the north the famous Ruta 40 connects with Ruta 143 in Pareditas crossing the lovely Uco Valley. From Córdoba and San Luis provinces, take Ruta 7 then Ruta 146.

There are only three reasons to come to San Rafael: to visit the wineries, to visit the Cañón del Atuel in the Valle Grande or to pass right through it towards other destinations. To make the most of a visit to the Cañón, one must have a car or be patient and willing to hitchhike everywhere. The town itself has little to offer, with no central plaza – or any other for that matter. Apart from the cathedral of San Rafael Arcangel (1935–52) on Avenida Belgrano, a block off Avenida San Martín, and a couple of museums, there is very little to keep anyone in San Rafael; however, the Valle Grande is spectacular, with accommodation, eateries and plenty of outdoor activities including rafting, fishing and walking along the river.

Car rental
Renta Autos 25 de Mayo 380; ☏ 424623; e rentaautos@infovia.com.ar
Renta Car San Rafael ☏ 15 530493, 423145; e info@rentacarsanrafael.com.ar
Localiza Rent a Car Av Balloffet 2480; ☏ 421995; e localizasanrafael@infovia.com.ar

Orientation
The centre of San Rafael is not marked by a plaza but is simply the intersection of the two major roads, which change their names upon crossing. Avenida San Martín leads northeast, Avenida H Yrigoyen northwest, Avenida El Libertador southwest, and Avenida B Mitre southeast.

Where to stay
For scenery and tranquillity, staying in the Valle Grande is recommended; however, there are several accommodation possibilities in the city. Among the nicest is **Terrazas Hotel Boutique** (*Maza 126;* ☏ *429474;* f *431481;* e *hotel.terrazas@speedy.com.ar*) which has a swimming pool, solarium and jacuzzi

and an internet café. Singles 69/90 pesos, doubles 90/120 pesos, triples 120/150 pesos (low/high season) plus tax. Buffet breakfast included.

The recommended budget option is at the HI-affiliated **Tierrasoles Hostel** (*Alsina 245;* ✆ *433449;* e *info@tierrasoles.com.ar*). Just five blocks from the bus terminal, it's owned and run by young people able to offer the best tips on activities in San Rafael. Dorms 15 pesos, doubles 40 pesos.

Where to eat
Along Avenida San Martín are several pavement restaurants and fast-food shops for sandwiches and pizza. **Tienda del Sol** (*Av Yrigoyen 1663;* ✆ *425022;* e *latienda@infovia.com.ar*) is a recommended restaurant. For a great ice cream go to **Heladería La Delicia** (*Buenos Aires 49;* ✆ *421103*) where you can sit in one of the few 'plazas' on the main street.

Practicalities
Tourist information is available at Avenida Yrigoyen and Balloffet (✆ *424217;* e *turismo@:slatinos.com.ar*).

The **Hospital Schetakow** is at Emilio Civit 155 (✆ *424290/1*). The **police** are at Barcala 480 (✆ *422164*). The **post office** is located on Avenida Libertador at Independencia. There are several banks along Avenida H Yrigoyen with ATMs, such as **Banco Nación** at no. 113 and **Banco Credicoop** at no. 140. **Banco Bansud** is at Avenida Libertador 36.

Museums
Museo de Bellas Artes de San Rafael Bernardo de Yrigoyen 148; ✆ 421735. *Open Mon–Fri 09.00–13.00, 16.30–20.30; free admission.*
Museo Municipal Ferroviario Plazoleta del Inmigrante, at Av San Martín and Av Rivadavia; ✆ 421293. City and railway history and also a public library in the former train station. *Open Mon–Fri 08.00–13.00, 15.00–20.00, w/ends 08.00–20.00; free admission.*

Los Caminos del Vino
As a nice day tour, consider walking along the Ave Yrigoyen from Champaíera Bianchi back towards San Rafael visiting the bodegas along the way. All require confirmation prior to arrival for tours but most will offer tastings for interested buyers.

Valentín Bianchi, Bodega Fundadora (*Ruta 143 on Valentín Bianchi near the airport;* ✆ *422046, 435600 or 435353;* e *informes@vbianchi.com; open for tours and tastings Mon–Sat 09.15, 10.15, 11.15, 14.15, 15.15 and 16.15; the tours are free and last 45 minutes*) are producers of reds, whites and sparkling wines.

On Ruta Provincial 165 you will find **Bodega Roca** (*La Pichana, Cañada Seca;* ✆ *497194; open Mon–Fri 07.30–16.50, sometimes at weekends*) and **Viñas de Altura** (*Ruta 165 s/n;* ✆ *497044*). Continuing on Avenida Balloffet, **La Vendimia** is located at Moreno 1498 (✆ *422833*).

Avenida Yrigoyen has several bodegas, including **Bodegas Suter** (*Av Yrigoyen 2850;* ✆ *421076; open Mon–Thu & Sat 09.00–16.00, Fri 09.00–15.00*), **Bodega Fincas Andinas** (*Av Yrigoyen 5800;* ✆ *430095*) and **Jean Rivier** (*Av Yrigoyen 2385;* ✆ *432675/6; open Mon–Fri 08.00–11.00, 15.00–18.00*). Jean Rivier produces fine examples of Chenin Blanc, Tocai Friulano, Torrontés, Malbec, Cabernet Sauvignon, Bonarda and Tempranillo.

Bodegas Goyenechea is not on this circuit but at the other end of the Valle Grande at Villa Atuel (✆ *470005; open Mon–Fri 08.00–12.00, 15.00–18.30*).

Valle Grande and Cañón del Atuel

To the southwest of San Rafael an unpaved road runs through the spectacular multi-coloured gorge of the Atuel river. Leave San Rafael by turning left off Avenida Yrigoyen on to Avenida Balloffet, which leads to Ruta 143 (Av Libertador also connects with Ruta 143). This makes a complete loop, crossing the Río Diamante twice; thus, if you also cross the river a second time, you have missed the exit to Ruta 173, which follows the Río Atuel for 74km, all the way to the large lake and dam at Embalse El Nihuil. Halfway, at km35, there is a wonderful view over the Embalse Valle Grande. At El Nihuil you can turn left to Villa El Nihuil where there are services and fuel, or turn right on Ruta 180 to reach a junction with Ruta 144; turn right here to return to San Rafael or left (southwest) to reach the junction with Ruta 40 towards Malargüe.

Where to stay

Within the first few kilometres of Ruta 173, you will find many accommodation options, ranging from campsites, to cabins, *posadas* and basic hotels. Free campsites are available and marked. In several areas by the river camping (and swimming) are forbidden, but this will be clearly signposted. These regulations are in place for ecological as well as safety reasons; there are several hydro-electric dams along this river that can cause rapid fluctuations in water level.

Cabañas & Parrilla at km30 (✆ *02627 424030;* e *agata@infovia.com.ar*), has accommodation and a *parrilla* restaurant.

MALARGÜE

Area code 02627

Malargüe is the only district in Mendoza province that does not produce wine. Instead, it is known for its *chivito* (young goat), seed potato and garlic. You can imagine what tasty cuisine comes from this combination. The goats are free-range, organic, grass-fed on the hills and therefore *chivitos malargüinos* are famous across the country for their quality. November and December are the ideal months to taste goat meat. *Chivipan* is a typical dish that local chefs take great pride in; it is a goat sausage cooked in wine and served as a type of sandwich. By the way, goat meat goes very well with *Mendocino* red wine, especially Merlot.

Getting there

By air

Malargüe has a small airport on Ruta 40 (✆ *470098*) with infrequent flights from Buenos Aires. There is a public bus that links it to the city (1.50 pesos) or beyond to Las Leñas (maximum bus fare 8 pesos).

By bus

Services to Retiro station in Buenos Aires are operated by TAC (✆ *471286*) and Expresso Uspallata (✆ *470514*). There are five services per day to Mendoza with Expresso Uspallata and Vientos del Sur (✆ *470455*). Malargüe's terminal is at Roca and Aldao.

By car

Ruta 40, the major highway that stretches from north to south along the Andes through the entire country, passes directly through the town of Malargüe. It forms the main street of the town, taking the usual name of Avenida San Martín. Ruta 188 is the shortest road between Buenos Aires and the Andes mountains; from Ruta 7 in Junín, Ruta 188 passes through General Alvear, Mendoza province.

Orientation
Malagüe is another simple linear town lacking even a central plaza. Instead, the clock tower is the focal point of 'downtown'. This town is tiny and Avenida San Martín quickly transforms itself back into Ruta 40.

Where to stay
There are several basic hotels in town, but if you prefer to be out of the centre, **Hostel Internacional Malargüe** is a remote hostel on 6ha of land. It is impossible to get to without a car, arranging a lift with the owners or having the stamina to hitch to the exit off the main road and walk a few kilometres. It is at Calle Prolongación Constitución Nacional, finca no. 65, Colonia Pehuenche (\ *15 402439;* e *info@hostelmalargue.net*). A couple of kilometres south of the city on Ruta 40 you will see the HI sign telling you to turn onto a road that looks more like a wide field and which will cross small streams and minor obstacles until arriving at another junction with an HI sign telling you to turn left. The third sign will tell you that you have arrived. The reward upon arrival is being in the countryside with horses and dogs and a great view of the Andes. There are four rooms with four bunks and a private bath. The common area is a large kitchen where the owners, a biologist and a guide who live next door, will serve you breakfast in the morning. Beds cost 20 pesos per person in a dorm (17 pesos in low season), and 60 pesos per person (54 pesos in low season) in a twin room. Prices are 3 pesos per person higher without HI membership.

Where to eat and drink
There are a few restaurants on the main street of town. **Casa de Comidas Doña María** (*Av San Martín 156;* \ *471655*) was recommended and did not disappoint, with excellent cheese *empanadas*.

Practicalities
The **Malargüe Hospital** is at Avenida Roca and Esquivel Aldao (\ *471746, 471048*). The **police station** is on the corner of San Martín and Inalican (\ *471105*). The **tourist office** is on Ruta 40 Norte, Parque del Ayer (\f *471659;* e *infoturismo@malargue.gov.ar*). There is a **bank** on Avenida San Martín at Inalican and the **post office** is on Saturnino Torres and Adolfo Puebla.

Highlights
The modern **Convention and Expo Centre** is a surprisingly large facility for such a small town. The **Chapel Nuestra Señora del Rosario** dates from 1887 and is a historic monument.

Museums
The **Park of Yesteryear** (Parque del Ayer) and the **Regional Museum of Malargüe** (\ *471054*) are situated on 10ha of land by Ruta 40 2km north of town. There is a historic forest of pines, cedars, cypress and tujas (*Libocedrus*) and two large poplar groves. The buildings remain from the original ranch, as well as a mill that has been declared a National Historic Monument. The museum has palaeontological, mineral, archaeological and cultural exhibits – the highlight is an ichthyosaur that was found locally. *Open Tuesday to Sunday year-round.*

Local specialities/special events
Two of Malargüe's top three festivals focus on food and agriculture. The **National Festival of the Goat** is one of the most important in Malargüe. Held in January, it is a showcase of food, wine, music, dancing and, of course, showing off the goats.

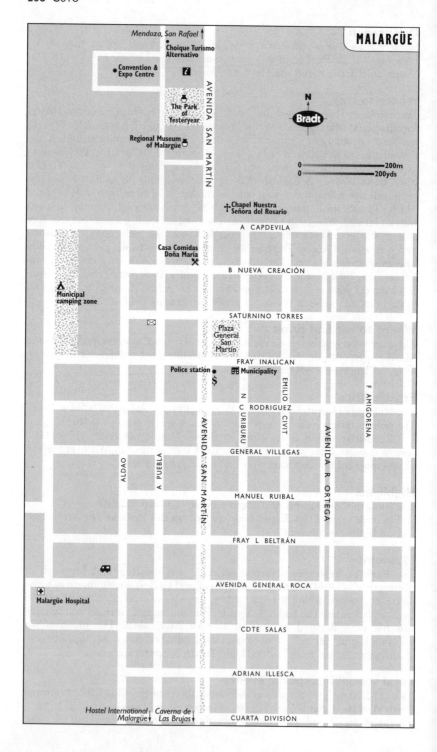

MALARGÜE

Mendoza, San Rafael ↑

Choique Turismo Alternativo

Convention & Expo Centre

The Park of Yesteryear

Regional Museum of Malargüe

AVENIDA SAN MARTÍN

N

Bradt

0 —————————— 200m
0 —————————— 200yds

† Chapel Nuestra Señora del Rosario

A CAPDEVILA

Casa Comidas Doña María ✗

B NUEVA CREACIÓN

Municipal camping zone

SATURNINO TORRES

Plaza General San Martín

FRAY INALICAN

Police station ● ✚ Municipality
$

EMILIO

Z

C RODRIGUEZ

CIVIT

URIBURU

F AMIGORENA

GENERAL VILLEGAS

AVENIDA SAN MARTÍN

AVENIDA R ORTEGA

ALDAO

A PUEBLA

MANUEL RUIBAL

FRAY L BELTRÁN

AVENIDA GENERAL ROCA

✚ Malargüe Hospital

CDTE SALAS

ADRIAN ILLESCA

Hostel International ↓ Caverna de ↓
Malargüe   Las Brujas

CUARTA DIVISIÓN

The **Regional Vintage Festival** takes place at the same time. The **Provincial Festival of the Lamb** is also in mid-January but is mainly a breeder's competition. The **Provincial Snow Festival** involves art exhibitions, musical shows and special events in **Valle de las Leñas**, the province's most important ski resort (*reached by* Ruta Provincial *222 off Ruta 40 north; see www.laslenas.com*). Skiing here costs 80–123 pesos per day, or 428–661 pesos per week (free to over-65s). In summer there's hiking, horseriding, climbing and rafting, and even scuba diving in glacial lakes at up to 2,300m!

Day trips and excursions
Choique Turismo Alternativo (*Ruta 40, km327, first floor;* ✆ *470391;* e *malargue@choique.net; www.choique.net*), located above the filling station convenience store, is a company run by a local who also runs the hostel, and knows the area intimately. They have various excursion packages, such as to the Caverna de las Brujas (40 pesos per person) or a six-hour horseriding trip (45 pesos per person). The **Caverna de las Brujas** (Cave of the Witches) has to be visited on an organised excursion, and is closed to children under four years of age. It is a cave at 1,830m in Monte Moncol, full of stalagtites and stalagmites and bizarre cave formations. It is located 63km from Malargüe, 8km off Ruta 40. Dress appropriately; the caves are damp (90% humidity) and cold (10°C).

San Luis Province
Area code 02652

The main sight of San Luis province, between Mendoza and Córdoba, is the Parque Nacional Sierra de las Quijadas, 130km from San Luis city in the northwestern corner of the province.

SAN LUIS
San Luis city was founded in 1596 by Martin de Loyala, governor of Chile. It's a small, modern city that serves as a good base for the Parque Nacional Sierra de las Quijados.

Getting there
By air
The airport of the city of San Luis is about 3km from the centre on Avenida Fuerza Aérea 3095 (✆ *422427*); to get there by taxi will cost about 3.50 pesos. Car rental is available at the airport with Hertz (✆ *437700*) and Avis (✆ *440288*). Services from Argentina are operated by Aerolíneas Argentinas (*Av 1ilia 472;* ✆ *425672;* e *luqgte@yahoo.com.ar*).

By bus
Several companies serve San Luis city by bus from Retiro station in Buenos Aires, with various levels of service throughout the day. The journey averages 12 hours but the duration and fare vary with the service provided. The cost can range greatly from 50 pesos for what is likely to be a long and uncomfortable journey to 120 pesos for an overnight ride with fully reclining seats and refreshments.

Parque Nacional Sierra de las Quijadas
To reach the park by car, take Ruta 147 northwest from San Luis towards San Juan. After 120km, at Hualtarán (where you must register at the ranger station and pay 12 pesos), turn onto a dirt road to Potrero de la Aguada, 8km west. Camping is permitted in certain areas; there is a basic store in the vicinity but no other services.

Some 150,000ha of dry chaco and montane biomes in this park were put under protection in 1991 along with important archaeological finds, including some 20 'ovens' that were probably used for firing pottery (an indication of a highly advanced society) in the area of an ancient village, and palaeontological remains (two pterosaurs or flying dinosaurs were found here, one with a lower mandible that functioned like a filter to scoop prey from water surfaces, much like a bird).

The special feature of the park is the Potrero de la Aguada, a large depression of strange geological formations in the midst of hills that create a natural amphitheatre. The plantlife is equally strange, particularly the gnarled chica that grows in shapes that speak of its discomfort in this dry harsh climate. There is also creosote bush, wattle, garabato, chica, cacti and bromeliads. Quebracho, *Prosopis* and yellow acacia are typical of the chaco. The Río Desaguadero flows west of the Quijadas range and has created a large floodplain. Chañar (*Geoffroea*) and other salt-resistant plants grow here. The fauna includes the guanaco, puma, collared peccary, mara, the fairy armadillo, rare species of tortoises, and birds such as the peregrine falcon, the crowned eagle, the yellow cardinal and the ultramarine grosbeak.

San Juan Province
Area code 0264

To the north of Mendoza is the province of San Juan, the country's second most important wine-producing area. Agriculture here is dependent on irrigation; elsewhere in the province is spectacular desert, exemplified by a famous provincial park.

SAN JUAN
Founded in 1562 but flattened in 1944 by an earthquake that killed over 10,000 people, the provincial capital of San Juan is now a modern service centre.

Getting there
By air
The airport is in 9 de Julio, east of the city of San Juan at km12 of Ruta 20 (\ 0264 425 4133). There is a daily flight from Buenos Aires with Aerolíneas Argentinas (*Av Libertador San Martín 215 Oeste;* \ 422 0205; f 427 4444; e *uaggte@aerolineas.com.ar;* open Mon–Fri 08.30–12.30, 16.30–19.30, Sat 09.00–12.30). *Remise* and taxi service to the city available with an approximate cost of 10 pesos.

Car rental at the airport is available from Hertz (\ 425 3962) and Avis (\ 425 4433).

By bus
Retiro station in Buenos Aires has almost a dozen departures per day to San Juan. The journey takes approximately 15 hours and the services range from basic to *supercama* with a ticket price of 60–135 pesos.

By car
The city of San Juan is right on Ruta 40. You can drive from Mendoza or from San Luis taking Ruta 147 followed by Ruta 20.

Where to stay
A couple of recommendations for places to stay in San Juan are, at one end of the scale, the five-star **Hotel Alkazar** (*Laprida Este 82;* \ 421 4965; f 421 4977; e *reservas@alkazarhotel.com.ar*) with singles at 130 pesos and doubles at 155 pesos, with buffet breakfast; and at the other, **Zonda Hostel** (*Laprida Oeste 572;* \ 420

1009; e info@zondahostel.com.ar) which has dorm beds for 18 pesos. This hostel is named for the El Zonda wind, the dry warm wind similar to a Chinook that blows through San Juan causing a rapid warming and often lasting several days.

Practicalities

The **tourist office** is at Sarmiento 24 Sur (⟍ *422 2431; www.turismo.sanjuan.gov.ar*), where you can also organise tours to the Ischigualasto Valle de la Luna Provincial Park. There are several **banks** downtown with ATMs and a **money exchange** office at General Acha 52 Sur. The **post office** is at Avenida Ignacio de la Roza 223 Este. The **police station** is at Entre Ríos 579 (⟍ *422 4240*). The **Hospital Marcial Quirogais** is at San Martín and Rastreador Calivar (⟍ *423 0880*).

Highlights

It's well worth going 26km north to La Laja to visit the university's **Museo Gambier** (*open Mon–Fri 08.00–20.00, Sat and Sun 10.00–18.00*), which houses a valuable collection of artefacts of the Ansilta and Huarpes cultures, and an Inca mummy found on the summit of Cerro del Toro.

Ischigualasto Valle de la Luna Provincial Park

Created in 1971, this park covers 60,369ha and contains a complete sedimentary record of the Triassic period, recording the important evolutionary transitions that brought about the first examples of mammalian species. The first accounts of fossil discoveries here were published in 1931, followed by the first palaeontological expedition in 1958. The park is now known to be one of the world's most important palaeontological reserves. A listing of the fossils discovered in the park is found at www.ischigualasto.com/principal.htm.

Ischigualasto is a native word meaning 'The place where the moon goes down', which has colloquially evolved to create the park's nickname: Moon Valley. The bizarrely geomorphed landscape is the result of wind and rain erosion upon the stratified rocks laid down over millions of years. Some of the natural sculptures have distinct forms such as birds and mushrooms that have lent them names such as the Pigeon or the Parrot. A 120m-deep gorge of red sandstone is a favoured habitat for the condor and other raptors.

There is no bus service to the park. You must have a car. The park is situated 80km from San Agustín del Valle Fértil and 300km from San Juan. To reach the park from San Juan city, head east on Ruta 141 and turn north onto Ruta 510. From Córdoba take Ruta 38 northwest and then Ruta 150. The park access is 20km from Los Baldecitos, which is at the intersection of Rutas 150 and 510. From here it's 3km to the park's visitor centre, here you'll have to pay an entry fee of 2 pesos and take a local guide (about 3 pesos) before setting out on the 40km circular drive. There's camping (but no shade) and a *comedor* at the visitor centre; you should bring all your water.

A couple of seasonal precautions: summer is the rainy season and the park's roads are often flooded. The park is hot by day and cold by night, so bring appropriate clothing, hats, sunscreen and other necessities to ensure your comfort.

The Wine Route of San Juan

There has been a viticultural industry in San Juan province since 1569, although it has not yet reached the heights of Mendoza. This is a short list of bodegas in San Juan that comprise the cream of the crop.

Bodegas y Vinedos Santiago Graffigna Colón 1342 Norte; ⟍ 421 4227. This producer of exceptional wines also runs a museum of wine-making, which is open Thu & Fri

09.00–13.00, Sat 09.00–14.00, Sun 10.00–20.00. There is a wine bar where you can pass a Fri or Sat night indulging in the wines of the bodega (21.00–02.00).

Fabril Alto Verde Ruta 40 south, entrance on Calle 13 and 14, Pocito; ☎ 421 2683, 492 1905; e altoverde@arnet.com.ar; www.fabrilaltoverde.com. This is a producer of organic wines.

Viñas de Segisa Aberastain and Calle 15, La Rinconada, Pocito; ☎ 492 2000; e segisa@saxsegisa.com.ar; www.saxsegisa.com.ar. The bodega of this traditional producer dates back to 1906.

Fábrica Miguel Más Calle 11 at 300m east of Ruta 40, Ing. Bruschi 520 Este; ☎ 422 5807; e miguelmas@infovia.com.ar. This producer is noted for excellent sparkling wines and for organic production.

Patagonia

8

The vastness of Patagonia soon becomes apparent once you start to travel across it, sandwiched between the 1,920km of the Cordillera de los Andes, the longest continuous mountain range on earth, and the 1,770km of the Atlantic coast. Only two main roads run north-south through Patagonia: Ruta 40, which parallels the Andes, and Ruta 3, which follows the coast. Both offer an incredible journey through vast empty landscapes that have a strange beauty. Sparsely populated but covering almost a third of Argentina's area, Patagonia is the furthest reach of South America. The northern boundary of Patagonia is more geographical than political but is generally accepted as being the Río Colorado. The Patagonian steppe, ecologically speaking, actually begins north of the river in La Pampa province and extends south along the coast to the Magellan Strait, between the Andean-Patagonian ecological zone to the west and the coastal zone to the east. Four provinces comprise Argentine Patagonia: Neuquén, Río Negro, Chubut and Santa Cruz, as well as Tierra del Fuego and the South Atlantic islands.

Many of the minor roads linking the coast to the mountains are unpaved and make you feel like a true explorer entering a landscape that few others have seen. Indeed, the Andean chain and the Atlantic coast demonstrate two completely different personalities that are for the most part completely disassociated from each other by the great expanse of central Patagonia. One exception is the Chubut Valley, where Welsh pioneers settled from Trelew on the coast all the way to the Andes. The following sections address a few of the distinct parts of Patagonia as a way to organise these differences – Andean Patagonia, the Chubut Valley and Coastal Patagonia, including Tierra del Fuego, Antarctica and the Malvinas/ Falkland Islands.

Neuquén Province

The interior of this province has four distinct regions. In its far northwest corner, it is marked by numerous volcanoes. Many are extinct and snow capped, offering excellent skiing and winter-sport opportunities. Some of these peaks are the highest in Patagonia and mountaineering expeditions are popular. To the south (but still on the western flank of the province) is the thermal region. Thanks to the volcanic zone underground geothermal water is plentiful and whether you are watching it spew in 15m geysers or soaking in their placid mineral-rich baths, 'oohs' and 'aahs' are sure to be uttered. To the east, the central region of the province is the steppe and dinosaur country. Palaeontologists have unearthed huge numbers of fossil remains in this area, believed to be just a tiny fraction of what is

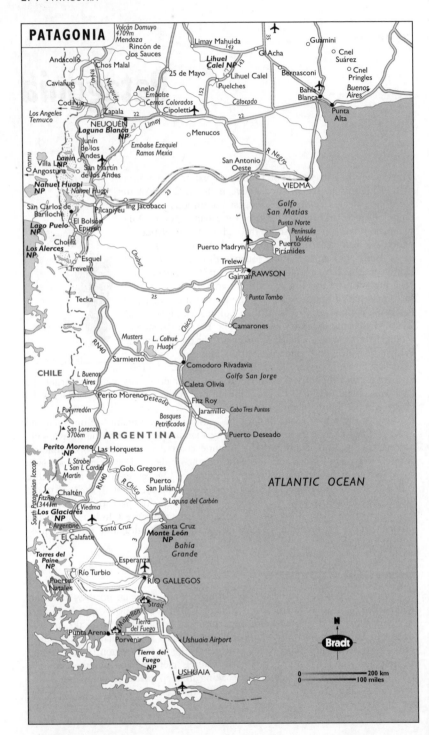

PATAGONIA

Volcán Domuyo
4709m
Mendoza
Rincón de
los Sauces
Limay Mahuida
Andacollo
Chos Malal
Lihuel
Calel NP
Gl Acha
Guamini
Cnel
Suárez
Caviahue
25 de Mayo
Lihuel Calel
Bernasconi
Cnel
Pringles
Codihue
Anelo
Puelches
Bahía
Blanca
Buenos
Aires
Los Angeles
Temuco
Zapala
Embalse
Cerros Colorados
Cipoletti
Colorado
Punta
Alta
NEUQUÉN
Laguna Blanca
NP
Limay
22
22
Menucos
R Negro
Junín
de los
Andes
Embalse Ezequiel
Ramos Mexia
San Antonio
Oeste
VIEDMA
Lanin
NP
Villa L
Angostura
San Martín
de los Andes
23
Golfo
San Matías
Nahuel Huapi
NP
L Nahuel Huapi
Punta Norte
Peninsula
Valdés
San Carlos de
Bariloche
Pilcaniyeu
Ing Jacobacci
23
Puerto Madryn
Puerto
Pirámides
Lago Puelo
NP
El Bolsón
Epuyén
Los Alerces
NP
Cholila
Chubut
Trelew
Gaiman
RAWSON
Esquel
Trevelin
Punta Tombo
Tecka
25
Chico
Camarones
Musters
L. Colhué
Huapi
CHILE
Sarmiento
Comodoro Rivadavia
Golfo San Jorge
L Buenos
Aires
Caleta Olivia
Perito Moreno
Deseado
Fitz Roy
Jaramillo
Cabo Tres Puntos
L Pueyrredón
Bosques
Petrificados
San Lorenzo
3706m
ARGENTINA
Puerto Deseado
Perito Moreno
NP
Las Horquetas
L Strobel
L San L Cardiel
Martín
Gob. Gregores
RN40
R Chico
Puerto
San Julián
ATLANTIC OCEAN
Chaltén
FitzRoy
3441m
L Viedma
Laguna del Carbón
Los Glaciares
NP
L Argentino
Santa Cruz
El Calafate
Santa Cruz
Monte León
NP
Bahía
Grande
South Patagonian Icecap
Esperanza
Torres del
Paine
NP
Río Turbio
Puerto
Natales
RÍO GALLEGOS
Magellan
Strait
Punta Arenas
Porvenir
Tierra
del Fuego
Ushuaia Airport
Tierra del
Fuego
NP
USHUAIA
N
Bradt
0   200 km
0   100 miles
RN40
Neuquén
Ororru

BIG FEET

The origin of the name Patagonia is nowadays most often explained as an elaboration from the Spanish word *pata* (meaning 'foot') due to Magellan meeting the very tall Tehuelche people, the first native group encountered in this region, and supposedly remarking on the large size of their footwear. This linguistic explanation is generally accepted without further question. However, the late great travel writer Bruce Chatwin was astute enough to point out that the suffix *gon* is absolutely meaningless in Spanish and so perhaps there was a more imaginative and credible explanation. And, it seems, he found one. He explains his theory in greater detail in his wonderful travelogue *In Patagonia* (1977), but the gist of it goes something like this:

The literary work *Primaleon of Greece* was published in Castille in 1512, seven years before Magellan set sail for South America, and Chatwin believed that Magellan must have read this book. At the end of Book II, Chatwin found reference to Knight Primaleon setting sail to a remote island where he discovered brutish people who ate raw flesh and wore animal hides. On the island lived 'a monster called the Grand Patagon, with the "head of a Dogge" and the feet of a hart, but gifted with human understanding'. The knight captured the beast and brought it back to his homeland for Queen Gridonia's royal collection. Magellan's voyage was chronicled by a rich tourist by the name of Pigafetta who had paid to come along; he wrote that the natives were naked giants seen dancing on the shores, singing with deafening voices, eating raw flesh and so forth. (He also wrote that the captain called these people *Pataghom*.) Magellan proceeded to capture two Tehuelche and attempted to bring them home as a gift for King Charles V. However, one escaped and the other died of scurvy while at sea. If this does not offer enough plausibility through similarity, Chatwin also drew parallels with Shakespeare's *The Tempest*. According to scholars, Shakespeare had read the account in Pigafetta's *Voyage* of the events at San Julián. He then wrote of the half-human beast Caliban, embittered by his stolen island, plague, lost language and slavery – thus echoing the pains of the colonised Americas. Caliban is referred to as the 'puppy-headed monster'. In 1592, when the Tehuelches attacked John Davis at Puerto Deseado, they were wearing battle masks of dog heads. It may be a stretch, but it is much more imaginative.

still to be found. The southernmost zone of Neuquén is the beautiful lake region. Protected by national park status but with better infrastructure than the rest of the province, this lovely area is the most visited by tourists.

CHOS MALAL

Area code 02948

Entering Patagonia across the Río Colorado from the north, Ruta 40 switchbacks and winds as it climbs a significant Andean pass. If driving, make sure that your car is well equipped for any eventuality as it is possible, even in the warm month of November, to meet a snowstorm at this high altitude. Finally, the road starts to descend, passing tiny villages and homesteads before reaching Chos Malal. This inconspicuous town is traditionally and historically the most significant in Neuquén province (having been the capital of the National Territory of Neuquén

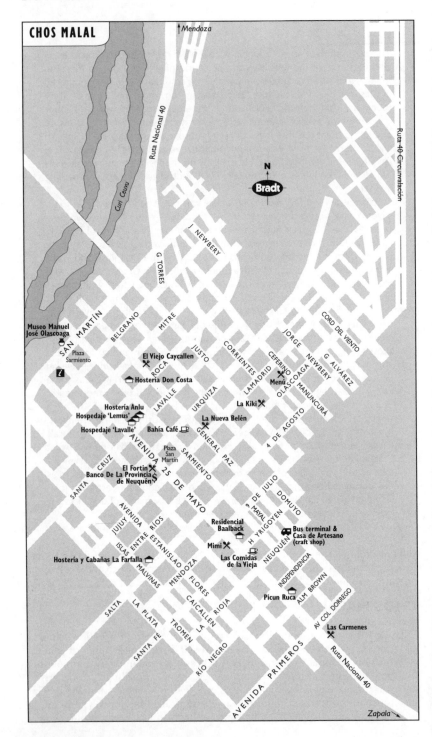

CHOS MALAL

↑Mendoza

Ruta Nacional 40

Curi Ceuvu

Ruta 40-Circunvalación

N

Bradt

J NEWBERY

G TORRES

CORD DEL VIENTO

SAN MARTIN

BELGRANO

MITRE

CORRIENTES

JORGE NEWBERY

G ALVAREZ

Museo Manuel
José Olascoaga

Plaza
Sarmiento

JUSTO

ROCA

CEFERINO

OLASCOAGA

MANUNCURA

El Viejo Caycallen

LAMADRID

Menú

Hostería Don Costa

LAVALLE

URQUIZA

La Kiki

4 DE AGOSTO

Hostería Anlu
Hospedaje 'Lemus'

La Nueva Belén

Hospedaje 'Lavalle'

Bahía Café

GENERAL PAZ

AVENIDA 25 DE MAYO

SANTA CRUZ

Plaza
San
Martín

SARMIENTO

El Fortin
Banco De La Provincia
de Neuquén

9 DE JULIO

DOMUYO

AVENIDA ENTRE RÍOS

JUJUY

9 MAYAL

H YRIGOYEN

Residencial
Baalback

Bus terminal &
Casa de Artesano
(craft shop)

ISLAS ENTRE RÍOS

Mimi

NEUQUÉN

Hostería y Cabañas La Farfalla

MENDOZA

FLORES

Las Comidas
de la Vieja

INDEPENDENCIA

MALVINAS

CAICALLEN

LA RIOJA

ALM BROWN

Picun Ruca

SALTA

LA PLATA

TROMEN

SANTA FE

RÍO NEGRO

AV COL DORREGO

Las Carmenes

Ruta Nacional 40

AVENIDA PRIMEROS

Zapala ↘

from 1887 to 1904) and still has the remains of old native settlements. Today it is the main urban base for the volcanic and thermal regions and the impressive Domuyo Volcano as well as the mountain sports at Cerro Wayle. If only passing through, it is a nice place to stop for a rest, to take a stroll or sit in its plazas full of trees. Men in traditional gaucho ponchos and boots can be seen riding their elegant mounts through town, and Plaza Sarmiento always has a few friendly vendors selling their art or crafts.

Getting there
By air
The nearest airport is at Neuquén; from Buenos Aires there are several flights a day (fewer at weekends) with Aerolíneas Argentinas/Austral and one daily with LAN Argentina, taking two hours. See page 284 for other flights and contact details.

By bus
Chos Malal's bus terminal is at Neuquén and General Paz (↘ 422676). Daily buses from Neuquén are operated by Cono Sur and Andes Mar (both ↘ 421800) and Transporte Amuche (↘ 421478).

By car
Arriving either from Mendoza to the north (130km from the provincial border) or from Zapala to the south, Ruta 40 will bring you directly to this small town sitting snugly in the beautiful Curi Leuvú Valley near its confluence with the Río Neuquén. Following Ruta 40 into Patagonia from the north by car is scenically gorgeous with ochre-coloured hills and canyons. The road is asphalt but in rough condition and very windy, climbing over small passes that often surprise you with a quick change of season from dry summer heat in the valley to sleet or snow at the top of the pass.

Orientation
There are two main plazas, Sarmiento and San Martín. The latter is where you will find the tourist office and most of the town's important buildings, such as the old military fort (see *Museums*), the parish church, public library and the cultural centre. A few blocks away is Plaza Sarmiento and between these two plazas are most of the hotels, cafés and services. There is a large gas station off Plaza Sarmiento.

Where to stay
There are a few options for basic inexpensive accommodation in Chos Malal.

Picun Ruca 25 de Mayo 1271; ↘ 421000
Hostería Don Costa Sarmiento 234; ↘ 421652
Hostería Anlu Lavalle 60; ↘ 421109; e anlu@comsat-mail.com
Hostería and Cabañas La Farfalla Salta 350; ↘f 421349
Residential Baalback 25 de Mayo 920; ↘f 421495
Hospedaje Lemus Lavalle and 25 de Mayo; ↘ 421133
Hospedaje Lavalle Lavalle s/n; ↘ 421732

Where to eat and drink
Restaurants
El Viejo Caycallen General Paz 345; ↘ 421373
Don Costa Sarmiento 234; ↘ 421652

El Fortín 25 de Mayo 586; ☎ 421187
Menú Ceferino Manuncurá 689; ☎ 42 245
Mimi 25 de Mayo 948; ☎ 421436
La Nueva Belén General Paz and Lamadrid; ☎ 422583
Las Carmenes Av Don Bosco; ☎ 421514. For *parrilla*.
La Kiki Olascoaga 518; ☎ 422217. For pizza.

Cafés and bars
Las Comidas de la Vieja 25 de Mayo and Irigoyen; ☎ 421939
Bahía Café Urquiza 110; ☎ 15 661722
Café Canay General Paz 579; ☎ 421660

Practicalities
The town's small tourist office, **Delegación Provincial de Turismo Zona Norte** (*25 de Mayo 89;* ☎ *421425;* e *turnorte@neuquen.gov.ar*) is big on information about the town and surrounding area.

There is no post office in Chos Malal, but there is a bank – the **Banco de la Provincia del Neuquén** (*25 de Mayo 540*). For shopping, aside from the vendors in the main plaza, there is a **Casa de Artesano** at General Paz and Neuquén.

Special events
If you time your trip well, you may arrive for the **Fiesta Provincial del Chivito, la Danza y la Canción,** held annually at the beginning of November. Women singing the traditional songs of the northern region of the province will reward you with music and get you dancing up an appetite for the feast of *chivito* (goat) that will surely reward you.

Museums
Museo Manuel José Olascoaga 25 de Mayo and San Martínon. On a small hill where the barracks of the IV Division of the 'Ejército Expedicionario' marks the site of the first fort installed in 1887 for General Roca's Campaign of the Desert. In this provincial historical museum you can see personal objects of Colonel Olascoaga, the first governor of the territory of Neuquén, fossil minerals, indigenous pieces and historical artefacts of the region. *Open Tue–Fri 07.30–13.00, 14.30–20.30; Sat and Sun 14.30–20.30; admission free.*

Day trips and excursions
If you have a car at your disposal, and preferably a 4x4 as the roads are rough, Ruta 43 from Chos Malal will take you to the **Cordillera del Viento** (mountain range of the wind) and the **Cordillera del Limite** (mountain range of the limit) and finally to the Provincial Park Domuyo where the famous **Domuyo Volcano** is located at the northern end of the Cordillera del Viento.

There are five major mountain chains in this area: Sierra del Cochico, Sierra del Aulinco, Chenque Mallín, Sierra de la Cruzada and the Cordillera del Viento. The last is distinguished by its height, with peaks up to 2,800m, and the variety of contrasting colours in its geology. Throughout the winter, thick snow covers the chain; in summer, it keeps some snow patches at the peaks. From Chos Malal take Ruta 43 to the little town of **Andacollo**. This one-time mining town saw the typical boom-and-bust cycle of the industry and saved itself by turning to agriculture. A 5km detour on Ruta 39 leads to the town of **Huinganco** amid a pine forest started with 250 saplings in 1971. Today there are a dozen forests that produce four million trees per year and employ 150 workers. There is also a fish hatchery, a producer of handmade sweets and regional jellies, and shops with tufa-stone carvings. From the town there is a nice hike to the foot of the Corona Hill and the Huingan Co Lagoon. Back on Ruta 43 you should continue to the town of **Las Ovejas** and the nearby **Cañada Molina Provincial Park**. Near the **Colo Michi Co** stream signs show the way to cave paintings that are among the most important in Patagonia. The Mapuche word for 'water' is *co*, so whenever you see 'Co' appended to a name, it signifies the presence of a stream or hot springs.

Before reaching Las Ovejas there is a junction where you can either remain on Ruta 43 towards the volcano, or turn left onto Ruta 45 to the **Lagunas de Epulauquén**. These two lagoons are small Andean lakes joined by a stream that offers excellent fishing for rainbow and brook trout, and close to a hundred species of birds have been recorded in the 7,450ha nature reserve, created in 1973 to protect the pellín oak and *Nothofagus* (lenga and ñire), unique this far north. Rustic camping is free along the shore of the lagunas.

Back on Ruta 43 and following the Río Neuquén you might notice the contrasting beige of the Río Varvarco staining its turquoise waters at the confluence of these two rivers. The little village of Varvarco is the closest town to the volcano and in a typical valley of this region where the traditional local music is sung. The scenery in the area is stunning, especially at the **Cajón del Atreuco** and **Los Bolillos** where the sandy volcanic toba stone has eroded into abstract formations.

Finally you will arrive at the thermal baths; the most important are El Humazo, Los Tachos and Aguas Calientes. The water ranges in temperature from 40 to 95°C and is famous for its reputed healing qualities and the blue algae that flourish in the waters.

Ever snow-capped, Domuyo Volcano (4,709m) is the highest peak in Patagonia. Marine fossils cover its bare slopes and hot thermal springs flow in its valleys where columns of steam, geysers and fumaroles spew and hiss and eject 15m-high jets of water. Domuyo attracts climbers as well as bathers. From here climbers can try, with guides, to reach the summit – it is not for the novice climber as it takes a couple of days with a rapid altitude change. The tourist office in Chos Malal can suggest guides and available excursions.

Another excursion from Chos Malal is to the **Parque de Nieve** (snowpark) of **Cerro Wayle**. This popular winter sports resort is 45km from Chos Malal, leaving the town on Ruta 2 and then following the gravel Ruta 37. The resort, opened in 1988 on the 3,296m Cerro Wayle, has two 300m Poma lifts and five ski runs. Alpine and Nordic skiing, snowboarding and snowbiking are available. From the central and southeastern runs you can see **Volcán Tromen** (3,968m). This volcano and an attractive lagoon are within Tromen Provincial Park, on the same Ruta 37 to Cerro Wayle.

Turning your sights south of Chos Malal on Ruta Provincial 6 you can visit the village of **El Cholar**. It is one of the oldest communities in the province, although the official founding date is given as 1910. The translation of the Mapuche name is 'yellow ravine' and this farming town is a little green oasis surrounded by ochre-coloured steppe. The 1895 schoolhouse and the old San Francisco mill from 1908 offer glimpses into this little village's past.

Continue to Cerro Caviahue, next to Lago Caviahue and the **Copahue Provincial Park**, with its thermal waters on the spurs of Copahue Volcano. The park was created to protect a pehuen (araucaria or monkey-puzzle) forest. The two main towns in the park, Copahue and Caviahue, are 19km apart. Copahue, reached by Ruta Provincial 21 and 26, is famous for its thermal springs resort with facilities for 2,500 users per day. In the winter there are 25km of ski runs for skiing and snowboarding.

ZAPALA
Area code 02942

Getting there
By air
Flights to Zapala are with LADE (*Uriburu 371;* ☎ *430134;* e *zapala@lade.com.ar*) from Bariloche, Chapelco and Neuquén on Wednesdays.

By bus
The bus terminal is located at Etcheluz and Uriburu (☎ *423191*). Most of the major bus companies including La Estrella, Andesmar, El Chevallier, Via Bariloche, TAC and others connect Zapala to nearby towns and major cities such as Neuquén, Mendoza and Bariloche.

By car
From the north or south Zapala is reached by Ruta 40; from Neuquén to the east take Ruta 22.

Orientation
Entering the city you will pass a roundabout amd then head down the main street, Avenida San Martín, hitting the main cross-street of Avenida Avellaneda just four

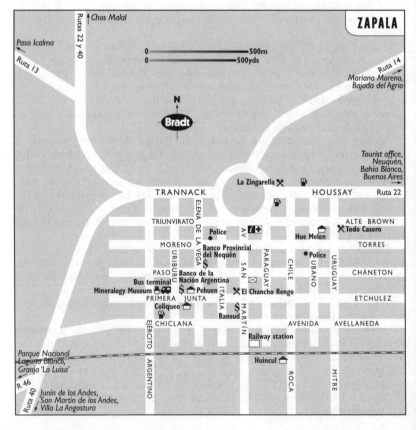

blocks later. All the restaurants, hotels, banks and services are within the few blocks on either side of San Martín leading up to Avellaneda.

Practicalities

The **tourist office** is located on Avenida San Martín s/n (✆ *421132;* e *turismo@zapaladigital.com.ar, munidesarrollo@yahoo.com.ar*). The **post office** (Correo Argentino) is at San Martín 324 and there are a few **banks** to choose from: Banco de la Nación Argentina (*Etcheluz 465;* ✆ *421361, 423203*), Banco de la Provincia del Neuquén (*Chaneton 410;* ✆ *422185*), Bansud (*Etcheluz 108;* ✆ *430786*).

LAGUNA BLANCA NATIONAL PARK

These 11,263ha of wetland are an oasis in the middle of the dry Patagonian steppe and form a crucially important habitat for many wetland species of birds, mammals and vegetation. Laguna Blanca is a large, shallow freshwater lagoon with a maximum depth of 6m, fed by several small permanent streams. There are also permanent freshwater lakes (including large oxbow lakes) and marshes on inorganic soils with vegetation that remains waterlogged for most of the growing season.

The significance of this aquatic bird habitat was recognised and it was protected as a national park in 1945. It was also recognised by the RAMSAR Convention on Wetlands, which placed Laguna Blanca on the worldwide list of Wetlands of International Importance in 1992.

Black-necked swans (*Cygnus melanocoryphus*) are the star attractions, but birdlife in general is abundant. Chilean flamingoes (*Phoenicopterus chilensis*) and white-tufted and silvery grebes (*Podiceps rolland* and *P. occipitalis*) can be seen, as well as upland geese (*Chloephaga picta*), southern widgeons (*Anas sibilatrix*), red shovelers (*A. platalea*), red-gartered coots (*Fulica arimillata*) and, of course, lake ducks (*Oxyura vittata*). Besides waterfowl, the lagoon is of vital importance to the endangered Patagonian frog (*Atelognathus patagonicus*), which is endemic to the basaltic basins of northern Patagonia. On land there are choique or lesser rhea (*Pterocnemia pennata*) and small lizards (*lagartija*). Mammals present include the vizcacha or chinchillón (*Lagidium viscacia*), the grey fox (*Dusicyon griseus*), armadillo (*Zaedyus pichi*) and the very shy cats, puma (*Felis concolor*) and Geoffrey's cat (*Felis geoffroyi*).

The gently rolling landscape is characterised by conical hills and deep ravines with steep cliff walls that make ideal nesting sites for the peregrine falcon (*Falco peregrinus*) as well as for condors and eagles. The persistent winds of the dry Patagonian steppe oblige plants to grow bent and twisted and many are covered in spines and thorns. They are hardy plants, adapted to resist the cold temperatures and snow in winter yet to conserve water during the hot dry summer.

Ancient human presence is of great significance in the park as well. Artefacts made by the early native peoples of this part of Argentina have been discovered in the area, and rock paintings typical of northern Patagonia are in the Salamanca cave on the edge of the park. These people were hunter-gatherers, subsisting on guanaco, fish and the plants of the region, making tools and utensils from basalt rocks and animal parts.

Where to stay

In the city, **Coliqueo** (*Etcheluz 159;* ✆ *421308*) has rooms for 25 pesos single; 48 pesos double, including breakfast. Across the street is **Pehuen** (*Etcheluz and E de la Vega;* ✆ *423135*) with similar, perhaps slightly higher, prices. **Hue Melen** (*Alte Brown 929;* ✆ *422391, 422407 or 422414;* e *hotelhuemelen@zapala.com.ar*) is the higher-priced hotel in town, though not much more expensive than the others, and also has a restaurant. **Huincul** (*Roca 311;* ✆ *431422*) is the budget option.

Señora Luisa runs the **Agroturismo Granja 'La Luisa'** (*Ayacucho 524, at km8 of Ruta Provincial 46, near Laguna Blanca National Park and 18km from Zapala;* ✆ *430635, 422684;* e *granjalaluisa@yahoo.com.ar*) which is surrounded by orchards and overlooks the spectacular San Domingo valley. (An agrotourismo is a working farm with guesthouse.) You can swim in the mountain-fed river or ride horses in the valley, then enjoy a full tea service of pastries, bread and preserves all made at the farm, for 30 pesos per person. Lunch and dinner each cost 40–60 pesos per person, all made from the products of her greenhouses, beehives, herb gardens and orchards. A cottage hosts up to eight people; two rooms with double beds and one room with a bunk bed and two single beds. The cost per person including breakfast is 60 pesos. If you are without a vehicle, two local buses (5 pesos) pass the agrotourismo: Alumine Viajes and Albus, leaving Zapala at 18.00 and 20.00, meaning that you must spend the night at the farm. These buses continue on the lake circuit for 150km. A minibus pickup from the airport or bus station can be arranged for around 30 pesos per person. Excursions to Laguna Blanca National Park cost 60 pesos on horseback or 50 pesos by minibus, with lunch included, or 70 pesos by horse or 60 pesos by minibus to the cave paintings.

Where to eat and drink

There are a few basic options for dining in Zapala: **El Chancho Rengo** (*Av San Martín and Etcheluz;* ✆ *422797*), **Huincul** (*Av Roca 311;* ✆ *422797*), **Todo Casero** (*Brown 1045;* ✆ *15 579130*), **Hue Melen** (*Brown 929;* ✆ *422414 or 422407*). **La Zingarella** is a *parrilla* on Houssay and Ruta 22.

Museums

Mineralogy Museum 'Dr Juan A Olsacher' Etcheluz and Ejército Argentino. This museum is dedicated predominantly to the mineralogy and palaeontology of Neuquén. It has a collection of over 2,000 mineral specimens, precious and semi-precious stones and fossils of plants and animals from the Holocene and Inferior Mesozoic. *Open Mon–Fri 08.00–15.00, 18.00–21.00; w/ends 18.00–22.00.*

Day trips and excursions

Parque Nacional Laguna Blanca is the prime destination of visitors to Zapala. The park office in Zapala (30km northeast of the park) is at Ejército Argentino 260 (✆ *431982;* e *lagunablanca@apn.gov.ar*). The best time of year to visit the park is from November to March. Take Ruta 40 and then Ruta Provincial 46. There is a camping and picnic area but be aware of the absence of shade and the strong winds that affect this zone. The visitor centre (*open weekends and holidays 09.00–18.00*) will provide interpretation of the natural and cultural history of the area. The park was established to protect important wetland habitat and is an excellent place to see a great variety of aquatic birds. There is no admission fee for this park.

NEUQUÉN

Area code 0299

Not scrambling for the attention of the tourist, Neuquén's personality is unaffected and honest. It is a pretty city with some lovely architecture, notably the

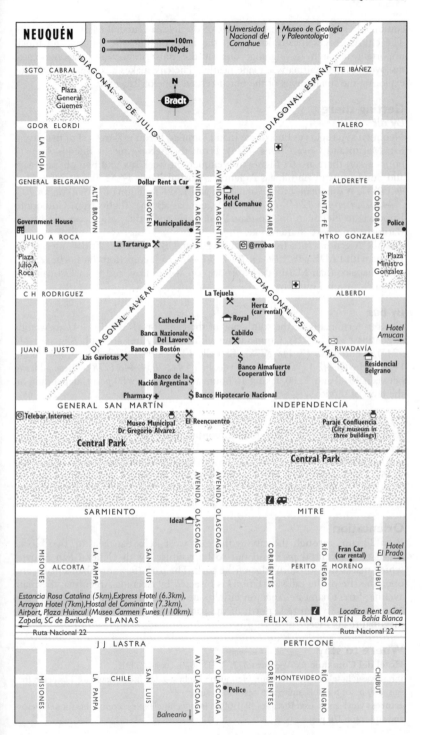

NEUQUÉN

0 ————— 100m
0 ————— 100yds

N
Bradt

↑ Unversidad Nacional del Cornahue   ↑ Museo de Geología y Paleontología

SGTO CABRAL
Plaza General Güemes
DIAGONAL 9 DE JULIO
DIAGONAL ESPAÑA
TTE IBÁÑEZ

GDOR ELORDI
TALERO

LA RIOJA
GENERAL BELGRANO
Dollar Rent a Car
ALTE BROWN
IRIGOYEN
AVENIDA ARGENTINA
AVENIDA ARGENTINA
Hotel del Comahue
BUENOS AIRES
SANTA FÉ
CÓRDOBA
ALDERETE

Government House
Municipalidad
Police

JULIO A ROCA
MTRO GONZALEZ

Plaza Julio A Roca
La Tartaruga ✕
@rrobas
Plaza Ministro Gonzalez

C H RODRIGUEZ
DIAGONAL ALVEAR
La Tejuela ✕
DIAGONAL 25 DE MAYO
ALBERDI

Hertz (car rental)
Cathedral ✝
Royal
Banca Nazionale Del Lavoro
Cabildo
Hotel Amucan

JUAN B JUSTO
Banco de Bostón
RIVADAVIA

Las Gaviotas ✕
Residencial Belgrano

Banco de la Nación Argentina
Banco Almafuerte Cooperativo Ltd

Pharmacy ✛
Banco Hipotecario Nacional

GENERAL SAN MARTÍN
INDEPENDENCIA

Telebar Internet
Museo Municipal Dr Gregorio Álvarez
El Reencuentro ✕
Paraje Confluencia (City museum in three buildings)

Central Park
Central Park

SARMIENTO
Ideal
MITRE

AVENIDA OLASCOAGA
AVENIDA OLASCOAGA

MISIONES
ALCORTA
LA PAMPA
SAN LUIS
CORRIENTES
RÍO NEGRO
Fran Car (car rental)
MORENO
Hotel El Prado
CHUBUT

PERITO

Estancia Rosa Catalina (5km), Express Hotel (6.3km),
Arrayan Hotel (7km), Hostal del Cominante (7.3km),
Airport, Plaza Huincul (Museo Carmen Funes (110km),
Zapala, SC de Bariloche PLANAS
Localiza Rent a Car,
FÉLIX SAN MARTÍN Bahía Blanca

Ruta Nacional 22
Ruta Nacional 22

J J LASTRA
PERTICONE

MISIONES
LA PAMPA
CHILE
SAN LUIS
AV OLASCOAGA
AV OLASCOAGA
CORRIENTES
MONTEVIDEO
RÍO NEGRO
CHUBUT

Police

Balneario ↓

combined Gothic and Romantic styles of the Iglesia Catedral María Auxiliadora. The city is geographically located in the heart of dinosaur country and much important research is ongoing; one of the most important palaeontological discoveries in Argentina was made nearby. The city makes a convenient base for exploring the small towns of the north-central zone of Patagonia.

Getting there
By air
Neuquén's Aeropuerto Presidente Juan Domingo Perón is 7km west of the city, at San Martín and Goya (✆ 444 0525). From the Aeroparque in Buenos Aires (2 hours away) there are six flights to Neuquén on weekdays and two on Saturdays and Sundays, with Aerolíneas Argentinas/Austral (*Santa Fé 52;* ✆ *442 2409–11 or 443 0841;* e *nqnadmin@aerolineas.com.ar*) and LAN Argentina (*Av San Martín 107;* ✆ *442 0124 or 444 1284*). Aerolíneas Argentinas also has flights from Comodoro Rivadavia to Neuquén on Monday, Wednesday and Friday afternoons, and from Bariloche on weekday afternoons.

LAN Argentina flies from Río Gallegos and Bariloche on Friday afternoons. Flights with LADE (*Av A Brown 1065;* ✆/f *443 1153*) come fom Bariloche, Zapala and Chapelco (San Martín de los Andes) on Wednesday; and from Ushuaia and Río Gallegos on Thursday.

By bus
The bus terminal is on the south side of the central park at Mitre 147 at Avenida Argentina (✆ 442 4903). Connections with Buenos Aires are with Albus (✆ 447 3745), Centenario (✆ 448 8778), El Valle (✆ 443 0959), Ko Ko (✆ 448 7606), Pehuenche (✆ 442 1951) and Via Bariloche (✆ 442 7054, 448 1778). These all leave between 18.00 and 22.00, taking 16 hours and costing 65–80 pesos, depending on the level of service.

By car
Ruta 22 comes from Bahía Blanca, continuing westwards towards Zapala or, forking left onto Ruta 237, Bariloche.

Car rental is available through Avis Chapelco (*Int Castro and Purrán;* ✆ *443 0216*), Dollar Rent a Car (*Belgrano 18;* ✆ *442 9875*), Fran Car (*Perito Moreno 354;* ✆ *443 6753*), Hertz (*Alberdi 193;* ✆ *15 581 8800*), Localiza Rent a Car (*Perticone 1035;* ✆ *442 8652*) and Transac Rent a Car (*Copahue 1075;* ✆ *440 0419*).

Orientation
Ruta 22 runs through the city as the east–west Félix San Martín, two blocks south of the central park and not to be confused with General San Martín, which marks the northern edge of the park. The park (far more than a plaza, and once the site of the railway station) is bisected by Avenida Argentina, the main avenue. Street names change on either side of this avenue and of General San Martín. The city centre is north of the park on Avenida Argentina, where four diagonal roads meet.

Where to stay
Hotel del Comahue Av Argentina 337; ✆ 443 2040; fax 447 3331; e reservas@hoteldelcomahue.com. Neuquén's highest-rated hotel. Rates are 173 pesos for sgls, 200 pesos for dbls, up to 286 pesos for a suite.
Express Goya and Costa Rica; ✆ 449 0100; e info@ehotelexpress.com. Dbls for 160 pesos and suites for 270 pesos.

Hostal del Caminante Ruta 22, km1227 (13km west); ➎ 444 0118; f 444 0119;
e hostal@satlink.com; www.patagonias.net/hostaldelcaminante; 13km west (and handy for the
airport). This 3-star place has sgls for 115 pesos, dbls for 135 pesos and triples for 160 pesos.

The following are slightly cheaper options:

Arrayán Hotel Alaska 7000, Ruta 22; ➎ 444 0044; e hotelarrayan@neunet.com.ar
El Prado Perito Moreno 488; ➎ 448 6000; f 448 6004
Amucan Tucumán 115; ➎ 442 5209; e reservas@amucanhotel.com.ar
Royal Av Argentina 143; ➎ 448 8902; e informes@royalhotel.com.ar,
www.royalhotel.com.ar. Rates are: sgl 86 pesos, dbl 117 pesos, triple 138 pesos and
quadruple 170 pesos. Parking is available for 10 pesos per day.
Ideal Av Olascoaga 243; ➎ 442 2431; e hotelidealneuquen@yahoo.com.ar. Sgls 30 pesos,
dbls 45 pesos, triples 60 pesos.

Budget options include **Residencial Belgrano** (*Rivadavia 87;* ➎ *447 4127*) and
Liberty Hostal (*Río Desaguadero 479;* ➎ *442 2485*).

Where to eat and drink
There are many restaurants and cafés in Neuquén. For *asado* try: **El Asador** (*Félix
San Martín 890;* ➎ *448 7735*), **El Reencuentro** (*General San Martín 29;* ➎ *443 1461*)
and **Estancia Rosa Catalina** (*J J Lasta 5300;* ➎ *449 0100*). Seafood is the speciality
at **Las Gaviotas** (*J B Justo 129*). **La Tejuela** (*Alberdi 59;* ➎ *443 4354*) offers meat
and seafood. **Cabildo** (*Rivadavia 68;* ➎ *442 9473*) and **La Tartaruga** (*Roca and
Irigoyen;* ➎ *442 3332*) are good choices for pizza.

Practicalities
Tourist information is available at the **Provincial Tourism Office**, Félix San
Martín 182 at Río Negro (➎ *442 4089; www.neuquentur.gov.ar*) and at the bus terminal.
　　The **post office** is at Rivadavia and Santa Fé, and there are a couple of internet
cafés, **Telebar Internet** (*San Martín 327*) and **@rrobas** (*Ministro González 17*).
　　There are several banks: **Banca Nazionale del Lavoro** (*Av Argentina 101;* ➎ *448
0815*), **Banco Almafuerte Cooperativo** (*Rivadavia 61;* ➎ *443 4101*), **Banco de
Boston** (*J B Justo 45;* ➎ *443 8101*), **Banco de la Nación Argentina** (*Av Argentina
80;* ➎ *443 7122*) and **Banco Hipotecario Nacional** (*Av Argentina 79;* ➎ *443 1945*).

Museums
Museo de Geología y Paleontología Buenos Aires 1400; ➎ 449 0300 ext 247. Exhibits
include dinosaurs as well as their closest relatives, birds and reptiles, and other finds from
the Cretaceous period and the Mesozoic era. Entry is through a mock-up of a mine. *Open
Mon–Fri 09.00–17.00, w/ends 16.00–20.00.*
Museo Carmen Funes Av Córdoba 55, Plaza Huincol, Ruta 22 at the intersection with
Ruta Provincial 17 (104km west of Neuquén); ➍f 446 5486. The museum's
palaeontologists continue field research, constantly adding specimens, of which the most
important are the remains of *Argentinosaurus huinculensis* – the largest herbivorous dinosaur
known (found by Guillermo Heredia in 1987). *Open Mon–Fri 08.30–20.00; w/ends and hols
15.00–19.00 (winter), 16.00–20.00 (summer).*
Museo Municipal 'Dr Gregorio Álvarez' General San Martín just off Av Argentina, in the
former Ferrocarril Sud railway station (built in 1901) displays specimens and information on
palaeontology as well as exhibits on archaeology and the cultural history of the region.
Paraje Confluencia City Museum In 3 houses at Colonia no. 6, in the former
Ferrocarril Roca railway yard, displays artefacts from pioneering days as well as
archaeological pieces up to 10,000 years old.

Shopping

The **Paseo de los Artesanos**, in front of the cathedral (Friday to Sunday afternoons), is a local arts and crafts market.

The Lakes District

With its lakes, mountains and forests, this part of Patagonia is a delight. Several adjoining national parks line the cordillera, along the Chilean border: Lanín, Nahuel Huapi, Lago Puelo and Los Arrayanes. A horizon of impressive Andean peaks forms a backdrop to the many beautiful lakes that characterise the area, the largest of which is Lago Nahuel Huapi. This lake, like every great lake, has its legendary sea monster. Those who claim to have seen the *Nahuelito* report a large beast moving like a long undulating piece of leather. Watch out for it while you are taking part in the many watersports, including windsurfing, diving and canoeing, that the lake encourages. Be especially careful when reeling in that 'big fish'!

JUNÍN DE LOS ANDES

Area code 02972

A few kilometres from the entrance to Lanín National Park, Junín de los Andes boasts pehuén forests and typical flora and fauna of Andean Patagonia. It is a place to encounter nature and fantastic scenery with the opportunity for a wide range of excursions. The many rivers and lakes surrounding it make it a fishing paradise. The fertile volcanic soil of the Chimehuín Valley has fostered a small agricultural and cattle-breeding community that was one of the earliest frontier towns, founded in 1883 as a progressive fortress in the so-called 'Conquest of the Desert'. Today, with the dominant presence of Lanín Volcano – 3,776m high and snow-capped year round – this quiet town is realising its potential for tourism.

Getting there

By air

Chapelco Airport is 22km south (closer to San Martín de los Andes than to Junín), but flights into the busier Bariloche airport may prove more convenient. From Buenos Aires, Aerolíneas Argentinas/Austral (*Capitán Drury 876 in San Martín de los Andes;* ✆ *427003/4;* e *austral@smandes.com.ar; open Mon–Fri 09.00–13.00, 16.30–20.30, Sat 09.00–13.00, 18.00–20.30*) offers five flights a week, taking an hour and 20 minutes. LADE (*San Martín bus terminal, at Villegas 231, Local 3;* ✆ *427672*) has flights from Buenos Aires on Thursday and Sunday, continuing to Bariloche, Calafate and Río Gallegos.

By bus

The bus terminal is at Olavarria and San Martín (✆ *492038*). TAC has a service from Buenos Aires (Retiro) every evening at 18.00, arriving in Junín de los Andes the next day at 14.30.

By car

Junín de los Andes lies on Ruta 234 from San Martín de los Andes to Aluminé; from Ruta 40, north or south, a sideroad leads west to Junín by way of the small town of La Rinconada.

Where to stay

There are a a few options for simple hotels: **Alejandro I** (*Ruta 234 and Chubut;* ✆/f *491182;* e *hotelalejandro1@fronteradigital.net.ar*), **San Jorge** (*Av Antartida*

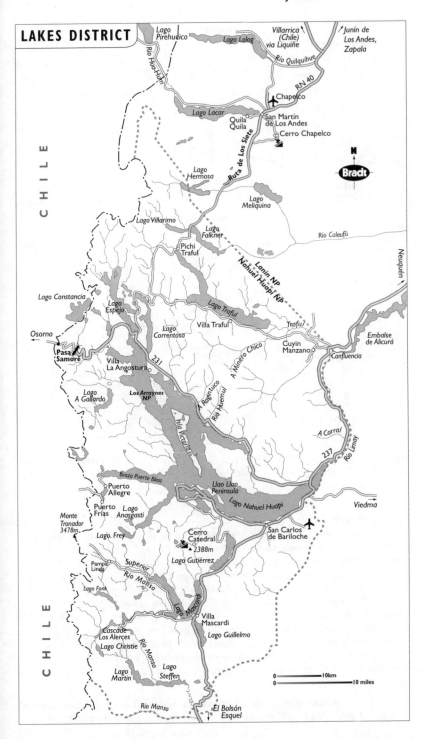

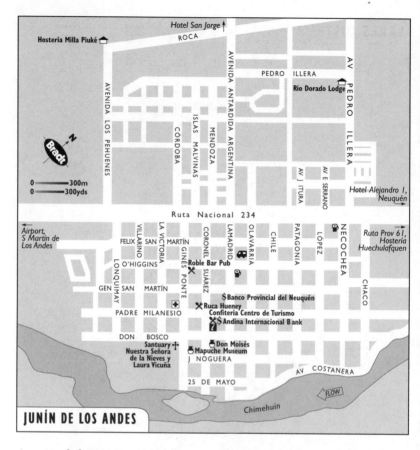

Hotel San Jorge
ROCA
Hostería Milla Piuké
AVENIDA LOS PEHUENES
AVENIDA ANTARDIDA ARGENTINA
PEDRO ILLERA
Río Dorado Lodge
AV PEDRO ILLERA
CÓRDOBA
ISLAS MALVINAS
MENDOZA
AV J ITURA
AV E SERRANO
Hotel Alejandro I, Neuquén
Ruta Nacional 234
Airport, S Martín de Los Andes
FELIX
VILLARINO
SAN VICTORIA
LA
MARTÍN
CORONEL
LAMADRID
OLAVARRIA
CHILE
PATAGONIA
LOPEZ
NECOCHEA
Ruta Prov 61, Hostería Huechulafquen
O'HIGGINS
GINÉS PONTE
Roble Bar Pub
SUAREZ
CHACO
LONQUIMAY
GEN SAN MARTÍN
Banco Provincial del Neuquén
PADRE MILANESIO
Ruca Hueney
Confitería Centro de Turismo
Andina Internacional Bank
DON BOSCO
Santuary Nuestra Señora de la Nieves y Laura Vicuña
Don Moisés
Mapuche Museum
J NOGUERA
25 DE MAYO
AV COSTANERA
FLOW
Chimehuin

JUNÍN DE LOS ANDES

Argentina; ✆/f *491147;* e *hotelsanjorge@jdeandes.com.ar*) and **Residencial Marisa** (*Rosas 360;* ✆ *491175*). A more upmarket choice is **Hostería Milla Piuké** (*Av Los Pehuenes and Roca;* ✆/f *492378*).

Fishing lodges

Río Dorado Lodge Pedro Illera 378/448; ✆ 491548; e info@riodorado.com.ar. Located outside town on a trout-stocked artificial lake, this is in the heart of fishing country and offers fly-fishing lessons, transport to fishing sites and streamside lunches. With tranquil surroundings, large rooms and a swimming pool, even the non-fisherman will enjoy staying here. Country b/fast, afternoon teas and weekly *asado* are offered. Rates start at 174 pesos sgl, 240 pesos dbl, and full packages are available on an individual basis.

Spring Creek Lodge Ruta Provincial 61, Valle San Cabao; ✆ 4795 4636; ✆/f 491286; e springcreek@fibertel.com.ar. Located in the national park. A little village of blue cabins set up in prime fishing territory. Rates include meals, beverages, an English-speaking guide, transportation to and from rivers, and horses for riding; 2,975 pesos per week (Sat–Sat) or 450 pesos per day per person for dbl occupancy, 3,995/600 pesos for sgl occupancy.

You can camp at **Camping Laura Vicuña**, on the island at the southeastern end of Ginés Ponte (✆ 491149; e campinglv@jandes.com.ar); there are plenty of other choices all along Ruta Provincial 61 and around Lakes Huechulafquen and Paimún, many of which are free.

Where to eat and drink

Ruca Hueney Padre Milanesio and Coronel Suárez; ☏ 491113; f 491319; e rucahueney@fronteradigital.net.ar; www.ruca-hueney.com.ar. This *parrilla* and restaurant specialises in venison, mushroom and trout, and has a fair wine selection in its bodega. It also offers take-away.

Río Dorado Lodge Pedro Illera 448; ☏ 491548; e consultas@riodorado.com.ar; www.riodorado.com.ar. Once per week the menu features a typical Patagonian dish, such as venison, trout, lamb or goat *asado*.

Hostería Huechulafquen Ruta Provincial 61, km51; ☏ 450760; e huechulafquen@laninsur.com.ar. Your meal will be enhanced by the wonderful view of Volcán Lanín from the dining room.

Roble Bar Pub Ponte 331; ☏ 15 618055. Has a simple bar menu.

Confiteria Centro de Turismo Padre Milanesio 590; ☏ 492555. A tea house and pastry shop.

Practicalities

The **tourist office** or Dirección Municipal de Turismo is at Coronel Suárez and Padre Milanesio (☏ *491160;* e *turismo@jdeandes.com.ar*). The **Banco Provincial del Neuquén** has an ATM at San Martín and Lamadrid (☏ *491164, 491168*). There's another bank, **Andina Internacional**, at Padre Milanesio 590 (☏ *491022*).

Highlights

Colegio María Auxiliadora is a school that was built at the beginning of the 20th century by missionaries from Chile intent upon converting the girls of the Mapuche community to Christianity. History tells of one girl named Laura Vicuña, who came from Chile with her mother and sister to Estancia Quilquihue where her mother was employed as a housekeeper. She learnt that her mother was also the mistress of the estancia owner. Deeply distressed, she decided to offer her life for the redemption of her mother's soul. Laura soon became gravely ill and on 22 January 1904, died at the age of 13. She is now remembered on an annual pilgrimage and revered as a true Christian example. The **Sanctuary Nuestra Señora de las Nieves y Laura Vicuña,** on the corner of Ginés Ponte and Don Bosco, is home to the mortal remains of Father Domingo Milanesio, the first member of the Salesian order to evangelise in the area. At the entrance is a macabre case displaying a vertebra of Laura Vicuña.

Museums

Mapuche Museum Ginés Ponte 540, with archaeological exhibits plus musical instruments, handicrafts and maps showing the location of the Mapuche communities. *Open Mon–Fri 09.00–19.00, Sat 15.30–20.00. Free admission.*

Don Moisés' Private Museum San Martín and Coronel Suárez 311; ☏ 491569. An estimated 400 pieces of textiles and garments, artefacts and artwork of the historical Mapuche communities are preserved here.

Shopping

Most of the inhabitants of Junín de los Andes are Mapuche or of part-Mapuche descent and therefore you may also find unique handicrafts of exceptional quality. At weekends there is the **Feria Artesanal Independiente** in Plaza San Martín, as well as the **Paseo Artesanal** in the centre (*open daily 09.00–13.00, 17.00–21.00*), where you can find many beautiful pieces.

Fishing
Trout-fishing in the area is excellent and lures anglers from around the world. Most of the best sites are within 30km of the town. Huechulafquen, Paimún and Tromen lakes and the rivers Quilquihue and Curruhue are recommended for their scenery and record-size trout. Fly-fishing is said to be best at the mouth of the Río Chimehuín as well as on the Limay, Aluminé and Collon Cura rivers for large rainbow, brook and brown trout and landlocked salmon; the Río Malleo for dry fly-fishing; and Lago Curruhue for salmon-fishing. Licences can be purchased at the tourist office (*30 pesos for a day, 150 pesos for a week*). A recommended local fishing guide is Angel Fontanazza and his family-run business **Flotadas Chimehuín** (*Ginés Ponte 143;* ✆ *491313;* e *info@fchimehuin.com.ar; www.fchimehuin.com.ar*).

Lanín National Park, Lake Huechulafquen and Lanín Volcano
A trip north from town along Ruta Provincial 61 will take you along the northern shores of Lago Huechulafquen, the largest lake in Lanín National Park. The eastern end of the lake connects to the mouth of the Río Chimehuín, a recommended spot for fly-fishing. At the western end of the lake are **Puerto Canoa** and a view of the wrinkled and all-the-more photogenic face of Volcán Lanín (3,776m). Excellent hikes begin at the trailheads here. Boat excursions from the Puerto Canoa tour lakes Huechulafquen, Paimún and Epulafquen. *Catamarán Jose Julian* departs daily at 11.00, 13.00, 15.00 and 17.00; 20 pesos. At various spots along the lakeshores are *hosterías*, restaurants and fishing lodges. Several days could be spent hiking around the lakes to enjoy the beaches of volcanic sand and the forests of raulí, roble pellín and coihue.

You can reach the main park entrance by Ruta 234; the Lahuen Co hot springs are on Ruta 62. From the bus terminal in town, Crucero del Norte/Cooperativa Litrán has departures to the park at 10.00, 15.30 and 18.30 daily; 12 pesos.

The national park office is at Padre Milanesio 590, local C (✆ *492748*), where you can pay your park admission fee (12 pesos).

LANÍN NATIONAL PARK
At the foot of the magnificent snow capped Lanín Volcano (3,776m), trees that grow nowhere else in the country thrive on the volcanic soils, including raulí and roble pellín, both types of *Nothofagus* or false beech. Also here is the lovely ñire, in an unusual location for this southern species of false beech. The araucaria or pehuén is commonly called the monkey-puzzle tree and is a gorgeously unusual primitive pine that is sacred to the Mapuche. It grows up to 45m and is topped with a parasol-like crown; the largest individuals are estimated to be over a thousand years old. Certain rare mammals also make their home in the park; the endangered huemul deer, the threatened Andean otter or huillín, the elusive puma and, the smallest deer in the world, the pudú. Glacial lakes more typical of the south are plentiful (24 to be precise) in this mountainous landscape and the icy waters contrast with the thermal springs steaming nearby. The park was established in 1937 and covers an area of 379,000ha. It borders Chile and the adjacent Nahuel Huapi National Park to the south.

SAN MARTÍN DE LOS ANDES
Area code 02972

Set on the eastern shore of Lago Lacar, this is a popular city for tourists interested in the great outdoors, especially fishing. Yet another town founded (in 1898) as a fort during Roca's campaign to 'tame the desert', it proved to be important economically due to its proximity to Chile. The town grew with the seemingly limitless supply of lumber from the forest until the Lanín National Park was established in 1937, but many of the original homesteads and buildings still stand.

Getting there
By air
Aeropuerto Carlos Campos (better known as Chapelco) is 20km north on Ruta 234 (↘ *428388, 428398*). From Buenos Aires Aerolíneas Argentinas/Austral (*Capitán Drury 876;* ↘ *427003/4;* e *austral@smandes.com.ar; open Mon–Fri 09.00–13.00, 16.30–20.30, Sat 09.00–13.00, 18.00–20.30*) offers five flights a week, taking an hour and 20 minutes. LADE (*San Martín de los Andes bus terminal, at Villegas 480 Local 3;* ↘ *427672*) has flights from Buenos Aires on Thursday and Sunday, comtinuing to Bariloche, Calafate and Río Gallegos. A taxi into town will cost about 12 pesos; you could also walk 1km to the highway to catch a Junín–San Martín bus.

More frequent flights serve the airport of Bariloche where you can rent a car; a group of San Martín tour companies have also recently launched the Puente Terrestre or Land Bridge, a minibus shuttle to Bariloche airport that leaves at 08.00, arriving at noon and returning at 15.30. Fares are 60 pesos single, 110 pesos return; reservations are required, through Turismo El Claro (*Coronel Díaz 751, San Martín de los Andes;* ↘ *420430;* e *puenteterrestre@smandes.com.ar; www.puenteterrestre.com.ar*).

By bus
The bus terminal is located on Villegas and Juez del Valle. Nueva Chevallier (↘ *427291*), Via Bariloche (↘ *422800*), TAC (↘ *428878*), Albus (↘ *428100*), Centenario (↘ *427294*) and El Valle UTE (↘ *423808, 422800*) each has a daily departure to Buenos Aires (23 hours). A Via Bariloche/Turismo Algarrobal bus leaves San Martín de los Andes for Bariloche via the Seven Lakes at 13.00 and via Rinconada at 15.30. From Bariloche departures for San Martín de los Andes are at 09.00 via Rinconada or at 11.30 via the Seven Lakes. In summer there are two other services via the Seven Lakes. Via Bariloche's office is in the terminal (↘ *422800, 423808*). Albus has one bus from Villa La Angostura leaving at 20.15, arriving at 22.30 (19 pesos).

By car
From the north take Ruta 41 from Junín de los Andes; from the south take Ruta 234 through the park or Ruta 237 and then Ruta 63. From Buenos Aires take Ruta 5 west to Santa Rosa in La Pampa (620km) followed by Ruta 35, Ruta 152 and finally Ruta 143 to Chacharramendi (190km); then take Ruta Provincial 20 (often referred to as the Ruta 'Conquista del Desierto') until it crosses the Ruta 151 at Colonia 25 de Mayo and then crosses the Río Colorado. This route will take you to the town of Cippoletti, in Río Negro, from where you take Ruta 22 to Neuquén. Continue to Ruta 237, turn onto Ruta 40 at Collón Cura and finally take Ruta 234 to San Martín de los Andes.

Orientation
Avenida Costanera borders Lago Lacar about half a dozen blocks west of the centre of town; the main plaza is surrounded by generals, colonels and explorers: Avenida Villegas, Avenida Peréz, Avenida Moreno and Avenida Belgrano.

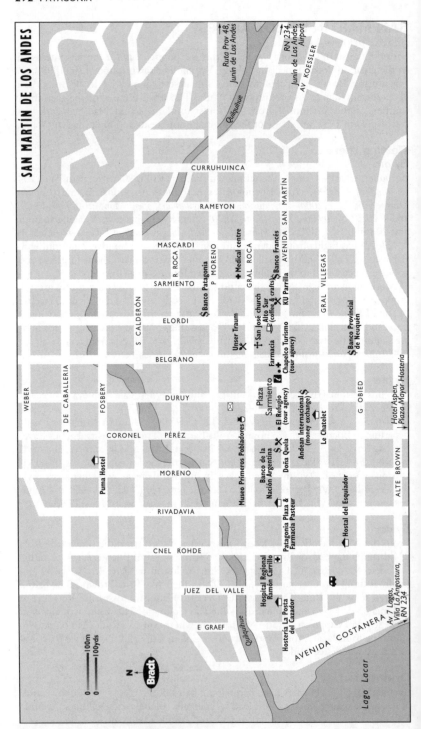

SAN MARTÍN DE LOS ANDES

Where to stay

Le Chatelet Villegas 650; ↘ 428294, 428296; e info@hotellechatelet.com.ar; www.hotellechatelet.com.ar. Built of stone and wood in the style typical of the region, this mid-sized hotel has a pool with gym and sauna and serves a large b/fast of regional delights. Rates start at 205/257 pesos sgl, 275/360 pesos dbl.

Patagonia Plaza Av San Martín and Rivadavia; ↘f 422280, 422284; e patagoniaplaza@smandes.com.ar; www.hotelpatagoniaplaza.com.ar. There are a pool and spa, restaurant and bar and parking. Rates start at 205/257 pesos sgl and 275/360 pesos dbl.

Plaza Mayor Hostería Pérez 1199; ↘f 427302; e plazamayor@smandes.com.ar; www.hosteriaplazamayor.com.ar. You will be comfortable here, with a solarium, swimming pool, bar and covered parking. In high season a dbl starts at 200 pesos, b/fast included.

Hostal del Esquiador Rohde 975; ↘ 427674; e info@hdelesquiador.com.ar; www.hdelesquiador.com.ar. This *hostería* has comfortable rooms and a common area with a fireplace. Tour guides based here can offer excursions or basic information. Sgl 160 pesos, dbl 175 pesos, with b/fast.

Hostería La Posta del Cazador Av San Martín 175; ↘f 427501, 427802; e laposta@smandes.com.ar; www.postadelcazador.com.ar. This alpine-style building is 20m from Lake Lacar. Rates change dramatically from low to high season, 60–133 pesos for a sgl, 78–133 pesos for dbl. Triples, suites and apts are also available.

Hotel Aspen Coronel Pérez 1127; ↘ 428426, 427475; f 427425; e aspen@smandes.com.ar. Sgls range from 97 pesos to 227 pesos between low season (Mar–Jun and Oct–Dec) and high season (Jul), with dbls from 174 pesos to 394 pesos.

Puma Hostel Fosbery 535; ↘ 422443; e puma@smandes.com.ar. Dorms are 23 pesos per person and a dbl with private bath is 68 pesos per night.

There is plenty of **camping** in the national park, along the lakes and at the hot baths.

Where to eat and drink

Doña Quela Av San Martín facing Plaza Sarmiento. Specialities include trout, pasta and venison.

KU Parrilla San Martín 1053; ↘ 427039; e ku@smandes.com.ar. Featured dishes are lamb, wild boar, chicken and *chivito* (young goat), cooked on the *parrilla*, of course.

Down Town Matias Arrayán Cerro Comandante; ↘ 425570. Situated over Curruhuinca Hill, very close to the centre but you'll still need a taxi or car as there's no direct route.

Arrayán Tea House ↘ 421699. Located 3km from the town centre on Calderón and Juez del Valle, with a great view overlooking Lake Lacar and the town. This is the leading tea house in San Martín.

Unser Traum In the centre, facing the San José church on Roca. German pastry shop and cafeteria.

Alto Sur Elordi near Plaza Sarmiento. A place to find handicrafts and sip a coffee.

Practicalities

Tourist information is available at the offices of the Secretaria de Turismo, Avenida San Martín and J M Rosas (↘ *425500 or 427347;* e *munitur@smandes.gov.ar; see also www.sanmartindelosandes.com.ar*).

To exchange money, **Andina Internacional** is at Cap Drury 876 (↘ *427871, 482392*), and there are several banks: **Banco de la Nación Argentina** (*San Martín 687;* ↘ *427292*), **Banco Provincial de Neuquén** (*Belgrano and G Obeid;* ↘ *427234*); **Banco Patagonia** (*P Moreno and Elordi;* ↘ *429531*), and **Banco Francés** (*San Martín and Sarmiento;* ↘ *425681*).

The **Hospital Regional Ramón Carrillo** is on San Martín and Colonel Rodhe (↘ *427211; in emergency dial 107*); there is a medical centre on Sarmiento 489

(↘ *427148*). **Farmacía del Centro** is at San Martín 896, at Belgrano (↘ *428999*); another centrally located pharmacy is **Farmacía Pasteur** (*San Martín and Rivadavia;* ↘ *422243*).

San Martín de los Andes Rent-a-Car is at Gen Villegas 459.

Travel agencies

El Refugio On the corner of Perez and San Martín, almost in front of the tourist office; ↘ 425140.

Chapelco Turismo San Martín 876; ↘ 427550

Chilco Capitán Drury 860, Local 5; ↘ 429030

Highlights

An old English double-decker bus called the Redbus operates a city tour, leaving from Plaza Sarmiento at 16.30 daily (↘ *15 550785*).

From the Bandurrias Hill, 4km down Ruta Provincial 48, a turn-off indicates a steep winding road to a mirador with a panoramic view of San Martín and the lake. There is also a footpath from town.

Museum

Museo Primeros Pobladores Juan M de Rosa St 760; ↘ 428676; e dpto.cultura@smandes.gov.ar. Many artefacts of the pioneer community are preserved in very good condition in this small museum. *Open Tue–Fri 10.00–16.00, 19.00–22.00, Sat and Sun 19.00–22.00; admission 1.50 pesos (free in low season).*

SPORT-FISHING SPECIES

Catch limits are published in the Annual Fishing Regulations. In Nahuel Huapi National Park, fly-casting, spinning and trawling are permitted with artificial bait only. *Season November to March.*

Rainbow trout/Trucha arco iris (*Oncorhunchus mykiss*). The flanks of this spectacularly colourful trout are boldly striped like the flag of Italy: green, red and white (just in the wrong order!). If the red is missing, as occurs in some variants, the fish is referred to as *plateada*, meaning silver coloured. It is black-spotted with a small head and long body with two dorsal fins. Introduced from North America, it is common in most lakes and streams and is favoured by anglers for its size (up to 10kg) and combativeness. Almost identical but migratory in habit is the steelhead trout, found in the Río Santa Cruz.

Brown trout/Trucha marrón (*Salmo trutta*). This trout is large (up to 15kg), rare, evasive, unpredictable, aggressive, cunning and generally difficult to catch, all of which make it the favourite of anglers. Its loins are dark brown, its flanks golden brown and its abdomen yellowish; it is spotted with green and brown above intermingling down its sides with red spots encircled in white.

Brook trout/Trucha de arroyo (*Salvelinus fontinalis*). Introduced from North America into Argentina around 1904, this species is sexually dimorphic: the male is larger with more prominent mandibula and brighter colouring, which is brown and green and occasionally black with undulating lines marking its upper body and red spots with white halos on its sides. Its lower flanks are orange (becoming quite bright on the males in the reproductive season) with a black and white border on its belly. It weighs about 1kg in rivers and streams but reaches up to 4kg in lakes. It crossbreeds with brown trout (producing what is

Day trips and excursions

A drive along Ruta Provincial 62 takes you to the **Termas de Lahuen Co** where you will find several small (about 2m wide) circular thermal pools and mudbaths. Along the way you will pass Lagos Curruhué Chico and Curruhué Grande, Lago Verde and the ancient black lavaflow (*escorial*) of **Volcán Achen Ñiyeu**.

Rafting the **Hua-Hum River** as it makes its way into Chile and ultimately to the Pacific Ocean is a true Patagonian adventure experience. Agencies in town offer excursions on these class II and III waters. Remember that you will enter Chile on this excursion; therefore, it is necessary to carry your passport. Yuco, at km47 on Ruta 48, is a centre for fishing and other water activities on this river, and there is free camping at Nonthué. The Chachín Waterfall is nearby. With your passport, you can also cross Lago Pirehueico by ferry to the Chilean village of the same name, 12km from the Hua-Hum border crossing.

Ruta 234, south from San Martín de los Andes towards Villa La Angostura, is also known as the *Ruta de los Siete Lagos* or **Seven Lakes Route**, a famed scenic drive through the lake country.

Cerro Chapelco (2,441m), a 20-minute drive from San Martín, is a small but important winter resort and ski school. There are 20 ski runs of various levels of difficulty through the forest and ravines, including black runs with jumps and moguls. For 2006 the resort has installed the most modern quad chairlift in Latin America (with heated seats). Ski passes cost 5–96 pesos per day, or 298–533 pesos for a week (free to over-70s).

often named 'tiger trout') and with American lake trout (producing 'splake').

Lake trout/Trucha de lago (*Salvelinus namaycush*). This is a dark grey or blackish-green fish spotted with white or yellow; its flanks and fins are orange during the spawning season. It is a large fish weighing in at up to 23kg. Its most distinctive feature is the highly forked tail.

Landlocked salmon/Salmón del Atlántico encerrado (*Salmo salar sebago*). This is a non-native species, introduced in the early 20th century. In its native environs it migrates between fresh and salt water at different stages of its life cycle. The name 'landlocked' refers to the fact that here it must remain permanently in fresh water. It is silver with black spots and colouring on its head and back, striping up the dorsal fins. It is often mistaken for a brown trout; the smaller mouth is one way to differentiate it. It is often only available for catch-and-release fishing.

Perch/Perca (*Percychtys* spp.). There are three species of native perch in the lakes of this region: *perca boca chica*, *perca bocona* and *perquina espinuda*. They have a single dorsal fin with strong radial bones, ventral fins and an extensible mouth. Its dark olive-green back fades down its flanks, becoming pale yellow on its abdomen. The largest, *perca bocona*, can surpass 4kg.

Pejerrey/Pejerrey Patagónico or Pejerrey de escama chica (*Patagonina hatchery* or *Odontesthes microlepidotus*). This is a native species from a family of both salt and fresh water species. It has a greenish dorsal fin becoming silver on its flanks with a reflective longitudinal band. Its weight averages 1kg. This is not a prized trophy fish but very popular for eating. Several species of this family are important ecomonically, such as the sea pejerrey or pejerrey bonaerense (*Odontesthes bonariensis*).

At **Laguna Verde**, near the isthmus of the Quetrihue Peninsula (about 500m along Quetrihue Boulevard from the port), you may take a pleasant walk along a floral interpretative walkway. This natural reserve is home to a large variety of flowers and attracts many bird species. Near the small pier you will see the **Arrayán of Love**, where a cypress and an arrayán tree grow intertwined in an enduring embrace.

You can find sailing trips on Lacar Lakes and Nonthué through various agencies in town. Catritre Beach on Lake Lacar has campsites with grills.

Near **Quila Quina Village**, 12km from town on Ruta 234, is the waterfall of the Arroyo Grande River, as well as the El Cipresal Trail with indigenous rock paintings and a thermal water fountain.

Birdwatching is very popular in San Martín de los Andes owing to the great variety of birds found in the area (some 243 species can be seen in the province of Neuquén). Trips are organised by the Patagonian Bird Assocation; enquire at the tourist office or ↘ 422022; www.avespatagonia.com.ar. Prices start at 150 pesos for a simple morning's birding; more elaborate programmes (up to eight days touring various areas) start at 800 pesos, including lodging, meals, transport and guides.

The **Centro de Ecologia Aplicada del Neuquén (CEAN)** in Valle San Cabao (*7km northwest on Ruta Provincial 61;* ↘ *491427;* e *peces@smandes.com.ar*) is a fish management and research station, and also a place to see plenty of animals such as llamas, coipos and river otters. Guided visits are available from 09.00 to 13.00 daily.

VILLA LA ANGOSTURA
Area code 02944
At the far south of the province of Neuquén on the shores of Lago Nahuel Huapi, Villa La Angostura is a small town that boasts two national parks: Nahuel Huapi National Park and Los Arrayanes National Park. It is the sort of town that offers the simple indulgences of a natural getaway, but also with options for elegant hotels and restaurants. Founded in 1932 when a radio station was established, it was boosted by the development of the nearby ski centre of Cerro Bayo and by the 'rich and famous' building summer homes and giving the village a more sophisticated atmosphere. However, the town remains small and pleasant, with buildings mostly of wood and rock and with a two-storey height limit on construction. In fact, in 2002 hundreds of residents blocked the construction of a large hotel proposed on the shore of Lago Nahuel Huapi in order to protect the arrayanes and coihues that grow there. Villa La Angostura offers a slower pace than the town of Bariloche, with many options for excursions and activities. However, as interest increases it creates the very thing it is trying to avoid and this town is finding it ever more difficult to maintain its quaint feel. The name Angostura meaning 'narrows' comes from being situated near the narrow isthmus that joins the Península de Quetrihue to the mainland.

Getting there
By *air*
Aerolíneas Argentinas (*Santa Fé 52;* ↘ *442 2409–11 or at the airport 444 0736;* e *nqnadmin@aerolineas.com.ar*), LADE (*Almirante Brown 163;* ↘ *443 1153 or at the airport 444 0817;* e *neuquen@lade.com.ar*) and LAN Argentina (*Quaglia 262, Local 13;* ↘ *442 3704 or at the airport 443 0002;* f *443 4470*) serve Bariloche airport, where you'll probably have to transfer into town before taking a car or bus to Villa La Angostura. Alternatively, buses from Bariloche to Villa La Angostura pass by the airport turning, 14 km east of the town.

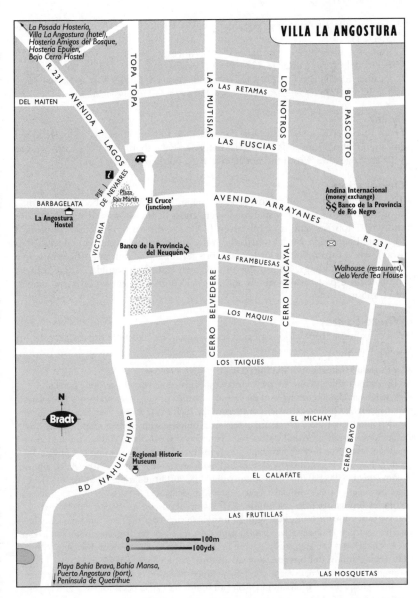

VILLA LA ANGOSTURA

La Posada Hostería,
Villa La Angostura (hotel),
Hostería Amigos del Bosque,
Hostería Epulen,
Bajo Cerro Hostel

TOPA TOPA

R 231

DEL MAITEN

AVENIDA 7 LAGOS

LAS MUTISIAS

LAS RETAMAS

LOS NOTROS

BD PASCOTTO

LAS FUSCIAS

PJE | DE NEVARRES

Plaza
San Martín

'El Cruce'
(junction)

AVENIDA ARRAYANES

Andina Internacional
(money exchange)
Banco de la Provincia
de Río Negro

BARBAGELATA

La Angostura
Hostel

VICTORIA

R 231

Banco de la Provincia
del Neuquén

LAS FRAMBUESAS

CERRO INACAYAL

Walhouse (restaurant),
Cielo Verde Tea House

CERRO BELVEDERE

LOS MAQUIS

LOS TAIQUES

N

Bradt

NAHUEL HUAPI

EL MICHAY

CERRO BAYO

Regional Historic
Museum

EL CALAFATE

BD NAHUEL HUAPI

LAS FRUTILLAS

| 0 ————— 100m
| 0 ————— 100yds

Playa Bahía Brava, Bahía Mansa,
Puerto Angostura (port),
↓ Península de Quetrihue

LAS MOSQUETAS

Across the border in Chile, the city of Osorno has several flights a day from Santiago and elsewhere in Chile, with LAN, Sky Airlines and Aerolíneas del Sur.

By bus
From Bariloche buses take an hour and a quarter to Villa La Angostura, charging 9 pesos. Via Bariloche/Turismo Algarrobal have eight departures a day from the Bariloche terminal, and Albus has six or seven. Buses to San Martín de los Andes via the Seven Lakes Route call at Villa La Angostura.

At the Villa La Angostura terminal are Via Bariloche (✆ *494 360*) and Albus (✆ *494721*).

Long-distance bus companies: Via Bariloche/El Valle (✆ *0800 333 7575*), Crucero del Norte (✆ *02944 435 999 in Bariloche, 011 4315 1652 in Buenos Aires*), Chevallier/Flecha Bus (✆ *02944 423 090 in Bariloche, 011 4313 9846 in Buenos Aires*) and TAC (✆ *02944 434 727 in Bariloche, 011 4313 362 in Buenos Aires*).

By car
From Buenos Aires, take Ruta 3 to Bahía Blanca, followed by Ruta 22 to Neuquén and then Ruta 237 towards Bariloche; before arriving there, Ruta 231 turns west to Villa La Angostura. From the north, take Ruta 40 then Ruta 237 and 231.

Orientation
The hub of town is something of a 'Y' shape. Ruta 237 West becomes Avenida Arrayanos as you enter town and is where most of the shops and restaurants are and where tourists tend to stroll. From El Cruce, the central junction, Boulevard Nahuel Huapi leads south towards the water and the various piers and docks (3km away), while turning north leads to the bus terminal, the tourism office and a few other public buildings. Continuing out of town Ruta 237/Avenida 7 Lagos follows the lakeshore past various hotels and *hosterías*. Without a car you'll need taxis to reach these.

Where to stay
You can choose from various elegant hotels along the lakeshore or rustic log cabins in the woods.

La Posada Hostería and Spa Ruta 231; ✆ 494450, 494368;
e laposada@bariloche.com.ar; www.hosterialaposada.com. This elegant little hotel is located several kilometres west on the lakeshore with a private beach and jetty. Their boat takes clients for fishing excursions or tours of the lake. Many rooms have lake views; there is an outdoor pool and a wonderful indoor spa, complete with exercise room, massage and a fabulous hot tub enclosed by glass walls with views over the lake. You can eat indoors or on the terrace. The hotel is surrounded by gardens and paths into the forest. A private 3-hole golf course is available to guests of La Posada and 3 other hotels nearby. A sgl standard room costs US$90/120 (low/high season), dbl US$100/140 and triple US$120/170. There are also superior suites with lake views, some with jacuzzis.

Villa La Angostura 6km east on Ruta 231, Puerto Manzano; ✆f 494307, 302341;
e reservas@bahiamanzano.com. With an incredible view over the lake, this large hotel has facilities such as tennis courts, a pool, a gym, day care, a private dock and more, and in case you still feel as if you are roughing it out in the woods it is only a 5-min drive into town!

Hostería Amigos del Bosque 6km east on Ruta 231, km55.5; ✆ 494977;
e amigosdelbosque@netpatagon.com; www.amigosdelbosque.com.ar. 12 rooms face Lago Nahuel Huapi on Puerto Manzano. Standard rooms start at 95 pesos low season, 112 pesos high, for sgls; 125–150 pesos for a dbl; but suites, at 230–290 pesos, have fireplaces, jacuzzi and lake views. One room is also fully equipped with facilities for the disabled.

Hostería Epulen ✆f 15 567612 or in Buenos Aires (011) 4922 8130;
e hosteria@epulen.com.ar; www.epulen.com.ar. This mountain-style inn has an excellent view of Lago Correntoso 300m away. Sgls 90 pesos, dbls 140 pesos, triples 170 pesos, b/fast included. A 50% deposit by bank transfer may be requested, especially in high season, the remainder to be paid in cash upon arrival.

Two recommended hostels in town are members of the Hostelling International association (with discounted rates on presentation of an HI hostel card).

La Angostura Hostel Barbagelata 157, 2 blocks from the terminal; ☎ 494834; e info@hostellaangostura.com.ar, hostellaangostura@yahoo.com.ar. A comfortable hostel with many communal areas and a pool table, library, TV, internet and a bar/cafeteria. Beds cost 20 pesos per person in dorms for 6 people with private bath; 21 pesos in dorms for 5 people; 22 pesos for 4; or 60 pesos for a dbl. B/fast is included.

Bajo Cero Hostel Río Caleufu 88; ☎ 495454; e info@bajocerohostel.com. This hostel is the out-of-town option, located 1.2km from the centre on the Seven Lakes road, in a forested area in a log-cabin-style building with a dining room with fireplace. Dorms 22 pesos per person, dbls 55 pesos. B/fast is included.

Where to eat and drink

Regional specialities include venison and wild boar, trout, mushrooms, pickles and smoked meats. At teatime there are many wonderful desserts to indulge in. Choosing any of the *hosterías* or the many fine establishments in town or along the lakeside, you will be treated to excellent local cuisine. Avenida Arrayanes has several restaurants on the main two blocks.

Walhouse Ruta 231, km56 above Río Bonito as you enter Villa La Angostura from Bariloche; ☎ 495123. This restaurant and tea house serves very well-made regional dishes.

Cielo Verde Tea House Av Arrayanes km2.6; ☎ 494919. Comes recommended by the local residents.

Practicalities

The **tourist office** is at the Secretaria Municipal de Turismo, opposite the bus terminal at Avenida Siete Lagos 93 (☎ *494124;* e *turismo@villalaangostura.gov.ar*). The **post office** is at Unifón, Avenida Arrayanes 235.

Money exchange is available at **Andina Internacional** on Avenida Arrayanes 256 (☎ *495197*); **Banco de la Provincia de Río Negro** on Avenida Arrayanes 275 (☎ *495220*), and **Banco de la Provincia del Neuquén** on Las Frambuesas 70 (☎ *494180*).

Museum

Regional Historic Museum Nahuel Huapi 1900. Has exhibits from the town's first school and post office, old woodworking tools, water navigation and mountaineering equipment and photographs. *Open Mon to Fri 10.30–17.30 (closes at 14.30 on Wed); Sat 14.30–17.30.*

Special events

The **Fiesta de los Jardines** takes place in February when a three-day adjudication takes place to reward the most beautiful garden of a private home and of a public locale or business. The award to the winners is exemption from property tax for a full year! The best thing about this festival is that glorious gardens are on display for the entire spring leading up to the event and the summer and autumn afterwards.

Also in February and March are the mountain bike and endurance racing championships. The **Fiestas Mayas** in May coincide with the anniversary of Villa La Angostura when cultural celebrations take place as well as sporting events such as a biathlon. There are skiing and snowboarding events in July and August, such as the **Fiesta de la Esquinieve**, dog-sledding with Siberian huskies in July, rugby championships in August, the **Liberty Triathlon** in September, the 42km **Adventure Marathon** in October, an antique car event in November and a fishing tournament and **National Trout Festival** in December.

Activities
In the forest
Canopy Villa La Angostura 📞 15 417817; e info@canopyargentina.com.ar; www.canopyargentina.com.ar. Adventures in the canopy of the forests provide exhilarating views from elevated platforms that you 'fly' between by hanging in a harness from a cable.
Centro Recreativo La Piedra Ruta 66, km200 (Cerro Bayo turning); 📞 15 562314; e sergiobroder@yahoo.com.ar. Adventure and family recreation options include a kids' park, trampolines, quad-biking, abseiling, rock climbing and hours on cables.
Free Bikes 📞 495047; e freebikes@netpatagon.com; www.freebikes.com.ar. Mountain bikes can be rented for excursions in various parts of the national park for 24 pesos.
Cabalgatas Correntoso 📞 15 510559, 15 604903; e info@cabalgatacorrentoso.com.ar; www.cabalgatacorrentoso.com.ar. Horseriding day trips as well as 2- to 4-day excursions are available through the forests and around the lake in the national park.

On the lake
Rather than an often-crowded and frenetic experience of the catamaran tour, you and a few friends can enjoy a more peaceful and private experience sailing with companies such as **Vela Aventura** (📞 *15 554153 or 494834; e veleaventura@yahoo.com.ar*). The cost is approximately 130 pesos for a group of four or five for a couple of hours on the lake (year-round).

Fishing
Great fly-fishing for brown and rainbow trout is to be had at the mouth of the Río Correntoso, which is reputedly the shortest river in the world (600m). The Río Bonito has infinite little bends and corners to fish along. Lakes such as Espejo, Correntoso and Nahuel Huapi are full of rainbow trout, brook trout, brown trout, perch, pejerrey and landlocked salmon. The best fish are found in the northern zone: Brazo Machete, Rincón and Ultima Esperanza.

Day trips and excursions
There are several sites of interest in the area, such as the cave paintings on Victoria Island, over 500 years old, and those in Cerro Leones, 80km away from the village.

Three kilometres from the centre of Villa La Angostura is El Puerto, site of the docks for the excursion boats and the national park office (where you must buy your 12 pesos admission ticket to visit **Los Arrayanes National Park**). This point is the neck of the **Península de Quetrihué**, narrow enough to walk across in a few minutes. Two boat companies operate excursions to the arrayán forest and natural reserve. Both go to the park, allowing you time to walk about with or without a guide; but one will circumnavigate the bay that is adjacent to the road where all the main hotels are located, and the other tours the opposite bay, which is less developed. The first, nearest to the park office, is **Greenleaf Turismo**, taking a route along the east side of the peninsula, parallel to Avenida Arrayanes (Ruta 231) and passing Messidor Castle, a replica French chateau and residence of the province's governor, the fronts of the many elite hotels such as the Hotel Angostura and the Messidor, as well as **Puerto Manzano**. This harbour is named after the apple plantations that were once in the area; today it is a popular location for swimmers, sunbathers and watersport enthusiasts owing to a large flat rock at the front of the bay that acts as a natural pier. The other company, **Catamarán Patagonia Argentina**, leaves from the dock near the Quetrihué viewpoint of Lago Nahuel Huapi and takes a more secluded route along the west side of the peninsula. In between the two ports is the entrance to the park by a path that can be taken on foot or by bicycle. It's an easy 12km

LOS ARRAYANES NATIONAL PARK

The beautiful and unusual arrayán or arrayanes (*Luma apiculata*) tree is a species of myrtle that is found as a lone tree or in rare groves throughout the area. One such grove is on Isla Victoria, in Parque Nacional Los Alerces, and another very small grove is just west of Llao-Llao. The unusually large grove protected by Los Arrayanes National Park is truly unique for its density of ancient arrayán trees. Century-old individuals are protected here. They grow very slowly, 150cm in 50 years; the oldest stand at almost 20m with trunks 50cm in diameter. If you look closely at the bifurcations of branches, the bark seems to wrinkle and crease, giving them their ancient and sage appearance. The cinnamon-coloured trunks contort and twist and the large base roots gnarl and turn over the surface of the earth, resisting the urge to dig deep. Instead they produce new suckers that may climb up other trees. This suckering ability can lead to a substantial grove of trees that are all clones of the same individual. From this point of view an arrayán grove can be classified as one of the largest organisms on earth.

One of their most interesting properties is that their endothermic bark is always cool to the touch. In the spring, the trees produce small white flowers, later sweet purple fruit, eaten by the indigenous peoples. The leaves have medicinal properties, being said to soothe muscle pain and intestinal infections when taken in an infusion.

The area of this park was once part of Nahuel Huapi National Park but was giving its own designation in 1971 in recognition of this rare and beautiful tree and this large grove that is unique in the world, at Península Quetrihué, on the north shore of Lake Nahuel Huapi. The park's total area is 1,753ha, of which just 20ha (at the southern tip of the peninsula) comprise the arrayanes forest.

The eco-system preserved in the park provides habitat for over 80 species of bird, 20% of which are migratory. The most significant is the Magellanic woodpecker (*Campephilus magellanicus*), the largest and most beautiful species of woodpecker and a symbol of Patagonia. The male has a bright red head and the female is all black with a distinctive top-knot feather curl on her head. The pair are never far apart from each other and you will likely hear them knocking before you spot them.

through a forest of coihues, cypress, notros and indigenous flora to the arrayán grove at the far tip of the peninsula. You can choose to take the boat in only one direction and walk 12km through the forest either to or from the park entrance. Be sure to buy your ticket in advance if you intend to return by boat as they will not sell you a ticket on the boat. You must buy the ticket for the park (12 pesos) on top of your ticket for the boat.

By **Brazo Ultima Esperanza** (Last Hope Arm), the '**Alerzal Milenario**' (Thousand-Year-Old Larch Forest) boasts specimens of alerce 3,000 years old, making them some of the oldest living things on the planet. From **Puerto Blest**, 16km from Villa La Angostura on Ruta 231, a footpath leads through the forest to *El Abuelo* (The Grandfather), a coihue that is over a thousand years old. Continuing along the path through the woods, you arrive at Puerto Alegre, where you can take a catamaran across Lago Frías from in front of the Echo Wall, a high rock formation that will shout back at you if you holler at it.

Along Avenida Arrayanes (Ruta 231) from El Cruce (ACA gas station) heading towards Bariloche, take the unpaved Ruta 66 for 5km to a 200m-long walkway through native forest that leads to the 35m-high **Río Bonito waterfall** with beautiful views of the river. Further along Ruta 66 you can also take the chairlift at **Cerro Bayo**; this ski centre has 20km of pistes and 200ha of off-trail skiing and is also a nice place for hiking or biking in summer. A refuge and snack bar is open year-round. Continuing along Ruta 231 towards Bariloche you will pass **Puerto Manzano**, already described on page 300.

NAHUEL HUAPI NATIONAL PARK

The arms of Lake Nahuel Huapi penetrate into the forests and mountains of Nahuel Huapi National Park, the largest and oldest in all of South America, established in 1934. Glaciation left many lakes, such as Traful, Mascardi, Gutiérrez and Guillelmo, but the largest is the eponymous Lago Nahuel Huapi, covering 55,700ha of the park's 710,000ha and reaching depths of 454m. The central island, Isla Victoria, hosts forests of native coihue and ñire and is full of deer.

It was the visionary motivation of explorer and naturalist Francisco 'Perito' Moreno that led to the founding of this national park. Piece by piece, its protected area grew to its current area through his efforts. The first protected area that he saw enacted, in 1903, was 7,000ha in the area of Puerto Blest; in 1922 he created the Parque Nacional del Sud, expanded in 1934 to include the entire area of the park today and endowed with the name of Parque Nacional Nahuel Huapi. It is one of the last strongholds for many endangered species, such as the huemul and pudú deer, and the *monito de monte*, a rare marsupial. Many wonderful birds have their old-growth forest habitat protected, such as the Magellanic woodpecker.

Three major biomes are represented within the borders of the park: the high Andean, Patagonian-Andean beechwoods and a portion of Patagonian steppe. The high Andean biome lies above 1,600m with sparse alpine vegetation adapted to cold, snow and wind. The Patagonian-Andean beechwoods are comprised of southern or false beech – lenga (*Nothofagus pumilio*) at higher elevations, evergreen coihue (*N. dombeyi*) at mid-elevations and the deciduous ñire (*N. antarctica*) below. They include a sector of Valdivian Forest at Puerto Blest, near the Chilean border, with high precipitation and particular species of cypress (*Pilgerodendron uviferum*), the redwood-like alerce (*Fitzroya cupressoides*), the proteaceous fuinque (*Lomatia ferruginea*), and two endemic podocarps – mañío macho (*Podocarpus nubigenus*) and mañío hembra (*Saxegothaea conspicua*). The south Andean otter or *hullin* (*Lutra provocax*) and the colonial tuco-tuco (a small rodent, *Ctenomys sociabilis*) are specific to this part of the park. as well as endemic species such as the Chall-huaco frog (*Atelognathus nitoi*). The eastern reaches of the park are a transition ecotone with the open, drier woods of cordillera cypress (*Austrocedrus chilensis*), such as those seen growing on the rocky slopes of the Valle Encantado. The Patagonian steppe further east, in the rain shadow of the Andes, is a semi-arid landscape of mesas, rolling hills and canyons covered by dry, yellowing grasses. Found here are puma, fox and guanaco and several birds of prey such as the black-chested buzzard-eagle (*Geranoaetus melanoleucus*) and the American kestrel (*Falco sparverius*).

One of the most popular day excursions in the area is to drive the **Ruta de los Siete Lagos** (Ruta 234) between Villa La Angostura and San Martín de los Andes. You will indeed pass seven lakes and also see several types of forest that offer spectacular scenery, especially in autumn. The first attraction is a detour to the **Inacayal Waterfall** and the **Belvedere Hill** viewpoints. Less than 1km west of town you will reach the Plazoleta de las Colectividades; turn right, continue to the last junction and turn left. This will lead you to the aptly named Cerro Belvedere (1,992m), a panoramic viewpoint over lakes Correntoso and Nahuel Huapi. It stands between two other peaks: Inacayal Hill (1,840m), which from your perspective will be to the right of Belvedere Hill, and Falso Belvedere (1,685m), which will be to the left. Between Falso Belvedere and Belvedere is **Cajón Negro**. Returning, a trail leads from the first hairpin bend for an hour towards the base of Inacayal Hill and the viewpoint over the Inacayal Waterfall.

Back on Ruta 234 you will pass the seven lovely lakes to arrive on the shore of Lago Lacar in San Martín de los Andes. You will have passed the junction with Ruta 231 that heads into Chile; about 300m along this road is a viewpoint over Lago Espejo. It's several kilometres further to the Argentine customs post, beyond which, about 100m before the Patojo stream, a trail leads to the 60m-high Santa Ana Waterfall. There's also a mirador offering views of the spectacular volcanic plug of Cerro Patojo. Unless continuing to Chile, you must indicate your interest in viewing the waterfall at the customs post where they will arrange for a National Park guide to escort you to the falls.

You can do this tour of the Seven Lakes by bicycle in several days, camping at various beaches and forests along the way.

Valle Encantado (enchanted valley) is at **Confluencia**, the meeting point of the Traful and Limay rivers, where the landscape of eroding rock formations morphs into strange hoodoo-like formations. The rivers reflect the conifers that fill the valley and appear to be wading knee-deep into the lake at the **Bosque Sumergido** (submerged forest). Erosion by the river has formed a natural amphitheatre at Rincón Grande (a ring of steep escarpments).

Villa Traful is located along Ruta Provincial 65 between Confluencia and Villa La Angostura. Here you can visit the picturesque area around Lago Traful (known for salmon fishing), with wooden houses surrounded by gardens, and hikes beyond through less pruned forests into the mountains to find views of waterfalls and lakes and great spots for camping.

Nahuel Huapi National Park
Park offices are in Bariloche on San Martín 24 (✆ *423 121* or *423 111; e pnhuapi@bariloche.com.ar or pnint@bariloche.com.ar*). There is a park admission of 12 pesos.

Río Negro Province
Escapes into nature lure visitors to this province in the Andean Lakes District, mainly identified with trout fishing on Lago Nahuel Huapi, skiing, summer hiking, horseriding and mountain climbing and every imaginable watersport.

BARILOCHE
Area code 02944
This alpine-style town cuddles up against the shores of Lago Nahuel Huapi and stares across at the wilderness of Nahuel Huapi National Park, the first national park in all of South America. San Carlos de Bariloche was founded in 1902, and

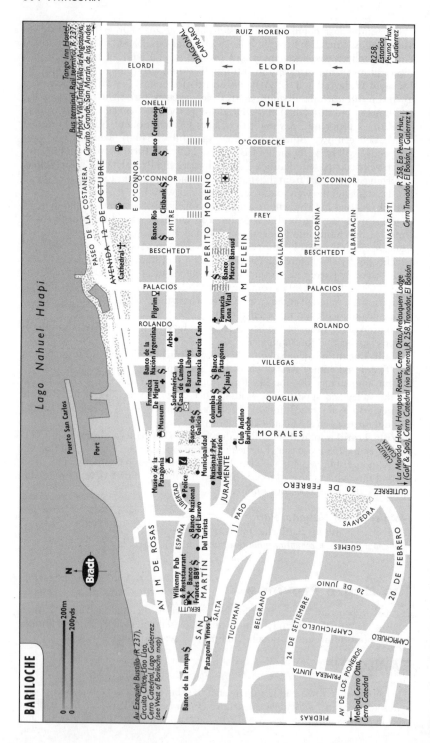

BARILOCHE

0 _____ 200m
0 _____ 200yds

Lago Nahuel Huapi

Puerto San Carlos

Port

N

Bradt

Av Ezequiel Bustillo (R237),
Circuito Chico, Llao Llao,
Cerro Catedral, Lago Gutierrez
(see West of Bariloche map)

Banco de la Pampa $

Patagonia Vinos $

Tango Inn Hostel;
Bus terminal, Rail terminal, R 237;
Airport, Villa Traful, Villa la Angostura;
Circuito Grande, San Martin de los Andes

RUIZ MORENO

ELORDI   ELORDI

ONELLI   ONELLI

Banco Credicoop $

O'GOEDECKE

Banco Rio $ J O'CONNOR

Citibank $

B MITRE

BESCHTEDT

Banco Macro Bansud $

PALACIOS   PALACIOS

Pilgrim

ROLANDO   ROLANDO

Arbol

Farmacia
Zona Vital

Banco de la
Nación Argentina $

Farmacia
De Miguel $

Sudamérica
Casa de Cambio $

Barca Libros

Farmacia Garcia Cano

Banco
Patagonia $ VILLEGAS

Jauja

Museum

Banco de
Galicia $

QUAGLIA

Columbia $
Cambio

Museo de la
Patagonia

Police

Municipalidad

National Park
Administration

Club Andino
Bariloche

MORALES

JURAMENTE

Wilkenny Pub
& Restaurant

Banco
Francis BBV $

Banco Nazional
Del Turista $

BERUTTI

20 DE FEBRERO

GUTIERREZ

CIRUZU
GALTA

La Morada Hotel, Harapos Reales, Cerro Otto, Arelauquen Lodge
(Golf & Spa), Cerro Catedral (via Pioneros), R 258, Tronador, El Bolsón

SAAVEDRA

GÜEMES

20 DE FEBRERO

20 DE FEBRERO

DIAGONAL CAPRARO

AVENIDA 12 DE OCTUBRE

PASEO DE LA COSTANERA

Cathedral

E O'CONNOR

PERITO MORENO

FREY

A M ELFLEIN

A GALLARDO

BESCHTEDT

TISCORNIA

ALBARRACIN

ANASAGASTI

R258,
Estancia
Peuma Hue,
L Gutierrez

R 258, Ea Peuma Hue,
Cerro Tronador, El Bolsón, L Gutierrez

AV JM DE ROSAS

ESPAÑA

SAN MARTIN

SALTA

TUCUMAN

BELGRANO

JJ PASO

LIBERTAD

CAMPICHUELO

24 DE SETIEMBRE

20 DE JUNIO

PRIMERA JUNTA

AV DE LOS PIONEROS

PIEDRAS

Meilpal, Cerro Otto,
Cerro Catedral

most of the first settlers were Swiss, German or northern Italian, explaining the Swiss-style chalets, fondue restaurants and chocolate shops that characterise this town and leave you guessing as to whether you are in the Alps or the Andes.

Getting there
By air
Bariloche's airport (↘ 426162) is 14km east of town. Unlike most cities in Argentina, Bariloche has direct domestic flights to many cities other than Buenos Aires.

Aerolíneas Argentinas (*Mitre 185;* ↘ *422144, 423091*) flies from Buenos Aires daily except Tuesday, with other flights from Córdoba, Esquel and El Calafate. LADE (*Villegas 480;* ↘ *423562;* e *bariloche@lade.com.ar*) flies from Buenos Aires to Bariloche daily, also calling at Mar de Plata, Chapelco, El Calafate and Río Gallegos. LAN Argentina (*Mitre 534;* ↘ *477755, 0810 999 9526*) also flies from Buenos Aires twice daily, and its parent company LAN flies to Bariloche from Santiago de Chile via Puerto Montt every Sunday year-round. Between December and February they put on additional flights (usually Mon, Thu and Fri). Coming from Chile, it's also possible to fly to Osorno and then take a bus the rest of the way to Bariloche.

From the airport there are shuttle buses (3 pesos) with Via Bariloche to the centre or public bus 72 that runs from the parking lot to downtown (1.50 pesos). Taxis and *remises* are at the front entrance to the terminal and charge about 15 pesos to take you downtown. Car rental is also available at the airport with Annie Millet-Hertz (↘ 430994) or Avis (↘ 431649; e *info@avisbariloche.com.ar*). Both have offices downtown, Avis at San Martín 162 (↘ 431648) and Hertz at Quaglia 352 (↘f 423457 or 15 581186; e *hertz@bariloche.com.ar*).

By bus
The main bus terminal and railway station are 3km east of the civic centre on Avenida 12 de Octubre. Via Bariloche/Turismo Algarrobal is the main regional operator, as well as offering local connections (↘ 427698). Of the major long-distance operators, Mar y Valle run services to Esquel, Trelew and Puerto Madryn; Don Otto/Transportadora Patagónica go via Esquel and Trelew to Río Gallegos; TUS serves Córdoba; Chevallier (↘ 423090), El Valle (↘ 0800 333 7575), TAC (↘ 434727) and TAM all serve Buenos Aires, and Andesmar serves Buenos Aires, La Plata, Mendoza, Neuquén, Esquel, Comodoro Rivadavia, and also Osorno, Valdivia and Puerto Montt in Chile, also reached by Bus Norte and TasChoapa. City buses connect the terminal to the centre, Villa Catedral and along Ruta 237.

By car
The town of Bariloche, surrounded by the Nahuel Huapi National Park, can be reached from the north, south or west: from Neuquén take Ruta 237; from Confluencia or El Bolsón Ruta 237; from Villa La Angostura Ruta 231. From San Martín de los Andes to the north, Bariloche can be reached either by routes 234 and 231 (known as the Seven Lakes Route – *Ruta de los Siete Lagos*) or by Ruta 63. There are two international crossings to Chile, one by Ruta 231 over the Paso Cardenal Samoré, the other using ground and lake transport on the *Ruta de los Siete Lagos*.

Orientation
The reference point is the civic centre, raised above the lake. The commercial area is to the east towards the lake mainly along Avenida Bartolomé Mitre. Following the lakeshore east on Avenida 12 de Octubre will take you past the cathedral to the

THE CRUCE DE LAGOS

The Lakes Crossing from Puerto Montt (Chile) to Bariloche is one of the most prestigious excursions in the Lakes District. Operating year-round except on Sunday (when the border is closed), a bus takes passengers from Puerto Montt, Puerto Varas and Ensenada to Petrohué, from where a luxury catamaran leaves at 11.00 for Peulla, about two hours away at the far end of Lago Todos Los Santos. From here a bus covers the 29km across the border to Puerto Frías, from where another boat goes to Puerto Alegre at the north end of Lago Frías. There's another bus for 3km to Puerto Blest, on Lago Nahuel Huapi, from where another boat goes to Puerto Pañuelo, for the final bus ride to Bariloche. The whole trip takes 12 hours and costs a staggering US$195; Chileans can pay US$65 less, but probably in the low season only. The alternative is to take the bus via Osorno, an easy six-hour trip on paved roads throughout that costs just US$8 – however, the scenery of the lakes justifies the cost of the Cruce de Lagos for many people. It is possible to stay overnight in Peulla, either continuing to Bariloche or returning westwards the next day. Fishing or hiking excursions at Peulla can also be booked.

It is possible to cut the cost by taking the public bus to Petrohué and paying on the boat (credit cards accepted) for the crossing of the lake. You can also pay for the remaining legs, although it's possible to hike or cycle between the legs (bikes are carried on the ferry at half the cost of an adult); from Puerto Pañuelo bus 20 will take you to Bariloche. You may also wish to bring sandwiches, as Peulla has only basic but pricey restaurants (lunch is not included in the fare). There are also various packages for day trips or overnight stays at Peulla, with horseriding, hiking and fishing available.

bus and railway stations and onwards to the airport. Heading west will take you through a suburban area and the beginning of the Circuito Chico tourist route.

Where to stay

The range of places to stay in Bariloche and throughout the surrounding areas of mountain and lakeside resorts is seemingly endless. They range from cosy inns to luxury hotels to rustic camping.

Hotels

Arelauquen Lodge Golf & Spa Ruta Provincial 82, Lago Gutiérrez; ✎ 467638, 467626; e reservas@arelauquenlodge.com; www.arelauquen.com. This is Bariloche's leading golf and country club, with an 18-hole golf course, polo fields and a natural reserve in its 700ha. It is on the lakefront, allowing various watersports. The accommodation is luxury class, with rates starting at US$123/173 plus 21% VAT.

Llao Llao Hotel & Resort Golf-Spa Av Ezequiel Bustillo km25; ✎ 448530, 445781; e llaollao@datamarkets.com.ar; www.llaollao.com. Built in 1940, this lovely cypress and green-stone building is one of Bariloche's treasures. It was revamped in order to host the 1995 Summit of the Americas (inc Fidel Castro of Cuba). This world-class hotel offers every convenience and local speciality or activity. Rates start at US$175/230 plus 21% VAT.

La Cascada Hotel Av Ezequiel Bustillo km6; ✎ 441088, 441046, 441023; e lacascada@infovia.com.ar. The rooms offer views of the lake and parkland as well as the nearby waterfall. There is a fine restaurant, a cafeteria, bar, solarium, swimming pool, sauna and gym. A standard dbl starts at approximately 335 pesos.

Hosterías

Pirámides Andinas Cureu, off Av Quilpo at km12.2 on Av Bustillo; ↘ 461018;
e piramidesandinas@hotmail.com; www.piramidesandinas.com. This beautiful guesthouse,
located 12km from the town centre with easy beach access, is a stunning glass and stone
pyramid built around a central tree. In addition to bedrooms in the main building, guests
can also stay in their own private pyramid cabin. The pyramids are surrounded by herb
gardens and ponds and have parillas and indoor and outdoor Jacuzzis. This facility is
ecologically friendly, using only biodegradable shampoos, soaps and detergents. Rates for 2
people are 170–200 pesos in the main pyramid, or 250–350 pesos for a cabin.
Nido del Condor Resort and Spa Av Bustillo km6.9; ↘ 442221; f 442292, or in Buenos
Aires ↘ 011 4315 2207, 4315 2210; e reservas@nidodelcondor.com.ar;
www.nidodelcondor.com.ar. A luxury resort and spa with cottage accommodation close to
the beaches and Cerro Catedral. There is a café and restaurant and a spa with a heated pool,
sauna and jacuzzi facing Lago Nahuel Huapi. Rates start at US$110 for a junior suite.
Villa Huinid Av Bustillo km2.6; ✓f 523523, 523524; www.villahuinid.com.ar. This hotel
seems like a little village on its own, situated within 17,000m² of forest and gardens. Rates
start at 120 pesos but double in high season.
Meli Hué B&B Km24.7 Circuito Chico (Ruta 237); ↘ 448 029; e meli-
hue@bariloche.com.ar. Rates start at 160 pesos for 2 people in low season. Call a week in
advance for rates and availability in high season. No children. Sip fresh lavender tea while
enjoying the best panoramic lake views.

Estancias

Estancia Peuma Hue Nahuel Huapi National Park, 25km south on Ruta 258; ↘ 15
501030, 15 504856, in Buenos Aires ↘ 011 15 5101 1392; e info@peuma-hue.com;
www.peuma-hue.com. On the south shore of Lago Gutiérrez and at the foot of Catedral
Sur, this 200ha estancia is a true Argentine paradise getaway. Just 27 guests can stay in the
luxury houses or log cabins surrounded by wilderness. Peuma Hue means 'place of dreams'
in Mapudungun. There is a garden, orchard and stables and tours can be arranged for
rafting, kayaking, trekking, paragliding, etc. They quote an all-inclusive rate in US dollars
that can be paid in pesos at the current exchange rate; US$165 plus 21% VAT per day
provides a dbl suite with lake view, airport transfer, four meals plus wine and activities on
the property (horseriding, trekking, use of dinghy on lake).

Hostels

Alaska Hostel Lilinquen 328; ↘ 461564; e info@alaska-hostel.com. Dorm beds 11–14
pesos, dbls 22–28 pesos, dbls in cabins 30–40 pesos, cabins shared by 6 80–110 pesos; rates
vary according to season (cheapest Mar–Jun, most expensive Jul–Aug). They've recently
added a downtown branch called **Periko's** at Morales 555; ↘ 522326; e info@perikos.com.
Tango Inn Hostel Av 12 de Octubre 1915; ↘ 430707; e info@tangoinn.com.ar,
www.tangoinn.com.ar. Close to the bus terminal, and quite a party place. Dorm beds cost 18
pesos, and sgls/dbls with private bath 54/63 pesos, with b/fast, kitchen and 24-hour internet.
La Morada Cerro Otto km5; ↘ 442349, 441711; e lamorada@bariloche.com.ar;
www.lamoradahostel.com. Claiming to be the 'highest hostel on the mountain', they are
not Hostelling International, but they do have great views. There is a winding road up the
mountain leaving Av Pioneros at km4.7, or you can take a footpath straight up. They offer
to pick up guests, however, if you phone ahead.

Mountain refuges

A rustic and traditionally European approach to staying in the mountains would be
to sleep in a backcountry refuge. These are under the management of the Club
Andino Bariloche; offices in Bariloche are at Calle 20 de Febrero 30 (↘ 424531,

www.clubandino.org; open Jan–Feb, Mon–Sat 8.30–14.00, 17.00–20.30, Sun 8.30–12.00, 18.00–20.00). The refuges are modest facilities but set in beautiful locations. Costs are always minimal but the less self-sufficient you are, the more you will have to pay for, ie: bedding, soap, food, etc.

Refugio Berghoff Cerro Otto; **e** casadeotto@bariloche.com.ar. Hot showers, restaurant.

Refugio Emilio Frey Cerro Catedral; **e** reffret@bariloche.com.ar. Hot water. Bar and restaurant. *Open year-round.*

Refugio 'Jakob' General San Martín Laguna Jakob, 16km into the backcountry behind Cerro Catedral **e** fidanis@bariloche.com.ar. Bar and restaurant. *Open mid-Dec to mid-Apr.*

Refugio López Cerro López; **e** info@bariloche.com.ar. Hot water. Bar and restaurant. *Open mid-Dec to mid-Apr.*

Refugio Italian Manfredo Segre Laguna Negra; **e** lagunanegra@ciudad.com.ar; www.geocities.com/lagunanegra. Hot water. Bar and restaurant. *Open mid-Dec to mid-Apr.*

Refugio J J Neumeyer Valle del Chall-Huaco; **Vf** 428995; **e** diversidad@speedy.com.ar, refneu@bariloche.com.ar. Hot water. Dormitories. Bar and restaurant. *Open year-round.*

Refugio Otto Meiling Cerro Tronador; **e** bestianelli@yahoo.com. Hot showers. *Open mid-Dec to mid-Apr.*

Refugio Reynaldo Knapp Cerro Catedral; **e** beamud@bariloche.com.ar, hosteria@hosteria-knapp.com.ar. Restaurant. *Open year-round.*

Where to eat and drink
Restaurants
Fondue and raclette, trout, venison and boar, home-brewed beer, smoked meats and cheeses, *bagna cauda* and Patagonian lamb are the specialities of this town whose cuisine is flavoured by French, German and Italian cultures.

Los Césares and **Café Restaurant Patagonia** Both located at the fantastic Llao Llao Hotel. Los Césares is a formal evening restaurant while the café is more informal and cosy and is also open during the day for tea.

Bucanero Palacios 187; **** 423674. Perhaps the best of the pizza places on this street.

Jauja Quaglia 366; **** 422952; **e** jauja@bariloche.com.ar. Extensive regional menu, with numerous choices of salads, boar and venison, seafood and fish, but to make things a bit easier for you, the lake trout in a cream and wild mushroom sauce is exquisite.

Cerveceria Blest, Bar and Restaurant Av Bustillo km11.6; **** 461026. The extensive menu offers something for everyone and the microbrews are excellent. There is also a speciality shop selling local products.

El Boliche de Alberto Villegas 347; **** 431433. Probably the best steak in town.

El Boliche de Alberto Pastas Elflein 163; **** 431084. A great option for vegetarians.

Luna de Oriente Av de los Pioneros km 3.9 y Boock; **** 442 574; **e** info@lunadeoriente.com. New (2007) Middle Eastern restaurant owned by an Armenian-Italian-Argentine-Greek couple. Patagonian lamb done Greek style comes recommended.

Bahia Serena Av Bustillo km 12.250; **** 524 614. Enjoy fresh trout while viewing the lake from which it was caught.

Bars and pubs
The after-hours scene is ever-changing in this energetic city and it is good to ask the locals where the latest popular bars are.

Patagonia Vinos Quaglia 146; **** 425372; **e** info@patagoniavinos.com.ar; www.patagoniavinos.com.ar. A nice wine selection with wine-tasting sessions available.

Wilkeny Pub and Restaurant Av San Martín 435; **** 42444. An Irish-style pub with live music twice a week.

Pilgrim Palacios 167; **** 421686. An Irish pub good for pizza and beer.

Practicalities

The **tourist office** is located in the civic centre, between Avenidas Libertad and B Mitre (℡ *423022;* f *426784;* e *secturism@bariloche.com.ar; open Mon–Fri 09.00–21.00*). One of the original buildings of the city, this long and lovely alpine-inspired building of stone and wood was designed by architect Ezequiel Bustillo who also built the Llao Llao Hotel. It houses the tourist office, the **post office**, the **police station** (℡ *422772*) and the **Museo de la Patagonia** (geology and wildlife, indigenous artefacts). In the plaza in front there is often a token St Bernard adding to the alpine ambiance … and looking somewhat in need of rescue himself as he lies panting in the Argentine summer sunshine.

There are both public and private hospitals in Bariloche. The public one, free of charge but not highly recommended, is **Hospital Zonal 'Dr Ramon Carrillo'** (*Perito Moreno 601;* ℡ *426100*). The private hospitals (not free) are **Hospital Privado Regional** (*20 de Febrero 594;* ℡ *423074*) and **Sanatorio San Carlos** (*Av Bustillo km1;* ℡ *429000*). Pharmacies in the centre include **Farmacía Zona Vital** (*Moreno and Rolando;* ℡ *420752*), **Farmacía Garcia Cano** (*Moreno 102;* ℡ *420859*) and **Farmacía De Miguel** (*Mitre 130;* ℡ *423025*).

Banks and exchange offices

Banco de Galicia Moreno 77; ℡ 427126, 427127
Banco Credicoop Mitre 762; ℡ 426205, 426388
Banca Nazionale del Lavoro San Martín 192; ℡ 423726, 429801
Banco de la Nación Argentina Mitre 178; ℡ 445923, 445922
Banco de la Pampa San Martín 662; ℡ 430912, 430913
Banco Francés BBV San Martín 336; ℡ 430325, 430326
Banco Róo Mitre 520; ℡ 423591, 422789
Banco Patagonia Moreno 127; ℡ 422600, 422829
Banco Macro Bansud Mitre 433; ℡ 421054, 423675
Citibank Mitre 694; ℡ 436301
Columbia Cambio Moreno 105; ℡ 425178, 425265
Sudamérica Casa de Cambio Mitre 63; ℡ 434555, 423270

Shopping

Arbol, on the main street, Mitre, between Villegas and Rolando and next to the Del Turista chocolate shop, has beautiful ceramics, leather and knitwear.

Barca Libros, on Quaglia, between Mitre and Moreno, has a good selection of books, including some in English and good natural history and regional sections.

Origin (*Av Bustillo, km3,850;* ℡/f *442640;* e *origin@bariloche.com.ar; open daily 09.00–21.00*) is an attractive shop with plenty of local wares, art and crafts from Patagonia and other parts of Argentina.

Harapos Reales at the Hotel Cerro Catedral (*Villa Cerro Catedral;* e *info@haraposreales.com.ar* or *haraposreales@fibertel.com.ar; open only in Jul and Aug*), makes and sells beautiful handmade one-off garments and art made from 100% natural and locally produced textiles, including silk, cotton, wool, fur and leather. See the Buenos Aires chapter for their main store and page 121 for their advert.

Near the civic centre there is a daily (except Wed) outdoor market where vendors sell leatherwork, ceramics, wood carvings, jewellery and woollen items.

Local specialities/Special events

CHOCOLATE! This tradition started with the Italian families that first immigrated here but the style and flavours of today are distinctly Argentine. There are several large chocolatiers on Avenida Mitre, between Quaglia and Palacios. The biggest is **Del Turista**, which could almost be considered a department store with areas of fresh pastries, a café, packaged goods and enormous gift boxes of various types of chocolates. It has an almost Disney feel to it but is not necessarily the best quality in town. Amazingly the clientele also supports a second location a few blocks away at San Martín 252. **Mamushka,** recognisable by the giant Ukrainian dolls, and **Rapa Nui** are both located on Avenida Mitre, the latter a personal favourite – try the layered chocolate and *dulce de leche* bombóm.

Sweets, fruit preserves, jams and smoked meats and cheeses have European origins but have adopted local ingredients such as *membrillo* fruit, *dulce de leche*, deer, boar and trout, and became regional specialties.

Bariloche is a haven for artists and artisans and you will find many shops selling locally made ceramics, sweaters and knitted items, and both traditional and modern jewellery and handicrafts. For example, **Belém** at km3.6 on Avenida Bustillo is a ceramic factory where you can watch craftsmen at work.

Ski races, parades and a torchlit evening ski descent are just a few of the events on the agenda for the five-day **Fiesta Nacional de la Nieve** (National Snow Festival), held in August to announce the official opening of the ski season.

Day trips and excursions

A cable-car ride up the ridge of **Cerro Otto** (entrance off Av Los Pioneros at km1, signposted to Piedras Blancas and Refugio Berghoff) for views of the town, lake and park is a relaxing approach to mountain climbing (25 pesos adults, 15 pesos kids). You can take the cable-car back down, or if you have a bit of energy to burn you may choose to descend through the forest hikes along the far side of the ridge to Golf Villa Arelauquen and Lago Gutiérrez. The cable-car takes mountain bikes, and in winter Cerro Otto is popular for cross-country skiing.

For a half-day scenic tour of the area, the **Circuito Chico** takes you through the lovely forests skirting Lake Nahuel Huapi along the **Llao Llao Peninsula**. Setting out along Avenida Bustillo, you'll pass the residential neighbourhood of Helipal, reclining on the slope of Cerro Otto, at km4, and Playa Bonita, meaning 'pretty beach', at km8. Continuing towards Llao Llao, pass the intersection to Cerro Catedral and Villa los Coihues on Lago Gutiérrez. At km17.5 you can take the chairlift to the top of **Cerro Campanario** and enjoy the view. There is a snack bar for refreshments at the top. Past Cerro Campanario is a loop around Lago Moreno Oeste, past Llao Llao and a panoramic view of the west shore of the lake looking towards Chile. City buses travel this route.

Villa Cerro Catedral (17km southwest of Bariloche) is a large ski resort, one of the most important in the country. **Cerro Catedral** ski centre (❧ 423776; e *info@catedralaltapatagonia.com or in Buenos Aires (011) 4780 3300 or 4896 0505;* e *infobue@catedralaltapatagonia.com*) can be visited year-round either to ski or take the various lifts up for the views and hiking. The cable-car and chairlifts take you from 1,050m to 2,010m. There are three main points that you can take lifts to: Punta Princesa, Piedra del Condór and Refugio Lynch. There are three chairlifts to Punta Princesa and Piedra del Condór, Tuesday to Friday 10.00–17.45 (last descent at 18.30), 24 pesos adults/16 pesos minors and seniors. The best view of Monte Tronador can be had from Refugio Lynch, reached by a cablecar and chairlifts, daily 10.00–18.30 (last descent at 19.00), 30 pesos adults/20 pesos minors and seniors. You can also hike from Refugio Lynch to Piedra del Condór (easy), to the Mirador del Rucaco (medium difficulty) or to the base of Cerro Catedral (difficult). Other activities can be enjoyed such as rock climbing, abseiling and mountain biking. There are many restaurants, hotels and lodges in the village. The ski season is from mid-June to September (high season is July); day passes for adult

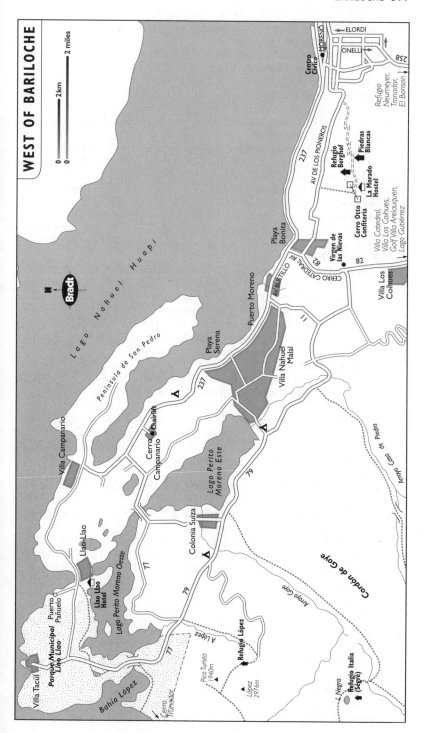

skiers are 55–95 pesos (low to high season), or 300–523 pesos for a week. Full details at www.catedralaltapatagonia.com.

Villa Mascardi is a small tourist resort on Lago Mascardi on Ruta 258 south to El Bolsón. **Monte Tronador** is the highest peak in the park at 3,478m; the base of the mountain can be reached by boat on Lago Mascardi or by car along a winding scenic drive. A couple of kilometres past Villa Mascardi at the south end of Lago Mascardi you should turn onto a dirt road that eventually divides: the left fork leads to the 20m-high Cascada de los Alerces. You drive through many kilometres of fire-burned forest, but the falls at the end are beautiful. Head right at the fork in the road to go to Tronador, 40km away along an extremely bad road, but it's worth it to see the hanging glaciers. Ice shears off the glaciers and you can hear avalanches in the distance. This section is a one-way road; you must go up by 14.00, when the traffic direction reverses for vehicles to begin descending. At Tronador there is a snack shop, restaurant, *parrilla* and a couple of hotels.

Bahía López is a windy bay at the base of Cerro López with piles of driftwood along the side of the lake. Although the wood is beautiful, collection is prohibited within the national park. There is a path up the mountain to the refuge and a rugged path to the summit.

Puerto Blest is at the far end of Lago Nahuel Huapi en route to Chile. You can take a ferry from Bariloche (*book at Palacios 263*) at 06.45 to Puerto Blest (arrive 09.00), Monday to Saturday October to mid-April; the rest of the year the departure is only Monday to Friday from Bariloche at 09.00 arriving at Puerto Blest at 11.30. From Puerto Blest departure is at 19.00 arriving in Bariloche at 21.00, Monday to Saturday October to mid-April; the rest of the year departure from Puerto Blest is at 16.30 arriving in Bariloche by 18.30.

The **Circuito Grande** is a full-day (240km) excursion east from Bariloche then north through the **Valle Encantado** to **Villa Traful**, a small town famous for salmon fishing on the lovely **Lago Traful** that is also popular for hiking and horseriding. It's a delightfully scenic drive.

A day trip to **Villa La Angostura** from Bariloche requires an early start to have time to see the town and take a trip to Los Arrayanes National Park. Via Bariloche (✆ 427698) buses depart from 08.00, with the last bus returning at 19.30. Albus (✆ 423552) runs at 07.30 and 11.15, with their last bus returning at 20.00. The cost with either company is 8 pesos one way.

Parque Cerro Leones and the **Cavernas del Viejo Volcán** are 15km from Bariloche on Ruta 237 and then another 1km on Ruta 23 (✆ 468200, 539909; e *cerroleones@bariloche.com.ar*). Take a guided tour and learn about the history, culture, geography, zoology, botany and geology of the zone. You can enter a cave that is 130m long and 30m wide and one of the most important in this zone. Inside you will see underground springs that feed a small subterranean lake. From the summit there's a stunning panoramic view. Allow yourself a couple of hours for this visit.

Fishing on Lago Nahuel Huapi and at the mouths of the Limay and Machete rivers and the Millaqueo, Vinagre, Coluco, Colorado and Castilla streams is a fisherman's dream. The lakes of Fonch, Hess, Los Moscos and Mascardi around Cerro Tronador and the Río Manso are ideal for fly-fishing for brown, rainbow and brook trout. The Río Limay is best for brown and rainbow trout, while the Pichi Leufu offers easy wading for beginners and has large brown trout. The Río Traful is good for landlocked salmon. Fishing licences are available for one day (30 pesos), one week (150 pesos) or for the full season, which is seven months, November to May (200 pesos). Note that the licence fee stated here is the tourist/foreigner rate; residents pay less. For more information ✆ 436210; e *pescaenrionegro@infovia.com.ar*, *permisosdepesca@infovia.com.ar*.

Fly-fishing tours can be arranged through Asoc. Guias Profesionales de Pesca de Parques Nacionales, contact Arturo Dominguez, Director of the Mel Krieger Foundation (*f: 441613 or 15 552237; e levalley@bariloche.com.ar*). Rates start at US$250 per day for two fishers varying with chosen lodging, meals, transfers and equipment.

Lake cruises are available for half-day or full-day trips, from Bariloche or Puerto Pañuelo. One option travels past Isla Centinela, where Francisco 'Perito' Moreno is buried, and onwards up the Blest arm of Lago Nahuel Huapi all the way to Bahía Blest. Another possibility is to sail to Península Quetrihué to visit the arrayán forest in Los Arrayanes National Park. The trip may continue to Puerto Anchorena on Isla Victoria. A full-day trip from Villa Mascardi takes you up the Tronador arm of Lago Mascardi, continuing on land through the Valle de los Vuriloches all the way to Pampa Linda and the Ventisquero Negro Glacier. A few kilometres further on you arrive at the foot of Monte Tronador. You can also have a day (or half-day) on a yacht with Aquanauta Charters (✆ 491088; e gustavosantamaria@hotmail.com), with scuba diving an option as well.

Rafting on the Manso River

Adrenaline-pumping or leisurely trips are both possible, on separate or combined tours! The river has three distinct sections: Inferior, Medio and Superior. The Manso rises on the slopes of Cerro Tronador and flows into the Mascardi, Los Moscos, Hess and Steffen lakes. The Manso Medio (Middle Manso) stretches from Lago Steffen to the Vellegas sawmill and is a Class III river. A significant part of the trip is a gentle float down the river with the time to take in the stunning scenery of transition forest (from Andean to the lush Valdivian) and even take a swim, but it eventually passes into canyons with some rapids that will give a few thrills. The Manso Inferior (Lower Manso) passes the Los Alerces Waterfall, among others, and eventually passes into Chile, joining with the Río Puelo and emptying into Lago Tagua Tagua and eventually into the Golfo de Ancud and the Pacific Ocean.

It is great fun to go rafting on the Manso River. Trips organised by many agencies in Bariloche take beginners on day trips. More experienced rafters can take the trip to the Chilean border along rapids and through narrow canyons.

EL BOLSÓN

Area code 02944

El Bolsón was a hippy town in the '60s, declaring itself a Nuclear-Free city; this style and attitude still prevails with the residents. Besides hippies there are also, reputedly, witches and, absolutely, there are elves. If you walk in the main plaza you might hear their mischievous laughter coming from the trees. In the summer months the small manmade pond in the plaza has paddle boats to rent.

El Bolsón sits in a narrow valley whose microclimate promotes crops of beer hops and berries. You can drive around the surrounding countryside and find local producers selling their organic products; alternatively, you can find many of the jams and jellies in town as well as visit the pubs selling microbrews.

Getting there
By air

Although there is a small airport here, Bariloche has a much better service and is only 130km away.

LADE (*Roca 446, casa 1;* ✆ *492206*) has flights to El Bolsón from Buenos Aires, Bariloche and Chapelco on Thursday, and from Esquel on Tuesday.

By bus

Buses connect from Bariloche in the north or Esquel in the south. AndesMar
(\ *430211*) comes from Bariloche once daily; Don Otto/Transportadora
Patagónica and Mar y Valle run from Trelew to Bariloche via El Bolsón.

By car

Ruta 258 links Bariloche and Esquel and passes through El Bolsón.

Orientation

Penned in by the Río Quemquemtreu on one side and Cerro Piltriquitrón on the
other, the layout of the town is uncomplicated; the motorway becomes the main
street of town, Avenida San Martín, and will lead you directly to the main Plaza
Pagano and the tourist office.

Where to stay

Morada del Sol Hostería and Spa North of town along Ruta 258 and heading west
towards Costa del Río Azul; \ 493201; e moradadelsol@elbolson.com;

LAND, LAND EVERYWHERE BUT NOT A SPOT TO OWN...

It is a twist on the words of Samuel Taylor Coleridge's *Rime of the Ancient
Mariner*, but the analogy is apt. To travel through Patagonia and feel
overwhelmingly alone is natural; to feel as though you are surrounded by
limitless land and wilderness seems obvious. Yet there is seemingly not
enough land here to house the few thousand Mapuche people who have
been displaced from their ancestral homeland. Patagonia encompasses an
area of over 770,000km^2 yet an estimated 90% is privately owned. This
came to international attention in 2002 when the well-known clothing
company Benetton came under fire. Luciano Benetton, the Italian textile
magnate, owns 900,000ha of land in Patagonia, producing wool and leather
for export and production overseas. Eight Mapuche families, discovered
'squatting' at Leleque (where they had worked loading wool and leather
onto trains), growing a vegetable garden and raising some animals, were
ordered to remove themselves from the private property – they
subsequently sued and lost. As compensation, Benetton constructed the
Leleque museum to 'narrate the history and culture of a mythical land'; there
are also plans to re-activate the railway to bring tour groups to the museum.

Adolfo Pérez Esquivel, who won the Nobel Peace Prize in 1980 for
campaigning against human rights abuses by the military regime, brought the
issue to public attention. Benetton agreed to donate some 2,500ha but the
Mapuche rejected the offer, refusing to accept as a gift what they claim has
always been theirs. In November 2005 Benetton upped the offer to 7,500ha.

In any case the problem of exporting raw materials and lack of
investment in infrastructure in Argentina remains fundamental. Recent
economic difficulties have put land prices at all-time lows and numerous
landowners have asked Conservación Patagónica to purchase their lands.
Other buyers are also looking to purchase large tracts of land in Patagonia
for oil development, mining, subdivision or for speculation. To seize any
private land, both chambers of the National Congress must pass legislation
stating that the property is of high value for the country. Passage of such
legislation is not easy and has rarely happened.

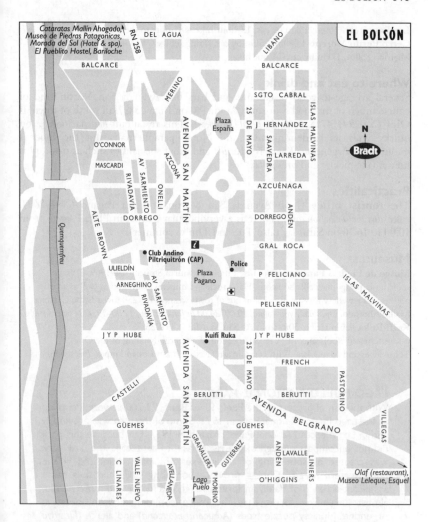

Map labels:

Cataratas Mallín Ahogado,
Museo de Piedras Patagonicas,
Morada del Sol (Hotel & spa),
El Pueblito Hostel, Bariloche

RN 258 · DEL AGUA

LIBANO

EL BOLSÓN

N

Bradt

BALCARCE · BALCARCE

SGTO CABRAL

MERINO

Plaza España

25 DE MAYO · J HERNÁNDEZ

ISLAS MALVINAS

O'CONNOR

SAAVEDRA · LARREDA

MASCARDI

AVENIDA SAN MARTÍN

AZCONA

AV SARMIENTO

RIVADAVIA

ONELLI

DORREGO

AZCUÉNAGA

ANDÉN

DORREGO

ALTE BROWN

Quenquenfreu

Club Andino Piltriquitrón (CAP)

GRAL ROCA

Police

ULIELDÍN

ARNEGHINO

AV SARMIENTO

RIVADAVIA

Plaza Pagano

P FELICIANO

ISLAS MALVINAS

PELLEGRINI

J Y P HUBE

Kuifi Ruka

J Y P HUBE

AVENIDA SAN MARTÍN

25 DE MAYO

FRENCH

PASTORINO

CASTELLI

BERUTTI

BERUTTI

AVENIDA BELGRANO

VILLEGAS

GÜEMES

AVENIDA SAN MARTÍN

GRANALLERS

GUTIERREZ

GÜEMES

ANDÉN

LAVALLE

LINIERS

Olaf (restaurant), Museo Leleque, Esquel

C LINARES

VALLE NUEVO

AVELLANEDA

P MORENO

Lago Puelo

O'HIGGINS

www.moradadelsol.com. This *hostería* is edged by rivers, forests and mountains. There is a full spa with indoor and outdoor pools and plenty of outdoor activities, such as paragliding, trekking and horseriding, to experience. Rates start at US$50 for a sgl.

El Pueblito Hostel, Barrio Luján (1km from Ruta 258); ☏ 493560;
e elpueblito@elbolson.com. A budget option with dorm beds for 12 pesos per person, dbls for 32 pesos, dbls in a cabin for 36 pesos or with a private bath 45 pesos.

Mountain refuges
These are managed by the Club Andino Piltriquitrón, Avenida Sarmiento and Roca in El Bolsón (☏ 492600).

Cerro Piltriquitrón 1,400m; 13km by car, 11-hour hike
Cerro Lindo 1,400m; 6km by car, 5-hour hike
Hielo Azul 1,500m; 8km by car, 4½-hour hike
Cajón del Azul 600m; 15km by car, 4-hour hike

Los Laguitos 1,100m; 15km by car, 12-hour hike – 8 hours to the Cajón del Azul
Cerro Perito Moreno 1,000m; 25km by car, skiing refuge
Motoco 850m, 17km by car, 7-hour hike

Where to eat and drink

Several average-to-good restaurants and bars line Avenida San Martín, and of course much of the food is organic. At km140 on Ruta 258, 7km south of town, is **Olaf** (✎ *02944 471550;* e *olaf@red42.com.ar*). This restaurant-*hostería* looks a bit quirky with its garden gnomes and Norse paraphernalia but the food is traditionally Argentine. There is a *parrilla* and other specialities such as trout, plus homemade pickles and preserves.

Practicalities

The **tourist office** is on Avenida San Martín at Plaza Pagano (✎ *492604;* e *sec_turismo@elbolson.com*). There is a very popular market in Plaza Pagano from 10.00 to 16.30 on Saturday (also Tue and Thu in summer).

Museums

Museo de Piedras Patagónicas (Museum of Patagonian Stones) ✎ 491969;
e piedrasdepatagonia@elbolson.com. Has a rock and mineral exhibition as well as artistic objects and jewellery for sale. It is 13km out of town west off RN258 towards the Cataratas Mallín Ahogado. *Open daily year-round, 10.00–20.00 in Jan and Feb, 11.00–19.00 in other months.*
Kuiñi Ruka Pablo Hube, 50m from Av San Martín; ✎ 491735;
e montefiejo@elbolson.com. A reconstruction of a typical dwelling of the Onas, Tehuelches and Mapuches. With ceramic artefacts such as vases and pipes. *Free admission.*

LAGO PUELO NATIONAL PARK

With the aim of protecting the Puelo River Basin, 23,700ha were identified as the Lago Puelo National Park in 1971. Some of the area was previously within Los Alerces National Park, created in 1937, but because this park did not encompass enough of the river basin to protect it, the new park was created as something of an annexe. The park is located in the northwestern part of Chubut province bordering Chile and thus has a significant acreage of Valdivian forest, which is a lusher and more humid, almost jungle-like, forest than the more common Andean forest in Argentina. Monkey-puzzle trees (*Araucaria araucana*) and alerce (*Fitzroya cupressoides*) are characteristic of this forest type, as well as tique (*Aexotoxicum punctatum*) and so-called hazel (*Geuvinia avellana*) and elm (*Eucryphia cordifolia*). The transition between this forest and the Andean-Patagonian forest of cypress, coihue, radal and arrayán is fascinating and ecologically important for its higher level of biodiversity and endemism. Lago Puelo itself is of course a beautiful lake within a glacial valley at 200m above sea level – a valley at this altitude is very rare in the Andes and allows for a special microclimate. There is an endemic trout, commonly called the creole trout, as well as the introduced rainbow. The abundant sweetbriar rose (*rosa mosqueta*), although lovely, is another exotic invasive species. The pudú, the huemul, red fox and puma are protected within the park, as is the ancient rock art left by the first inhabitants of this region. Most of the paintings are red geometrical symbols that some anthropologists have suggested may have signalled pathways through the forest.

Museo Leleque 80km south of El Bolsón at km1440 of Ruta 40, on the grounds of the Benetton estancia; ℩ 02945 455141. From the road, you will only see a sign for the museum. The short drive on a dirt road to the museum takes you instantly from a long highway drive onto a quiet and somehow intimate country road. The sudden increase in bird life once off the highway is impressive, as is the view of the extensive pampas. In the 4 exhibition rooms are displays and installations with artefacts, art, clothing, tools, etc from the indigenous Tehuelche people and early European pioneers. There is a replica of the *boliche* – a multi-functional room for public services such as a general store, post office, restaurant and bar. The museum is located on the site of the last skirmish by federal troops against the Tehuelche in 1888. Ironically, it is with the current estancia owners, Benetton, the Italian clothing manufacturer, that the remaining Tehuelche are struggling to maintain a right to live and work on their historic lands, winning much international attention in recent years. *Open Thu–Tue 11.00–17.00, Jan and Feb to 19.00; closed May, Jun and Sep.*

Day trips and excursions

El Hoyo, 14km south of El Bolsón on Ruta 258, is proud of its great production of tulips and lilies, as well as cherries, boysenberries and other soft fruits; commercial fields radiant with colourful spring blossoms make a drive in the countryside spectacular. A further 28km from El Hoyo brings you to **Epuyén**, where great fishing can be had on the lake of the same name. The Swiss-owned Refugio del Lago Epuyén (℩ *02945 499025;* e *sophie@elbolson.com*) is a great stopover, with rooms, cabins, camping, a pier and boats, and great food (trout from the lake, and a *flan casero* made with goat's cheese, above all).

Lago Puelo National Park and townsite are a 39km-round trip from El Bolsón on Ruta 258 plus a section of secondary road entering the park. There is a recreational area within the park with services such as camping (both organised and free sites), horse rental, hiking trails and boat excursions. Remember that the west shore of the lake is a National Reserve closed to public use; check the regulations with the park administration. Park admission is 12 pesos.

The beautifully restored **Juana de Arco** (℩ *493415, 15 602290;* e *juanadearco@ red42.com.ar; www.interpatagonia.com/juanadearco*), built in 1931, makes excursions along the lake to the Chilean border.

Santa Cruz Province

Santa Cruz is the second-largest province in Argentina but boasts the lowest population density. Sheep are the most numerous residents; they do quite well on the large estancias of dry grassland interspersed with semi-desert zones, high tablelands (*mesetas*) and sheltered valleys. The Santa Cruz section of the Andean chain invites mountaineers to ascend its famous summits and cross its numerous glaciers. Cerro Torre has a 1,500m-high face and the north face of FitzRoy is 3,441m high. The South Patagonian Ice Field is the third-largest single expanse of ice on earth (only Antarctica and Greenland surpass it in scale). The spectacular breaking of the ice bridge that forms when the Perito Moreno Glacier reaches the far shore of the lake has been occurring increasingly often. For these reasons among others, the mountains of Santa Cruz are attracting more and more tourists, causing the tiny and obscure settlements nearby to grow hugely from year to year.

EL CALAFATE
Area code 02902
This small town seemingly plonked in the middle of nowhere is the base for the many tourists visiting the famous Los Glaciares National Park. Its population grew five-fold,

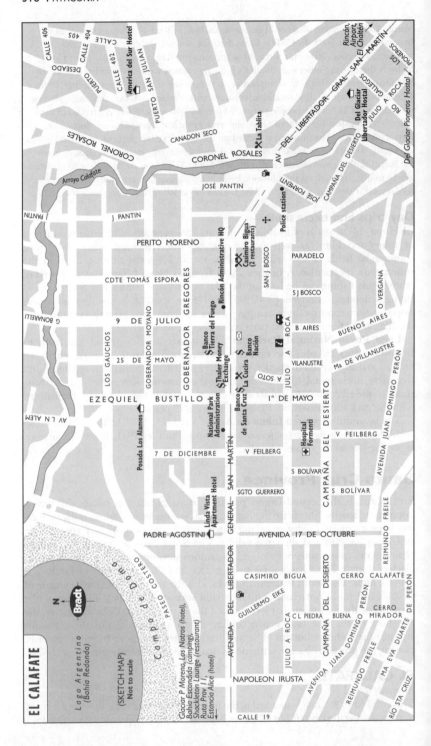

EL CALAFATE

(SKETCH MAP)
Not to scale

Lago Argentino
(Bahía Redonda)

Glaciar P Moreno, Los Notros (hotel),
Bahía Escondida (camping),
Shackleton Lounge (restaurant)
Ruta Prov 11,
Estancia Alice (hotel)

to 10,000 inhabitants, just between 2002 and 2004, owing to the new airport and the breaking of the Perito Moreno Glacier, bringing tourists in droves. Of course, it being one of the most beautifully sited cities in the province, many government officials, including the governor, have weekend homes here. Completely surrounded by private land, the town is simply becoming denser instead of spreading, giving an inappropriate sense of claustrophobia in such an empty landscape. Yet the town has a wonderful location on Lago Argentino, the largest lake in the country and the third-largest in South America with a surface area of 1,560km² (60km long and 14–20km wide) and depths of up to 1km; it is at its highest in February and freezes over in June, allowing ice-skating. The wonderful blue, green and grey shades of its waters are due to so-called 'glacier milk', fine dust, silica and minerals resulting from the abrasive action of the glaciers. The town is named after the calafate bush, whose delicious purple berries are said to promise your return to Patagonia if you eat them. Its little yellow blossoms and the bright red ones of the notro characterise the springtime woodlands. Glaciar Perito Moreno is in an evergreen region of lenga, coihue, canelo and guinda. As for fauna, it is worth mentioning the huemul and the ñandú or rhea, which runs in big groups on the tableland area.

Getting there
By air
Direct flights are available from Buenos Aires, Ushuaia, Trelew or Bariloche to El Calafate. The new El Calafate airport (*16km east of town on Ruta Provincial 11;* ☏ *491230 or 491220*) opened in 2000, allowing Boeing 737s to reach Calafate for the first time. It has good connections with major destinations in Patagonia; northern cities are reached mainly through Buenos Aires.

Aerolíneas Argentinas (*9 de Julio 57, Local 1;* ☏ *492815;* e *arventas@cotecal.com.ar; open Mon–Sat 09.30–12.30, 16.00–20.00*) flies daily from Buenos Aires with some flights also serving Trelew and Ushuaia. LADE (*Roca 1004;* ☏ *491262;* e *ladecalafate@cotecal.com.ar*) flies to El Calafate on Monday and Friday from Buenos Aires (Aeroparque) via Comodoro Rivadavia, continuing south to Río Gallegos and Ushuaia; there are flights to Esquel on Tuesday, returning on Wednesday, and to Bariloche on Monday, Tuesday and Friday. LADE's office is in the bus terminal. Remember that when flying out of this airport you will have to pay a tax of 18 pesos.

From the airport a shuttle bus to your hotel (12 pesos each way) is operated by Trans Patagonia Express (☏ *493766, 491498;* e *reservapatagonia@cotecal.com.ar*). Remise service (28 pesos one way, 50 pesos return) is provided by Cóndor (*25 de Mayo 51;* ☏ *491655;* e *remiscondor@calafate.com; www.remiscondor.calafate.com*). Rental Cars are available in town with On Rent a Car (☏ *493788*), Servi Car 4x4 (☏ *492541*) and Alquisur (☏ *02966 15 634475*). There is an ATM at the airport, but it is unreliable.

By bus
The bus terminal is at the top of Avenida Roca. There are several buses from Río Gallegos, taking three and a half hours: Interlagos (☏ *491179*) has one service on Monday, Wednesday and Friday; TAQSA (☏ *491843*) has two daily connections, with an additional service on the days that Interlagos does not run. Freddy Representaciones (☏/f *491273; also at Libertadores 1345;* ☏/f *492671;* e *freddy@cotecal.com.ar*) also has a daily connection. In the other direction, each operator has a departure at about 02.00, plus one or two afternoon services. All charge 30 pesos for a one-way ticket. Schedules change between winter and summer, and arrival times cannot be accurately determined due to the wind.

Freddy Representaciones can also book connecting tickets from Río Gallegos with long-distance operators such as Andesmar, Don Otto and El Pinguîno, to destinations such as Punta Arenas (Chile), Ushuaia, Los Antiguos, Puerto Madryn, Buenos Aires and points north; it is far cheaper, quicker and more comfortable to take this route to Bariloche rather than the so-called 'direct' service via El Chaltén and Ruta 40. This is a tourist service operated by El Chaltén Travel, costing 165 pesos to Perito Moreno or 265 pesos with a connection to Bariloche, which is worthwhile if you want to see the ancient outlined paintings of hands at the Cueva de los Manos.

TAQSA also has a daily service to Puerto Natales in Chile, as does Turismo Zaahj except on Mondays. See below for services to El Chaltén and the Glaciar Perito Moreno.

By car
Ruta Provincial 11 links El Calafate to the interminable (but slowly being brought up to a fair standard) Ruta 40; it's 316km to Río Gallegos.

Orientation
The main street running east–west through town, Avenida del Libertador, has most of the main offices, shops, restaurants, etc. Running parallel to the south is Avenida Roca where the bus terminal and the tourism office are located.

Where to stay
Hotels
Los Notros Ruta Provincial 11, facing the glacier; ☎ 499510/11; e info@losnotros.com. This luxury hotel is the only one situated on the Magellan Peninsula next to the park and in front of the Perito Moreno Glacier itself. It has decadent views of the glacier, as well as decadent accommodation and restaurant. Rates per person start at US$1,320 sgl, US$930 in a dbl, US$885 in a triple for 2 nights' accommodation with all meals. If this is beyond your budget, keep in mind that a similar view is available for 7 pesos per night at the nearby campsite!
Posada Los Alamos Gobernador Moyano and Bustillo; ☎ 491144; f 491186; e posadalosalamos@posadalosalamos.com. The hotel is fully serviced and offers practically every comfort and convenience, inc a golf course with 3 raised greens and a 9-hole putting green, plus tennis courts. Book at least a month in advance in high season; rates are US$104 sgl, US$111 dbl.
Linda Vista Apart Hotel Av Padre Agostini 71; ☎ 493598 or in Buenos Aires (011) 4963 9637; e calafate@lindavistahotel.com.ar. Comfortable and homely but fully equipped cabins that sleep 4 people for 320 pesos.
Los Dos Pinos 9 de Julio 358; ☎ 491271; e losdospinos@cotecal.com.ar. Simple but adequate rooms for 70 pesos sharing a bathroom and kitchen, or 100 pesos with private bathroom.

Hostels
Del Glaciar Pioneros Hostel Los Pioneros 251; ☎f 491243; e info@glaciar.com. The hostel has a very open and friendly atmosphere with common areas and a good little restaurant at the back. Dorm beds cost 18-22 pesos with shared or private bath, and rooms with private bath cost 46/76 pesos sgl, 55/80 pesos dbl in low season (Apr–mid-Oct)/high season (mid-Oct–Mar). Tours to local attractions organised.
Del Glaciar Libertador Hostel Av del Libertador; ☎f 491792; e info@glaciar.com. Under the same management as the nearby Glaciar Pioneros hostel, this hostel is in a new building with rooms opening onto an inner courtyard. Dorm beds cost 14/19/27 pesos, a sgl with private bath 73/93/183 pesos, a dbl with private bath 79/111/200 pesos in low season (Jun–Aug)/ mid-season (Sep–mid-Oct) and high season (Oct–Mar). Triple and quadruple rooms also available. Tours to local attractions organised.
Hostal Calafate Gobernador Moyano; ☎ 492450; e calafatehostel@cotecal.com.ar; www.hostelspatagonia.com. A large cheery log cabin with dorm beds (27 pesos, or 24 pesos

with HI card), standard rooms with bathrooms for 85 pesos sgl, 110 pesos dbl, 140 pesos triple and 160 pesos quadruple, plus superior rooms for 110 pesos, 130 pesos or 180 pesos (sgl, dbl or triple), all with b/fast included. If it's otherwise full it's not worth taking up the offer of the *refugio*, ie: the floor of the attic over the restaurant, with loud music except from after midnight to 0500. There's internet access, plus a variety of competitively priced tour packages.

América del Sur Hostel Puerto Deseado s/n; ℣f 493525; e info@americahostel.com.ar; www.americahostel.com.ar. A new hostel with panoramic views of lake and mountains (but not close to centre) with a fireplace and restaurant. Dorms 30 pesos, dbls with private bath 130 pesos.

Estancias

Rincón Av del Libertador 1080; ℺ 491965; e info@estanciarincon.com.ar, estanciarincon@cotecal.com.ar; www.estanciarincon.com.ar. There is also an office in Buenos Aires; ℺ (011) 4393 7440, 4326 5482; e estanciarincon@redesdelsur.com. Rincón offers you a chance to stay on a typical Patagonian estancia surrounded by stunning scenery on the bank of the Río Santa Cruz 60km east of El Calafate. On Ruta 40 midway between the Perito Moreno Glacier and the FitzRoy sector of the national park, it offers convenient access to all the main points of interest. At the estancia there are opportunities to explore the steppe and see guanacos, rheas, fox and abundant birdlife, petroglyphs, fossils and petrified forests. Excursions can also be arranged to go fishing, horseriding, four-wheel-driving and cycling. Demonstrations are given of sheepdog work and sheep shearing and wool processing. Patagonian lamb and trout and Argentine wines are the usual culinary highlights.

Estancia Alice Ruta 11, km22; ℺ 491793 (in Buenos Aires 011 4312 7206); e elgalpon@estanciaalice.com.ar, www.estanciaalice.com.ar. This estancia encompasses some 80,000ha located by the Laguna de los Pájaros and Lago Argentino. All rooms look onto the lake or the Andes. Visitors can watch traditional farm activities such as sheep shearing and wool baling, and the kelpie dogs working the flocks. An ancient indigenous camp on the property is being excavated by archaeologists from La Plata University. Lodging is comfortable and dining includes lamb *asado*, homemade breads and preserves. Excursions can be arranged for horseriding, 4x4 and trekking with Cerro Frías (see below). Only 15 mins from town on the way to the glacier.

Camping

Bahía Escondida 7km from Glaciar Perito Moreno; ℺ 491002 after 14.00. Facilities include electricity in the bathrooms at night, hot showers and firewood for sale; 8 pesos per person.

Where to eat and drink

Casimiro Bigua has two excellent restaurants on Av del Libertador. The Restaurant, Grill and Wine Bar is at no. 963 (℺ *492590, 15 4531 9297*) and serves beautifully prepared and presented dishes with attention to local ingredients, blending the traditional with the gourmet, and the menu is quite helpful in suggesting the appropriate wine from their fine selection to accompany your meal. The Parrilla and Asador is a more casual venue just down the street at no. 993 (℺ *493993*) with a fantastic *parrilla* specialising in Patagonian lamb, presented in the front window with full honours, while the kitchen is also in open view at the back. Email either location at casimiro@cotecal.com.ar.

Shackleton Lounge Av del Libertador 3287; ℺ 493516; e info@shackletonlounge.com. Shackleton's is probably the best spot in town for afternoon tea or an evening cocktail while enjoying the best view of Bahía Redonda from the upper lounge, which also has a small photographic gallery and slideshow presentations. The restaurant on the main level specialises in Patagonian cuisine. Shackleton of course refers to Sir Ernest Shackleton, the Irish explorer who led the 1914–16 Antarctica expedition aboard HMS *Endurance*. The ship apparently didn't have the endurance expected and got trapped and crushed among the ice floes. 28 crew were left stranded for 5 months, but all survived, thanks to Shackleton's epic voyage in a tiny whaleboat to South Georgia and the subsequent efforts of the Chilean navy.

La Cucina Av del Libertador 1245; ☏ 491758. Closed on Tue. A superb range of homemade pastas and sauces (many vegetarian) and good wine.

La Tablita Coronel Rosales 28; ☏ 491065; e latablita@cotecal.com.ar. The name means 'little piece of wood', which refers to the wooden plate that your *asado* is served on. The lamb comes highly recommended.

Practicalities

Tourist information is available at the Centro de Informes, Julio Roca 1004 (☏/f 491090, 491466; e info@elcalafate.gov.ar). The **post office** is the Correo Argentino (*Av del Libertador 1133;* ☏ 491012). There are a few banks in town, some with ATMs: **Banco de Santa Cruz** (*Av del Libertador 1285*), **Banco Tierra del Fuego** (*25 de Mayo 34*) and **Banco Nación** (*Av del Libertador 1133*). You can also change money at **Thaler Money Exchange** (*Av del Libertador 1242;* ☏ 493245; e thalercalafate@cotecal.com.ar, www.cambio-thaler.com).

The **Hospital Formenti** is at Roca 1487 (☏ 491001/3) and the best pharmacy is **Minich** at the corner of Libertador and Espora (☏ 49180). The **police station** is at Avenida del Libertador 819 opposite the YPF gas station (☏ 491077 *or in emergencies 101*).

Shopping

El Calafate is probably the most expensive city in Argentina for shopping, owing in part to its isolation, but also to the high level of tourism that has developed in recent years. You would be wise to buy necessities such as film, toiletries, etc. prior to your arrival, and most souvenirs and typical items such as cowboy hats or *maté* gourds, even bird guides and similar tourism books, can be found in other cities for considerably lower prices. Most of the shops are along the main street, Avenida del Libertador, at the east end of which is a beautiful new crafts market, with steppe grasses on the roof.

Day trips and excursions
Los Glaciares National Park

The **Glaciar Perito Moreno** is the most visited part of the park, with an elaborate construction of boardwalks that attempt to safely offer you every possible view of the spectacular ice. There are a few options for visiting. You can drive yourself there by taking Ruta 11. There are also several tour buses for transport to and from the glacier. Cal-Tur departs daily from the bus terminal at 07.00 and 15.00, returning at 11.00 and 19.30; TAQSA departs daily at 08.00 and 15.00, returning at 15.30 and 20.00 (both charge 40 pesos for a round trip). A recommended tour is offered through the HI hostels, listed on page 54, where you can be guided on a trail that will show you additional views of the glacier without the crowds on the boardwalks. The tour also includes a boat excursion to see the front of the glacier from the water. Refreshments are available for purchase on board. You can even order a scotch (the local still is named Old Smuggler) with glacial ice – the only time you will drink a scotch on the rocks, when the rocks are older than the scotch! Extended excursions to view the Upsala Glacier are also available. Admission to the park (which is closed in winter) costs 60 pesos for foreigners. There is a small café and toilets. There are no rubbish bins in the park; you must take your rubbish away with you.

Cruceros MarPatag (☏ 011 5031 0756; e glaciars@crucerosmarpatag.com; www.crucerosmarpatag.com) gives you the opportunity to spend two full days and one night aboard the *Leal*, a 20m cruiser exploring the Spegazzini, Onelli, Upsala and Perito Moreno glaciers. The ship sleeps 14 passengers in seven cabins, each with

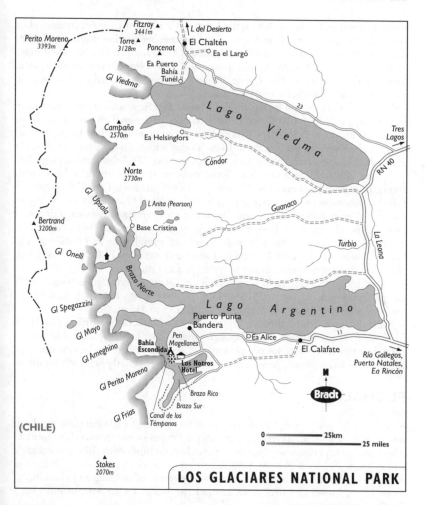

LOS GLACIARES NATIONAL PARK

private bath; there is hot water, a kitchen (meals are included in the excursion) and a lounge area. A broad external bridge and wide windows in the cockpit provide excellent vantage points for viewing the glaciers. This trip is offered from around July to the end of May and departs on Monday, Wednesday or Friday. The cost is US$395 per passenger in double occupancy, US$540 as a single. An option to sleep onboard the night prior to the excursion costs US$70 and US$90.

Boat trips to the Perito Moreno Glacier are also offered by René Fernández Campbell (*Av del Libertador 867;* ☎ *491428*). Another wonderful option is the all-day catamaran cruise covering 70km from Puerto Bandera to the Upsala Glacier (the largest in the park, covering 600km²) and to Puerto Las Vacas where there's a three-hour stop. There's a restaurant, and you can either walk 800m through lenga forest to Lago Onelli, at the foot of the Onelli Glacier, or hike to the Refugio Onelli, used by scientists observing the glacier's retreat (up to 60m per year). The return may take in a detour to the Spegazzini Glacier, which rises up to 125m above water level in places.

Upsala Glacier and **Estancia Cristina** (*reservations at 9 de Julio 69;* ☎ *491034 or 491133;* e *info@upsalaexplorer.com.ar; www.estanciacristina.com*) is a historic outpost located near the Upsala Glacier on the Cristina Channel of Lago Argentino in Los Glaciares National Park. It was one of the pioneering ranches with over 20,000 sheep at its peak and is one of the remotest outposts catering to adventurers exploring southern Patagonia. The peaks of **Cerro Norte**, only climbed once, loom over the estancia. The *Upsala Explorer* will take you cruising through the icebergs to view the glacier from the water.

Visiting El Chaltén and hiking around **Mount FitzRoy:** with an early start a day trip is possible, but you will not be able to hike in far enough to see the main attractions up close. At least one overnight is recommended to then be on the trail bright and early to the glaciers above **Lago Torre**, which is a fairly tough trek to do in a rush. A couple of days is needed to see this area (see *El Chaltén* section, page 328).

Glacier and trekking tours are offered through the Hostels del Glaciar with **Patagonia Backpackers**. The Moreno Glacier Alternative Tour (78 pesos) is a full-day excursion to the glacier and includes a boat ride to the face of the Perito Moreno Glacier and a hike through the forest on a private path to see a different view of the glacier away from the crowds of tourists on the boardwalks. The Supertrekking is a two-day trip with a night of camping in El Chaltén to the Glacier Torre under Cerro Torre. Food and transport from El Calafate included, 399 pesos. Find more information at www.glaciar.com.

Horseriding, trekking or 4x4 excursions on Estancia Alice can be booked with **Cerro Frías** (*Cte Espora 159;* ⤏ *492808 or 493434;* e *cerrofrias@cotecal.com.ar; www.cerrofrias.com*). Rates per person range from 75 to 115 pesos.

Fully outfitted fishing trips are organised by **Los Glaciares Fishing** (⤏ *011 15 5117 9551, 15 5494 1530;* e *info@losglaciaresfishing.com; www.losglaciaresfishing.com*). Half-day trips cost 320 pesos per person or 250 pesos per person in a group; full-day trips are 400 pesos per person, 350 pesos each for two, 310 pesos each for three.

EL CHALTÉN
Area code 02962
Situated in the northern or FitzRoy sector of Los Glaciares National Park, this little town with a few hundred residents services the needs of the thousands of tourists who come to experience the beauty of these famous mountains, lakes, woodlands and glaciers. Founded only in 1985 following a border dispute with Chile, it is Argentina's youngest town. It is considered the centre of trekking and climbing in Santa Cruz, luring climbers from around the world to the formidable Cerro FitzRoy and Cerro Torre.

Getting there
Most tourists arrive from El Calafate, where there are an airport and major bus connections; however, access is also possible from the north along the very rough and remote Ruta 40.

By bus
There are daily buses between El Calafate and El Chaltén, in the early morning and the early evening, returning at the same sorts of times. The one-way fare is 45 pesos; round trip 80 pesos (return tickets may be open or for a fixed date). The journey currently takes about five hours, but with the completion of roadworks it should soon be four hours or less.

CalTur ⤏ 02902 491842; e terbuscaltur@cotecal.com.ar. Calafate to Chaltén daily at 07.30 and 18.00; Chaltén to Calafate 06.00 and 18.00.
Los Glaciares ⤏ 02902 491158. Calafate to Chaltén daily at 08.00; Chaltén to Calafate 18.00.

LOS GLACIARES NATIONAL PARK

This park is made famous by the 35km-long, 5km-wide and 60m-high Perito Moreno Glacier, probably the first thing that comes to mind when thinking of the national parks of Argentina. Even larger is the Upsala Glacier, 60km long and 50m high. In the park's northern sector, Mount FitzRoy challenges mountain climbers from around the world to reach its 3,375m summit. A few thousand years ago the entire area of the park was covered by glaciers, and the still-enormous icefields that remain (2,600km² of icefields from which 47 major glaciers descend) and the huge glaciated valleys and moraines suggest the intensity of such an ice age. When the climate warmed, the glaciers began melting and retreating to their current strongholds on the mountains. This retreat continues as the climate warms, indeed at an accelerating pace.

The area receives about 8m of precipitation per year, more than the Amazon rainforest, but in the form of snow. The Perito Moreno Glacier moves at a rate of 1.5–2m per day; however, the front of the glacier calves off at an equal rate so that the glacier remains more or less at the same location. The famous breaking of the Perito Moreno Glacier occurs when the ice crosses the Canal de los Témpanos that connects the Brazo Rico to Lago Argentino and meets the opposite shore. Thus the Brazo Rico is cut off and its water level rises as it continues to receive rainwater and melting ice and snow from the mountains and glaciers. Eventually the pressure of water begins to push past the point of contact of the glacier with the land, creating a small tunnel. This tunnel increases in size until the ice above it becomes an ice bridge that eventually wears thin and breaks in a spectacular event of tons of crashing ice. The first known breaking occurred in 1917 – the only evidence being the sudden flooding of a 700-year-old forest. In 1940 the first breaking actually recognised by geologists at the time of its event brought it to the attention of tourists. Since then the phenomenon has taken place every two to four years (with gaps from 1956 to 1970 and 1991 to 2004); scientists cannot predict with accuracy when the next break will occur. Surprisingly, in the 1950s when this swelling of the lake was causing the flooding of the estancias, the local people tried to break the ice bridge by force. First they tried using salt, then carbon. Then they called in the Air Force to bomb it! They were all futile efforts; it will only break when it is ready, by the true force of nature. The park was founded in 1937, and its 717,800km² area was designated a UNESCO World Heritage Site in 1981. Thirty per cent of this great park is covered in glaciers – 365 individual glaciers in total. The 13 largest of those on the Atlantic watershed are the Perito Moreno, Marconi, Viedma, Moyano, Upsala, Agassiz, Bolado, Onelli, Peineta, Spegazzini, Mayo, Ameghino and Frías glaciers.

Chalten Travel ☏ 02902 491833; e chaltentravel@cotecal.com.ar. Calafate to Chaltén daily 08.00 and 18.30; Chaltén to Calafate 06.30 and 18.00.
TAQSA ☏ 02902 491843. Calafate to Chaltén 08.00, Tue and Fri 02.30; Chaltén to Calafate 18.00, Wed and Sat 08.40.

By car

Ruta 40 onto Ruta Provincial 23; 220km from El Calafate. *Remise* service to the airport in El Calafate is possible with Remis Chaltén Móvil (☏ 493061).

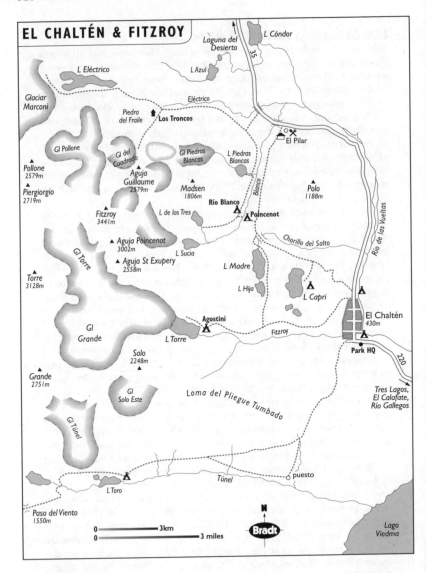

EL CHALTÉN & FITZROY

Orientation

El Chaltén is a little mountain town between the rivers Las Vueltas and FitzRoy; it should present very little difficulty in getting around. Arriving by bus, you should stop at the national park information office for an excellent introductory talk, before crossing the bridge, passing the tourist information office and entering 'downtown'. Following the main Avenida San Martín north you will arrive at the Hostería FitzRoy. Buses terminate at this *hostería* in El Chaitén.

Where to stay

Los Cerros Offices in Buenos Aires; ☎ 011 4814 3934; f 011 4815 7645;
e info@loscerrosdelchalten.com. This luxury hotel opened in 2005; it is situated on a hill

overlooking the village and surveying the splendour of the surrounding forests and mountains. Standard rates range from US$220, sgl or dbl per night, to US$1,320 sgl or US$1,670 dbl, for 2 nights with FB, inc transfer from El Calafate airport, all meals (not alcohol) and excursions.
Hostería FitzRoy Inn Av San Martín 520; ✆ 493062. This building acts as the town's main *hostería*, restaurant and bus terminal. It is located at the foot of the main trails, beside the Río de las Vueltas. The dining room offers continental and American b/fast and a lunchbox service. In high season (Dec–Mar) a sgl room costs 240 pesos with b/fast, 250 pesos with b/fast and dinner; a dbl room costs 264 pesos or 288 pesos.
El Puma Hostería Lodge Lionel Terray 212; ✆ 493095; e hosteriaelpuma@infovia.com.ar; www.elchalten.com/elpuma. Owned by one of the leading local mountain guides, the lodge has a prime location at the start of the trails. Rates are subject to currency fluctuations, but are about 280 pesos for a sgl, and 325 pesos for a dbl; packages with excursions are also available.
Hostería El Pilár 16km north on Ruta Provincial 23; ✆ 493002; www.hosteriadelpilar.com.ar. By the Río Eléctrico bridge on the road to the Laguna del Desierto, with a fine restaurant, this is owned by a local climber and makes a great base for hikes to the Piedra del Fraile and the Piedras Blancas Glacier. Dbl rooms cost 332 pesos, with b/fast and transfers from El Chaltén.

A few well-run hostels in El Chaltén are Hostelling International affiliates.

Albergue Patagonia Travellers' Hostel Av San Martín 493; ✆ 493019; e patagoniahostel@yahoo.com.ar. This budget option is conveniently located close to the trailheads with helpful staff for planning excursions. There are small dorm rooms for 21 pesos per person with shared bathroom, a comfortable dining room with b/fast and lunchboxes available.
Rancho Grande Hostel Av San Martín 635; ✆ 493005; e reservas@hostels.org.ar. There is a simple restaurant and bar and both continental and American b/fast is available in the morning. Dorm rates are 21 pesos for HI members; sgls and dbls with private baths are also available with prices ranging from 58–84 pesos.
Cóndor de los Andes Hostel Av Río de las Vueltas y Halvorsen; ✆ 493101; e reservas@hostels.org.ar. Dorm beds 18–21 pesos; dbls with private bathroom 90–100 pesos.
Posada Poincenot San Martín s/n; ✆ 493 005; e infochalten@chaltentravel.com. Dorms are available for 18 pesos and dbls with private bathrooms start at 90 pesos.

Estancias
Bahía Túnel c/o Caminoabierto Expeditions; ✆ 493043, 493081; e bahiatunel@hotmail.com. 16km from El Chaltén on Ruta 524 on the shores of Lago Viedma, the house is open Nov–Apr and has 3 dbl rooms. There is also a restaurant that features local specialities such as lamb goulash and trout. You can arrive by car or by boat (on the Viedma Glacier tour) from El Chaltén. 180–200 pesos per person per night in a dbl room with shared bath.
Estancia Helsingfors Contact in Buenos Aires; ✆ 011 4315 1222; e info@helsingfors.com.ar. Located 180km from El Calafate and 170km from El Chaltén or 30km by boat from El Chaltén, the lodge was built by Swedish pioneer Alfred Ranström in the early 20th century on the shores of Lago Viedma with views of Mount FitzRoy, and named after his hometown. In the '60s it was bought by its present owners who now offer accommodation in 8 dbl and triple rooms, 6 with Jacuzzi, as well as hearty traditional cuisine. While at the lodge, guests are taken on a boat tour of Lago Viedma, the Viedma Glacier and Laguna del Morro, and horseriding or trekking up the RamstromStream to Laguna Azul in FitzRoy. The estancia takes guests from mid-Oct to mid-Apr. Payment is requested in advance (30% upon booking and remainder 25 days prior to arrival; partial refunds for cancellation up to 7 days in advance). Dbl rooms cost US$396 and sgls US$240. Meals, activities and ground transfer (to/from El Calafate) included.

Where to eat and drink

Hostería FitzRoy Inn Av San Martín 520; 𝒱f 493079.

Bahía Túnel 16km from El Chaltén on Ruta 524; ℩ Caminoabierto Expeditions at 493043/81; e bahiatunel@hotmail.com. This restaurant and tea house offers views over Lago Viedma and a menu focusing on local traditional recipes and ingredients.

El Bodegón de Chaltén – Cerveza Artesanal Av San Martín s/n; ℩ 493109. 2 unfiltered, additive- and preservative-free traditional beers, a dark, turbid bock and a blond pilsner, are produced according to a traditional recipe from Bohemia. This pub also serves up a good ambiance plus pizza.

Practicalities

Tourist information is at the Centro de Informes de El Chaltén, Avenida Costanera s/n (by the bridge) (℩ *493011;* e *sfchalten@infovia.com.ar*). There are no postal services or bank machines in El Chaltén, nor is there reception for mobile phones. There are a couple of *locutorios* for telephone and fax services, and one on Avenida San Martín offering internet access.

Day trips and excursions

Day hikes along the well-maintained trails of **Los Glaciares National Park** can be self-guided only on certain trails and up to certain points of some trails unless you have experience and the necessary equipment. To get as far as **Glaciar Torre**, you will have to cross a river by a Tyrolean crossing, dangling in a harness from a cable. You would be wise to hire a guide who can take you in one day up to the glacier and back (be sure of your fitness as it is a long hike with many hills, and crossing the river by ropes and harness takes abdomenal strength). With a guide you can also trek on the glacier. Alternatively, there are two-day excursions that take a longer loop, with a night in a tent at the base camp. You can reserve these excursions through the HI hostels in either El Chaltén or El Calafate.

In addition, a recommended tour agency is **Camino Abierto** (*Calle San Martín s/n;* ℩ *493043;* e *ventas@caminoabierto.com.ar; www.caminoabierto.com.ar*). With excellent guides, they offer adventure tours, trekking and camping expeditions, horseriding and other activities. Custom-designed treks are possible for small groups.

Lago del Desierto (37km north of El Chaltén): fishing, camping, trekking, mountain biking. Boat trips (45 pesos) are available two or three times a day (November to March), taking half an hour to cruise the length of the lake; you can hike back if you choose. The **South Patagonian Ice Field** (Campo de Hielo Patagónico Sur), the third-largest ice mass after Antarctica, is hiding behind the huge granite walls. At the south end of the lake is a campsite run by Tito Ramírez (℩ *02962 490370*), Nearby a path leads up by a streambed for 3km to a lake by the Glaciar del Huemul, with stunning views of the mountains.

Perito Moreno National Park

This national park is serviced by the town of Gobernador Gregores, which is the largest town nearby but is still 220km away. This is the only town in the area where fuel is available for cars. It can be reached by LADE flights but there's no onward transportation. From Gobernador Gregores you must take Route Provincial 25 for about 130km, mostly on gravel, then an additional 90km on secondary route 37. You can also reach the park on Ruta 40 from the town of Perito Moreno, but this is a long hard drive on a poor road. In summer tourist buses leave daily for the towns of Perito Moreno and Los Antiguos via Ruta 40, with Chalten Travel

(✎ *492212, 491833*) from El Calafate bus terminal at 08.00 (198 pesos, with a change of buses at La Leona), from El Chaltén Rancho Grande hostel at 08.30 (165 pesos), or from the Tango Inn in Bariloche at 07.00 (150 pesos). It is still 90km from Ruta 40 to the entrance of the park; there is no public transport to the park itself. Once you reach the park, admission is free and rough camping areas are available but there are no services – you must bring all your own supplies, especially fuel. South of the town of Perito Moreno, still on Ruta 40, is the **Cueva de las Manos** (Cave of the Hands), one of the most famous examples of pre-Columbian rock art in the country.

GLACIATION

A man who keeps company with glaciers comes to feel tolerably insignificant by and by. The Alps and the glaciers together are able to take every bit of conceit out of a man and reduce his self-importance to zero if he will only remain within the influence of their sublime presence long enough to give it a fair and reasonable chance to do its work.

A Tramp Abroad

A glacier is a large mass of ice and snow in constant movement, its speed determined by the degree and volume of the slope. Glacier ice is formed when ice crystals become crushed and compressed under the weight of centuries of accumulated snow. The crystals first form pellets and as they increase in density, hardness and transparency air is expelled and they become a crystalline mass of stunning bright blue hues.

Types of glacier found in the area:

Indiansis Enormous horizontal ice sheets, such as the South Patagonian Ice Field of 17,000km^2.

De Circo Found at the tops of mountain ranges.

De Valle Flowing through well-defined valleys.

Piedemonte Valley glaciers that widen into a fan-like form upon reaching the plains.

Compound An accumulation of smaller glaciers joining onto the flanks of a larger one, which therefore increases in volume along its course.

Other definitions:

Calving Large pieces of ice breaking off the front of a glacier when it makes contact with a body of water. The Upsala, Moreno, Spegazzini glaciers on Lake Argentino and the Viedma Glacier on Lake Viedma are examples.

Moraines The accumulation of rocks, sand and clay carried by a glacier. Their positions reveal the former extent of the glacier and classify the moraine as either lateral, central or terminal.

Erratic boulders Rocks of different sizes dropped by a glacier when it recedes.

Icebergs Chunks of floating ice that have calved from a glacier. Only one-eighth of their size is visible above the surface of the water.

PERITO MORENO NATIONAL PARK

In 1937, 115,000ha were designated as national park in recognition of the palaeontological and archaeological treasures found in the area and also in honour of the man who instigated the national park movement in Argentina, Francisco 'Perito' Moreno (1852–1919). There are three vegetation zones in the park: Patagonian steppe, Andean-Patagonian forest of lenga trees and high mountains, plus two lake systems. The mountain ranges run north-south and east-west, creating amphitheatres and deep glacier valleys. Some glaciers are at over 900m elevation.

There are eight lakes in total, into which non-native trout were never introduced; therefore the native species thrive. There are also large groups of guanaco and a relative abundance of the endangered huemul deer whose numbers are dangerously low elsewhere in Argentina and Chile. They summer on the alpine slopes above treeline and winter in the lower woods. Predatory species include the puma, red fox and raptors, notably the Andean condor, black-chested buzzard eagle and great horned owl. Other birds in the park include ñandú or lesser rhea on the steppe and a great diversity of wetland species such as flamingos, great grebes, black-necked swans, flying steamer duck, spectacled duck and upland geese.

Long before the Tehuelche people came to this region, the prehistoric inhabitants were primitive cave-dwelling hunter-gatherers, identified by anthropologists by the rock art still remaining on the cave walls and under rocky riverside overhangs. The most important can be found at Casa de Piedra Hill, where there are seven caverns. Archaeological remains such as tools and arrowheads were also found. The people moved with the seasons and came to this area in the late spring when the higher elevations and colder climate led to guanaco calving a month later than elsewhere in the region, therefore extending their hunting season for the young guanacos or *chulengos*. There is no further trace of these peoples after AD1750 when a mini-ice age affected this region.

ESQUEL
Area code 02945

Esquel lies in a hollow along the flanks of the Esquel Range, with Cerros Esquel (2,145m), La Hoya (2,100m) and Nahuel Pan (2,240m) prominent. Bordering the Patagonian Desert, Esquel seems to be a town right out of the Wild West, with century-old houses lining the streets and lots of people on horseback, including plenty of Argentine cowboys or gauchos. Once goose-hunting territory until the goose was placed under protected status, the area now embraces the ideals of wildlife and wilderness guardianship due to its close proximity to Los Alerces National Park. The lakes in the region are great for fly-fishing, rafting and canoeing. Winter delivers great quantities of snow to Esquel's famous **La Hoya Ski Centre**, a mere 17km from the town centre, with some of the best snow conditions in South America. It's popular with families, but is also used for training by national teams from the northern hemisphere. The National Ski Festival takes place over one week in September. In the summer the resort is popular for mountain biking, hiking and horseriding. It can be reached by minibus for 5 pesos. In summer there's little rain and 17 hours per day of sunlight.

Getting there
By air
Esquel's airport lies 25km east, with taxis and minibus shuttles available. Aerolíneas Argentinas (*Fontana 408;* ☎ *453614*) flies from Buenos Aires to Esquel on Monday, Wednesday and Friday LADE (*Alvear 1085;* ☎ *452124*) connects from Bariloche on Saturday, Tuesday and Thursday, from Buenos Aires on Tuesday and twice on Thursday (one via Bariloche). There are also flights from El Bolsón and Paraná on Thursday, and El Calafate, Puerto Madryn, Río Gallegos and Mar del Plata on Tuesday.

By bus
The terminal is at Alvear 1871. AndesMar (☎ *450143*) has a daily bus from Bariloche, taking 4 hours 15 minutes (24 pesos) calling at El Bolsón after three-and-a-half hours into the journey (17 pesos). Don Otto/Transportadora Patagónica (☎ *453012*) and Mar y Valle (☎ *453712*) run from Bariloche to Trelew via Esquel.

By car
The city can be reached along Ruta 40 or Ruta 258 from Bariloche, or Ruta 25 from Trelew. Car rental is available through Avis (*Fontana 331;* ☎ *455062*) and local companies.

Where to stay
Casa del Pueblo Hostel San Martín 661; ☎ 450581; e albergue@ciudad.com.ar. Dorm beds are 13 pesos, sgls with private bath 40 pesos, dbls 52 pesos and triples 60 pesos.
Cabañas Lorien Los Ñires 1123; ☎ 452568, 15 695460; e lorienesquel@hotmail.com. In the nearby *barrio* of Villa Ayelen on Ruta 259. Has clean, new cabins in a quiet location.

Where to eat and drink
Mamá Inés Teahouse and Restaurant Av Alvear 161; ☎ 456336, 15 690707. Features the typical Welsh tea of the area, as well as fondue, stews, pastas, meat, fish and other dishes.

Practicalities
Tourist information is available at the Secretaría de Turismo de la Municipalidad de Esquel, Avenida Alvear and Sarmiento (☎ *451927, 453145;* e *infoturismo@esquel.gov.ar, securismo@esquel.gov.ar; www.esquel.gov.ar*). Hiking in Los Alerces National Park, as well as snow-shoeing and cross-country skiing in winter, can be arranged with *Quehumanque* at Roca 691 (☎ *451869;*

THE CHUBUT VALLEY – THE WELSH IN PATAGONIA
The *Mimosa* set sail from Liverpool with 150 Welshmen and as many dreams of finding prosperity in the new frontiers of Argentina. After two long months at sea they landed at Golfo Nuevo in Chubut province on 28 July 1865. They founded the village of Rawson, the present capital of the province, and subsequently Trelew, Gaiman and Dolavon. They pioneered westward in search of the fertile soils that would support their crops and their futures; they were led to their promised land, the Chubut Valley. Their communities spread all along the valley and the towns of Esquel and Trevelin were founded at the foot of the Andes. The rich soils and moderate climate of the valley allowed them to plant fruit orchards and wheat fields – flour mills are characteristic of their communities.

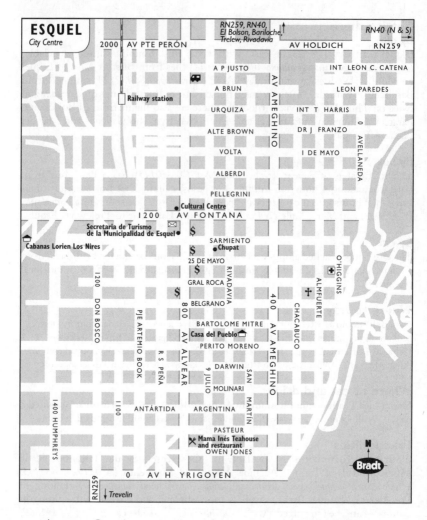

e *quehumanque@speedy.com.ar*). Esquel has surprisingly good bike shops, with Shimano parts.

Museums

Museo Lituano Olgbrun Located in a *barrio* outside town called Villa Ayelén, on Ruta 259, km2,700; ➲ 450536, 15 504983. This private collection features the history of Baltic immigration to the Chubut Valley, by means of literature and artefacts from around 1890. There is also a small salon dedicated to science and the discoveries of Francisco Moreno, the great Patagonian explorer of the time. A side business run by the proprietors is the making and selling of metalwork (in iron, bronze and silver), ceramics and homemade foods ranging from cakes to salmon and smoked cheese.

Shopping

Rural fairs are common in Esquel but there is a large one held in January to trade livestock and agricultural supplies. Several stores (known as *talabarterías*) sell riding tackle and ranch equipment such as ornate stirrups and hand-tooled saddles, braided rawhide ropes and cast-iron cookware.

Chupat 9 de Julio 1033; ⟍ 453 651; e juliolituano@yahoo.com.ar. You can find almost any kitchen object imaginable hand-carved from wood. There are typical craft items as well, such as scoops carved from cow horns, *portamaté* and some ironware.

Day trips and excursions

The dozens of rivers and lakes of the Comarca de los Alerces (District of the Larches) create a perfect setting for sport-fishing, rafting or lake excursions or witnessing the diversity of flora and fauna – especially various species of salmon. Fly-fishing enthusiasts from all over the world come to the Rivadavia, Futaleufú and Cholila rivers to catch perch and rainbow and brown trout. The Comarca de los Alerces is also where Butch Cassidy and the Sundance Kid, the famous outlaws, once hid out.

THE OLD PATAGONIAN EXPRESS OR 'LA TROCHITA'

This semi-retired old steam train now runs mainly for the interest of tourists but still captures the nostalgia and romance of its past with the local people who fought to keep it running when the government wanted to retire it for good. It first ran in 1922 from Esquel to El Maitén (165km, with another 237km to Ingeniero Jacobacci opened only in 1945) and its steam locomotives are some of the oldest still operating in South America. The rails are a mere 750mm apart and the trains travel at a maximum speed of 60km/h (more often 30–40km/h, and only 5km/h uphill) across an imposing curving landscape of the Andean foothills. Many towns and water stations (these locomotives can consume as much as 100 litres of water per km) were established to supply the train. The line was almost closed in 1992, but a public outcry fortunately allowed it to continue chugging and it became a National Historical Monument in 1999. Paul Theroux's 1978 literary success, *The Old Patagonian Express*, describes the author's train trip from Boston (US) to Esquel – the southernmost point of the Argentine railway network; this contributed hugely to its becoming a viable tourist attraction at last. In 2004 fake hold-ups by 'outlaws' on horseback were staged, until a tourist had a heart attack.

The tourist train leaves on Saturday at 10.00, and on other days in summer, and travels for just 45 minutes from Esquel to Nahuel Pan and back. From El Maitén (east of El Bolsón) trains run south to Leleque on Tuesday and Saturday in season, leaving at 11.30 and taking an hour and 45 minutes each way, with time to visit the museum at Leleque. The regular *Trochita* (which carries *indígenas*) leaves El Maitén on Wednesday at 11.00, reaching Esquel at 17.30, and returning on Thursday at 11.00. There are three Baldwin locomotives (from Philadelphia) and three Henschels (from Germany), all built in the early 1920s; the carriages, heated by a wood stove in winter, also date from the 1920s, except for first-class carriages and a buffet built in the 1960s.

For further information and private charters, contact Viejo Expreso Patagónico La Trochita at the station (*open Mon–Sat 08.00–18.00*), Pellegrini 841, El Maitén, Chubut (⟍f 02945 495190; e *latrochita@epuyen.net.ar; www.latrochita.org.ar*); you can also call El Maitén's tourist office (⟍ 495016). Esquel station, at Roggero and Urquiza (⟍f 451403), is open at the same times.

Following Ruta 40 to the tiny town of **Tecka** (100km) is a direct route on mostly asphalt road, but most of the points of interest are on Ruta 34 between Tecka and Trevelin (see under *Excursions from Trevelin*). It is sensible, however, to take Ruta 40 in one direction so as not to double back on the secondary route, which is in worse condition.

TREVELIN
Area code 02945
Trevelin is a small village 23km southeast of Esquel and was founded around 1860 during the period of Welsh immigration into this valley. They realised the fertility of this valley enabled them to grow their crops and they soon built a large mill. This famous mill gave the town its name – Trevelin means 'town of the mill' in Welsh. This mill is now the **Museo Galés** or Welsh Museum.

The valley between Esquel and Trevelin is lovely where the river cuts through the plateau, creating red and white ravines called the **Valle de los Altares** and **Valle de los Mártires** (the Valleys of the Altars and the Martyrs) – the latter referring to an ambush in 1884 during which natives killed a group of young Welshmen. John Evans was the sole survivor and was saved only by a heroic leap of his horse, Malacara, over the steep ravine; this story is presented at the **Cartref Taid** (Grandfather's House) **Museum** at the entrance to town (480108; e *cleycelta@cybersnet.com.ar*). Malacara – the name, meaning 'ugly face', comes from a disfiguring blaze on the horse's head – became a legend. He died in 1909, aged 31 years, and his tomb and bronze plaque are in a tree-shaded garden setting in the village. The **Dique Embalse Florentino Ameghino** is the dam and artificial lake in the valley.

There are a few tour guides available through the tourism office, and fishing guides are also available. The most popular fishing, both fly-fishing and spinning, is to be had on the Río Futaleufú (this is a Mapuche name meaning 'great' or 'grand' river) – which is considered one of the world's top rafting rivers on the Chile side of the border. The fishing season runs from November to April.

Getting there
Numerous buses per day connect Trevelin with Esquel for a few pesos. Any buses connecting Trevelin with the north or with Buenos Aires must first pass through Esquel, which is 25km north on Ruta 259.

Where to stay
Estancia La Paz Located 50km from Esquel airport and 10km from Trevelin on the way to the Futaleufú Dam, in the southern part of Los Alerces National Park; 452758; e estancialapaz@lapazpatagonia.com.ar. It has waterfront cabins with endless acreage to explore on horseback or on foot, as well as excellent fishing right at your front door.
Casa Verde Hostel Los Alerces s/n; 480091, 15 691535; e casaverdehostel@ciudad.com.ar. A member of Hostelling International, this is a small and cosy hostel overlooking the town. There are a couple of dorm rooms at 18 pesos per person, and dbls at 55 pesos and triples at 67 pesos, all with private bathrooms. A cabin is also available that is suitable for a family or small group. Discounts available for HI members. B/fast is 4 pesos extra.
Residencial Estefania Perito Moreno and 13 de Diciembre; 480148; e santidoc@ciudad.com.ar. Basic, clean, around 50 pesos for a dbl. The front reception is closed after 22.00; guests are provided with a code to open the back door after this time.

Where to eat and drink
Restaurant Patagonia Celta Molino Viejo and 25 de Mayo; 480722, 15 687243. Recommended by the locals.

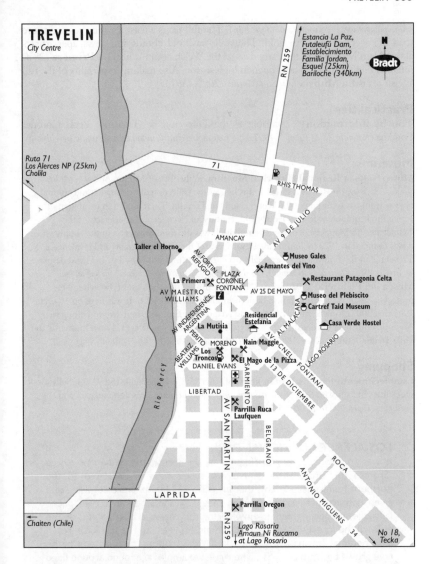

Amantes del Vino Owen Jones 1496; ☏ 450521, 15 505081;
e amantesdelvino@hotmail.com. If you want a nice meal, a good bottle of wine and even a
fine cigar, you will love it here. With very little nightlife in Trevelin, this establishment
offers a place to relax and spend an evening chatting over a bottle or two of Malbec served
in the antique glasses of the proprietor Leonardo's grandmother.

There are two *parrillas* in town: **Parrilla Oregon** (*Av San Martín and Laprida;*
☏ 480408) and **Parrilla Ruca Laufquen** (*Av San Martín and Libertad;* ☏ 480400).
For fast food try **Los Troncos** (*on Av San Martín between Moreno and Evans*); and
for pizza, **El Mago de la Pizza** (*Av San Martín 247;* ☏ 480788).

Welsh biscuits and tea are served in most cafés in the Welsh towns. Among the
best-known is **Nain Maggie** (*Perito Moreno 179;* ☏ 480232; e nainmaggie@hotmail.com;

www.patagoniaexpress.com/nainmaggie.htm). The full tea is a feast for the eyes and more than the average belly can hold! The walls have old photos and newspaper articles about Nain Maggie and the early days of the Welsh community. **La Primera** (*28 de Julio and Fortín Refugio*) is only open in high season. Also making a speciality of the full Welsh tea is **La Mutisia** (*Av San Martín 170;* ❧ *480165*).

Practicalities

Tourist information is available at the Dirección de Turismo, Plaza Coronel Fontana (*Rotonda 28 de Julio;* ❧ *480120;* e *turismotrevelin@ciudad.com.ar; www.trevelin.org*).

Museums

Museo Galés or **Regional Historical Museum**, in the former Molino Andes at Molino Viejo 488; ❧ 480189. Created in 1971, this houses the collection of documents and cultural objects from the founding of the Welsh colony in Trevelin. There is also an exhibition of agricultural equipment from the early 20th century and a collection of artefacts of the Tehuelche and Mapuche peoples. The mill itself was the most important in the county when it was founded in 1922 by John Daniel Evans, one of the first immigrants and residents of Trevelin, but the flour industry gradually declined. The mill was closed in 1953 and destroyed by fire in 1972. *Open daily in summer, closed Mon and Tue in winter, it takes about half an hour to visit.*
Museo del Plebiscito 1902 (School '18' Museum) 9km southeast of Trevelin. This protects a small rural schoolhouse built of mud and cane in 1896. It was here on 16 Oct 1902 that 300 colonists, mostly Welsh and Mapuche, expressed their will to belong to Argentina during a border dispute with Chile; indeed the whole area is now known as the Valle 16 de Octubre. *Open daily 11.00–20.30 in summer and 11.00–18.30 in winter.*

Shopping

Establecimiento Familia Jordán km60 of Ruta 259; ❧ 15 687554, 15 692324. Sells local specialities inc smoked fish, pâtés, caviare, wines and liqueurs, oils and vinegars and preserves. *Open 09.00–12.00, 15.00–20.00.*

LOS ALERCES NATIONAL PARK

It was to protect the grandfathers of the forest, the *lahuán* or alerce (Spanish for larch, although *Fitzroya cupressoides* is unrelated to the northern hemisphere larch), that in 1937, 263,000ha were set aside and given national park status. *Lahuán* means 'grandfather' in the Mapuche language, respecting and acknowledging this majestic tree's status as the elder of the forest. It can live for thousands of years and its trunk can reach a diameter of 3m and a height of 60m. With variations, the diameter of the tree grows by 1mm per year. The largest examples are found around Lago Menéndez, the largest lake in the park. Many stunning lakes decorate the landscape swirling their blue and silver rivers and streams through the sweeping Andean-Patagonian forests of larch, lenga and coihue. The huemul is practically a mystical, legendary creature of these forests. This deer is precariously close to extinction and many wildlife groups and biologists are working for its comeback; however, competition from introduced European deer and fragmentation of its habitat have sorely compromised its population. The tiny pudú is another endangered deer protected by this national park. Ancient rock paintings by the native peoples that once lived in this region can be seen at sites on the Río Desaguadero: the Alero del Shamán and the Interpretation Path.

Taller el Horno Escondido Fortín Refugio 77, off Plaza Coronel Fontana; ↘ 480719;
e elhornoescondido@yahoo.com.ar. A family of artisans produce original pieces of wood
and metal such as knives and *matés*.
Amaun Ñi Rucamó at the Mapuche village of Lago Rosario (see excursion below). This is
a workshop producing gorgeous woollen items. You can watch the women spinning the
wool and working on the looms. The wools are dyed with the pigments of local herbs such
as cafayate berries and *maté*.

Day trips and excursions
Circuito Complejo Hidroeléctrico Futaleufú
Over a distance of 18km, this drive will take you past the extreme southern end
of **Los Alerces National Park**. The hydro-electric complex was built between
1973 and 1978 at the head of the Futaleufú River, to provide electricity to the
ALUAR aluminium factory near Puerto Madryn. The aluminium is
manufactured for export, but the surplus is used locally in the region. You can
take a two-hour guided tour of the complex. At the top of the dam there is an
excellent panorama of the artificial lake, Amutui Quimey (*Lost Beauty* in the
Mapudungun language, referring to the valley that was flooded by the dam),
which was once several smaller lakes (Quiñé, Epú, Culá and Situación) that
merged when the valley was flooded.

Circuito Ruta 259, Trevelin to the Paso Internacional Futaleufú
You can cover this 45km route in approximately four to five hours, but six to eight
hours are recommended to take advantage of the many viewpoints and points of
interest. This popular tourist circuit offers many camping possibilities and places
to spend the night. The route will take you to the **Nant Y Fall Waterfalls**, a
Welsh name meaning 'Stream of the Falls', where the natural drainage of Lago
Rosario and the Río Corintos (a tributary of the Futaleufú) forms a series of large
waterfalls. The last three falls are the most impressive; they are within 400m of
each other inside a provincial reserve. **Molino Museo Nant Fach** (22km from
Trevelin) is the next point of interest, the site of the original establishment of the
old family-run and semi-industrial mills of Trevelin at the end of the 19th and
beginning of the 20th centuries.
Further along the route, you will arrive at the **Estación de Piscicultura**, a
research station for the production and farming of trout and salmon.
Approximately 500m before the Chilean border you will arrive at the Puente
Internacional where there is a lovely view of the Río Futaleufú. **La Balsa** is the
antique raft on which you would have had to cross the river until the 80s when the
bridge was built. The town of Futaleufú is just across the border in Chile.

Circuito Ruta 17, Trevelin to Lago Rosario
This long (24km) and winding dirt road will take you from the centre of town to
Lago Rosario. Don't let the short distance deceive you as the road conditions make
for slow driving and you will need about an hour to reach the lake. There is a
switchbacking climb at the beginning that offers a good view of the pastoral valley.
The road continues to undulate until the final hilltop gives you the view over the
lake. The lake is lovely but difficult to reach as the shoreline is all private land (be
sure to ask for permission). However, you can see plenty of birdlife from the road,
including flamingoes, ibis, black-necked geese, etc. The road ends at the Mapuche
reserve where you should visit **Amaun Ñi Rucamó**, the local workshop where
you can buy beautiful and unique woollen products made by the native artists (see
more under *Shopping*, on previous page).

Circuito Ruta 34, Trevelin to Tecka

Close to the town of Trevelin (9km) you will find the **School '18' Museum** (see *Museums*, on previous page) and, 6km further, **Piedra Holdich**, a memorial to the British arbitrator who came to resolve the sovereignty dispute between Chile and Argentina over the Welsh and Mapuche in this area. Crossing the Nahual Pan Stream and continuing on the route known as the *Huella de los Rifleros* (Trail of the Riflemen) you will see the source of the Río Corintos in the middle of a spectacular area where the forest opens to shrubs and low plants and a display of magnificent rock formations. The area is windy and makes for excellent thermals, which condors and eagles love to ride. Your chances of seeing them are better in the spring. The route continues for another 45km to the junction of Ruta 34 with Ruta 40, which is mostly asphalt to the town of Tecka. At Tecka you can visit the **Mausoleo del Cacique Inacayal** (Mausoleum of Chief Inacayal). This is a monument to the final resting place of the Mapuche who fought for the freedom of this village. There are two options for your return route: if you do not wish to backtrack along the secondary roads, Ruta 40 is asphalt to Esquel.

Circuito Ruta 71, Trevelin through Los Alerces National Park to Cholila

To reach the park from the south, take Ruta 259 followed by Ruta Provincial 71. You will pass **Villa Futalaufquen** and the national park office where you can pay your 12 pesos admission fee and get information and fishing licences. The village has a filling station, cafés, accommodation and a few shops. The park has hiking trails and opportunities for excursions on horseback or mountain bike and more accommodation options from camping to hostels to cabins. Day-long boat excursions are available from Puerto Chucao to **Lago Menéndez**. Leaving the park and heading north to El Bolsón and Bariloche, you will join Ruta 258. The northern exit from Los Alerces National Park is by an inconspicuous road into a valley seemingly right out of an old cowboy film. The dusty little town of **Cholila** was a former refuge of the notorious bandits Butch Cassidy and the Sundance Kid between 1901 and 1905.

GAIMAN

Area code 02965

The early Welsh settlers were mostly tradesmen and labourers and the name Gaiman means 'sharpening stone' in the Tehuelche language. This is one of the most traditional of the Welsh towns in the Chubut Valley and most of the residents are descendants of the early pioneers and still speak a bit of the Welsh language, if not fluently. Children study Welsh in school and take part in exchange programmes with children from Wales; Welsh teachers also come here on exchanges. As often happens when immigrant cultures are isolated for many generations from their homeland, they hang onto traditions more strongly. Today, many of the ancient Welsh songs, poetry, folklore and even dialect are being returned by the Argentine Welsh back to Wales where much has been lost over the years. The culture is celebrated in August at the **Eisteddfod** or Welsh Arts Festival, with traditional music and dance.

Getting there

By air

From Trelew airport (see page 341) it is possible to take a taxi directly to Gaiman for around 18 pesos (a half-hour journey).

By bus

Most travellers arrive in Gaiman from Trelew on a Linea 28 de Julio bus that runs frequently and costs just a few pesos. The ride takes under an hour and it's a local

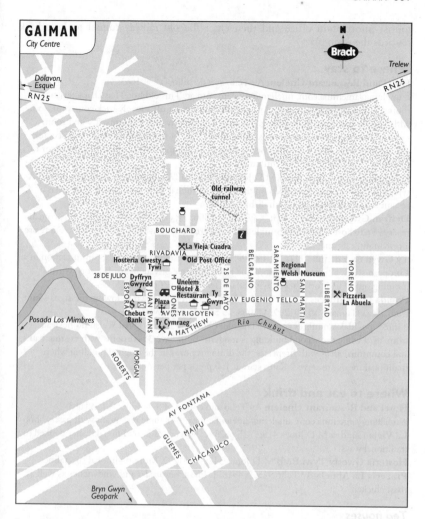

GAIMAN
City Centre

Trelew
RN25

Dolavon,
Esquel
RN25

Old railway
tunnel

BOUCHARD

La Vieja Cuadra
RIVADAVIA
Old Post Office
Hosteria Gwesty
Tywi
28 DE JULIO
Dyffryn
Gwyrdd
Unelem
Hotel &
Restaurant   Ty
Gwyn
Plaza
YRIGOYEN
Chebut
Bank
Ty Cymraeg
A MATTHEW

Posada Los Mimbres

Rio Chubut

BELGRANO
SARAMIENTO
Regional
Welsh Museum
AV EUGENIO TELLO
SAN MARTIN
LIBERTAD
MORENO
Pizzeria
La Abuela

25 DE MAYO
ESPORA
JUAN EVANS
M JONES
AV

ROBERTS
MORGAN

AV FONTANA
MAIPU
GUEMES
CHACABUCO

Bryn Gwyn
Geopark

bus allowing you to disembark wherever you choose. Dolavon, another Welsh town, is just 19km further on the same bus route. Arriving at Gaiman, getting off before the main plaza, at the bakery on Belgrano, will allow you to then walk a couple of blocks up a slight hill to the tourist office. Disembarking instead at the plaza (at a little corner store where you can buy your return ticket) will put you within walking distance of most that the town has to offer.

By car
Gaiman is a short drive on Ruta 25 from Trelew or Dolavon. A taxi from Trelew to Gaiman costs approximately 18 pesos.

Orientation
Gaiman is a small town with a central plaza; head south to the river and the tea houses, north to the historic buildings and the tunnel, east down the main Avenida Eugenio Tello then north on Belgrano (heading back towards Trelew) towards the

tourist information office and then enter the old railway tunnel to loop back towards the main plaza.

Where to stay

Hotel and Restaurant Unelem Av Tello at 9 de Julio; ☎f 491663; e unelem@argentina.com, unelem@unelem.com.ar. This old hotel has characteristic rooms, either in the main original part of the building or off a lovely back courtyard, some with antique furniture or panelling. The rooms have private bathrooms, TV and room service. The proprietor organises excursions throughout the surrounding area to see, for example, the Cañadon del Valle, the Florentine Ameghino dam and petrified forest, or to go rafting or canoeing on the Chubut River.

Hostería Gwesty Tywi B&B M D Jones 342; ☎ 491292; e gwestywi@infovia.com.ar. A typical Welsh colonial-style B&B on the most traditional street in Gaiman. It also has a restaurant boasting typical Welsh dishes.

Dyffryn Gwyrdd Av Tello 103; ☎ 491777, 15 406591; email infodw@dwhosteria.com.ar, reservas@dwhosteria.com.ar. Simple and comfortable rooms with private baths. There are a restaurant, café and snackbar.

Ty Gwyn Av 9 de Julio 111; ☎f 491009. This tea house offers quaint accommodation in a European style. The rooms overlook the river and have private baths. B/fast is worth jumping out of bed for. A room with b/fast is 90 pesos per person.

Posada Los Mimbres Chacra 211, by the river 6km from town following the signs south from Plaza Gaiman; ☎f 491299, 443088, 15 530773, 15 673841; e info@posadalosmimbres.com.ar. The older building is an original Welsh homestead from 1879 while the second building is modern. Both have 3 bedrooms with ensuite baths, and communal areas with fireplaces; the dining room is in the original building where traditional meals are served. Rates start at 100 pesos per person.

Where to eat and drink

Hotel and Restaurant Unelem Av Tello and corner of 9 de Julio; ☎f 491663; e unelem@argentina.com, unelem@unelem.com.ar. A simple restaurant with pastry shop.

La Vieja Cuadra M D Jones 418; ☎ 15 682352. Specialises in traditional dishes cooked in traditional ways.

Hostería Gwesty Tywi B&B M D Jones 342; ☎ 491292. More traditional specialities.

Pizzería La Abuela Av Tello 915; ☎ 491871. Pizza, *empanadas* and sandwiches as well as roast chicken.

Tea houses

Ty Gwyn Av 9 de Julio 111; ☎f 491009. Surrounded by lovely gardens with a view of the river. The full tea service includes the typical spicy Welsh fruitcake (*torta negra* or black cake), apple and lemon pies, nut and chocolate cakes and homemade bread with butter and regional jams and jellies.

Ty Cymraeg Mathews 74; ☎ 491010; e tycymraeg@infovia.com.ar. A lovely way to pass an afternoon in Gaiman is to walk along the river and then visit this tea house for a decadent afternoon tea. The full tea service is excellent and the house and gardens overlooking the river are lovely.

Practicalities

The **tourist office** is a few blocks north up Belgrano at Rivadavia (☎ *491571; e informes@gaiman.gov.ar; www.gaimanweb.com.ar, www.gaiman.gov.ar/turismo/turismo.htm; open Mon–Sat 09.00–20.00, Sun 14.00–20.00*). They are shy on printed materials but keen to offer assistance. The original **post office** is on Jones, a couple of blocks north of the central plaza; and the Chubut Bank is just west off the central plaza.

Museums

Welsh Regional Museum 28 de Julio 705 at Sarmiento, in the old railway station. Recounts the way of life of the Welsh pioneers. The little gift shop sells souvenirs and books and cute little hand-knit tea cosies. *Open Mon–Fri 16.00–20.00.*

Anthropological Museum On the west side of the tunnel. Interprets the different cultures that inhabited Patagonia before the arrival of European immigrants. *Open daily 14.00–20.00, also Mon–Fri 09.00–13.00; admission 1 peso.*

Day trips and excursions

Bryn Gwyn Palaeontological Park (ƴf *432100;* e *info@mef.org.ar to the Museo Paleontológico Egidio Feruglio in Trelew, www.mef.org.ar; open 10.00–18.00 Sep–Mar; 11.00–17.00 out of season; admission 8 peso*) is 8km south of town and a must-see if you are in Gaiman. If you do not have a car you will have to take a *remise* (9 pesos each way), which can be arranged at the store that sells the bus tickets. The drive to the park alone is stunning as you approach the badlands. The park is set up for a self-guided tour of the geology that represents 40 million years of geological change from when the area was a vast savanna similar to that of Africa. There are fossils of crabs, seals, dolphins, penguins and various now-extinct species either left in situ or with moulds and replicas placed where the fossil was found. The walk ends by ascending a hill that was once the sea bed and is covered in fossilised oyster beds. The panoramic view from here is incredible. Avoid this excursion in the midday heat; you will be outdoors and exposed for at least two hours. Wear sunscreen and a hat and carry water.

Dolavon, on Ruta 25 from Gaiman, known as the 'town of the waterwheels', is a small Welsh farming town. The flourmills and Welsh chapels are its main features. The Chubut River is only 5km away and has excellent fly-fishing.

The **Bosque Petrficado Florentino Ameghino** is an area of 58-million-year-old fossilised tree trunks (lauracea from the Palaeocene era) lying as proof that a forest once stood where today is desert. Another 22km from the Petrified Forest are the red rock canyon and kaolin quarries of **Valle Alsina** and **Florentino Ameghino Dam.** This is a popular place for fishing for rainbow and brown trout, Patagonian kingfish, perch and carp. You can go canoeing on the artificial lake within the canyon walls which ends at a small village with some services. The countryside offers hiking, horseriding and rock-climbing adventures.

TRELEW

Area code 02965

One of the first Welsh pioneers was Lewis Jones, who in 1886 promoted the railway to connect the Welsh Chubut Valley with the Golfo Nuevo. Trelew is named after him and means Lewistown in Welsh. The town is set in a lush valley full of farms and flanked on one side by the Atlantic Ocean and the other by the badlands, which are geologically and palaeontologically fascinating and fossil-rich. Served by a major airport and located conveniently for all the points of interest in the area – Playa Unión, Punta Tombo, the badlands, the Welsh towns and Península Valdés – Trelew is the most important city in the lower valley. Although it is an easy transfer from Trelew airport to Puerto Madryn (the nearest city to Península Valdés), many of the points of interest on the coast are much more easily visited from Trelew and at least one night's stay is recommended here before moving north to Puerto Madryn.

Getting there
By air
The Aeropuerto Almirante Zar, the only major airport in the region) is close to town; a taxi costs around 8 pesos. There is also an airport shuttle directly to Puerto Madryn.

Aerolíneas Argentinas (*25 de Mayo 33;* ✆ *420210;* f *420222;* e *reladmin@ aerolineas.com.ar; open Mon–Fri 09.00–12.30, 16.00–20.00, Sat 09.30–13.00*) flies daily (except Tuesday) from Buenos Aires.

LADE (*stand 12/13 at the bus station, Urquiza s/n;* ✆ *435740;* e *trelew@lade.com.ar*) has flights from Buenos Aires and Comodoro Rivadavia on Tuesdays, and on Thursdays its amazing omnibus flight from Mar del Plata, Bahía Blanca and Viedma to Bariloche, El Bolsón and Esquel, among other stops.

By bus

Trelew's terminal is at Urquiza and Lewis Jones, facing the Laguna Cacique Chiquichano. From Buenos Aires' Retiro terminal, long-distance bus services to Trelew are offered by various companies: AndesMar, Don Otto-Transportadora Patagónica, El Condór, El Pingüino, QuéBus, Ruta Patagónica, TAC, TUS and a few others. The journey takes around 20 hours and costs 35–60 pesos depending on the level of service. Some of these buses continue south to Comodoro Rivadavia and Río Gallegos, and others continue north from the capital to Rosario and Córdoba. Don Otto and Mar y Valle both operate services to Esquel, El Bolsón and Bariloche. Mar y Valle (✆ *432329*) and Linea 28 de Julio (✆ *436223*) run roughly hourly to Puerto Madryn (7 pesos).

By car

Trelew lies directly on Ruta 3, following the Atlantic coast.

Orientation

The central square is Plaza Independencia, surrounded by eucalyptus trees and full of activity at weekends. The main streets are 25 de Mayo and San Martín and the central avenue is Avenida Fontana (note that street names change on either side of this avenue).

Where to stay

Hotel Libertador Rivadavia 31; ✆f 420220, 426026; e hlibertador@infovia.com.ar; www.hotellibertadortw.com. Probably the finest hotel in town is this 4-star with all services, restaurant, parking, etc. Sgls 78 pesos, dbls 96 pesos, suites 115 pesos.

Hotel Rayentray San Martín 101; ✆ 434702/3/6; e rcvcentral@ar.inter.net; www.cadenarayentray.com.ar. With restaurant, pool and spa. Sgls 90 pesos, dbls 110 pesos, triples 130 pesos.

Hotel Centenario San Martín 150; ✆ 420542, 426111; f 423491; e hotelcentenario@yahoo.com.ar; www.hotelcentenario.com.ar. Sgls 70 pesos, dbls 80 pesos, suites 90 pesos.

Hotel Cheltum Av Yrigoyen 1385; ✆ 429700; ✆f 431066; e cheltum@internet.siscotel.com. Sgls 40 pesos, dbls 60 pesos, triples 80 pesos.

City Hotel Rivadavia 254; ✆f 433951. Sgls 35 pesos, dbls 50 pesos, triples 70 pesos.

Hotel Touring Club Av Fontana 240; ✆f 433997/98; e htouring@ar.inter.net. This classic landmark is a historical building with marble staircase and antique furniture. It is high on ambiance and fair on price, with rates starting at 40 pesos for a sgl, 60 pesos dbl, 80 pesos triple and 90 pesos quadruple, but rates change with season and availability.

Hotel Galicia 9 de Julio 214; ✆ 433802; f 433803; e hotelgalicia@arnet.com.ar; www.hotel-galicia.com.ar. Sgls 50 pesos, dbls 60 pesos, triples 80 pesos.

Residencial Argentino Moreno 93; ✆ 436134. 20 pesos for sgls, 35 pesos for dbls.

Residencial Rivadavia Rivadavia 55; ✆ 434472; f 423491, 424344; e hotelriv@infovia.com.ar, hotel_Rivadavia@hotmail.com; www.cpatagonia.com/rivadavia. Rates start from 27 pesos per person.

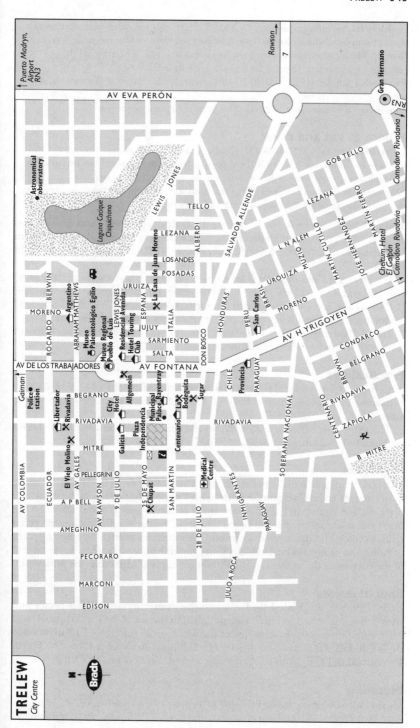

TRELEW
City Centre

N

Bradt

Residencial Avenida Lewis Jones 49; 📞 434172. Sgls, dbls and dorm-style rooms with shared bathrooms. The accommodation is modest and clean and the reception is very friendly. The location is very convenient for the bus terminal, the centre and the palaeontology museum. 15 pesos for a sgl; 25 pesos for a dbl.

San Carlos Sarmiento 758; 📞 421038; e caricarzeppa@infovia.com.ar. Another budget option.

Provincia Av Fontana 565; 📞 420944. This starts at 15 pesos per person.

Where to eat and drink

Libertador Rivadavia 31; 📞/f 420220, 426026. A nice hotel restaurant.

El Viejo Molino Gales 250; 📞 428019. A popular restaurant ingeniously located in an old flourmill dating from 1910, giving an authentic flavour of this Welsh city.

Allgemein Av Fontana 233; 📞 435777. Traditional and international cuisine are served in this simple restaurant with an appreciation for niceties such as cloth napkins.

Three choices for *parrilla* in Trelew are **El Galpón de Don Juan** (*Av Yrigoyen 2252;* 📞 *15 682814*), **Don Pedro** (Ruta 25 at the intersection of Ruta 3) or **Gran Hermano** (*Josian Williams before the traffic circle on the Rawson road;* 📞 *15 688270, 15 670086*).

For pizza, **La Casa de Juan** (*Moreno 360;* 📞 *421534*) has an excellent reputation, but **Chupat** (*25 de Mayo 518;* 📞 *428494*) and **La Bodeguita** (*Belgrano 374;* 📞 *436276*) also come recommended. **Sugar** (*25 de Mayo 247;* 📞 *435978*) is located off the main plaza and is a popular place to come for a drink or a light meal.

Hotel Touring Club (*Av Fontana 240;* 📞/f *433997/98*) has a no-frills yet somehow stylish bar with great ambiance.

Practicalities

Entretur is Trelew's official **tourist office** located at Mitre 387 (📞 *420139, 426819;* e *eturismotw@ernet.com.ar; open daily 08.30–21.00; closing at 20.00 w/ends in low season*).

The main **post office** is at 25 de Mayo and Mitre, while most **banks** are found off Plaza Independencia on Belgrano, 9 de Julio and Rivadavia.

Highlights

The bus terminal is actually in the midst of many of the city's highlights. Flanking it on one side is the **Cacique Chiquichano Lagoon**, full of aquatic birds such as black-necked swans, and at its north end is an astronomical observatory. To the other side of the terminal is the large Plaza del Centenario with benches and green space to enjoy on a quiet sunny afternoon, although this is often the meeting point of rallies and protests as well, which change the ambiance somewhat. At the far end of the park from the terminal is the **Palaeontological Museum** (see *Museums*).

Special events

Every October, the **Eisteddfod** is a two-day competition of Welsh poetry and choral singing, based on the Eisteddfodau in Wales. **Gwyl y Glaniad** is a commemoration of the first landing of the Welsh on 28 July 1865. **El Aniversario de la Ciudad** commemorates the city's founding on 20 October 1886. The **Fiesta Provincial del Pingüino** celebrates this adored flightless bird in October.

Museums

Museo Paleontológico 'Egilio Feruglio' Av Fontana 140; 📞/f 420012, 432100; e info@mef.org.ar. This excellent museum is internationally recognised for its high-quality

exhibits and interpretation and ongoing research. You will learn about the palaeontological history of Argentina over the last 65 million years and see over 17,000 Patagonian fossils, with 30 dinosaur skeletons inc the carnotosaurus, the only known horned meat-eating dinosaur. You can take a guided tour or watch palaeontologists reconstruct skeletons; there's also a good café. *Open 10.00–20.00 Sep–Mar (10.00–18.00 out of season); admission 15 pesos.*
Museo Regional Pueblo de Luis Av Fontana and 9 de Julio; ✆ 424062. An interpretative museum of the Welsh and indigenous cultures. *Open Mon–Fri 07.00–13.00, 15.00–21.00 Dec–Feb, 07.00–13.00, 14.00–20.00 Mar–Nov.*

Day trips and excursions
The easy day trip to **Gaiman** (see page 338) for Welsh tea and the Bryn Gwyn Palaeological Park in the badlands is a must-do. The bus takes under an hour and the little town has just enough to offer to fill a day. The park is highly recommended, but if you are visiting in the heat of summer, avoid midday heat. The park is a large, self-guided, unsheltered hike. Wear a hat and sunscreen and carry water.

From the fishing port of **Rawson**, the provincial capital city, Toninas Adventure, Frente al Muelle (✆ 483472, 15 689836) makes boat excursions to see the *toninas* or Commerson's dolphins. These small dolphins are gorgeous with bold black and white colouring and playful habits such as bowriding with the boat. Usually seen in twos or threes, pods as large as eight can come and race around your boat.

Punta Tombo (107km) has the largest nesting colony of Magellanic penguins in South America – over half a million birds. Their nesting grounds cover an immense area that is crossed by a path for tourists. The penguins seem to be unperturbed by human presence, as long as you are always courteous and give them the right of way when your paths cross. The walkway leads up to the shoreline where you can watch the penguins playing in the surf. When the chicks hatch in November you can observe the diligent parents trekking back and forth from the sea to the nest to feed them by regurgitating fish.

You can take an excursion with almost any of the tour agencies in town to visit both the *toninas* and Punta Tombo; all excursions leave by 09.00 so book the night before.

Further south down the coastline (251km from Trelew) are **Cabo dos Bahías** and **Puerto Camarones**. Here you can observe a large Magellanic penguin colony, sea lions and fur seals and a diversity of seabirds. In addition to sea lions and elephant seals, **Punta León** is an important habitat for many species of seabirds of scientific interest, including imperial cormorants and kelp gulls.

PUERTO MADRYN
Area code 02965
Founded by Parry Madryn in 1865, today Puerto Madryn is one of the busiest towns on the coast with the infrastructure to support the ever-increasing numbers of tourists coming to see the abundant wildlife of Península Valdés.

Getting there
By air
Until about 22.15, buses run from Puerto Madryn to the airport of Trelew, which has good services throughout the country. The small airport at Puerto Madryn is used only by LADE (*Av Roca 119;* ✆ 451256; e *pmadryn@lade.com.ar*), with flights from Buenos Aires and Comodor Rivadavia on Tuesdays. Aerolíneas Argentinas (for bookings out of Trelew) is at Avenida Roca 427 (✆ 450938; f 451998; e *arpmy@arpmy.com.ar*).

By bus

From Trelew, which is served by buses along Ruta 3, Mar y Valle/Linea 28 de Julio (↘ *472056*) run roughly hourly to Puerto Madryn (7 pesos). Mar y Valle also has day and night services to Esquel and Bariloche. Don Otto/Transportadora Patagónica (↘ *451675*) operates services between Buenos Aires and Comodoro Rivadavia, with some continuing as far as Río Gallegos. Lider Patagonia (*also* ↘ *451675*) connects Puerto Madryn with Mar del Plata and the coastal cities along the way. Other long-distance services are run by Andesmar/Central Argentino (↘ *473764*), El Condór (↘ *454465*), El Pinguïno (↘ *456256*), QueBus (↘ *455805*), TAC (↘ *457542*) and TUS (↘ *451962*).

Locally, Mar y Valle has a service at 08.55 (from Trelew at 07.45) to Puerto Pirámides on Península Valdés (arriving at 10.20); this returns to Puerto Madryn at 11.00, heading back to Puerto Pirámides at 17.00 and returning to Trelew via Puerto Madryn at 19.00.

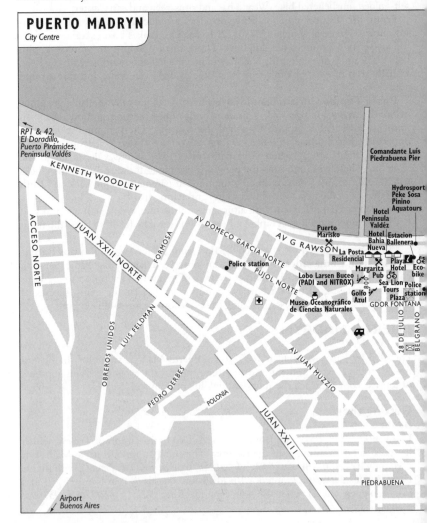

The terminal is just north of the centre (behind the former railway station, which is to become a museum – trains ran to Trelew from 1889 to 1961); there are an ATM, free WCs, tourist information, and several tour operators taking bookings for trips to Península Valdés.

By car

Puerto Madryn is 65km north of Trelew. From the north or south of the country you should take Ruta 3 to Trelew; from the Chubut Valley area take Ruta 28. Car-rental agencies in Puerto Madryn include Avis, Hertz, Fiorassi, Motor Home Time, Rent A Car Patagonia, Sigma and Localiza.

Orientation

Most of what will interest you in Puerto Madryn, including most of the travel agencies, restaurants, hotels, etc, is along the beachfront Boulevard Brown, and

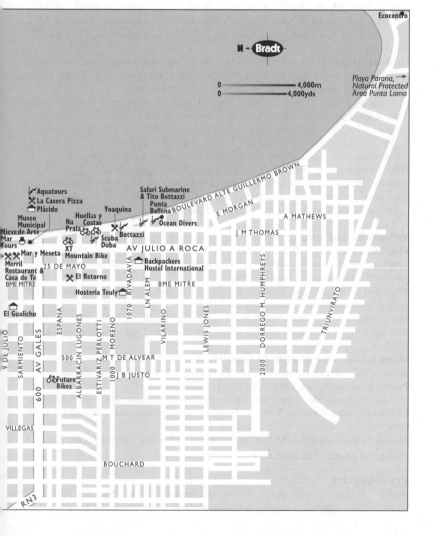

the next street inland, Avenida Roca, which is lined with shops and includes a mall.

Where to stay

Hotel Península Valdés Av Roca 155; ☎ 471292, f 452584; e info@hotel-peninsula-valdez.com. Elegant rooms, some with sea view, a spa, gym and 24-hour room service will make your stay more than comfortable. Rates start at 200 pesos for sgl or dbl with or without the sea view. B/fast included, parking not.

Hotel Bahía Nueva Av Roca 67; ☎ 451677, 450045, 450145; e hotel@bahianueva.com.ar. A room with a sea view is possible at the very comfortable and friendly hotel. The common areas include a bar and pool table, internet corner and sitting room. American b/fast is served and parking is available. Rates start at 133 pesos for a dbl.

Playa Hotel Av Roca 187; ☎ 451446; e playahotel@playahotel.com.ar. Rooms with ocean view are available at this clean and simple hotel. 145 pesos sgl or dbl with view; 120 pesos without. B/fast not included.

La Posta Residencial Av Julio Roca 33; ☎ 472422; e ricardoantin@infovia.com.ar. Simple accommodation close to the beach. Rates start at 50 pesos for a sgl and 60 pesos for a dbl, with b/fast included.

Hostería 'Teuly' Rivadavia 355; ☎ 471715; e teulypatagonia@hotmail.com. This residence is a little off the beaten track but sweet. B/fast is included and Señora Betty and the whole family plus dog are very friendly. Sgls 20 pesos with private baths.

El Gualicho Marcos Zar 480; ☎ 454163; e info@elgualicho.com.ar; www.elgualicho.com.ar. This HI hostel and former railway house has recently expanded to offer private rooms as well as dorms. There is a large backyard for *asados*, a communal kitchen and ample common areas to relax in and meet with other travellers. It is a 5-min walk to the beach and 10 mins to the bus terminal. Rates start at 18 pesos for members (20 pesos for non-members).

Hostel Viajeros Gob Maiz 545; ☎ 456457; e info@hostelviajeros.com; www.hostelviajeros.com. Dbls 55 pesos, triples 66 pesos, beds 22 pesos in 3-bed dorms, 20 pesos in 4-bed dorms; communal kitchen and recreation areas. Expeditions can be organised for wildlife watching and visiting local sites of interest.

Where to eat and drink

Plácido Av Roca 506; ☎ 455991; e placido@placido.com.ar. An elegantly presented restaurant with reasonable prices for excellent dishes: pastas, meat, fish and seafood. Try to get one of the tables with a view of the sea.

Yoaquina Bd Brown 1050; ☎ 456058. Extensive menu with many seafood choices; and the great view will make slow service tolerable.

Mar y Meseta Av Roca 485; ☎ 458740. Nice menu and equally pleasant staff.

Ambigú Av Roca 97 at Saenz Peña; ☎ 472541. Excellent pizza in a stylishly adapted historic building.

Merril Restaurant & Casa de Té Av Roca at 28 de Julio; ☎ 457436. Many large windows in one of the halls provide views of the sea and create a wonderful dining atmosphere.

Puerto Marisko Rawson 77 (near the long pier); ☎ 450752; e Jorge@puertomarisko.com.ar. Excellent seafood selection and *parrilla* at excellent prices.

La Casera Pizza Roca 561; ☎ 457777. Excellent pizza and *empanadas*, also available to take away.

Margarita Pub Saenz Peña 15; ☎ 475871. International cuisine daily and ethnic menu on Wed. Good bar for a *trago* (long drink).

Practicalities

Puerto Madryn's city hall and tourist office are at Avenida Roca 223 (☎/f 453504 or 456067; e informes@madryn.gov.ar or www.turismo.madryn.gov.ar). The tourist office is very helpful and with plenty of information printed in English. The **post office** is on the corner of Belgrano and Gobernador Mais.

Bicycle rental

An excellent way to get around town and to nearby points of interest such as the Ecocentre is by bicycle; the distances to nearby beaches however are substantial and you should know your level of fitness before embarking on a long trek in the hot weather. For example, it's a 38km trip from Puerto Madryn to the popular beach of El Doradillo to whalewatch, and 40km to Punta Loma to see the sea lions (passing Punta Este after 25km). Given the headwinds and rough roads, an average cyclist won't manage more than about 10km/hr.

Ecobikes 25 de Mayo 309; ☎ 02965 454411, 15 408593; e ecobikes@madryn.com
El Gualicho M A Zar 480; ☎ 454163
El Retorno Mitre 798; ☎ 458044
Future Bikes Juan B Justo 683; ☎ 15 665108
Huellas y Costas Bd Brown and Perlotti; ☎ 15 680515
Backpackers Hostal Internacional 25 de Mayo 1136; ☎ 474426
Na Praia Bd Brown 860 on the beach; ☎ 455633; e napraia@napraia.com.ar. They also rent windsurfers and kayaks.
Sea Lion Tours 25 de Mayo 141; ☎ 474703
XT Mountain Bike Av Roca 742; ☎ 472232

Museums

Ecocentro Puerto Madryn Julio Verne 3784; ☎ 457470; e cultura@ecocentro.org.ar, www.ecocentro.org.ar. Come to visit and buy the guidebook! This impressive interpretative centre is professional and educative and is situated atop cliffs that grant stunning views of the sea, south of the town beyond the Monumento al Indio Tehuelche. There are 3 levels: the main level has all the interpretative exhibitions; the top level is a reading room reached via the library but where the view is too beautiful to keep your eyes on a book; and the lower level is a kids' room full of interpretive and educative games. Shuttles run 3 times a day from the tourist office on Av Roca. *Open Tue–Sun Oct 1–Dec 14 11.00–19.00, Dec 15–Mar 14 17.00–21.00, Mar 15–Sep 30 15.00–20.00; admission 15 pesos.*
Museo Oceanográfico y de Ciencias Naturales Chalet Pujol, Domecq García at Menéndez; ☎ 451139. This museum will teach you all about the flora and fauna of Patagonia. *Open Mon–Fri 09.00–12.00, 16.00–20.30, Sat and Sun 16.00–21.00.*
Museo Municipal de Arte Av Roca 444; ☎ 453204. This claims to be the only museum of modern art in Patagonia, with some interesting visiting shows. *Open Mon–Fri 10.00–13.00, 18.00–21.00, Sat and Sun 18.00–21.00; admission free.*

Special events

Fiesta Nacional del Cordero (a celebration of lamb, inevitably involving an *asado* or two) in January, **Marine Fauna Week** in June and the **Fiesta del Buceo** (Diving Festival) in December are fun events to take part in.

Activities
Diving

Puerto Madryn and Península Valdez are considered to be the capital of *el buceo* (diving) in Argentina. Underwater encounters with seals and dolphins are unforgettable experiences. There are also several marine parks created out of sunken buses and boats.

Aquatours Av Roca 550; ✆ 451954, 455985; e aquatours@aquatours.com.ar; www.aquatours.com.ar
Bottazzi Bd Brown 1070; ✆ 474110; e info@titobottazzi.com, www.titobottazzi.com
Golfo Azul Mitre and Yrigoyen; ✆ 471649
Lobo Larsen Buceo (PADI) Yrigoyen 144, Local 1; ✆ 15 516314, 15 681004;
e info@lobolarsen.com, www.lobolarsen.com
Madryn Buceo (PADI and NITROX) Balneario Nativo Sur, 3rd Rotunda; ✆ 15 513997;
e madrynbuceo@madrynbuceo.com, www.madrynbuceo.com
Ocean Divers Bd Brown on the 1st and 2nd rotundas; ✆ 472569
Patagonia Buceo Balneario Mamina, Bd Brown; ✆ 452278, 15 661160;
e patagoniabuceo@yahoo.com.ar
Puerto Madryn Buceo Balneario Nativo Sur; ✆ 15 513997
Safari Submarino Complejo Krill, 1st Rotunda; ✆ 474110, 473800
ScubaDuba Bd Brown 893; ✆ 452699; e scubadub@infovia.com.ar and info@scubaduba.com.ar

Whale and wildlife watching

Many of these companies have similar packages for wildlife watching throughout the peninsula and compete with each other. Rates change according to season and demand, but start at 50–100 pesos for 40- to 90-minute outings. You would be wise to shop around to find what company best suits your interests, although there is not much difference between the most popular excursions. Not all have English-speaking guides, so make sure to check if you do not speak Castellano. Although every experience is unique, I had very considerate guides and enjoyable excursions with Flamenco, Bottazzi and Cuyun Co.

Cuyun Co Turismo Av Roca 165; ✆ 454950
Estación Ballenera Av Roca 297; ✆/f 458824; e estacionballenera@infovia.com.ar
Factor Patagonia 25 de Mayo 186, Local 3; ✆/f 457079; e factorpm@infovia.com.ar.
factorpatagonia@hotmail.com
Flamenco Tour Av Roca 331; ✆ 455505, 15 402282, 15 404065, 15 699540;
e ventas@flamencotour.com; www.flamencotour.com
Hydrosport Av Roca 297; ✆ 458824, 495065
Moby Dick ✆ 15 518397
NieveMar Tours Av Roca 549; ✆/f 455544. They also have an office in Trelew.
Peke Sosa Av Roca 297; ✆ 495010, 15 680852
Pinino Aquatours Av Roca 297; ✆ 458824
Punta Ballena 2 Bajada al Mar; ✆ 495112, 495012
Tito Bottazzi Balneario Krill; ✆ 458223, 474110, 495050

Playa Flecha and **El Doradillo** (15km north) beaches are both recommended spots to relax on the sand and perhaps see a whale.

Day trips and excursions

Southwest of Puerto Madryn a long winding gravel road will bring you in 17km to the **Punta Loma** nature reserve (admission 4 pesos), a colony of about 400 sea lions; lacking a car or taxi, there are organised tours to take you there in combination with other destinations such as **Punta Ninfas**, further along the coast. Here there is a famous lighthouse and the **El Pedral Estancia**, being developed as a private reserve for elephant seals and sea lions. The old estancia house is beautiful with comfortable stylish rooms, an elegant dining room and library and a lovely long gallery that looks out over the sea. There is a big fireplace and several gas stoves that heat the building. The modern guesthouse, also heated with gas stoves, sleeps 12 people. There is a package available for three nights plus excursions and services; ☏ 011 4311 1919; e info@burcoadventure.com.

PENÍNSULA VALDÉS

On the coast of Chubut is the incredible wildlife haven of Península Valdés and nearby points. The peninsula itself was designated a UNESCO World Heritage Site in 1999 for its wildlife, most importantly the southern right whale (*Eubalaena australis*), which comes to breed in **Golfo Nuevo** and **Golfo San José** between June and mid-December. The whale itself was declared a Natural Monument by the Argentine government in 1984. The coastline near **Caleta Valdés** from **Punta Norte** to **Punta Hércules** has also been named a Natural Monument – sea lions and some 40,000 elephant seals (with approximately 10,000 pups born each year between August and November) breed along this 200km stretch of coast.

Puerto Madryn is the main base for visitors to Península Valdés. If you are not taking a tour but arriving independently, take the paved Ruta Provincial 2 north for 18km and turn right to cross the **Carlos Ameghino Isthmus**, a narrow spit of land with views of Golfo Nuevo to the south and Golfo San José to the north. You'll have to pay 35 pesos to enter the Península Valdés Provincial Park. A little east of the park gate, the Interpretative Centre is open daily from 08.00 to 20.00, with wildlife displays and an observation tower. Driving the peninsula can be hazardous if the unpaved roads are muddy, so pay attention and realise the distances are deceptive; the peninsula is large. From Puerto Madryn to Puerto Pirámides is 100km; to Punta Norte 170km, Caleta Valdés 140km and Punta Delgada 174km. Throughout the peninsula are numerous shorebirds such as oystercatchers and pelicans and most conspicuously the cormorants. There are also guanaco, mara, armadillo and rheas not far inland.

Isla de los Pájaros, a seabird reserve to the north of the isthmus, is closed to visitors but visible through a telescope. It is an important breeding habitat for at least ten different seabird species. To watch the island from the observation station seems like a scene from a certain Hitchcock film – the sky above the island throbs with the silhouettes of the birds.

Puerto Pirámides

Puerto Pirámides is the only village on the peninsula. It was founded by the Spanish in 1774 but in 1810 the inhabitants fled from native attacks. It later became a port for salt from the **Salina Grand** and **Salina Chica**, which cover an area of 35km² and 12km², respectively, at 42m below sea level. Sadly, it was also a major centre for whaling and trading of seal skins. Back in the 19th century these shores hosted over 700 whaling ships; and the right whale was hunted to the brink of extinction for the exploitation of its blubber for oil. Thankfully, the port left behind these bloody exploits to become the centre of one of the most important wildlife reserves in Argentina. Hunting the right whale was banned worldwide in 1935; protection measures were taken here in 1937 and expanded in 1982. Catamarans now leave from Puerto Pirámides on whale watching tours and the current whale population is estimated at around 2,000. The time to see the whales is between June and mid-December when around 700 (as they only breed every three years) congregate at Península Valdés to mate and give birth. It is possible to stay at Puerto Pirámides; there is food and lodging, but no bank. The tourist office (on the first road down to the beach) is open from 08.00 to 20.00 daily. One place to find accommodation is at the Cabañas en el Mar (☏ *495049, 15 661629;* e *cabanas@piramides.net, www.piramides.net*) where there are several fully equipped pyramidal cabins just off the main street. If you are staying in the village without a car, there is a sea lion colony only 4km away that makes a nice bicycle excursion.

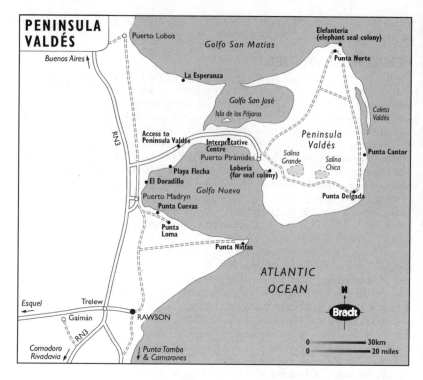

Elephant seals bring the tourist paparazzi to **Punta Delgada Nature Reserve**. They seem to lie on the beach and pose for the cameras with bored vanity. **Faro Punta Delgada, Hotel de Campo** (↘ *02965 15 406304;* f *458444;* e *delgada@puntadelgada.com; www.puntadelgada.com*) is located above the elephant seal colony; the hundred-year-old lighthouse is a stoic sentinel and landmark for the hotel. Originally, this was a post office and naval messhall; today, it is an exclusive romantic hotel, restaurant and boutique surrounded by coastal wildlife and beauty yet with the comfort of luxury accommodation. Rates start at US$110 for a single in low season.

The inlet of **Caleta Valdés** is an elephant seal colony; near its southern end at **Punta Cantor** there's a self-service restaurant (at the former Estancia La Elvira) and some paths, including the Sendero del Lolita (named after a Chilean schooner wrecked here in 1905). Just north there's a car-park and viewpoint with penguins nesting just across the fence.

Punta Norte is a breeding site for elephant seals; sea lions are seen in spring as well as seal-pup hunting orcas during high-tide (mid-February to mid-April). Boardwalks extend about 4km south along the beach. The parks main entrance has a gift shop and a restaurant. Accommodation available at nearby **Estancia la Ernestina** (↘ *92965 661 079;* e *info@laernestina.com.ar*). Excursions and meals included in rates, sgl US$190, dbl US$340, tpl US$490. Open September 15 to April 20.

Other wildlife and eco-tourism options
Viedma and Carmen de Patagones — Rio Negro Province
On opposite banks at the mouth of the Río Negro, about 450km north of Puerto Madryn, are the twin towns **Carmen de Patagones** and **Viedma**, both founded

in 1779 by Francisco de Viedma. Carmen de Patagones is one of the oldest Spanish settlements and being the southernmost city in Buenos Aires province makes it the gateway to Patagonia. Viedma, south of the river, is the smaller, less glamorous of the two, but yet the capital of Río Negro province. In 1879 it was the residence of the governor of Patagonia, making it an important political and administrative centre for the south. A century later, President Raúl Alfonsín's administration suggested it become the new federal capital, calling it the Argentine Brasília owing to the high economic and political interests in the area. The logistics and bureaucracy involved in such a project ensured it remains only a suggestion. These are small cities with many hotels, restaurants, banks and other conveniences.

Thirty-two kilometres from Viedma is Patagonia's oldest lighthouse, at **Balneario El Condór**, a popular resort with campsites and guesthouses. Thousands of sea lions colonise the beaches on the north coast of Golfo San Matías; they can be seen at the **Reserva Faunística de Punta Bermeja** (60km from Viedma on Ruta Provincial 1), which is also commonly referred to as La Lobería. The spring mating season is when you can see the most numbers and the most action. Like a rowdy nightclub scene, the males fight over the females but are not content with finding one mate, gathering harems of up to ten females each. By December the females are giving birth.

The **Río Negro** flows into a narrow valley that contrasts with the surrounding desert and is home to a thriving fruit industry (apples, pears and grapes). These are shipped out of the port of San Antonio Oeste (263 km north of Puerto Madryn), near **Las Grutas**, a popular seaside resort where the sea has eroded numerous caves into the cliffs. Some of these majestic rock walls are 20m high and store archives of marine fossils spanning millions of years. The sandy beaches and clear warm waters are favoured by divers, while sport-fishing and whalewatching are also popular.

COMODORO RIVADAVIA
Area code 0297

The largest town on the Patagonian coast is Comodoro Rivadavia, a boom city whose 150,000 inhabitants live almost exclusively off the oil and petrochemicals industries. On 13 December it celebrates Petroleum Day. Despite this it is also very proud of the fact that 10% of its electricity is generated by the country's largest wind turbine complex. If you have the misfortune to get stuck here, make sure you have a few novels left unread and head for the beach, Rada Tilly, 10km south of the city (south of which is the Punta Marqués sea lion reserve).

Getting there
By air
The airport (✆ 454 8093) is 9km north of the city, reached hourly by bus no. 6. Aerolíneas Argentinas (*Rivadavia 156;* ✆ *444 0050;* f *447 3302;* e *crdcomerc@aerolineas.com.ar; open Mon–Fri 09.00–12.30, 15.30–20.00, Sat 09.00–13.00*) has three flights a day Monday to Friday (just one at weekends) from Buenos Aires. LAN Argentina (✆ *0810 9999 526 – local rate, press 8 for English*) started services from Buenos Aires in October 2005, just twice a week at first but building up to twice a day in summer.

LADE (*Rivadavia 360;* ✆ *447 0585;* e *crivadavia@lade.com.ar*) has an amazing omnibus flight along the coast from Buenos Aires on Thursdays, calling at seven towns including Mar del Plata and Trelew, as well as from El Calafate and Esquel on Sunday, Río Grande, Río Gallegos and El Calafate on Tuesday, Río Gallegos, San Julián and Puerto Deseado on Wednesday and Friday, and Ushuaia on Friday.

By bus

Comodoro Rivadavia is the main interchange point for travellers along the Atlantic coast and heading into the interior of Patagonia, with most national companies offering services, especially north-south along Ruta 3. These include Andesmar (✆ 446 8894), Don Otto-Transportadora Patagónica (✆ 447 0450), El Condór (✆ 447 2485), El Pingüino (✆ 447 9104), La Unión (✆ 446 2822), Co-op Sportman (✆ 444 2988) and TAC (✆ 444 3376). The terminal is at Pellegrini 730 at Almirante Brown (*one block from the seafront;* ✆ 446 7305).

By car

Comodoro Rivadavia is on Ruta 3, 1,839km south of Buenos Aires, 384km south of Trelew and 945km north of Río Gallegos. Heading inland on Ruta 26, it's 619km to Esquel.

Cars can be rented from Avis (✆ 454 8483) and Hertz (✆ 454 8999), both at the airport, and Budget (*Moreno 864;* ✆ 444 0008; e *comodoro@budgetargentina.com*), Europcar (*Yrigoyen 2778;* ✆ 448 6962; e *europcar_patagonia@uolsinectis.com.ar*), Lider (*Rivadavia 439;* ✆ 446 1400) and Localiza (*Rivadavia 535;* ✆ 446 3526; e *reservas@localiza.com.ar*).

Orientation

Ruta 3 follows the coast through the city. Avenidas Rivadavia and San Martín run inland from the port, on a small headland, with the viewpoint of Cerro Chenque (once a Tehuelche cemetery) immediately to the north.

Where to stay

There's little reason to stop (as overnight buses are the best way to cover the great expanses of Patagonia), but the **Residencial Azul** is a clean and comfortable two-star place at Sarmiento 724 (✆f 447 4628), and the **Austral Plaza** at Moreno 725 (✆ 447 2200; f 447 2444; *www.australhotel.com.ar*) is a good four-star. The **Hotel Comodoro** (*9 de Julio 770;* ✆ 427300) lives on its reputation as the party-place of the early-20th-century oil boom and is overpriced, although it's worth visiting the bar. There are various cheaper *hospedajes* on Belgrano, and camping is available at Rada Tilly.

Where to eat and drink

In the centre of town, acceptable restaurants include **La Rastra** (*Rivadavia 348*), **Bom-Bife** (*España 832 at Rivadavia*) and **Giuletta** (*Belgrano 864*).

Practicalities

The city's **tourist office** is at Rivadavia 430 (✆f 447 4111; *open Mon–Fri 08.00–20.00 Dec–Mar, 08.00-15.00 Apr–Nov*). The **police** are at Rivadavia 101 (✆ 446 2778), and the regional **hospital** at Avenida Yrigoyen 950 (✆ 444 2287, *emergency* ✆ 107). The **post office** is at San Martín and Moreno. Money can be changed at **Thaler** (*San Martín 272;* ✆ 446 2679) and **Turismo Ceferino** (*9 de Julio 880;* ✆ 447 3805), and the **Banco de la Nación** is at San Martín 108 (✆ 449 9417).

Highlights

Other than the cathedral, at Rivadavia and Belgrano, there are few notable sights. However, there are a few museums, of which the most interesting is the **Museo Nacional del Petróleo** (*San Lorenzo 250, Barrio General Mosconi;* ✆ 455 9558; *open Tue–Fri 09.00–12.00, 15.00-20.00, Sat and Sun 15.00–20.00, closes 18.00 in winter; admission 3.50 pesos*), which is visible from the main road 3km north of the centre

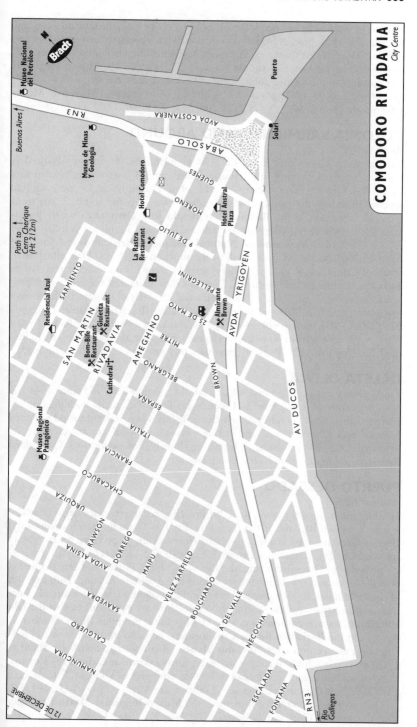

COMODORO RIVADAVIA
City Centre

Museo Nacional del Petróleo

Buenos Aires

RN3

RN3

Museo de Minas Y Geología

AVDA COSTANERA

ABASOLO

Puerto

Solari

GÜEMES

Hotel Comodoro

MORENO

Path to Cerro Chenque (Ht. 212m)

9 DE JULIO

Hotel Anstral Plaza

SARMIENTO

La Rastra Restaurant

PELLEGRINI

Residencial Azul

SAN MARTIN

Giulietta Restaurant

RIVADAVIA

AVDA YRIGOYEN

Bom-Bife Restaurant

Cathedral

25 DE MAYO

Almirante Brown

AVDA BROWN

AMEGHINO

MITRE

Museo Regional Patagónico

ESPAÑA

BELGRANO

BROWN

ITALIA

AV DUCOS

FRANCIA

CHACABUCO

URQUIZA

RAWSON

AVDA ALSINA

DORREGO

MAIPU

SAAVEDRA

VELEZ SARFIELD

BOUCHARDO

CALGUERO

A DEL VALLE

NAMUNCURA

NECOCHA

12 DE DICIEMBRE

ESCALADA

FONTANA

RN3

Río Gallegos

and can be reached by bus no. 5. Established in 1987 by YPF, the state oil company, it covers the whole process from the formation of oil deposits to their extraction and refining. You can also see the rig that made Argentina's first major oil strike in 1907 (while drilling for water, it should be said). There's also the **Museo Regional Patagónico**, in the former public baths at Rivadavia and Chacabuco (↘ 447 7101; *open Mon–Fri 09.00–19.00; admission free*), and the rather cramped **Museo de Minas y Geología** (*Abásolo 1015;* ↘ *445 2178; open Mon–Fri 09.00–13.00; admission free*).

COLONIA SARMIENTO AND AROUND
Area code 0297
Not far from Comodoro Rivadavia (150km inland on the road to Esquel) is Colonia Sarmiento, centre of a farming community of Boer origin, nestled in a lush valley between lakes Musters and Colohué Huapi, home to many wildlife species, including the beautiful black-necked swan. To the south, 32km from Colonel Sarmiento, is the **Bosque Petrificado José Ormachea** where proto-araucaria trees were buried in volcanic ash and fossilised 70 million years ago. The similar (but older) **Monumento Natural Bosques Petrificados** is 82km west from km2063 on Ruta 3 (just south of the junctions to Puerto Deseado, 160km south of Comodoro Rivadavia). This is scrubby steppe, with bunchgrass, calafate and cacti; wildlife includes guanaco, Darwin's rhea, mara, red and grey foxes, cats, armadillo and lizards. There's a 1km path, and no water or camping. There are a few places to stay in Colonia Sarmiento, including Residencial Ismar, Patagonia 248 (↘ *489 3293*), with doubles for 33 pesos, and Los Lagos, Roca y Alberdi (↘ *489 3046*), with rooms from 30 pesos to 45 pesos; there are also campsites, including the Club Deportivo (↘ *489 3103*), near the entry into town from the main road.

CALETA OLIVIA
Caleta Olivia was founded in 1901 as a wool-exporting port, and since 1944 has been the centre of a major oil and natural gas field, with many nodding donkey pumps visible. You may find yourself changing buses here to head inland to Perito Moreno and Los Antiguos, and perhaps cross into Chile to travel along its wonderful Carretera Austral. There's an hourly bus service to Comodoro Rivadavia, 75km north, and a few cheap hotels.

PUERTO DESEADO
Area code 0297
Heading south along the coast, Ruta 281 branches east to arrive at Puerto Deseado, a superb natural harbour at the mouth of the Río Deseado, which drains Lago Buenos Aires. It served as a resting-place before tackling Cape Horn for navigators such as Magellan, Schouten, Lemaire, John Davis and Thomas Cavendish (indeed it's named after Cavendish's ship, the *Desire*), as well as Fitzroy and Darwin, and is now the home port for fishing boats working in the western Atlantic. With a wealth of coastal wildlife, its tourist appeal is becoming recognised, and you can take boat trips on the estuary (where Commerson's dolphins are common) to visit the **Isla Pingüinos nature reserve**, a colony of Magellanic penguins (from October to April), and the **Barranca de los Cormoranes**, home to imperial, rock and red-legged (or grey) cormorants. At **Cabo Blanco** (80km north) a lighthouse (built in 1916) overlooks a fur seal colony, and a bit further north, at **Cabo Tres Puntos**, there's a sea lion colony. Tours can be booked through Los Vikingos, Estrada 1275 (↘ *487 0020*) or Darwin Expediciones, Embarcadero Muelle Gipsy (↘ *15 624 7554*).

The town has a couple of museums: the **Museo Regional Mario Brozisky** near the sea at Colón and Belgrano (*open Mon–Fri 10.00–17.00; free admission*), which has an interesting display of items from HMS *Swift*, wrecked in 1770 and found only in 1982, and the **Museo Padre José Beauvoir**, at the Salesian College, opposite the former station at 12 de Octubre 577 (*open Mon–Fri 09.00–12.00, 15.00–18.00, Sat & Sun 15.00–18.00; donation*), which has a large but badly displayed collection of indigenous artefacts. Two important events are the pilgrimage to the cavern of Lourdes (25km west) in mid-February and the shark fishing tournament at the end of February.

Where to stay
The **Albergue Municipal** or **Town Hostel** at Colón and Belgrano (✆ 487 0260) has dorm beds and private rooms. There's also **Residencial Los Olmos** (*Gobernador Gregores 849;* ✆ 487 0077) and, rather better, the **Hotel Isla Chaffers** (*San Martín and Moreno;* ✆ 487 2246). There's also a municipal campsite (✆ 487 0579) on the costanera.

Where to eat and drink
El Pingüino (*Piedrabuena 958*) is a decent *parrilla*, while **Puerto Cristal** (*España 1698*) is a more run-of-the-mill restaurant.

Practicalities
Tourist information is available at San Martín 1120 (✆ 487 2261; e *turismo@puertodeseado.com.ar*) and from an old railway carriage outside the former station, all that remains of the line that once brought wool for export. The closest major airport is at Comodoro Rivadavia, but LADE (*Don Bosco 1519;* ✆ 487 2674; e *pdeseado@lade.com.ar*) has flights from Comodoro to Puerto Deseado and Río Gallegos on Monday and Wednesday, returning north on Wednesday and Friday. There are three buses a day from Comodoro Rivadavia with La Unión (✆ 487 0188) – be sure to get off in the centre rather than going all the way to the terminal.

PUERTO SAN JULIÁN
Ruta 3 reaches the coast again at Puerto San Julián, situated in a bay between Cabo Curioso and the sandy beaches of Punta Desengaño, 420km from Comodoro Rivadavia and 353km from Río Gallegos. It faces **Gibbet Point**, where both Magellan and Drake executed mutinous crew members; from December to March Commerson's dolphins can be seen here, and almost 5,000 Magellanic penguins come to breed on an island reserve. The town's new Centur tourist information centre is at San Martín 500 at 9 de Julio and the Costanera (✆ 452353, 452750; e *sanjulian@santacruz.gov.ar; www.sanjulian.gov.ar*), where you should ask about boat trips to Banco Cormorán or Isla de los Pingüinos.

LADE (*San Martín 1552,* ✆ 02962 452137; e *sanjulian@lade.com.ar*) has flights from Comodoro Rivadavia and Puerto Deseado to Río Gallegos on Monday and Wednesday, returning north on Wednesday and Friday.

RÍO GALLEGOS
Area code 02966
With a population of 82,000, Río Gallegos is half the size of Comodoro Rivadavia but equally dull, although it should be mentioned that the museum has moved to new premises and is worth a visit. Tours to penguin colonies are also well worthwhile in season. Its name means Galician River – this is not the part of Patagonia colonised by the Welsh or Gales (although oddly there is a noticeable population of *gitanos* or gypsies, who dominate the used-car business). The capital

of President Kirchner's home province, Santa Cruz, it was founded in 1885 and boomed in the early 20th century when its wool barons became immensely wealthy. Thanks to tourism and high lamb prices it is currently booming again.

Getting there

The last town on Argentina's mainland Atlantic coast, this is the jumping-off point for Tierra del Fuego, as well as Punta Arenas and the Torres del Paine in Chile. Buses down Ruta 3 take at least 36 hours to get here from Buenos Aires, without a lot of real scenery along the way, so it's worth considering flying.

By air

The recently modernised airport (◥ *442340/4*), with its 3.5km runway, one of the longest in the area, is 6km west of town, passed by all traffic towards El Calafate and the north. There are taxis and a minibus shuttle, and micro no. 1 to Barrio Consejo will take you most of the way there.

Aerolíneas Argentinas (*Av San Martín 545;* ◥ *422020, airport 442059;* f *420181;* e *rglgte@aerolineas.com.ar*) has two to four flights a day from the Aeroparque in Buenos Aires (taking 3¼ hours if you're lucky enough to get a non-stop flight), LADE (*Fagnano 53;* ◥ *422316;* e *rgallegos@lade.com.ar*) has flights from Buenos Aires on Tueday (4 hours) and Friday (5½ hours), as well as Comodoro Rivadavia (Mon, Tue, Wed, Fri), El Calafate (Tue) and Río Grande and Ushuaia (Mon, Tue, Thu, Fri).

LAN Argentina (◥ *0810 9999 526 – local rate, press 8 for English*) started services from Buenos Aires in October 2005, just twice a week at first but building up to twice a day in summer.

By bus

The bus terminal (◥ *442159*) is on Ruta 3 opposite the end of Eva Perón, 3km from the centre: to get there take micro B 'Terminal' on Avenida Roca. Heading into town, the pick-up is to the right across Charlotte Fairchild.

The main operators north along Ruta 3 towards Buenos Aires are Andesmar (◥ *442195; also to Córdoba*), Don Otto-Transportadora Patagónica (◥ *442160*), El Pingüino (◥ *442169*). and ViaTAC (◥ *442042*). All have one or two departures per day between about 16.30 and 21.30, spending two nights on the road. Don Otto also serves Bariloche, while Co-op Sportman (◥ *442595*) and TAQSA (◥ *442194*) have evening departures for Los Antiguos, on the Chilean border near Perito Moreno.

There are several buses from Río Gallegos to El Calafate, taking about three and a half hours: Interlagos/El Pingüino (◥ *442169*) has one service on Monday, Wednesday and Friday; TAQSA/Quebek (◥ *442194*) has three daily departures (picking up at the airport by reservation only) with additional service on the days that Interlagos/El Pingüino does not run. Freddy Representaciones also has a daily connection. In the other direction, each operator has a departure from El Calafate at about 02.00, plus one or two afternoon services. All charge 30 pesos for a one-way ticket. Schedules change between winter and summer, and arrival times cannot be accurately determined due to the wind. TecniAustral (◥ *442427*) has departures to Ushuaia at 08.45 Monday to Saturday year-round.

For the Torres del Paine area of Chile, El Pingüino has departures to Punta Arenas at 13.00 daily and to Puerto Natales at 11.00 on Saturdays, in summer; Buses Ghisoni (◥ *442687*) goes to Punta Arenas at 08.30 on Thursday and 12.00 on Tuesday, Friday and Sunday. Bus Sur goes to Puerto Natales at 17.00 on Tuesday and Friday; and TAQSA goes to Río Turbio (near the border crossing to Puerto Natales) at 13.30 and 20.00 daily. The through buses from Puerto Montt (Chile) to Punta Arenas are now allowed to stop here for passengers, although not

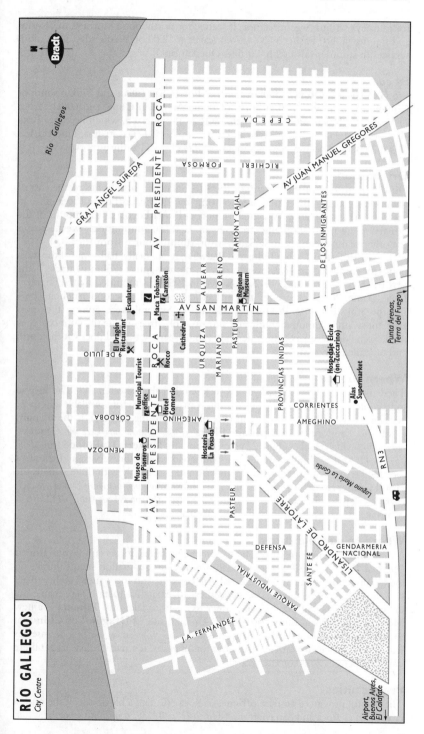

RÍO GALLEGOS
City Centre

Brandt

Río Gallegos

GRAL ANGEL SUREDA

AV PRESIDENTE ROCA

CEPEDA

FORMOSA

RICHIERI

AV JUAN MANUEL GREGORES

DE LOS INMIGRANTES

Escalatur

Maca Tobiano
El Carretón

ALVEAR

MORENO

RAMÓN Y CAJAL

Regional Museum

El Dragón
Restaurant

9 DE JULIO

AV SAN MARTÍN

Cathedral

ROCA

Rocco

URQUIZA

MARIANO

PASTEUR

Punta Arenas,
Tierra del Fuego

Municipal Tourist
office

Hotel
Comercio

CÓRDOBA

AMEGHINO

PROVINCIAS UNIDAS

Hospedaje Elcira
(in Zuccarino)

Alas
Supermarket

CORRIENTES

AMEGHINO

Museo de
los Pioneros

MENDOZA

AV PRESIDENTE

Hostería
La Posada

Laguna María La Gorda

R N 3

PASTEUR

LISANDRO DE LA TORRE

DEFENSA

SANTE FÉ

GENDARMERIA
NACIONAL

PARQUE INDUSTRIAL

J.A. FERNANDEZ

Airport,
Buenos Aires,
El Calafate

for journeys within Argentina, nor, it seems, for northbound journeys to Osorno and Puerto Montt: Pacheco (✆ 442765) leaves at 12.00 on Wednesday, with more services in summer (also with Turibus/Queilen Bus).

By car
Río Gallegos is on Ruta 3, 350km south of Puerto San Julián and 770km south of Comodoro Rivadavia, 278km north of Punta Arenas in Chile, and 600km from Ushuaia. It's 316km from El Calafate by Ruta Provincial 5, which becomes Ruta 40. Cars can be rented from Avis, at the airport (✆ 457171), Cristina, Libertad 123 (✆ 425709) and Localiza, Sarmiento 237 (✆ 424417) and at the airport.

Orientation
On the south side of the estuary of the Río Gallegos, the city lies to the east of the narrow-gauge railway that used to bring low-quality coal from Río Turbio to the docks (now replaced by a modern port at Punta Loyola at the mouth of the estuary). The main shopping street, Avenida Roca, running east–west, crosses the other main street, Avenida San Martín, running north from Ruta 3.

The RFIRT (Río Turbio Industrial Railway), incidentally, had some of the most powerful steam locomotives ever to run on narrow-gauge (750mm) tracks – the first batch of Mitsubishi 2-10-2s delivered in 1956 was modified by the engineer Livio Dante Porta for greater thermal efficiency, and a second batch in 1964 incorporating his 'Gas Producer Combustion System' were among the most efficient steam locomotives built, and almost smoke-free despite the poor coal they used. Some of these locos, now derelict, can be seen by the old docks at the north end of Calle Mendoza.

Where to stay
There are quite a few cheapish hotels in town, but they're often full. The helpful tourist information desk at the bus terminal can advise on what's available and make bookings. A good budget option, just six blocks from the terminal, is the friendly, clean and comfortable **Hospedaje Elcira** (*Pasaje Zuccarino 431, off Corrientes;* ✆ *429856*), which charges about 22 pesos per person; **Hostería La Posada** (*Ameghino 331;* ✆ *436445*) is also recommended, with good rooms and service and excellent food, and charges 50 pesos. Rather grander (though still only with three stars) is the **Hotel Comercio** (*Roca 1302;* ✆ *420601;* e *hotelcomercio@informacionrgl.com.ar*), which charges 130 pesos for a double. **Camping** is available at the ATSA site (✆ *442310*) at Asturias and Yugoslavia, west of the bus terminal.

Where to eat and drink
Although the menus might not be to foreigners' tastes, locals still favour **Rocco** (*Av Roca 1157;* ✆ *420203*), a traditional *parrilla* whose reputation stands or falls on the quality of the meat and its charcoal grill cooking, and the waiter's ability to get it to the table at its best. It also has good alternatives such as pasta. There is an ever-increasing number of pizza places, either to eat in or take out. **Tijuana** is a new Mexican take-away at Entre Ríos 385 (✆ *436777*), and **El Dragón/Los Chinos** at 9 de Julio 27 is the best bet for vegetarians and those who enjoy stuffing themselves with a self-service all-you-can-eat buffet for 18 pesos. It's always busy, so get there when it opens at 20.00 or after 23.00.

Practicalities
The helpful provincial **tourist office** is at Roca 863, half a block east of the central crossroads of Roca and San Martín (✆ *436920/17, 442159;* e *infotur@santacruz.gov.ar,*

www.santacruz.gov.ar; open Mon–Fri 09.00–19.00, Sat and Sun 10.00–15.00). There's also an excellent municipal office for tourism and the environment, on the corner of Roca and Córdoba (\ *436920, 429764;* e *turismo@riogallegos.gov.ar, www.riogallegos.gov.ar; open Nov–Easter Mon–Fri 09.00–20.00*), which also runs the tourist information centres in the *carretón* (a typical estancia worker's caravan) at Roca and San Martín (*open daily in summer 10.00–20.00, Sat & Sun closed 14.00–16.00*) and at the bus terminal (\ *442159; open daily 07.00–21.00 year-round, in principle*).

If you're crazy enough to cycle, the inevitable repairs can be carried out by Galaxi, on Calle Ameghino at Pasteur (*open Mon–Sat 14.00–21.00, and mornings from 11.00 with luck*).

Highlights

The **cathedral**, built in 1889 by the Salesian Juan Bernabé with just five helpers, faces Plaza San Martín, a block south of Roca, on San Martín. The **Museo Regional Padre Molina** and the provincial cultural centre are at Ramón y Cajal and San Martín (*open Mon–Fri 10.00–20.00, Sat and Sun 11.00–19.00; admission free*); the museum has displays of archaeology (with indigenous artefacts) and palaeontology (with models of local dinosaurs and extinct mammals in lifelike settings), as well as a programme of contemporary art. Perhaps more interesting is the **Museo de los Pioneros** at El Cano and Alberdi (*open daily 10.00–20.00; admission free*): built in about 1890, this was the home of Arthur Fenton, the colony's first doctor and an ancestor of its curator, Pamela Mackenzie.

Excursions

Cabo Vírgenes (named on the feast day of the 10,000 Virgins martyred with St Ursula by the Huns), 135km south of Río Gallegos, is worth visiting from October to March, when 80,000 pairs of Magellanic penguins come to breed. It's easiest to take a tour with Maca Tobiano, opposite the Anónima supermarket at Roca 998 at Fagnano (\f *422466;* e *macatobiano@macatobiano.com*) or Escalatur, at Alberdi and San Martín (\ *420001;* e *escalatur@internet.siscotel.com.ar, escalatur@speedy.com.ar*). Costing 83 pesos per person (with a minimum of four, with a bilingual guide in high season only), plus 7 pesos entry fee, these include a stop at the lighthouse on the cape, where you can visit the **Estancia Monte Dinero**'s Al Fin y al Cabo tea shop (*not always open*). With two days advance booking you can also stop at the estancia, still owned by the Fentons, for lunch and a sheep-herding show by their collies and Australian kelpies. You can also drive yourself, and indeed stay at the estancia (\f *428922, 426900;* e *turismo@montedinero.com.ar*) for US$40 single, US$60 double with breakfast, or US$90 per day with full board.

In addition to Monte Dinero, it's possible to spend a few days at many other estancias in Santa Cruz, where you will be the guests of the owners in the traditional style, with organic home-grown food and doubtless an *asado* of lamb before you leave, and activities such as horseriding with the gauchos, fishing, or simply watching the farmwork. Some especially interesting estancias include Helsingfors (see page 327); Stag River near Río Turbio; Alta Vista and Nibepo Aike, southwest of El Calafate; and La Oriental, in the Parque Nacional Perito Moreno. **Stag River** (*c/o Sarmiento 178, 9400 Río Gallegos;* \ *15 621069, 02966/422466;* e *stagriver@southern.com.ar*), owned by the Johnston family, is best known for its fantastic trout fishing in the headwaters of the Río Gallegos and for the *criollo* horses they breed. **Alta Vista** (*AP 17, 9405 El Calafate;* \f *02902/491247, in Buenos Aires 4489 9146;* e *altavista@cotecal.com.ar*), 33km southwest of El Calafate, is part of the famous Estancia Anita and ideally placed for visiting the Parque Nacional Los Glaciares. **Nibepo Aike** (*Estudio Contable*

MONTE LEÓN NATIONAL PARK

The country's newest national park, granted official status in October 2004, is the Parque Nacional Monte León, 210km north of Río Gallegos. An estancia founded in 1920 by the Braun-Menéndez family, the great sheep magnates of Argentina and Chilean Patagonia, it was bought largely with funds from Yvon Chouinard, owner of the US outdoor clothing company Patagonia, and donated to the Argentine government. Its 61,700ha cover steppe and coastal eco-systems, which are still home to 11,000 sheep plus cattle, guanaco, puma, foxes, rhea, martinetas, owls, upland goose and flamingoes inland, and 60,000 Magellanic penguins, grey cormorants, fur seals and sea lions along the coast. Offshore you may see southern right whales and Commerson's dolphins.

This is the first coastal-marine national park on the Argentine mainland, and is recognised not only for its coastal biodiversity but also for the many palaeontological sites. The area was once home to the Tehuelche people, hunter-gatherers who subsisted principally on the guanaco, but also on birds, shellfish, small animals and the occasional sea lion. Although the arrival of Europeans on these shores had mostly negative impacts, one man, Francisco Moreno, came to this area in the late 19th century doing the exploratory work that fired his passion for preserving the natural wonders of Argentina for future generations. He was the impetus for national park designation in Argentina that has continued to today with Monte León becoming the country's 26th national park.

Tours are not yet available (indeed there's no electricity yet), but this will not remain the situation for long, as it is predicted to become one of the country's most popular eco--tourism destinations. There is free camping, and better accommodation is available in Puerto Santa Cruz, 50km north. Contact the municipal tourism office (*Av Piedrabuena 531;* ☎ *02962 498301 or 498252;* e *mpsc@santacruz.gov.ar*).

Jansma, Perito Moreno 229, 9400 Río Gallegos; ☎ *02966/422626;* e *nibepo@speedy.com.ar; www.nibepoaike.com.ar*), tucked away in the hills near the Brazo Sur of Lago Argentino (and, unusually, raising Hereford cattle as well as sheep), offers spectacular views best appreciated on horseback, with their trained guides. Hiking, fishing and boat trips to the Perito Moreno Glacier are also available. **La Oriental** (*Casilla 51, 9310 Puerto San Julian;* ☎/f *02962/445 2445;* e *elada@uvc.com.ar*) is in one of the remotest and least spoilt areas of Patagonia, allowing day-long horse rides in the wilderness, with great views of condors and Cerro San Lorenzo, the highest peak in the southern Andes.

There are plenty of others – see www.estanciasdesantacruz.com or www.scruz.gov.ar/turismo/espa/estancia.htm, or call at the Centro de Informes Estancias Turísticas de Santa Cruz at Suipacha 1120 in Buenos Aires; ☎ 011 4325 3098.

Territory of Tierra del Fuego

The archipelago of Tierra del Fuego is separated from Patagonia by the Magellan Strait. Magellan supposedly named the archipelago 'Land of Smoke' in 1520 and then Charles V reasoned that there was no smoke without fire and changed its name to 'Land of Fire'.

The total area of the archipelago is 73,746km², about two-thirds Chilean and one-third Argentine. An infinity of rocks and islets! The mainIsla Grande is 48,100km², half of which is Chilean.

Immigrants came first as missionaries, then in larger numbers to follow the gold rush and then the first oil strikes. Sheep-breeding is the principal activity today in the north of the Isla Grande or Big Island, although up to an acre and a half of this poor scrubby land is needed per head of livestock.

Isla Grande is divided into three different landscape zones: the southern zone is mountainous with beautiful deep valleys, lush forests and a maritime coast. The capital, Ushuaia, is in this zone. The central zone is between the mountains and the steppe, where there are many opportunities for watersports on lakes Fagnano, Escondido, Yehuin and Chepelmut or for exploring the surrounding countryside. The northern zone is the Patagonian plateau, rough and treeless, with many ranches and significant oil and gas exploitation. Many important rivers flow through this zone towards the Atlantic Ocean, making fishing a popular activity. The coastline from Bahía San Sebastián to Cabo San Pablo is also of international importance as a migratory bird habitat.

USHUAIA
Area code 02901
The capital of Tierra del Fuego, this is the world's southernmost city and the main base for Antarctic tourism. The first immigrants arrived over a hundred years ago; it is interesting to see the many original family homes built by Italians, Spaniards, Lebanese, Croats and others. The average summer temperature in January is barely 10°C; however, there are almost 18 hours of daylight! Temperatures are erratic and unpredictable throughout the year but the winter temperature in July can reach –20°C, although the average is usually not below zero. The winter daylight hours are much reduced – as little as seven hours a day. Being at such an exposed tip of the continent subjects the town to frequent and often strong winds, but these keep the skies generally clear and blue.

Getting there
By air
Flying into the Malvinas Argentinas International Airport on a clear day is a spectacular visual experience. The landscape, seemingly void of human habitation, is also treeless and seemingly barren of significant vegetation, but this is far from the case. What vegetation exists paints itself across the landscape with streaks and blotches of greens and yellows dramatically accentuated by the bright blue-green lakes scattered here and there. The most majestic aspect is the sight of the mountains – you will most likely fly directly over their snowcapped peaks and observe them soften in altitude and character as you fly towards the end of the continent before turning back to land. The approach over Ushuaia Bay is thrilling; the dazzling blue waters and the sensation of arriving at the end of the world will fill you with a sense of adventure and freedom. The modern airport that welcomes you is impressively sited on a 12,000-year-old glacial moraine in the Beagle Channel. From Buenos Aires there are daily flights (3½ hours direct) to Ushuaia, and others from Córdoba, Mendoza and all major cities in Patagonia.

Aerolíneas Argentinas/Austral (*Roca 116;* ✆ *421091, 421218;* f *431291;* e *ushgte@aerolineas.com.ar; open Mon–Fri 09.30–17.00, Sat 09.30–12.00*) connects daily from Buenos Aires; the flexible fare is US$105 each way. LADE (*Av San Martín 452;* ✆ *421123;* e *ushuaia@lade.com.ar*) flies to Ushuaia from Buenos Aires and El Calafate on Monday, Wednesday and Friday, and from Río Gallegos on Monday and Wednesday. LAN Chile (*www.lan.com*) flies from Santiago, Puerto Montt and Punta Arenas in summer only on Monday, Wednesday and Saturday; the official return fare from Punta Arenas is US$99, but there may be good deals on the website.

There is no bus service from the airport, so you will have to walk (about 4km) or take a taxi or *remise* (approximately 9 pesos, but be sure to negotiate your fare in advance; *remises* tend to have a flat rate while taxis have unpredictable meters). Remember that when flying out of the airport you will have to pay an airport tax of 13 pesos.

By bus

There are no direct buses from Buenos Aires to Ushuaia, but only as far as Río Gallegos, in Santa Cruz province. Several companies can take you from the capital to Río Gallegos for about 150 pesos (depending on service quality), departing in the evening, generally between 18.00 and 22.00 and arriving about 36 hours later; then you'll have to take another bus from Río Gallegos to Ushuaia, for about 50 pesos. This service from Río Gallegos to Ushuaia runs only from October to March; in winter you'll have to fly, or take a bus towards Punta Arenas and wait at the turning to the Primera Angostura ferry.

Likewise, from El Calafate you must either take the four-hour bus ride to Río Gallegos and then get a plane or bus to Ushuaia, or go by bus via Puerto Natales and Punta Arenas in Chile, and from there to Ushuaia. There are buses most days (several a day in summer, but try to book in advance) from El Calafate to Puerto Natales, a frequent service from there to Punta Arenas (hourly in summer from 08.00 to 20.00), and an early-morning departure most days from there to Ushuaia (perhaps changing in Río Grande). The Punta Arenas–Ushuaia leg takes 12 hours and costs 90 pesos.

The main bus offices are: Bus Sur-Líder (*Gobernador Paz 921;* ✆ *436421; www.bus-sur.cl*), Tolkeyen (*Maipú 237;* ✆ *437073, 427354*) and Techni Austral (*25 de Mayo 50;* ✆ *02901/423396*).

By car

The only way in is by Ruta National 3, paved most of the way. To enter Tierra del Fuego, however, it is necessary to cross into Chile to take a ferry. The main crossing is at the Primera Angostura (First Narrows) from Punta Delgada on the continent to Bahía Azul on the island (30 minutes); the other crossing is from Punta Arenas to Porvenir (just one crossing per day; 2½ hours).

Orientation

The main street through the centre of Ushuaia is San Martín, parallel to the waterfront Avenida Maipú. At the main dock are Plazas 25 de Mayo and 12 de Octubre with the historic Obelisk. At the other end of Avenida Maipú is the Yacht Club and a bridge that crosses to the site of the Anglican Missions, separating Bahía Encerrada (Closed Bay) from the main bay. Avenida Maipú continues along the water until it turns and becomes Avenida Malvinas Argentinas, leading to the airport.

Several bus companies run from stops on Avenida Maipú to many of the area's tourist destinations.

Where to stay

Las Hayas Hotel and Resort Camino Glaciar Martial, km3; ✆ 430710, f 430719; e lashayas@overnet.com.ar. This 5-star hotel is the most exclusive in Ushuaia and offers all comforts. Sgls and dbls US$130, triples US$156.

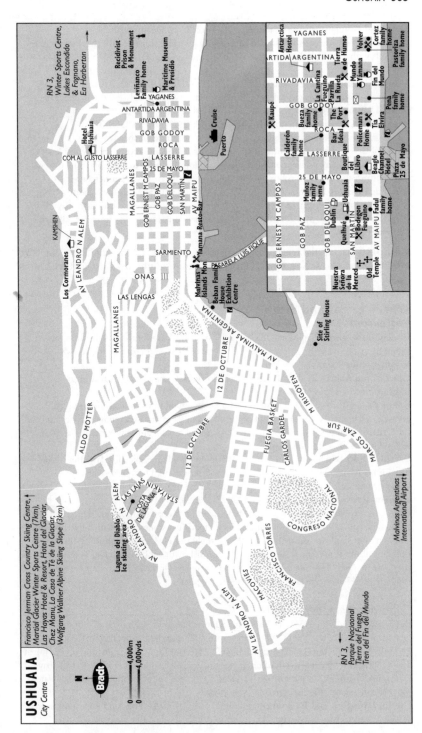

USHUAIA
City Centre

Bradt

N

0   4,000m
0   4,000yds

Francisco Jerman Cross Country Skiing Centre,
Martial Glacier Winter Sports Centre (7km),
Las Hayas Hotel & Resort, Hotel del Glaciar,
Chez Manu, La Casa de Té de la Glaciar;
Wolfgang Wallner Alpine Skiing Slope (3km)

RN 3,
Winter Sports Centre,
Lakes Escondido
& Fagnano,
Ea Harberton

Recidivist
Prison
& Monument

Maritime Museum
& Presidio

Leviñanco
family home

YAGANES

ANTARTIDA ARGENTINA

RIVADAVIA

GOB GODOY

ROCA

LASSERRE

25 DE MAYO

SAN MARTIN

GOB DELOQUI

GOB PAZ

GOB ERNEST M CAMPOS

MAGALLANES

KAMSHEN

Los Cormoranes

AV LEANDRO N ALEM

SARMIENTO

ONAS

LAS LENGAS

MAGALLANES

ALDO MOTTER

AV LEANDRO N ALEM

AV LEANDRO N ALEM

LAS LAJAS

COSTA DE LAGUNA

STAIAXIN

Laguna del Diablo
Ice skating area

12 DE OCTUBRE

12 DE OCTUBRE

FUEGIA BASKET

CARLOS GARDEL

MACACHINES

FRANCISCO TORRES

CONGRESO NACIONAL

MARCOS ZAR SUR

MI IRIGOYEN

AV MALVINAS ARGENTINA

Site of
Stirling House

Beban Family
House
Exhibition
Centre

PASARELA LUIS FIQUE

Malvinas
Islands Mon

Yamana Resto-Bar

AV MAIPU

Puerto

Cruise

Hotel
Ushuaia

COM. AL GUSTO LASSERRE

RN 3,
Parque Nacional
Tierra del Fuego,
Tren del Fin del Mundo

Malvinas Argentinos
International Airport

Inset map:

YAGANES

Antarctica
Hostel

PARTIDA ARGENTINA

RIVADAVIA

GOB GODOY

ROCA

LASSERRE

25 DE MAYO

GOB ERNEST M CAMPOS

GOB PAZ

GOB DELOQUI

SAN MARTIN

AV MAIPU

Kaupé

Bueza
family
home

Calderón
family
home

La Cantina
Fueguino
Parilla

La Rueda

Tierra
de Humos

Mundo
Fin del
Mundo

Yamana

Volver

Cortez
family
home

Pastoriza
family home

Peña
family
home

The
Port

Bar
Ideal

Policeman's
Home

Tia
Elvira

Boutique
del
Libro

Beagle
Channel
Hotel

Plaza
25 de Mayo

Muñoz
family
home

Quelhué

Bodegon
Fueguino

Dublin

Ushuaia

Fadul
family
home

Nuestra
Señora
de la
Merced

Old
Temple

Hotel del Glaciar Camino Glaciar Martial, km 3.5; ☎ 430640; f 430636;
e delglaciar@speedy.com.ar. Located in a stunning setting atop the hills overlooking the
bay. Sgls with a view of the bay US$179, with a view of the glacier US$159; dbls US$340
and US$318.
Beagle Channel Hotel Av Maipú 547; ☎ 421117, 421119; f 421120;
e reservas@hotelcanalbeagle.com.ar. The best hotel downtown. Sgls 300 pesos, dbls 330 pesos.
Hotel Ushuaia Lasserre 933; ☎ 430671, 423051, 431134, 424217;
e hotelushuaia@yahoo.com.ar. Sgls US$80, dbls US$110, triples US$130.
Los Cormoranes Kamshen 788; ☎ 423459; e loscormoranes@speedy.com.ar. It's a bit of
an uphill trek to this hostel, but you'll be greeted by a friendly receptionist with plenty of
helpful advice, many international travellers with lots of stories to share and a nice view of
the bay from the common room upstairs. Dorm beds for 22 pesos per person.
Antartica Hostel Antártida Argentina 270; ☎ 435774; e antarcticahostel@hotmail.com;
www.antarcticahostel.com. A well-received new hostel in a central location (handy for the
Presidio), with dorms and dbl rooms costing 14 pesos per person. Pleasant bar, kitchen and
free internet.

Camping is available at La Pista del Andino (*Alem 2873;* ☎ *435890;*
e *lapistadelandino@infovia.com.ar*), and at the Rugby Club, just west at Ruta 3 km.4
(☎ *435796*).

Where to eat and drink
Restaurants
Bodegón Fueguino San Martín 859; ☎ 431972. Come here for the best lamb in town.
Prepared in various creative and delicious ways, but the one prepared with herbs is
mouthwateringly superb.
Chez Manu Martial 2135; ☎ 423253. This upscale restaurant offers a great meal
accompanied by a great view.
Kaupé Roca 470; ☎ 422704. The most exclusive restaurant in town, ideal for a special
occasion. Obviously at the pricey end of the scale, but the menu and reputation are excellent.
La Cantina Fueguina San Martín 326; ☎ 421887. Casual seafood restaurant; the *picada*
seafood dishes are recommended.
Parrilla La Rueda San Martín 193; ☎ 436540. An excellent choice for Argentine *asado*.
Tía Elvira Maipú 349; ☎ 424725. Great seafood served amid local bric-a-brac.
Volver Maipú 37; ☎ 423977. All kinds of fish, served in a casual homely setting.
Yámana Resto-Bar Luis Pedro Fique 121; ☎ 432090, 15 616245;
e info@centrobeagle.com; www.centrobeagle.com. A Yámana dining experience will be re-
created for you as you dine upon king crab or shellfish at stone tables with a live fire using
harpoons and shells for eating utensils. At the replica of HMS *Beagle* a historic film about
Yámana culture is presented (in English and Spanish with subtitles in other languages) on a
large screen. *Open Tue–Sun 12.00–24.00, reserve ahead for the show (13.45–20.30) and transfer
(remise or taxi, 5 mins from downtown); show price 60 pesos.*

Cafés and bars, light meals
Bar Ideal San Martín 393; ☎ 437860. This popular bar and restaurant is one of the oldest
establishments in town; the building dates from 1937 and the bar opened in 1953.
La Casa de Té de la Glaciar Martial 3560; ☎ 434699. Out of the centre and up the hill at
the upmarket Hotel del Glaciar, offering elegant ambiance and a great view over the bay.
Cafetería Ushuaia San Martín 783; ☎ 422568. Come here for a coffee or hot chocolate
and a tantalising selection of handmade chocolates.
Dublin Irish Pub and Restaurant 9 de Julio 168; ☎ 430744. You can find Guinness here
as well as microbrew and regional beers, other drinks, food, coffee and cakes.

Practicalities

The municipal **Tourist Information Board** has three branches: the main office in the town's first library at San Martín 674 (✆ *432000, free 0800 331476;* e *muniush@tierradelfuego.ml.org*), and others on the tourist pier at Plaza 12 de Octubre and at the airport, which open only when ships or planes are due. There's also the provincial office at Maipú 505 (✆ *423340;* f *430694;* e *info@tierradelfuego.org.ar*). There are many travel agents in town hanging the distinctive blue 'I' for Information, but the real tourist boards are those listed here, both well run and with plenty of excellent brochures and information.

The main **post office** is at San Martín and Gobernador Godoy, in a historical building dating back to 1933. The first post office was established on Avenida Maipú in 1891 but unfortunately burned down. Several banks and internet cafés are to be found along San Martín, as well as a good sports and bike shop, **DTT Ushuaia Sport** at San Martín 1258 (✆ *434939*).

Highlights

The port: the ships that are forever docked in the bay include the tugboat *Saint Christopher*, sent in 1943 to rescue a stranded ship; it ran aground itself and was damaged beyond repair, despite being named after the patron saint of travellers.

A walking or double-decker bus tour of the **Original Family Homes** is an alternative approach to seeing the city. There are over a dozen original buildings in the centre of Ushuaia, each with a unique story to tell. To see them all on foot takes stamina, but to see the majority of them you can start by circling the block along Avenida Maipú between Belgrano and Piedrabuena. Continue along Maipú for a while to enjoy the port until you reach the Salomón family home at no. 737. This is one of the oldest buildings and still looks as it did between 1913 and 1970 when it functioned as a general goods store. Turn up Fadul to the house of the Fadul family at no. 156; Señores Fadul and Salomón both came from Lebanon in 1913 and each opened general goods stores. Turn right and walk to Deloqui and 25 de Mayo and the Muñoz family home. This house was built by a Croatian carpenter, Juan Nirici, in the 1930s, and became the home of the Chilean consul. At Deloqui 402 is the Calderón family house, of typical Fuegian design, covered by corrugated metal against the wind. Next, head one block down Avenida Roca to the corner of San Martín and Ideal Bar, which was once the Bueza family home. The house was built in 1937 by Señor Bueza, who opened the bar in 1953. You may wish to take a break here for refreshments.

Return to Maipú and the Policeman's Home at no. 367, built in about 1920. This was the Ramos family home and another general store; in 1937 it passed to the Mata family and then the government, as a police station and small prison. It is suggested that the strange engravings on the doors were made by prisoners. The Pena home is at Maipú 263; it was built in 1928 and housed the Magistrates Court and the Customs Office until it went back to private use. At Maipú 91 is one of the most characteristic Fuegian houses, built in 1918 by the Pastoriza family. They had come in 1913 along with a group of 400 people intent upon working in a sardine- canning factory. The factory failed due to a shortage of sardines, but the family stayed on and built this home that is now declared a cultural heritage site. The Cortéz family home at Maipú 37 (the Volver Restaurant) was built in 1898 by Ramón Cortéz, the second director of the prison and the first chief of Ushuaia's police department, and his wife, María Sánchez Caballero, the first schoolteacher in town. When the prison closed in 1947, the remaining prisoners were held in this house. When it became a private residence again, it was home until 1985 to Mrs Rafaela Ishton, one of the last Selk'nam people (see page 34). In 1990 it became a coffee shop and later a popular restaurant. Now would be an appropriate time to see the actual Presidio or Recidivist Prison, now a National Historic Monument at Gobernador Paz and Yaganes (see details under *Museums*) and the adjacent Blanco family home. Señor Blanco was the prison accountant and the house, named Villa Julieta after his daughter, was built for him by the convicts. It was bought and sold several times and was even relocated, having originally been on Fadul and Deloqui streets. The porch, arched roof and triangular windows are characteristic of old Fuegian architecture. End your tour with the Leviñanco home at Gobernador Paz 56 and see one of the most beautiful Fuegian houses in town, built in about 1926.

At the far end of Ushuaia Bay, at the bridge over Bahía Encerrada, is the **Monumento Islas Malvinas** (commemorating the 1982 Falklands conflict) and the National Army Square and Monument to General Guëmes.

Three Christian institutions were established in the early days of Ushuaia: the **Old Temple** was built in 1886 and consecrated on 24 December 1898; **Nuestra Señora de la Merced Church** was built in 1949, with presbytery, apse and bell tower; and the site where the Anglican missionaries settled is on the far side of the bay beyond the bridge. The monument erected here marks the site of Stirling House, established in 1869.

Museums

Museo Mundo Yámana Rivadavia 56; ☎ 422874; e mundoyamana@infovia.com.ar. To learn about the Yámana peoples and the theories concerning the arrival of the first inhabitants of Tierra del Fuego, this museum presents an excellent interpretative collection of photos, maps, textual plaques and a 1:15 scale reproduction of a Yámana village. *Open daily 10.00–20.00; admission 5 pesos.*

Museo del Fin del Mundo Av Maipú and Rivadavia; ☎ 421863; f 421201; e museo@tierradelfuego.org.ar. Beautifully organised, the Museum of the End of the World has 6 rooms on different themes: artefacts of the aboriginal groups and the first voyagers to Tierra del Fuego; a replica of an old grocery store; items from the old prison; an impressive collection of over 180 mounted bird specimens from the area; a library; and a quaint little gift shop. *Open Mon–Sat 09.00–20.00 in summer, 12.00–19.00 in winter; admission 10 pesos.*

Presidio and Maritime Museum Gobernador Paz and Yaganes; ☎ 437481. The Presidio or former prison now houses an impressive array of exhibits about the murderers, anarchists and revolutionaries who once inhabited it, as well as model ships, a replica of a Yámana canoe, and a full-size copy of the 'Lighthouse at the End of the World', as described by Jules Verne in his novel of the same name. *Open daily 09.00–20.00, closed Mon Easter–Oct; admission 15 pesos.*

Exhibition Centre, Bebán Family House Maipú and Plüschow. A prefabricated house brought from Sweden in 1913 and now used for temporary exhibits. *Open Tue–Fri 10.00–20.00; w/ends 16.00–20.00; admission free.*

Shopping

Boutique del Libro 25 de Mayo 62; ☎ 432117; e info@antartidaypatagonia.com.ar. The best shop in town for books in English on Antarctic expeditions, Patagonia, travel guides, maps, posters, videos, etc.

Tierra de Humos San Martín 246/281; ☎ 433020, 433050; e terra1@impsat1.com.ar. This store offers a selection of typical Argentine and Fuegian objects such as *maté* gourds, ceramics, crafts, leather goods and souvenirs.

Quelhué San Martín 771; ☎ 435882; e quelhue@ciudad.com.ar. This wine and speciality store has a very good selection of Argentine wines and gifts. It sells spirits and some speciality foods as well. The staff are very helpful with your wine selection.

Activities
Diving
Diving is not only possible but popular in Tierra del Fuego. Experienced guides will know when and where dives can take place, since conditions change quickly owing to the erratic winds at the tip of the continent. Wind speed and direction and water currents are important factors. In addition, the water is cold and it is in the winter months that the diving is best! In the winter there is less wind, the sea is calmer and the water is clearer – because it is colder and thus there is less vegetation. Warmer water in the summer causes increased plankton growth. Water temperature in winter is about 2–4°C; in summer it reaches 8–10°C. You definitely need a drysuit to dive here.

Horseriding
The Centro Hípico Fin del Mundo (↘ 15 569099; e *info@centrohipicoushuaia.com.ar; www.centrohipicoushuaia.com.ar*) organises a wide array of horseback expeditions and day trips in the forest, along the coast, in the hills and to sites of special interest.

Winter sports
Winter sports include alpine and Nordic or cross-country skiing, snowboarding, sledging, ski mountaineering, ice climbing, snow-shoeing, ice skating, dog sledding and snowmobile riding.

Wolfgang Wallner Alpine Skiing Slope (Club Andino Ushuaia) 3km from town. The slope is 859m long at a 30° angle. There is a ski lift and a cafeteria at the base.
Francisco Jermán Cross-country Skiing Centre (Club Andino Ushuaia), 5km from town on the way to the Martial Glacier. The tracks are 2.5–7.5km long.
Laguna del Diablo ice-skating rink In the Andino neighbourhood, the block surrounded by Alme, Las Lajas, Staiyakin and Costa de Laguna streets. Public use free of charge.
Martial Glacier Winter Sports Centre 7km from town at the end of the road leading to the glacier. The slope is 1,130m long with a double chairlift. Ski lessons and clothing and equipment rental are available.

Summer activities include fishing, hiking, biking, canoeing and horseriding.

Fishing
In the lakes and rivers of Tierra del Fuego, record-size brown, rainbow and stream trout attract fishing enthusiasts from around the world. A fishing licence is required, of which there are two kinds – one is for use in all the national parks of Patagonia, the other is only for Tierra del Fuego. Only two fishing techniques are permitted: spinning (*cucharita*) with a 1.7m rod, a frontal reel, nylon fishing line 0.25–0.30mm and only artificial bait and simple hook – no battery-operated baits or lures allowed; or fly-casting (*mosca*) with a flexible rod for lines no. 6–8. Trolling is completely prohibited. The season is from November to March, and depending on area and time of year catch-and-release may be required. To go fishing, you may either take a fishing excursion through one of the agencies in town, pay a fee to fish at a private *coto* or go to a free public fishing area.

Day trips and excursions
Boat tours on the Beagle Channel go to **Seal Island**, **Bird Island**, **Les Eclaireurs Lighthouse** and other places, departing from the tourist pier twice a day. These trips, costing from about 60 pesos for two hours (more in high season), are wonderful ways to get out and see wildlife up close as well as spectacular scenery. Each company, with their office kiosks set up at the pier, has slightly varying tours

with different itineraries, services, size of boats (and therefore number of tourists squeezed onto the boat with you) and length of trip. Another question to ask is whether you will disembark from the boat at any time or if you will remain on board for the duration of the tour. One company that had an excellent guide on board able to identify every bird pointed out to him, was **Canoero Catamaranes** (\ 15 513291; e *losyamanas@arnet.com.ar*). Another reputable company is the **Tres Marias** (\/f 421897, 15 611074; e *marias3@satlink.com*), whose captain, Hector Monsalve, is a long-time resident and the only one with permission to visit one of the islands in the channel. He takes a maximum of ten passengers on his small old boat, which is better for wildlife viewing, but this is not a luxury cruise!

Tour agencies
Compañia de Guias de Patagonia Gob Campos 795; \/f 437753, 15 618426; e lacompania@arnet.com.ar; www.companiadeguias.com.ar
Nunatak Adventures \ 443968, 15 513463; e nunatak@tierradelfuego.org.ar. Nunatak is a group of professional guides without a formal office. They specialise in trekking, ice-trekking, canoeing, kayaking and mountain biking.
Canal Rivadavia 82; \ 437395; www.canalfun.com. This company has excellent tours that include kayaking, sailing, trekking and 4x4 off-road adventures. The tours link with wildlife or cultural experiences, such as visiting the beaver colonies, Gable Island and Harberton Estancia, Tierra del Fuego National Park and the lakes.
Kams \ 15 618907, 15 616523; e pluspatagonia@kams.com.ar. Makes tailor-made trips to wildlife and anthropological sites. They offer some standard programmes, for instance to the lighthouse, Penguin Island and Harberton Estancia, but also go to Lapataia Bay, Remolino Farm, Redonda Island and Cucharita Bay.
Wintek Expeditions e isladelosfuegos@speedy.com.ar; www.wintekexpeditions.com.ar. This independent professional group has a diverse range of expeditions.

Martial Glacier
The glacier is 7km by road from the centre. Pasarela, Body, Feder, Gonzalo, Costa del Sur, Kaupen, La Paloma and Lautaro run tour buses to the roadhead for 5 pesos each way; then a chairlift (*daily 10.00–16.00; 10 pesos*) will take you up to the glacier.

Parque Nacional Tierra del Fuego
Access to the **Tierra del Fuego National Park** is via Ruta 3, 11km to the west of Ushuaia. Inside the park there is an organised campsite, near Lake Roca, as well as many free camping areas and several hiking paths well laid out on a map provided at the park gate when you pay your 12 pesos park fee. The highway ends at Lapataia, 3,063km from Buenos Aires and a thousand from Antarctica; there's a flagpole and a small car-park, and virtually nothing else.

There are several hikes through this park, as well as canoeing on the lakes. The **Pampa Alta Trail** (4.9km) is a medium-difficulty trail taking about an hour to hike. You will have a panoramic view of the Beagle Channel and Pipo Valley. Start at Bahía Ensenada campsite and go either along the Arroyo Piloto or take a shortcut from Ruta 3. The **Senda Costera** (Coastal Trail; 6.5km) takes you along the shores of Lago Roca, the Río Lapataia and both Lapataia and Ensenada bays, through the forest of coihue (*Nothofagus betuloides*) and canelo (*Drimys winteri*). At 'the post office at the end of the world' at Bahía Ensenada you can have your passport stamped for 3 pesos. The **Hito XXIV Trail** (4km each way) is an easy hike along the northeast shore of Lago Roca (starting from the Lago Roca car-park) to the Argentine-Chilean border. The **Cerro Guanaco Trail** (4km) is a tough

TIERRA DEL FUEGO NATIONAL PARK

Created in 1960 to protect the 63,000ha of the southern tip of the Andes, the sub-Antarctic false beech forests, and the southernmost reach of the Magellanic biogeographical zone, this park holds the distinction of being the southernmost national park in the world. Lenga and the evergreen coihue are the dominant tree species of the cool and damp Magellanic forests. The park encompasses the area from north of Lake Fagnano to the coast of the Beagle Channel, along the border with Chile. Eras of glaciation have etched the landscape with mountain chains and deep valleys. Winds off the sea and the Andes keep the temperatures moderate and rarely below freezing in winter, but rarely above 10°C. The mean precipitation is 700mm per year with no real peak period other than a slight rise in August, and winter snowfall is abundant in the mountains. Peat-bogs are common in Tierra del Fuego, occurring when accumulations of dead plant matter such as sphagnum moss and aquatic grasses build up in damp valleys where low temperatures and slow-moving acidic waters prevent decomposition. After several centuries the weight of the upper layers forces oxygen out of the compressed lower layers that thereby form peat. Tierra del Fuego has very limited animal diversity, with only 20 species of mammals and 90 birds. There are no amphibians. What wildlife there is though is abundant and several species are unique; the Fuegian red fox (*Dusicyon culpaeus lycoides*) is the best example.

Introduced species take their toll on the island. Most loved and hated is the beaver (*Castor canadensis*). It has become an attraction with tourists and there are tours specifically to see the beavers' dams, but they are a menace to the natural ecology and especially the riparian systems. These animals along with rabbits, muskrats and the mainland grey fox were all introduced for supposedly economic reasons for their pelts. There are also rats and other rodents that made their way onto the island from ships, as well as insects and plant species introduced by tourists. Island ecology is fragile, however, and after centuries of a unique evolution based on isolation from mainland species, it cannot quickly adapt to invaders. These introduced species have altered the natural landscape and ecological balance.

Along the coastal shores wildlife is ever-present, whether it be one of the sheldgeese (upland, kelp or ashy headed) or cormorants (you may be fortunate to see the the imperial cormorant up close and glimpse its stunning blue eyes) or any of the numerous coastal birds such as the oystercatcher or the entertaining flightless steamer ducks, churning their legs ferociously to carry them along the water. There are also particular coastal plants such as the sea pink (*Armeria* spp.). Crustaceans and shellfish are abundant and important economically.

The presence of several tribal groups on the island before the arrival of Europeans goes back some 10,000 years. Ancient middens exist on the beaches of the Beagle Channel and Lago Roca where remains of shells and bones tell of the diet of these peoples. They stayed near the shorelines and used canoes made of the bark of lenga trees for hunting sea lions, collecting molluscs and transporting themselves throughout the area. They were completely integrated into this seemingly hostile environment and clothed themselves in little more than a sea lion pelt; for the most part they were comfortable naked and simply applied the fats and greases from the animals to their skin to repel water.

hike up the mountain (970m above sea level) to take in the view of the Fuegian Range and the peat-bog valley. This hike also starts from the Lago Roca car-park but diverts uphill right after crossing the Arroyo Guanaco.

In addition, there are several gentle and relatively short hikes in the Lapataia area. The **Paseo de las Islas** (600m) takes you along the shores of the rivers Lapataia and Ovando and crosses the Cormoranes Archipelago. The **Laguna Negra** path (950m) visits a peat-bog in formation. The **Mirador Lapataia** path (1km) offers panoramic views of Bahía Lapataia, intersecting with the **Paseo del Turbal** (2km), an alternative approach to Bahía Lapataia through the peat-bog and beaver habitat. It will also connect to the **Castorera** (beaver colony) trail (400m) that leads to a beaver dam, following the Los Castores stream. The **Sendero de la Baliza** or Beacon Trail (1.5km) will also enter beaver territory.

Bus companies Eben Ezer, Pasarela, Kaupen, Gonzalo, Body, Weekend and Bella Vista have various schedules for transportation to the park for 10–20 pesos round trip depending on drop-off point. The earliest departure is at 08.30 and the last return is at 20.00, both with Eben Ezer.

The 11m-high **Les Eclaireurs Lighthouse**, Argentina's southernmost lighthouse, is on one of the Les Eclaireurs islets marking the entrance of Ushuaia Bay (not to be confused with the 'Lighthouse at the End of the World', actually on Isla de los Estados or Staten Island) and is powered by solar energy.

On the way to Harberton Estancia are areas of beaver habitat where you can arrange with a guide to try to see a busy beaver at work. They are crepuscular animals, active in the early morning and at dusk; they are also an introduced species and have caused significant damage to the natural ecology and riparian systems.

Harberton Estancia is the oldest estancia in Tierra del Fuego and the oldest buildings and the stone piers have been declared National Historic Monuments. Founded by Thomas Bridges and his wife Mary Ann Varder in 1886, today their great-great-grandchildren still live at the estancia, which has a guesthouse, tea house and museum. Bridges' biography is fantastically interesting from the start; as an infant he was found abandoned on a bridge by an Anglican missionary, who adopted him. At the age of 13 he and his family went to Keppel Island in the Falklands to work with the settlers there. At 21 he came to Tierra del Fuego and was soon fluent in the Yámana language. He set up a mission at Ushuaia in 1870 and was named the 'Father of Tierra del Fuego'. Sixteen years later he moved to Harberton with his family and began working his estancia.

You can take a guided tour of the estancia (15 pesos) and visit the museum (*open daily 10.00–19.00, 15 Oct–15 Apr; admission 5 pesos*). Catamaran tours to the estancia and a nearby penguin rookery cost about 60 pesos round trip from Ushuaia; you'll see hundreds of Magellanic penguins and a few king penguins, from November to March; you may also see seals, sea lions, petrels, cormorants, kelp geese and the occasional black-browed albatross. There is, however, no time allocated to take the full estancia tour. You may prefer to rent a car to come to the estancia independently and arrange to take the boat to visit the penguins. Reserve in advance (❨ *422742;* f *422743;* e *estanciaharberton@tierradelfuego.org.ar; www.estanciaharberton.com; open Mon–Fri 13.30–17.00*).

Lakes **Escondido, Fagnano** and **Yehuin** are respectively 60km, 100km and 160km north of Ushuaia. The watershed of Lago Fagnano is important stream trout habitat and there are campsites, hostelries and cabins on the shores of the lake. Nearby Tolhuin is referred to as 'The Heart of the Island' and is the smallest village in Tierra del Fuego. To reach Lago Yehuin, take Ruta 3 and then the picturesque Ruta Provincial 21. Other nearby lakes are Chepelmut and Yakush, where there is trout fishing, boat trips and wildlife watching. Continuing on Ruta

21 will take you to the coast at Cabo San Pablo, near the outlet of the Ladrilleros and San Pablo rivers.

Several bus companies run to Escondido and Fagnano lakes from town at various times and locations for approximately 35–60 pesos.

The **Tren del Fin del Mundo** (\ *431600;* f *437696;* e *reservas@ trendelfindelmundo.com.ar; www.trendelfindelmundo.com.ar*) is a historic convict train that still travels on part of its original route of a hundred years ago. Its proper name is *Ferrocarril Austral Fueguino* (Southern Fuegian Railway) and it took the prisoners into the forest to cut wood for fuel and building material. Today the railway allows visitors to see otherwise inaccessible areas of the Tierra del Fuego National Park. The 6km line runs along the Río Pipo and the Cañadón del Toro, crosses the Puente Quemado (the remains of the original 'Burnt Bridge' still lie below the new one), stops at Estación Cascada de la Macarena for passengers to view the Macarena Waterfall and the river valley where a reconstruction of an aboriginal settlement can be visited, and takes a second stop inside the park at the remains of an old sawmill. Trains start from Estación del Fin del Mundo, 10km from Ushuaia on Ruta 3, heading west towards the park; buses (Pasarela, Costa del Sur or Kaupen) run to the station from the corner of Maipú and 25 de Mayo for around 10 pesos. Departures are at 09.30, 12.00, 15.00 and 17.00 (but only at 10.00 in winter), returning from Estación Parque Nacional at 10.40, 13.10, 16.10 and 18.40 (only at 11.10 in winter). Confirm departure times in advance, as some are conditional requiring a minimum number of passengers. Fares are 50 pesos for adults and 18 pesos for children. Reserve tickets in advance.

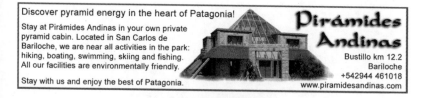

Appendix 1

PATAGONIAN WILDLIFE GUIDE
English name (Spanish or local name)
Latin or scientific name

Dogs
Foxes
Argentine grey fox/little grey/Patagonian grey (zorro gris chico/zorro patagónico)
Pseudalopex griseus/Dusicyon griseus
Shoulder height: 30–45cm; Length: 42–68cm plus 30–35cm tail; Weight: 4kg
The fox is shy but commonly seen at dusk and dawn and is likely to cross your path at night so drive with caution on rural roads. Except in spring when part of a family unit that consists of two parents and five to six kits, the fox is a solitary creature. It will take almost any small prey, such as rodents, birds (and their eggs), insects and lizards, and will also eat berries and mushrooms. This small fox has relatively large ears and a pointed muzzle, and though named the grey fox, its colouring is non-uniform with a blending of tawny head and extremities, yellow under-fur and white facial and chest accents. Sadly, the grey fox is prized for its fur and renowned, often unfoundedly, as being a livestock threat and thus often classified as vermin; the poor creature seems to be the subject of trapping and hunting practically wherever it roams, often without restriction. This species' status in Argentina varies from rare, locally common to stable depending upon region, throughout Patagonia from Río Negro to the Magellan Strait, where it was introduced to Tierra del Fuego, and northwest to Catamarca. The skin trade is an important source of income for people in rural Argentina, with thousands of culpeos (*Dusicyon culpaeus*) and grey fox hunted for their fur annually in Patagonia; more than one million grey foxes were killed in the 1980s, with the most pelts coming from Argentina, more than 100,000 in 1987 alone.

Similar species:
The red fox (also known as the South American or culpeo fox (zorro Colorado; *Pseudalopex culpaeus/Dusicyon culpaeus magellanicus*) is found throughout Patagonia, though rare on the coast, and along the Andes and beyond Argentina. This nocturnal fox is larger and stockier than the grey (L: 60–115 plus 30–45cm tail; W: 5–13kg) with rustier colouring; a subspecies is the endemic Fuegan red fox, *D.C. lycoides*, that it is hypothesised was the fox introduced by the Yaghan peoples to the Falkland Islands, called the *warrah* or the Falkland Islands wolf; sadly, it was hunted to extinction. The grey or pampas fox (zorro gris común/zorro gris pampeano; *Pseudalopex gimnocercus/Dusicyon gimnocercus*) ranges throughout Argentina but especially in the Río Negro region. It is similar in colouring but varies in size from the Argentine grey (L: 60–115cm plus 30–45cm tail; W: 5–13.5kg).

Cats

Puma/cougar/mountain lion (puma)

Puma concolor/Felis concolor

Length: female 86–131cm; male 102–154cm plus 63–96cm tail
Weight: females 29–64kg; males 36–120kg.

Puma

This cat is the most geographically dispersed and found throughout the Americas, from the northern Rocky Mountains in Canada all the way to southern Patagonia, but is not on Tierra del Fuego. Different subspecies of puma correspond to different areas in its range; the subspecies of Patagonia is the largest in Argentina. Historically found on the coast, it is now rare, but it can be found almost anywhere else in Patagonia, from the forested Andes to the open steppe. This cat is easily recognisable merely by its size; in addition it has light brown pelage with black markings around the muzzle and at the tips of the ears and tail. The wild fare of this large cat includes guanacos, rheas, geese, maras and the introduced European hare, but numerous domestic sheep dotting the landscape inevitably enter the cat's diet, causing frequent shootings of pumas by ranchers.

Similar species:

The jaguar (yaguareté/tigré/overo; *Panthera onca*) is not found in Patagonia but only within the subtropical forests in Argentina's northeast and there is little chance of confusing the tawny coloured puma with the distinctly spotted or black coat of the jaguar (melanistic colouring common in spotted cats, typically occurring in populations that inhabit dense dark forests to offer more camouflage; the spots are visible in strong light). However, the jaguar is the only other large cat (H: 50–80cm; L: 112–240cm plus 17–30cm tail; W: 55–160kg – females not generally more than 100kg) in Argentina similar to the puma. Where the puma's extensive range does encroach on that of the jaguar these cats would directly compete for prey (jaguars prey upon tapirs, peccaries, fallow deer, paca, snakes, lizards, rodents, birds and occasionally monkeys, fish – it is a great swimmer – and even fruit) but this is curbed by at least a couple of factors: the jaguar prefers wetter areas, the puma drier; and the jaguar is active by day while the puma has more nocturnal behaviour. The jaguar is an endangered species threatened by habitat loss and poaching. This cat is the largest in the Americas and third-largest in the world; its name derives from the Gurani *yaguara*, probably meaning 'beast that kills its prey in one bound'.

Small cats

Pampas cat (gato de pajonal); Geoffroy's cat (gato montés); kodkod/guigna (gato hiuña/guiña)

Oncifelis colocolo/Felis colocolo; Oncifelis geoffroyi; Oncifelis guigna; Felis geoffroyi

Shoulder height: 30–35cm; 15–30cm; 25cm;
Length: 45–70cm body plus 22–32cm tail; 45–75cm body plus 25–38cm tail; 40–50 plus 20–25cm tail
Weight: 3–7kg; 3–8kg; 1.5–2.7kg

These small Argentine cats all have wide handsome faces and beautiful markings (spots and stripes, banded tail) accenting otherwise pale fur. The pampas cat has the largest and pointiest ears of the three but can demonstrate a stark variance of pelage, from bold to the most subtle markings (bolder only on the legs) and three varieties of colouration to its shaggy coat: silvery grey with reddish stripes, red with black markings or solid black. It is also a more robust cat than the other two species listed here. Geoffroy's cat has a sleek coat with uniform, distinct spots covering its entire body that make it a target for the skin trade. The kodkod is the smallest felid in the western hemisphere and has long fur with black spots; it has 10–12 black bands on its tail, a white or spotted face and black ears with a white spot in the centre; pure black individuals are not uncommon. The pampas cat ranges throughout Patagonia, a more expansive range than the other small cats, but it is uncommon and its population unknown. Geoffroy's cat ranges through the foothills and river valleys of central to northern Patagonia and though reportedly locally common, it is rarely seen and poached for the pelt trade. The kodkod is found in the limits of the Andean-Valdivian and Magellan forests of Neuquén, Río Negro, Chubut and Santa Cruz. It is on the IUCN Red List as a vulnerable species, in moderate to high risk of extinction. All these cats are solitary and nocturnal, feeding on small prey, such as rodents, lizards, birds and insects.

Similar species:
Found only in northeast Argentina, at the southernmost extent of its range that reaches north to Texas, the jaguarundi (yaguarundí; *Herpailurus yaguarondi*) is is a rare and beautiful animal, with a sleek dark coat and agile movements and an almost otter-like physique with a round head and ears, and round pupils, like that of pantherine cats, rather than slitlike. It is a medium-sized cat (H: 25–35cm; L: 55–70cm plus 50cm tail; W: 4–8kg). It is solitary, hunting (birds, rabbits, rodents) and hiding in dense thickets and brush, ideally near water; one reason for its threatened status is the extensive clearing of shrubland for farming or settlement.

Note If you are lucky enough to see one of Argentina's wild cats, you should report it to the relevant provincial wildlife authorities for their records.

Weasel family
Patagonian/Humboldt's hog-nosed skunk (zorrino patagónico)
Conepatus humboldtii
Length: 30–50cm plus 20–40cm tail
Weight: 2–4kg
Found throughout Patagonia and unmistakeable by sight or smell, hog-nosed skunks are named for their broad bald pink noses. This stocky skunk may be of brown or black colouring on its back between two bold white stripes that extend from the forehead down its sides. The short but full tail is white with shading towards grey owing to dark under-fur. Skunks feed on insects and small vertebrates but will also incorporate vegetable matter and carrion into their diet. This is the only skunk species in Patagonia; a similar species is the common skunk or Molina's hog-nosed skunk (zorrino común) – *Conepatus chinga* (L: 30–50cm plus 20–40cm tail; W: 2.5–4.5kg) found only in northern Argentina. Skunks are protected by national law in Argentina

Patagonian weasel (huroncito); Little/lesser grison (hurón menor)
Lyncodon patagonicus; *Galictis cuja*
Length: 30–35cm plus 12–30cm tail
Weight: 2–2.5kg
At a quick glance, or even a quick whiff, you might first think that you have encountered a skunk when seeing the Patagonian weasel. It is very similar in colouring to a skunk (black face, neck, underbelly and front legs, dark charcoal grey dorsal and tail with a wide white stripe extending from the forehead down either side of the neck and halfway down the lower sides of the body) and, like all members of this family, it produces strong-smelling secretions for scent-marking its territory. However, the Patagonian weasel is easy to identify by its long slender body frame, but it is not easy to spot and one would be exceptionally lucky to see one. It is active at night in its habitat of dry scrubby steppe and hilly terrain, but owing to its elusiveness little is known about it. The lesser grison, on the other hand, is very active (diurnal) and more frequently seen, but only ranges in the north of Patagonia (the Patagonian weasel is distributed throughout Patagonia; both range further north). It bounds along through the bushes and seems to be always busily in search of something – probably food, which is small prey such as rodents and lesser cavies. It is slender but larger and with a longer

tail than the Patagonian weasel, similar in colour but the white is mainly on the forehead, possibly extending just down the neck.

Patagonia/southern river otter (huillín/lobito de río común)
Lontra provocax
Length: 65–70 plus 35–45cm tail
Weight: 6–10kg
This rare and endangered species is found only in three small populations, each isolated from the other. One is in Nahual Huapi National Park, a second is in the Beagle Channel and Bahía Lapataia in Tierra del Fuego and the third is on Staten Island. Reasons for its decline are attributed to trapping, introduced species that compete with its prey species, and other introduced weasel species, such as the American weasel, that compete directly for the same ecological niche. The Patagonian river otter is nocturnal with aquatic habitats: lakes, rivers, marshes and streams where it stays near the banks where there is dense foliage. It feeds mainly on crustaceans. It is dark in colour. This is the only otter in Argentina; the marine otter or southern sea otter (nutria marina/chingungo; *Lontra feline*) is a very small remnant population on the east coast of Tierra del Fuego after being introduced to the Falkland Islands.

Armadillos
Pichi (pichi)
Zaedyus pichiy

Armadillo

Length: 26–33cm plus 10–14cm tail
Weight: 1–2kg
As cute as its name sounds, this little armadillo is relatively common and frequently seen. It is solitary and active by day, toddling about the steppe, typically digging about in search of food (vegetation, carrion, spiders and insects) or skilfully digging deeper burrows (up to 2m deep) with its long claws. The outer 'shell' of armadillos is made of scutes, which are actually thin bone plates in the skin, the only mammal with such a characteristic. Fossilised scutes up to fifty million years old have been found in South America. If unable to burrow as an escape mechanism, an armadillo will hold fast onto the ground with its long strong claws and pull its carapace edges flat to the ground, tucking under its head and tail. Some, such as the pichi, will roll up into a ball. Pichi scutes are dark brown with pale lateral edges that form a rather rounded carapace that extends over the head with the ears barely protruding from underneath. The eight central bands are articulated. Sparse hairs cover the scutes while thicker brown fur grows from the undersides of the carapace and coarse yellowish fur covers its belly. The tail and strong legs are hairless and covered with scales.

Larger hairy armadillo (peludo/quirquincho grande)
Chaetophractus villosus
Length: 22–40cm plus 9–17cm tail
Weight: 2kg
This species is the largest armadillo and it ranges from north-central Argentina into western Patagonia. The banded portion of carapace has 18 bands, seven or eight of which are articulated. The armadillo derives its name from the abundance of hair growing from between its scutes and the thick light-coloured fur covering its undersides. Feeding strategies of this animal are somewhat distasteful – burrowing under carcasses to obtain maggots and other insects and scavenging upon carrion – making it remarkable that it is poached (illegally hunted, not the cooking method) for a human food source. It is nocturnal in high summer, diurnal the rest of the year. Generally there are two offspring per litter, one male and one female. This is one of the most common armadillos captured for zoo specimens and can live in captivity for up to 30 years.

Rodents
Mice (ratón)

With so much of Patagonia being open grasslands, there are naturally many species of field mice – too many to list comprehensively in this guide. To list but a few of the more noteworthy would include the pampas field mouse (ratón pajizo; *Akodon molinae*), the bay-tipped field mouse (ratón hocico bayo; *A. xanthorinus*) and the Patagonian field mouse (ratón Patagónico/campestre; *A. iniscatus*), which has also apparently performed certain tasks to merit it the alternative common English name of intelligent field mouse. All of these mice are about 8–10cm in body length with a 3–5cm tail.

Other species of mice in Patagonia include: the unique and easily recognisable long-tailed mouse (ratón colilargo; *Oryzomys longicaudatus*), which measures an impressive 22cm in length owing to its remarkably long tail that is over twice the length of its body and from which it derives its name; the rabbit-rat (ratón conejo; *Reithrodon physodes*), named for its large oval-shaped ears; the leaf-eared mouse (ratón orejudas; *Phyllotis* spp.) also named for its oversized auricles; the white-eared vesper mouse (laucha bimaculada; *Calomys musculinus*), which is a cute tiny mouse (7cm plus 7cm tail) with little white tufts of fur that sometimes are seen behind the ears; and of course the introduced house mouse that, along with the old-world rats such as the Norway rat, has established throughout the Americas.

Common chinchillón/mountain vizcacha/pilquin
(chinchillón común/vizcacha serrana/pilquín)
Lagidium famatinae/L. viscacia/L. boxi
Length: 45cm plus 40cm tail

Chinchillón

Found in the Andean foothills, vizcachas are members of the exclusively South American Chinchillidae family, but despite the confusion in common names the chinchilla itself is extinct in Argentina. Vizcachas are pale yellow or grey with a black-tipped tail and long, furry, rabbit-like ears. They are active at dawn and dusk and do not hibernate. Well adapted to rough mountainous habitats with sparse vegetation, they will eat almost any plantlife they encounter, from grass to moss to lichen.

All members of this family are famous for their long soft fur and suffer from over-hunting for their pelt, which has led to the extinction of some species, although others, such as the chinchilla of northern Chile (Chinchilla lanigera), are widely bred in captivity.

Similar species:
The orange chinchillon (chinchillón anaranjado; L. wolffsohni), found only in Santa Cruz province and southern Chile is extremely rare, with too little information to judge whether its population remains viable.

Coipo/nutria (coipo)
Myocastor coypus
Length: 47–57cm plus 35–40cm tail
Weight: 5–10kg

Native to South America the coipo inhabits freshwater, even brackish, marshes, ponds and rivers. It builds vegetative platforms upon which it enjoys resting, feeding (roots, shoots, leaves) and grooming for extensive periods; it also builds extensive burrows in the soil or through dense vegetation or it may take over abandoned muskrat houses. It is physically adapted to a semi-aquatic habitat by having webbed toes (actually only the back feet and only four out of the five toes), water-repellent fur and the ability to remain submerged for several (up to ten) minutes. Owing to its long thin, rather than paddle-shaped, tail it resembles a muskrat more than a beaver. It is gregarious in nature with social groups of a few to over a dozen members comprised of related adult females and their offspring and one adult male.

Similar species:
The North American beaver (castor; *Castor canadensis*) was introduced during the fur trade era and it has survived very well and now competes with the coipo for habitat as well as being quite destructive with its dam-building tendencies, which are not part of the ecology in Argentina – the coipos build platforms, but are not as high-impact on trees and waterways as beavers are. However, the beaver is popular with wildlife watchers and there are tours to see them and/or their dams in locations such as Tierra del Fuego.

Tuco tuco (tuco tuco)
Ctenomys spp.
Length: 16–25cm plus 6.5–8cm tail
Weight: 18–23g
The tuco tuco is a vegetarian rodent very similar in appearance and behaviour to the ground squirrel. In Argentina, there are approximately 16 species, varying only slightly in size and colouring (grey to brown); some have limited and specific geographic ranges while others overlap their territories with other species over a greater area. The Patagonian tuco tuco (tuco tuco patagónico; *C. haigii*) is widespread throughout southwestern Argentina, preferring the open treeless areas of the Andes; Magellan's tuco tuco (tuco tuco magallánico; *C. magellanicus*) and the Fuegian tuco tuco *(C.m.fueginus)* are endemic to the Magellan forest and Tierra del Fuego, respectively. The Patagonian tuco tuco is rarely above ground, but when it is, it is noted for repeatedly calling its name 'tuc!' The sociable tuco tuco (tuco tuco sociable; *C. sociabilis*) is above ground much more often but only at dusk and dawn and is recognised by a black and white moustache; it is found in the Río Negro and Neuquén provinces.

Marsupials
Patagonian opossum (comadrejita patagónica)
Lestodelphys halli
Length: 13–15cm plus 8–10cm tail
Weight: 70–80g
Out of the 76 South American opossums, this species is the only one in Patagonia, one of two in Argentina. The Patagonian opossum is the farthest south marsupial in the Americas, but also farther south than in Australia as well. This opossum lives in a cold and dry temperate zone atypical of other opossums that tend to occur in tropical and neotropical areas. Another anomaly with this species is that the females do not have the neo-natal pouch that is a primary feature of the marsupial order, which includes kangaroos and wombats. The Patagonian opossum is very rare and critically endangered, seldom seen and understudied. This species is believed to be carnivorous and terrestrial, judging mainly by physiological factors in the skull, teeth, feet and tail that appear most adapted to these life strategies. The Patagonian steppe also lacks trees; therefore, this animal would live in areas of grass and shrub.

Similar species:
The only other Argentine opossum is the dwarf mouse-opossum, also known as the South American desert mouse opossum or the small/velvety fat-tailed opossum (marmosa común; *Thylamys pusilla*), but it does not occur in Patagonia. It lives in the temperate drylands of neotropical northern Argentina. It is known by several common names, which give insights into the characteristics of this little rodent. For example, 'fat-tailed' refers to its ability to store fat reserves in its tail, which becomes visibly engorged, during times of low resource availability, 'velvety' refers to its soft plush fur and 'mouse' refers to its size (L: 10cm plus 11cm tail; W: 18g). It is grey-brown with a white underbelly and has large ears and large black eyes.

Monito de monte (monito de monte/colocolo/chimaihuén)
Dromiciops australis
Length: 8–13cm plus 9–13cm tail
Weight: 17–31g

This nocturnal, semi-arboreal South American marsupial's common name translates to 'little mountain monkey'. It lives in the Andean forests of Argentina and Chile and is an excellent climber. It makes nests of sticks, moss, leaves and grass about 20cm in diameter, in which to have its young; like most marsupials, the young are born premature and enter a fur-lined pouch to nurse and continue developing. When they are more mature, they are carried on the mother's back. It has dense silky brown fur, white undersides and patches, short round ears and black rings around the eyes. The monito de monte eats insects and small invertebrates and sometimes fruit and stores fat from this high-protein diet in its tail – enough to double its body weight to sustain it during winter hibernation. This species is of special interest because it is the only member of its family, Microbiotheriidae, and is believed to be more closely related to Australian marsupials than any South American family.

Maras and cavies

Mara/Patagonian hare (mara o liebre patagónica)
Dolichotis patagonum
Length: 70–80cm plus 40–50cm tail
Weight: 8–16kg

Patagonian hare

Though the common names refer to the mara as a hare (liebre), it is not. The introduced European hare (liebre Europea; *Lepus europaeus*) is found in Argentina but it is a lagomorph, a different family from cavies and maras. The mara seems a cross between a rabbit and a small deer. It moves by leaping into the air from all four of its longish legs somewhat like an antelope. It has largish ears and a distinct white rump patch. Breeding pairs mate for life and tend to avoid other pairs. However, when they reproduce, which is two or three times per year, they raise the young in communal dens with up to 15 other pairs but do not permit more than one female at a time in the den while nursing, and have to take turns and locate their own young by scent, not permitting others to nurse. The partners seem to chatter to each other continuously with low- and high-volume whistles. The mara ranges from central Argentina to southern Patagonia in the pampas grasslands and steppe.

Patagonia lesser cavy (cuís chico)
Microcavia australis
Length: 22cm
Weight: 250–300g

The subfamily Caviinae (cavy) includes the genuses *Microcavia* and *Cavia*. The latter are the guinea pigs and the lesser cavy is very similar in appearance – a small creature, with a robust body, no visible tail and a head that is a third of its body length; it has large dark eyes encircled by a white ring and big ears. They are hystricomorphs, akin to porcupines; and their teeth are in constant growth, requiring gnawing and chewing to keep them short. With polygynous behaviour, there is typically one male with a small harem of females. The precocious young are born weighing a mere 30g but are covered in fur, open-eyed, able move about and eat solid food on the first day of life. They nurse for a few weeks from any lactating female in the harem. At about one month of age, the offspring are weaned and fully independent. Owing to their great similarity also in life strategies, *Microcavia* and *Cavia* ranges never overlap; the lesser cavy is found from Santa Cruz through western Argentina up to Jujuy.

Ungulates

Pudú (pudú)

Pudu puda
Height: 25–43cm
Length: 60–85cm

Pudu

The pudú is the smallest deer in the world. It has a minimal range in the temperate Andean rainforests of Argentina and more extensively in Chile. The coat is long coarse fur that has an overall pale brown colouring but with a reddish brown colour to the mid-back and facial accents. It has short

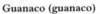

legs, small eyes and ears and an inconspicuous tail. The males have spiky antlers. They are solitary except during the rut. A single white-spotted fawn is born weighing less than a kilogram and will not wean until three months of age. At six months, the females are sexually mature, whereas the males are not mature until 18 months. They feed on fruit, ferns, sapling bark and leaves in the forest, and rise up on the hind legs to graze from trees. The pudú is an endangered species, threatened by habitat loss and competition with introduced roe and fallow deer. Apparently it becomes easily afflicted with parasites transmitted by domestic dogs.

Guanaco (guanaco)

Lama guanicoe

Guanaco

Height: 1.1–1.2m to the shoulder; 1.8–1.9m to the top of head
Length: 1.2m
Weight: 115–140kg

A member of the camel family, the guanaco has the characteristic two padded toes with hooves more resembling nails, a long neck, shaggy fur and dextrous cleft lips. It inhabits the high grasslands up to 4,000m from southern Peru down into southern Chile and central and southern Argentina east to Tierra del Fuego and was introduced to the Falkland/Malvinas Islands; it is the only camelid in Patagonia. Breeding season is in late summer or early autumn, near to which time the young are also born after a gestation of almost a full year. One 10kg precocious *chulengos* (newborn) is born, rarely twins, able to run within hours of its birth. Adult guanacos can run at speeds up to 60km/h. Guanacos form three forms of social structure: groups of male bachelors, solitary males and family units (one male with a harem of females and offspring, the male beginning to drive off male young at 6–12 months of age who then form the male troops, the solitary males typically being the old guanacos that have been usurped of their harems). Some of their more interesting behavioural traits include their nasty habit of spitting, which is a defensive strategy only; the attack is forewarned by the laying back of the ears and lifting the chin. They enjoy dust bathing, which likely reduces parasites, and use common dung heaps (latrines), which also serve as territorial markers (a dominant male presides over a 1–5km^2 range). Guanaco populations are drastically reduced from habitat loss from human as well as natural causes such as climate change reducing graze lands. Guanacos have also long been hunted for their meat and fur. Their natural predator is the puma, but the puma population is also greatly reduced and more guanacos die of starvation than from predation.

Similar species:
There are only six species of camelids in the world, four of which are in South America. The vicuña (*Vicugna vicugna*) is the only other wild camelid other than the guanaco but its range is in the far northwest in the high Altoplano region. The other two camelid species are the llama (*Lama glama*) and the alpaca (*Lama pacos*) which exist only in domesticated form.

Huemul/Chilean huemul/southern Andean deer (huemul)
Hippocamelus bisulcus
Height: 80–90cm
Length: 140–175cm (females smaller than males)
Weight: 50–100kg (females are smaller than males)
This highly endangered species (perhaps 1,000–2,000 individuals) on the IUCN Red List is deserving of particular attention in Argentina. Its numbers originally plummeted owing to over-hunting, but current threats include habitat loss, competition with the introduced red deer (*Cervus elephus*), disease from domestic livestock, predation by domestic dogs and roadkill. It is rarely seen, even by researchers. It is very vocal (snorts, whinnies, grunts), and hearing it is more likely than seeing it. It has short legs, with the hind legs appearing somewhat bent; the pelage is coarse brown fur, with a black tail that is white underneath, with a white rump. Distinct facial features include a large black nose, small eyes and large ears lined with white fur. Males have 35cm-long antlers that are bifurcating and shed each year. The deer's four-chambered stomach efficiently digests a wide variety of forest vegetation. The southern Andean deer's habitat is in forests of the southern Andes of Chile and western Argentina; several conservation projects are underway in both countries to try to ensure its survival (see page 85 for one example). It is featured on the Chilean coat of arms, even more reason for that country to be concerned for its welfare.

Similar species:
Hippocamelus antisensis, the northern Andean/huemul deer (also known as turuka, taruga, guamal or Peruvian huemul), is found further north; the ranges of the two species are separated by a large gap.

Bats
Vesper bats (murciélagos chicos)
Two mouse-eared or little brown bats: the Argentine mouse-eared bat (murciélago común; *Myotis levis*), and the larger (L: 11cm; WS: 24cm) mouse-eared bat (murciélago oreja de ratón; *M. chiloensis*) that is only found where its territory overlaps from Chile into the Argentine Valdivian forest. The Argentine species is small (L: 5cm; WS: 22cm) and fairly common and widespread throughout Argentina, found in varied habitats from towns to forests. These nocturnal insectivores echo-locate to hunt and the metallic 'clicking' produced is audible, while their ultrasound is not. They fly in a seemingly erratic pattern as they chase insects. They roost and breed under roof overhangs and hibernate in winter. The lesser large-eared bat (murciélago orejón chico; *Histiotus montanus*) is from a different genus. It has large grey ears and grey wings and measures L: 6cm; WS: 24cm. It roosts in small colonies, inside caves, on cliffs and under roof overhangs and also hibernates in winter.

Mexican free-tailed bat (moloso común)
Tadarida brasiliensis
Length: 9–11cm
Wingspan: 24cm
Weight: 10–15g
Named 'free-tailed' because the patagium (flying membrane) does not extend to the tip of the tail, it is the only species of free-tailed bat in Argentina. It is present only seasonally and migrates, rather than hibernates, between summer and winter sites that extend up to 1,300km. It is abundant in its breeding grounds in Texas and New Mexico; nonetheless, it is quite common in Patagonia in varied habitats from grasslands to forests, river valleys and cities and towns. It roosts in caves or trellises but only in colonies during the breeding season, where their numbers can reach the millions. This bat has a bad reputation as a

rabies carrier, and while it sees higher incidences of the disease than other bats, skunks, foxes and raccoons pose greater risk for human contraction; the odds of contracting rabies from a bat have been estimated at about one in a million. Only recently has education on this animal shown its value in controlling insect pests – a large colony of up to a million individuals is claimed to be able to consume 6,000–18,000 tons of insects in a single evening. The highest cause of mortality in these bats is pesticide poisoning. Heavy metals such as mercury, selenium and lead have been recorded in their tissues; organochlorides and PCBs (polychlorinated biphenyl) are in high concentrations in some populations; DDE (a metabolite of DDT, the well-known organochloride pesticide) is blamed for the collapse in the famous colony in Carlsbad Caverns, New Mexico, from 8–9 million in the 1930s to about 200,000 now.

Marine mammals
Pinnipeds
Southern elephant seal (elefante marino del sur)
Mirounga leonina
Length: 4–5m (male), 2–3m (female)
Weight: 2,400–4,000kg (male), 500–900kg (female)
These true seals (phocids, also called the 'earless' seals, which is a key diagnostic feature – the ears are hidden whereas the fur seals, or otoriids, including the two species listed next, have visible ears) come ashore only to rest or breed; the

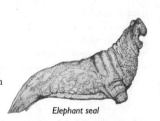
Elephant seal

only continental breeding colony occurs on Península Valdés. Most of the behavioural study on these species is during the mating season when they are easily observed on land, otherwise they may not come ashore for weeks at a time, preferring to rest floating in the water. Most of their time in the water, however, is spent diving – they spend 90% of their time underwater and can dive down to 1,500m and stay below the surface for up to two hours. This species is greatly sexually dimorphic, the significantly larger adult male providing for the common name by its large proboscis. Both adults are slate grey; pups are born black and will moult to grey prior to weaning at about three weeks. Adult females belong to harems during the breeding season with typically 10–20 females with a single dominant bull. The bulls arrive on shore in late August to start competing for hierarchy, the fights mainly in the form of posturing, biting and making impressively loud snorts from their bulbous noses in a symphonically tuba-like performance. Once all the shoving and snorting and machismo has achieved satisfactory results, the females begin arriving on shore and form harems (typically 10–20 females, but up to and over 100 has been observed but this is difficult for the male to maintain). The females give birth and 18 days later are receptive to rebreed; the subsequent pup will be born 11 months later. After breeding, the males return to sea, weaning begins, then the females return to the sea to feed (and regain the third of the original body weight lost while nursing the pup) and finally the pups venture off to sea – by December they are all off the beach. They will all return at various stages, however, to moult; the first in November, the last in March, males typically in February, and the moulting process takes two to three weeks. When on land, they move in an ungainly fashion by 'inchworming' along on their bellies. In the water, on the other hand, they are extremely agile and fast (maximum speed 20–25km/h). They are the top carnivore in their food chain, preying on squid, fish and crustaceans, with no natural predators of their own. They can live 20–25 years.

Southern sea lion (lobo marino de un pelo/del sur)
Otaria flavescens/O. byronia
Length: 2.3–2.6m (male), 1.8–1.9m (female)
Weight: 350kg (male); 150–200kg (female)
At the end of December, the aggressive territorial and hierarchical battles between the males begins. The heavily maned male is almost always posturing with his nose aloofly pointing

skyward, and battles with other males are mostly in the form of thrusting their heads at each other, roaring and grunting; the fights rarely involve physical contact but bites do occur. The established harems are of pregnant, birthing and nursing females. A week after the female has arrived on shore, a single pup is born, and a week after that, she mates again, and returns to the sea to feed but returns to nurse, locating her own pup in the crowd by calling to it and recognising its lamblike bleat in return and confirming its identification by smell. Although male pups are slightly larger than the females, they do not reach sexual maturity until six years of age, compared to the females' four. They are both, however, at full adult size at around eight years. Colonies move from mating/birthing grounds on protected beaches along the coast to wintering grounds further south. They feed on fish, squid, crustaceans and sometimes even penguins – almost any meat source smaller than themselves. Observations have been made of them hunting small fur seals. They are in turn preyed upon by orcas and sharks, and puma when on land when the pups are a particular target.

Southern sea lion

Similar species:

The South American fur seal (lobo marino de dos pelos; *Arctocephalus australis*) is rarely seen but can be observed on some Patagonian islands and will occasionally come ashore on the mainland. They also form large gregarious colonies on very steep rocky shores and coastal cliffs and can sometimes mix within sea lion colonies. This seal is smaller than the sea lion (L: 1.4m and 1.9m; W: 50kg and 159kg – males larger than females), with a pointier snout, very visible ears and fine dark grey pelage. Outside of the breeding season it prefers to stay in the water, floating with flippers extended out of the water to keep cool or swimming quickly and porpoising out of the water.

Cetaceans

Baleen whales are comprised of three families: the grey (Eschrichtiidae), the rorquals (Balaenopteridae) and the rights (Balaenidae). Hypothetically, two rorquals could occur in this territory, but no data exists to either repute or support whether the fin whale (rorcual común; *Balaenoptera phusalus*) or humpback whale (yubarta/ballena jorobada; *Megaptera novaengliae*) frequent Argentina's shores. The only representative of the Balaenidae family in Argentina's surrounding waters, aside from rare visitors, is the southern right whale – the star of the Patagonian whale watching industry. All the toothed whales that occur off Argentina's coast, other than the sperm whale (cachalote; *Physeter macrocephalus*), which has only been seen by passing ships far offshore, are members of the ocean dolphin family (Delphinidae). Owing to the confusion of common names, few realise that the orca and the bottlenose dolphin are in the same family. There are only half a dozen species of porpoises in the world, which look similar to a dolphin but smaller and never with a beaked mouth; two porpoises can be found in Argentine waters: Burmeister's porpoise (marsopa espinosa; *Phocoena spinipinnis*) is common year-round; the spectacled porpoise (marsopa de anteojos; *Phocoena dioptrica*) is a rare to accidental visitor.

Southern right whale (ballena franca austral)
Balaena glacialis australis or *Eubalaena australis*
Length: 12–16m
Weight: 27–73 tones (females larger); calf is born weighing approximately 4 tons and is 5.5m long.
Until international protection was established in 1935, the right whale suffered from intense hunting and its numbers remain threatened; for the northern right whale, however, protection came too late, its numbers remain critically low and it is feared that it will become

extinct. Despite man's offences against this gentle creature, it tolerates close and quite non-discreet human presence. The whale migrates annually south to Península Valdés to its mating and calving grounds (between June and November), the most sensitive time in its life cycle; yet, at this time, several boats per day circle about them with excited tourists. Mothers are nursing and teaching their calves important survival and socio-behavioural skills, at the same time they are warding off love-struck males of their constant advances. Yet, whale-watching increases education as well as appreciation for the whales and does more good than harm if done with conscientious tour companies. Today the greater threat to these and many marine creatures is habitat damage especially in the form of direct disturbance via coastal industrial activities and hazardous oceanic dumping that leads to bioaccumulation of toxins and kill-offs throughout the food chain; climate change is also a concern as it directly affects the plankton populations on which these whales feed. This whale is a pleasure to observe, as its gregarious behaviour results in such frequent spectacles as jumps, fin slaps, head bobs and fantastic breaches as well as the classic fluke shot prior to a dive. The body is robust with the head measuring a third of its full length. The body is black, with a white belly patch. Distinctive white patches on the head are called callosities, a natural thickening and roughening of the skin in growths on top of which are a layer of parasitic crustaceans called cyamids, which give the white colouration. These markings are like a fingerprint, an identification marking that is unchanging throughout life, which is estimated to be between 50 to 70 years on average.

Orca/killer whale (orca)

Orcinus orca
Length: 7–9m
Weight: average 7–9 tons (males larger than females)
The orcas most commonly seen off Argentina's shores live in pods, and hunt fish, birds, especially penguins, turtles, crustaceans and seals. In March and April at Punta Norté on Península Valdés, they make a gory spectacle of themselves by lunging onto the shore to snatch up sea lion pups. The orca has not historically been hunted for meat but, unfortunately, to a disturbingly high rate for the aquarium trade. With greater public scrutiny, this inhumane 'hunt' on marine mammals will hopefully end one day as well. Unmistakeable in its black-and-white colouration, it is probably the most internationally well known since it is one of the most dispersed marine mammals, inhabiting every ocean in the world in both temperate and tropical zones. Interestingly, females can live up to 60 years but males rarely over 30. Each female can give birth to a calf only once every ten years.

Similar species:
Occasionally the long-finned pilot whale (calderón o ballena piloto; *Globicephala melaena*) is observed off Argentina's shores. It is 6m in length and almost black in colour. It is famous for mass strandings in Chubut, the worst in recent history was in Bahía Bustamante in 1991 when over 400 individuals stranded. The cause of these events is unknown.

Commerson's dolphin (tonina overa)

Cephalorhynchus commersonii
Length: 15m
Weight: 30–40kg
This beautiful little dolphin is distinctly black and white – black at tip and tail (head and pectoral fin, and tail and dorsal fin) with a pure white 'shawl' across its back and down its flanks. It is typically seen in groups of two to 12 individuals and is very gregarious, breaching frequently and bowriding with boats. It eats fish and squid; it, like many small dolphin species, is illegally hunted for crab bait.

Similar species:
Several other dolphin species are seen in various locations around Argentina's shores but with varying frequencies. The bottlenose dolphin (tonina; *Tursiops truncates*) is a well-known dolphin. Another victim of the aquarium trade, it is 3–4m in length and common off the shores of Chubut. The dusky or Fitz Roy's dolphin (delfín oscuro/de Fitz Roy; *Lagenorynchus obscurus*) is seen around Península Valdés; it has lovely swirls of paler colours running along its 1.7–2m body length that vary in design with each individual. There is also the common dolphin (delfín común; *Delphinus delphis*) named accordingly for being widely distributed in waters around the world; and Peale's dolphin (delfín austral; *Lagenorhynchus australis*), seen when crossing the Magellan Strait.

Birds

Upland goose (canquén común)
Chloephaga picta
Length: 54–70cm
In this commonly observed, sexually dimorphic species the male is white with heavy black striping on its back and sides, and a black bill and legs, whilst the female has a brown head and neck, a white body with black stripes, and a black bill and yellow legs. When in flight, they both show black primaries on white wings.

Between October and January the breeding pair establishes a nesting territory. The nest is built on the ground, in grass and near water, making it extremely vulnerable to predation – especially from the increased populations of mink. In addition to this, these ground nests are often built in agricultural fields and destroyed during harvests.

Similar species:
The upland goose is frequently associated with the smaller (53–55cm) ashy- headed goose (canquén rea cauquén de cabeza gris; *Chloephaga poliocephala*). Both the male and female have an ash-coloured head and chest, orange and black legs, a black bill, and part of the back is brown, whilst the rest of the body is white with black striping.

Flying steamer duck (pato vapor volador)
Tachyeres patachonicus.
Length: 68cm
So-called for the distinct churning of its legs as it attempts to alight from the water, this species puts in an enormous amount of effort in generally doing little more than run on the surface of the water. Despite its ungainly locomotory advances, the duck is not an unattractive bird. It has a portly body, mottled grey-brown colouring, a white belly and orange bill. The female has a browner head and a white stripe leading from the eye.

Similar species:
The white-headed steamer duck (*T. leucocephalus*) is found around the Peninsula Valdés area, whilst the flightless steamer duck (*T. pteneres*) is found in Tierra del Fuego. These two species are slightly larger (80cm long) than the flying steamer duck but similar in coloration.

Buff-necked ibis (bandurria baya)
Theristicus caudatus
Length: 57cm
The ibis is characterised by its long, thin, downward-curved beak that it uses to probe the ground in search of invertebrates. It produces a very distinctive call, like the metallic honk of an old-fashioned bicycle horn. This species has a buff-coloured head, a black face, pink legs and a body with a grey band across its chest. It makes a short migration between its wintering grounds in the pampas to its breeding and nesting grounds in the marshlands

of Patagonia, where it builds a platform nest on the ground or on cliff faces along the coast.

Similar species:
The white-faced ibis (cuervillo de Cañada; *Plegadis chihi*) is not common but can be observed. It is completely dark brown in colour with a white stripe outlining its face.

Chilean flamingo (flamenco austral)
Phoenicopterus chilensis
Length: 110–70cm
Almost everyone is familiar with this large pink bird, found throughout Argentina. It is easily identified by its pink body, yellow legs, and black bill with yellow base. Black primaries can be seen on the wings when the bird is in flight. Flamingos are waders, often seen standing on one leg and, most commonly, head down sifting the water and mud for invertebrates and plankton. They are always found in flocks, ranging from a few dozen to a thousand birds. A colony breeder, numerous raised mud nests (40cm wide) are built side by side with a single white egg (rarely two) laid within. Once the chicks are old enough to exit the nest they are raised in crèches. Juvenile flamingos are grey to white in colour with dark legs and bill.

Black-browed albatross (albatros ojeroso)
Diomedea melanophyrs
Wingspan: 2.2m
This majestic seabird is black from wingtip to wingtip, with white underwings bordered in black. The tail and eyebrow are also black, but the rest of the body is pure white. The bill is yellow and the legs and feet pale grey. This pelagic bird comes ashore only to breed or if the winds are excessively strong. It swoops onto the water to catch fish, squid and crustaceans. By holding its wings outstretched and very straight it can catch the wind currents, allowing it to cover great distances with minimal effort. Breeding colonies are found in Tierra del Fuego and the Falkland/Malvinas islands, and other sub-Antarctic islands.

Similar species:
Although the wingspan of this albatross is remarkable, it is dwarfed by that of the wandering albatross (albatros errante; *D. exulans*) whose wingspan is a staggering 3.5m – the greatest of all birds – but whose nearest colonies are in the Antarctic. The royal albatross (albatros real; *D. epomophora*), with a wingspan of 3m, is rare and breeds on sub-Antarctic islands. These two species are whiter with only black wingtips and edges; the wandering albatross has black outer tail feathers. A fourth species is the grey-headed albatross (albatros de Cabeza gris; *D. chrysostoma*) with a wingspan of 2m and similar in markings to the black-browed although with a grey head; it is also a rare visitor found further south in the Antarctic.

Imperial cormorant (cormorán imperial)
Phalacrocorax atriceps
Length: 57–60cm
A cormorant's distinctive posturing makes it easy to distinguish; its legs are positioned far back on its body, so it has quite an upright stance. The two races of this species – the less common blue-eyed or southern race (*Phalacrocorax atriceps atriceps*) and the abundant king or northern race (*Phalacrocorax atriceps albiventer*) – are only distinguishable by how high the white plumage of the cheek is in relation to the eye (that of the latter species is lower) before it descends down the chin, neck and underbelly. The rest of the bird is black with a crown of black plumes on its head in breeding season. The eye is a brilliant blue. The bill is dark brown

with a yellow caruncle, the legs are pink and the toes webbed. Courtship involves a lot of head bowing and preening. They are monogamous breeders but colonial nesters, mixing with other species of cormorants as well as other colonial nesters, such as penguins and albatrosses, if in their range. Nests are built out of seaweed and guano and parents take turns sitting on the nest to protect the vulnerable eggs from predators, while the other feeds. Two to four chicks hatch during the months of November and December.

Similar species:
Several species of cormorant can be found in Patagonia. The rock (cormoràn roquero/de cuello negro; *P. magellanicus*) is 50cm high, and the rarely seen guanay (cormorant guanay; *P. bougainvillii*) is a whopping 80cm. Both are black with the white only reaching to the base of the neck. The 50cm-tall red-legged cormorant (cormoràn gris; *Phalacrocorax gaimardi*) is grey and white and the frequently seen neotropic cormorant (biguà; *Phalacrocorax olivaceous*) is uniformly dark all over and 63cm tall.

South American tern (gaviotín sudamericano)
Sterna hirundinacea
Length: 38cm
This is the most commonly observed tern throughout the length of coastal Patagonia and is a year-round resident. It has an elegant long forked tail, a black cap, a long straight pointed red beak and red legs. Its body is pale, with a white underbelly and light-grey coloration across the back and wingtips. Outside of breeding season the black cap recedes leaving a white forehead and flecking in the back and the beak can darken to almost black. This tern forms great flocks that swoop over the water in search of fish. They roost and nest on rocky outcrops and islands, sometimes mixing with other species of tern. Two chicks hatch per nest and once they leave the nest are raised in crèches.

Similar species:
There are several species of South American tern. However, the only two you're likely to observe are the royal tern (gaviotín real; *Sterna maxima*) or the cayenne tern (gaviotín pico amarillo; *Sterna superciliaris/eurygnatha*). The royal has black legs and is larger (44cm) with a much broader bill. The cayenne (40cm) has a yellow bill and black legs.

Great grebe (huala)
Podiceps major
Length: 60–77cm
The courtship rituals of the great grebe are enchanting; the pair seem to dance on the water intertwining and bowing their long graceful and emblazoned red necks either side of each other. Breeding takes place near lakes or on the ocean; they never come ashore and even build floating nests on the water, on which they also mate. Typically there are three chicks to a brood and they frequently travel from the nest atop the back of one of the parents, who co-operatively rear the chicks.

The bill is long, straight, pointed and dark in colour blending to the dark-grey head colour that extends down the back of the neck and onto the back and wings. The underbellies are white and the distinctive cinnamon-brown front of its neck and chest turns white outside of the breeding season.

Similar species:
All the other grebe species observable in Patagonia are small and almost podgy-looking with short dark bills. They include the white-tufted grebe (macá común; *Podiceps Rolland*), the silvery grebe (macá plateado; *Podiceps occipitalis*), the hooded grebe (macá tobiano; *Podiceps gallardoi*) and the rarely seen pied-billed grebe (macá pico grueso; *Podilymbus podiceps*).

Magellanic penguin (pingüino patagónico)
Spheniscus magellanicus
Height: 50–70cm

Penguin

Vast breeding colonies of this penguin can be visited on Peninsula Valdés and other key areas of Patagonia. They are unperturbed by human presence and will wander past you, oblivious, during the breeding season. The parents take turns travelling between the ocean and the nest to fish and feed the young, of which there are two per clutch. The breeding pair are monogamous and the breeding colony is located at the same site every year. The males arrive first and prepare the nest, which they dig out like a small burrow and preferably under a large bush. The season for observing the nesting colonies on Peninsula Valdés is between October and December. They have distinctive black-and-white patterning, with a black stripe encircling the border of the white bib, and a white circle outlining each side of the face and joining under the chin. The bill is black with a white band prior to the tip. The gravest threat to this penguin species are oil and hydrocarbon spills, which kill thousands every year.

Similar species:
Other species of penguin are either rare visitors or found in small colonies in southern Patagonia and Tierra del Fuego. The macaroni penguin (pingüino frente dorada; *Eudyptes chrysolopus*) is 45cm with a broad single eyebrow of golden plumes that extend in length back from the eyes. The gentoo penguin (pingüino pico rojo; *Pygoscelis papua*) is 48cm with a key diagnostic of an orange bill and a black head with a white eyebrow. The rockhopper penguin (pingüino penacho amarillo; *Eudyptes crestatus*) is 40cm with yellow eyebrows extending into fine yellow plumes and an orange bill.

Darwin's or lesser rhea (choique)
Pterocnemia pennata
Height: 95–120cm

This large, flightless bird is a cousin of the ostrich. It is round-bodied and decadently feathered with long, buoyant, brown-grey plumes. It has a long neck and small head (that it does not bury in the ground!) with a straight flat beak. Its long powerful legs make it a strong runner, capable of reaching speeds of up to 60km/h. The claws at the ends of its three toes (per foot) and a talon on its heel are formidable weapons – never approach a rhea, for if it doesn't flee it will probably fight. When it does choose to flee, it will run in a zig-zag motion, or enter dense vegetation and lie flat to the ground to hide. When at rest, it sits back on its tarsi and sleeps with its neck slung over its back and its head buried into its feathers. The lesser rhea is found in the Patagonian steppe; it prefers to be near water during the breeding season, but otherwise lives in arid open plains.

The most interesting aspect of the rhea is its reproductive strategy. During courtship the male of this otherwise-silent species will make a drumming noise to attract females, breeding with several, but on average four. He builds a large nest scratched out of the dirt and built up with grasses and twigs (50cm wide) and defends this with a threatening hiss from all except his harem of females, which come at intervals to lay their eggs. Each female will lay ten–12 bright-green eggs (bleaching to white after a couple of days) – one a day every two days – which results in at least 20–60 eggs (600g each) per clutch. The female then searches for a new mate while the male is left to sit on the nest to incubate the eggs, which takes about 42 days. Synchronous hatching is induced by the cries of the chicks from within the eggs. The chicks are able to leave the nest within the first day of hatching and forage on their own. The male takes on more of a guardianship role, protecting the chicks from danger, but not brooding them. After the breeding season, in winter, they will form flocks of about 20–30 individuals, consisting of males, females and chicks.

Rhea numbers are dwindling because they are hunted for their meat and skins (its toes are considered good-luck charms and are sometimes used to make the handle of the gaucho's knife or facón), and farmers often shoot them because they cause significant damage to their crops. Fences built to confine cattle and keep out the flightless rheas limit the birds' movements, threatening their ability to expand to new territories and thus prevent genetic bottle-necking.

Similar species:

A subspecies, *P.p.garleppi*, is found in the high, open dry puna of the high Andean plateau in the northwest of the country. The greater rhea (ñandú; *Rhea americana*) is the larger of the two species, reaching 180cm tall and the largest amongst South American birds. The greater rhea ranges across the northeastern expanse of Argentina, avoiding the open grasslands, preferring the neotropical region.

Elegant crested tinamou (martineta/copetona común)
Eudromia elegans
Height: 40cm

Atop its long neck, this bird holds high its elegantly white-striped head (eyebrow and cheek leading to the neck) to show off its striking crest of black plumes – even the chicks have a crest. The overall body colour is mottled brownish-grey, striped and streaked in pattern above, becoming muted and pale on its underparts, with pale legs. Comparable to a European partridge in body shape and behaviour, the tinamou has short legs and, although a ground forager, is capable of flight. Similar to the rhea (to which it is distantly related) the male establishes a 2–6ha breeding territory, mates with several females, builds a nest in which all his mates deposit their eggs, incubates the eggs and rears the chicks.

Similar species:

The Patagonian tinamou (keú patagónico; *Tinamotis ingoufi*) is slightly shorter (35cm) and Darwin's tinamou (perdiz chica pálida; *Nothura darwinii*) is even smaller (25cm). Neither are commonly seen, the Patagonians' range is limited to the Santa Cruz province and Darwins' to the north of the Chubut province. Both lack the crest on the head, though the Patagonian has the white facial stripes that extend down its neck.

Southern lapwing (tero tero/tero común)
Vanellus chilensis
Height: 33cm

Frequently seen and even more frequently heard calling its name 'terro terro', this bird is practically a Patagonian mascot. It is usually seen in pairs, although also in loose flocks, standing about or running from some perceived threat – it is a nervous and excitable bird. It nests on the ground and one of the pair will run around as a decoy to lure predators away from the nest. The colouration and markings on the lapwing are distinctive and handsome. It has black head plumes, a black face around the black-tipped orange bill, a black chest and a black band across the tail feathers. The belly is white and the rest of the bird is grey and brown. The legs are orange.

Burrowing parrot/Patagonian Conure (loro barranquero)
Cyanoliseus patagonus
Length: 42–45cm

This gregarious parrot once nested in huge colonies all over Patagonia, but these large colonies are very vulnerable to persecution, and are increasingly rare, having disappeared from many parts of its range. This parrot is a colonial nester, typically digging into the sides of sandstone cliffs. The world's largest known colony of burrowing parrots is in Viedma in northern Patagonia with over 6,000 nests. However, scientists have noted a decline in recent years. They are threatened by nest poachers, who sell the embryos (which are considered a delicacy) to restaurants and the hatched chicks to the pet trade. They are also occasionally shot by farmers who regard them as pests.

When in flight, their blue wings and vibrant red and yellow bellies are fully displayed. Their overall colouring is olive green with a grey breast. The irises and the ring around the eye are white in mature adults. The beak is black and the feet are pale. It ranges from central Patagonia to northwest Salta.

Similar species:
The austral parakeet (cachaña; *Enicognathus ferrugineus*) has a dark-green body, 31cm long, with a black border to the crown and back feathers and a short hooked bill. The wings are a metallic blue, the tail and belly red. They range throughout southern Patagonia and are the southern most representative of the parrot family. The rarely seen monk parakeet (cotorra; *Myositta monacha*) is smaller (20–27cm) with a green body, a pale-grey belly and blue tips on the wings.

Magellanic woodpecker (carpintero magallánico)
Campephilus magellanicus
Length: 36cm
This woodpecker is not easy to spot, but easy to identify with an almost pure black body, a white bar across the wings, and the conspicuous red around the bill on the female and entirely red head on the male; the female has a 'curl' of feathers atop her head, looking very much coiffured. The magellanic woodpecker lives exclusively in the southern beech forests of the Andes. It relies on old-growth trees in which it can create cavities to nest in; in turn, several other species can take advantage of these cavities for shelter or nests. Thus, the population of this species acts as a good ecological indicator of the health of old-growth forest ecology. Its large home range requires significant areas of old growth forest to remain protected. It is the largest woodpecker in South America, but you are more likely to hear it drumming on the trees in search of insects, larvae and eggs, before you see it. It tends to remain within the 5–15m tree canopy boundary, and the male and female remain in close proximity to one another.

Burrowing owl (luchucita pampa)
Speotyto cunicularia
Length: 25cm
This burrowing bird takes over abandoned mara or armadillo burrows in open fields. In the season in which the parents are rearing the chicks, the owls are seen with their heads popping out of the burrow or standing around the entrance. Mainly diurnal, they feed on small rodents and large insects. Their colouring is an overall mottled brown-grey with small white spots, and some barring on the chest. The burrowing owl is a characteristic bird of the open grasslands, in arid or semi-arid regions of Patagonia and north into the pampas.

Similar species:
At night, the owl most commonly seen is the great-horned owl (ñacurutú; *Bubo virginianus*); it is widespread all the way to northern Canada. Its key features are its high ear tufts. It is much larger (50cm) than any other owl in Patagonia, of which there are few. Two other possible owl sightings would be the barn owl (lechuza de campanario; *Tyto alba*) or the short-eared owl (lechuzón de campo; *Asio fammeus*). The barn owl (36cm) gets its name for nesting in barns or abandoned buildings; it has a characteristic white heart-shaped face with black eyes and pale bill. The short-eared owl has a similar look to the burrowing owl, but is darker with a more pronounced facial disc and larger (38cm); it is a ground nester, not a burrower,

and nocturnal. The austral pygmy owl (*Glaucidium nanum*) is only 20cm long and found in Tierra del Fuego and the southern Andean forests.

Andean condor (condor)
Vultur gryphus
Length: 95cm; wingspan: 3m

Seen soaring on the thermals throughout Andean Patagonia, the condor is a symbol of the majesty of this region. The condor, the largest bird of prey in the world, creates a large black silhouette with finger-like primaries characteristic of all vultures. If seen from relative proximity the white collar is a key diagnostic feature as well as the white undersides of the wings and the red featherless head; males have a prominent caruncle. They are scavengers and do not have the airborne agility of predatory raptors, instead they glide over the landscape on the lookout for carcasses.

Condor

Pairs mate for life, nesting on high and bare Andean cliffs and co-operatively raise one chick every two to three years. Chicks do not fledge until six months of age, relying on the parents for the first two years of development and do not reach sexual maturity until seven to eleven years of age. In hopes to sustain the population of this critically imperilled species, scientists state that a breeding pair should survive until two of their offspring in turn reproduce, which implies a lifespan of 25–30 years. In captivity, the condor has lived in excess of 70 years. The factors that impede the condor from reaching its full life expectancy include poaching, pesticide poisoning, predation of young and limited food supply. Because they mate for life, the loss of a partner has devastating effects on the surviving mate and chick as well as the chance for future offspring. Several conservation organisations, including the Buenos Aires Zoological Garden, are working to save this species from extinction.

Similar species:

The turkey vulture (jote de cabeza colorada; *Cathartes aura*) is frequently observed in Patagonia. Its black wings stretch to 170cm and have white borders; its body is otherwise black and it has a red head with a yellow nape. The black vulture (jote cabeza negra; *Coragyps atratus*) lacks the red head and the wings in flight have a white 'window' near to the ends of the 140cm wingspan.

Chimango caracara (chimango)
Milvago chimango
Length: 37cm

Seen in abundance, this scavenger and opportunist hunter of small vertebrates is found throughout the grasslands, wooded areas and outer urban areas of Patagonia and north beyond Argentina, but prefers to be near a water source and avoids very arid areas. It builds a conspicuous nest in trees in which it lays two eggs. It has a long neck and legs and an overall brown coloration, pale on the belly and with darker barring on the back, wings and tail.

Similar species:

The crested caracara (carancho común; *Polyborus plancus*) has a very distinctive black cap and a bare, flesh-coloured face that blends into its large orange beak that is blue-tipped. Its long neck, tail and the ends of its wings are white barred with black. The body is black. It is a large (55cm) scavenger that hunts small rodents, birds and lizards. It also builds a conspicuous nest in trees and is found in the grasslands, wooded areas and foothills of the Andes. The white-throated caracara (carancho araucano; *Polyborus albogularis*) is 47cm long with less interesting colouration; it's black with a white chest.

Black-chested buzzard eagle (aquila mora)
Geranoaetus melanoleucos
Length: 60cm (females can be up to 70cm)
This large raptor stands in a class of its own. It is very robust and difficult to confuse with another bird. Despite its name, it is neither a buzzard nor an eagle, but a member of the hawk family. The head, chest, back and tail are a dark blue-grey and the tail has a greyish-white tip. The underparts are white, the bill black and the legs yellow. It preys mainly on birds and small mammals and its call is a series of short whistle-like screeches. It nests high in Andean cliffs or in tall trees if necessary. The large nests are used for several years. It ranges throughout Andean Patagonia down to Tierra del Fuego.

Similar species:
The red-backed hawk (aguilucho común; *Buteo polyosoma*) is also found in Andean Patagonia. It is 44–52cm in length with the female larger than the male; it is mostly grey above and white below, but with a red area on the shoulders that gives it its name. It can also be identified by its long, shrill, screeching call, typical of hawks, as it soars above the ground in search of prey. When not in flight it is typically observed perched on telephone poles or fence posts; it builds a large platform nest atop bushes or trees a few metres above ground. Both of these hawks are legally protected, yet are frequently shot none the less.

Puma

Appendix

LANGUAGE
Pronunciation
The official language of Argentina is Spanish, locally known as Castellano, and spoken with a distinct pronunciation most notable in the diphthongs 'll' and 'y' (see below).

Vowels
Spanish vowels are typically short and soft and do not change their quality of length from word to word, as is the case in English.

a   'ah', such as in 'cat' (eg: *pata*).
e   'eh', such as in 'pet' (eg: *gente*).
i   'ee', such as in 'feet' (eg: *oficina*).
o   'oh', such as in 'low' (eg: *lo*).
u   'oo', such as in 'june' (eg: *mucho gusto*).

Diphthongs
In order to make the long 'i' sound, you must pronounce the diphthong 'ai' or 'ay', such as in 'ride' (eg: *aire*).

Other diphthongs are:

'au'   'ow', such as the sound you make when you stub your toe, or say the word 'out' (eg: *aullar* or *auto*).
'ei' or 'ey'   such as in 'prey' (eg: *sies*).
'eu'   is not pronounced in English (eg: Europa (the 'e' and the 'u' are both pronounced, as opposed to the English pronunciation that combines the two vowels into a hard 'u' sound as in the word 'your').
'oi' or 'oy'   such as in 'boy' (eg: *estoy*).

Consonants
c   as in 'cat' when before an 'a', 'o' or 'u'
ce, ci   'sey' and 'see' as in 'second' and 'single' (eg: *cena* and *cinco*).
ch   the same as in English as in 'church' (eg: *che*).
d   as in 'dog', except when between vowels when it is pronounced like 'th' as in 'that'
g   as in 'got'
ge, gi   harsh 'h' at the back of the tongue on the soft palate, not pronounced in English (eg: *gente*).
gue, gui   'geh' and 'ghee' as in 'gay' and 'geese' (eg: *guerra* and *guia*).
h   always silent
j   hard 'h' at the back of the tongue on the soft palate, not pronounced in English (eg: *jardín*).
ll   somewhere between 'ch' and 'zh', not pronounced in English (eg: *llamar*).

ñ	like the 'ni' sound in 'onion'
q	'k' as in 'king'
r, rr	a single 'r' is pronounced strong, while the double 'rr' is rolled
s	soft as in the word 'soft', except before b, d, g, l, m or n it becomes hard such as in 'nose'
v	almost like 'b' as in 'boy' but somewhat softer, almost a blend between the sound of a 'b' and a 'v'
y	the same as 'll', somewhere between 'ch' and 'zh', not pronounced in English (eg: *yo*).
z	's' as in 'song'
b, f, k, l, m, n, p, t, x	These letters are pronounced as they are in English; k, w and x do not exist in the Spanish alphabet, therefore most encounters of these letters are within English words that have been adopted into the language, such as the metric 'kilo', 'whiskey' and 'xilofono' (xylophone); .

Vocabulary
Commonly used Spanish words throughout the text

gran	great
río	river
cordilleras	Andean chains
pampas	term derived from the Quechua word *bamba*, meaning 'upland meadow'
piso	floor, flight or level of a building

Numbers

0	*cero*	19	*diez y nueve*
1	*uno/una* (m/f)	20	*veinte*
2	*dos*	21	*veinte y uno*
3	*tres*	22	*veinte dos*
4	*cuatro*	30	*treinta*
5	*cinco*	40	*cuarenta*
6	*sies*	50	*cincuenta*
7	*siete*	60	*sesenta*
8	*ocho*	70	*setenta*
9	*nueve*	80	*ochenta*
10	*diez*	90	*noventa*
11	*once*	100	*cien*
12	*doce*	101	*ciento y uno*
13	*trece*	200	*doscientos*
14	*catorce*	1,000	*mil*
15	*quince*	10,000	*diez mil*
16	*diez y seis*	100,000	*cien mil*
17	*diez y siete*	1,000,000	*un millón*
18	*diez y ocho*		

Dates

January	*enero*	July	*julio*
February	*febrero*	August	*agosto*
March	*marzo*	September	*septiembre*
April	*abril*	October	*octubre*
May	*mayo*	November	*noviembre*
June	*junio*	December	*diciembre*

Sunday	*domingo*	Thursday	*jueves*
Monday	*lunes*	Friday	*viernes*
Tuesday	*martes*	Saturday	*sábado*
Wednesday	*miercoles*		

today	*hoy*	evening/night	*la noche*
tomorrow	*mañana*	last night	*anoche*
morning	*la mañana*	week	*semana*
tomorrow morning	*mañana por la mañana*	month	*mes*
yesterday	*ayer*	year	*año*
afternoon	*la tarde*		

(*Buenas tardes* = Good afternoon)

Time

What time is it?	*¿Qué hora es?*
01.00	*Es la una*
02.00	*Son las dos*
12.00 (noon)	*Es mediodía*
24.00 (midnight)	*Es medianoche*

Note The 24-hour clock is used rather than am and pm; therefore, instead of 3pm you would say '*a las 15*' ('*a las quince*') or in the evenings and mornings you can say '*a las seis de la mañana*' or '*a las seis de la tarde*'. Later than six would be '*a las diez de la noche*'.

01.05	*Es la una y cinco*
02.10	*Son las dos y diez*
03.15	*Son las tres y cuarto*
04.20	*Son las cuarto y veinte*
05.30	*Son las cinco y media*
06.40	*Son las siete menos veinte*
07.45	*Son las ocho menos cuarto*

Personal pronouns

Argentina has a few idiosyncrasies not spoken in other Spanish-speaking countries.

- *Yo* only has a pronunciation difference in Argentina
- The informal singular *tú* has been replaced with *vos*. Formal singular is *usted*.
- The informal plural *vosotros* has been replaced with *ustedes*. *Ustedes* is used throughout Latin America and understood though seldom used in Spain, and *vosotros* is understood in Argentina, but these variants indicate where you have learnt the language.

yo	I		*ello*	it
vos	you (singular informal)		*nosotros*	we (masculine or mixed gender)
usted	you (singular formal)		*nosotras*	we (feminine)
ustedes	you plural		*ellos*	they (masculine or mixed gender)
él	he/it		*ellas*	they (feminine)
ella	she/it			

Object/reflexive pronouns

me	me/myself
te	you/yourself
le/se	him, you formal/himself
lo/se	it/itself
la/se	her/it, you formal/herself

nos us/ourselves
os you plural/yourselves
les/los/se them, you plural formal masculine or mixed/themselves
las/se them, you plural formal feminine/themselves

Present tense

Regular vowels end in -ar, -er and -ir and conjugate as follows:

hablar: to speak

hablo	I speak	*hablamos*	we speak
hablas	you speak	*hablan*	you (plural) speak
habla	he or she speaks	*hablan*	they speak

vender: to sell

vendo	I sell	*vendemos*	we sell
vendes	you sell	*venden*	you (plural) sells
vende	he or she sells	*venden*	they sell

vivir: to live

vivo	I live	*vivimos*	we live
vives	you live	*viven*	you (plural) live
vive	he or she speaks	*viven*	they live

Note Remember from above that the personal pronouns in Argentine Spanish are variant – the second singular uses *vos* and the second plural uses *ustedes* – therefore, where traditional Spanish would conjugate *vostoros* (*habláis, vendéis, vivéis*), but with *ustedes*, the verb is conjugated with *–en* ending.

Basic vocabulary

good morning	*buenos días*	please/thank you	*por favour/gracias*
good afternoon	*buenas tardes*	you're welcome	*da nada*
goodnight	*buenas noches*	excuse me	*disculpe*
goodbye	*adiós*	sorry	*los sientos*
hello	*hola*	a pleasure to meet you	*mucho gusto*
well/very well/good	*bien/muy bien/bueno*	open/closed	*abierto/cerrado*
bon voyage	*buen viaje*	large/small	*grande/pequeño*
yes/no	*sí/no*		
of course	*claro*		

Questions

where?	*¿Dónde?* Eg: *¿Dónde está calle Moreno?* (Where is Moreno street?)
who?	*¿Quién?*
what?	*¿Cómo?*
when?	*¿Cuándo?*
why?	*¿Por qué?*
how?	*¿Cómo?* Eg: *¿Cómo se llama?* (What is your name?, but literally: How do you call yourself?)

Directions

here/there	*aquí/ahí*	straight/ahead	*derecha/adelante*
left/right	*izquierda/derecha*	block	*cuadra*
north/south	*norte/sur*	corner	*esquina*
east/west	*este/oeste*	street/avenue	*calle/avenida*
northeast	*noreste*	road/highway	*camino/autopista*
northwest	*noroeste*		

Transport

bus	city-to-city bus is an *autobús*; inner city bus is *coletivo*		
bus terminal	*teminal*	airport	*aeropuerto*
bus stop	*parade*	boat	*barca*
railway station	*estación de tren*	dock	*muelle*
platform	*plataforma*	return ticket	*pasaje ida-y-vuelta*
Where does this bus go?	*¿A dónde va este autobús/ coletivo?*	I want to get off at…	*Quiero bajar (me) a …*
I want to go to…	*Quiero ir a …*	Stop please	*Parada, por favour*

Accommodation

Do you have a room?	*¿Hay un cuarto?*	Do you have anything cheaper?	*¿Hay algo más barato?*
May I see the room?	*¿Puedo veder lo cuarto?*		
What does it cost?	*¿Cuánto cuesta?*		
single room	*sencillo*	air conditioned	*aire acondicionado*
twin room	*doble*	key	*llave*
double room	*matrimonial*	sheets	*sábanas*
with private bathroom	*con baño privado*	towel	*toalla*
		soap	*jabón*
hot/cold water	*agua caliente/agua fría*	toilet paper	*papel higiénico*
shower	*ducha*		

Shopping

I want	*Quiero*	Give me a (half)	*Póngame (medio)*
I would like (to eat)	*Quisiera (comer)*	expensive	*caro*
How much does it cost?	*¿Cuánto cuesta?*	cheap	*más caro, económica*
		too much	*demasiado*

Food and drink

Enjoy your meal	*Buen provecha*	bread	*pan*
bill	*cuenta*	butter	*mantequilla*
beer	*cerveza*	fish	*pescado*
wine	*vino*	meat (without meat)	*carne (sin carne)*
milk	*leche*	potatoes	*patatas*
water	*agua*	vegetables	*legumbres*
juice	*jugo*	fruit	*frutas*
tea/coffee	*té/café*	knife/fork/spoon	*cuchillo/tenedor/cuchara*

Slang

One of the favourite means of expression among Argentines is the insult; however, to call a person a name that some cultures would deem to be politically incorrect is in Argentina a term of endearment. Of course, this colourful language is used only among friends and would not go down well with a new acquaintance. For example, to call a friend 'fatso' or *gordo* is common. Also, *che* or *hombre* are affectionately used names.

Appendix

FURTHER INFORMATION

History
Lewis, D K *The History of Argentina* New York, Palgrave Macmillan, 2003
Lewis, C M *Argentina: A Short History* Oxford, One World Publications, 2002
Luna, F A *Short History of the Argentines* Buenos Aires, Grupo Editorial Planeta SAIC, 2000

Buenos Aires
Santoro, D *Tri-Dimensional Guide to Buenos Aires* Buenos Aires, Self-published, 2003
Bernhardson, W *Moon Travel Guides to Buenos Aires* Emeryville, CA, Avalon Travel Publishing, 2003. Written by a local Argentine and the website has many practical links and sources of information.
Luongo, Michael *Frommers Buenos Aires* Hoboken, NJ, John Wiley & Sons, 2005

Literary works
Borges, J L *Selected Poems* New York, Penguin Group, 1999. Translated into English by Alexander Coleman.
Chatwin, Bruce *In Patagonia* First published in the UK by Jonathan Cape Ltd, 1977. A travelogue of odd facts and amusing stories from the author's sojourns throughout Patagonia.
Darwin, Charles *Voyage of the Beagle* First published in 1839, reprinted by several contemporary publishers)
Galeano, E *Genesis – A Memory of Fire* New York, W W Norton & Co, 1998. Originally published in Spanish in 1982, it is a sombre and poetic account of the history of the Americas at the arrival of the Europeans; poetry.
Hudson, William Henry *Idle Days in Patagonia* 1893, reprints by several contemporary publishers. An illustrated account of the flora and fauna of Patagonia written by this Argentine-born English author and naturalist. Included among his many other works is *The Naturalist in La Plata* (1892).
Morgan, Eluned *Dring'r Andes* (Climbing the Andes). Printed in 1909, this out-of-print collectable is about the valley in Chubut, called Cwm Hyfrwd in Welsh.
Moreno, Francisco P *Perito Moreno's Travel Journal: A Personal Reminiscence* Buenos Aires, El Elefante Blanco, 2002. Personal recollections of the author 30 years after the events, as well as original diary entries from the times of his travels as one of the first explorers in Patagonia. *Viaje a la Patagonia Austral* was published by the author in 1876 and *Una Excursión al Neuquén, Río Negro, Chubut Y Santa Cruz* in 1898 (reprinted by El Elefante Blanco in 1999).
Theroux P *The Old Patagonian Express: By Train Through the Americas* Boston, Houghton and Mifflin, 1979. Classic on the journeys of the author on the historical train *La Trochita*.

Natural history
Canals G R *Mariposas Bonaerenses/Butterflies of Buenos Aires* Buenos Aires, LOLA, 2000. Published in both Spanish and English, 348 pages.

Chebez and Rumboll, *Fauna Misionera/Misiones Fauna* 2nd ed, Buenos Aires, LOLA, 2001. Catalogue of the vertebrates of Misiones, 318 pages with illustrations.

Couve E and C Vidal, *Birds of Patagonia, Tierra del Fuego & Antarctic Peninsula, The Falkland Islands & South Georgia* Punta Arenas, Chile Editorial Fanntastico Sur Birding Ltda, 2003. Photographic field guide of over 430 spp. illustrated with colour photographs and range maps.

Diaz N I and J Smith-Flueck *The Patagonian Huemul: A Mysterious Deer on the Brink of Extinction* Buenos Aires, LOLA, 2000. History and the present situation, in English and Spanish; 158 pages with photos, maps, tables and bibliographies.

Eisenberg J F and K H Redford *Mammals of the Neotropics, vol 2 – The Southern Cone* Chicago, University of Chicago Press, 1992. Chile, Argentina, Uruguay and Paraguay.

Harris A *Guide to the Birds and Mammals of Coastal Patagonia* Princeton University Press, 1998. Hard cover; 185 spp of birds, 61 spp mammals, range maps on each spp., colour illustrations and line drawings.

Lahitte B and J A Hurrell *Trees of the Rio de la Plata* Buenos Aires, LOLA, 1999. Published in both Spanish and English, 300 pages of species accounts with illustrations.

Morrone J J and S R Junent *The Diversity of Patagonian Weevils* Buenos Aires, LOLA, 1995. An illustrated checklist of the Patagonian Curculionoidea, published in Spanish and English in 189 pages.

Narosky T and Yzurieta D *Birds of Argentina and Uruguay, A Field Guide* Buenos Aires, Azquez Mazzini Editores, 2003. Published in collaboration with the Asociacion Ornitologica del Plata, one of the most highly recommended bird guides for Argentina.

Santiago G de la Vega *Natural History Handbooks* Contacto Silvestere Ediciones, 2003. Soft cover, black and white with colour insert of illustrations, 128 pages, this series of simple guidebooks is organised in chapters about ecology and natural systems with an overview approach. See also *Iguazú, the laws of the jungle* and *Patagonia, the laws of the forest*.

Smith N et al *Flowering Plants of the Neotropics* New Jersey, Princeton University Press, 2004. Coverage of 250 families between the tropics of Cancer and Capricorn, with colour illustrations and line drawings.

See LOLA (Literature of Latin America) www.thebookplace.com/lola for an extensive list of natural history, and some social history, books on Argentina written in Spanish.

Websites of interest

www.shinkal.com Online market promoting fair trade artisan works from all over Argentina.

www.argentinewines.com/bodegas/bodegas.asp Website dedicated exclusively to wine-lovers; bodegas, history and links among other information.

www.aaadir.com Directory of banks, credit unions and financial information on the internet.

www.oanda.com Currency converter with daily and historic exchange rates.

www.meteofa.mil.ar National Meteorological Service, in Spanish.

www.gobiernoelectronico.ar/sitio_ingles/our_country/nuestro_pais.htm Geo-political information about Argentina, sourced from www.igm.gov.ar/ in Spanish.

www.mrecic.gov.ar Ministry of External Relations, International Commerce and Culture, with links to foreign ministries, embassies and consulates.

www.turismo.gov.ar and **www.turismo.gov.ar/eng/menu.htm** National tourism authority.

www.greenvolunteers.org Directory, online network and guidebook series for volunteer projects in Argentina and around the world for alternative vacations that allow you to participate in conservation, development and cultural heritage projects.

www.ilam.org/ar/ar.html Argentina Directorio de Museos y Parques.

www.museosargentinos.org.ar/museos Museums of Argentina.

www.metrovias.com.ar Information on the subway system in Buenos Aires.
www.mrecic.gov.ar Ministry of External Relations, International Commerce and Culture, with links to foreign ministries, embassies and consulates.
www.museosargentinos.org.ar/museos Museums of Argentina.
www.oanda.com Currency converter with daily and historic exchange rates.
www.onlinenewspapers.com/argentin.htm Links to the online editions of around 100 Argentine newspapers.
www.pagina12.com.ar/diario/principal/index.html Alternative Buenos Aires newspaper.
www.paginasamarillas.com.ar Online Yellow Pages directory for the country.
www.panda.org/about_wwf/where_we_work/latin_america_and_caribbean/country/argentina World Wildlife Fund projects in Argentina.
www.plataforma10.com Argentine bus companies and schedules (Spanish).
www.ripioturismo.com.ar Tour agency website packed with info.**www.ruta0.com** Information on road travel, routes, conditions and services (Spanish).
www.shinkal.com Online market promoting fair trade artisan works from all over Argentina.
www.toandfrom.org/airport/argentina.html How to get to and from the airports by various forms of public and private transport.
www.turismo.gov.ar and **www.turismo.gov.ar/eng/menu.htm** National tourism authority.
www.welcomeargentina.com Popular website for general information.

Index

Page numbers in bold indicate major entries; those in italic indicate maps

Limerick
County Library